HEAVYWEIGHT

HEAVYWEIGHT

A Family Story of the Holocaust, Empire, and Memory

Solomon
J. Brager

WILLIAM MORROW
An Imprint of HarperCollins*Publishers*

For information, address HarperCollins Publishers, 195 Broadway, New York, NY 10007.

HarperCollins books may be purchased for educational, business, or sales promotional use. For information, please email the Special Markets Department at SPsales@harpercollins.com.

FIRST EDITION

Library of Congress Cataloging-in-Publication Data has been applied for.

ISBN 978-0-06-320595-6

24 25 26 27 28 LBC 5 4 3 2 1

For Talia and Ezra, new and newer

THE LEVI FAMILY

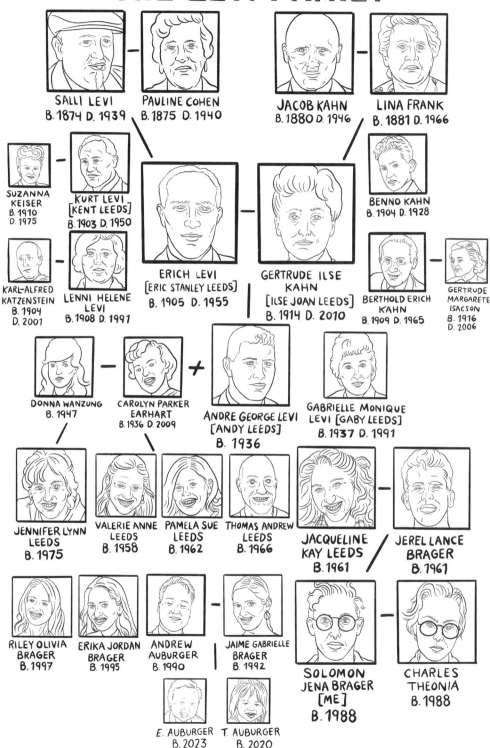

SALLI LEVI
B. 1874 D. 1939

PAULINE COHEN
B. 1875 D. 1940

JACOB KAHN
B. 1880 D. 1946

LINA FRANK
B. 1881 D. 1966

SUZANNA KEISER
B. 1910 D. 1975

KURT LEVI
[KENT LEEDS]
B. 1903 D. 1950

BENNO KAHN
B. 1904 D. 1928

KARL-ALFRED KATZENSTEIN
B. 1904 D. 2001

LENNI HELENE LEVI
B. 1908 D. 1991

ERICH LEVI
[ERIC STANLEY LEEDS]
B. 1905 D. 1955

GERTRUDE ILSE KAHN
[ILSE JOAN LEEDS]
B. 1914 D. 2010

BERTHOLD ERICH KAHN
B. 1909 D. 1965

GERTRUDE MARGARETE ISACSON
B. 1916 D. 2006

DONNA WANZUNG
B. 1947

CAROLYN PARKER EARHART
B. 1936 D. 2009

ANDRE GEORGE LEVI
[ANDY LEEDS]
B. 1936

GABRIELLE MONIQUE LEVI [GABY LEEDS]
B. 1937 D. 1991

JENNIFER LYNN LEEDS
B. 1975

VALERIE ANNE LEEDS
B. 1958

PAMELA SUE LEEDS
B. 1962

THOMAS ANDREW LEEDS
B. 1966

JACQUELINE KAY LEEDS
B. 1961

JEREL LANCE BRAGER
B. 1961

RILEY OLIVIA BRAGER
B. 1997

ERIKA JORDAN BRAGER
B. 1995

ANDREW AUBURGER
B. 1990

JAIME GABRIELLE BRAGER
B. 1992

SOLOMON JENA BRAGER
[ME]
B. 1988

CHARLES THEONIA
B. 1988

E. AUBURGER
B. 2023

T. AUBURGER
B. 2020

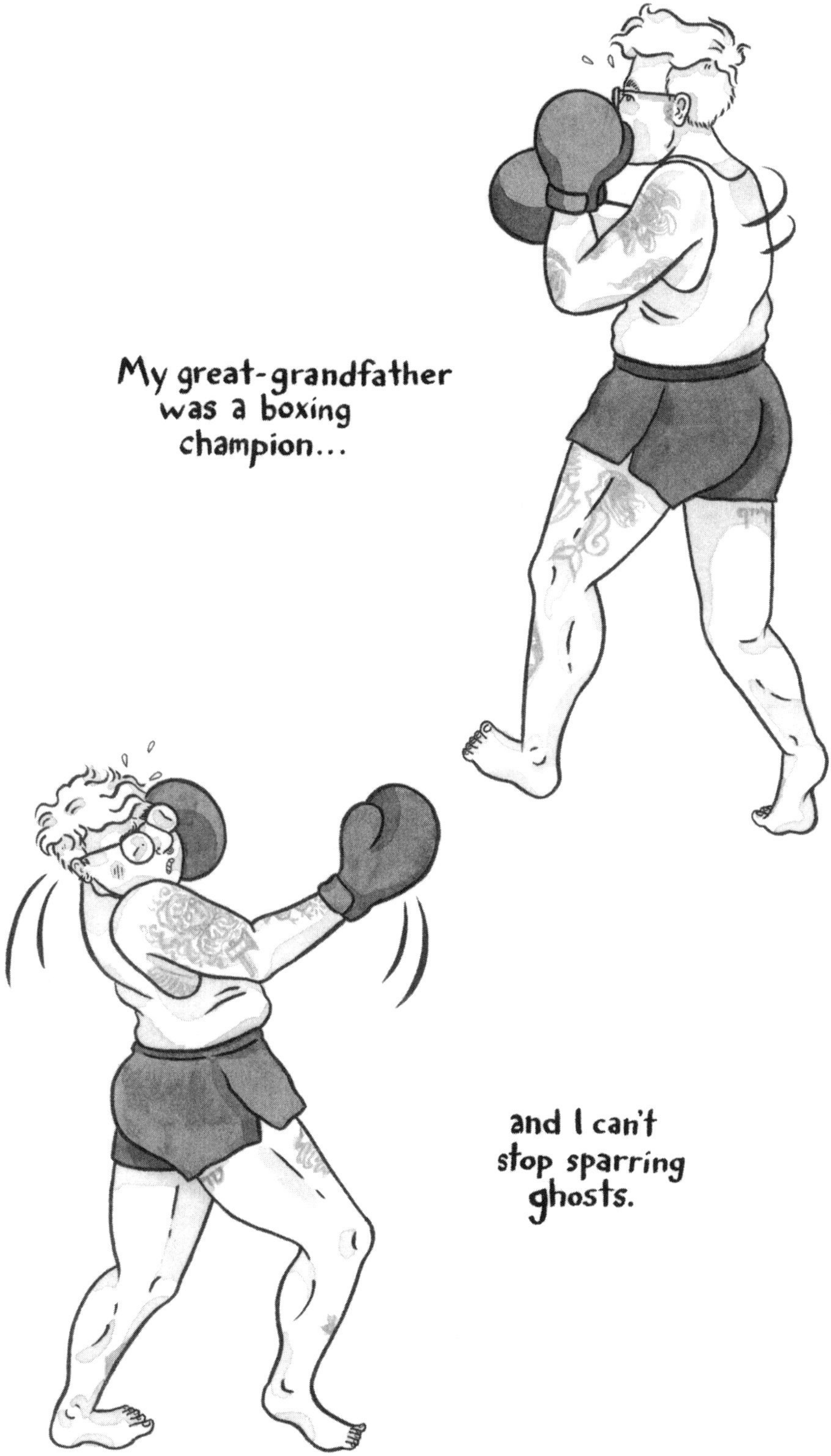
My great-grandfather was a boxing champion...
and I can't stop sparring ghosts.

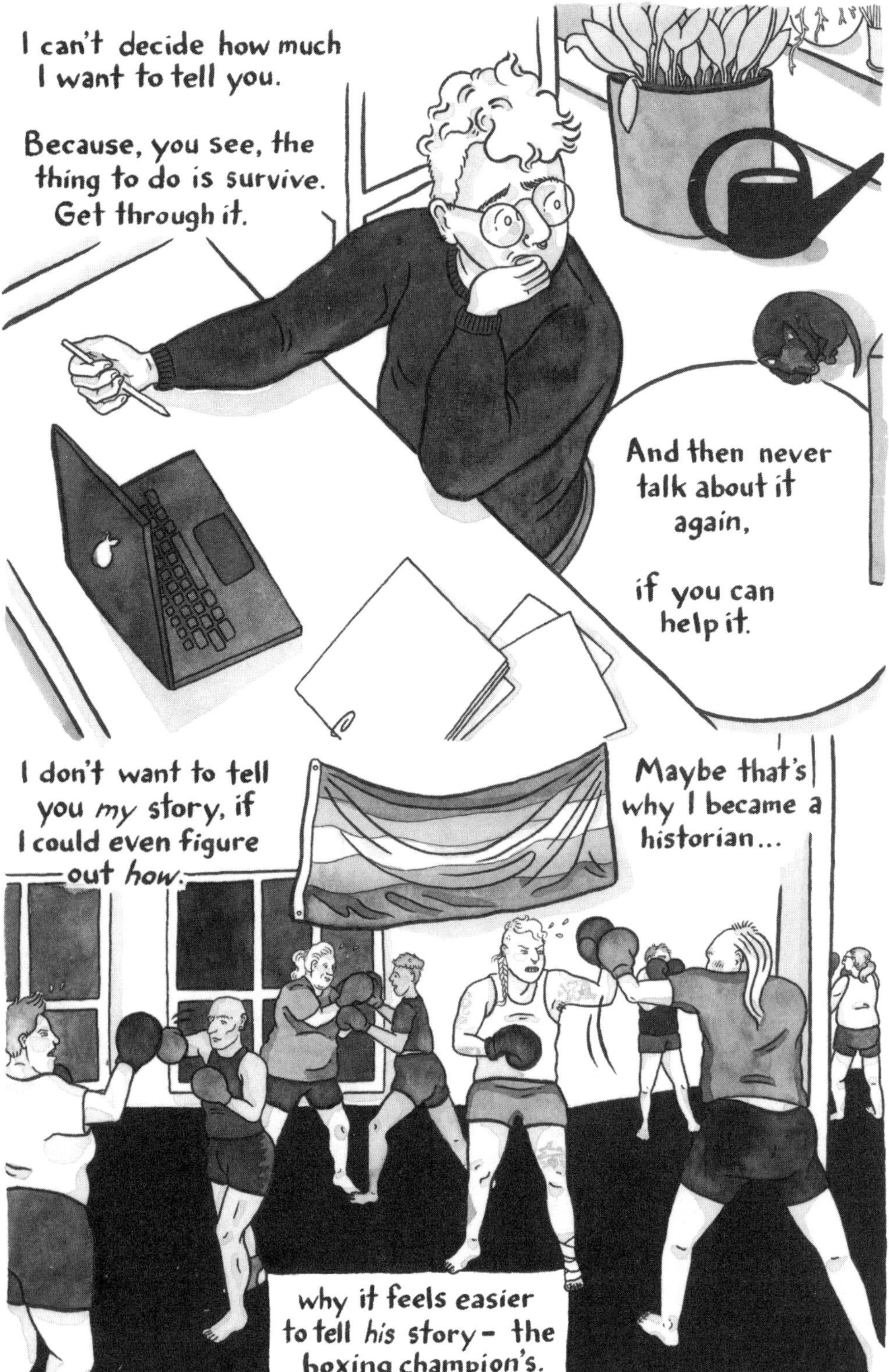
I can't decide how much I want to tell you.
Because, you see, the thing to do is survive. Get through it.
And then never talk about it again,
if you can help it.
I don't want to tell you *my* story, if I could even figure out *how*.
Maybe that's why I became a historian...
why it feels easier to tell *his* story – the boxing champion's.

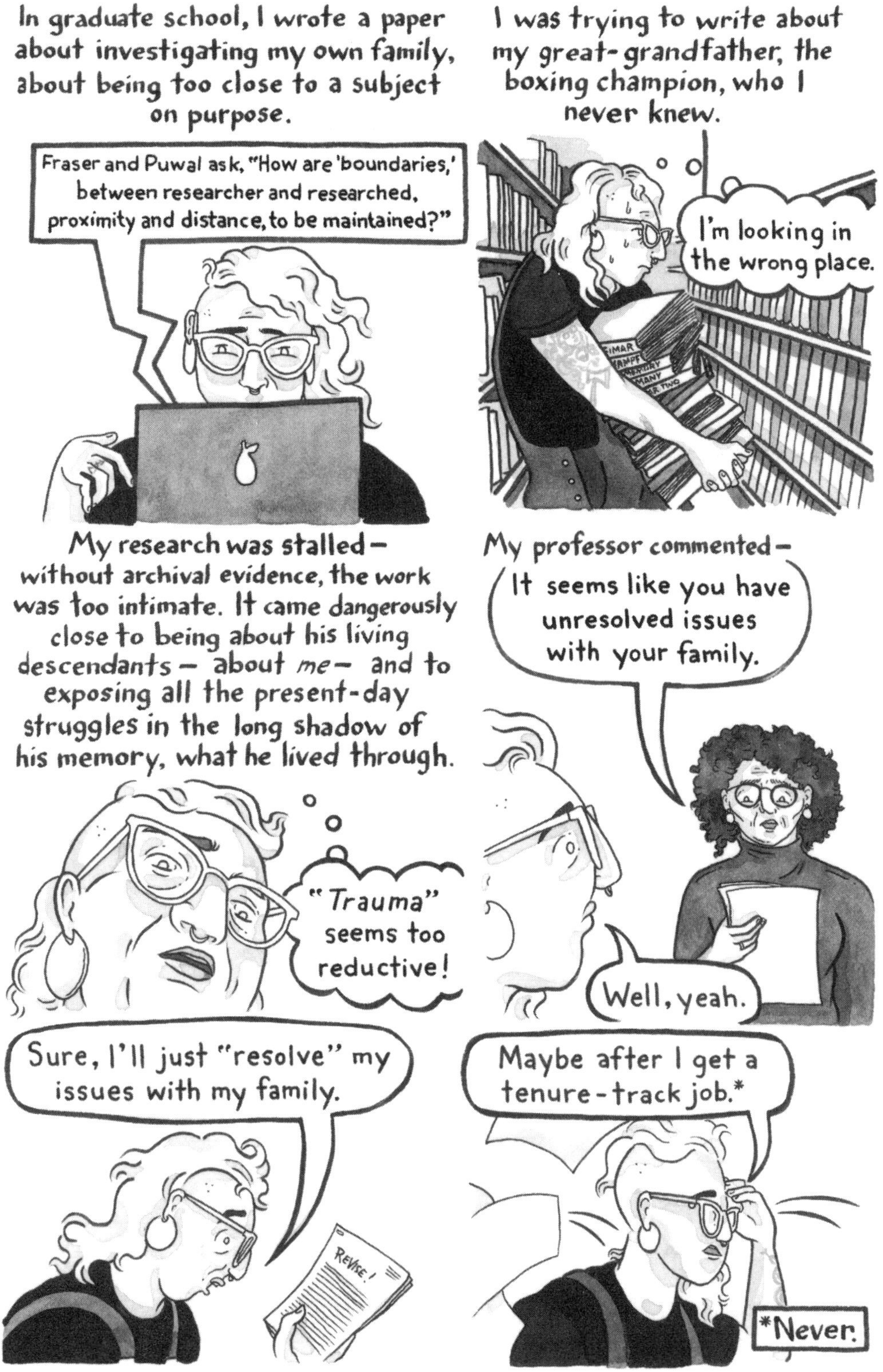
In graduate school, I wrote a paper about investigating my own family, about being too close to a subject on purpose.
Fraser and Puwal ask, "How are 'boundaries,' between researcher and researched, proximity and distance, to be maintained?"
I was trying to write about my great-grandfather, the boxing champion, who I never knew.
I'm looking in the wrong place.
My research was stalled— without archival evidence, the work was too intimate. It came dangerously close to being about his living descendants— about *me*— and to exposing all the present-day struggles in the long shadow of his memory, what he lived through.
"Trauma" seems too reductive!
My professor commented—
It seems like you have unresolved issues with your family.
Well, yeah.
Sure, I'll just "resolve" my issues with my family.
REVISE!
Maybe after I get a tenure-track job.*
*Never.

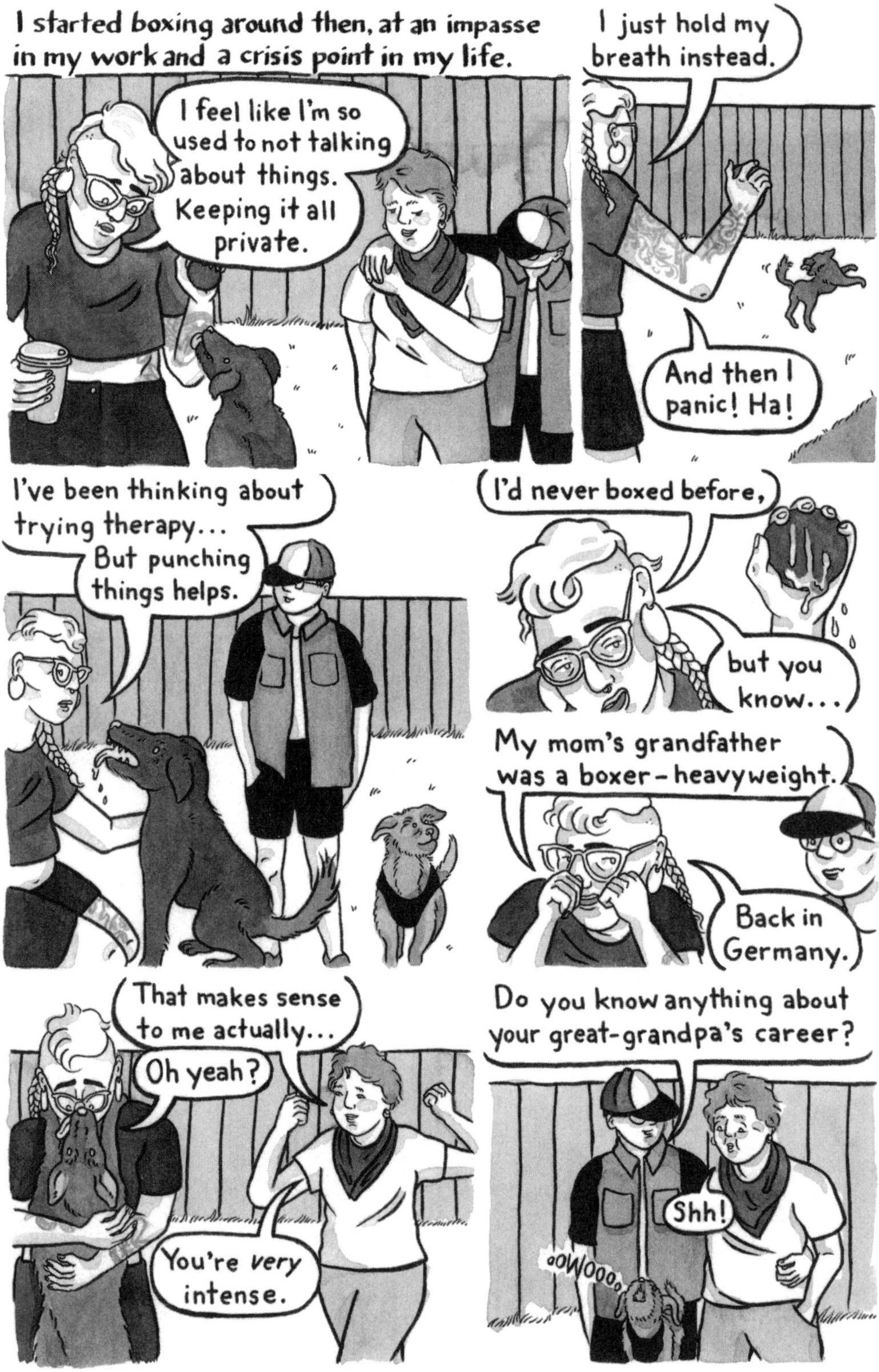
I started boxing around then, at an impasse in my work and a crisis point in my life.
I feel like I'm so used to not talking about things. Keeping it all private.
I just hold my breath instead.
And then I panic! Ha!
I've been thinking about trying therapy...
But punching things helps.
I'd never boxed before,
but you know...
My mom's grandfather was a boxer - heavyweight.
Back in Germany.
That makes sense to me actually...
Oh yeah?
You're *very* intense.
Do you know anything about your great-grandpa's career?
Shh!
oOWOOo

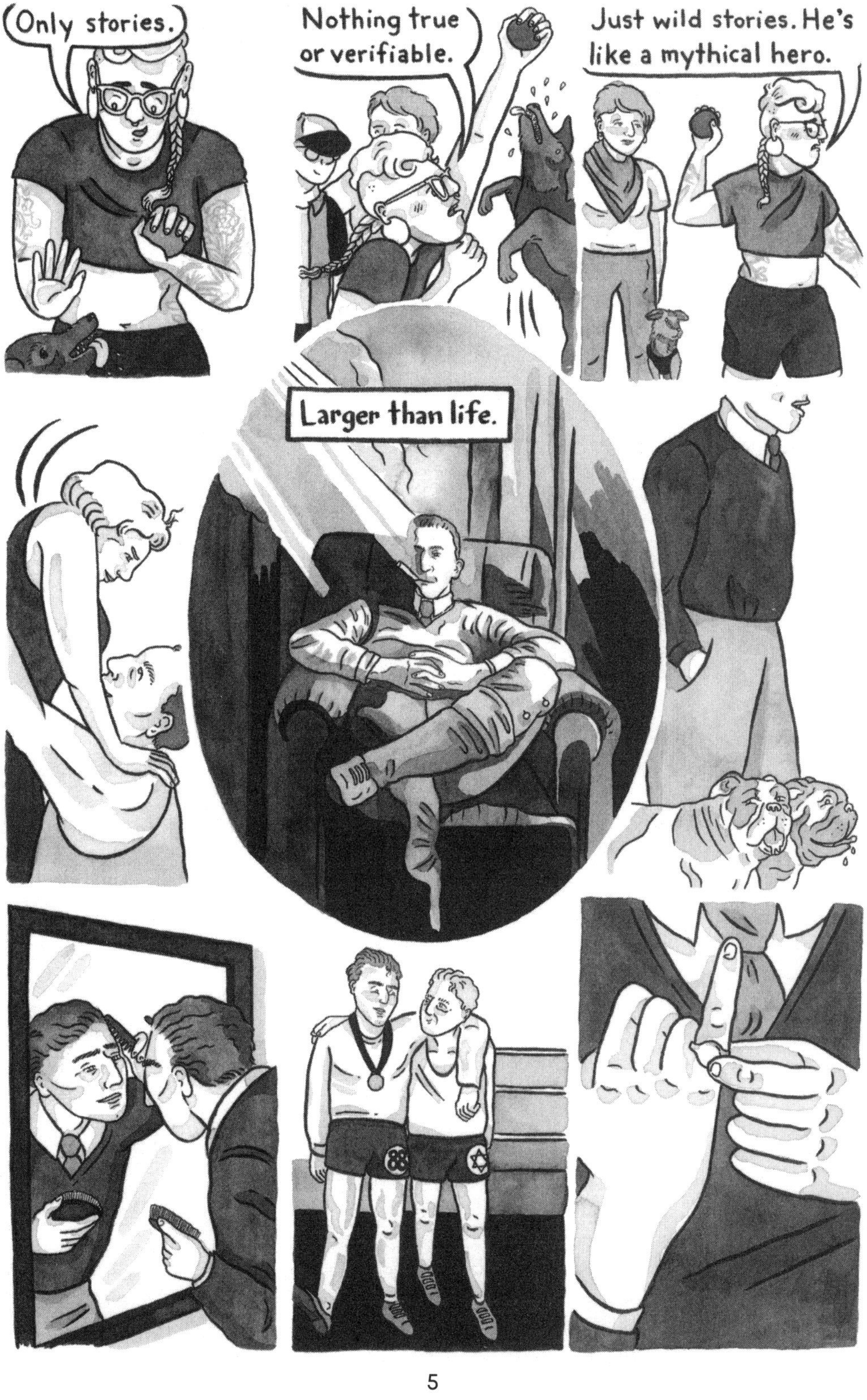
Only stories.
Nothing true or verifiable.
Just wild stories. He's like a mythical hero.
Larger than life.

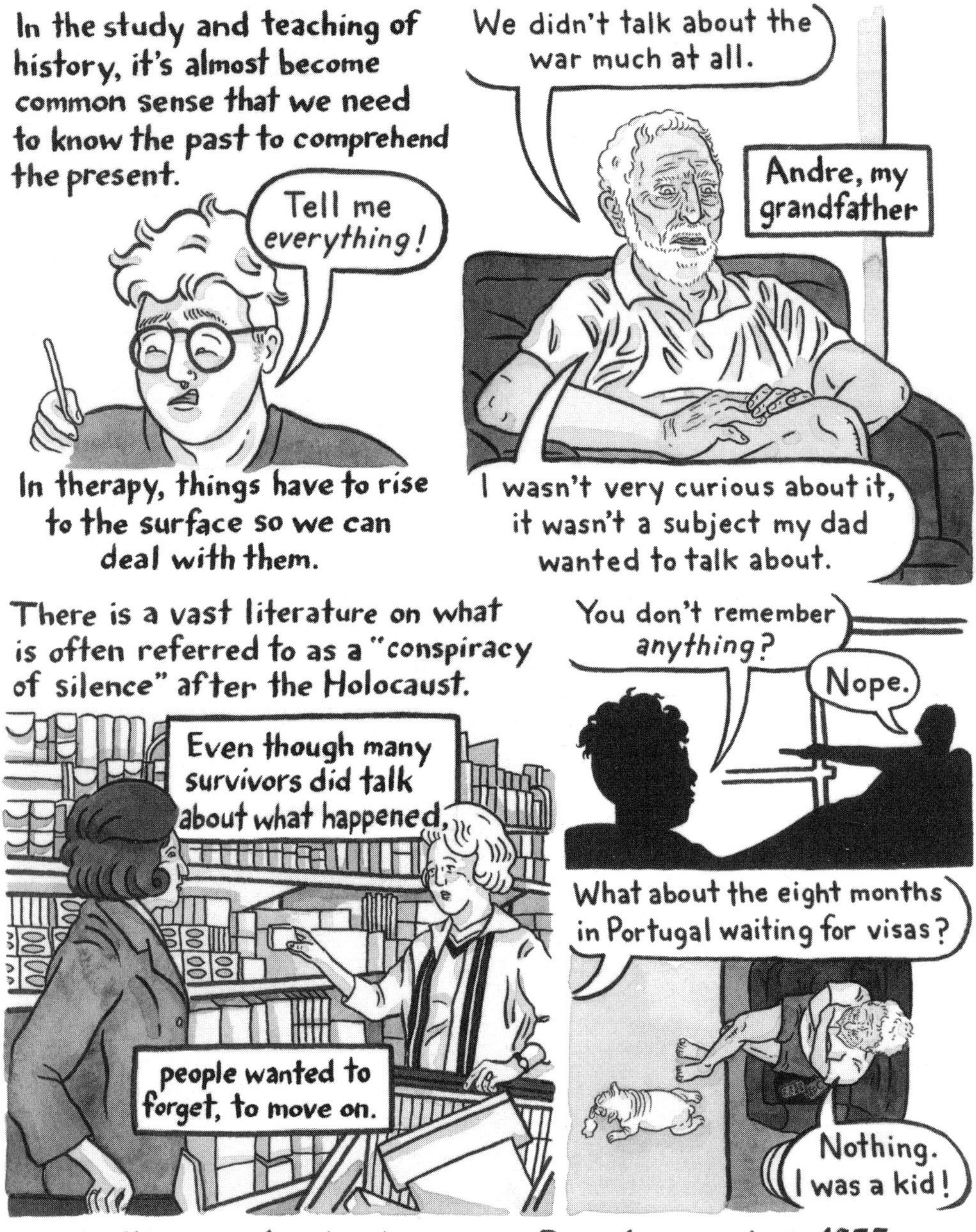
In the study and teaching of history, it's almost become common sense that we need to know the past to comprehend the present.
Tell me *everything*!
In therapy, things have to rise to the surface so we can deal with them.
We didn't talk about the war much at all.
Andre, my grandfather
I wasn't very curious about it, it wasn't a subject my dad wanted to talk about.
There is a vast literature on what is often referred to as a "conspiracy of silence" after the Holocaust.
Even though many survivors did talk about what happened,
people wanted to forget, to move on.
You don't remember *anything*?
Nope.
What about the eight months in Portugal waiting for visas?
Nothing. I was a kid!

The author and Auschwitz survivor Primo Levi wrote in 1955–

Yet the silence prevails... That they should keep silent about this in Germany, that the Fascists should keep silent, is natural and, all things considered, not unwelcome to us... But what shall we say about the silence of the civilized world, about the silence of culture, about our own silence in front of our children... It is not due simply to weariness... It is shame. We are men, we belong to the same human family to which our torturers belonged. Confronted by the enormity of their guilt... we are not able to feel exempt from the accusation... We are the children of the Europe where Auschwitz exists...

Robert Krell, a child survivor and psychiatric researcher, wrote in 1985—

> The older survivor possesses a memory of family and tradition, daily life and habits, the smells and sounds of a past. The children of survivors receive fragments of such memories, some more, some less. Their survivor-parents, protective of them, may withhold not only details of the war but also of prewar life and their own precious memories.
>
> The child survivors may have no memory. Too young to have partaken of a foundation for life, too traumatized to experience a childhood, too preoccupied with survival to reflect on its impact, the child survivors were not blessed with the opportunity for the systematized, chronological collection of ordinary personal history.

What do you remember from your earliest years?

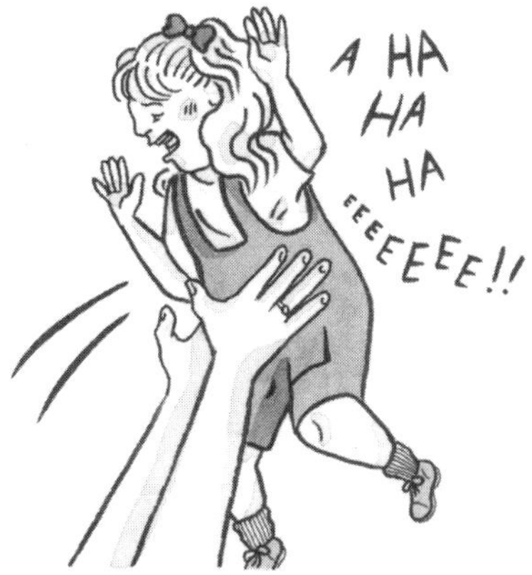
A HA
HA
HA
EEEEEEEE!!

How many of those memories are in your body, and how many are implanted stories?

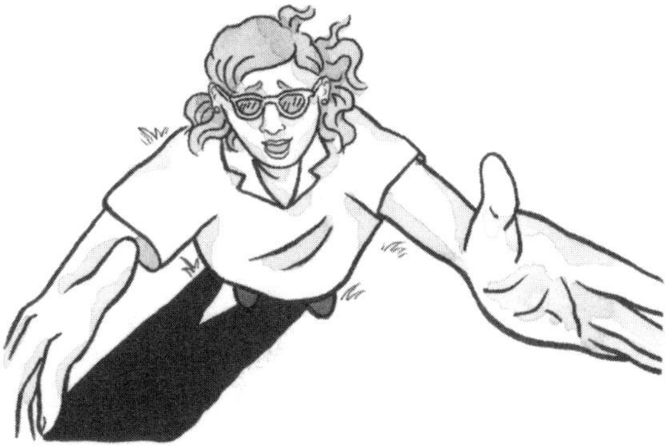

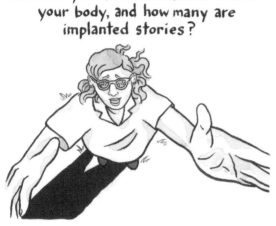

Would I remember this if I hadn't been told?

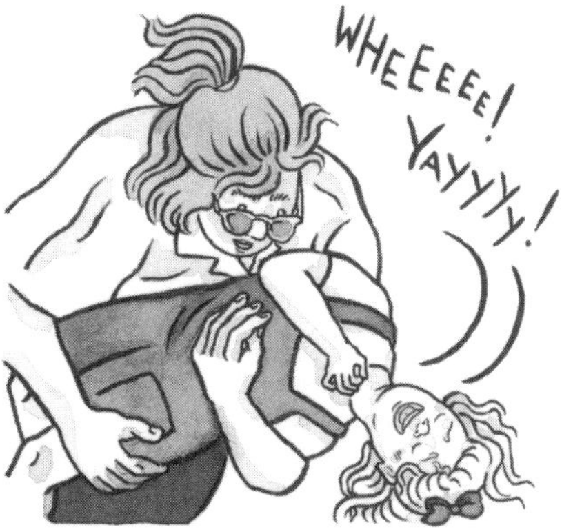
WHEEEEEE!
Yayyyy!

My grandfather and his sister spent their earliest childhood on the run. My grandfather says he remembers nothing...

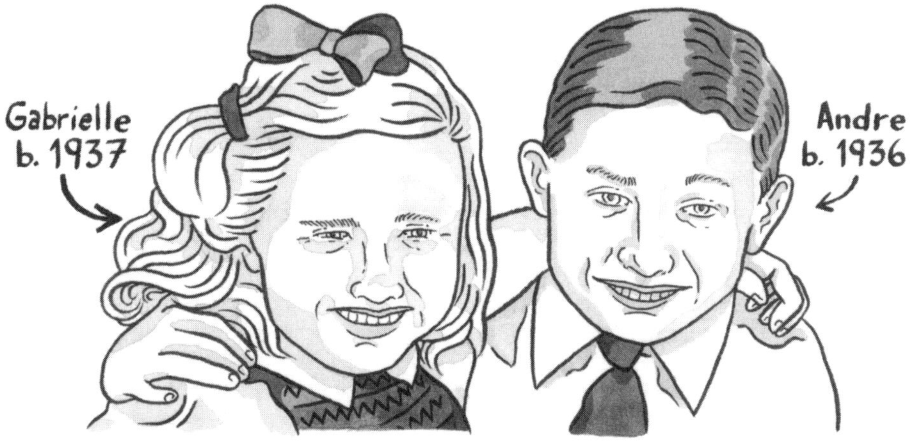
Gabrielle
b. 1937
Andre
b. 1936

(It's nearly impossible for me to imagine my grandfather *crying*.)

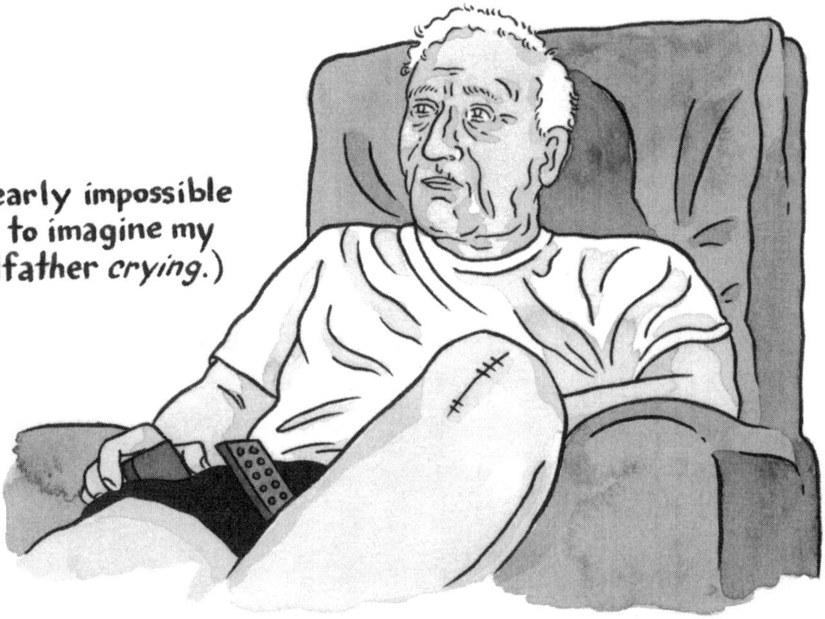

Sometimes, we remember nothing and are still wounded. Things *come up*. This is sometimes referred to as *haunting*.

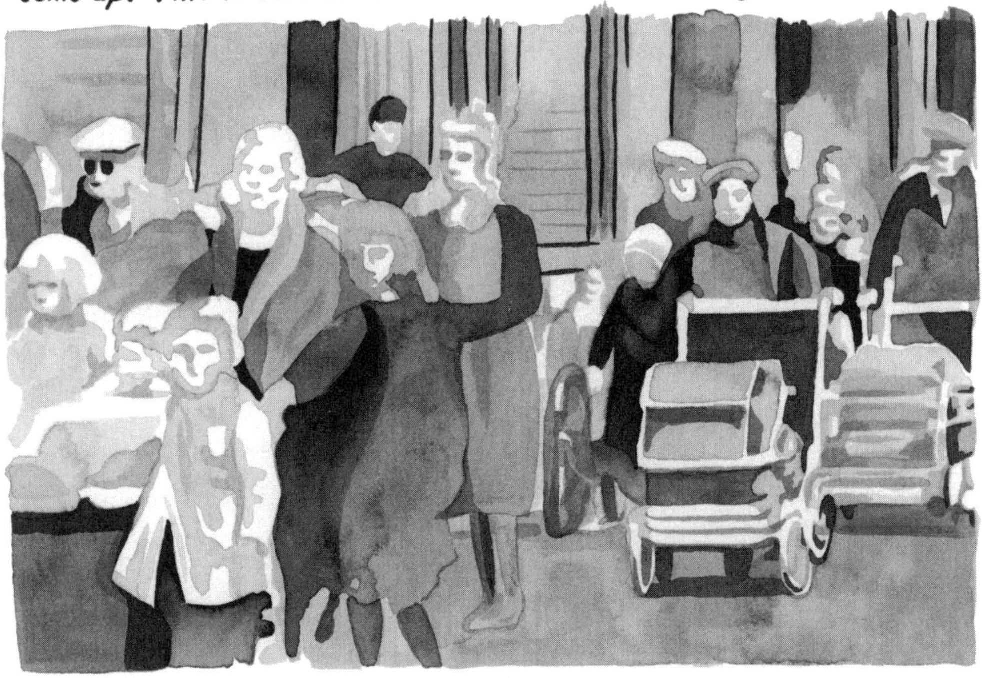

The stories I grew up with were my oma's.

My great-grandmother outlived her first husband by over 50 years. She held his memories, and her own, and her children's...

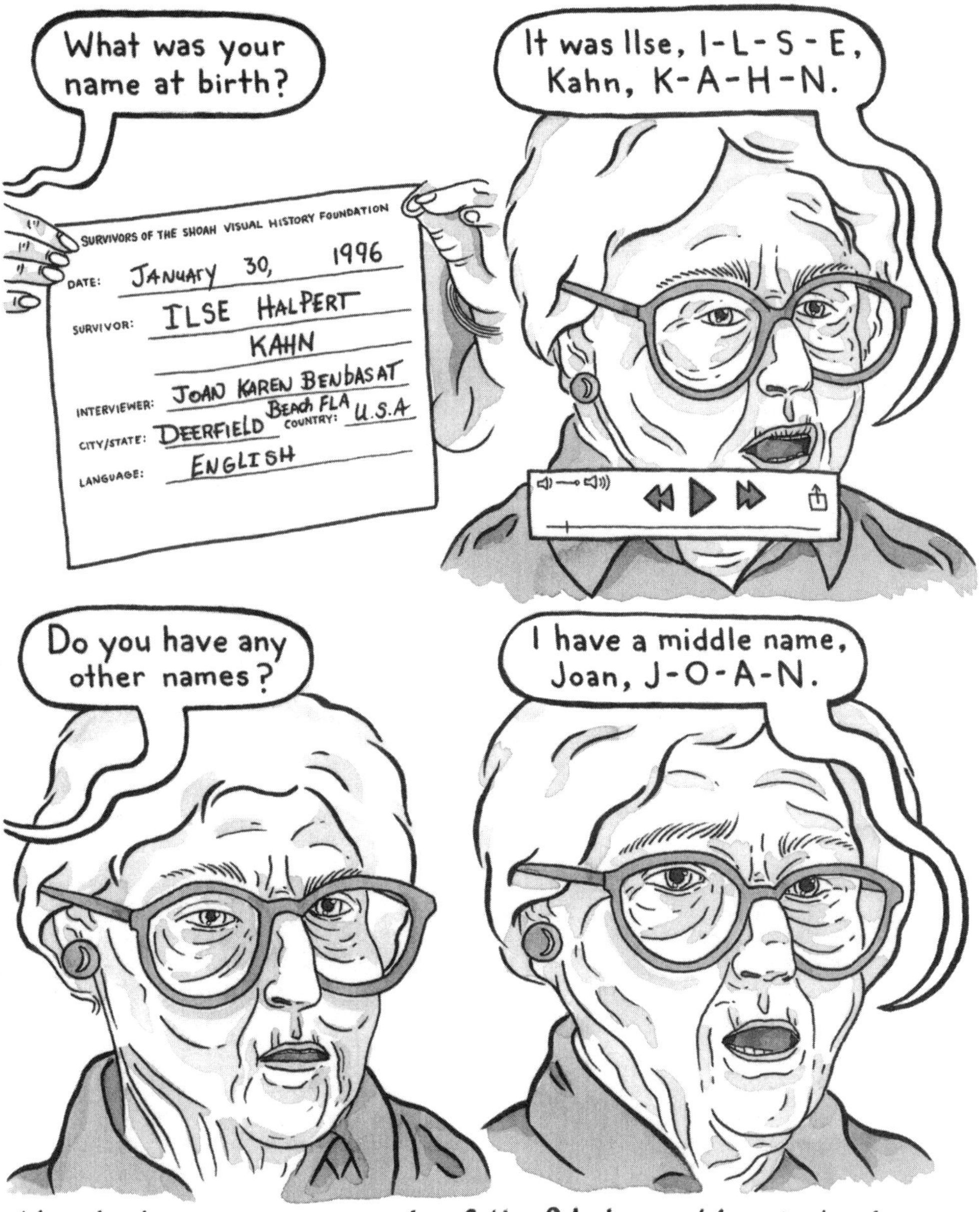
What was your name at birth?
SURVIVORS OF THE SHOAH VISUAL HISTORY FOUNDATION
DATE: JANUARY 30, 1996
SURVIVOR: ILSE HALPERT KAHN
INTERVIEWER: JOAN KAREN BENBASAT
CITY/STATE: DEERFIELD BEACH FLA COUNTRY: U.S.A
LANGUAGE: ENGLISH
It was Ilse, I-L-S-E, Kahn, K-A-H-N.
Do you have any other names?
I have a middle name, Joan, J-O-A-N.

Her testimony was episodic, full of holes and heroic deeds. I don't know how much she left out intentionally or what she had forgotten on purpose.

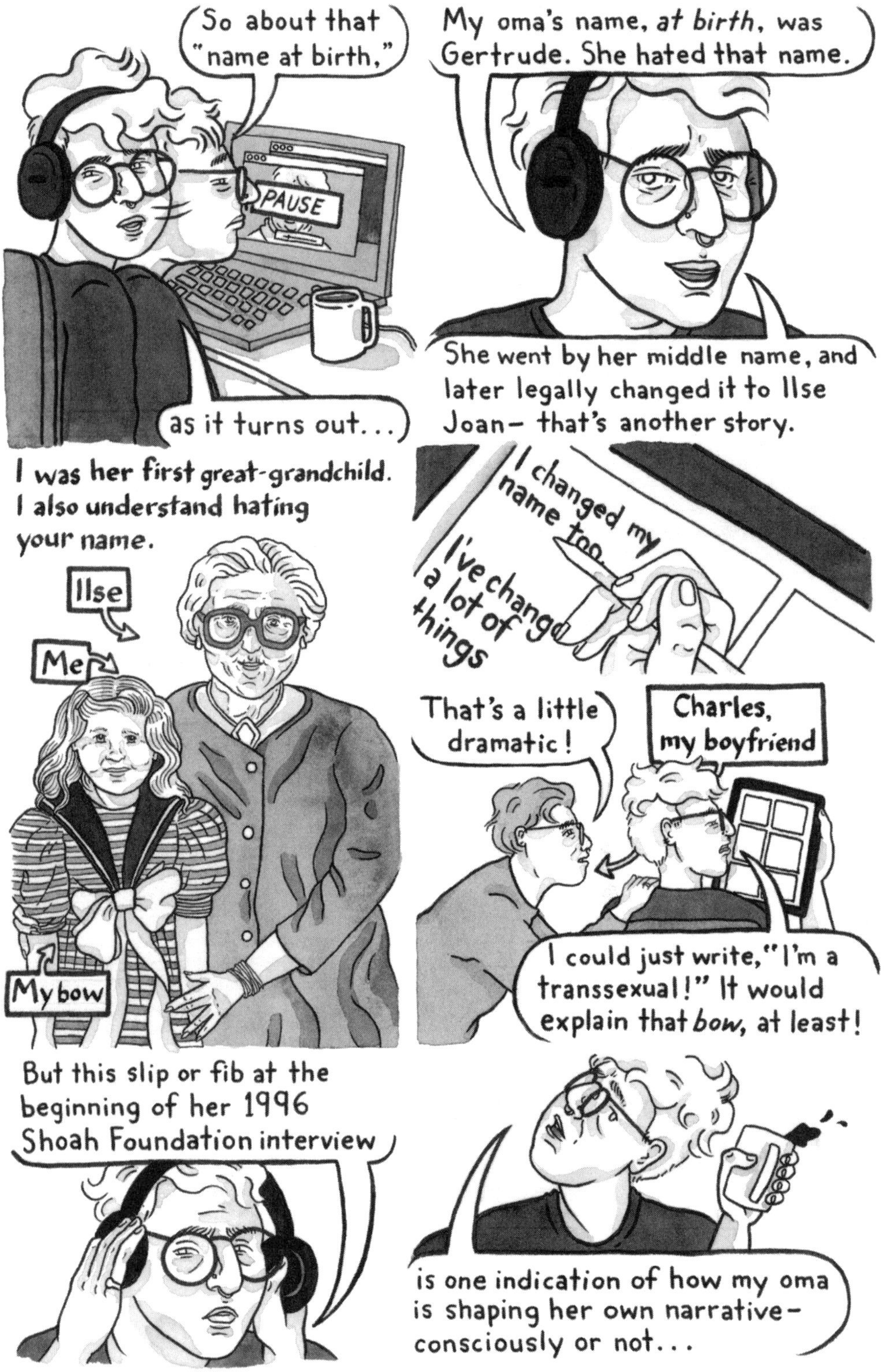
So about that "name at birth,"
PAUSE
as it turns out...
My oma's name, *at birth*, was Gertrude. She hated that name.
She went by her middle name, and later legally changed it to Ilse Joan— that's another story.
I was her first great-grandchild. I also understand hating your name.
I changed my name too.
I've changed a lot of things
Ilse
Me
My bow
That's a little dramatic!
Charles, my boyfriend
I could just write, "I'm a transsexual!" It would explain that *bow*, at least!
But this slip or fib at the beginning of her 1996 Shoah Foundation interview
is one indication of how my oma is shaping her own narrative— consciously or not...

My opa never got to tell his story.

Scholar Marianne Hirsch coined the term "postmemory" to describe ties to the past "mediated not by recall but by imaginative investment, projection, and creation..."

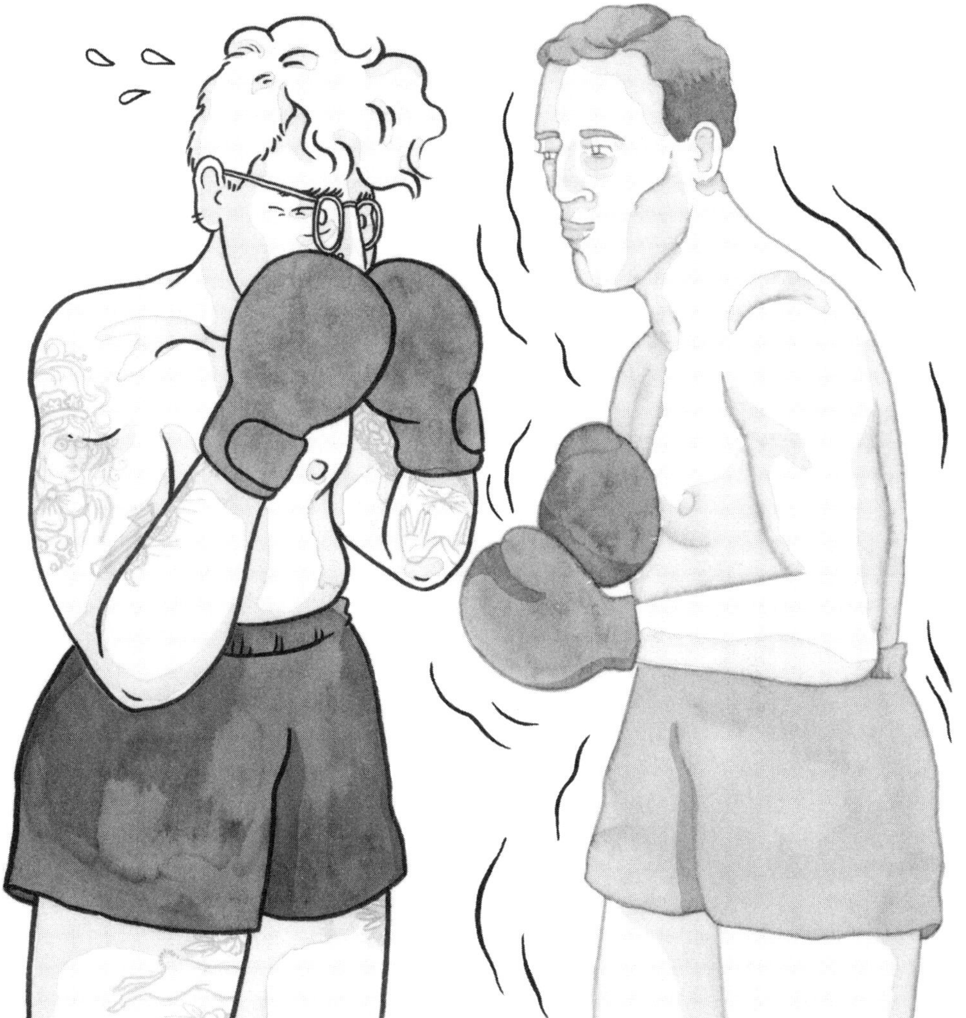

The thing is – I am steeped in my oma's account, but I am looking for *him* in *her* archive. And, it turns out, for myself in him.

His name was Erich Levi.

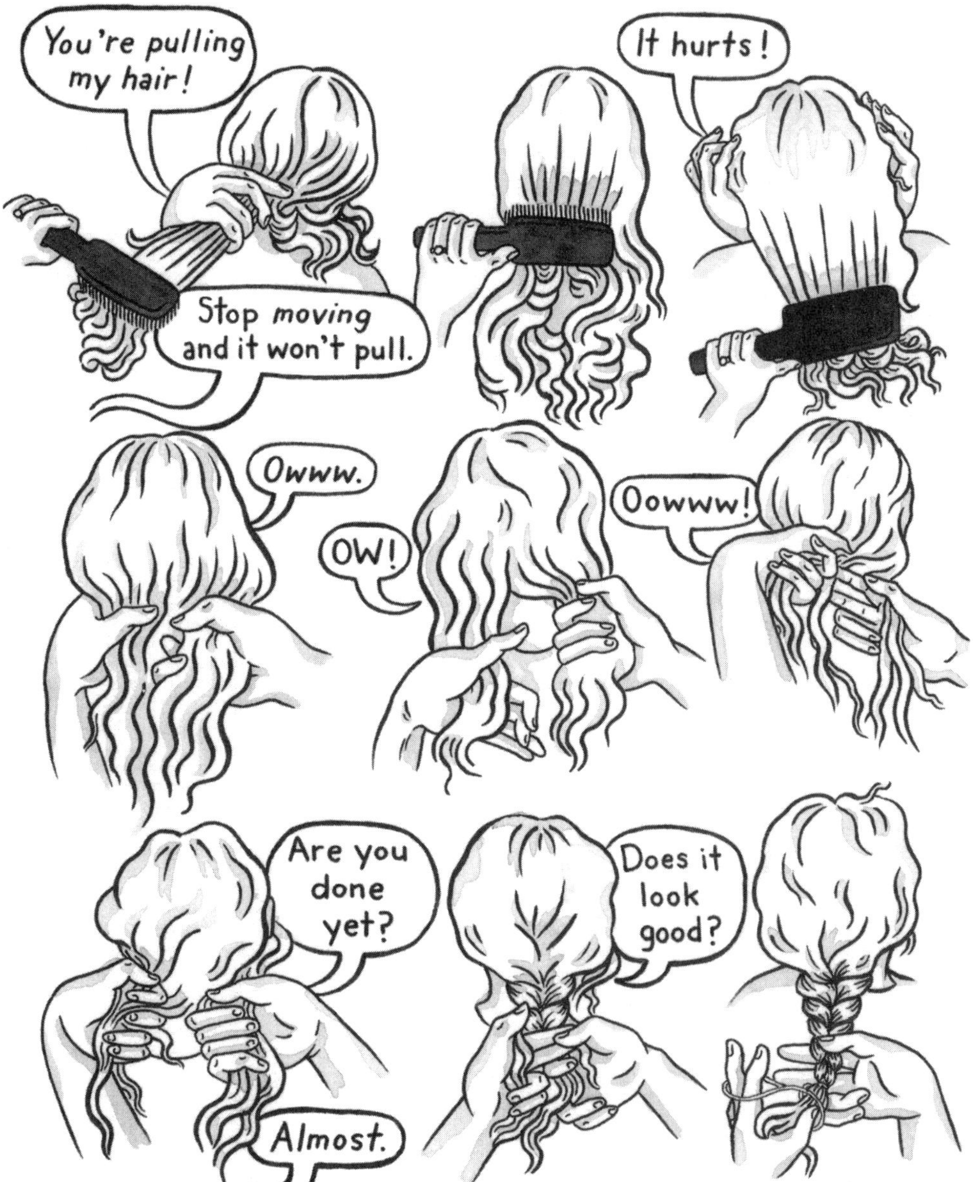
You're pulling my hair!
Stop moving and it won't pull.
It hurts!
Owww.
OW!
Oowww!
Are you done yet?
Almost.
Does it look good?

PART 1

TRAUMA TIME TRAVEL

I'm the oldest of four kids — my parents are *very* attached to the idea of having four *girls*. We are still working on this.

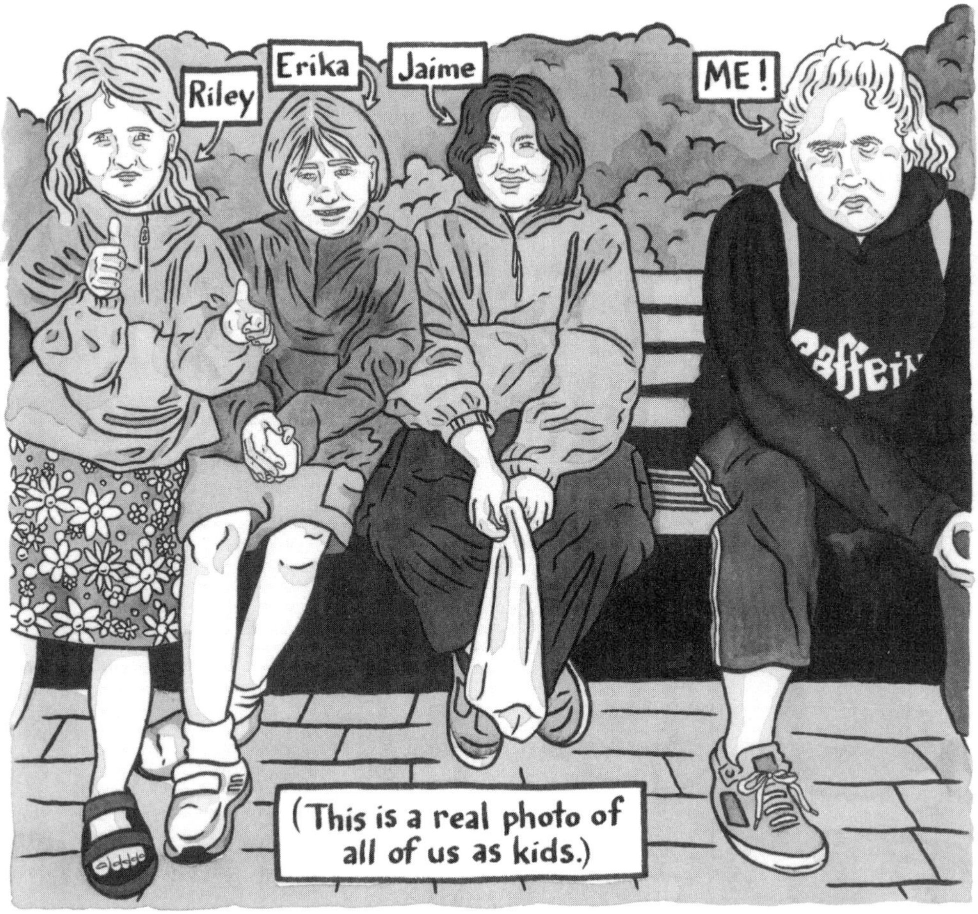
Riley
Erika
Jaime
ME!
(This is a real photo of all of us as kids.)

It's literally their license plate, to this day.

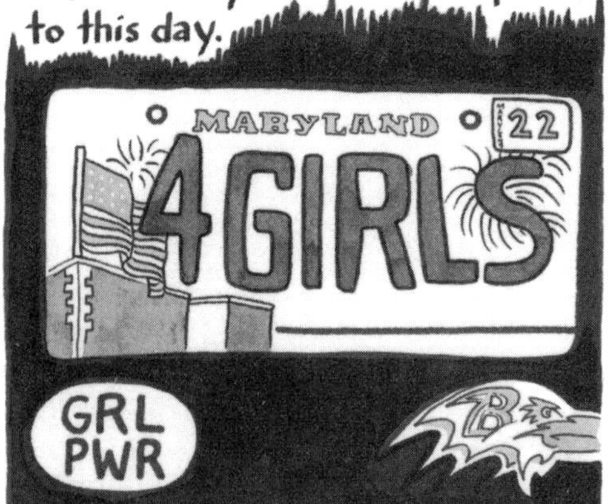
MARYLAND
22
4GIRLS
GRL PWR

My gender is far from the only thing they find perplexing about me...

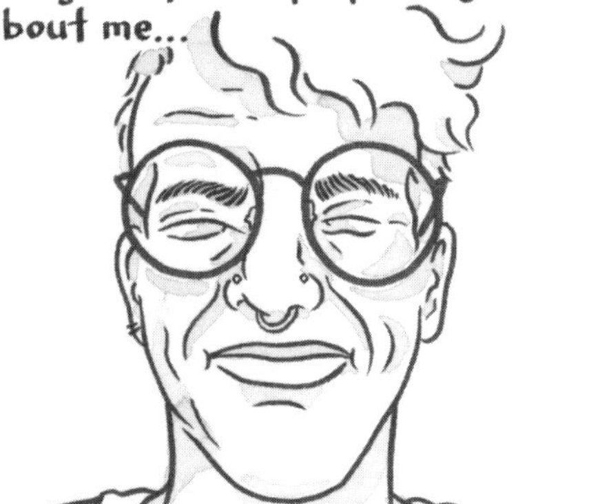

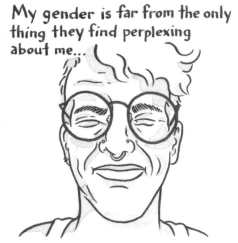

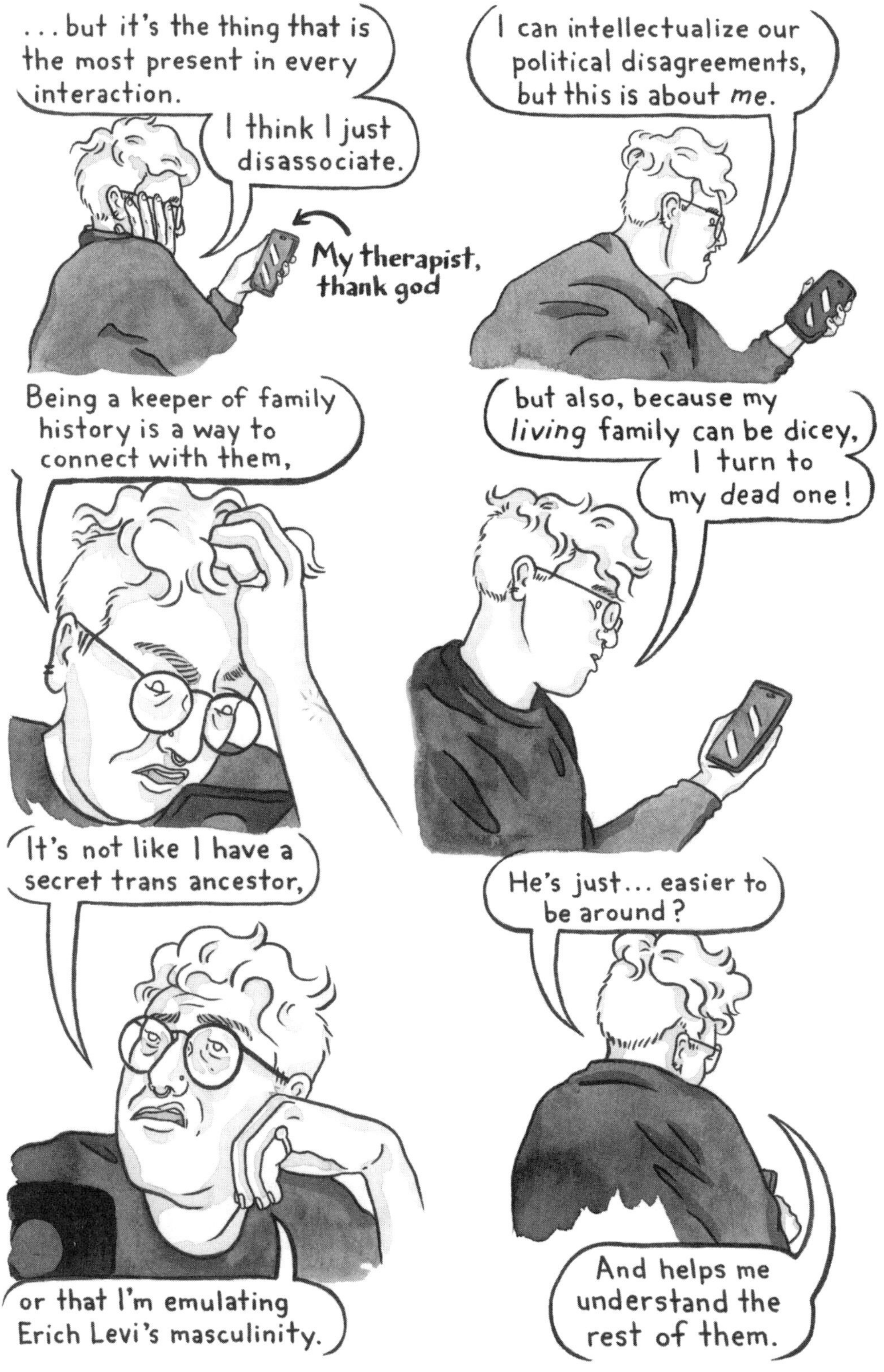

...but it's the thing that is the most present in every interaction.
I think I just disassociate.
My therapist, thank god
I can intellectualize our political disagreements, but this is about *me*.
Being a keeper of family history is a way to connect with them,
but also, because my *living* family can be dicey,
I turn to my *dead* one!
It's not like I have a secret trans ancestor,
or that I'm emulating Erich Levi's masculinity.
He's just... easier to be around?
And helps me understand the rest of them.

Before I understand the details of my specific family history, as a child, I was fairly convinced that, if I wasn't vigilant,

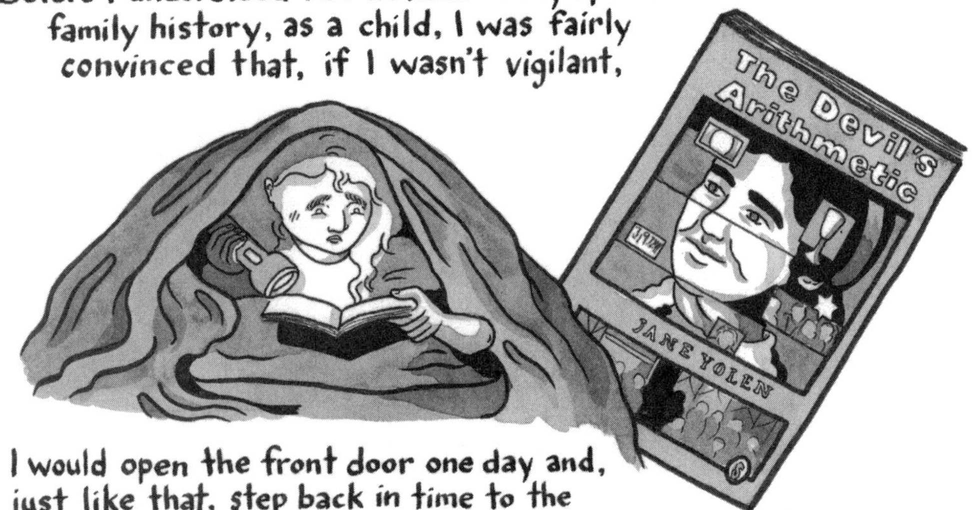
The Devil's Arithmetic
JANE YOLEN

I would open the front door one day and, just like that, step back in time to the Holocaust, where I would, paradoxically, have to sacrifice myself and die in a concentration camp in order to save my own ancestor, so I could then be born.

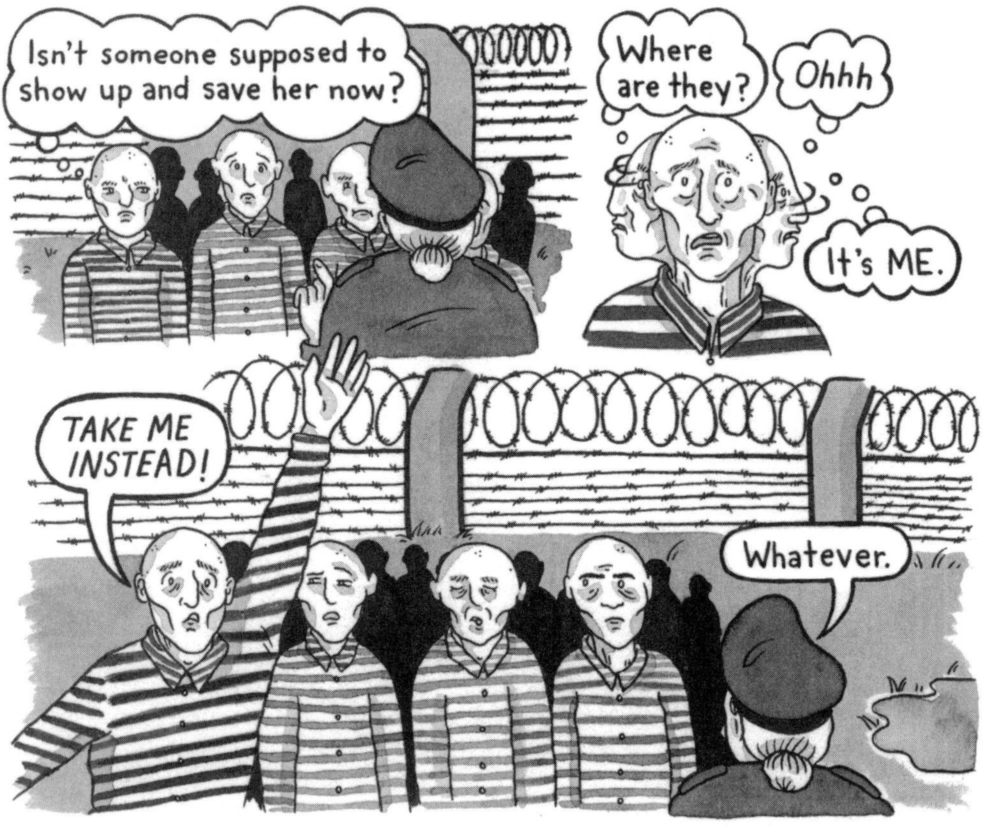
Isn't someone supposed to show up and save her now?
Where are they?
Ohhh
It's ME.
TAKE ME INSTEAD!
Whatever.

This is one way, maybe, to think about intergenerational trauma—

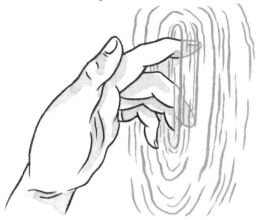

like time travel we didn't want, much less ask for...Like,

the skin between now and then is a little bit thin...

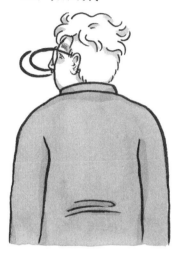

For a while, I thought this lived in my body, a little time capsule

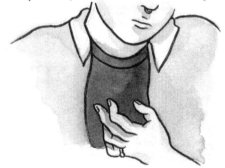

that could explain why things felt so... heavy.

I'm having a hard time.

For a while, I felt like I was full of ghosts.

Sometimes I wonder in what ways I would be different if I never learned the story.

But I don't remember a time when I didn't know about genocide.

Still my therapist

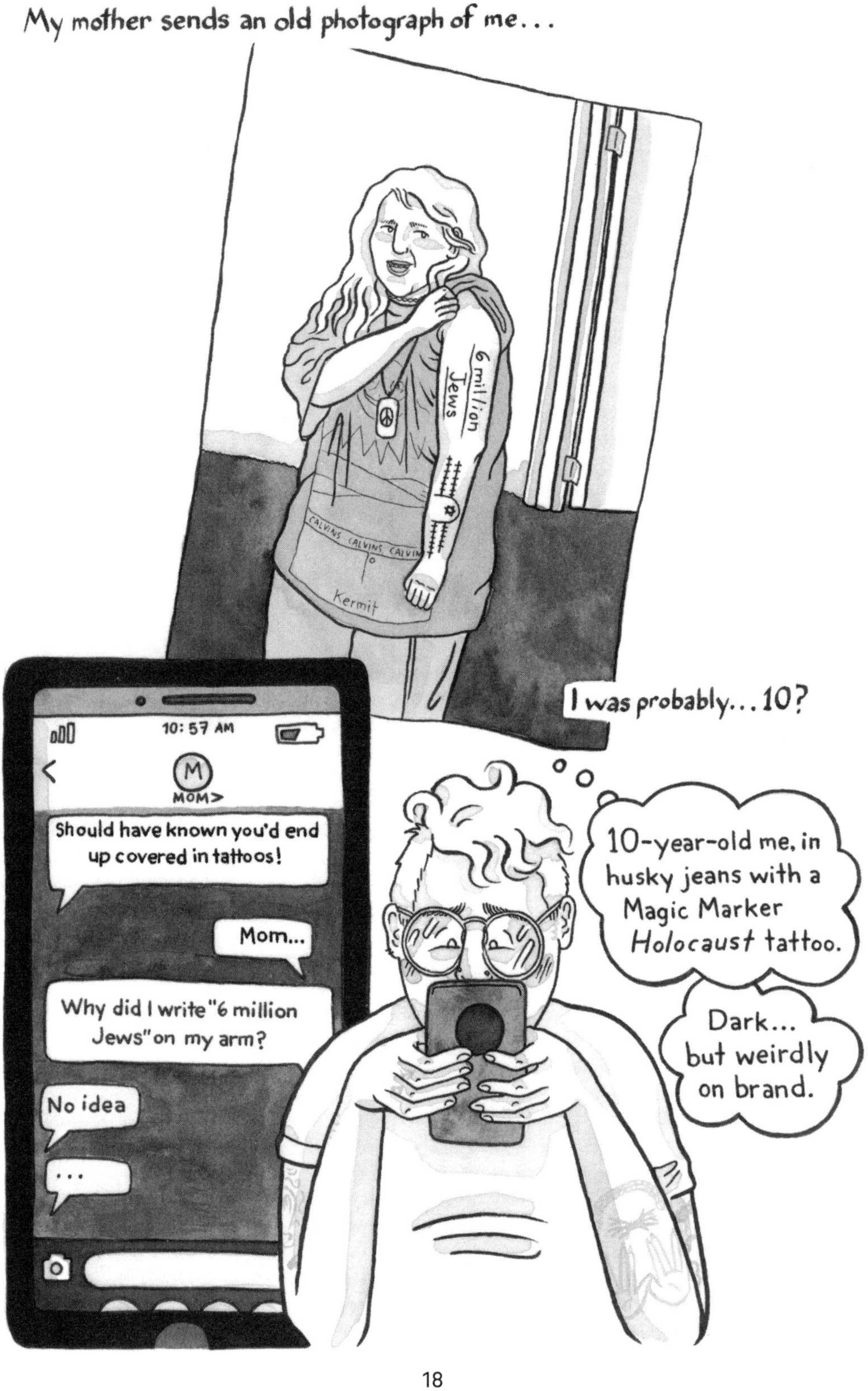
My mother sends an old photograph of me...
6 million Jews
CALVINS CALVINS CALVINS
Kermit
I was probably... 10?
10:57 AM
M
MOM>
Should have known you'd end up covered in tattoos!
Mom...
Why did I write "6 million Jews" on my arm?
No idea
...
10-year-old me, in husky jeans with a Magic Marker *Holocaust* tattoo.
Dark... but weirdly on brand.

I remember, at recess —

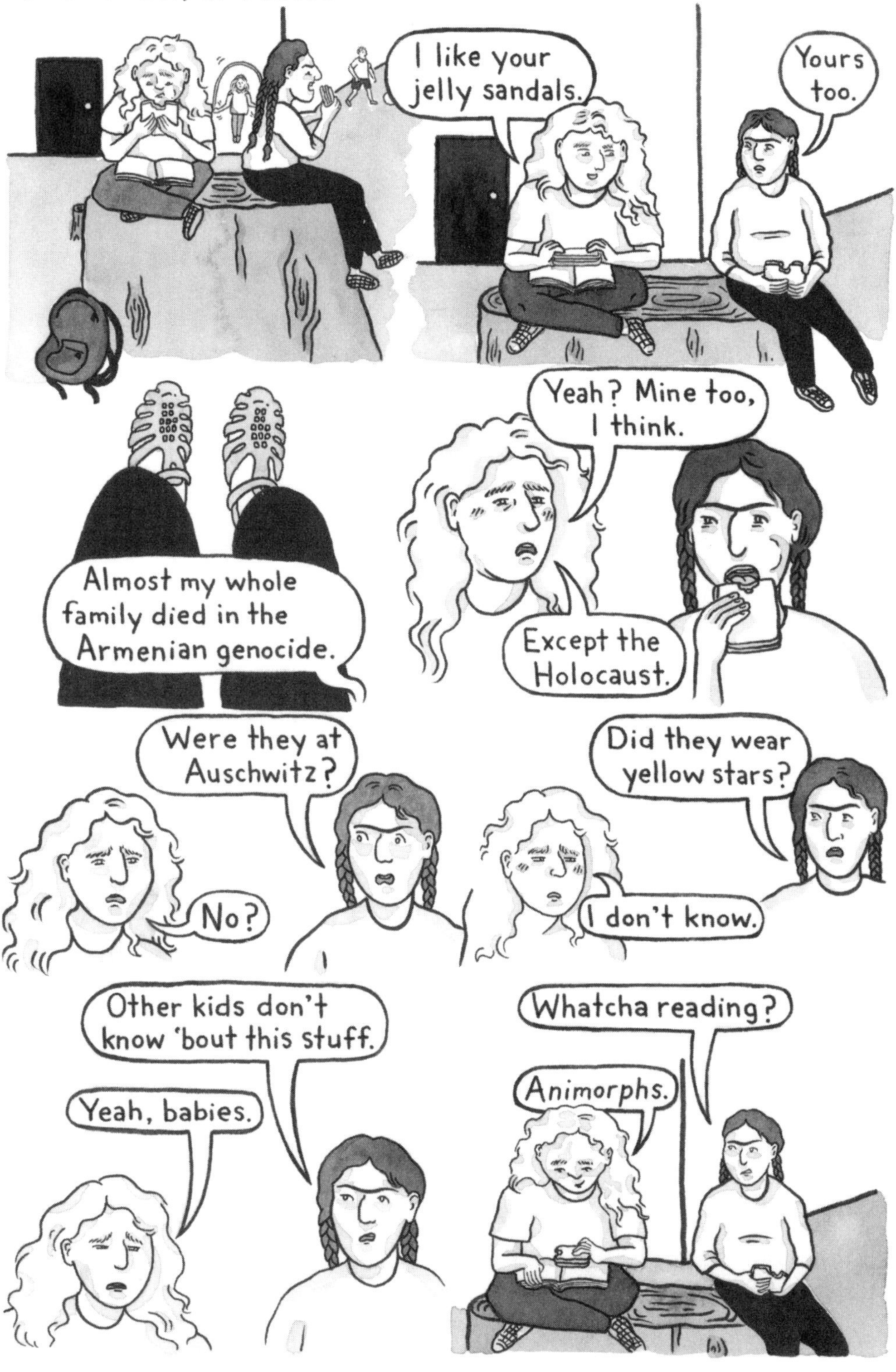
I like your jelly sandals.
Yours too.
Almost my whole family died in the Armenian genocide.
Yeah? Mine too, I think.
Except the Holocaust.
Were they at Auschwitz?
No?
Did they wear yellow stars?
I don't know.
Other kids don't know 'bout this stuff.
Yeah, babies.
Whatcha reading?
Animorphs.

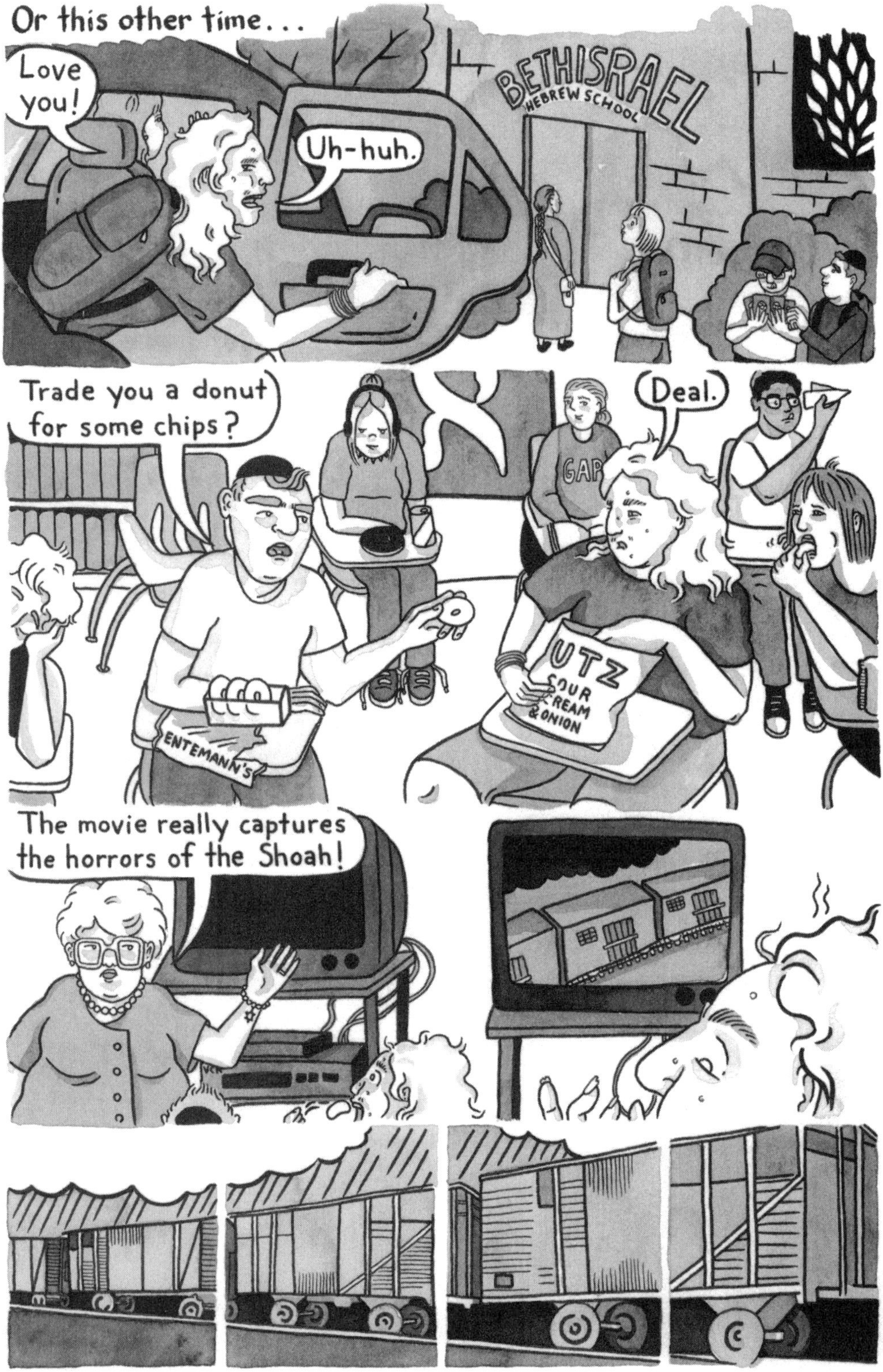

Or this other time...
Love you!
Uh-huh.
BETH ISRAEL HEBREW SCHOOL
Trade you a donut for some chips?
Deal.
GAP
UTZ SOUR CREAM & ONION
ENTEMANN'S
The movie really captures the horrors of the Shoah!

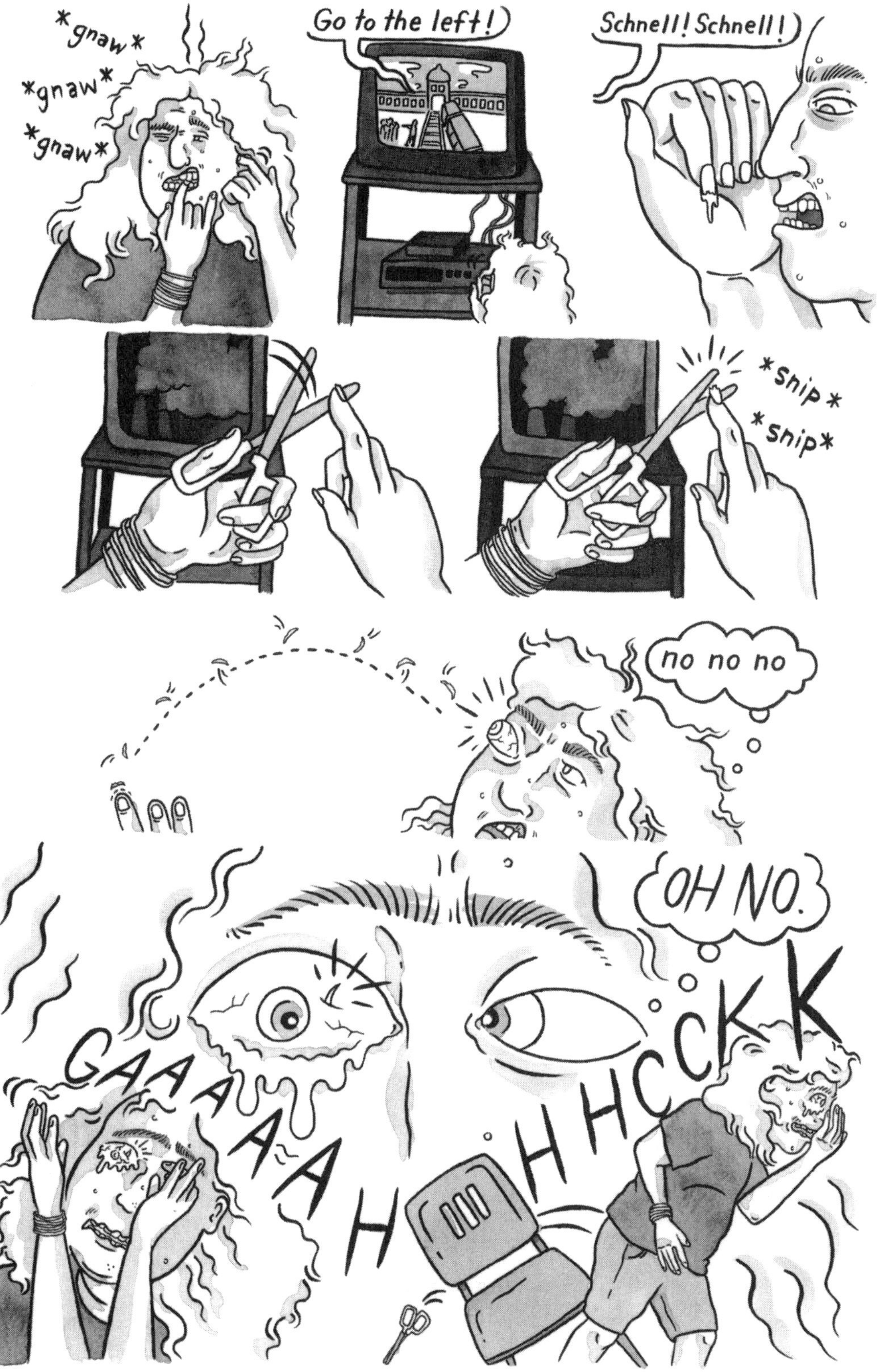
gnaw
gnaw
gnaw
Go to the left!
Schnell! Schnell!
snip
snip
no no no
OH NO.
GAAAAAHHHCCKK

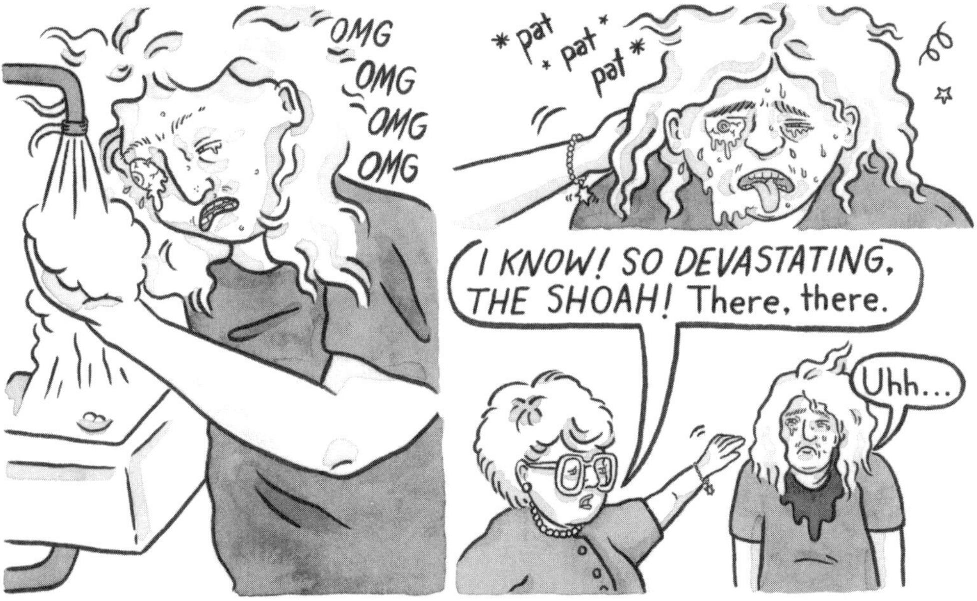
OMG
OMG
OMG
OMG
* pat * pat * pat *
I KNOW! SO DEVASTATING, THE SHOAH! There, there.
Uhh...

There was just... constant exposure.

Holocaust memorialization was an omnipresent and inherent part of my Jewish childhood.

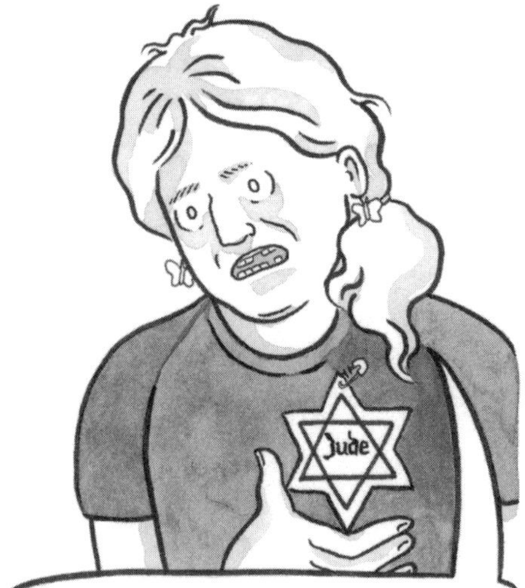
Jude
It's Yom HaShoah so I gotta wear this to remember six million Jews, okay– ya want one? I got more. Only if you're Jewish, duh. The message is like, NEVER AGAIN, okay?

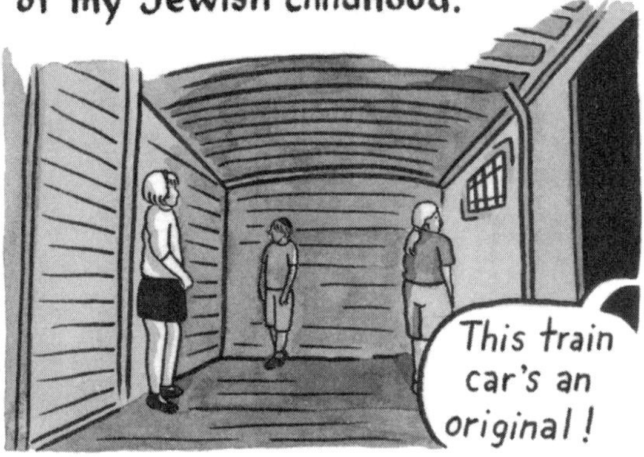
This train car's an original!

It made me kind of morbid.

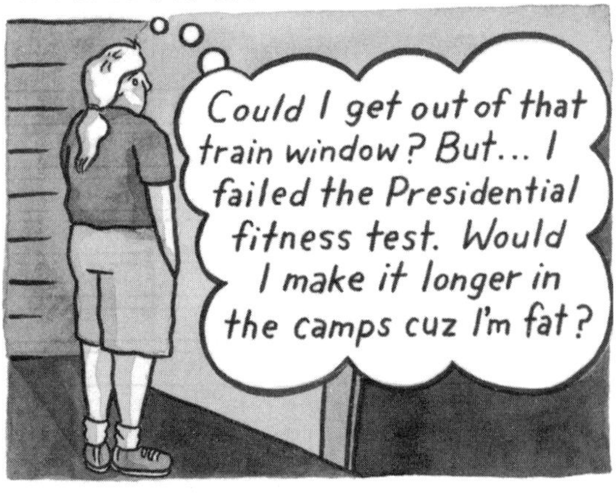
Could I get out of that train window? But... I failed the Presidential fitness test. Would I make it longer in the camps cuz I'm fat?

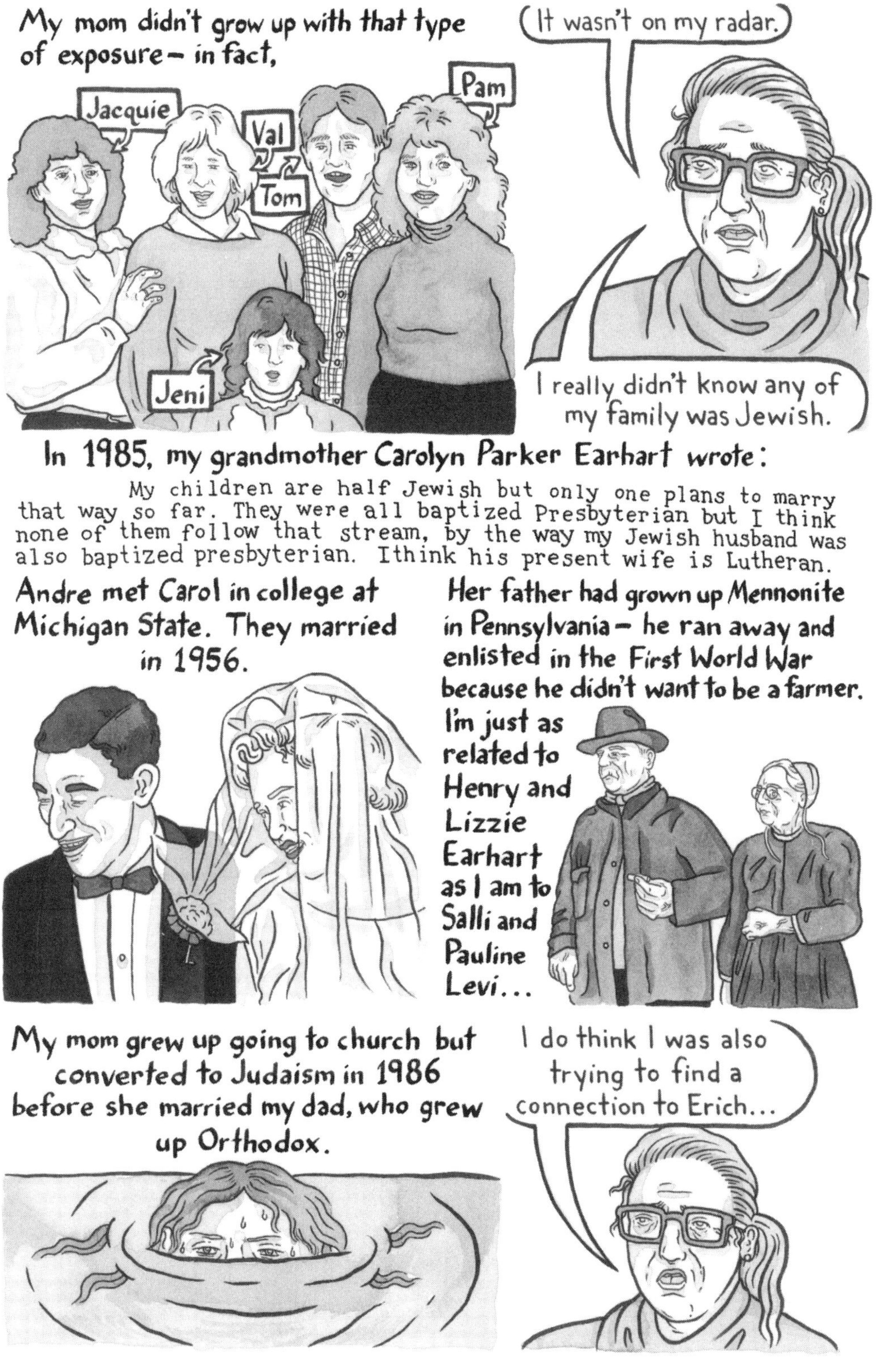
My mom didn't grow up with that type of exposure – in fact,
Jacquie
Val
Tom
Pam
Jeni
It wasn't on my radar.
I really didn't know any of my family was Jewish.
In 1985, my grandmother Carolyn Parker Earhart wrote:
My children are half Jewish but only one plans to marry that way so far. They were all baptized Presbyterian but I think none of them follow that stream, by the way my Jewish husband was also baptized presbyterian. Ithink his present wife is Lutheran.
Andre met Carol in college at Michigan State. They married in 1956.
Her father had grown up Mennonite in Pennsylvania – he ran away and enlisted in the First World War because he didn't want to be a farmer.
I'm just as related to Henry and Lizzie Earhart as I am to Salli and Pauline Levi...
My mom grew up going to church but converted to Judaism in 1986 before she married my dad, who grew up Orthodox.
I do think I was also trying to find a connection to Erich...

My oma said in her Shoah Foundation testimony:

When I came to America, I didn't know anymore who I was. And perhaps also that's why I turned against the religion, because I felt, if I'm being persecuted for that, I don't want any part of it.

But even with my lachrymose Jewish education, I grew up with a fierce pride in being Jewish and developed a strong antipathy toward the idea that Jewish identity was about inhabiting victimhood or in any way defined by antisemitism.

Conversely, my family connection to the Holocaust is not precisely the same as my family connection to Jewish identity, which includes my dad's Yiddish-speaking grandparents, who arrived in Baltimore before World War I.

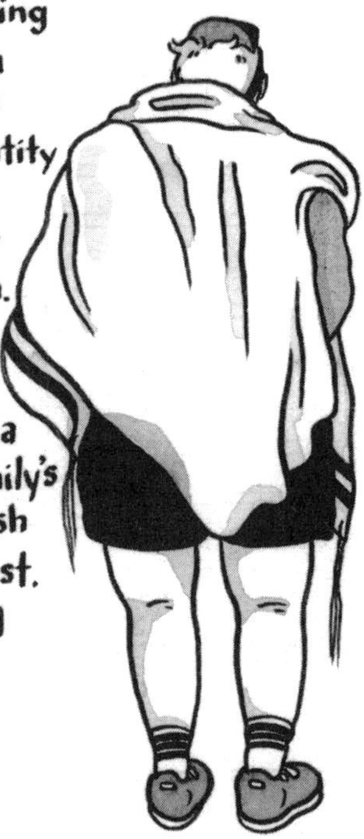

It still feels weird that a lot of my extended family's only relationship to Jewish identity is the Holocaust. Most of them are still practicing Christians.

Most of all, my Jewish identity is about being a part of living Jewish community, and practicing Judaism.

And also...

Literary critic Harold Bloom wrote of Kafka and Freud— "...their Jewishness consists in their intense obsession with interpretation... You don't have to be Jewish to be a compulsive interpreter, but, of course, it helps."

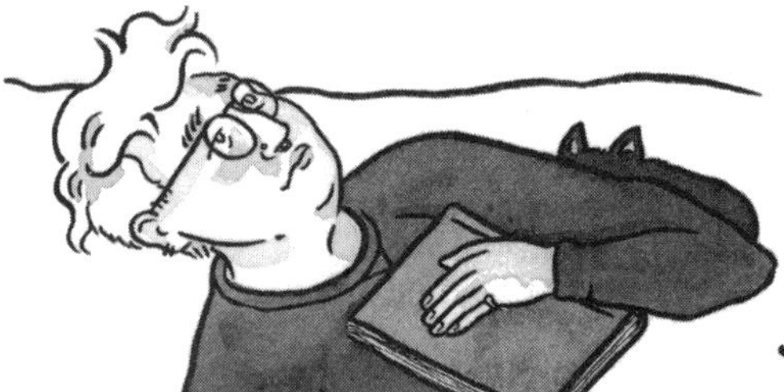

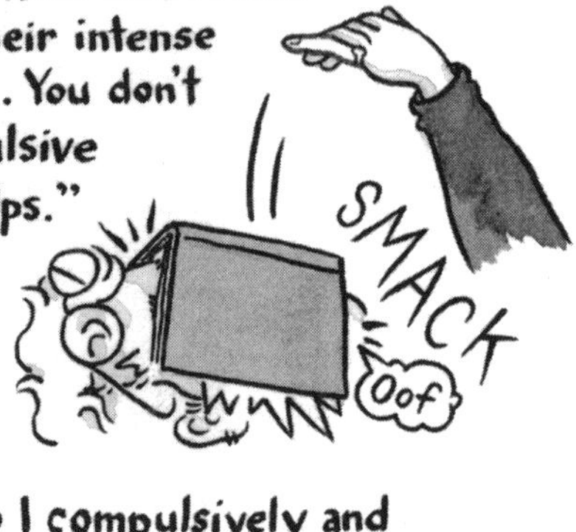
SMACK
Oof

So I compulsively and Jewishly interpret *everything* to *death*, always!

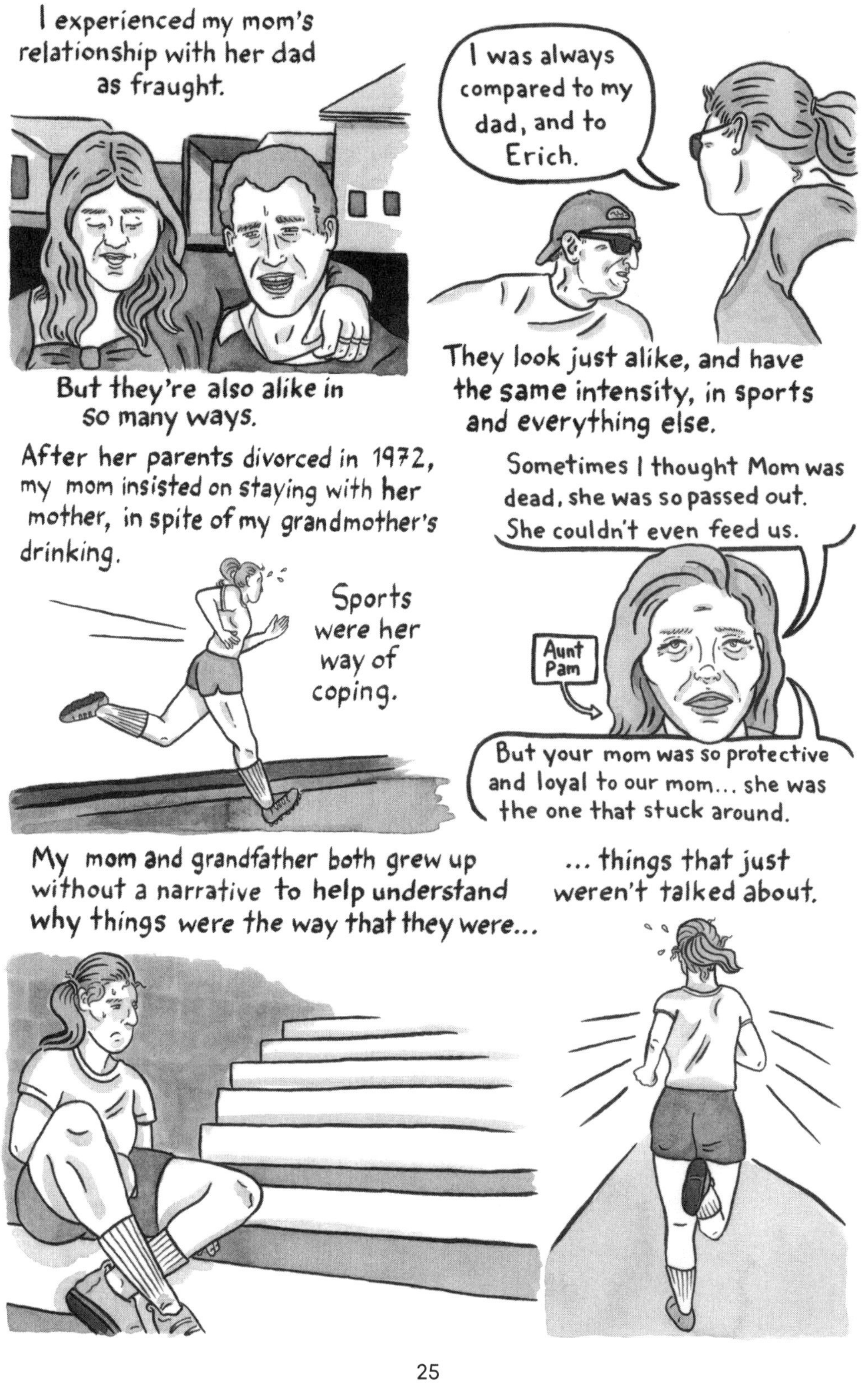
I experienced my mom's relationship with her dad as fraught.
But they're also alike in so many ways.
I was always compared to my dad, and to Erich.
They look just alike, and have the same intensity, in sports and everything else.
After her parents divorced in 1972, my mom insisted on staying with her mother, in spite of my grandmother's drinking.
Sports were her way of coping.
Sometimes I thought Mom was dead, she was so passed out. She couldn't even feed us.
Aunt Pam
But your mom was so protective and loyal to our mom... she was the one that stuck around.
My mom and grandfather both grew up without a narrative to help understand why things were the way that they were...
... things that just weren't talked about.

Meanwhile I'm out here practically *screaming*,

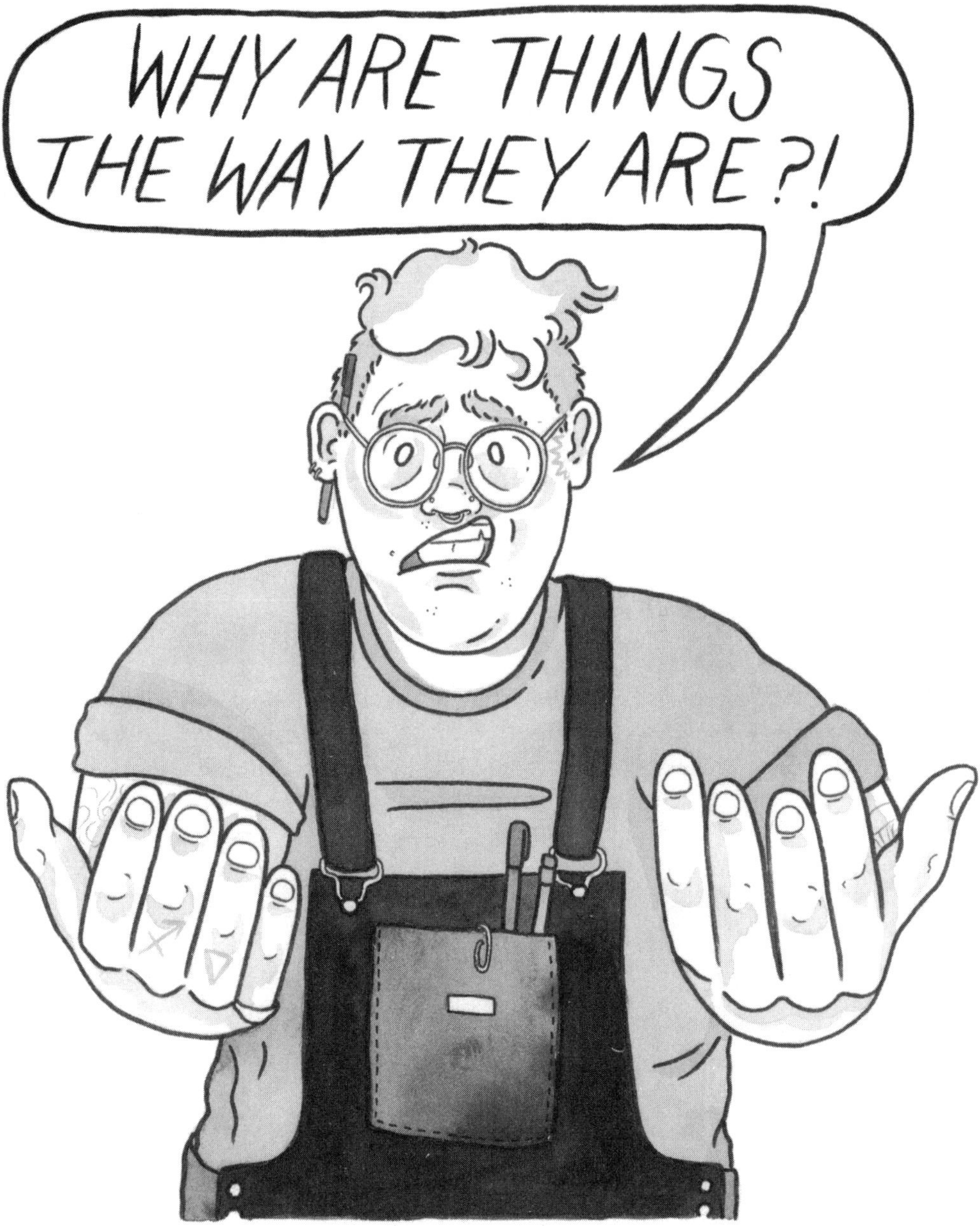
WHY ARE THINGS THE WAY THEY ARE?!

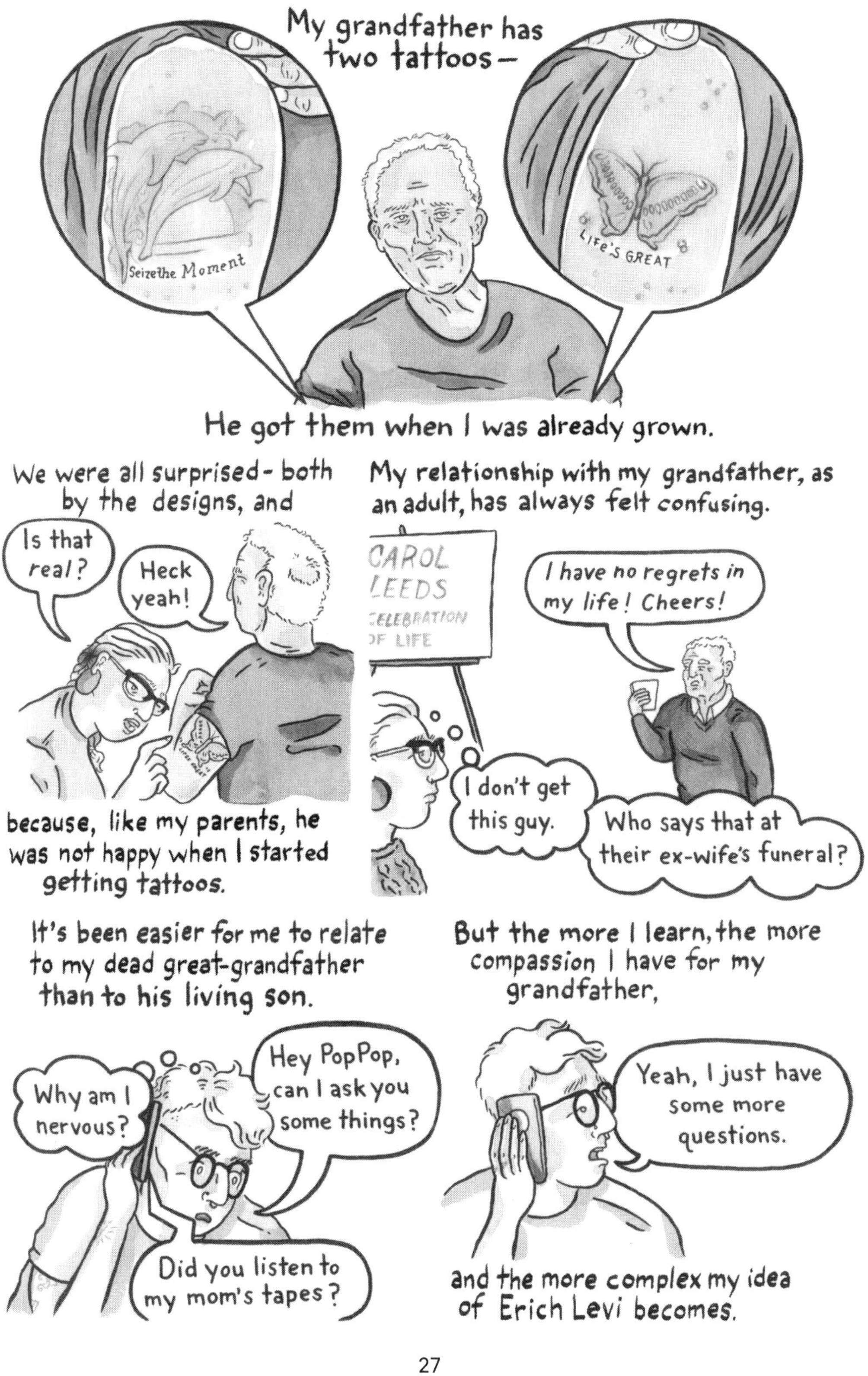

My grandfather has two tattoos–
Seize the Moment
LIFE'S GREAT
He got them when I was already grown.
We were all surprised– both by the designs, and
Is that real?
Heck yeah!
because, like my parents, he was not happy when I started getting tattoos.
My relationship with my grandfather, as an adult, has always felt confusing.
CAROL LEEDS CELEBRATION OF LIFE
I have no regrets in my life! Cheers!
I don't get this guy.
Who says that at their ex-wife's funeral?
It's been easier for me to relate to my dead great-grandfather than to his living son.
Why am I nervous?
Hey PopPop, can I ask you some things?
Did you listen to my mom's tapes?
But the more I learn, the more compassion I have for my grandfather,
Yeah, I just have some more questions.
and the more complex my idea of Erich Levi becomes.

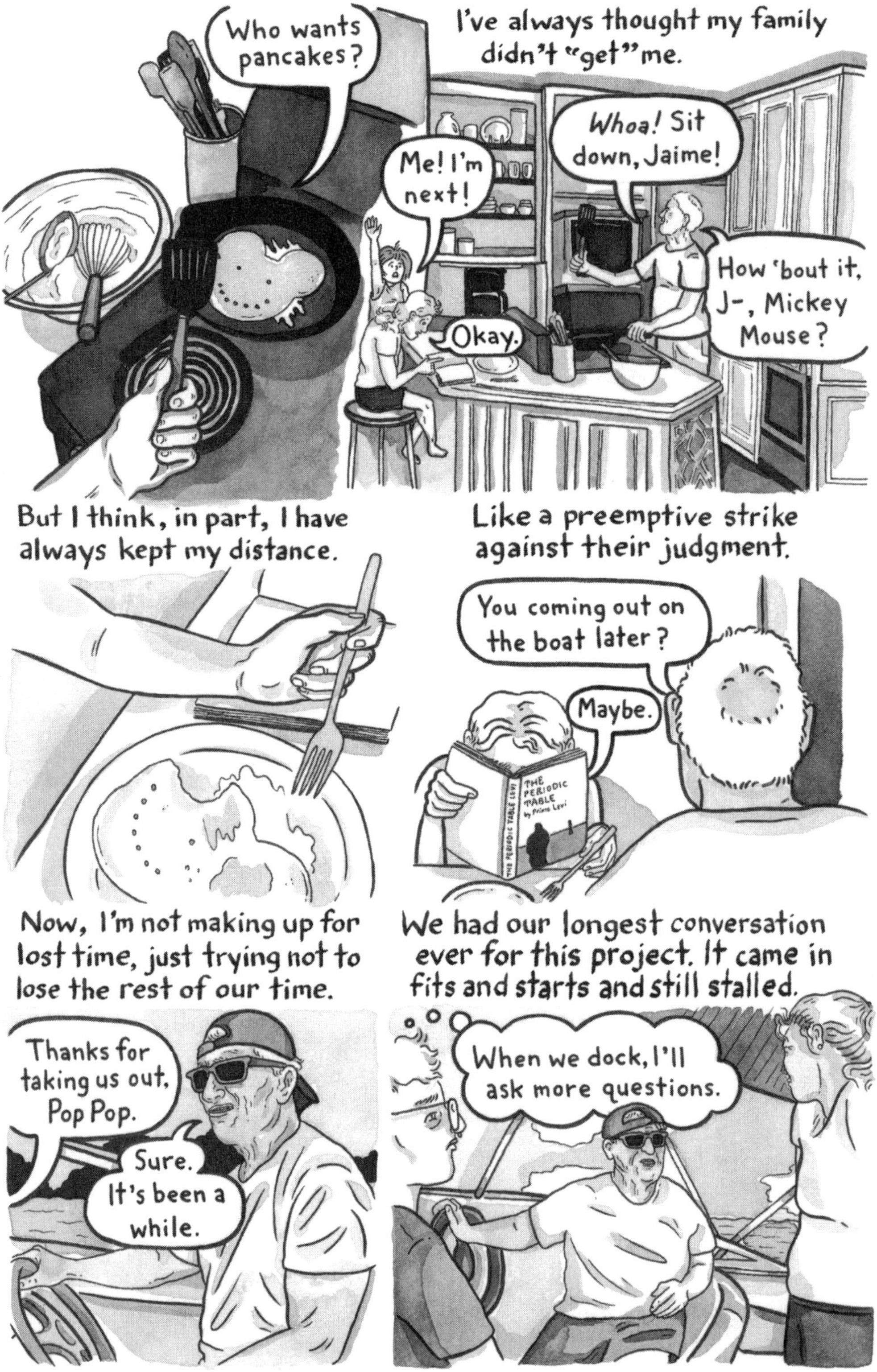
Who wants pancakes?
I've always thought my family didn't "get" me.
Me! I'm next!
Whoa! Sit down, Jaime!
How 'bout it, J-, Mickey Mouse?
Okay.
But I think, in part, I have always kept my distance.
Like a preemptive strike against their judgment.
You coming out on the boat later?
Maybe.
THE PERIODIC TABLE
Now, I'm not making up for lost time, just trying not to lose the rest of our time.
We had our longest conversation ever for this project. It came in fits and starts and still stalled.
Thanks for taking us out, Pop Pop.
Sure. It's been a while.
When we dock, I'll ask more questions.

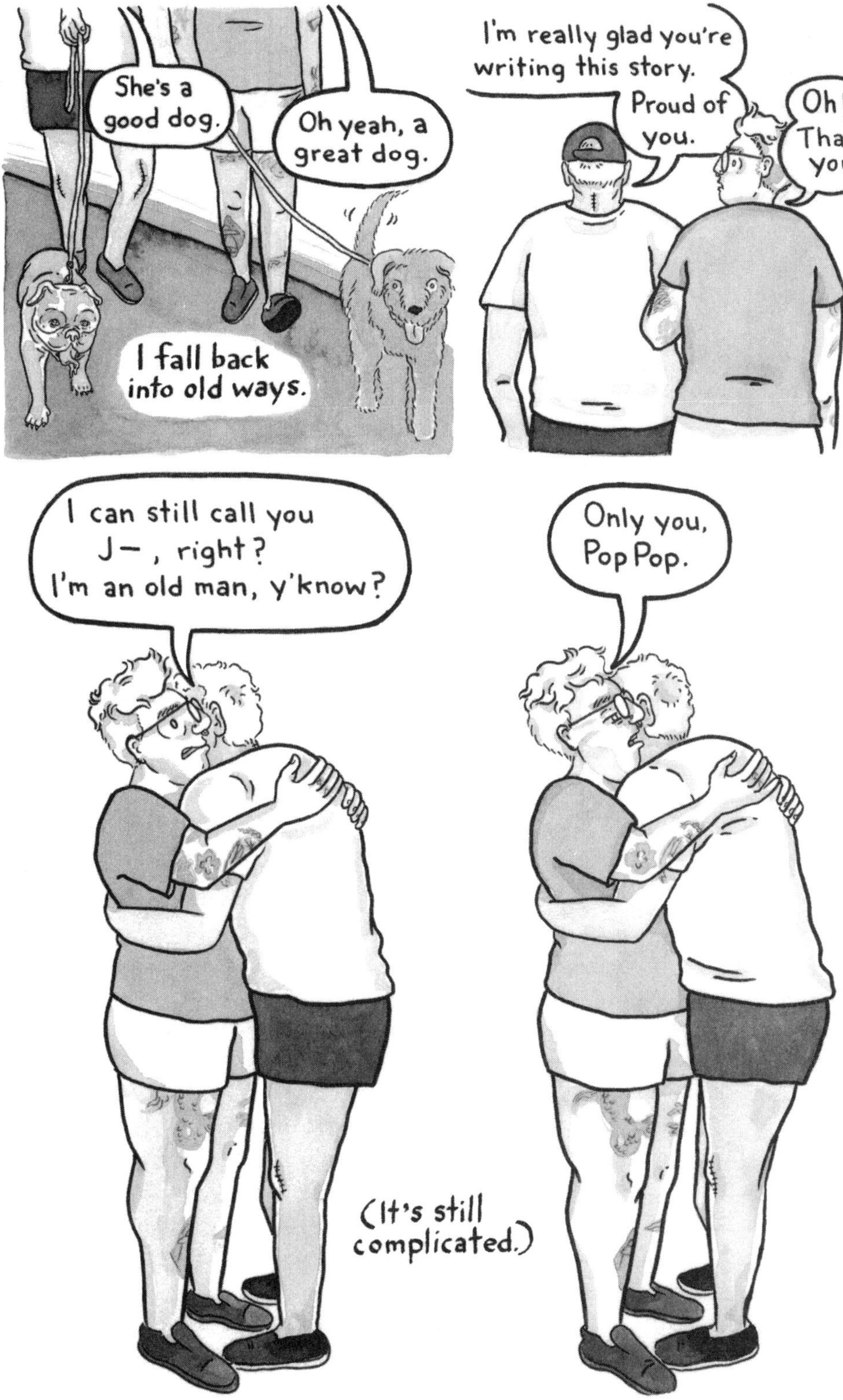
She's a good dog.
Oh yeah, a great dog.
I fall back into old ways.
I'm really glad you're writing this story.
Proud of you.
Oh! Thank you.
I can still call you J—, right? I'm an old man, y'know?
Only you, Pop Pop.
(It's still complicated.)

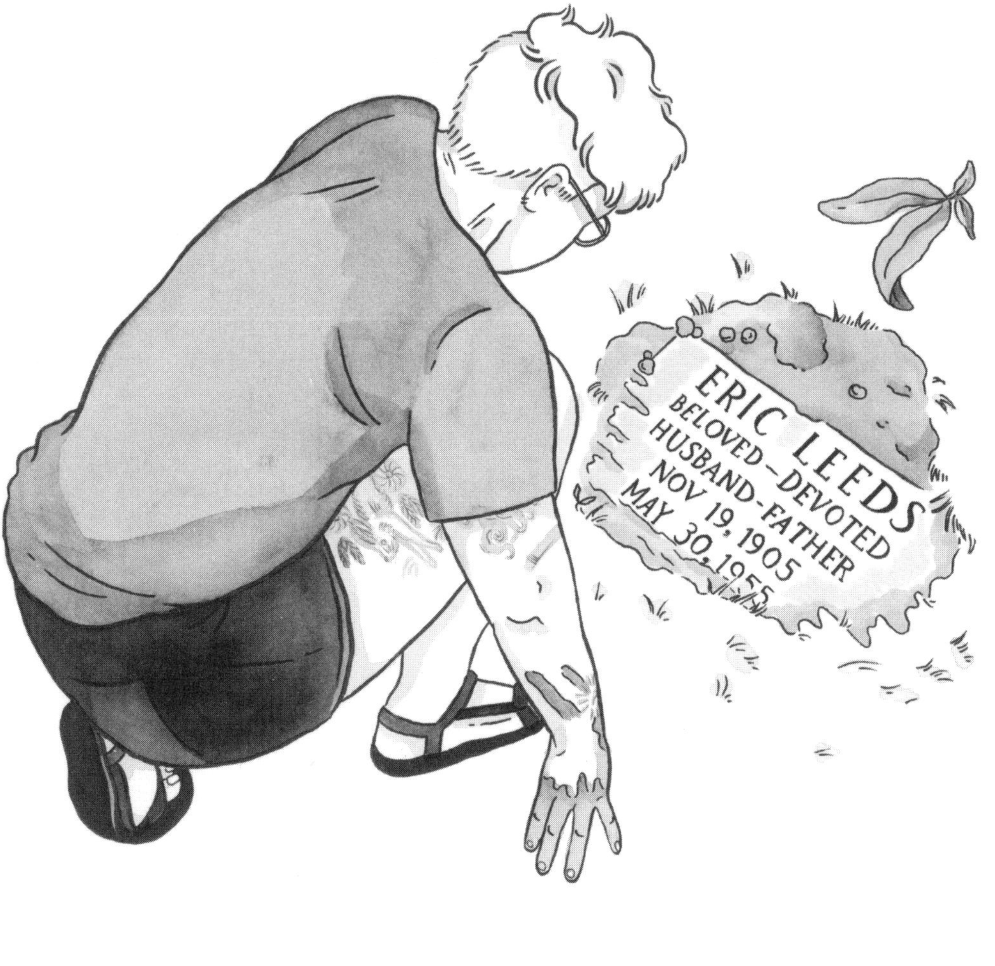
ERIC LEEDS
BELOVED – DEVOTED
HUSBAND – FATHER
NOV 19, 1905
MAY 30, 1955

PART 2

UNBURIED

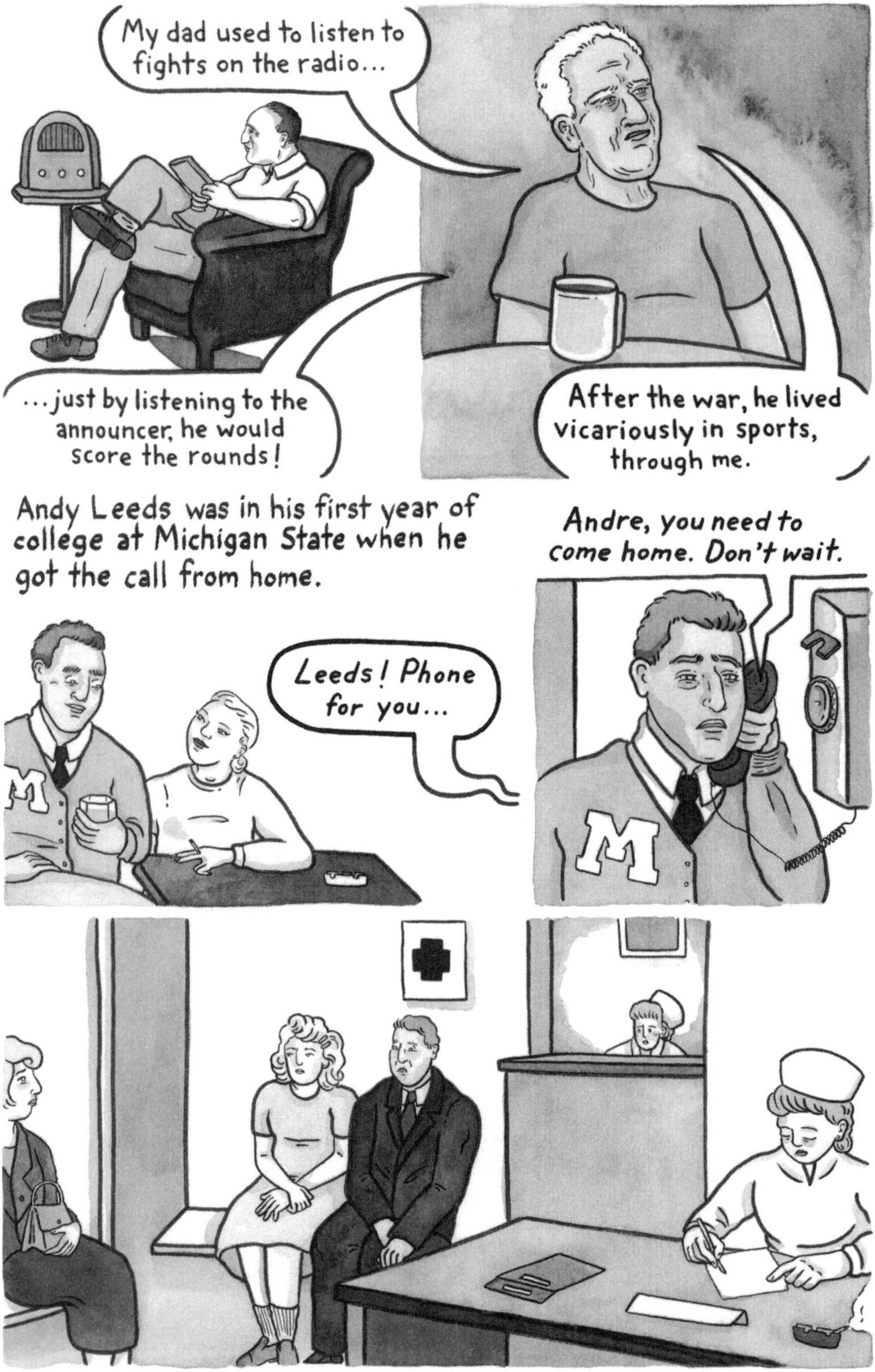
My dad used to listen to fights on the radio...
...just by listening to the announcer, he would score the rounds!
After the war, he lived vicariously in sports, through me.
Andy Leeds was in his first year of college at Michigan State when he got the call from home.
Leeds! Phone for you...
Andre, you need to come home. Don't wait.

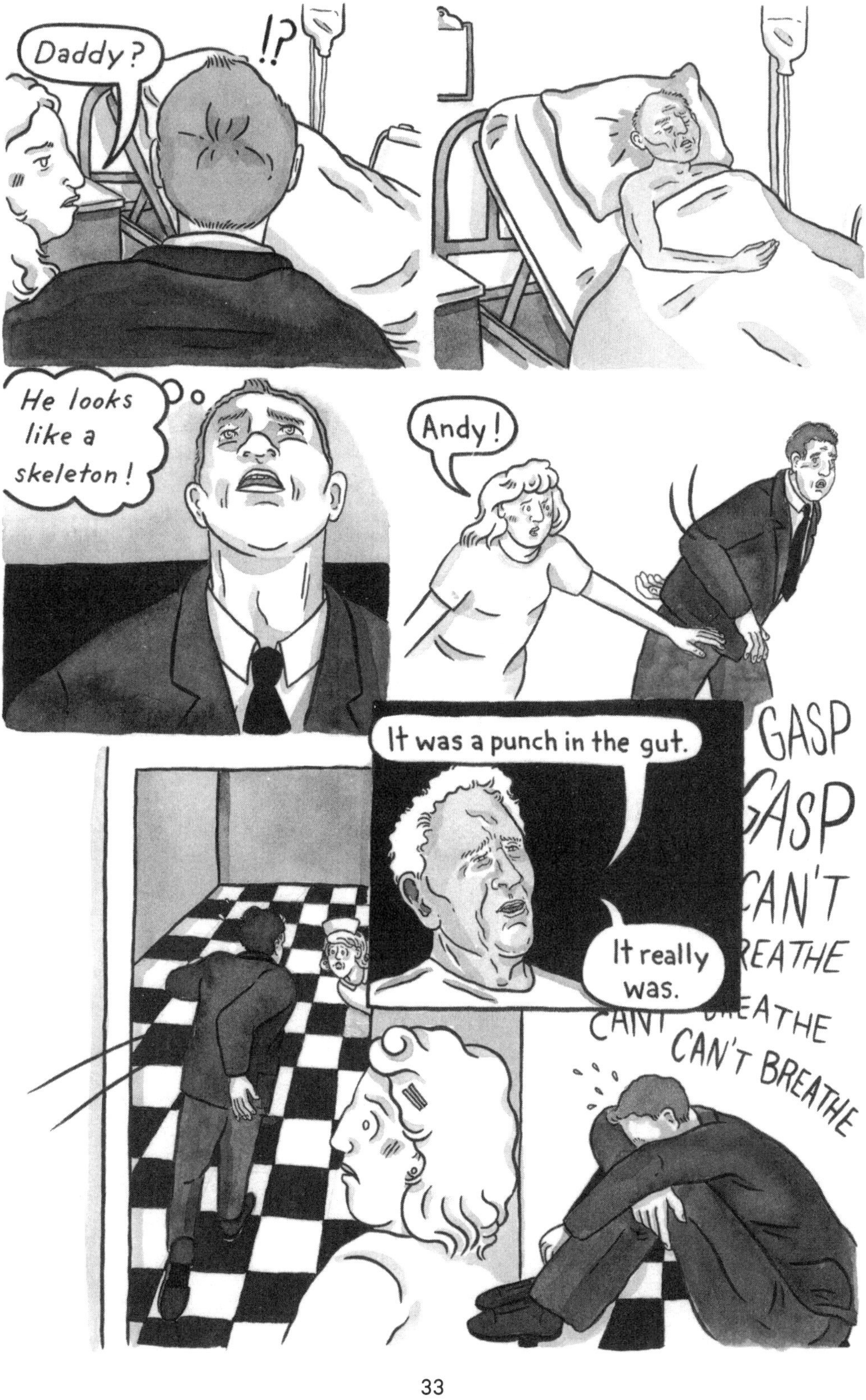
Daddy?
!?
He looks like a skeleton!
Andy!
It was a punch in the gut.
It really was.
GASP
GASP
CAN'T
CAN'T BREATHE

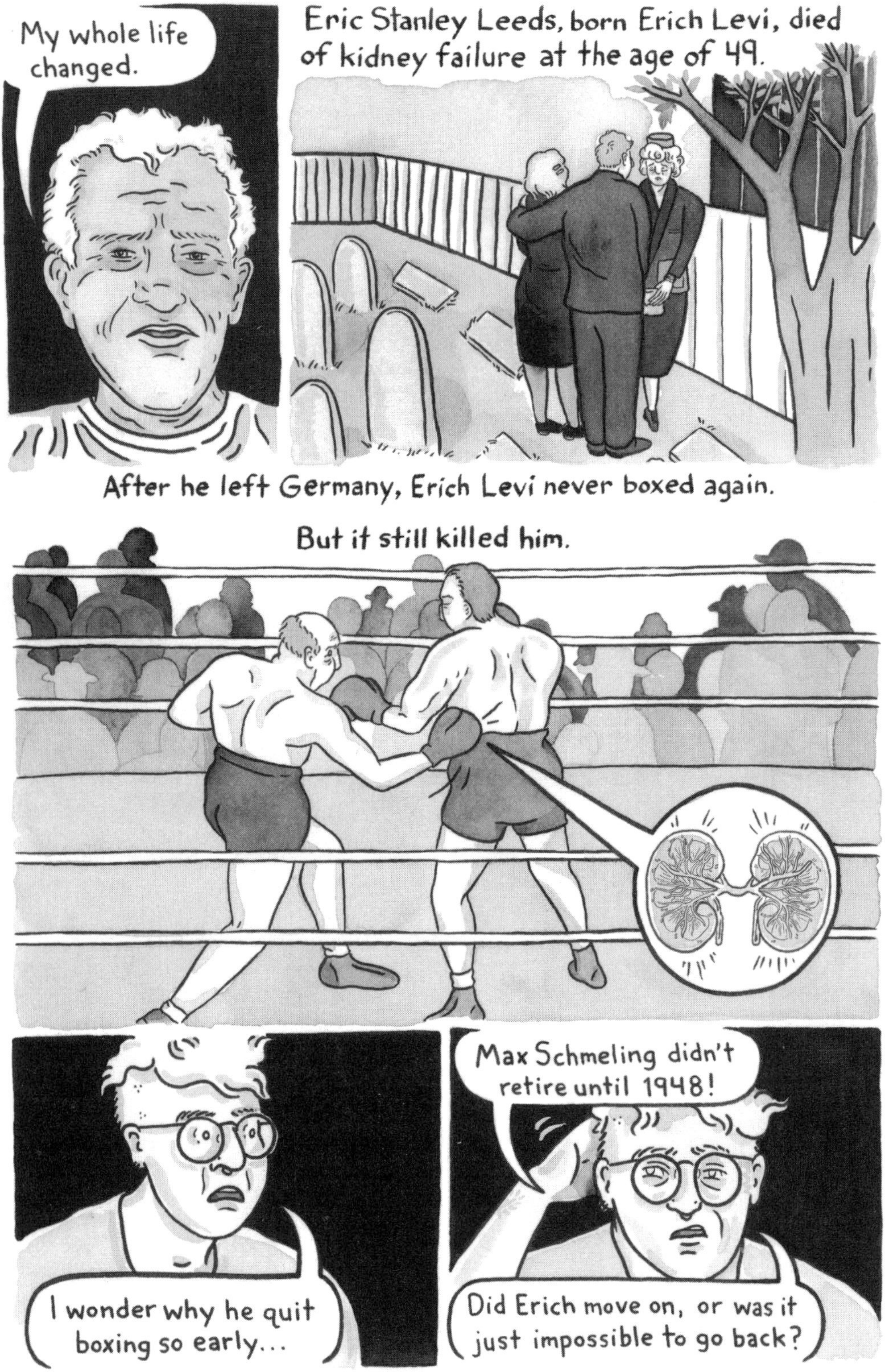
My whole life changed.
Eric Stanley Leeds, born Erich Levi, died of kidney failure at the age of 49.
After he left Germany, Erich Levi never boxed again.
But it still killed him.
I wonder why he quit boxing so early...
Max Schmeling didn't retire until 1948!
Did Erich move on, or was it just impossible to go back?

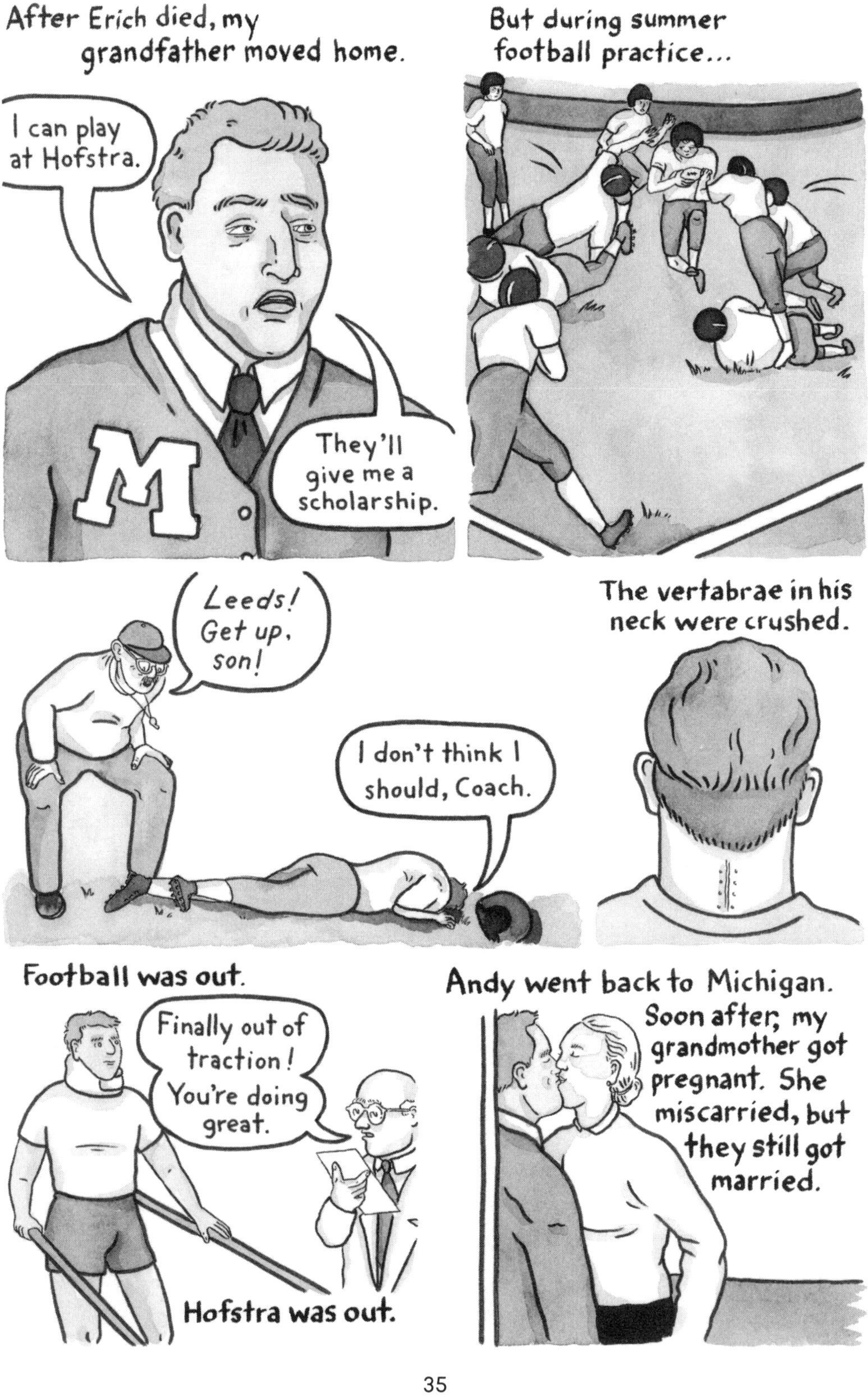
After Erich died, my grandfather moved home.
I can play at Hofstra.
They'll give me a scholarship.
But during summer football practice...
Leeds! Get up, son!
I don't think I should, Coach.
The vertabrae in his neck were crushed.
Football was out.
Finally out of traction! You're doing great.
Hofstra was out.
Andy went back to Michigan.
Soon after, my grandmother got pregnant. She miscarried, but they still got married.

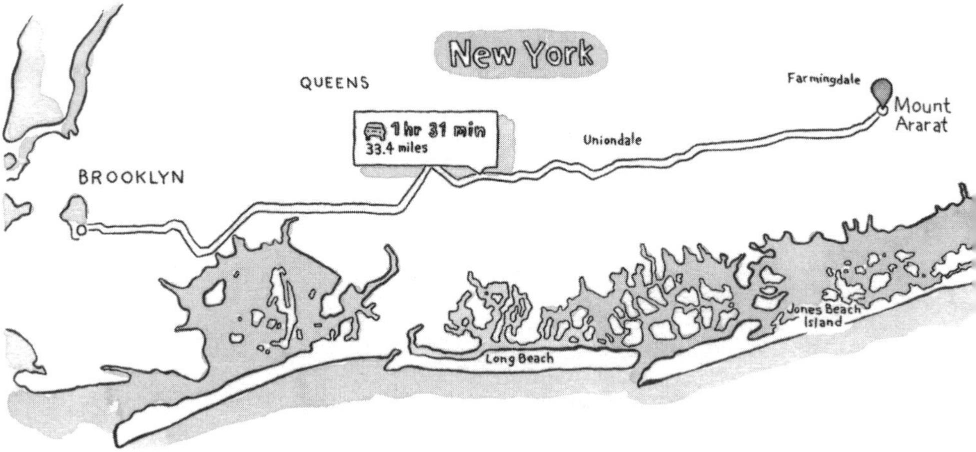
New York
QUEENS
Farmingdale
Mount Ararat
1 hr 31 min
33.4 miles
Uniondale
BROOKLYN
Jones Beach Island
Long Beach

I'd had the papers for Erich's grave plot for years, but I didn't realize how close it was to Brooklyn, out on Long Island.

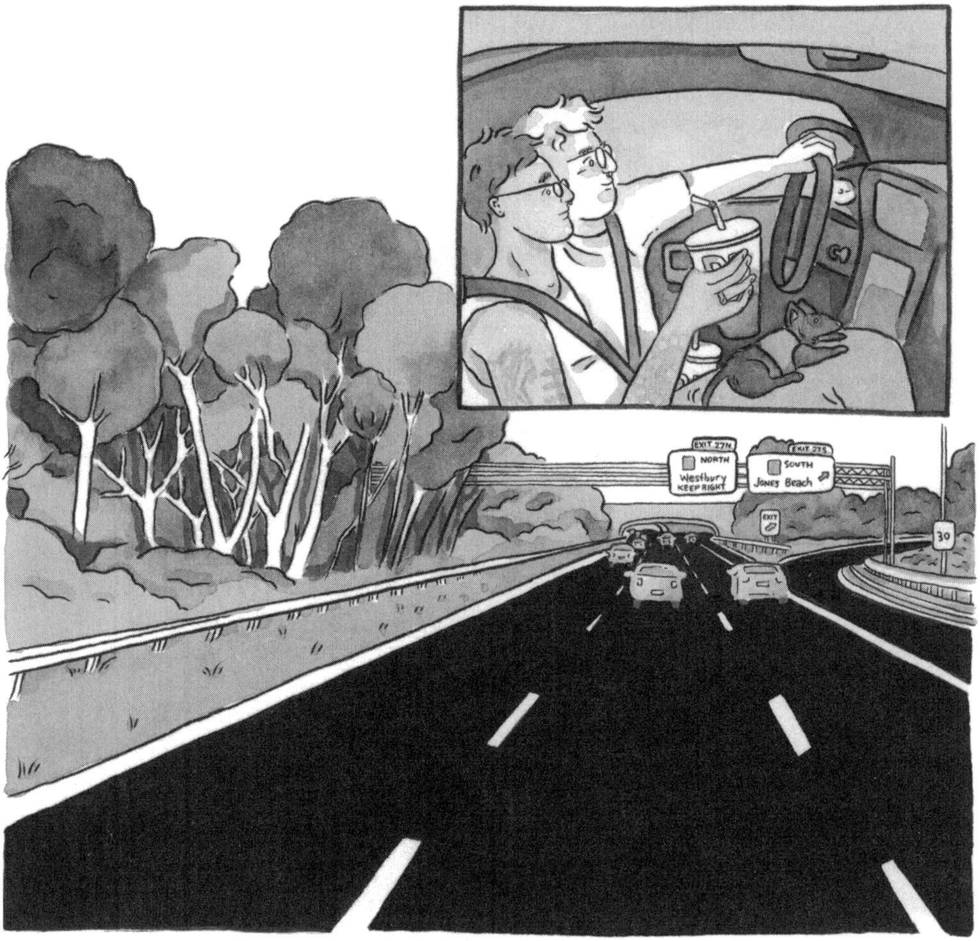
NORTH
Westbury
KEEP RIGHT
SOUTH
Jones Beach
30

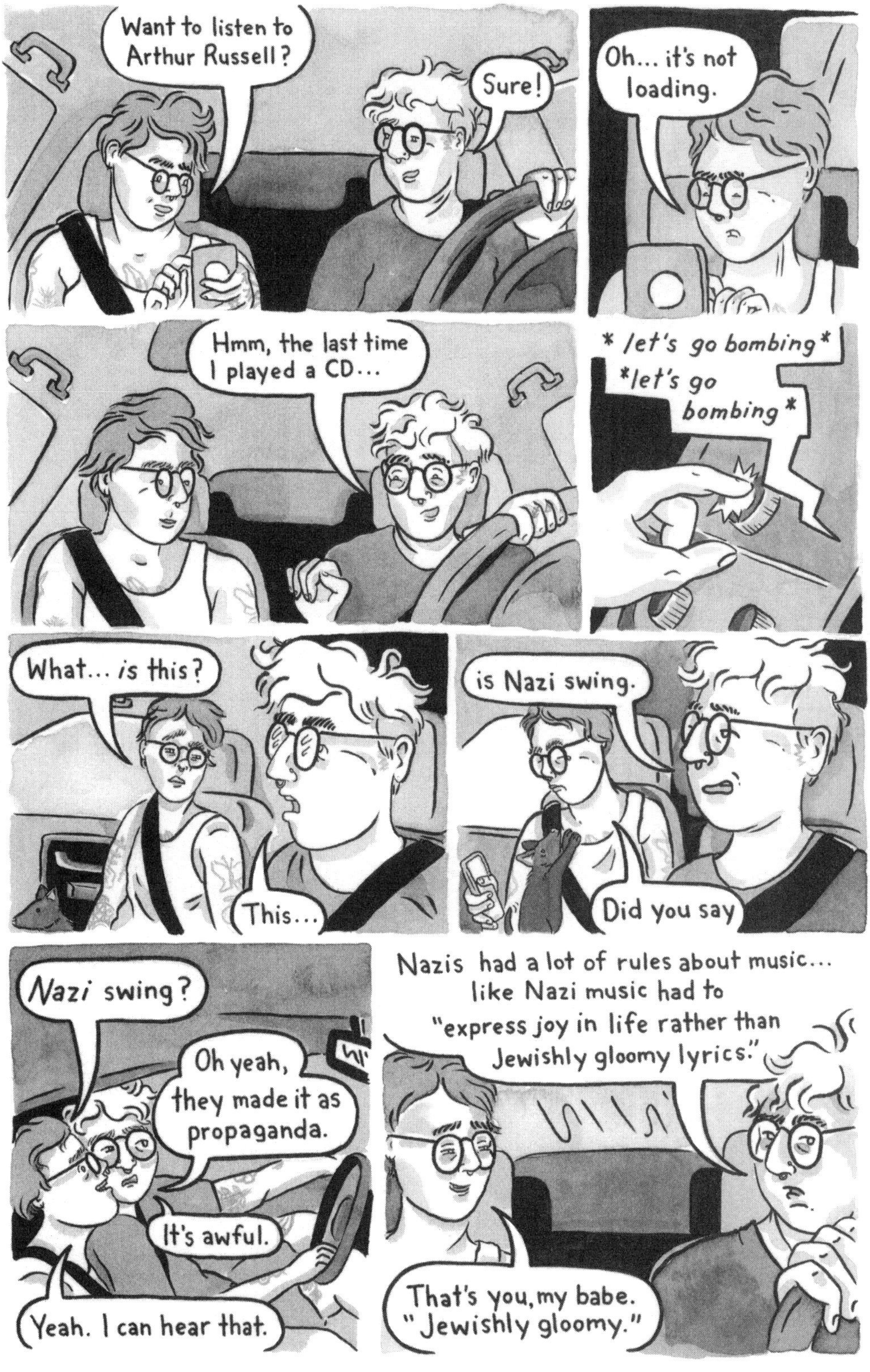
Want to listen to Arthur Russell?
Sure!
Oh... it's not loading.
Hmm, the last time I played a CD...
let's go bombing
let's go bombing
What... is this?
This...
is Nazi swing.
Did you say
Nazi swing?
Oh yeah, they made it as propaganda.
It's awful.
Yeah. I can hear that.
Nazis had a lot of rules about music... like Nazi music had to "express joy in life rather than Jewishly gloomy lyrics."
That's you, my babe. "Jewishly gloomy."

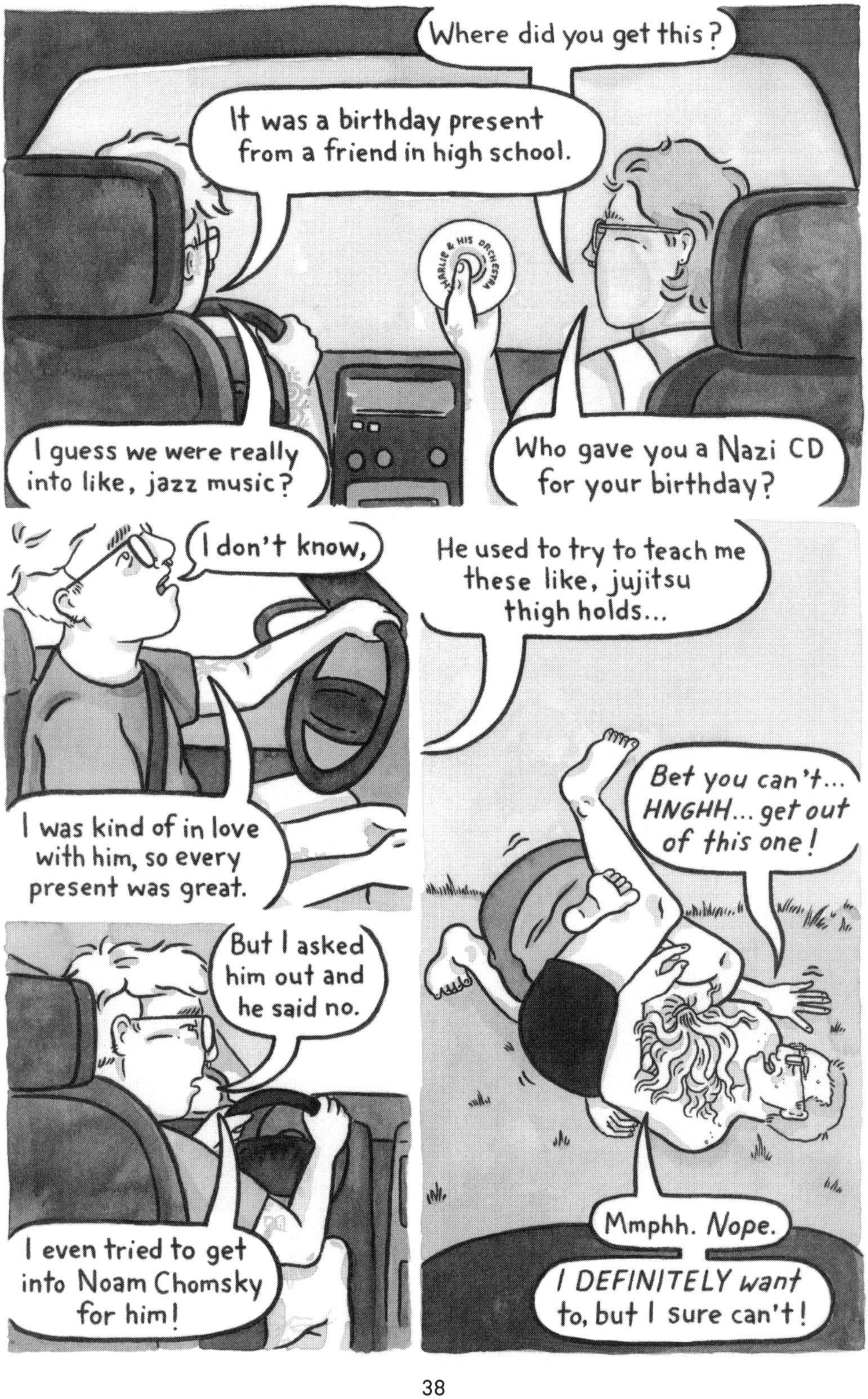
Where did you get this?
It was a birthday present from a friend in high school.
CHARLIE & HIS ORCHESTRA
I guess we were really into like, jazz music?
Who gave you a Nazi CD for your birthday?
I don't know,
He used to try to teach me these like, jujitsu thigh holds...
I was kind of in love with him, so every present was great.
Bet you can't... HNGHH... get out of this one!
But I asked him out and he said no.
I even tried to get into Noam Chomsky for him!
Mmphh. Nope.
I DEFINITELY want to, but I sure can't!

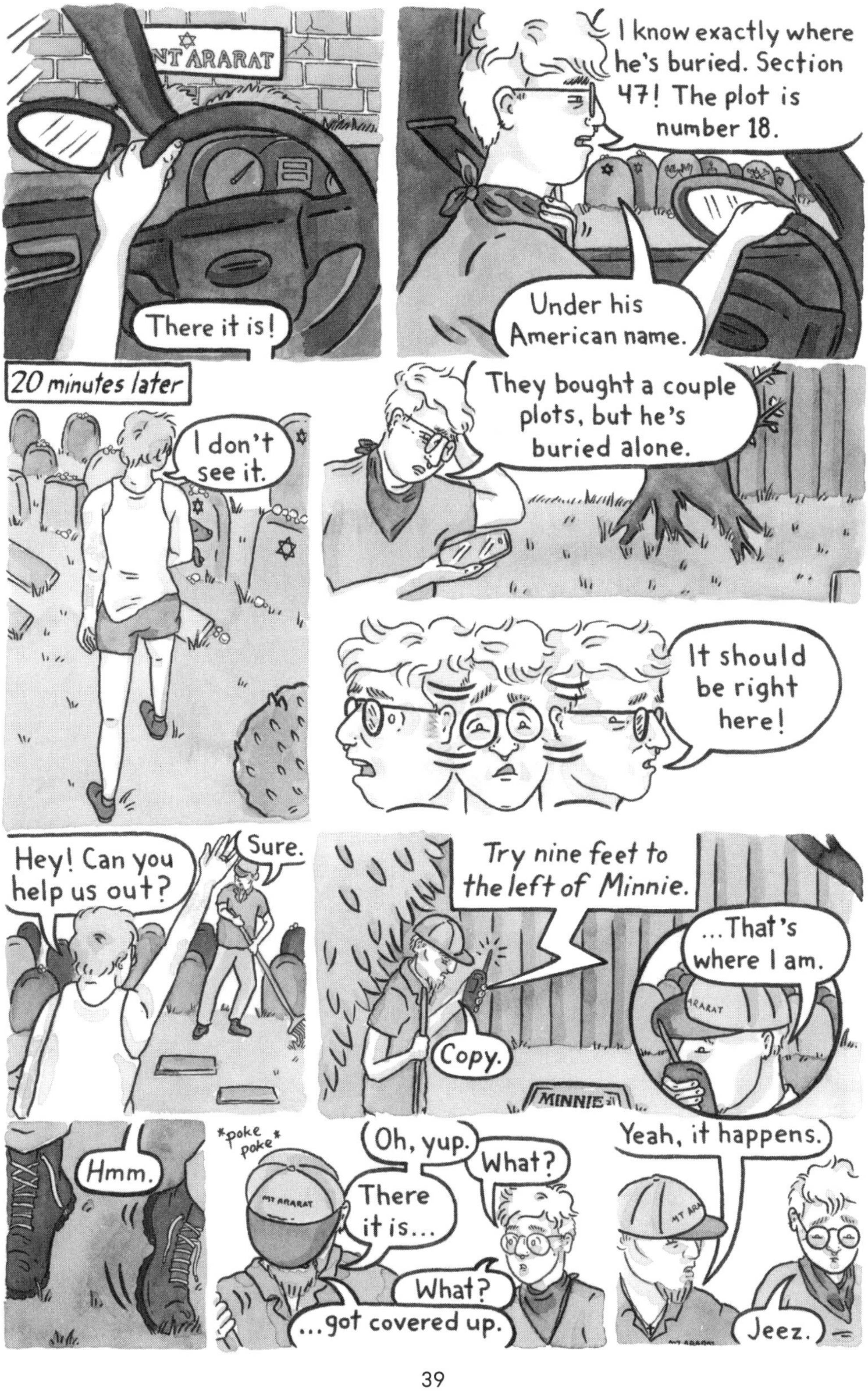
NT ARARAT
There it is!
I know exactly where he's buried. Section 47! The plot is number 18.
Under his American name.
20 minutes later
I don't see it.
They bought a couple plots, but he's buried alone.
It should be right here!
Hey! Can you help us out?
Sure.
Try nine feet to the left of Minnie.
Copy.
...That's where I am.
ARARAT
MINNIE
Hmm.
poke poke
MT ARARAT
Oh, yup.
There it is...
What?
What?
...got covered up.
Yeah, it happens.
Jeez.

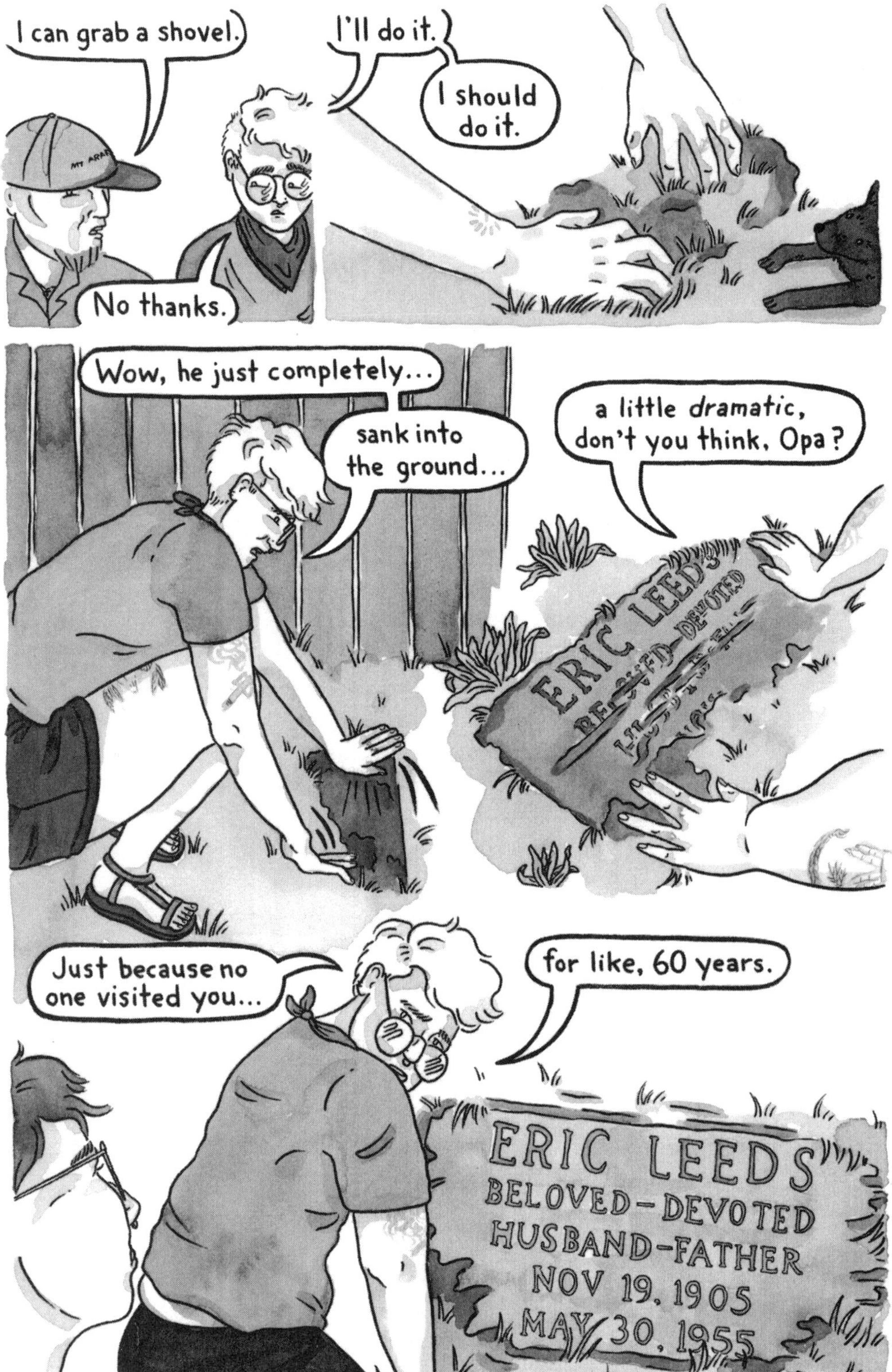

I can grab a shovel.
No thanks.
I'll do it.
I should do it.
Wow, he just completely...
sank into the ground...
a little *dramatic*, don't you think, Opa?
ERIC LEEDS
Just because no one visited you...
for like, 60 years.
ERIC LEEDS
BELOVED-DEVOTED
HUSBAND-FATHER
NOV 19, 1905
MAY 30, 1955

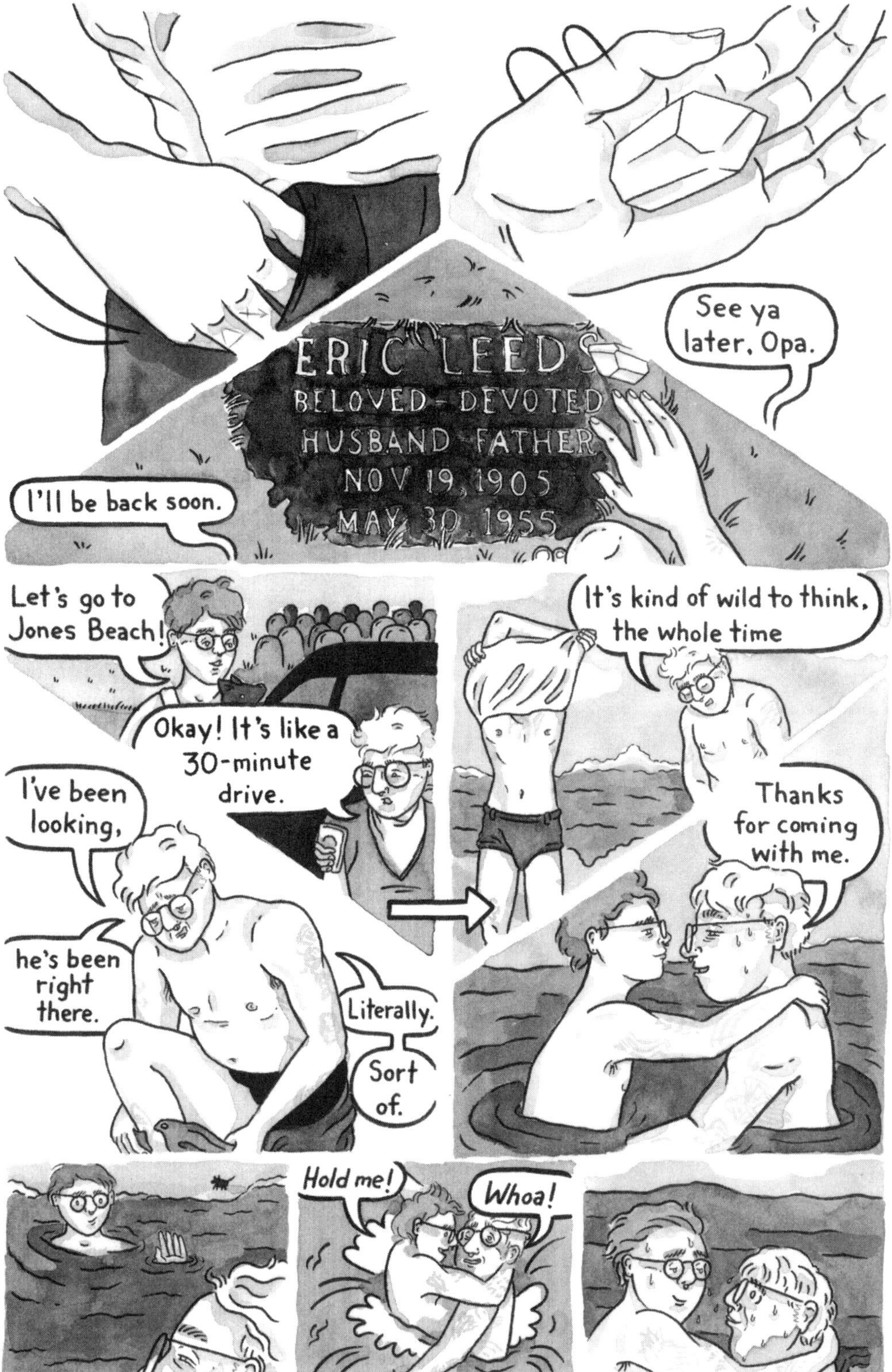

ERIC LEEDS
BELOVED - DEVOTED
HUSBAND FATHER
NOV 19, 1905
MAY 30, 1955
See ya later, Opa.
I'll be back soon.
Let's go to Jones Beach!
Okay! It's like a 30-minute drive.
It's kind of wild to think, the whole time
I've been looking,
he's been right there.
Literally.
Sort of.
Thanks for coming with me.
Hold me!
Whoa!

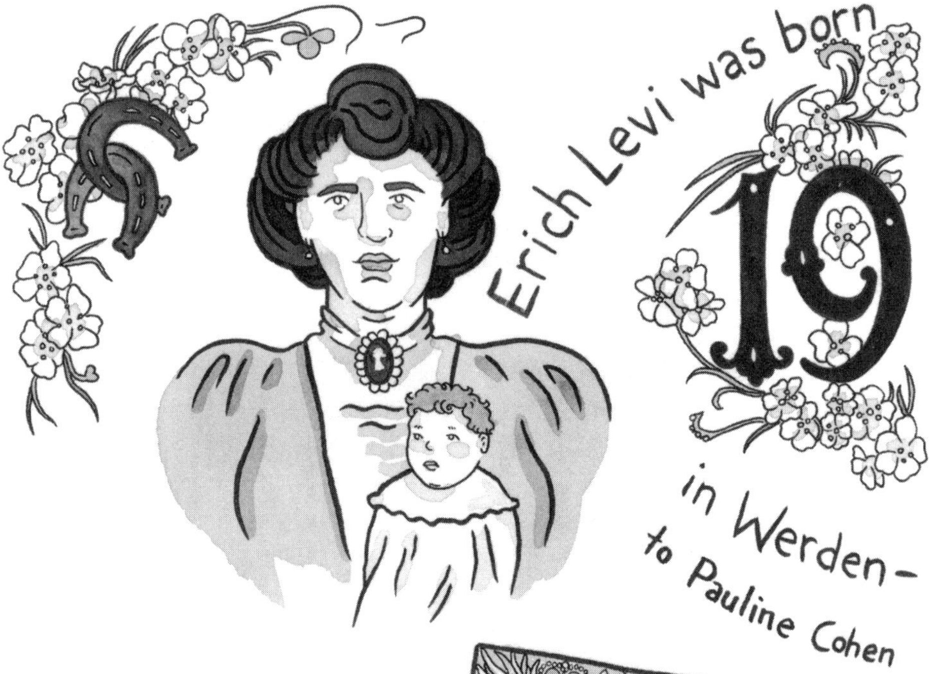
Erich Levi was born
19
in Werden-
to Pauline Cohen

It was the height of the German colonial empire.

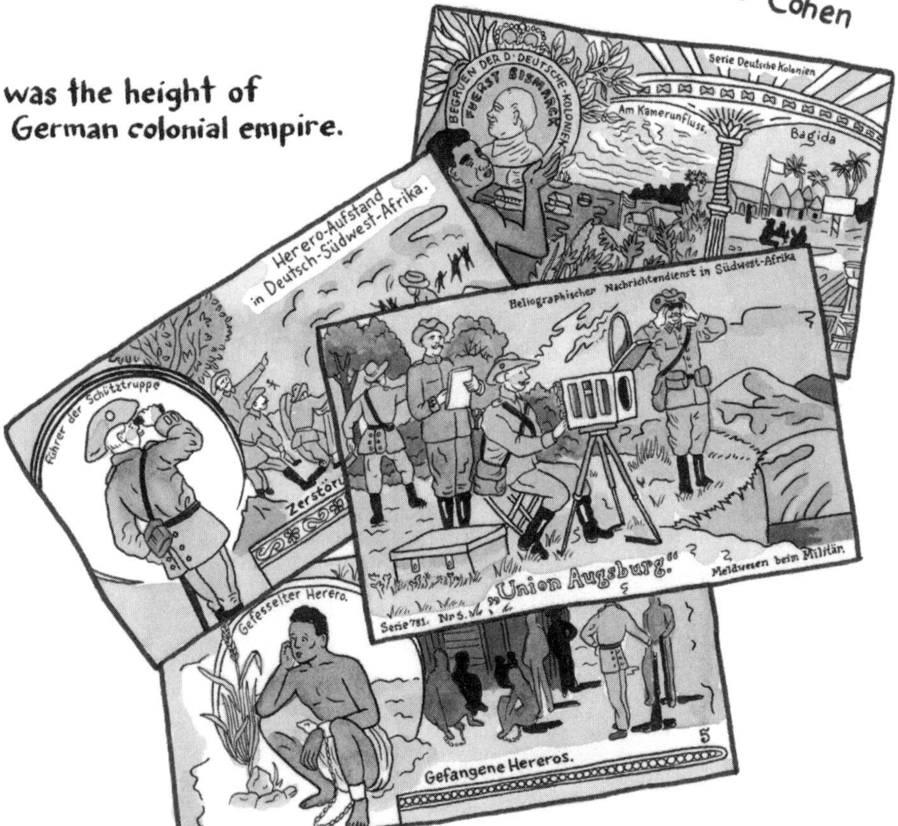
Serie Deutsche Kolonien
FUERST BISMARCK
Am Kamerunfluss
Bagida
Herero-Aufstand in Deutsch-Südwest-Afrika.
Heliographischer Nachrichtendienst in Südwest-Afrika
Führer der Schutztruppe
Zerstöru
"Union Augsburg"
Meldwesen beim Militär
Serie 781. Nr 5.
Gefesselter Herero.
Gefangene Hereros.
5

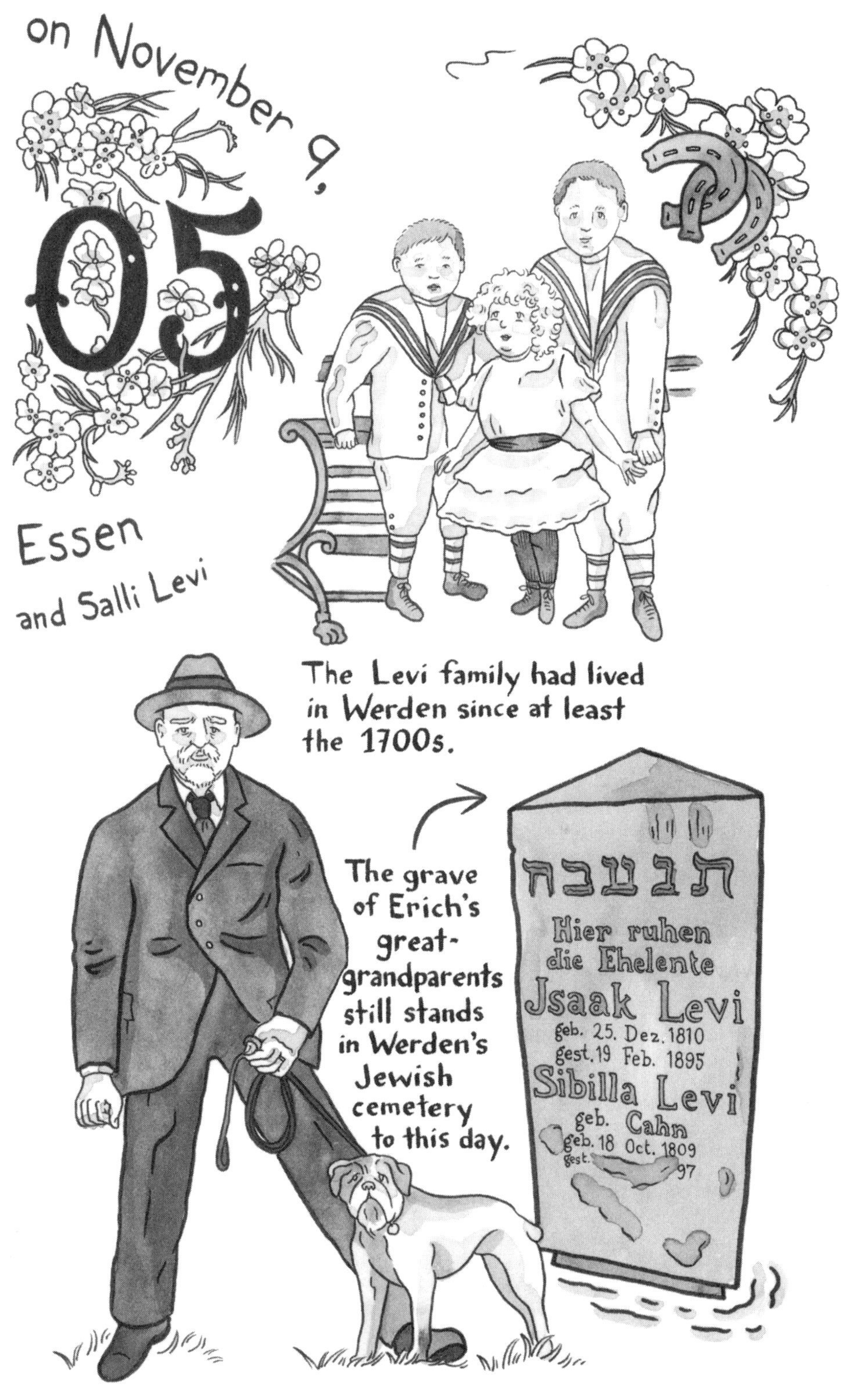
on November 9,
05
Essen
and Salli Levi
The Levi family had lived in Werden since at least the 1700s.
The grave of Erich's great-grandparents still stands in Werden's Jewish cemetery to this day.
Hier ruhen die Ehelente
Jsaak Levi
geb. 25. Dez. 1810
gest. 19 Feb. 1895
Sibilla Levi
geb. Cahn
geb. 18 Oct. 1809
gest.
97

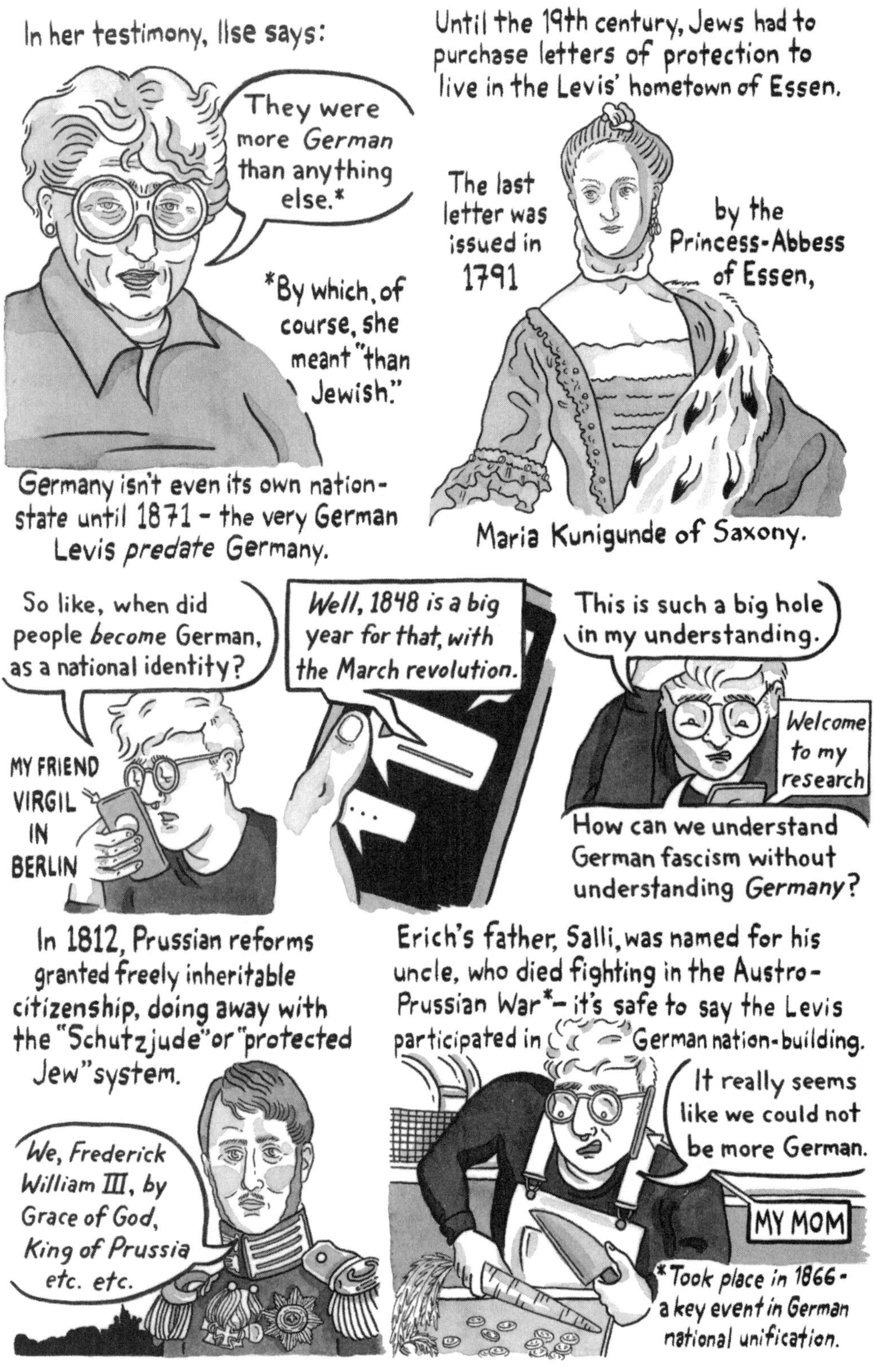
In her testimony, Ilse says:
They were more *German* than anything else.*
*By which, of course, she meant "than Jewish."
Germany isn't even its own nation-state until 1871 - the very German Levis *predate* Germany.
Until the 19th century, Jews had to purchase letters of protection to live in the Levis' hometown of Essen.
The last letter was issued in 1791
by the Princess-Abbess of Essen,
Maria Kunigunde of Saxony.
So like, when did people *become* German, as a national identity?
MY FRIEND VIRGIL IN BERLIN
Well, 1848 is a big year for that, with the March revolution.
This is such a big hole in my understanding.
Welcome to my research
How can we understand German fascism without understanding *Germany*?
In 1812, Prussian reforms granted freely inheritable citizenship, doing away with the "Schutzjude" or "protected Jew" system.
We, Frederick William III, by Grace of God, King of Prussia etc. etc.
Erich's father, Salli, was named for his uncle, who died fighting in the Austro-Prussian War* - it's safe to say the Levis participated in German nation-building.
It really seems like we could not be more German.
MY MOM
**Took place in 1866 - a key event in German national unification.*

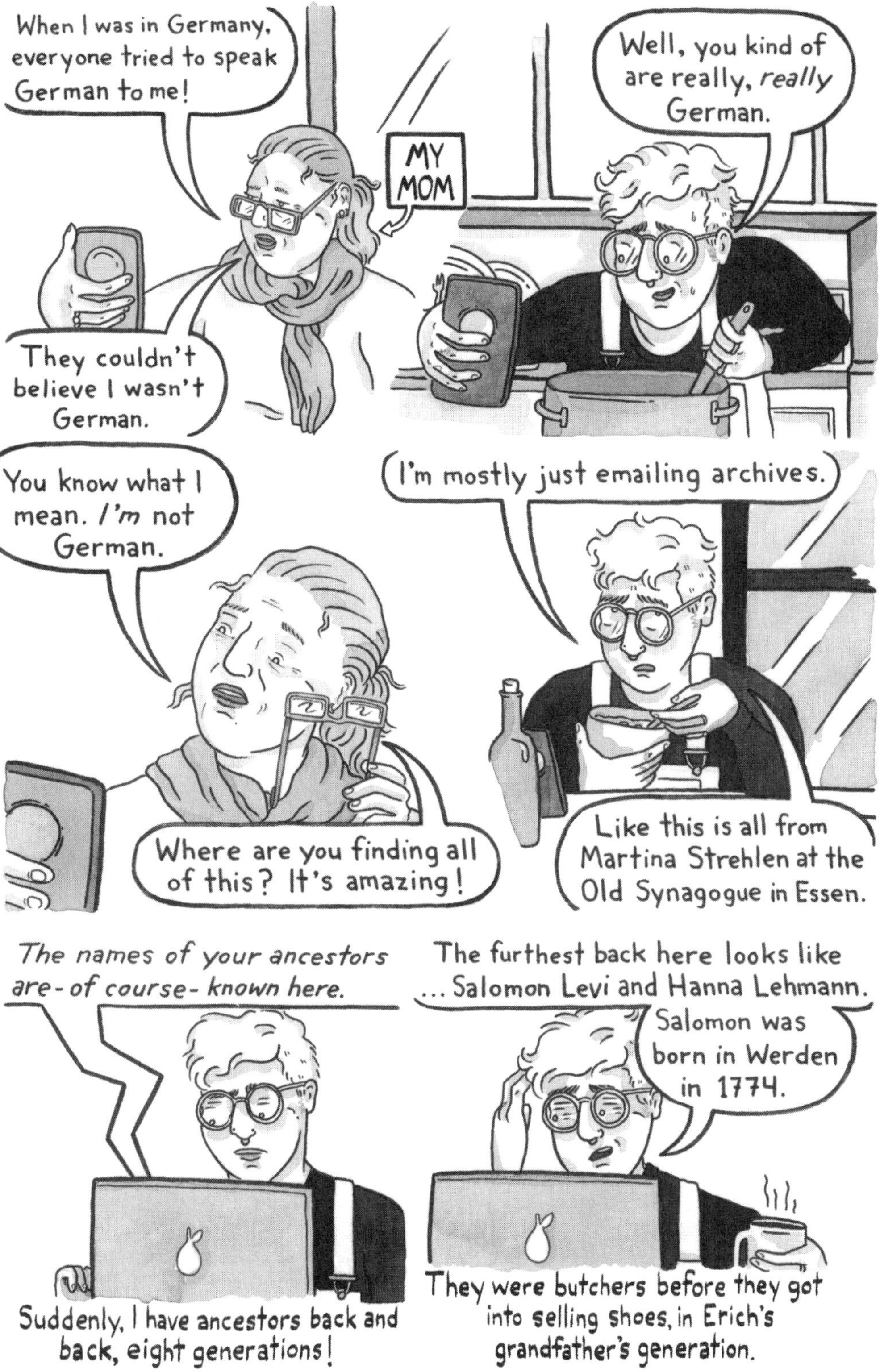
When I was in Germany, everyone tried to speak German to me!
MY MOM
Well, you kind of are really, *really* German.
They couldn't believe I wasn't German.
You know what I mean. *I'm* not German.
I'm mostly just emailing archives.
Where are you finding all of this? It's amazing!
Like this is all from Martina Strehlen at the Old Synagogue in Essen.
The names of your ancestors are- of course- known here.
The furthest back here looks like ... Salomon Levi and Hanna Lehmann.
Salomon was born in Werden in 1774.
Suddenly, I have ancestors back and back, eight generations!
They were butchers before they got into selling shoes, in Erich's grandfather's generation.

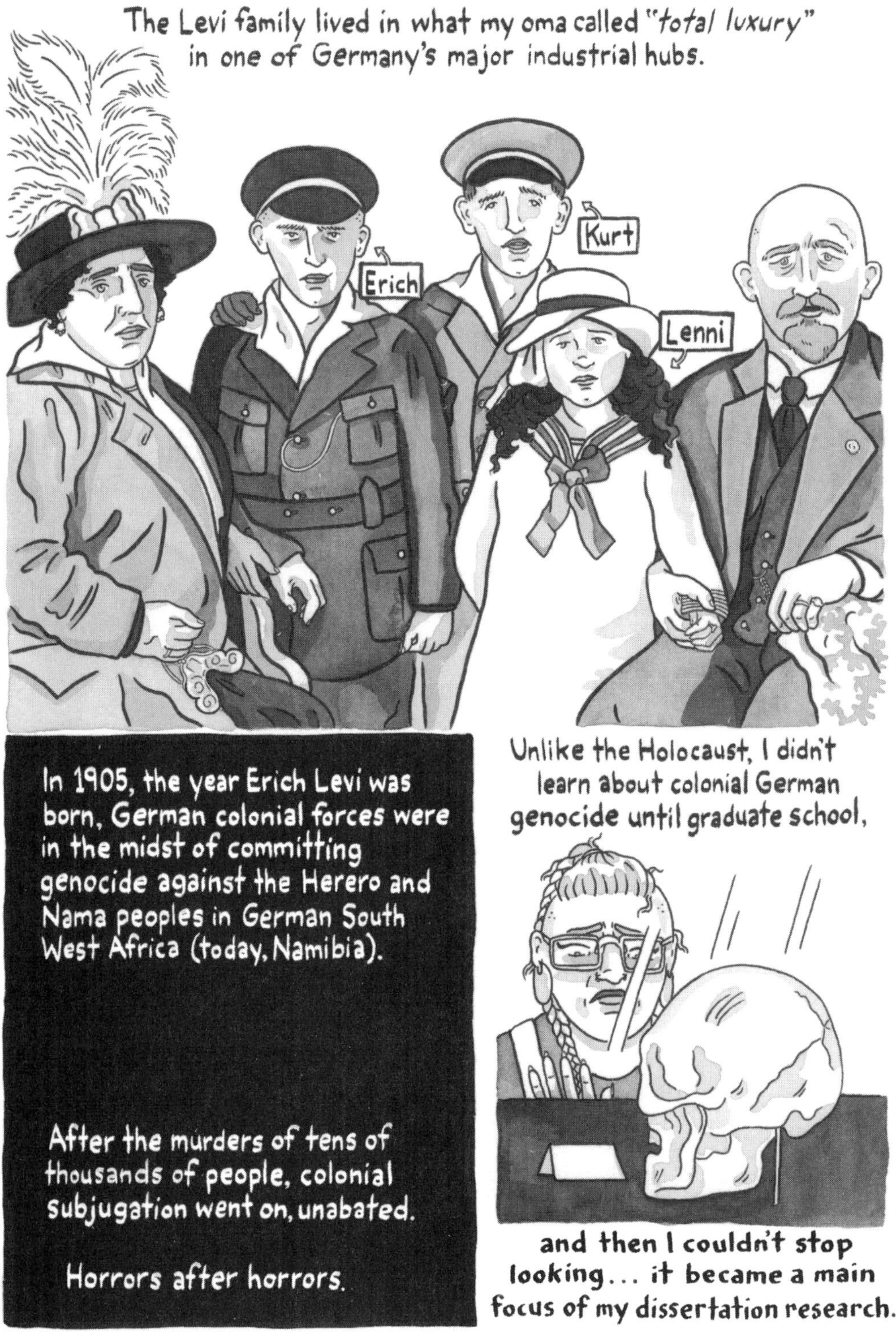
The Levi family lived in what my oma called "*total luxury*"
in one of Germany's major industrial hubs.
Erich
Kurt
Lenni
In 1905, the year Erich Levi was born, German colonial forces were in the midst of committing genocide against the Herero and Nama peoples in German South West Africa (today, Namibia).
After the murders of tens of thousands of people, colonial subjugation went on, unabated.
Horrors after horrors.
Unlike the Holocaust, I didn't learn about colonial German genocide until graduate school,
and then I couldn't stop looking... it became a main focus of my dissertation research.

Erich Levi was the middle child of three.

He had blue eyes.

I know little about his childhood, but I do know he grew up a bourgeois child of the German Empire.

This is the world he was born into.

The year of his birth also marks the start of the **Maji-Maji Rebellion** in Germany's East Africa Tanganyika colony,

a pan-Indigenous response to German forced labor practices in the production of cotton as a cash crop.

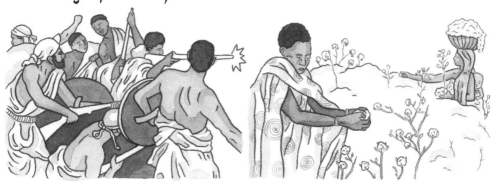

The reprisal tactics of the German colonial forces, including man-made famine, led to an estimated 250.000 deaths.

Fifteen Germans died.

Historian Robin D.G. Kelley writes in his introduction to Aimé Césaire's *Discourse on Colonialism*, "radical black intellectuals... understood fascism not as some aberration from the march of progress, an unexpected right-wing turn, but a logical development of Western civilization itself... imperialism gave birth to fascism."

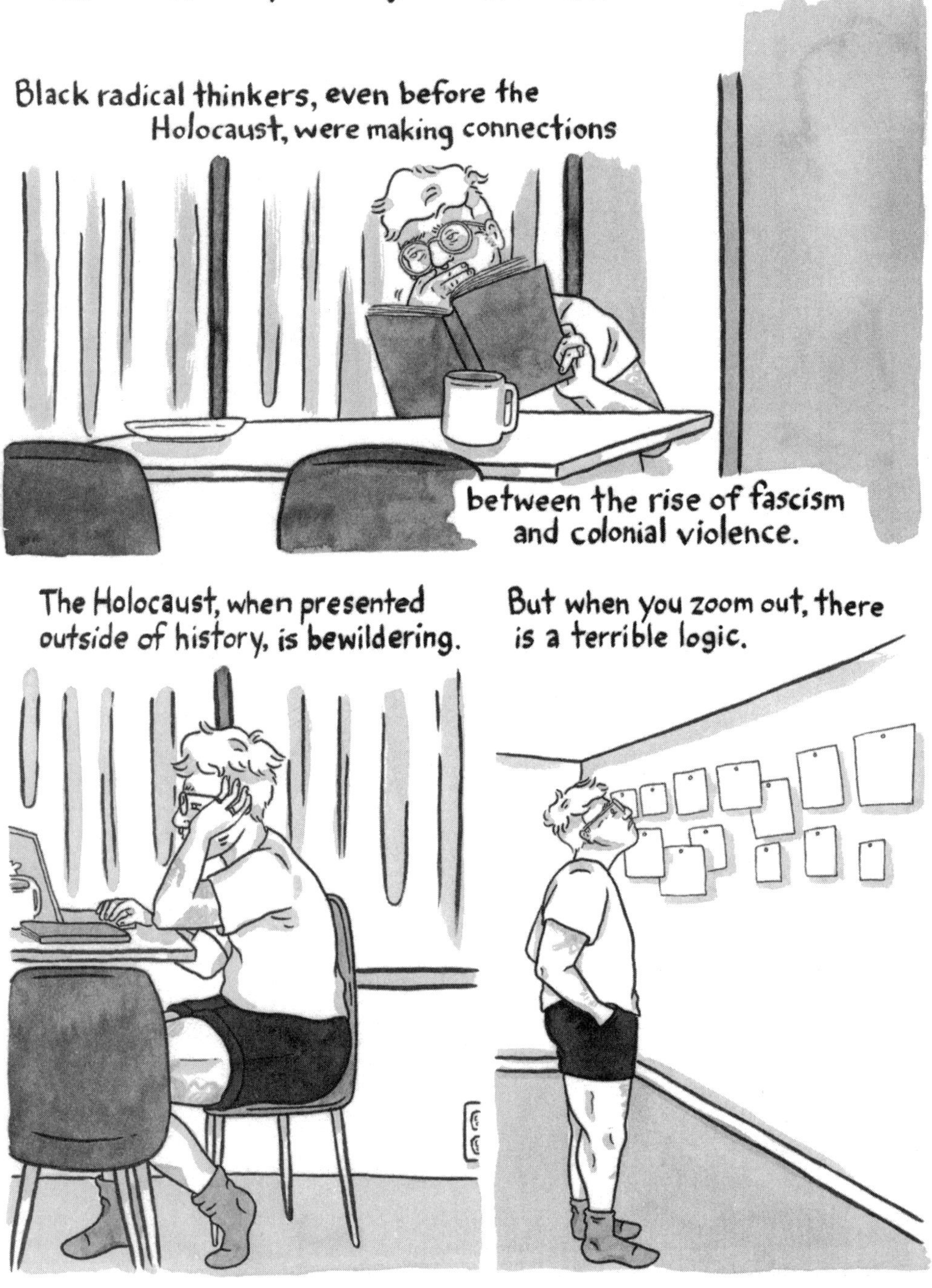
Black radical thinkers, even before the Holocaust, were making connections
between the rise of fascism and colonial violence.
The Holocaust, when presented outside of history, is bewildering.
But when you zoom out, there is a terrible logic.

Ralph Bunche

The doctrine of Fascism, with its extreme jingoism, its exaggerated exaltation of the state and its comic-opera glorification of race, has given a new and greater impetus to the policy of world imperialism which had conquered and subjected to systemic and ruthless exploitation virtually all of the darker populations of the earth.

French and British Imperialism in West Africa, 1936

Aimé Césaire

...before they were its victims, they were its accomplices; that they tolerated that Nazism before it was inflicted on them, that they absolved it, shut their eyes to it, legitimized it, because, until then, it had been applied only to non-European peoples; that they have cultivated that Nazism, that they are responsible for it...

Discourse on Colonialism, 1955

W.E.B. DuBois

There was no Nazi atrocity - concentration camps, wholesale maiming and murder, defilement of women and ghastly blasphemy of childhood – which Christian civilization or Europe had not long been practicing against colored folk in all parts of the world in the name of and for the defense of a Superior Race born to rule the world.

The World and Africa, 1947

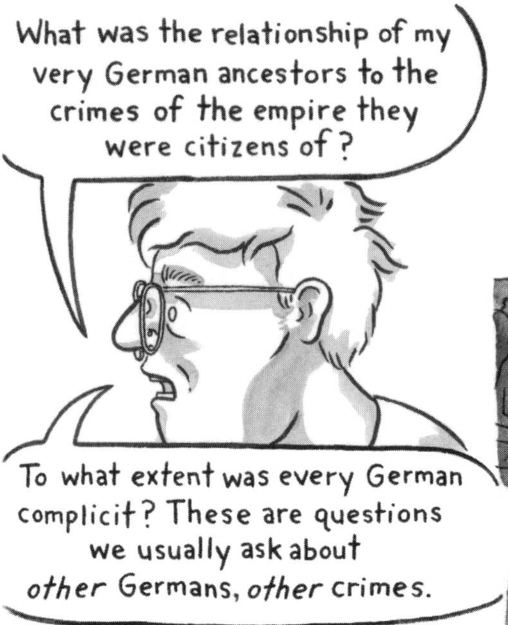
What was the relationship of my very German ancestors to the crimes of the empire they were citizens of?
To what extent was every German complicit? These are questions we usually ask about *other* Germans, *other* crimes.

During the genocide, a postcard was available for purchase in Germany that depicted soldiers packing the skulls of murdered Herero into crates to be sent to collectors in Europe and the U.S.

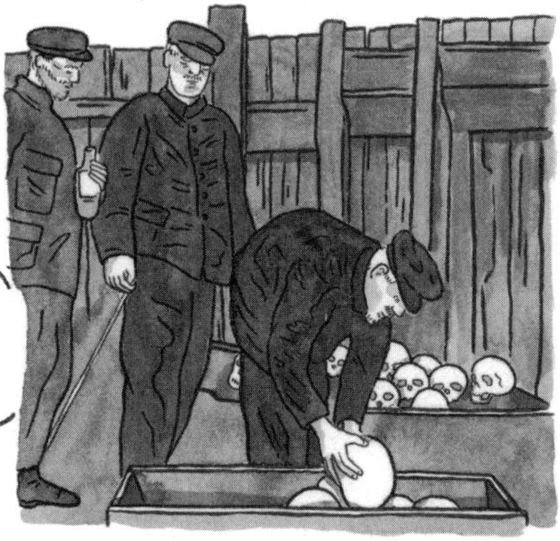

In 1906, a German magazine, *Der Wahre Jakob*, ran a cartoon about the colonies that sardonically reveals a knowledge of the mass killing.

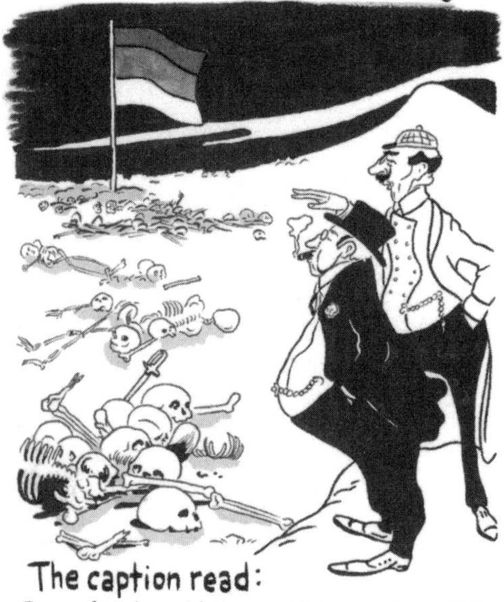

The caption read:

Even if it hasn't brought in much profit and there are no better quality goods on offer at least we can use it to set up a bone grinding plant.

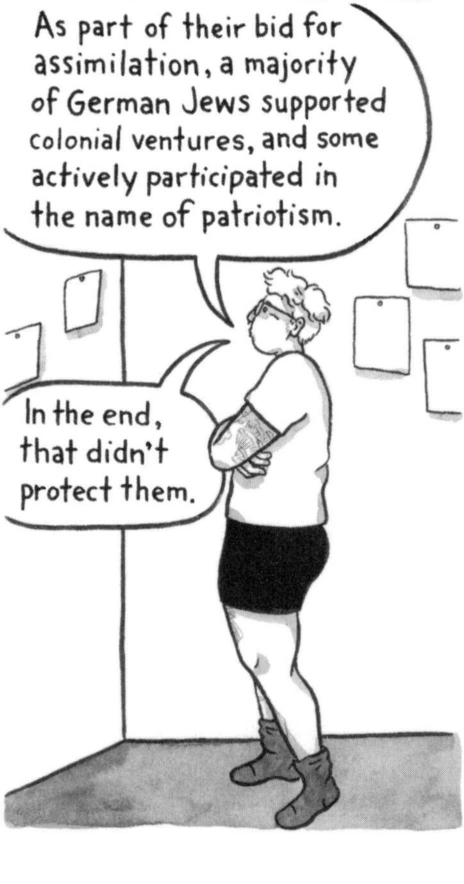
As part of their bid for assimilation, a majority of German Jews supported colonial ventures, and some actively participated in the name of patriotism.
In the end, that didn't protect them.

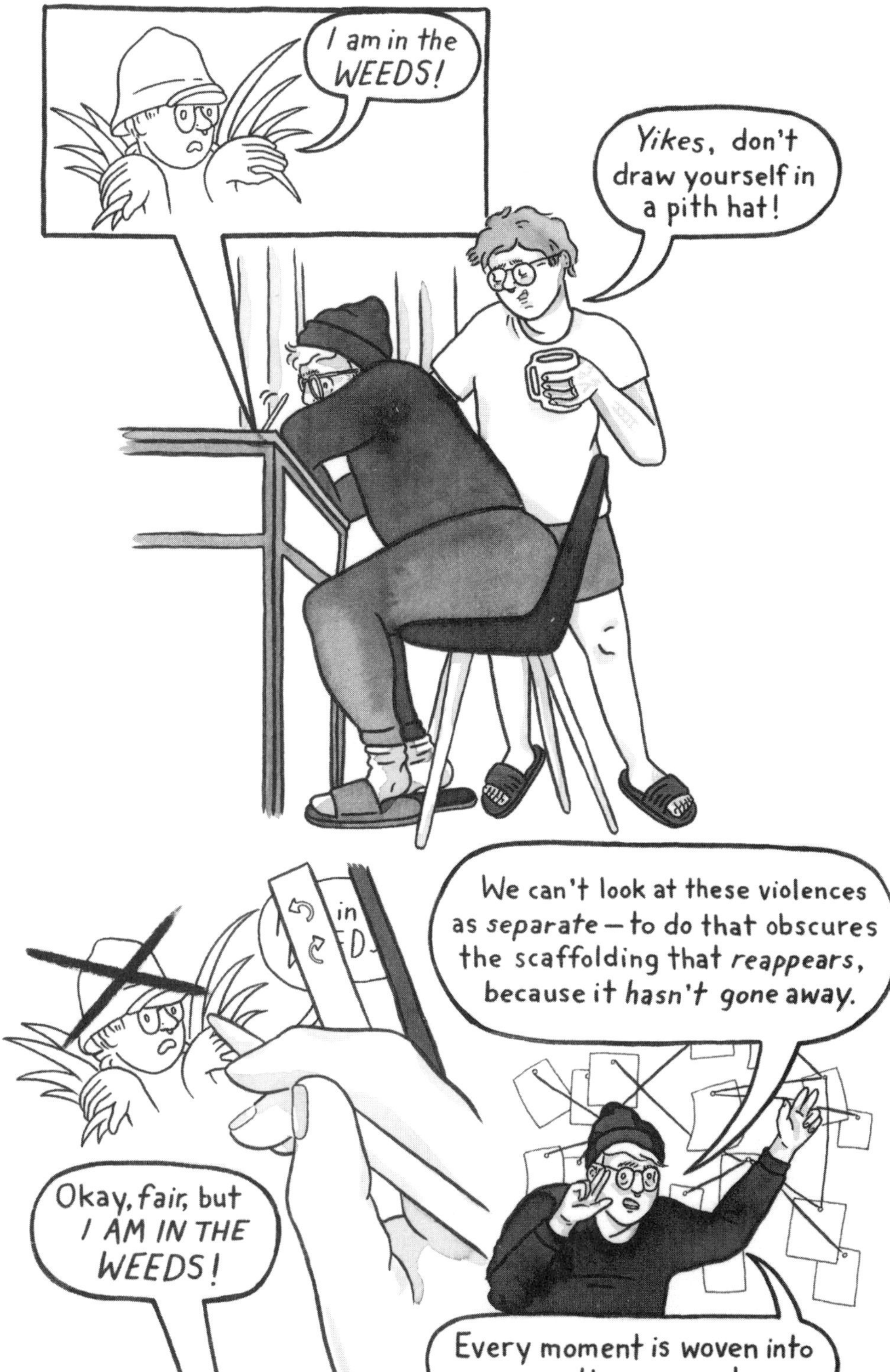
I am in the WEEDS!
Yikes, don't draw yourself in a pith hat!
We can't look at these violences as *separate* — to do that obscures the scaffolding that *reappears*, because it *hasn't gone* away.
Okay, fair, but I AM IN THE WEEDS!
Every moment is woven into every other moment.

My oma, Gertrude Ilse Kahn, was born on August 23, 1914, on the Rhine River in Neuwied. Her father was away fighting in World War I.

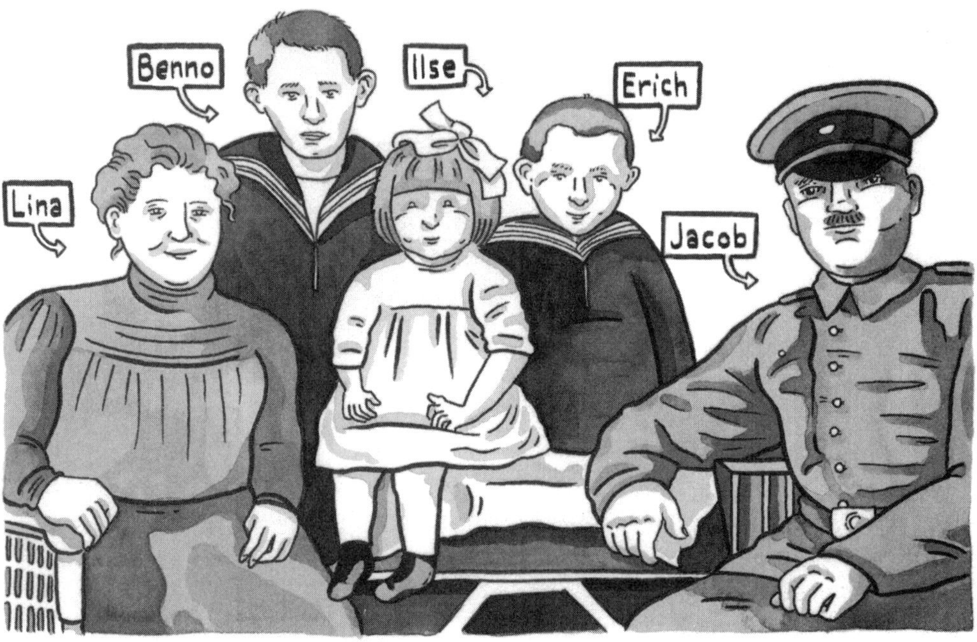
Benno
Ilse
Erich
Lina
Jacob

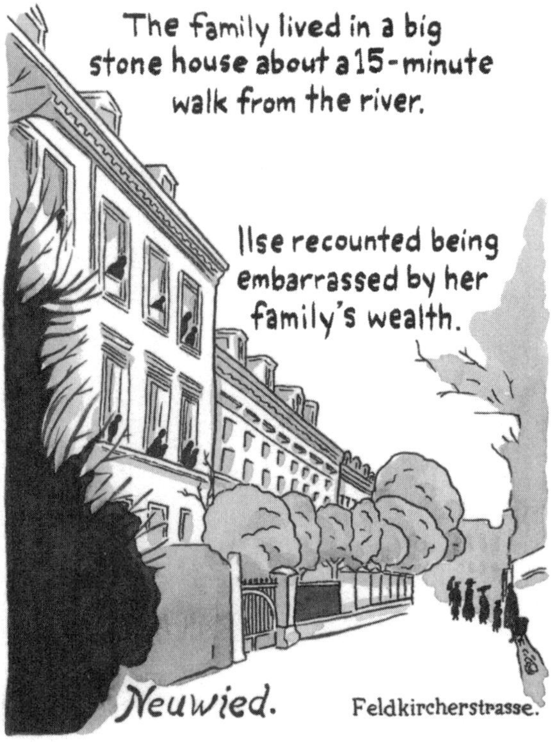
The family lived in a big stone house about a 15-minute walk from the river.
Ilse recounted being embarrassed by her family's wealth.
Neuwied.
Feldkircherstrasse.

She asked her chauffeur to drop her off a few blocks away from school

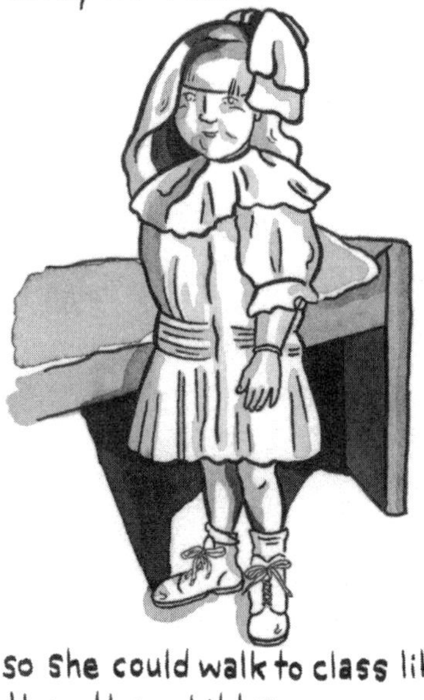

so she could walk to class like the other children.

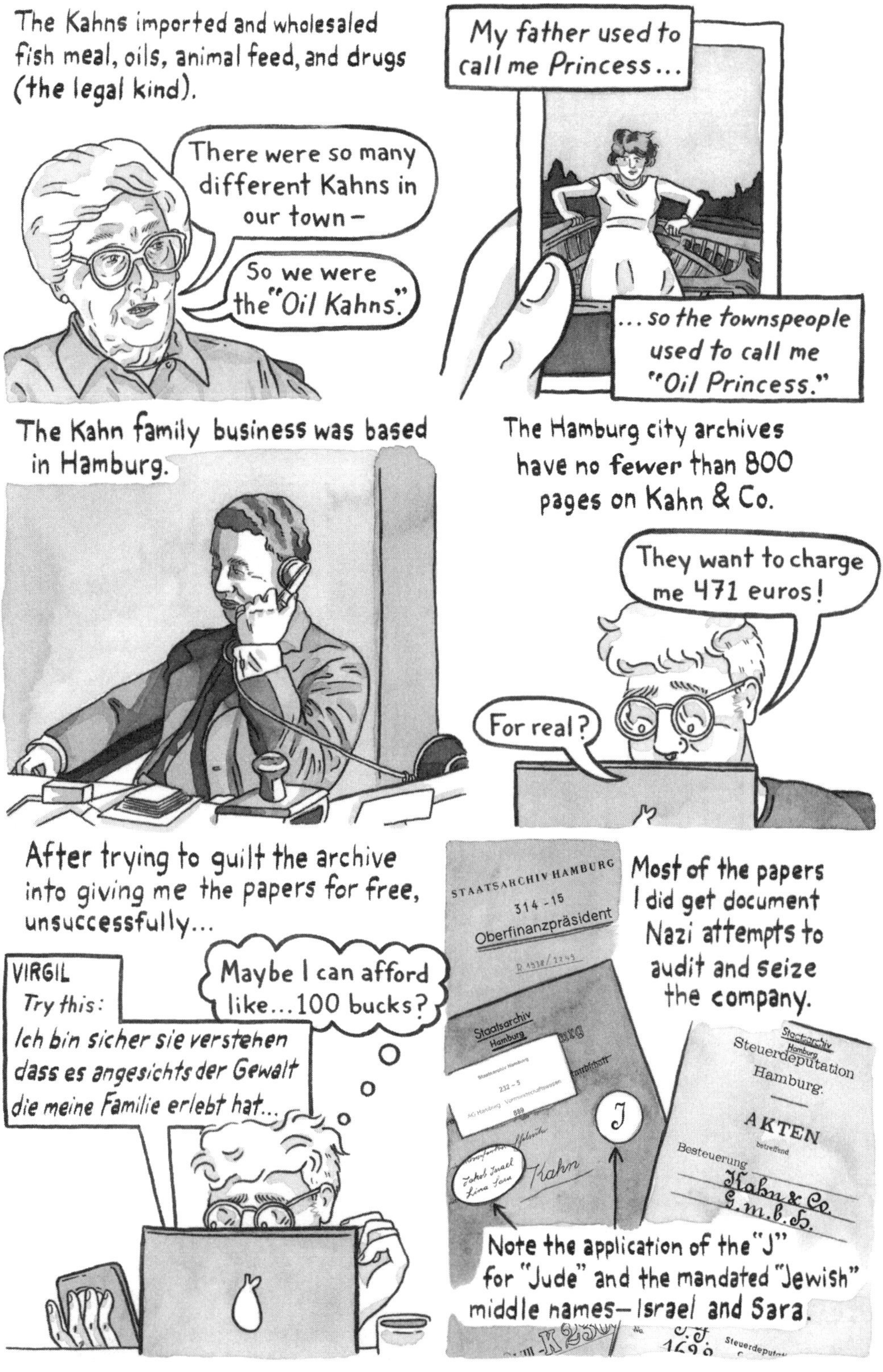
The Kahns imported and wholesaled fish meal, oils, animal feed, and drugs (the legal kind).
There were so many different Kahns in our town –
So we were the "Oil Kahns."
My father used to call me Princess...
...so the townspeople used to call me "Oil Princess."
The Kahn family business was based in Hamburg.
The Hamburg city archives have no fewer than 800 pages on Kahn & Co.
They want to charge me 471 euros!
For real?
After trying to guilt the archive into giving me the papers for free, unsuccessfully...
VIRGIL
Try this:
Ich bin sicher sie verstehen dass es angesichts der Gewalt die meine Familie erlebt hat...
Maybe I can afford like...100 bucks?
Most of the papers I did get document Nazi attempts to audit and seize the company.
STAATSARCHIV HAMBURG
314 - 15
Oberfinanzpräsident
Staatsarchiv Hamburg
Kahn
J
Staatsarchiv Hamburg
Steuerdeputation
Hamburg.
AKTEN
betreffend
Besteuerung
Kahn & Co.
G.m.b.H.
Note the application of the "J" for "Jude" and the mandated "Jewish" middle names – Israel and Sara.

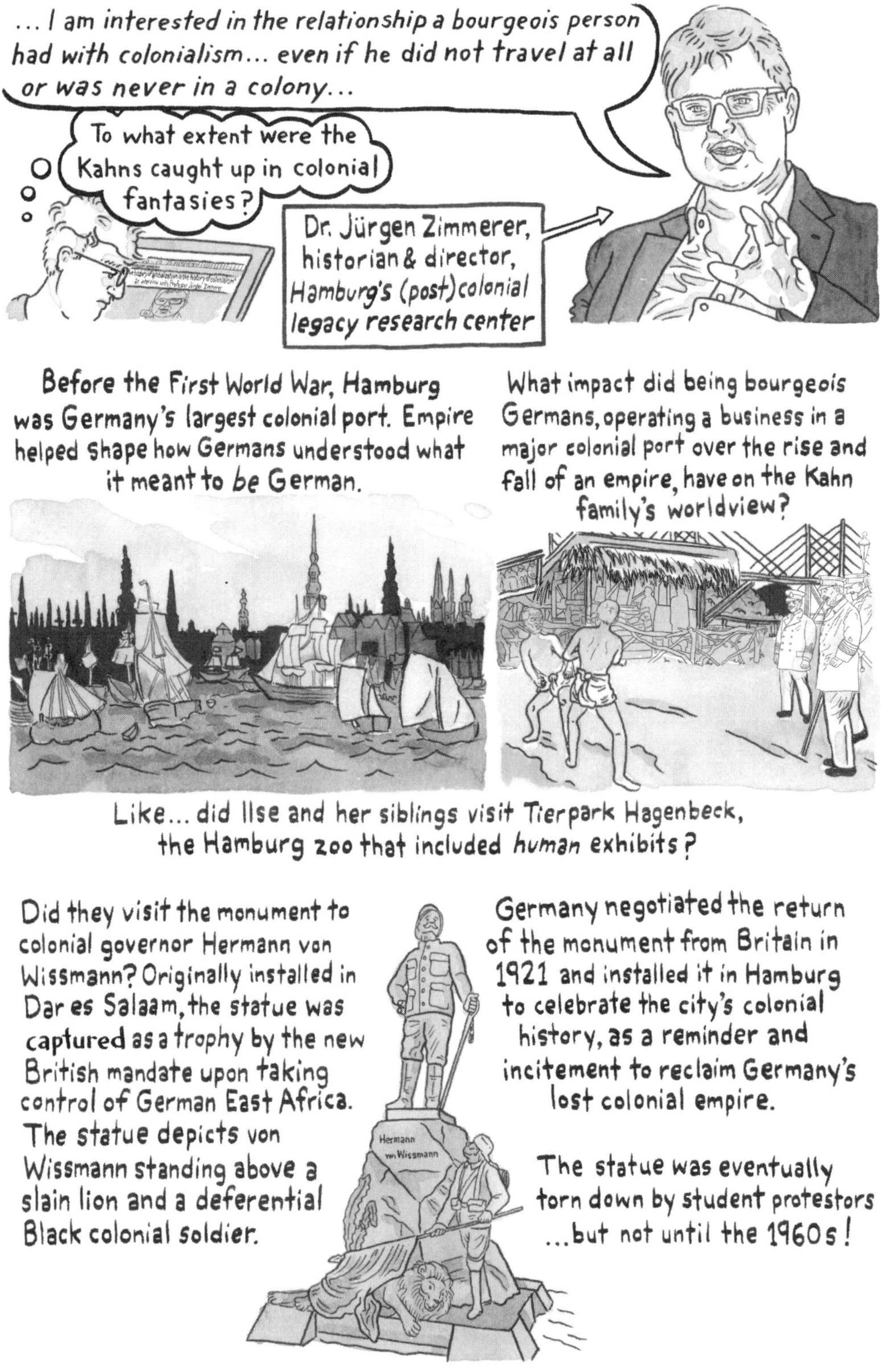
... I am interested in the relationship a bourgeois person had with colonialism... even if he did not travel at all or was never in a colony...
To what extent were the Kahns caught up in colonial fantasies?
Dr. Jürgen Zimmerer, historian & director, Hamburg's (post)colonial legacy research center
Before the First World War, Hamburg was Germany's largest colonial port. Empire helped shape how Germans understood what it meant to *be* German.
What impact did being bourgeois Germans, operating a business in a major colonial port over the rise and fall of an empire, have on the Kahn family's worldview?
Like... did Ilse and her siblings visit Tierpark Hagenbeck, the Hamburg zoo that included *human* exhibits?
Did they visit the monument to colonial governor Hermann von Wissmann? Originally installed in Dar es Salaam, the statue was captured as a trophy by the new British mandate upon taking control of German East Africa.
The statue depicts von Wissmann standing above a slain lion and a deferential Black colonial soldier.
Hermann von Wissmann
Germany negotiated the return of the monument from Britain in 1921 and installed it in Hamburg to celebrate the city's colonial history, as a reminder and incitement to reclaim Germany's lost colonial empire.
The statue was eventually torn down by student protestors ...but not until the 1960s!

The year before Ilse was born, in 1913, the researcher Eugen Fischer, who would later become an architect of Nazi racial policies, published his book *Die Rehobother Bastards*.

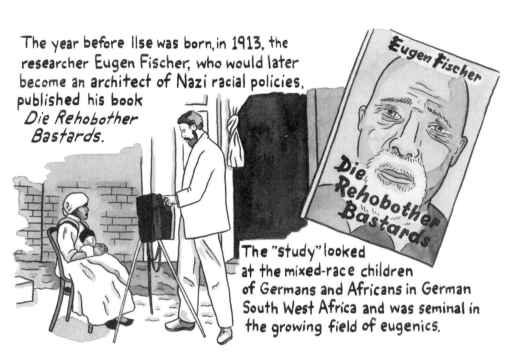

Eugen Fischer

Die Rehobother Bastards

The "study" looked at the mixed-race children of Germans and Africans in German South West Africa and was seminal in the growing field of eugenics.

Widely read in the U.S. and Britain as well as Germany, the study used the relatively new technology of photography to create "evidence" of degeneration through racial mixing...

In September 1933, the *New York Times* writes of Fischer's research—

Professor Fischer makes no bones about the concern of the new regime about "race." Just as, during the World War, a lot of confusion arose over the German word kultur, so now "race research" encounters a similar danger.

Ordinarily the German term for "race research" would be equivalent to genetics. But Professor Fischer candidly stated that the new Germany emphasized the racial factor. The object of German attempts at eugenics is not so much to produce a superior race as to produce a German race.

Professor Fischer sympathized with this aim. Briefly, his argument is similar to that advanced in the United States for preserving national parks free from outside plants, for keeping them in their natural state.

and tried to use photography to "expose" mixed-race phenotypes.

Fischer and his ilk were very anxious about the idea of racial passing

DENIES REICH SEEKS TO IMPROVE RACE

Scientist Says Purity Rather Than Superiority of Stock Is Aim of Hitlerites.

MOVE A BOON TO SCIENCE

In 1916, the influence of antisemitic circles in the military led to a census of Jewish soldiers in the German army by the War Ministry.

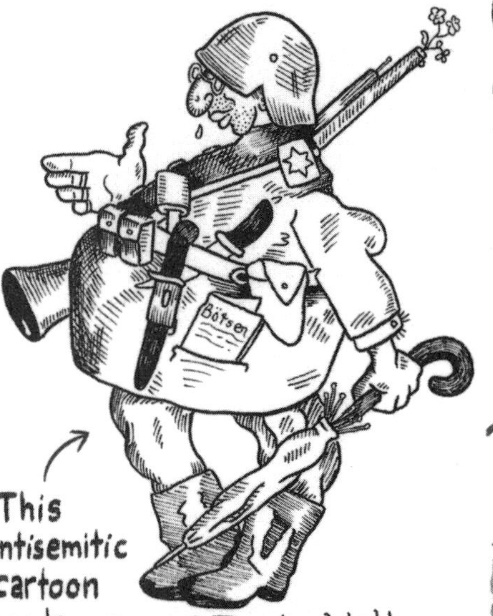
Bötsen

This antisemitic cartoon reads — Der jud. Frontsoldat!
Geht mer als letzter hinaus
ist mer als erster zu Haus.

"The Jewish soldier on the front! Always the last to go out and the first to go home."

Antisemites hoped the census would reveal that Jewish Germans avoided front line duty or serving at all.

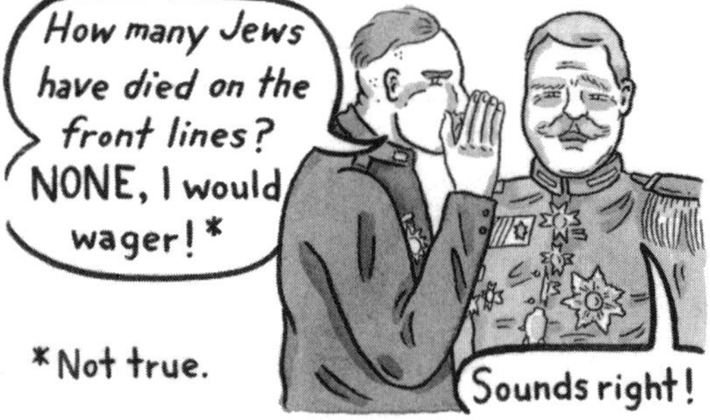
How many Jews have died on the front lines? NONE, I would wager! *
Sounds right!

*Not true.

When the inquiry failed to uncover any Jewish wrongdoing the census was never released...

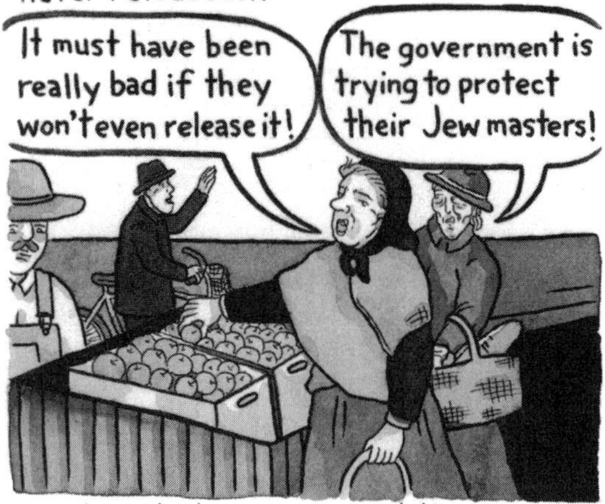
It must have been really bad if they won't even release it!
The government is trying to protect their Jew masters!

With Germany's defeat, some German nationalists popularized the "stab-in-the-back" theory to blame the loss of the war on a supposed betrayal of Germany by Jews and Marxists.

On top of the Great War, the whole world was dealing with a flu pandemic that would kill an estimated 50 million people worldwide. In 1918 the German Army reported 14,000 flu-related deaths. Around 287,000 Germans died of the flu in total. The First World War took the lives of an estimated two million German soldiers and over 750,000 German civilians.

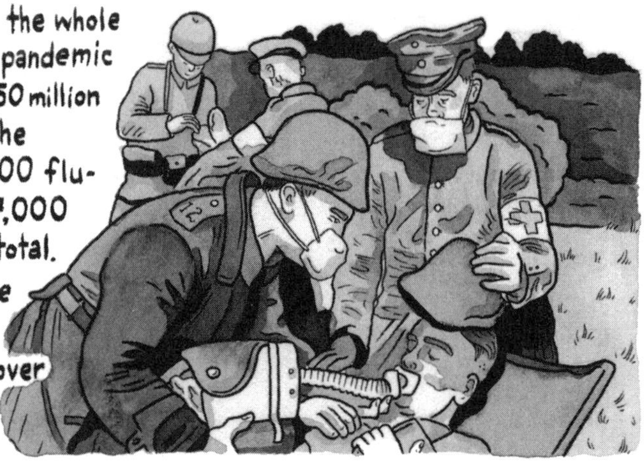

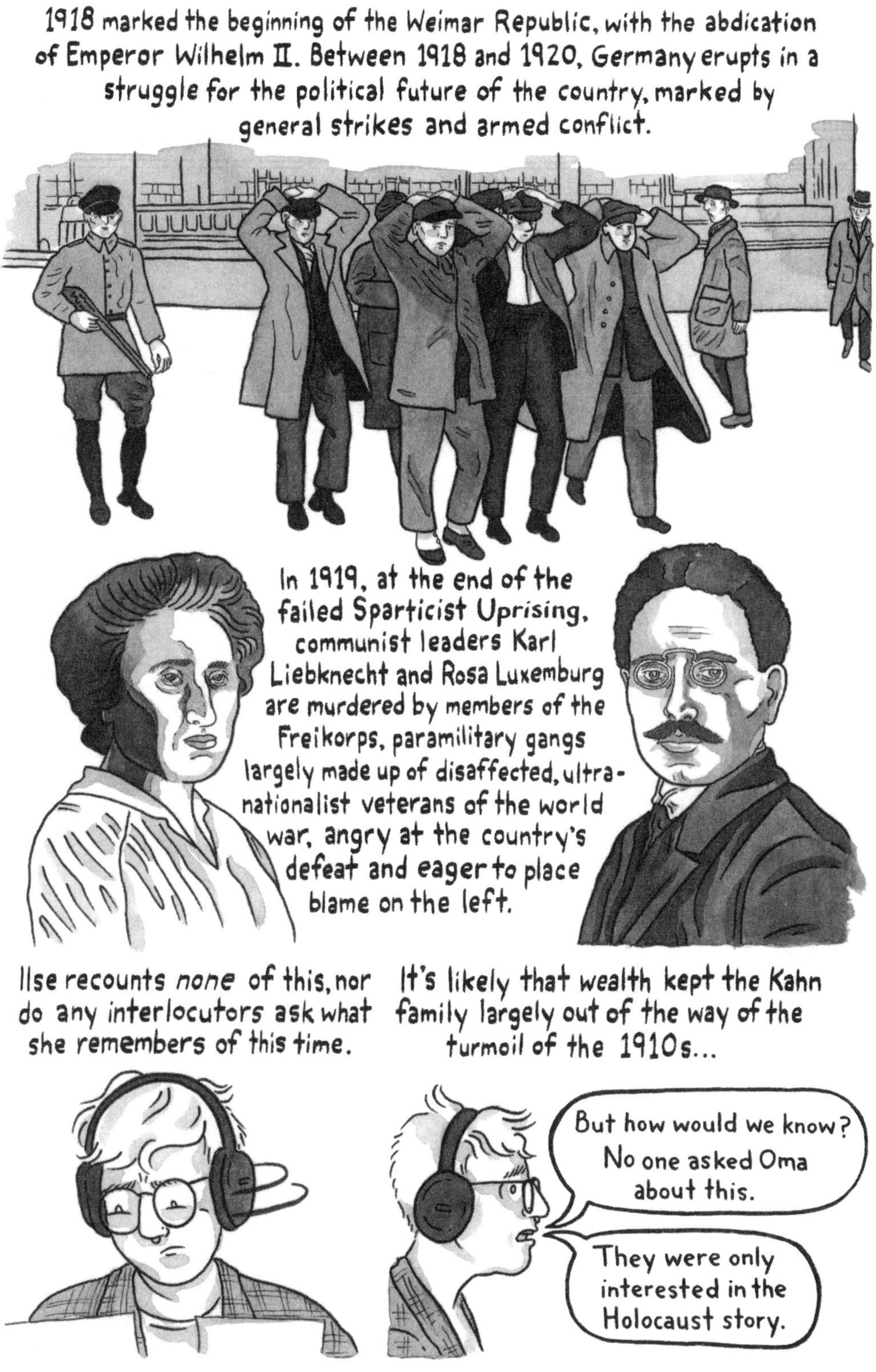
1918 marked the beginning of the Weimar Republic, with the abdication of Emperor Wilhelm II. Between 1918 and 1920, Germany erupts in a struggle for the political future of the country, marked by general strikes and armed conflict.
In 1919, at the end of the failed Sparticist Uprising, communist leaders Karl Liebknecht and Rosa Luxemburg are murdered by members of the Freikorps, paramilitary gangs largely made up of disaffected, ultra-nationalist veterans of the world war, angry at the country's defeat and eager to place blame on the left.
Ilse recounts *none* of this, nor do any interlocutors ask what she remembers of this time.
It's likely that wealth kept the Kahn family largely out of the way of the turmoil of the 1910s...
But how would we know? No one asked Oma about this.
They were only interested in the Holocaust story.

I remember studying hyper-inflation in Weimar Germany in school...sort of.

Paper money was so worthless, people used it for kindling.

The reproductive rights activist and eugenicist Margaret Sanger wrote from Berlin in 1920 —

I am constantly hungry; nothing satisfies except eggs, and these cost over two marks each. Fruit is plentiful just now, plums especially, but potatoes and other vegetables are both scarce and expensive. Meat is rationed to half a pound a week for each person, milk is obtained only by a doctor's certificate as Germany's cows were given over to France.

But the Kahns' wealth seems to have been largely protected from inflation —

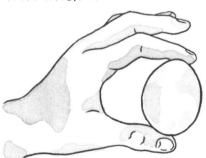

they weren't relying on paper money, regular paychecks, or the volatile stock market.

Neuwied, like Essen, is in the Rhineland, which was occupied by France after World War I.

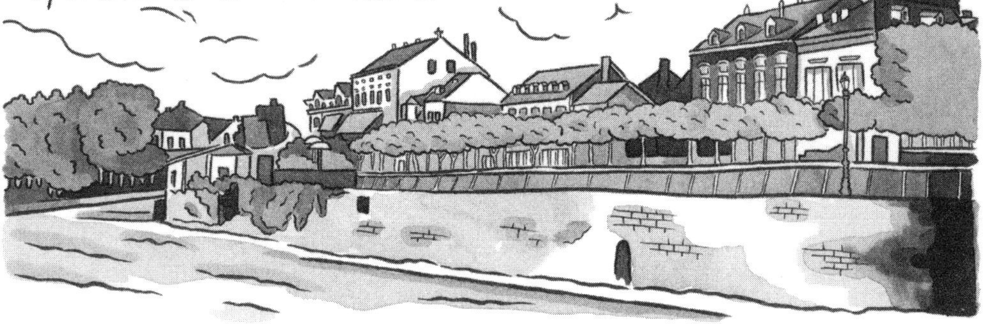

During the war, more than half a million combatants and over 200,000 noncombatant workers came from the French colonies. After Germany's defeat, soldiers from the colonies made up about 14% of the occupying force in Germany.

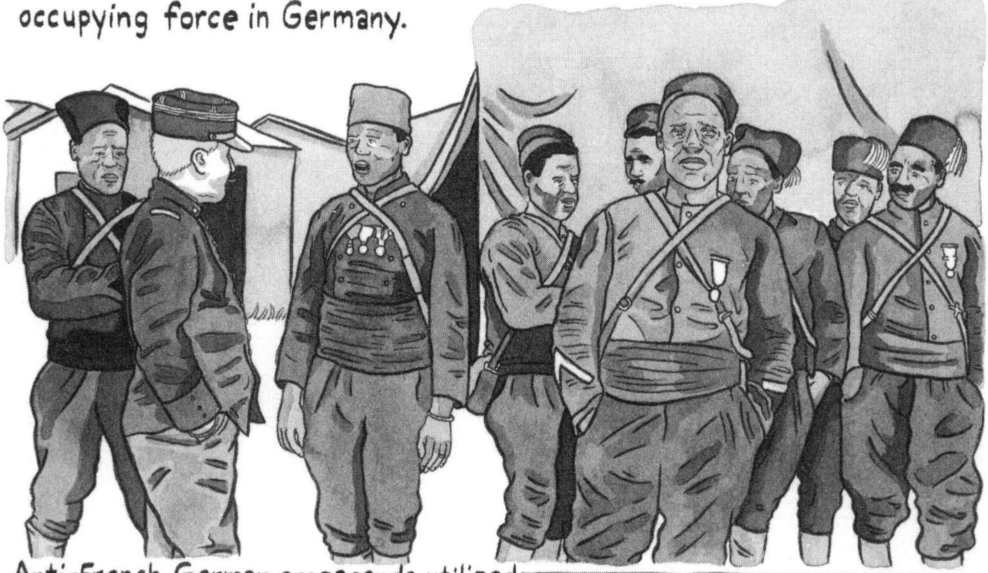

Anti-French German propaganda utilized familiar racist tropes – the mythical bogeyman of the savage Black rapist, threatening the purity of white women...

and thus the white race.

The "*Black French soldiers*" in this image are actually *white Germans* in costumes and blackface makeup.

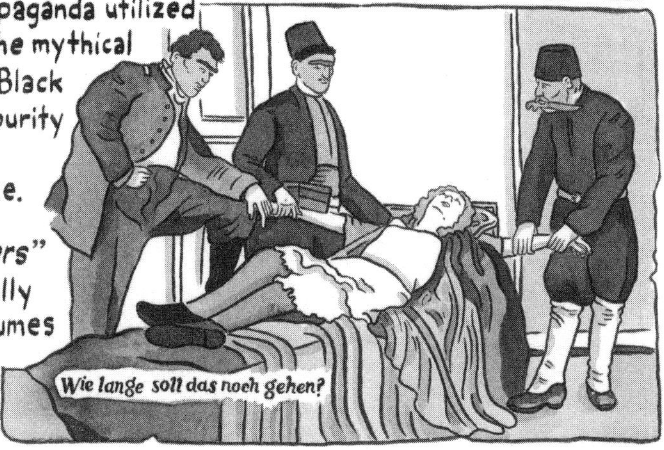
Wie lange soll das noch gehen?

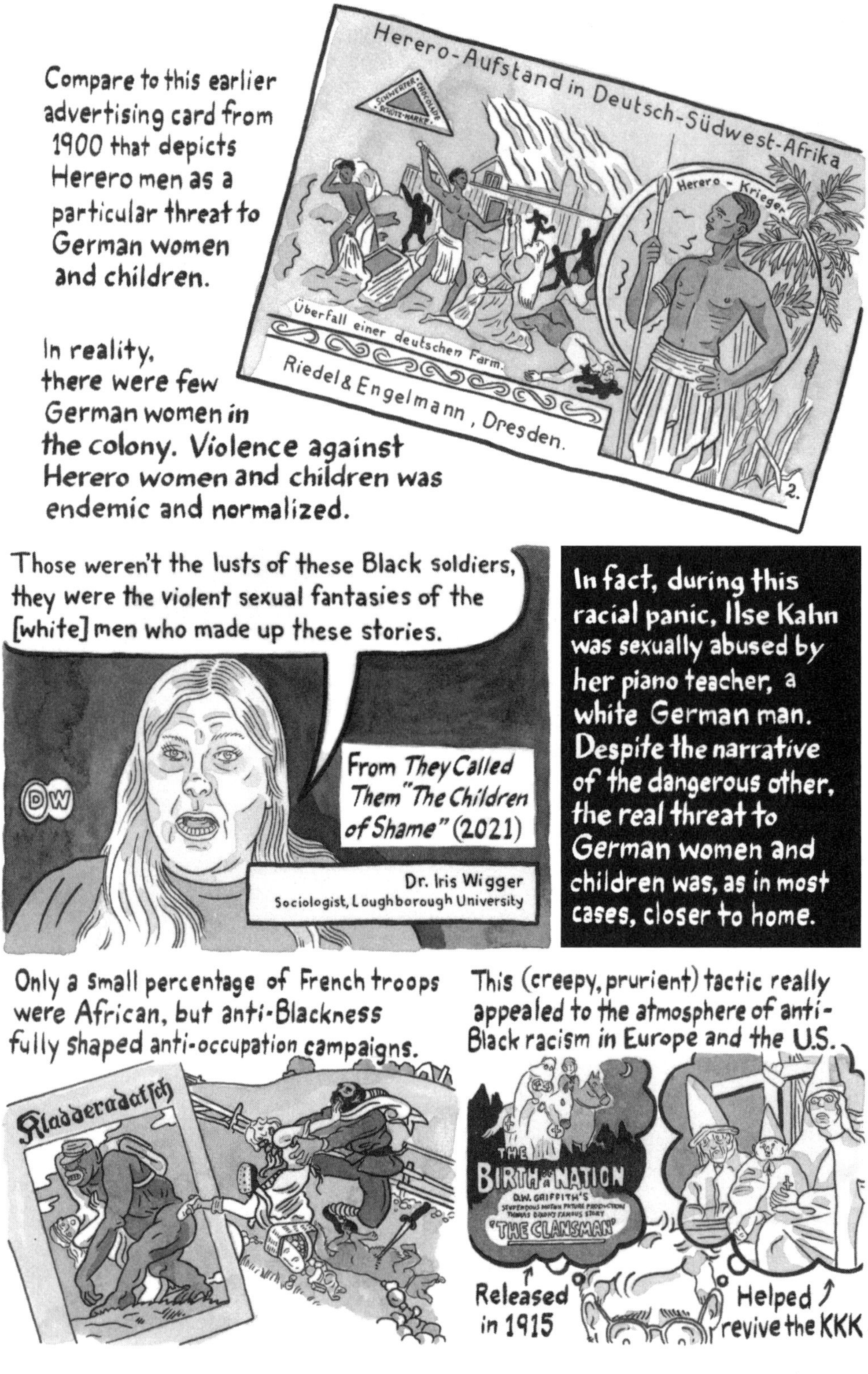
Compare to this earlier advertising card from 1900 that depicts Herero men as a particular threat to German women and children.
Herero-Aufstand in Deutsch-Südwest-Afrika
Herero - Krieger
Überfall einer deutschen Farm.
Riedel & Engelmann, Dresden.
2.
In reality, there were few German women in the colony. Violence against Herero women and children was endemic and normalized.
Those weren't the lusts of these Black soldiers, they were the violent sexual fantasies of the [white] men who made up these stories.
DW
From They Called Them "The Children of Shame" (2021)
Dr. Iris Wigger
Sociologist, Loughborough University
In fact, during this racial panic, Ilse Kahn was sexually abused by her piano teacher, a white German man. Despite the narrative of the dangerous other, the real threat to German women and children was, as in most cases, closer to home.
Only a small percentage of French troops were African, but anti-Blackness fully shaped anti-occupation campaigns.
Kladderadatsch
This (creepy, prurient) tactic really appealed to the atmosphere of anti-Black racism in Europe and the U.S.
THE BIRTH OF A NATION
D.W. GRIFFITH'S
STUPENDOUS MOTION PICTURE PRODUCTION
THOMAS DIXON'S FAMOUS STORY
"THE CLANSMAN"
Released in 1915
Helped revive the KKK

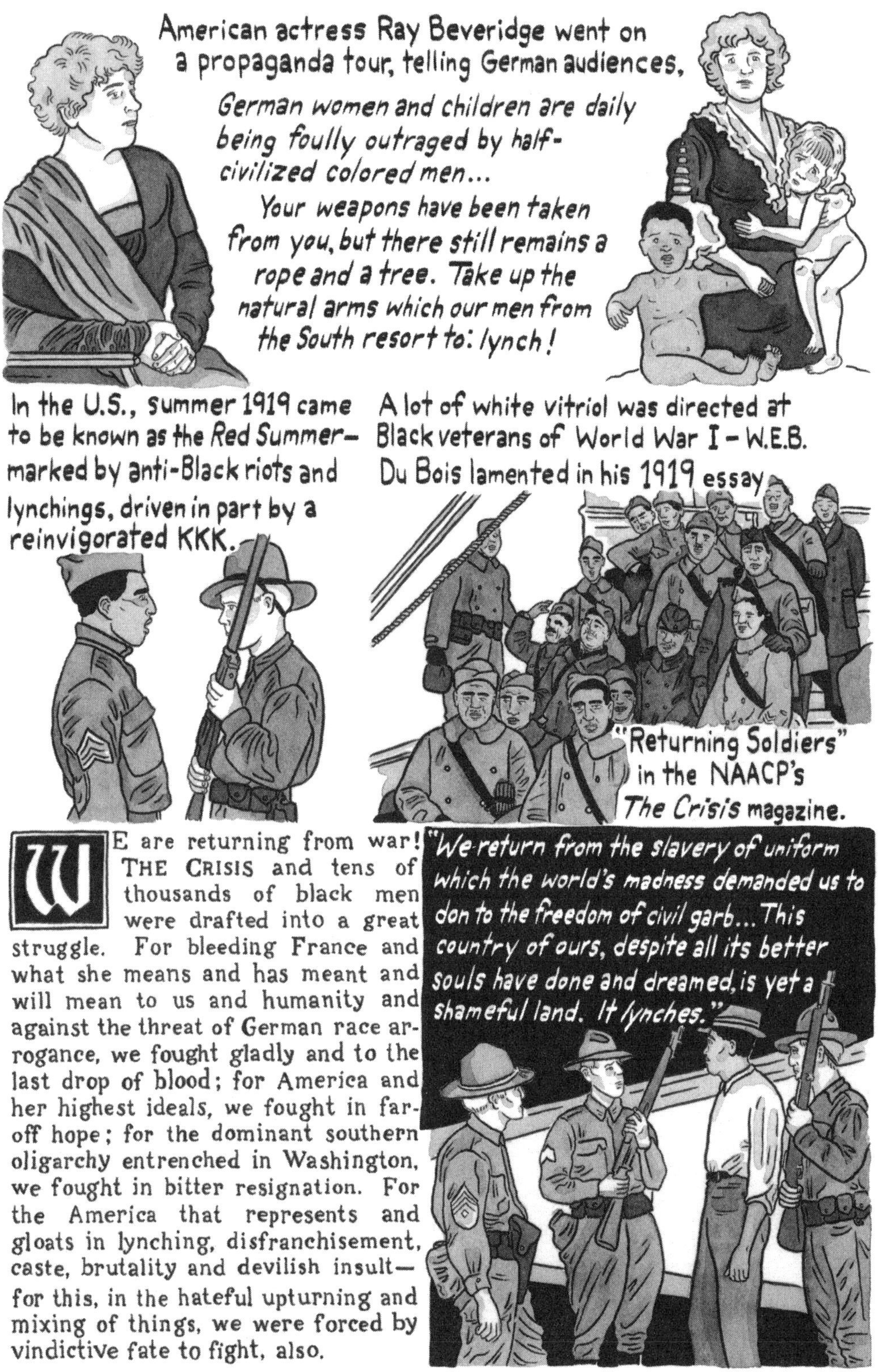

American actress Ray Beveridge went on a propaganda tour, telling German audiences,

German women and children are daily being foully outraged by half-civilized colored men...

Your weapons have been taken from you, but there still remains a rope and a tree. Take up the natural arms which our men from the South resort to: lynch!

In the U.S., summer 1919 came to be known as the *Red Summer*— marked by anti-Black riots and lynchings, driven in part by a reinvigorated KKK.

A lot of white vitriol was directed at Black veterans of World War I – W.E.B. Du Bois lamented in his 1919 essay

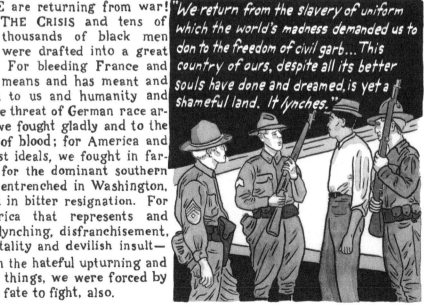

"Returning Soldiers" in the NAACP's *The Crisis* magazine.

E are returning from war! THE CRISIS and tens of thousands of black men were drafted into a great struggle. For bleeding France and what she means and has meant and will mean to us and humanity and against the threat of German race arrogance, we fought gladly and to the last drop of blood; for America and her highest ideals, we fought in far-off hope; for the dominant southern oligarchy entrenched in Washington, we fought in bitter resignation. For the America that represents and gloats in lynching, disfranchisement, caste, brutality and devilish insult— for this, in the hateful upturning and mixing of things, we were forced by vindictive fate to fight, also.

"We return from the slavery of uniform which the world's madness demanded us to don to the freedom of civil garb... This country of ours, despite all its better souls have done and dreamed, is yet a shameful land. It lynches."

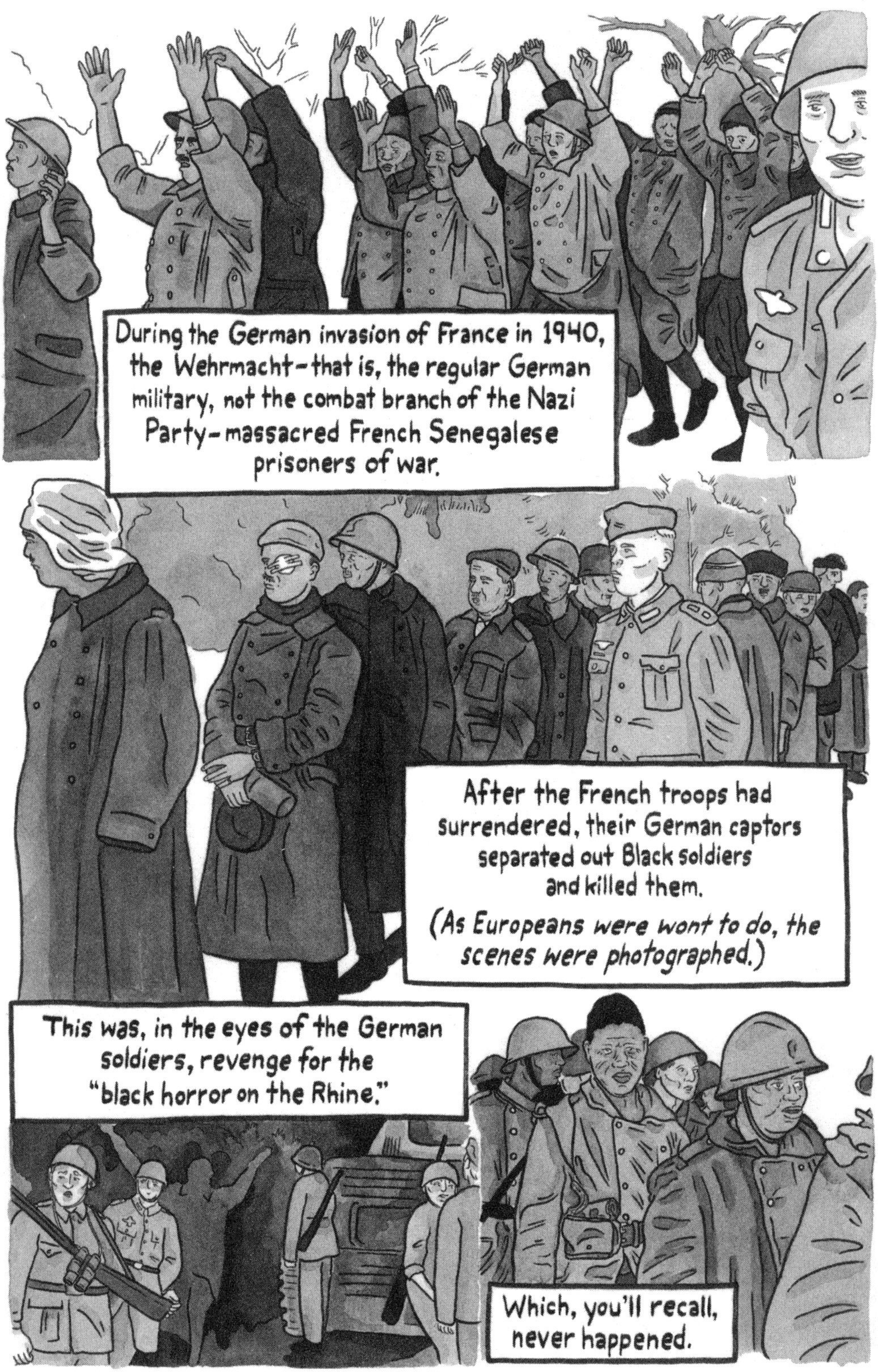
During the German invasion of France in 1940, the Wehrmacht—that is, the regular German military, not the combat branch of the Nazi Party—massacred French Senegalese prisoners of war.
After the French troops had surrendered, their German captors separated out Black soldiers and killed them.
(As Europeans were wont to do, the scenes were photographed.)
This was, in the eyes of the German soldiers, revenge for the "black horror on the Rhine."
Which, you'll recall, never happened.

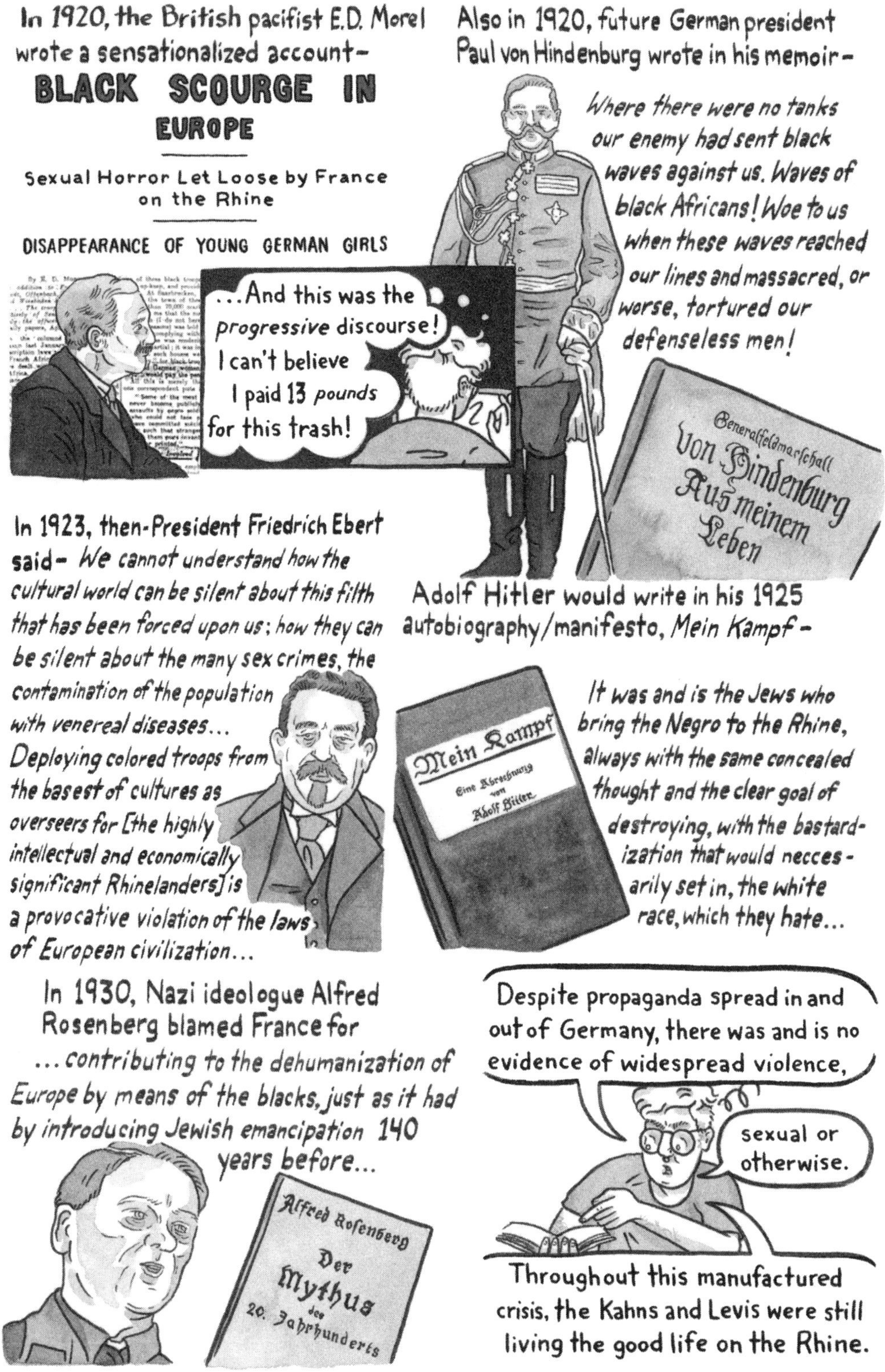
In 1920, the British pacifist E.D. Morel wrote a sensationalized account–
BLACK SCOURGE IN EUROPE
Sexual Horror Let Loose by France on the Rhine
DISAPPEARANCE OF YOUNG GERMAN GIRLS
...And this was the *progressive* discourse! I can't believe I paid 13 *pounds* for this trash!
Also in 1920, future German president Paul von Hindenburg wrote in his memoir–
Where there were no tanks our enemy had sent black waves against us. Waves of black Africans! Woe to us when these waves reached our lines and massacred, or worse, tortured our defenseless men!
Generalfeldmarschall von Hindenburg Aus meinem Leben
In 1923, then-President Friedrich Ebert said– *We cannot understand how the cultural world can be silent about this filth that has been forced upon us; how they can be silent about the many sex crimes, the contamination of the population with venereal diseases... Deploying colored troops from the basest of cultures as overseers for [the highly intellectual and economically significant Rhinelanders] is a provocative violation of the laws of European civilization...*
Adolf Hitler would write in his 1925 autobiography/manifesto, *Mein Kampf*–
Mein Kampf Eine Abrechnung von Adolf Hitler
It was and is the Jews who bring the Negro to the Rhine, always with the same concealed thought and the clear goal of destroying, with the bastard-ization that would necces-arily set in, the white race, which they hate...
In 1930, Nazi ideologue Alfred Rosenberg blamed France for
...contributing to the dehumanization of Europe by means of the blacks, just as it had by introducing Jewish emancipation 140 years before...
Alfred Rosenberg Der Mythus des 20. Jahrhunderts
Despite propaganda spread in and out of Germany, there was and is no evidence of widespread violence,
sexual or otherwise.
Throughout this manufactured crisis, the Kahns and Levis were still living the good life on the Rhine.

There were already conversations in the 1920s about sterilizing Afro-German children. This was not yet legal in Germany, but was very popular in the U.S.– and was upheld by the Supreme Court in the 1927 case *Buck v. Bell*.

Upon gaining power, the Nazis soon fixated on the tiny population of mixed-race children in the Rhineland.

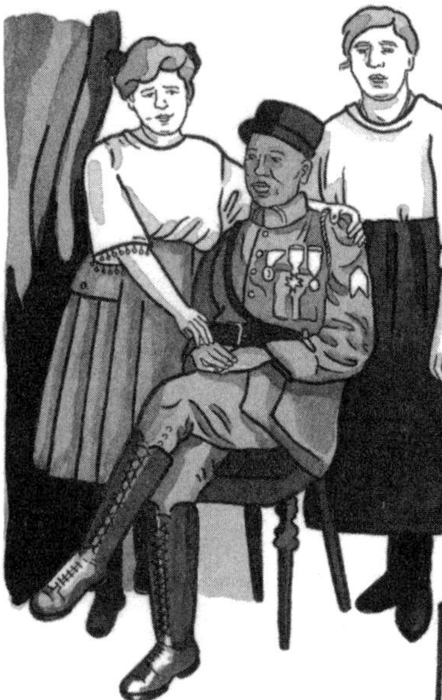

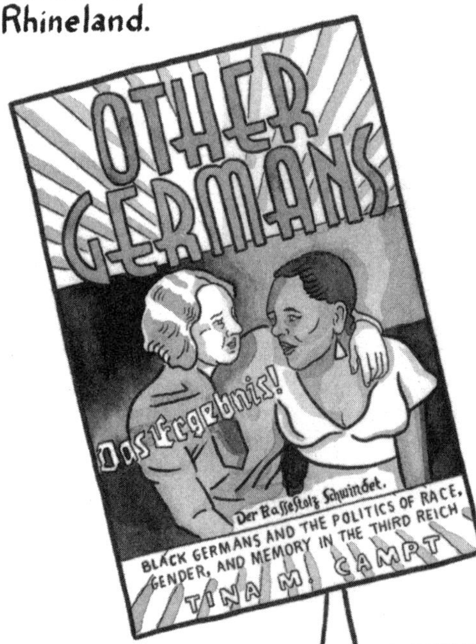
OTHER GERMANS
Das Ergebnis!
Der Rassestolz Schwindet.
BLACK GERMANS AND THE POLITICS OF RACE, GENDER, AND MEMORY IN THE THIRD REICH
TINA M. CAMPT

> . . . in the service of racial purity, this regime produced the same subjects it regulated, administered, and indeed ultimately sought to destroy.

In April 1933, cabinet minister Hermann Göring – whose father was a colonial governor in German South West Africa – ordered local authorities to collect demographic data on Black Germans. In 1937, the Gestapo formed Special Commission No. 3 – Eugen Fischer was on the board. Their task was to find and sterilize mixed-race people.

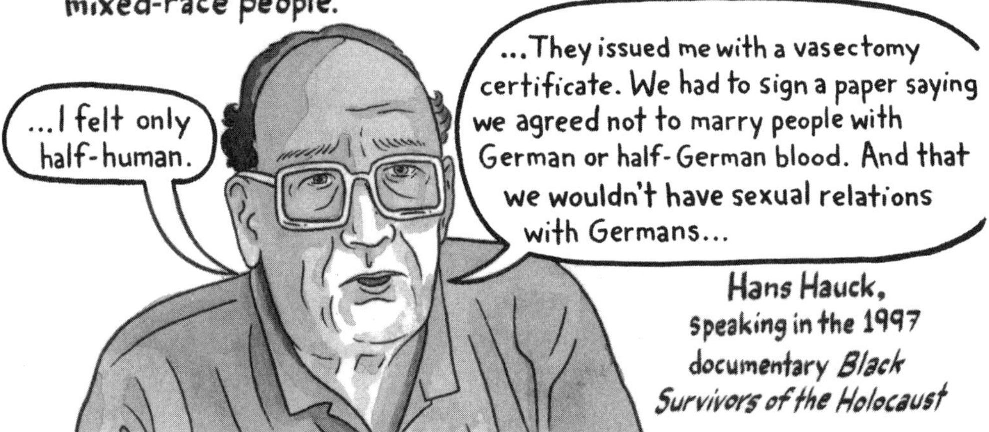
...I felt only half-human.
...They issued me with a vasectomy certificate. We had to sign a paper saying we agreed not to marry people with German or half-German blood. And that we wouldn't have sexual relations with Germans...

Hans Hauck, speaking in the 1997 documentary *Black Survivors of the Holocaust*

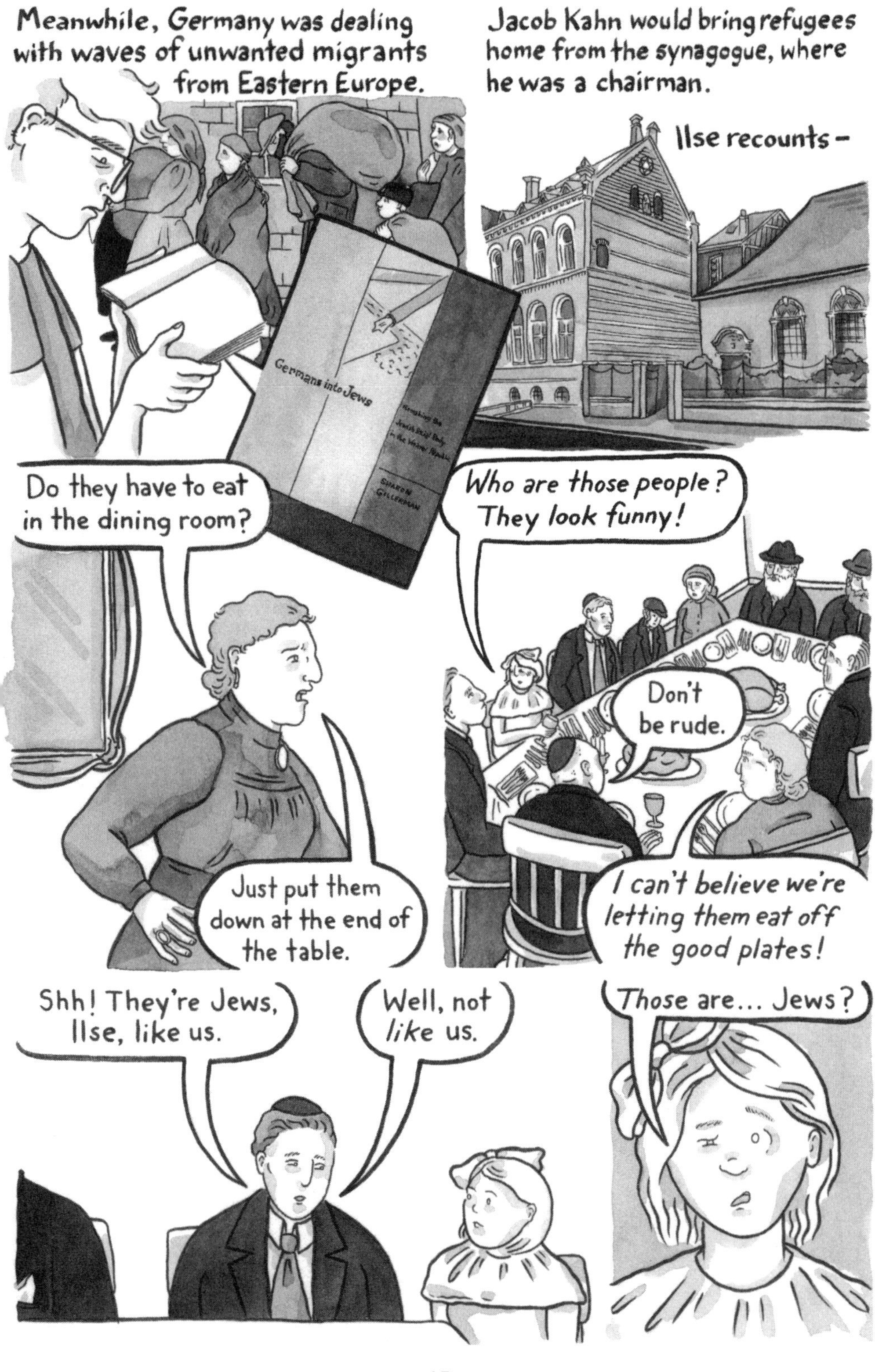

Meanwhile, Germany was dealing with waves of unwanted migrants from Eastern Europe.
Germans into Jews
SHARON GILLERMAN
Jacob Kahn would bring refugees home from the synagogue, where he was a chairman.
Ilse recounts –
Do they have to eat in the dining room?
Who are those people? They look funny!
Don't be rude.
Just put them down at the end of the table.
I can't believe we're letting them eat off the good plates!
Shh! They're Jews, Ilse, like us.
Well, not like us.
Those are... Jews?

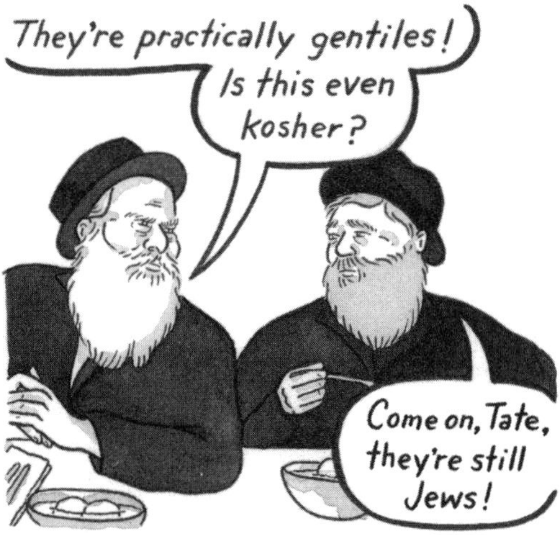
They're practically gentiles!
Is this even kosher?
Come on, Tate, they're still Jews!

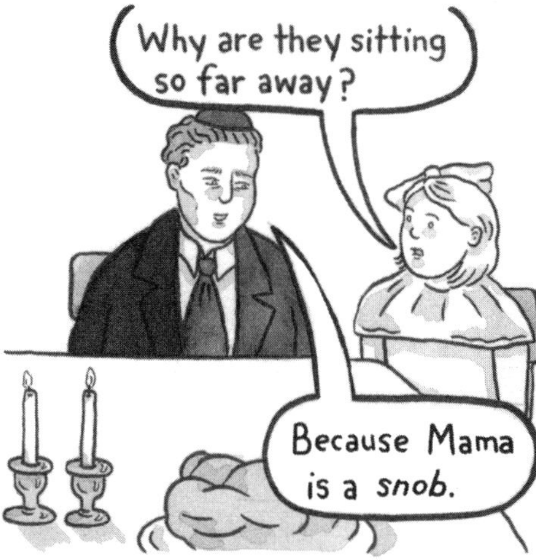
Why are they sitting so far away?
Because Mama is a *snob*.

The concerns of the Jewish community in Germany in the 1920s were, in part, very similar to those I grew up with in the U.S. in the 1990s,

Columnists in the Jewish press frequently fielded questions from mothers seeking advice on how to handle their children's antisemitic classmates.

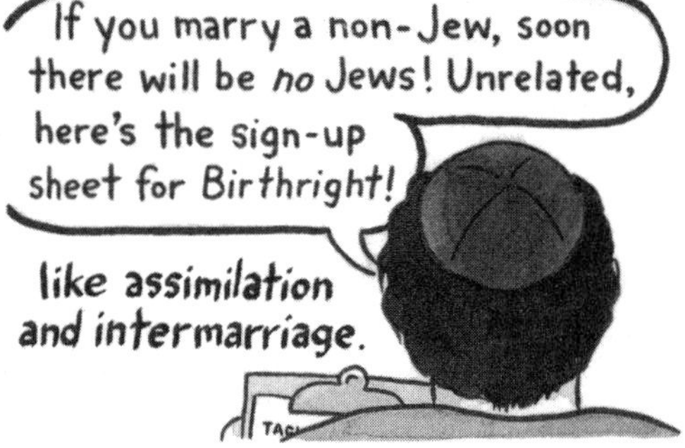
If you marry a non-Jew, soon there will be *no* Jews! Unrelated, here's the sign-up sheet for Birthright!
like assimilation and intermarriage.

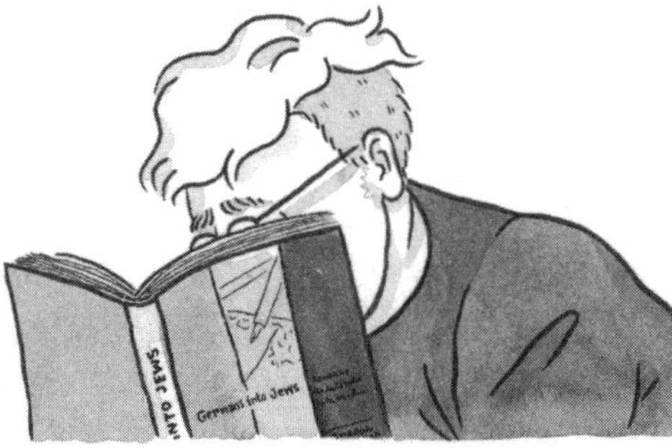
Germans into Jews

Benno Kahn died in a car crash in 1928. Ilse missed a year of school after his death...

Even so, Ilse was an average German teenager. She loved hiking and films and was on a swim team.

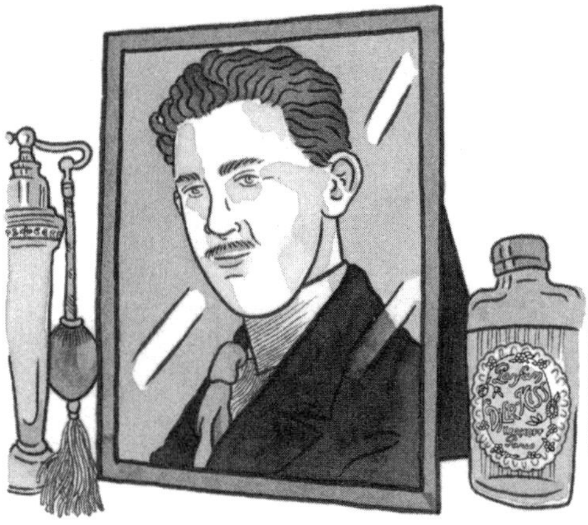

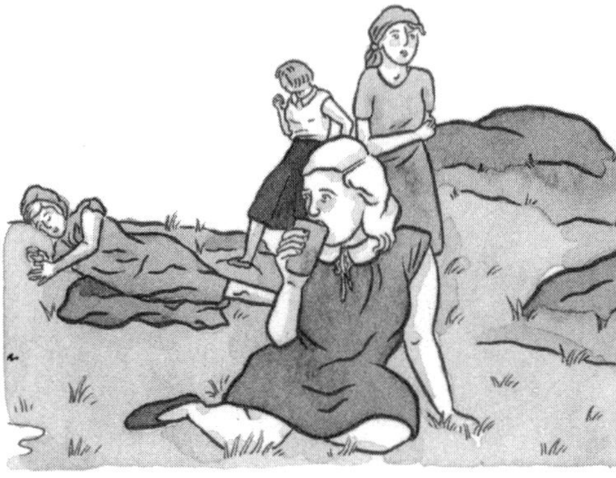

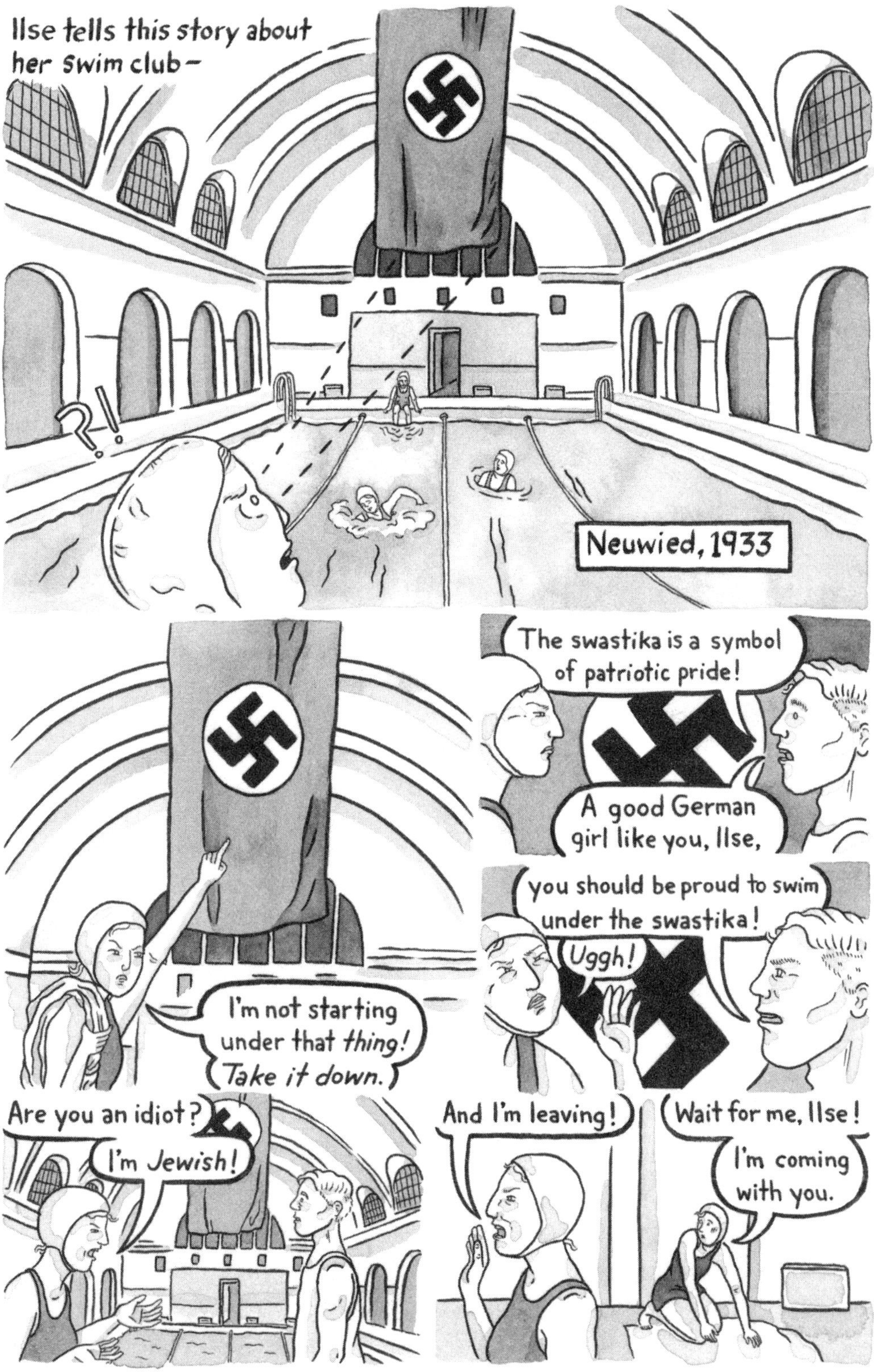

Ilse tells this story about her swim club –
?!
Neuwied, 1933
I'm not starting under that *thing*! *Take it down.*
The swastika is a symbol of patriotic pride!
A good German girl like you, Ilse,
you should be proud to swim under the swastika!
Uggh!
Are you an idiot?
I'm *Jewish*!
And I'm leaving!
Wait for me, Ilse!
I'm coming with you.

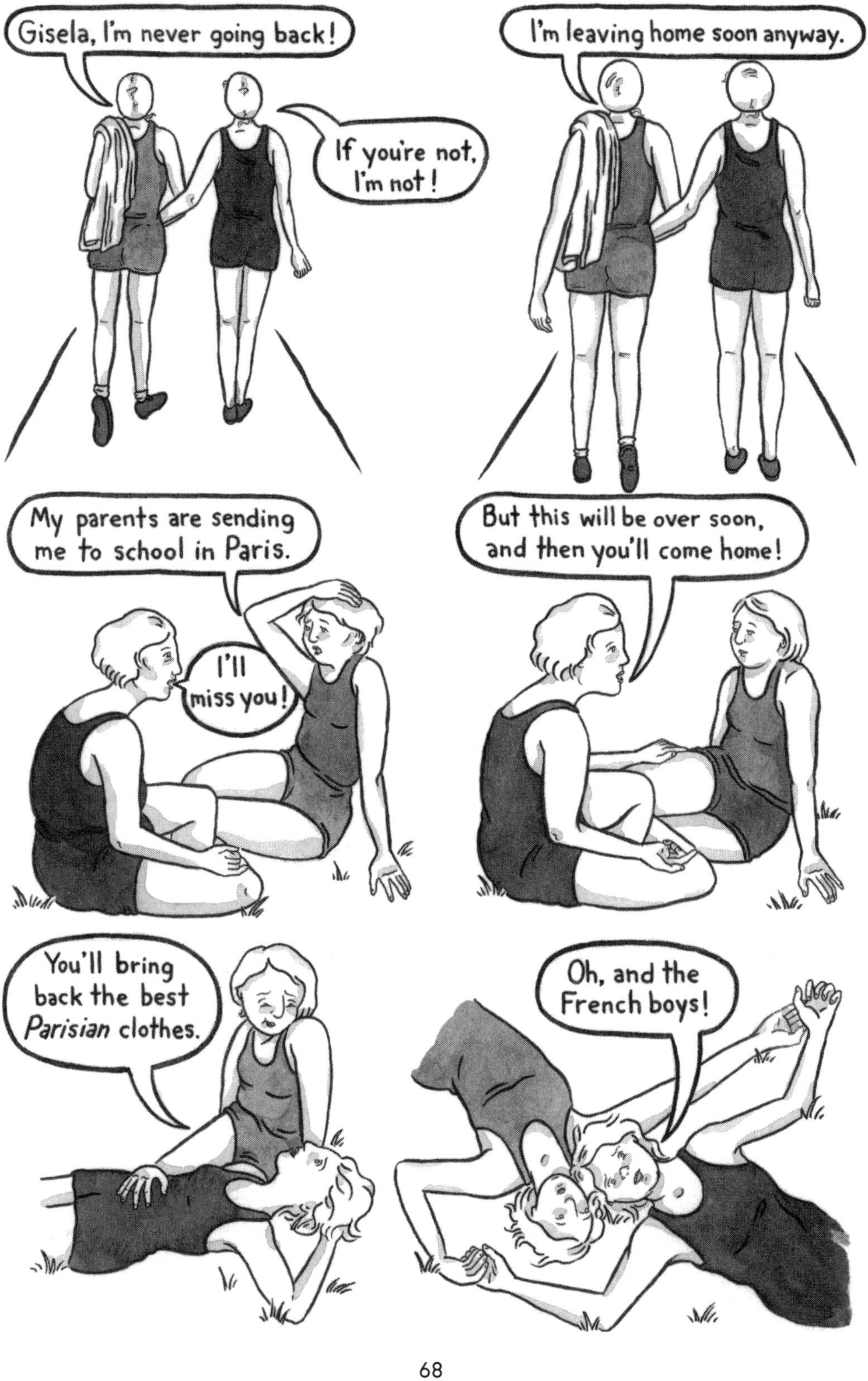
Gisela, I'm never going back!
If you're not, I'm not!
I'm leaving home soon anyway.
My parents are sending me to school in Paris.
I'll miss you!
But this will be over soon, and then you'll come home!
You'll bring back the best *Parisian* clothes.
Oh, and the French boys!

In 1933, Germany passed the Law against Overcrowding in Schools and Universities, which limited enrollment of non-Aryan students in public schools.

Ilse left to study in Paris—

a course in French language and literature at the Sorbonne.

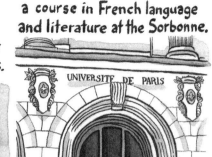

By the 1930s, the student population of the Sorbonne had tripled from its pre-World War I numbers.

Things are just getting worse at home.

My parents think Hitler will be out by next year!

A huge number of students died during the Great War. In the '30s, 41% of those enrolled were women.

Back in Germany, university students in the Nazi Party occupied the Institute of Sexology in Berlin

and burned its research library and archives.

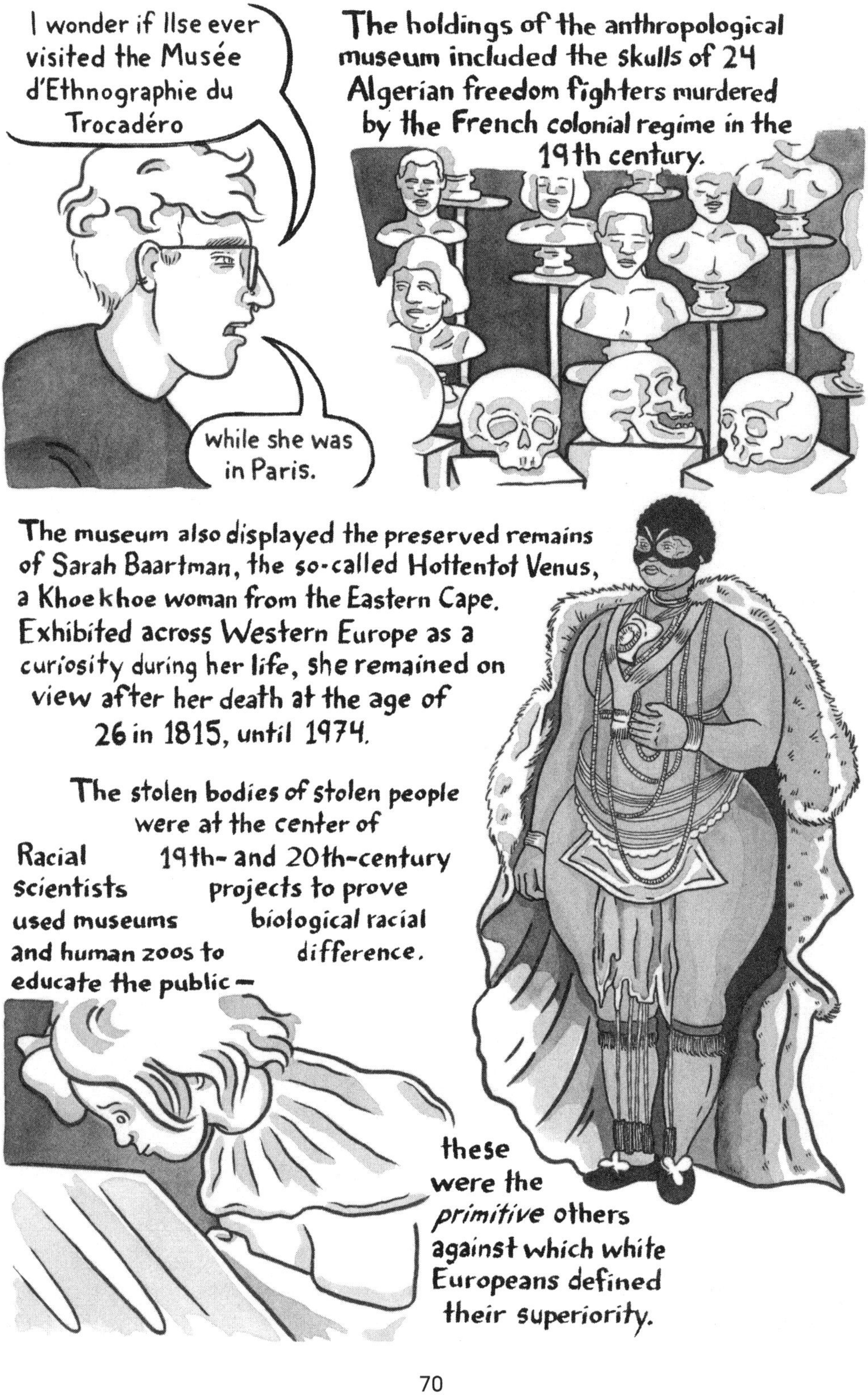

I wonder if Ilse ever visited the Musée d'Ethnographie du Trocadéro
while she was in Paris.
The holdings of the anthropological museum included the skulls of 24 Algerian freedom fighters murdered by the French colonial regime in the 19th century.
The museum also displayed the preserved remains of Sarah Baartman, the so-called Hottentot Venus, a Khoekhoe woman from the Eastern Cape. Exhibited across Western Europe as a curiosity during her life, she remained on view after her death at the age of 26 in 1815, until 1974.
The stolen bodies of stolen people were at the center of
Racial scientists used museums and human zoos to educate the public —
19th- and 20th-century projects to prove biological racial difference.
these were the *primitive* others against which white Europeans defined their superiority.

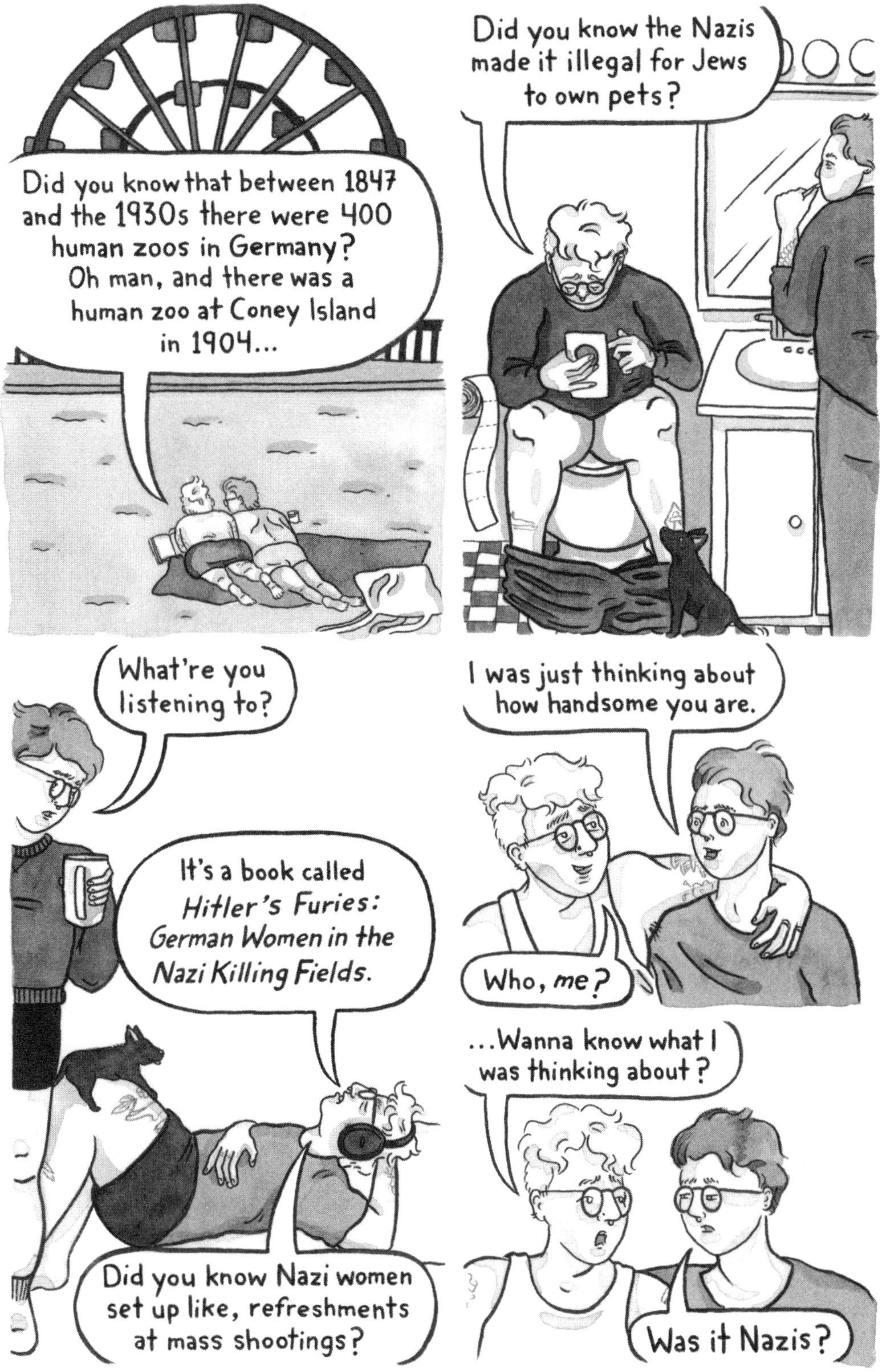

Did you know that between 1847 and the 1930s there were 400 human zoos in Germany? Oh man, and there was a human zoo at Coney Island in 1904...
Did you know the Nazis made it illegal for Jews to own pets?
What're you listening to?
It's a book called *Hitler's Furies: German Women in the Nazi Killing Fields.*
Did you know Nazi women set up like, refreshments at mass shootings?
I was just thinking about how handsome you are.
Who, *me*?
...Wanna know what I was thinking about?
Was it Nazis?

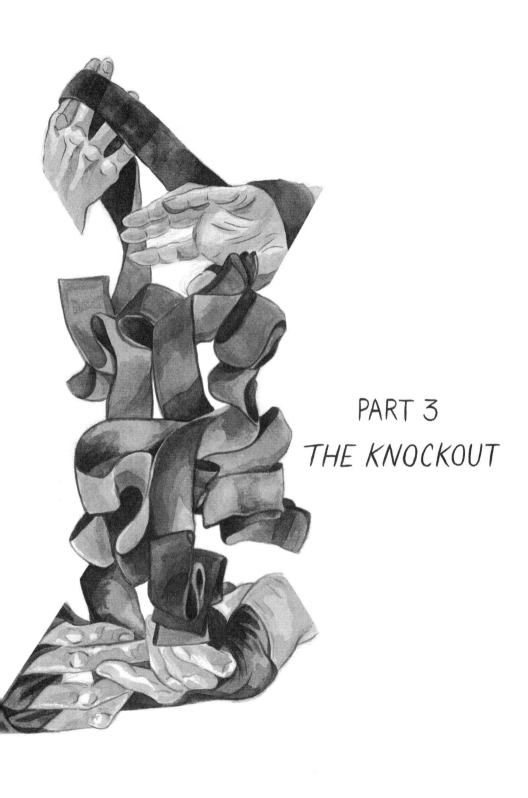

PART 3

THE KNOCKOUT

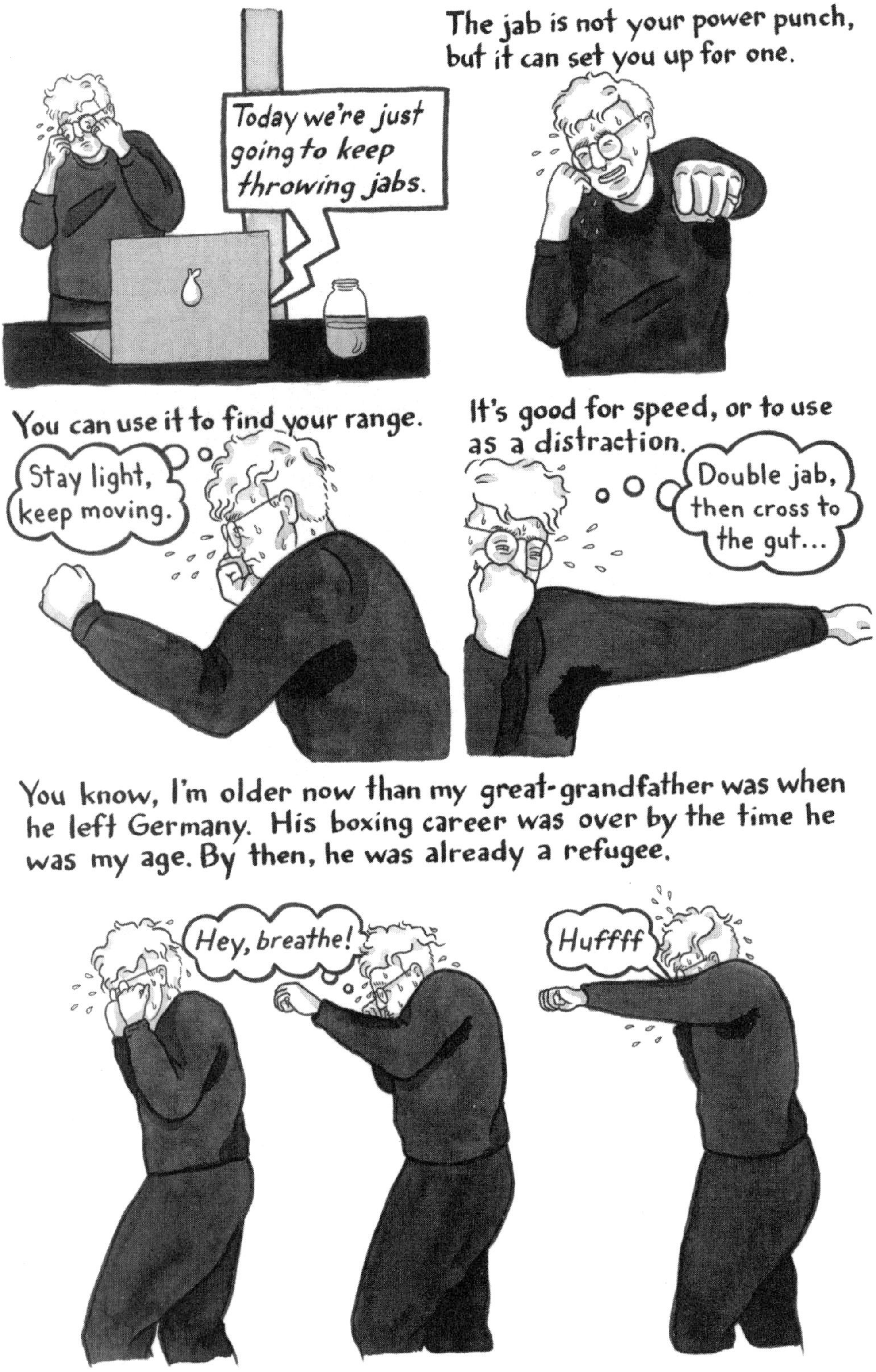
Today we're just going to keep throwing jabs.
The jab is not your power punch, but it can set you up for one.
You can use it to find your range.
Stay light, keep moving.
It's good for speed, or to use as a distraction.
Double jab, then cross to the gut...
You know, I'm older now than my great-grandfather was when he left Germany. His boxing career was over by the time he was my age. By then, he was already a refugee.
Hey, breathe!
Huffff

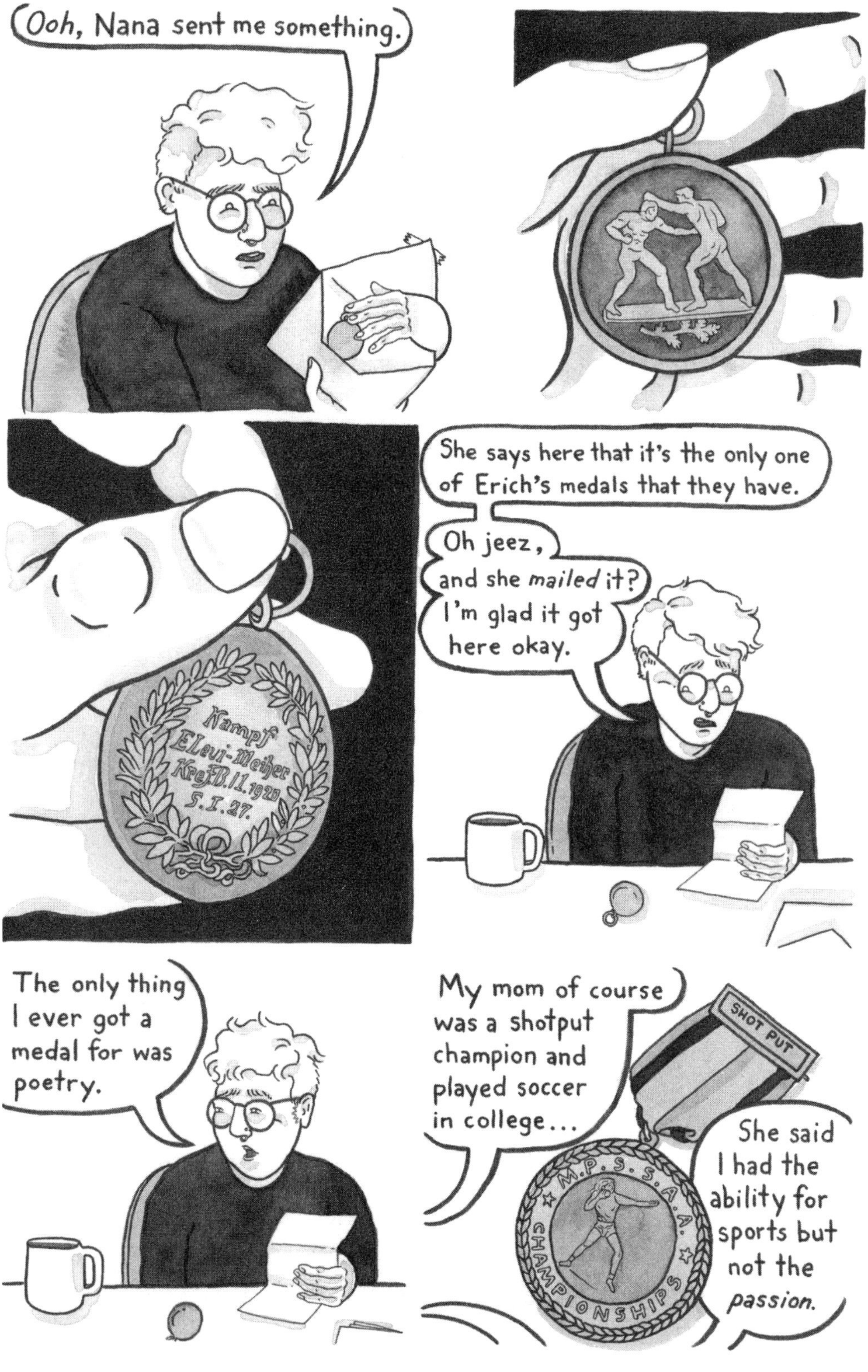
Ooh, Nana sent me something.
She says here that it's the only one of Erich's medals that they have.
Oh jeez, and she *mailed* it? I'm glad it got here okay.
The only thing I ever got a medal for was poetry.
My mom of course was a shotput champion and played soccer in college...
SHOT PUT
M.P.S.S.A.A. CHAMPIONSHIPS
She said I had the ability for sports but not the *passion*.

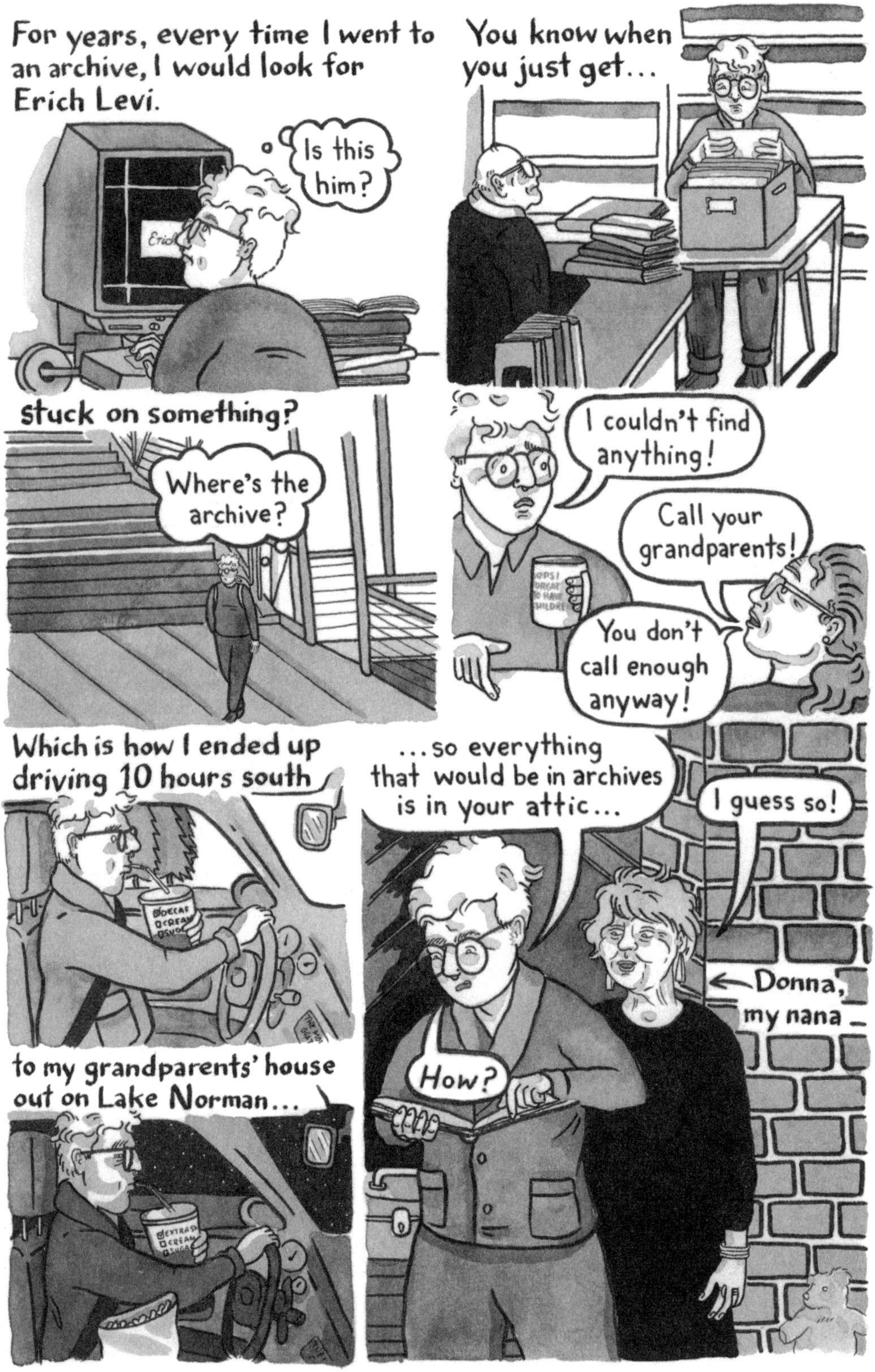
For years, every time I went to an archive, I would look for Erich Levi.
Is this him?
Erich
You know when you just get...
stuck on something?
Where's the archive?
I couldn't find anything!
Call your grandparents!
You don't call enough anyway!
Which is how I ended up driving 10 hours south
to my grandparents' house out on Lake Norman...
...so everything that would be in archives is in your attic...
I guess so!
Donna, my nana
How?

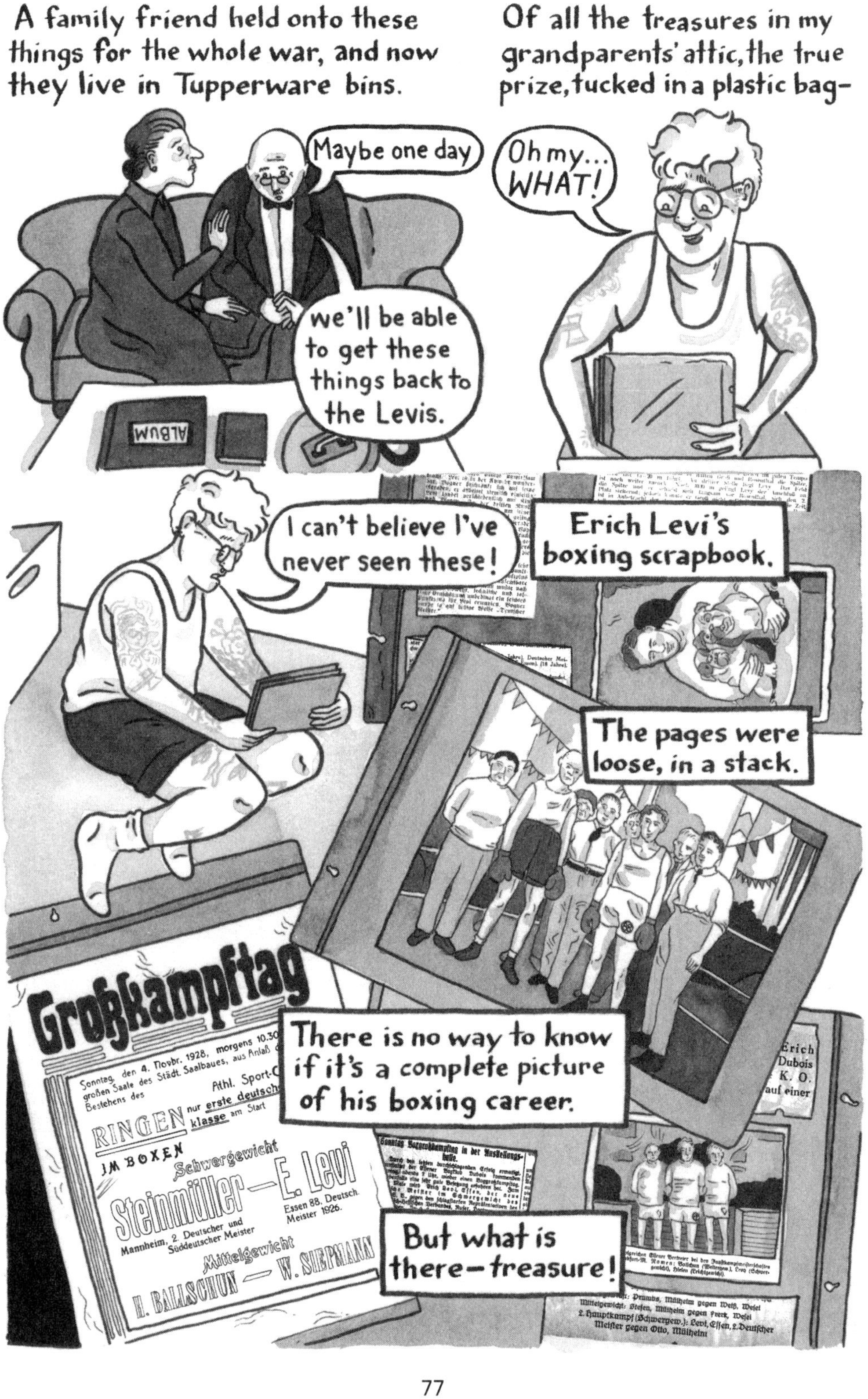
A family friend held onto these things for the whole war, and now they live in Tupperware bins.
Maybe one day
we'll be able to get these things back to the Levis.
ALBUM
Of all the treasures in my grandparents' attic, the true prize, tucked in a plastic bag-
Oh my... WHAT!
I can't believe I've never seen these!
Erich Levi's boxing scrapbook.
The pages were loose, in a stack.
Großkampftag
Sonntag, den 4. Novbr. 1928, morgens 10.30
großen Saale des Städt. Saalbaues, aus Anlaß
Bestehens des
Athl. Sport-C
RINGEN nur erste deutsche klasse am Start
IM BOXEN
Schwergewicht
Steinmüller — E. Levi
Mannheim, 2. Deutscher und Süddeutscher Meister
Essen 88. Deutsch. Meister 1926.
Mittelgewicht
H. BALLSCHUN — W. SIEPMANN
There is no way to know if it's a complete picture of his boxing career.
Erich
Dubois
K. O.
auf einer
But what is there—treasure!
Mittelgewicht: Stefen, Mülheim gegen Freck, Wesel
2. Hauptkampf (Schwergew.): Levi, Essen, 2. Deutscher
Meister gegen Otto, Mülheim

In the clippings in Erich's scrapbook, I get a portrait of my opa as a fighter.

A clipping from 1924, when he was 18, says he is "wonderful on defense."

He's described as an "intelligent fighter..." "technically superior..."

"... the Essener was very fast on his feet and blocked every single one..."

"E. Levi, Essen 88, wore down [his opponent] with fine, excellent lefts in such a way that the other gave up the hopeless fight..."

He was good!

Not undefeated or anything, but a solid, respected fighter with a good record.

"The German champion Levi 88 impresses with clear punches..."

He delivered a bunch of knockouts...

"Levi did with [his opponent] what he wanted and [same] could not apply one blow..."

"...delivered the best fight of the evening..."

"...justifies the hope he will represent the colors of the city of Essen in a worthy manner."

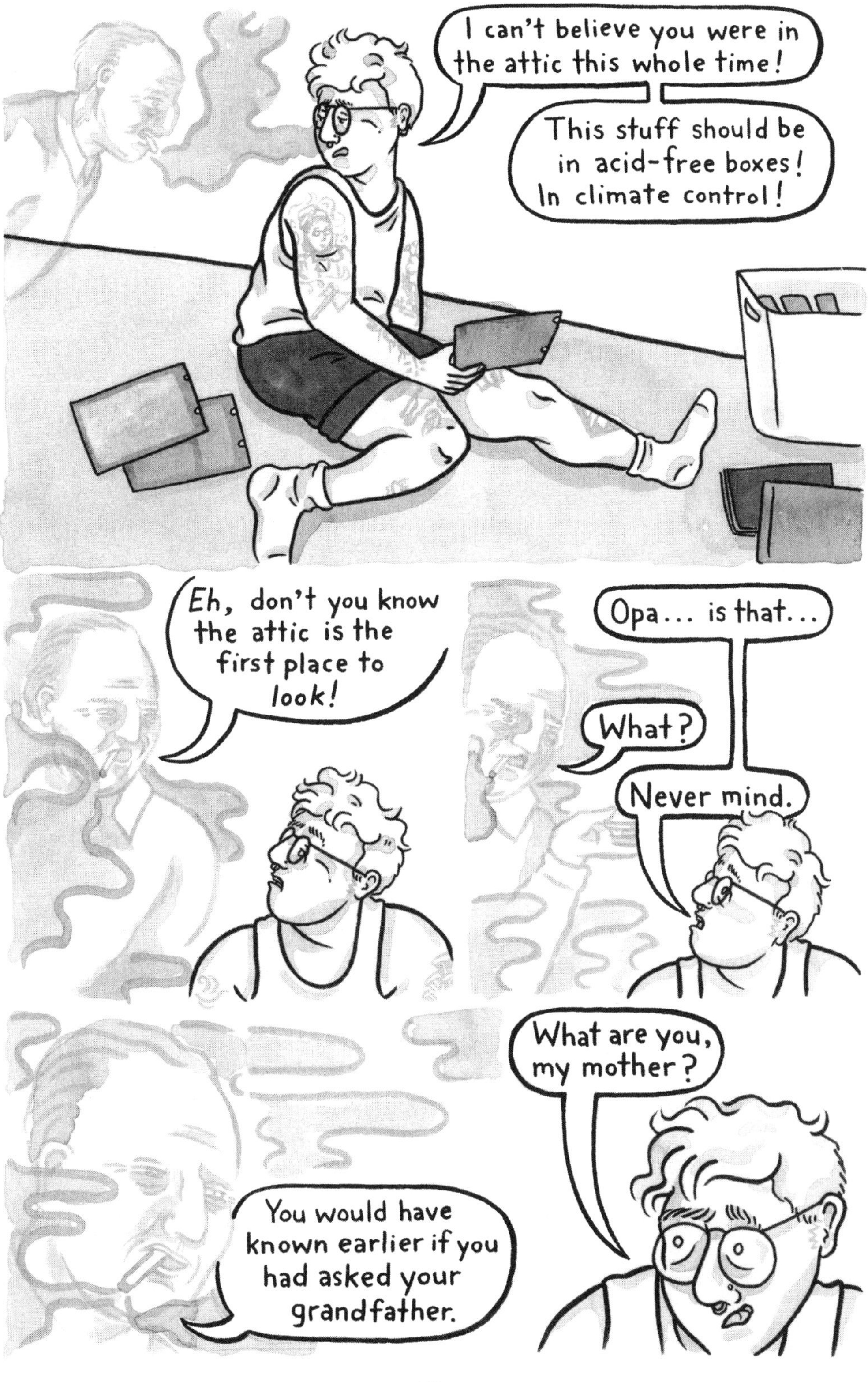
I can't believe you were in the attic this whole time!
This stuff should be in acid-free boxes! In climate control!
Eh, don't you know the attic is the first place to look!
Opa... is that...
What?
Never mind.
What are you, my mother?
You would have known earlier if you had asked your grandfather.

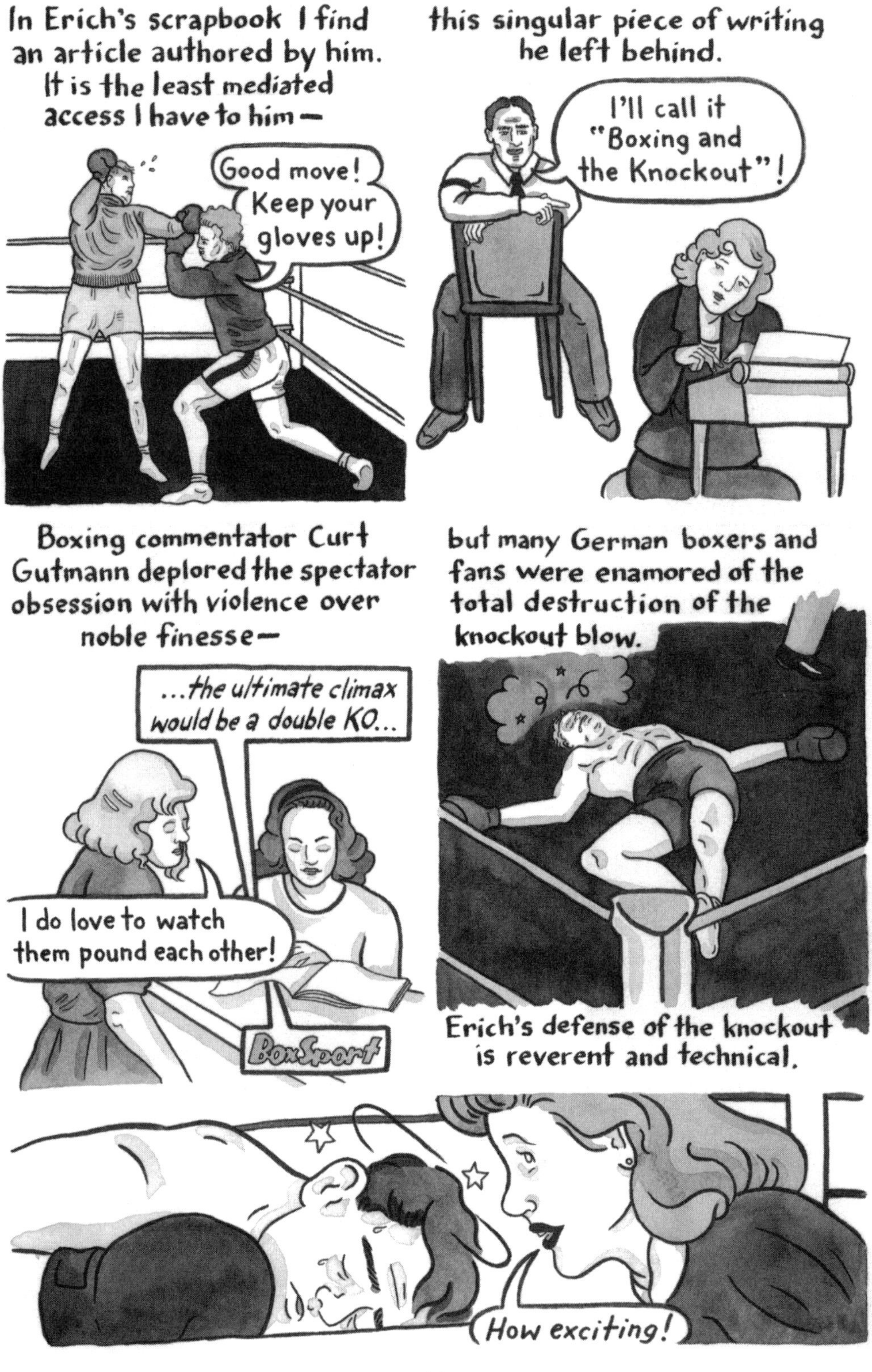
In Erich's scrapbook I find an article authored by him. It is the least mediated access I have to him—
Good move! Keep your gloves up!
this singular piece of writing he left behind.
I'll call it "Boxing and the Knockout"!
Boxing commentator Curt Gutmann deplored the spectator obsession with violence over noble finesse—
...the ultimate climax would be a double KO...
I do love to watch them pound each other!
BoxSport
but many German boxers and fans were enamored of the total destruction of the knockout blow.
Erich's defense of the knockout is reverent and technical.
How exciting!

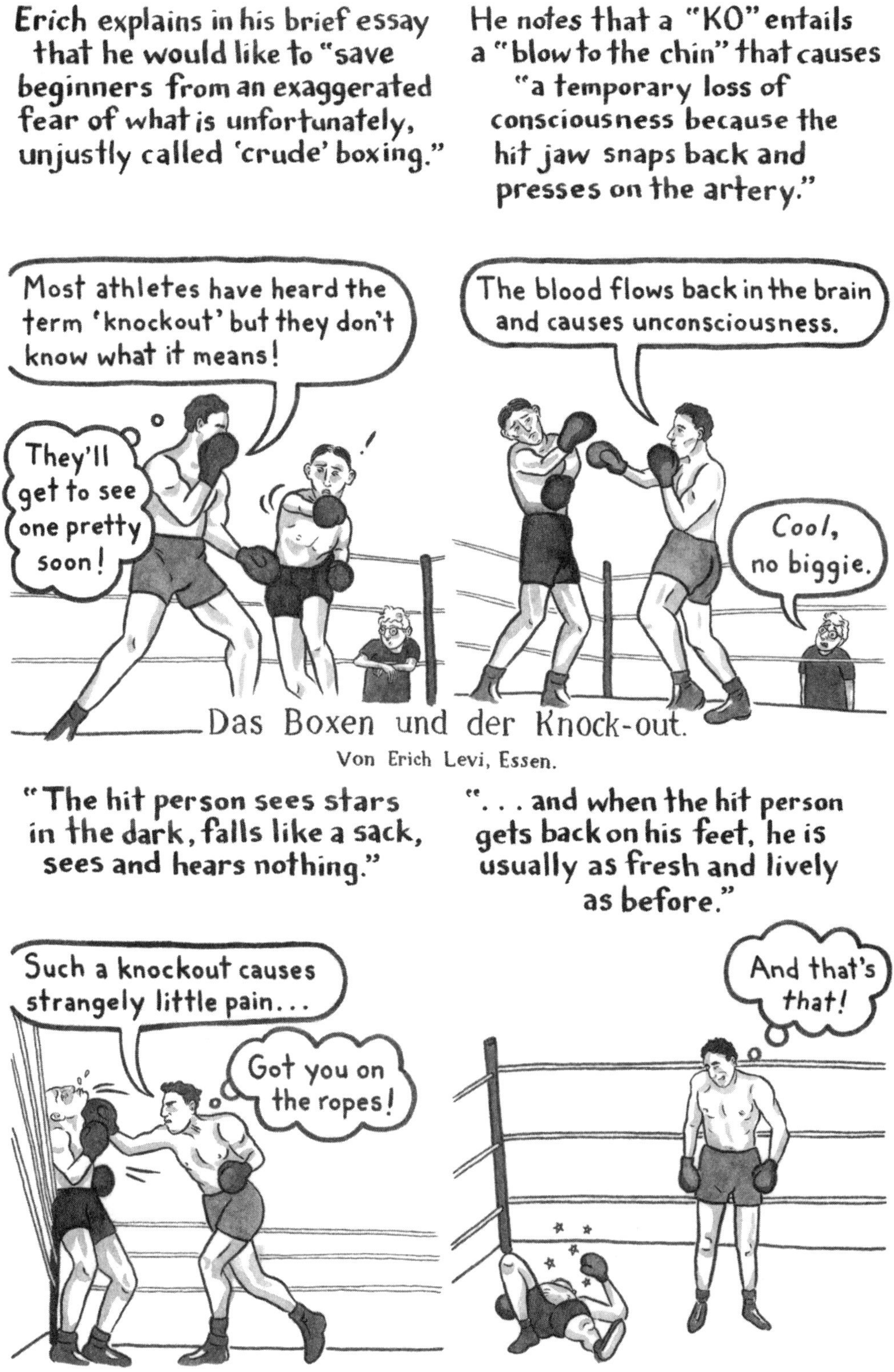
Erich explains in his brief essay that he would like to "save beginners from an exaggerated fear of what is unfortunately, unjustly called 'crude' boxing."
He notes that a "KO" entails a "blow to the chin" that causes "a temporary loss of consciousness because the hit jaw snaps back and presses on the artery."
Most athletes have heard the term 'knockout' but they don't know what it means!
They'll get to see one pretty soon!
The blood flows back in the brain and causes unconsciousness.
Cool, no biggie.
Das Boxen und der Knock-out.
Von Erich Levi, Essen.
"The hit person sees stars in the dark, falls like a sack, sees and hears nothing."
". . . and when the hit person gets back on his feet, he is usually as fresh and lively as before."
Such a knockout causes strangely little pain...
Got you on the ropes!
And that's that!

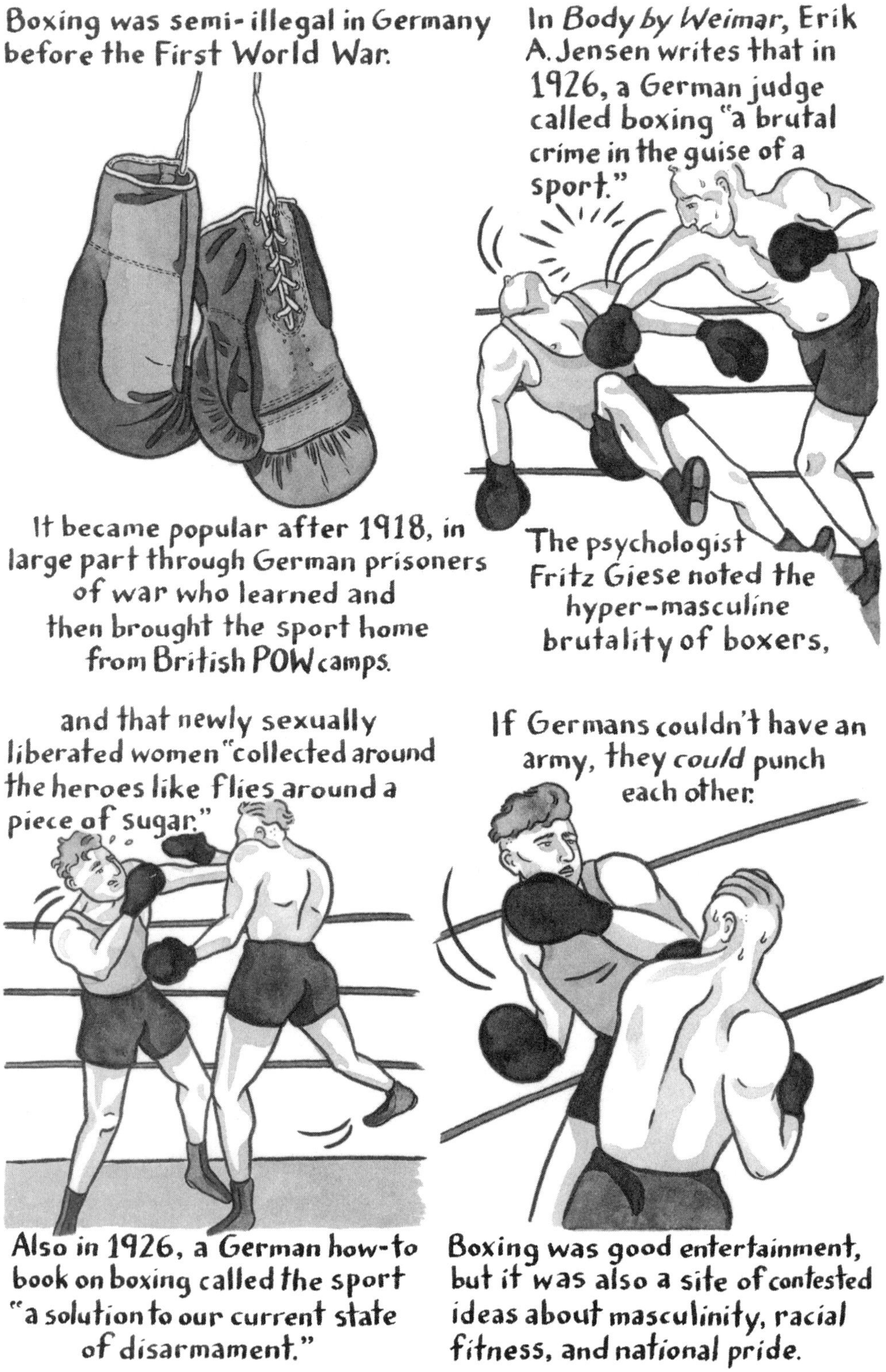
Boxing was semi-illegal in Germany before the First World War.
It became popular after 1918, in large part through German prisoners of war who learned and then brought the sport home from British POW camps.
In *Body by Weimar*, Erik A. Jensen writes that in 1926, a German judge called boxing "a brutal crime in the guise of a sport."
The psychologist Fritz Giese noted the hyper-masculine brutality of boxers,
and that newly sexually liberated women "collected around the heroes like flies around a piece of sugar."
Also in 1926, a German how-to book on boxing called the sport "a solution to our current state of disarmament."
If Germans couldn't have an army, they *could* punch each other.
Boxing was good entertainment, but it was also a site of contested ideas about masculinity, racial fitness, and national pride.

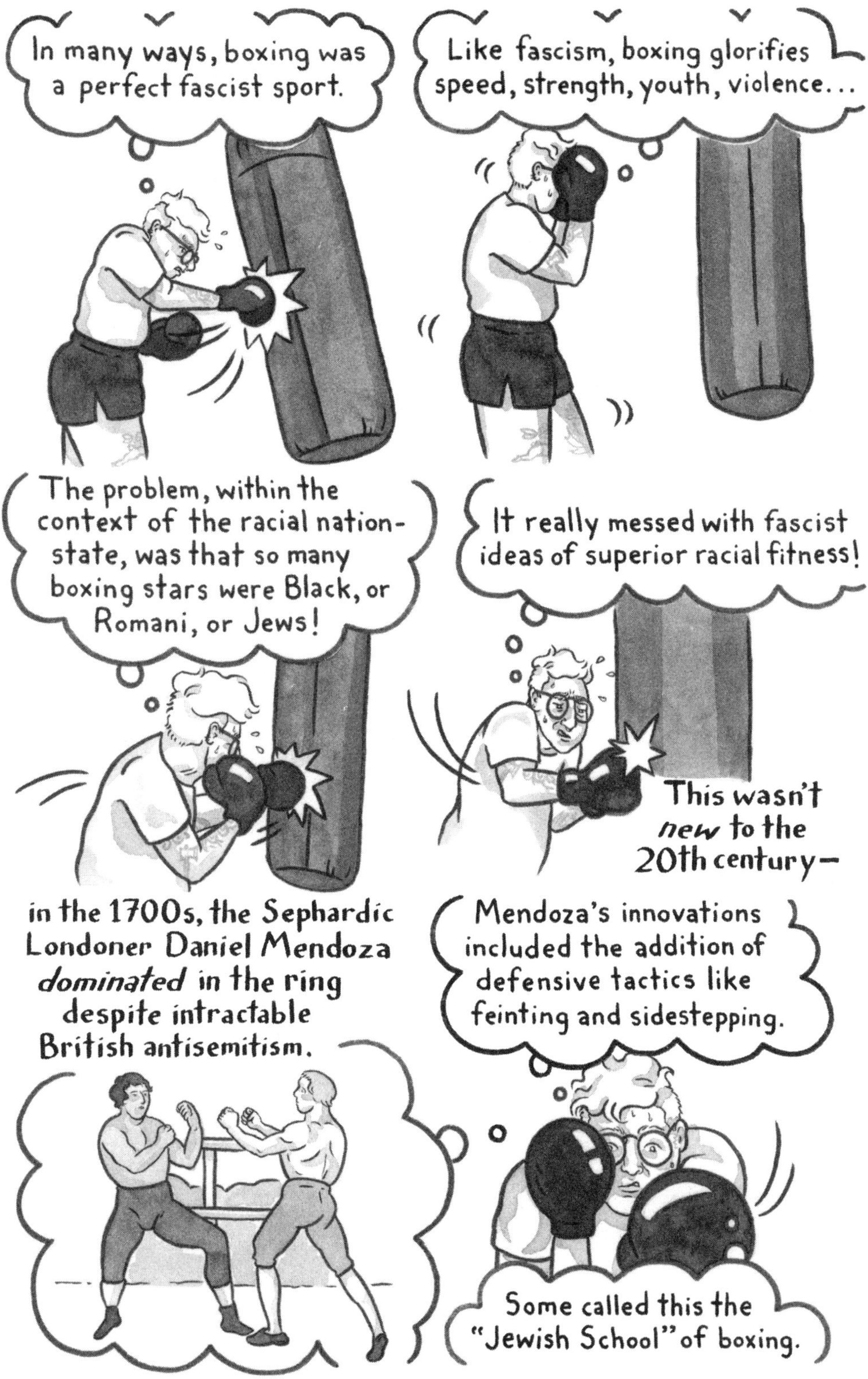

In many ways, boxing was a perfect fascist sport.
Like fascism, boxing glorifies speed, strength, youth, violence...
The problem, within the context of the racial nation-state, was that so many boxing stars were Black, or Romani, or Jews!
It really messed with fascist ideas of superior racial fitness!
This wasn't *new* to the 20th century—
in the 1700s, the Sephardic Londoner Daniel Mendoza *dominated* in the ring despite intractable British antisemitism.
Mendoza's innovations included the addition of defensive tactics like feinting and sidestepping.
Some called this the "Jewish School" of boxing.

German Jews also made an argument for Jewish dominance in the sport via positive eugenics.

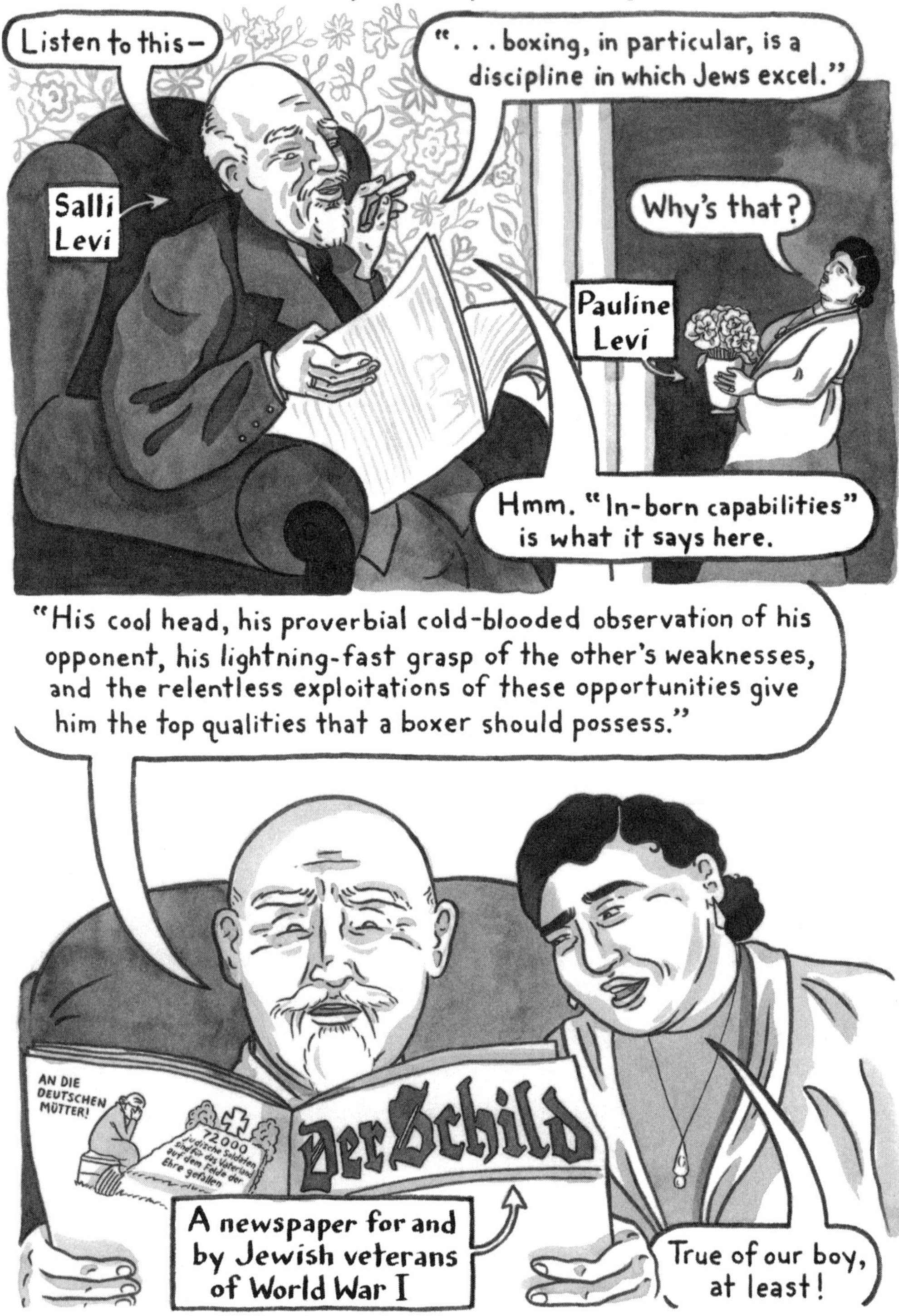
Listen to this–
". . . boxing, in particular, is a discipline in which Jews excel."
Salli Levi
Why's that?
Pauline Levi
Hmm. "In-born capabilities" is what it says here.
"His cool head, his proverbial cold-blooded observation of his opponent, his lightning-fast grasp of the other's weaknesses, and the relentless exploitations of these opportunities give him the top qualities that a boxer should possess."
AN DIE DEUTSCHEN MÜTTER!
72000 jüdische Soldaten sind für das Vaterland auf dem Felde der Ehre gefallen
Der Schild
A newspaper for and by Jewish veterans of World War I
True of our boy, at least!

Essen, during the Revolution and after, was a stronghold of Marxist politics.

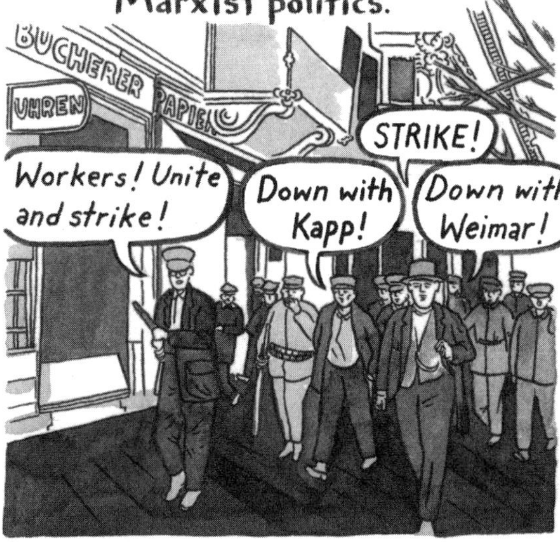
BUCHERER
UHREN
PAPIER
Workers! Unite and strike!
Down with Kapp!
STRIKE!
Down with Weimar!

It was also one of the Ruhr cities occupied by France in 1923 after Germany failed to pay levied war debt.

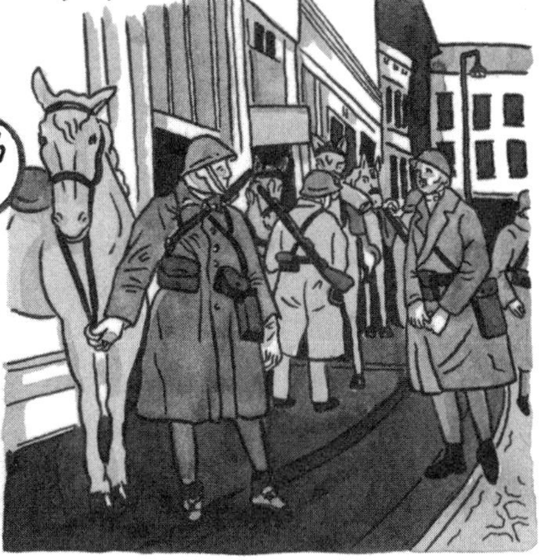

In 1923, in response to a rise in antisemitic violence, young Jews in Essen, Erich Levi among them, decided to start a Jewish sports club. They called it Hakoah (הכח) — Hebrew for "the Strength" — likely after the Viennese powerhouse club of the same name.

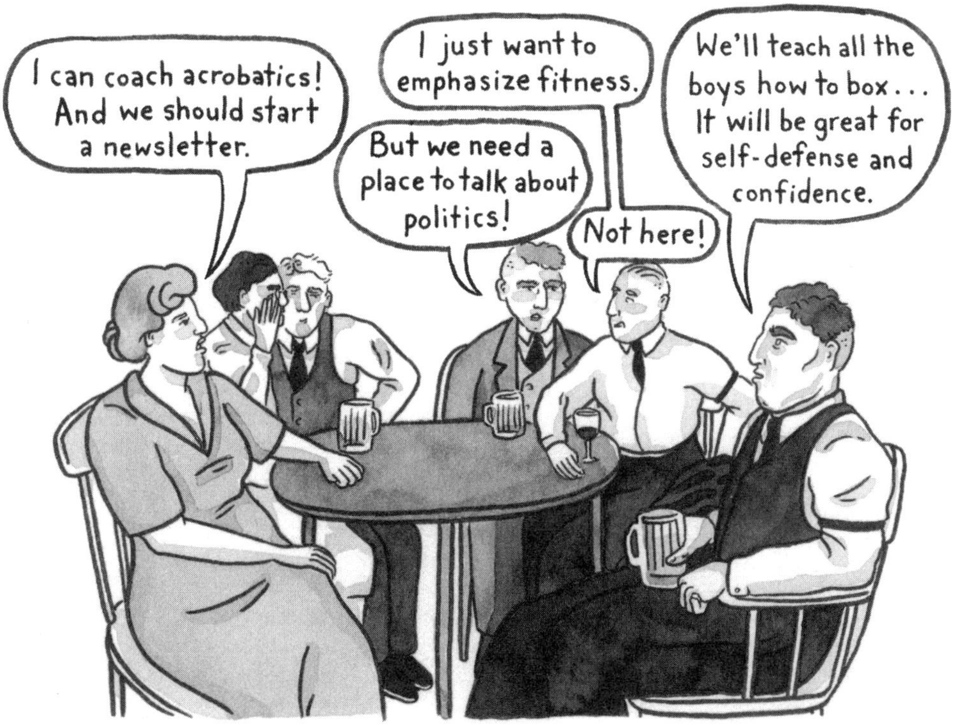
I can coach acrobatics! And we should start a newsletter.
I just want to emphasize fitness.
But we need a place to talk about politics!
Not here!
We'll teach all the boys how to box . . . It will be great for self-defense and confidence.

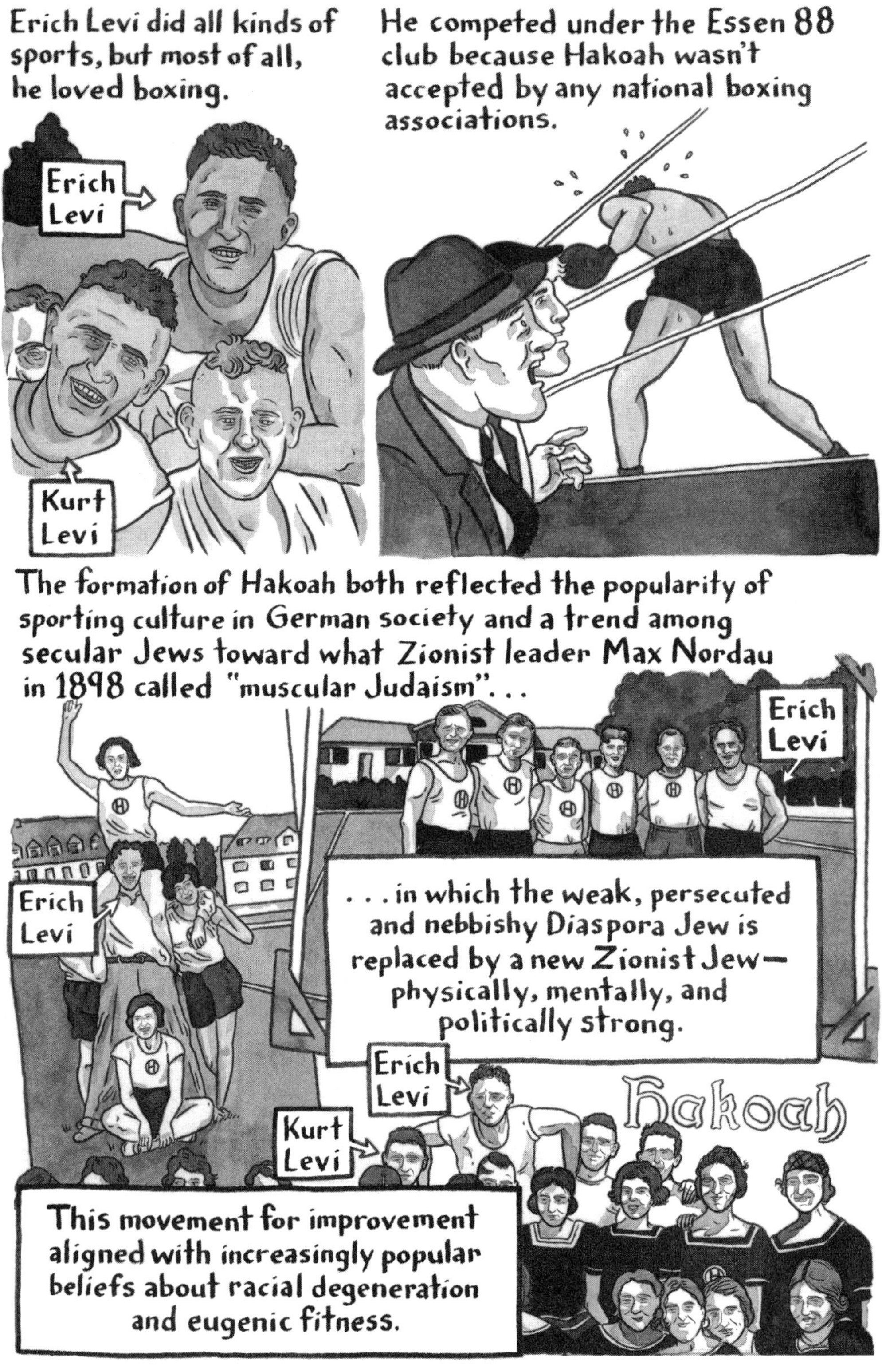
Erich Levi did all kinds of sports, but most of all, he loved boxing.
Erich Levi
Kurt Levi
He competed under the Essen 88 club because Hakoah wasn't accepted by any national boxing associations.
The formation of Hakoah both reflected the popularity of sporting culture in German society and a trend among secular Jews toward what Zionist leader Max Nordau in 1898 called "muscular Judaism"...
Erich Levi
Erich Levi
...in which the weak, persecuted and nebbishy Diaspora Jew is replaced by a new Zionist Jew—physically, mentally, and politically strong.
Erich Levi
Kurt Levi
Hakoah
This movement for improvement aligned with increasingly popular beliefs about racial degeneration and eugenic fitness.

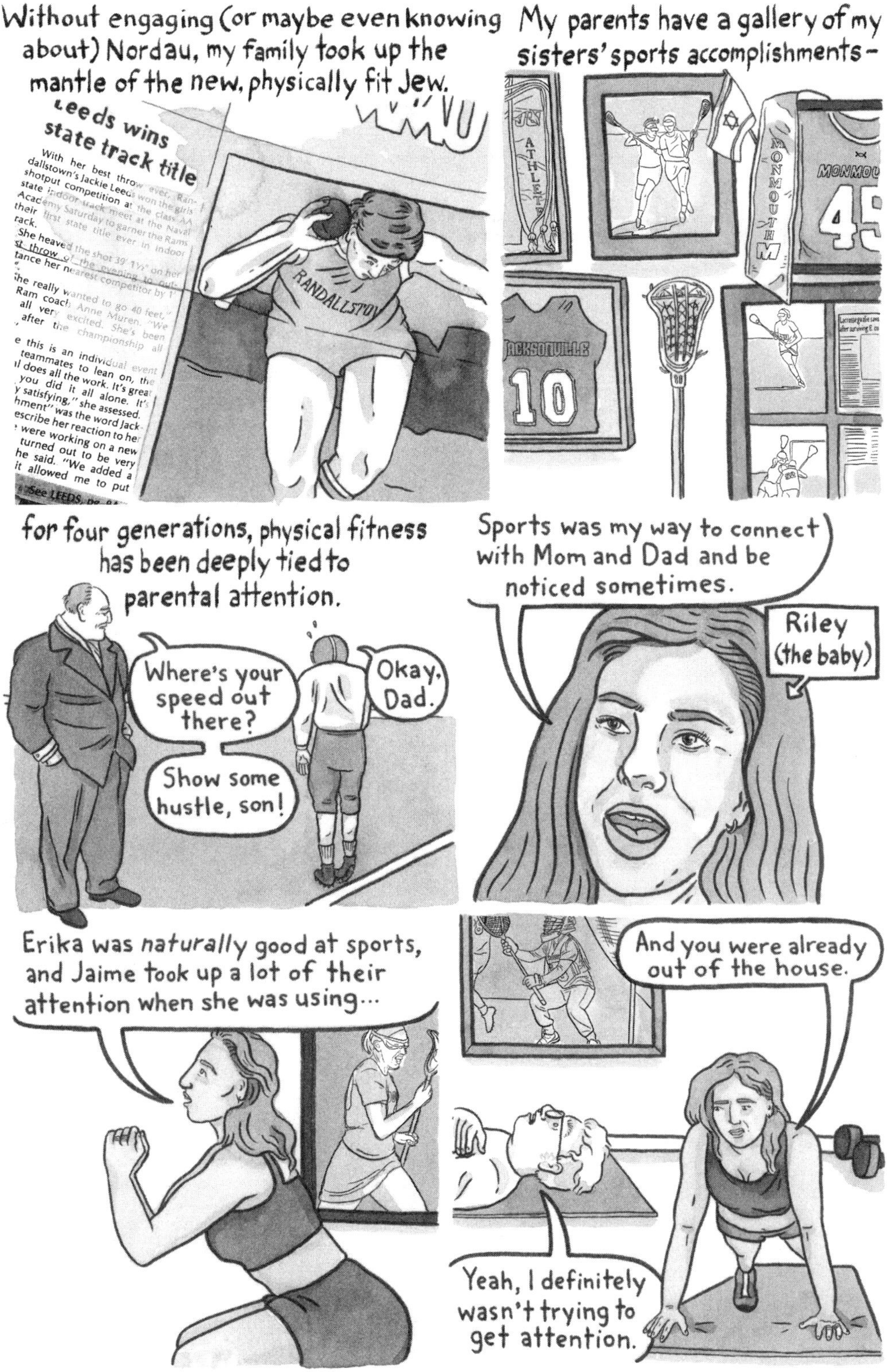
Without engaging (or maybe even knowing about) Nordau, my family took up the mantle of the new, physically fit Jew.
Leeds wins state track title
RANDALLSTOW
My parents have a gallery of my sisters' sports accomplishments -
ATHLETE
MONMOUTH
MONMOU
45
JACKSONVILLE
10
for four generations, physical fitness has been deeply tied to parental attention.
Where's your speed out there?
Show some hustle, son!
Okay, Dad.
Sports was my way to connect with Mom and Dad and be noticed sometimes.
Riley (the baby)
Erika was *naturally* good at sports, and Jaime took up a lot of their attention when she was using...
And you were already out of the house.
Yeah, I definitely wasn't trying to get attention.

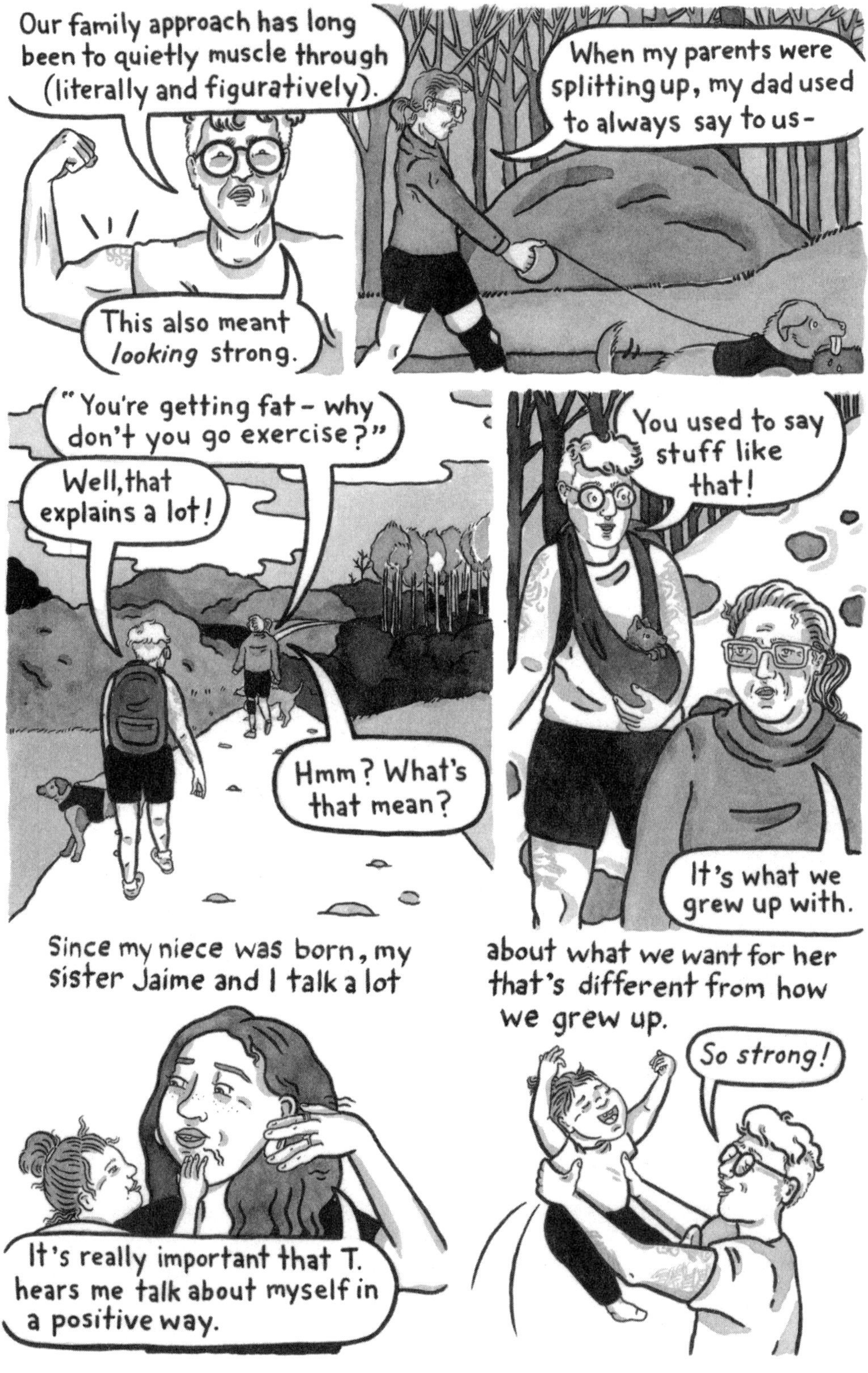
Our family approach has long been to quietly muscle through (literally and figuratively).
This also meant *looking* strong.
When my parents were splitting up, my dad used to always say to us-
"You're getting fat - why don't you go exercise?"
Well, that explains a lot!
Hmm? What's that mean?
You used to say stuff like that!
It's what we grew up with.
Since my niece was born, my sister Jaime and I talk a lot
about what we want for her that's different from how we grew up.
It's really important that T. hears me talk about myself in a positive way.
So strong!

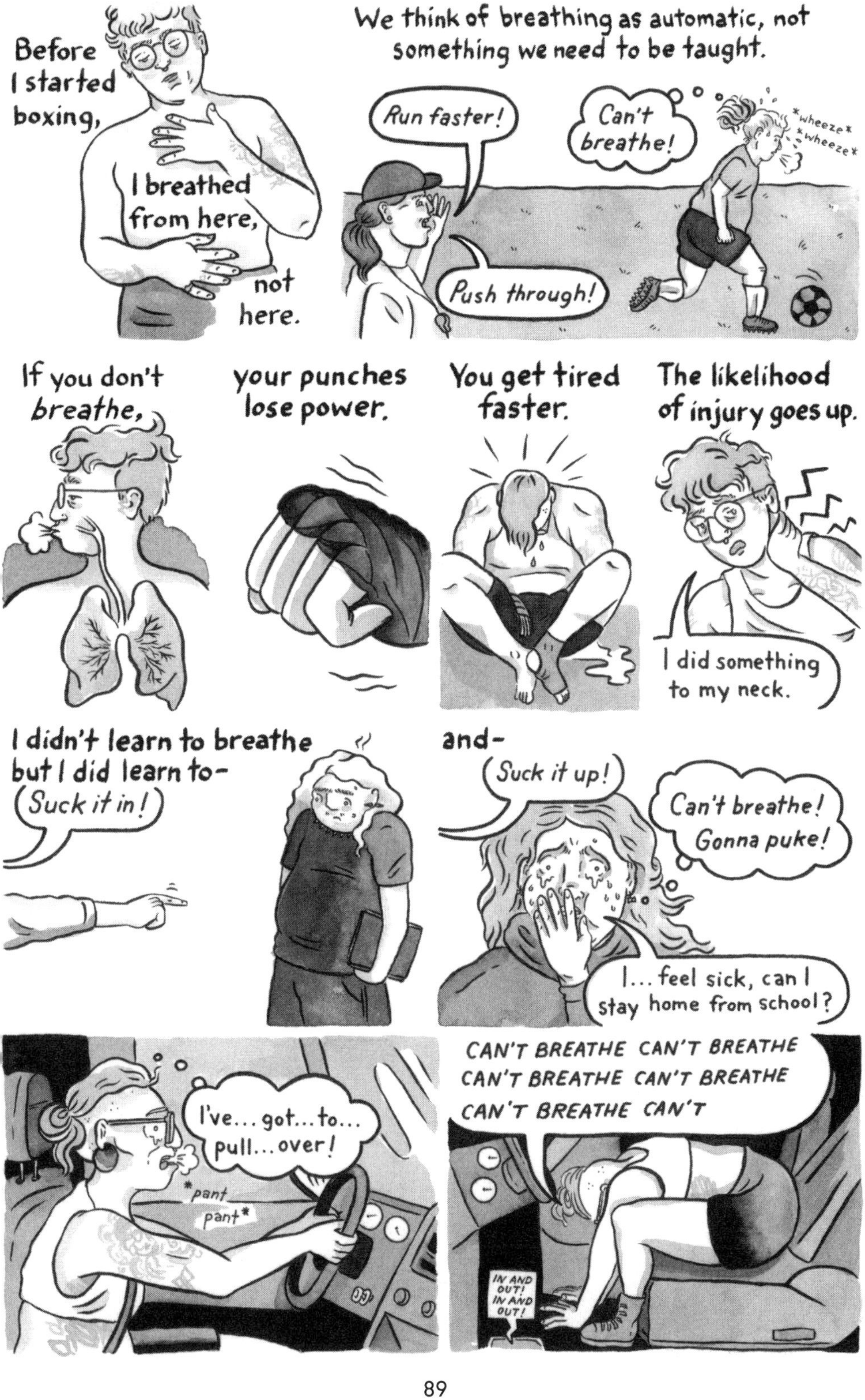
Before I started boxing,
I breathed from here,
not here.
We think of breathing as automatic, not something we need to be taught.
Run faster!
Push through!
Can't breathe!
wheeze
wheeze
If you don't *breathe*,
your punches lose power.
You get tired faster.
The likelihood of injury goes up.
I did something to my neck.
I didn't learn to breathe but I did learn to–
Suck it in!
and–
Suck it up!
Can't breathe! Gonna puke!
I... feel sick, can I stay home from school?
I've... got... to... pull... over!
*pant
pant*
CAN'T BREATHE CAN'T BREATHE
CAN'T BREATHE CAN'T BREATHE
CAN'T BREATHE CAN'T
IN AND OUT! IN AND OUT!

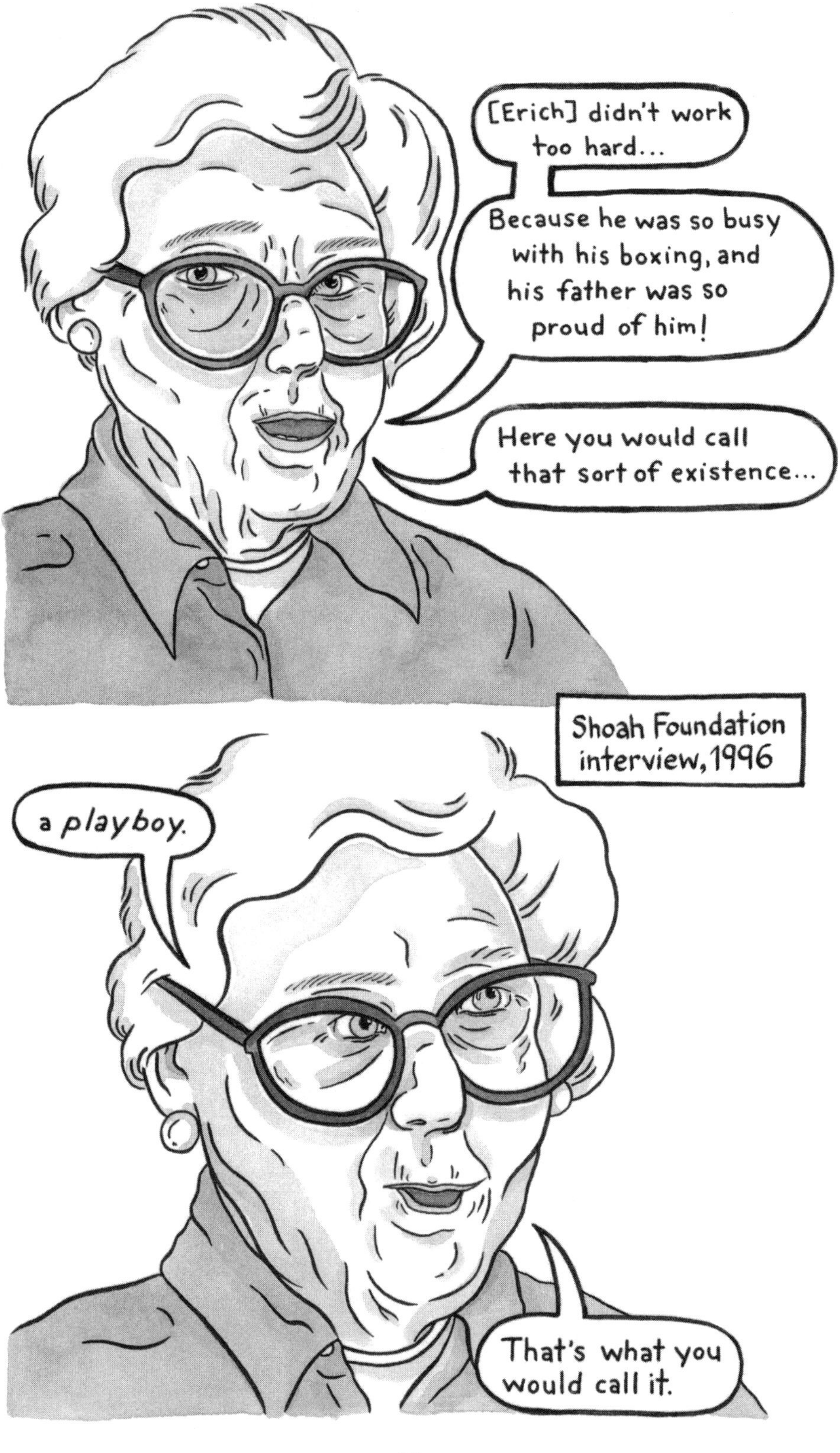
[Erich] didn't work too hard...
Because he was so busy with his boxing, and his father was so proud of him!
Here you would call that sort of existence...
Shoah Foundation interview, 1996
a *playboy.*
That's what you would call it.

He even fought Max Schmeling

and did win the fight!

Even though Erich Levi and Max Schmeling were born the same year...

there is no evidence beyond Ilse's testimony that they ever met in the ring.

Schmeling went pro in 1924, while Levi stayed amateur his entire career.

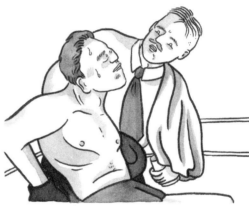

Both of their names appear in the same bout announcement, but for different fights, in different towns...

But who knows? Maybe they sparred or something.

... the German half heavyweight champion Max Schmeling... a real hope in German boxing and a son of the West...

It's easy to imagine that, from exile in Antwerp, Erich listened to Max Schmeling's historic 1938 fight against Joe Louis in New York, a rematch of their 1936 bout.

In the U.S., the fight was presented as a battle between freedom and fascism.

I wonder who Erich would have rooted for.

I wonder what happened to Erich's teammates.

How many of them survived?

Did Erich think of them?

...Louis out — and Louis missed with a left swing but in close brought up a hard right uppercut...

...Schmeling is down... Schmeling is down! The count is four... It's... and he's up...

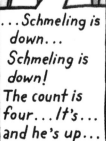

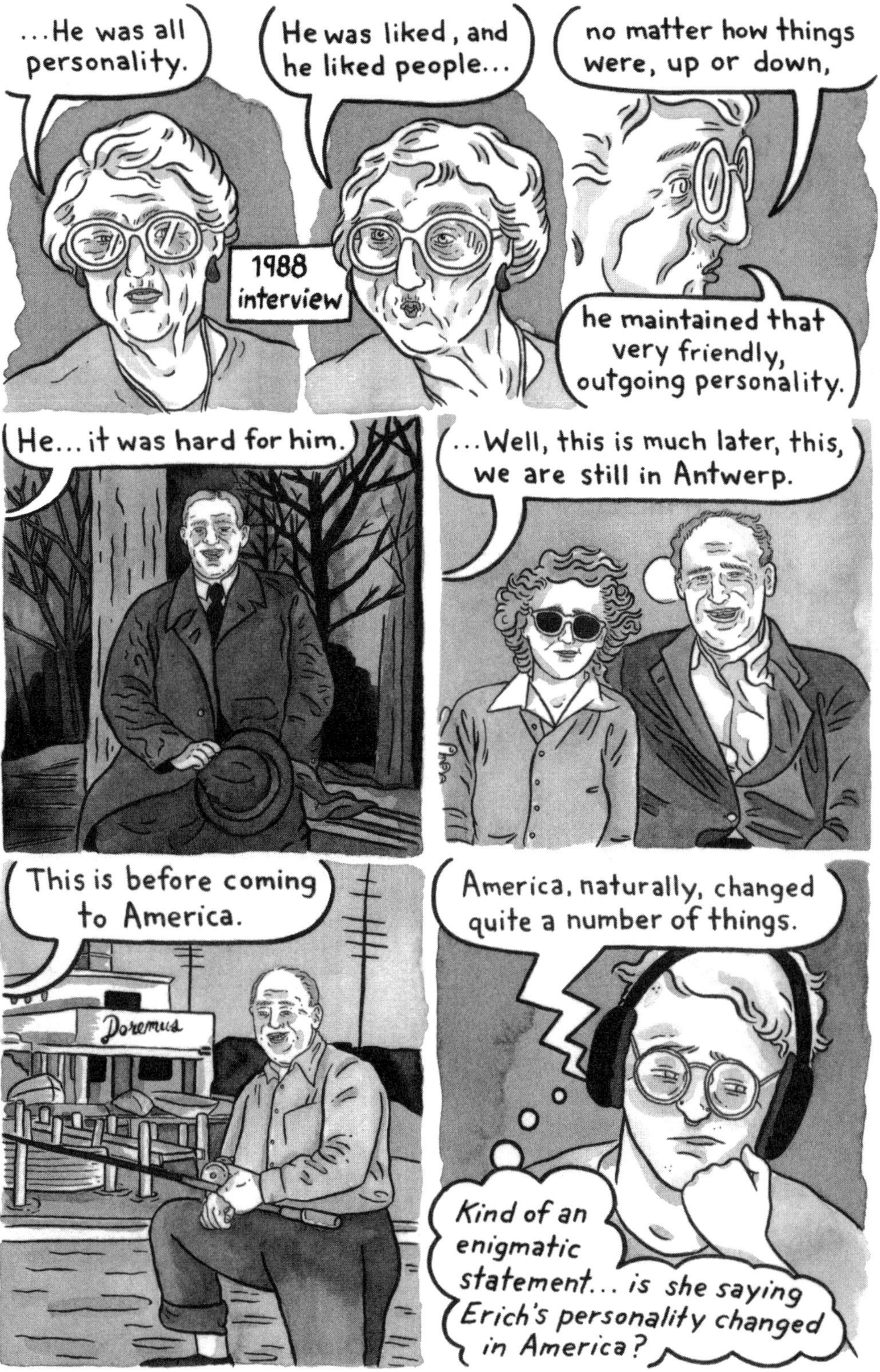
...He was all personality.
He was liked, and he liked people...
no matter how things were, up or down,
1988 interview
he maintained that very friendly, outgoing personality.
He... it was hard for him.
...Well, this is much later, this, we are still in Antwerp.
This is before coming to America.
Doremus
America, naturally, changed quite a number of things.
Kind of an enigmatic statement... is she saying Erich's personality changed in America?

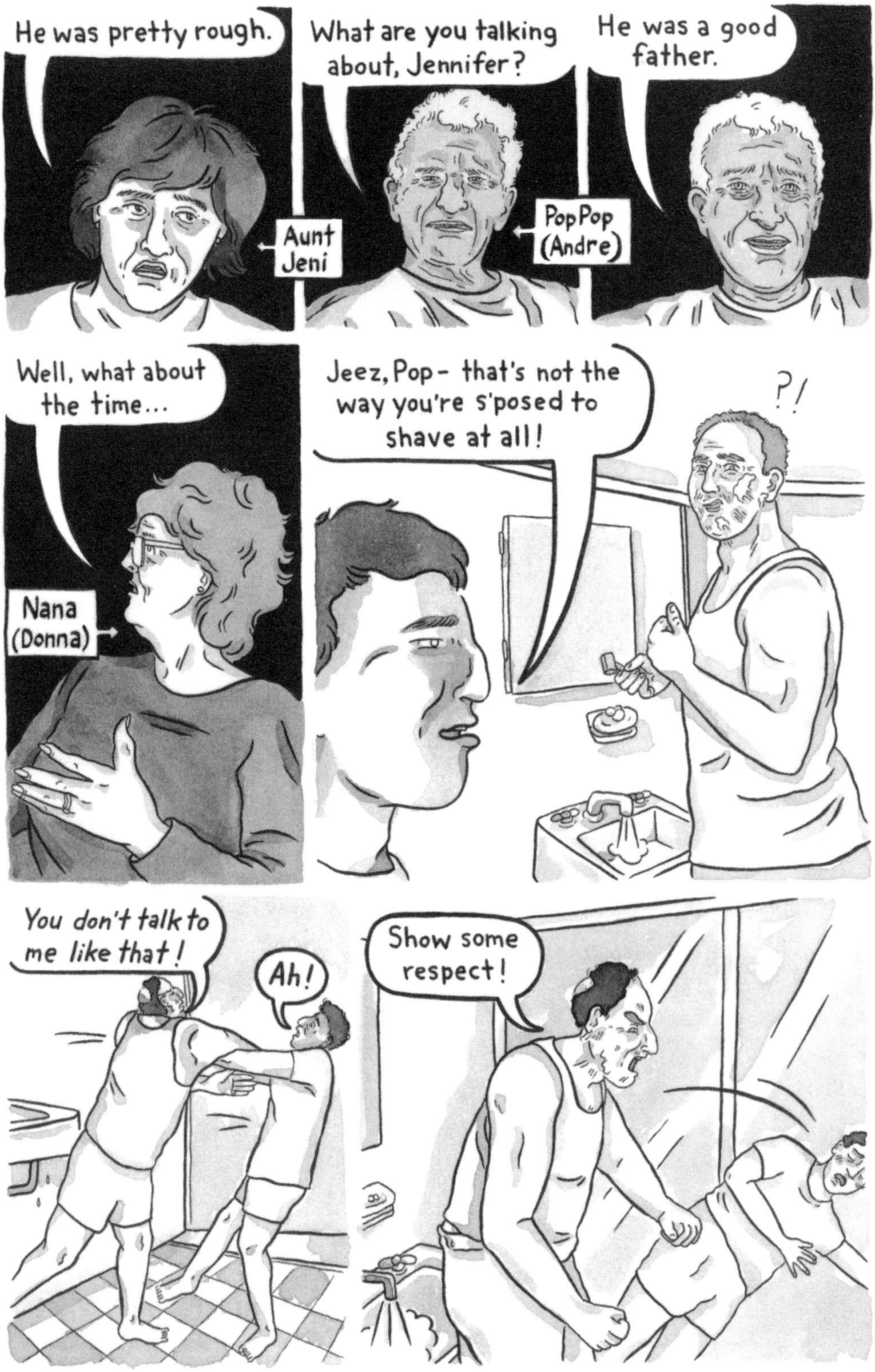
He was pretty rough.
Aunt Jeni
What are you talking about, Jennifer?
PopPop (Andre)
He was a good father.
Well, what about the time...
Nana (Donna)
Jeez, Pop- that's not the way you're s'posed to shave at all!
?!
You don't talk to me like that!
Ah!
Show some respect!

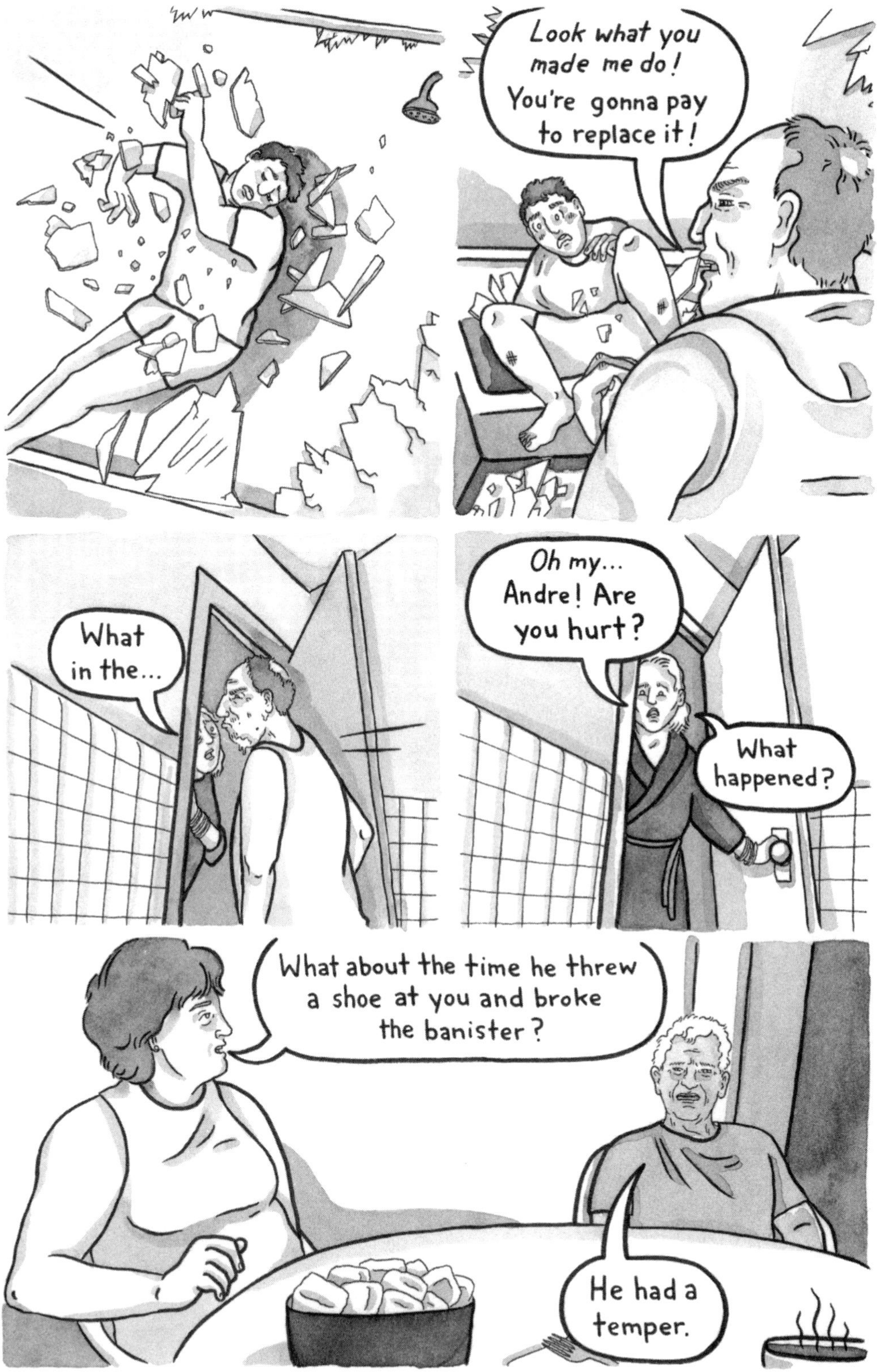
Look what you made me do! You're gonna pay to replace it!
What in the...
Oh my... Andre! Are you hurt?
What happened?
What about the time he threw a shoe at you and broke the banister?
He had a temper.

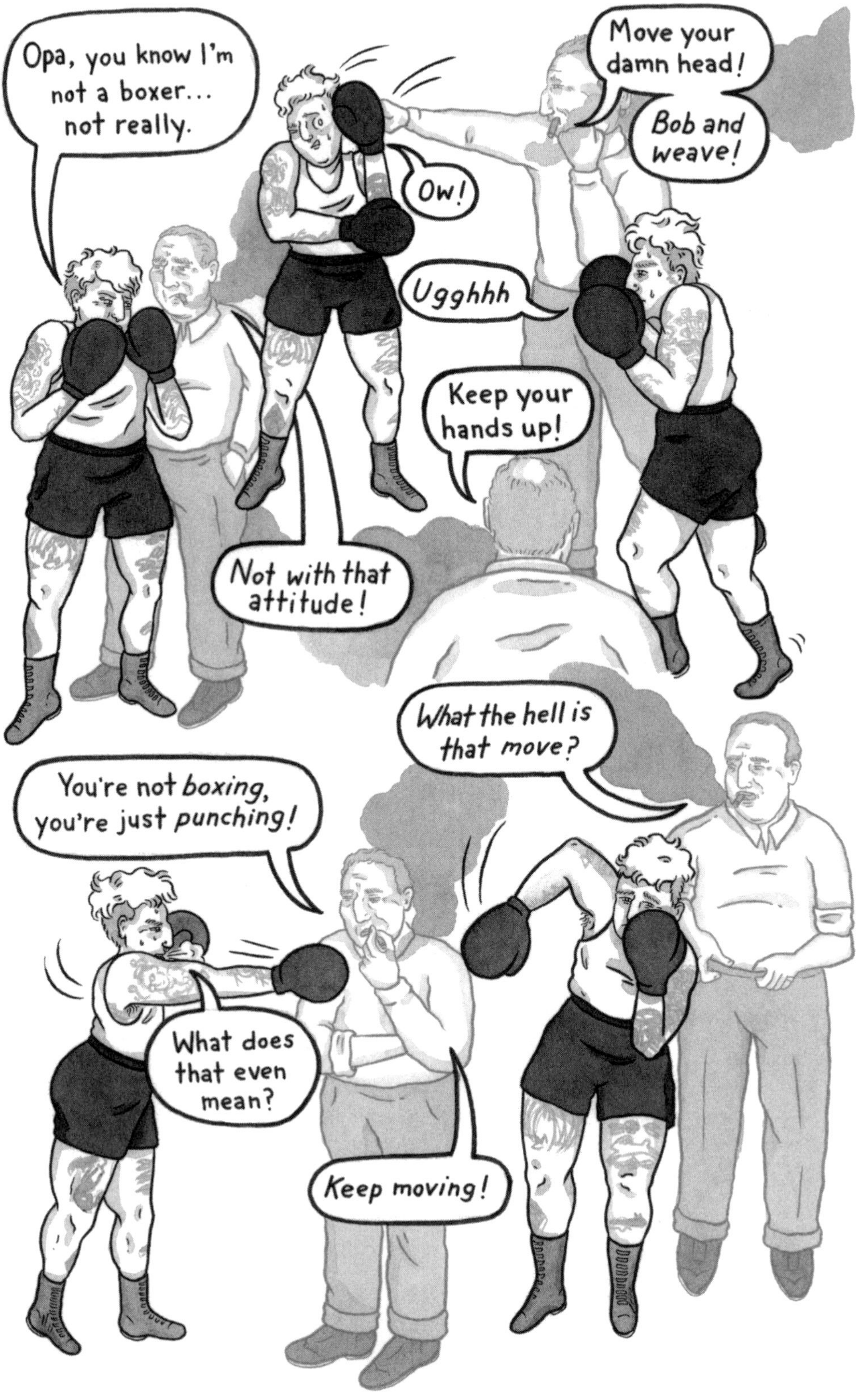
Opa, you know I'm not a boxer... not really.
Not with that attitude!
Ow!
Move your damn head!
Bob and weave!
Ugghhh
Keep your hands up!
You're not *boxing*, you're just *punching*!
What does that even mean?
Keep moving!
What the hell is that *move*?

In pursuit of understanding my great-grandfather, I start to research other contemporary boxers...

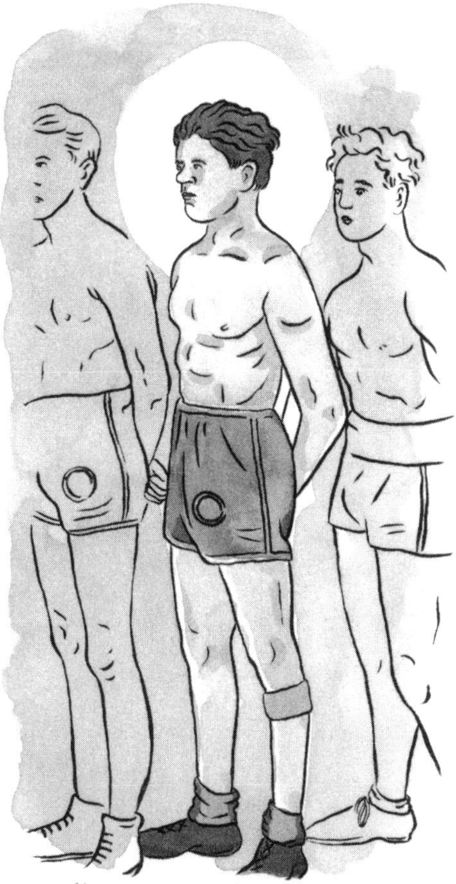

I get *hung up* on the German Sinti boxer Johann Trollmann–

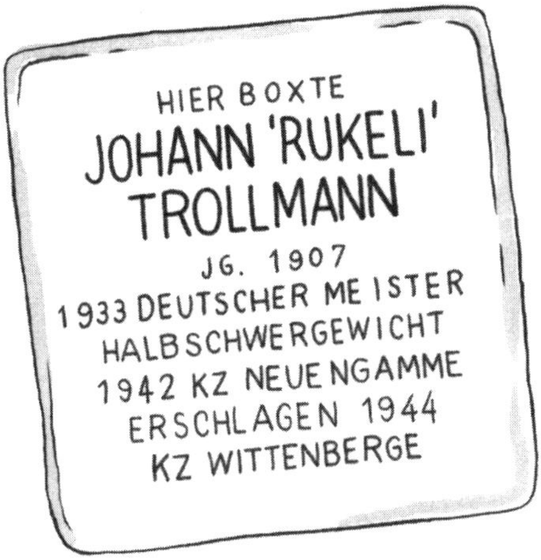

HIER BOXTE
JOHANN 'RUKELI' TROLLMANN
JG. 1907
1933 DEUTSCHER MEISTER
HALBSCHWERGEWICHT
1942 KZ NEUENGAMME
ERSCHLAGEN 1944
KZ WITTENBERGE

This is what Erich's life and death might have been, maybe, if he wasn't so privileged... and lucky.

Trollmann was two years younger than Erich Levi, born into a working-class Sinti family in Hanover.

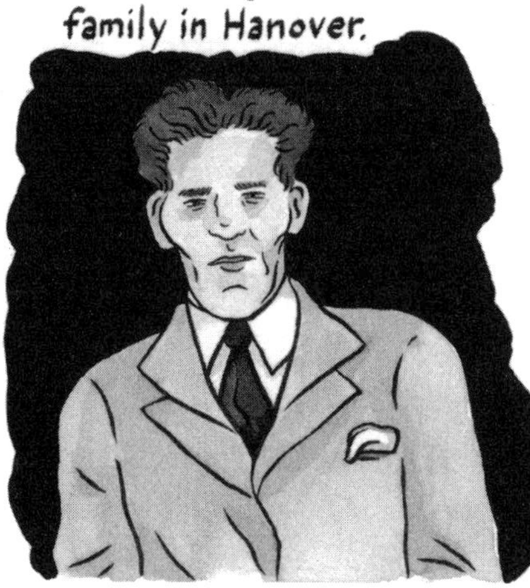

Before Nazism, by 1929, every German state had laws that required Roma and Sinti people to prove that they had regular employment or face up to two years of forced labor.

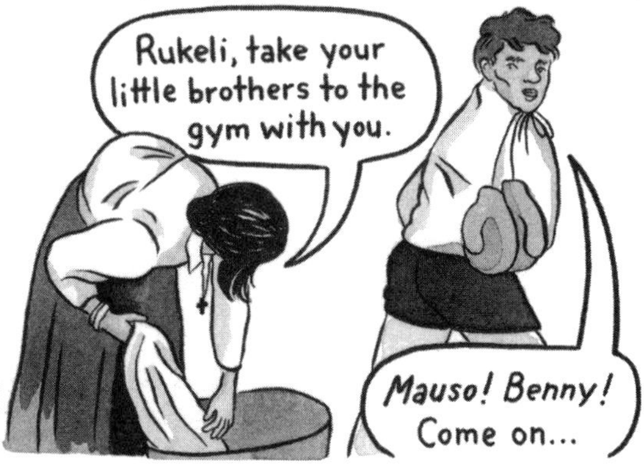

Rukeli, take your little brothers to the gym with you.
Mauso! Benny! Come on...

In 1928, Trollmann joined a Workers Sports Club, run by Marxists. The workers clubs rejected nationalism and *never* sang the national anthem.

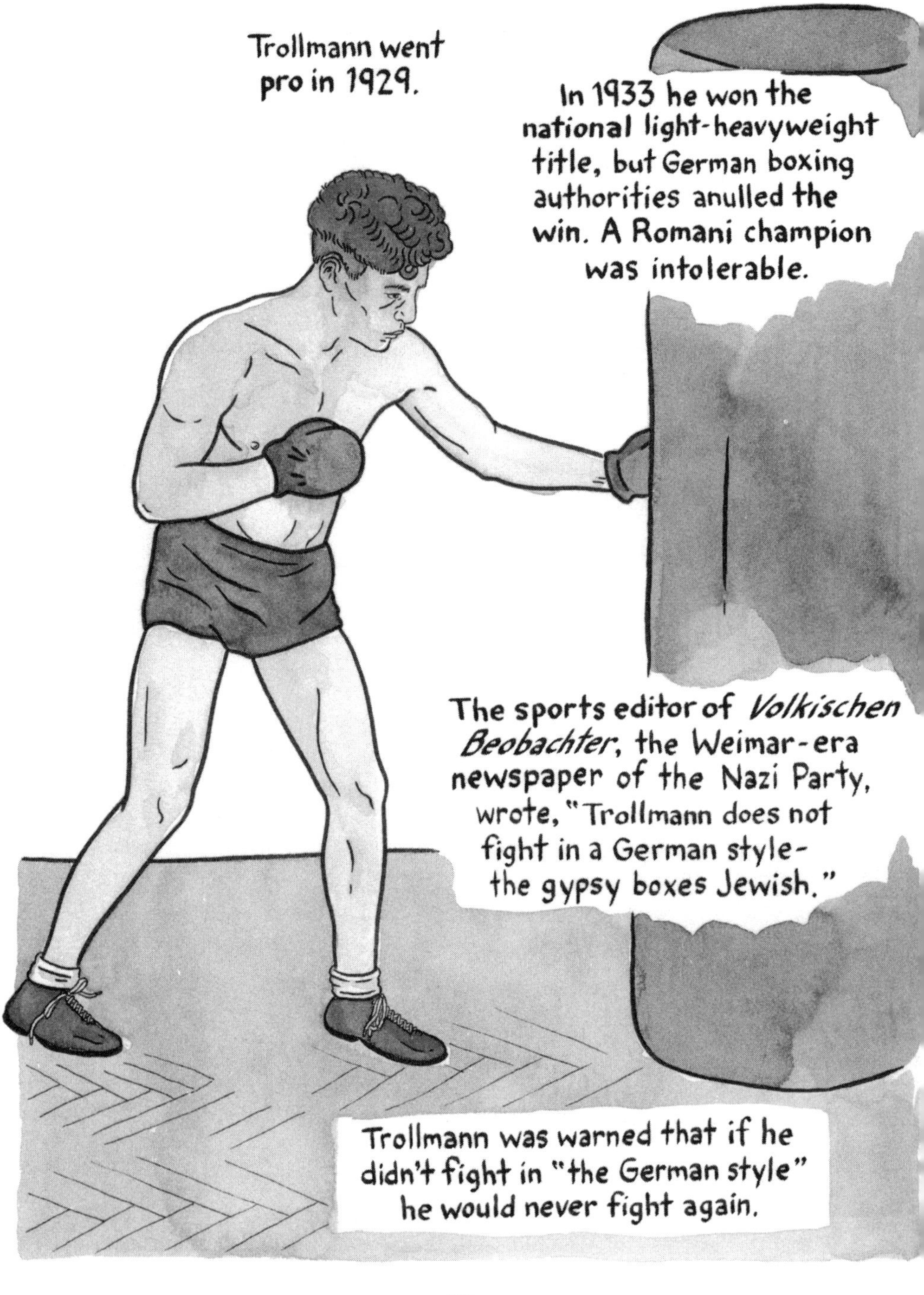
Trollmann went pro in 1929.
In 1933 he won the national light-heavyweight title, but German boxing authorities anulled the win. A Romani champion was intolerable.
The sports editor of *Volkischen Beobachter*, the Weimar-era newspaper of the Nazi Party, wrote, "Trollmann does not fight in a German style- the gypsy boxes Jewish."
Trollmann was warned that if he didn't fight in "the German style" he would never fight again.

Trollmann showed up to his next fight ready to box in the *German* style –

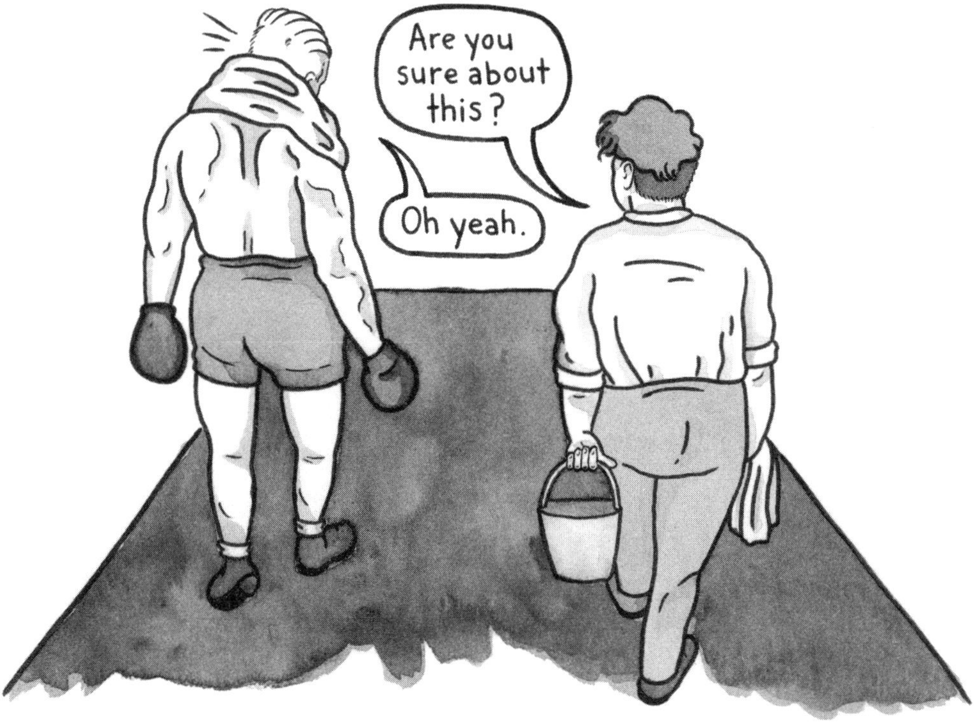
Are you sure about this?
Oh yeah.

He dyed his hair bright blond.

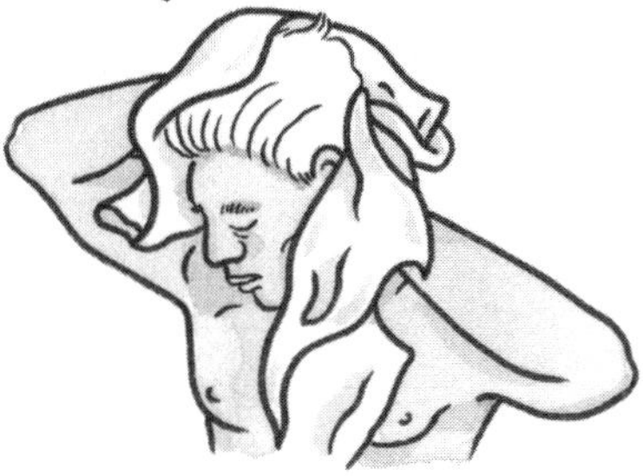

And powdered himself white.

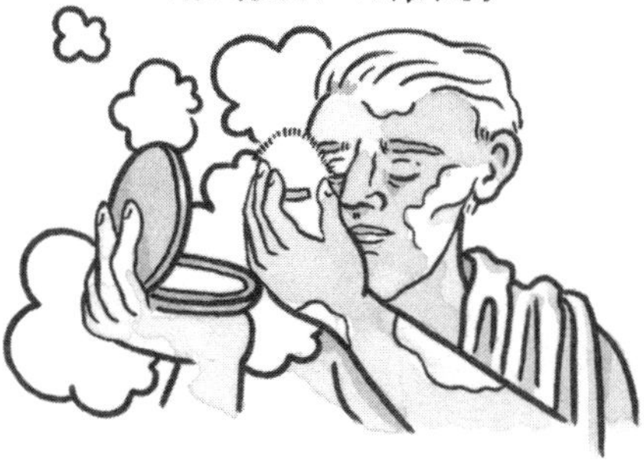

He refused to move his feet in the ring and stayed stiff,

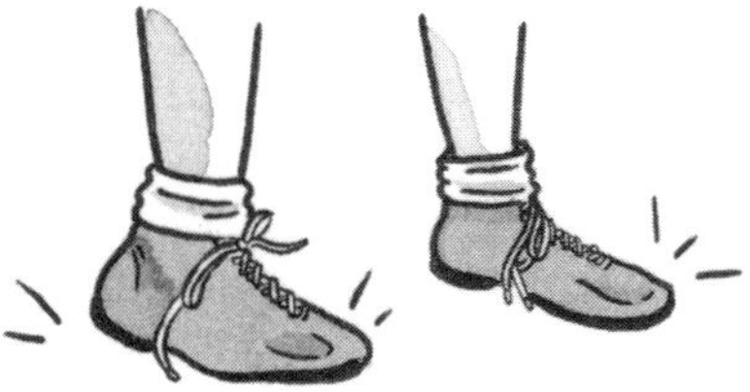

straight, and upright. He lost the fight. *(But you know, won...)*

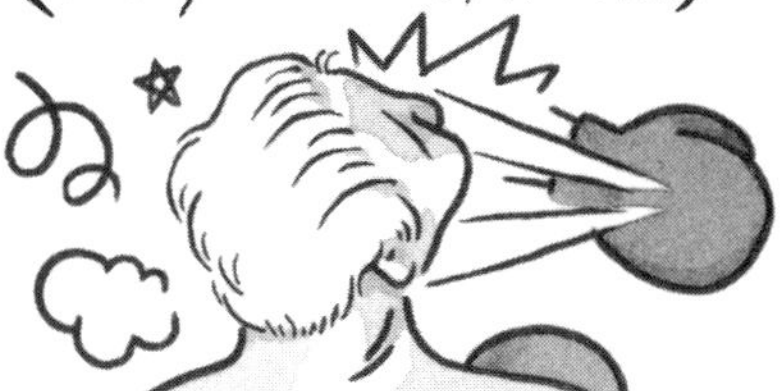

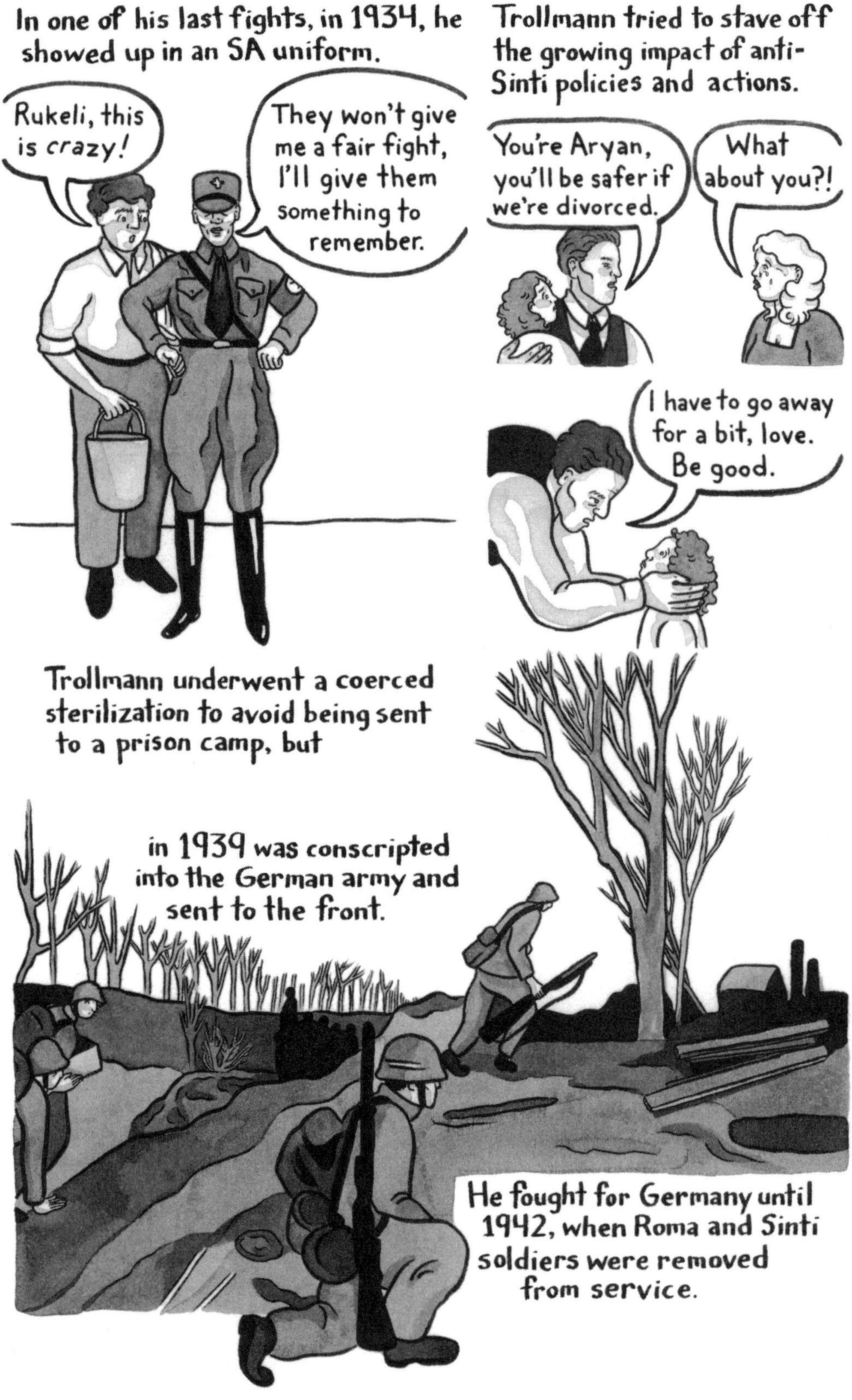
In one of his last fights, in 1934, he showed up in an SA uniform.
Rukeli, this is *crazy*!
They won't give me a fair fight, I'll give them something to remember.
Trollmann tried to stave off the growing impact of anti-Sinti policies and actions.
You're Aryan, you'll be safer if we're divorced.
What about you?!
I have to go away for a bit, love. Be good.
Trollmann underwent a coerced sterilization to avoid being sent to a prison camp, but
in 1939 was conscripted into the German army and sent to the front.
He fought for Germany until 1942, when Roma and Sinti soldiers were removed from service.

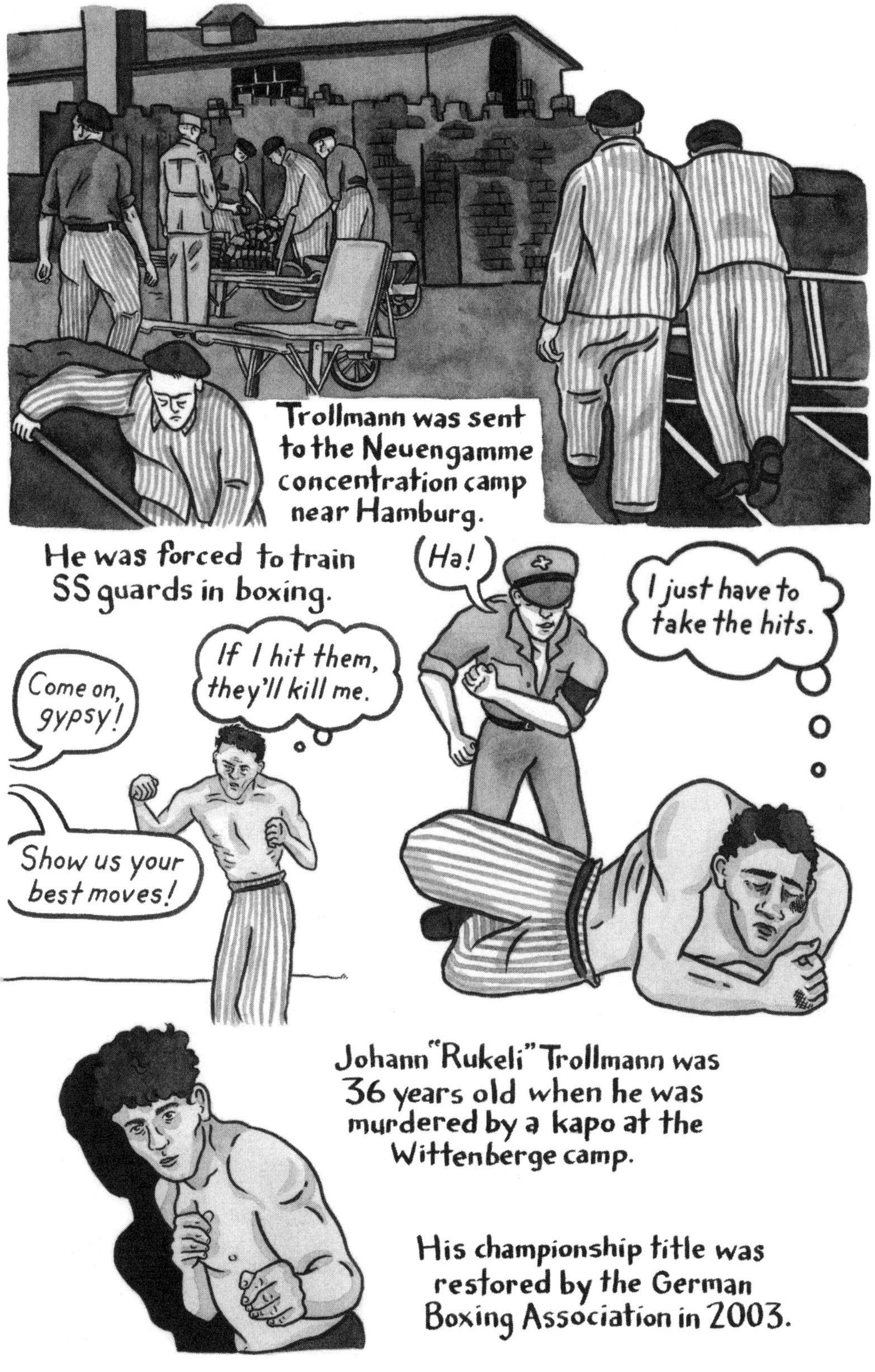
Trollmann was sent to the Neuengamme concentration camp near Hamburg.
He was forced to train SS guards in boxing.
Come on, gypsy!
Show us your best moves!
If I hit them, they'll kill me.
Ha!
I just have to take the hits.
Johann "Rukeli" Trollmann was 36 years old when he was murdered by a kapo at the Wittenberge camp.
His championship title was restored by the German Boxing Association in 2003.

Trollmann's fighting style reminds me of Jack Johnson—a 1977 feature in *Big Book of Boxing* magazine describes—

> Johnson experienced great joy and satisfaction in taunting a victim. Often times he purposely pulled his punches so that a man would be stunned and cut, but not knocked senseless. He loved to chide opponents by mocking them and to leave a portion of his body exposed as a target and grin: "hit here, boy."

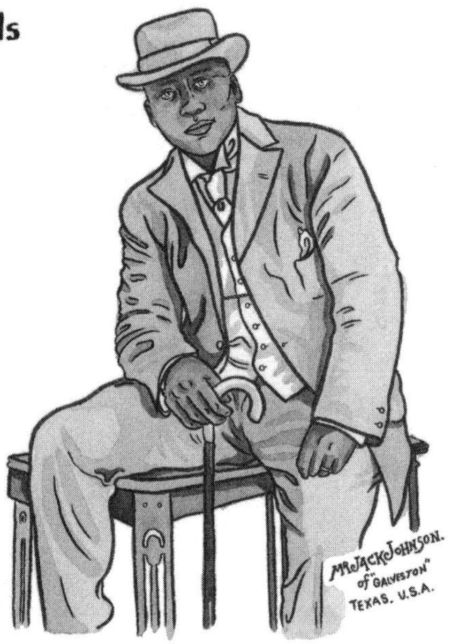

MR. JACK JOHNSON. of "GALVESTON" TEXAS. U.S.A.

After Jack Johnson won the world heavyweight championship in 1908, matches were set up all over the world between Black and white fighters. These fights were presented as "Darwinian struggles."

Jim Jeffries, the world champion from 1899 to 1905, once said of Johnson—"I will never box a colored fighter, and I won't change my mind."

But Jeffries came out of retirement in 1910 to reclaim the title as the "Great White Hope." Johnson beat him, soundly.

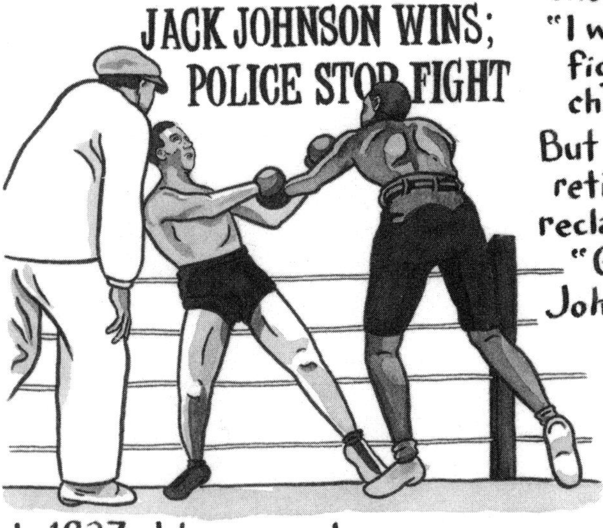

JACK JOHNSON WINS;
POLICE STOP FIGHT

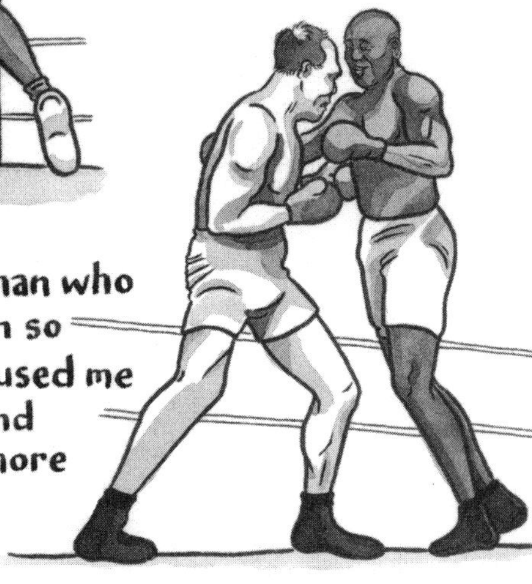

In 1927, Johnson wrote—"This 'crusade' to find a white man who could beat me had been carried on so bitterly and intensely that it caused me much trouble and sorrow and persecution. . . nobody was more relieved than I was when it finally came to an end."

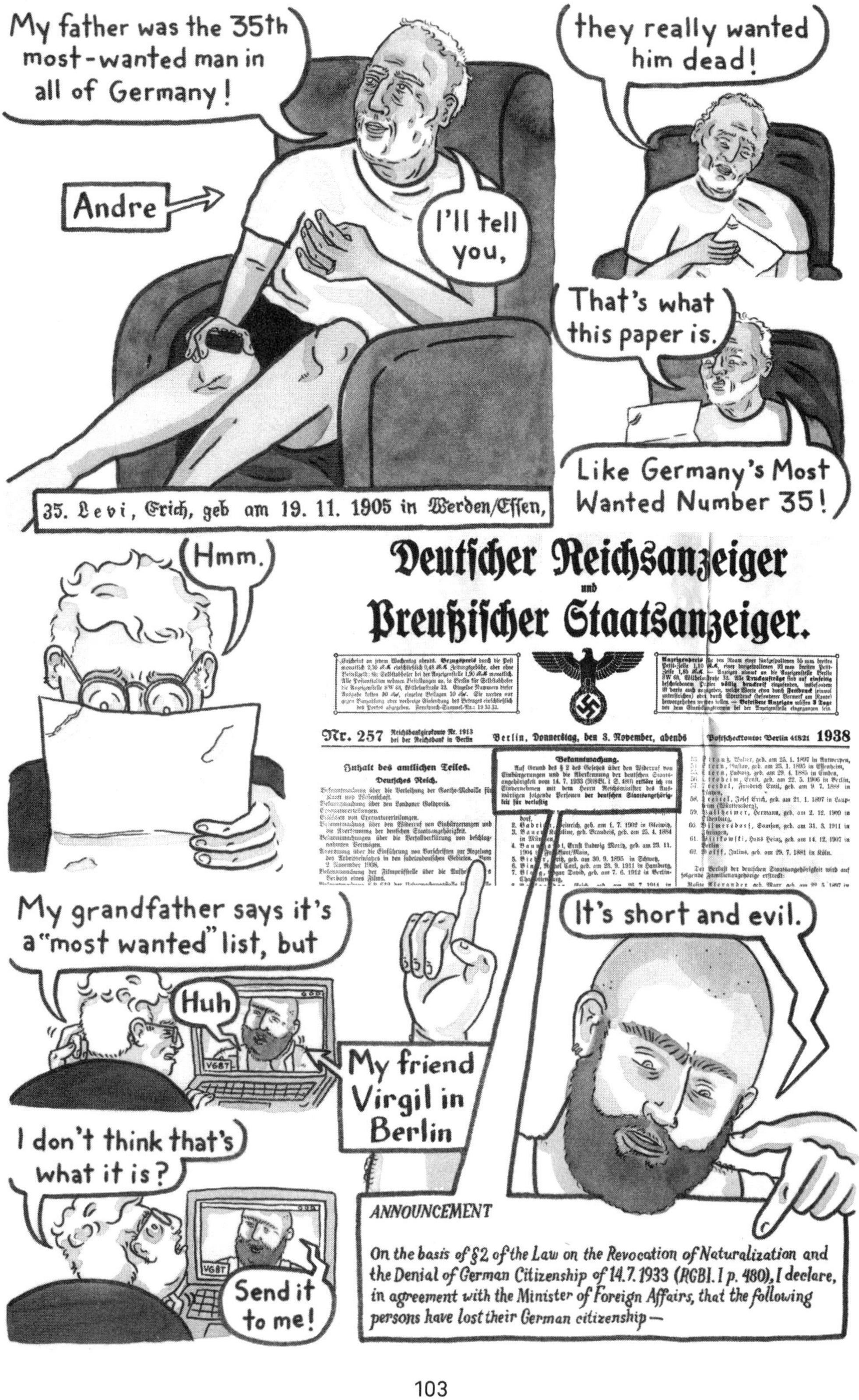

My father was the 35th most-wanted man in all of Germany!
Andre
I'll tell you,
they really wanted him dead!
That's what this paper is.
Like Germany's Most Wanted Number 35!
35. Levi, Erich, geb am 19. 11. 1905 in Werden/Essen,
Hmm.
Deutscher Reichsanzeiger
und
Preußischer Staatsanzeiger.
Nr. 257
Berlin, Donnerstag, den 3. November, abends
1938
Bekanntmachung.
Inhalt des amtlichen Teiles.
Deutsches Reich.
My grandfather says it's a "most wanted" list, but
Huh
My friend Virgil in Berlin
It's short and evil.
I don't think that's what it is?
Send it to me!
ANNOUNCEMENT
On the basis of §2 of the Law on the Revocation of Naturalization and the Denial of German Citizenship of 14.7.1933 (RGBl. I p. 480), I declare, in agreement with the Minister of Foreign Affairs, that the following persons have lost their German citizenship—

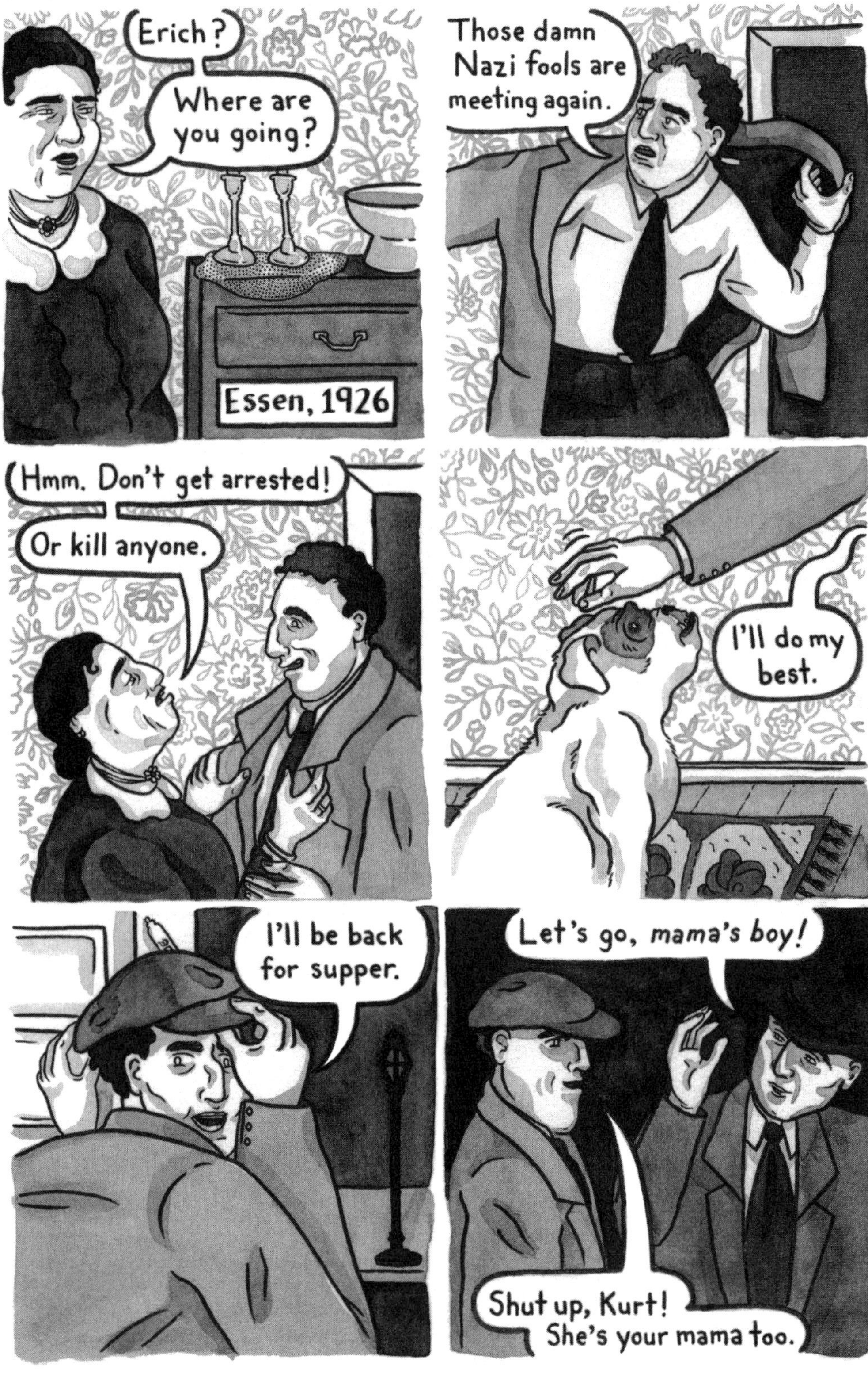
Erich?
Where are you going?
Essen, 1926
Those damn Nazi fools are meeting again.
Hmm. Don't get arrested!
Or kill anyone.
I'll do my best.
I'll be back for supper.
Let's go, *mama's boy*!
Shut up, Kurt! She's your mama too.

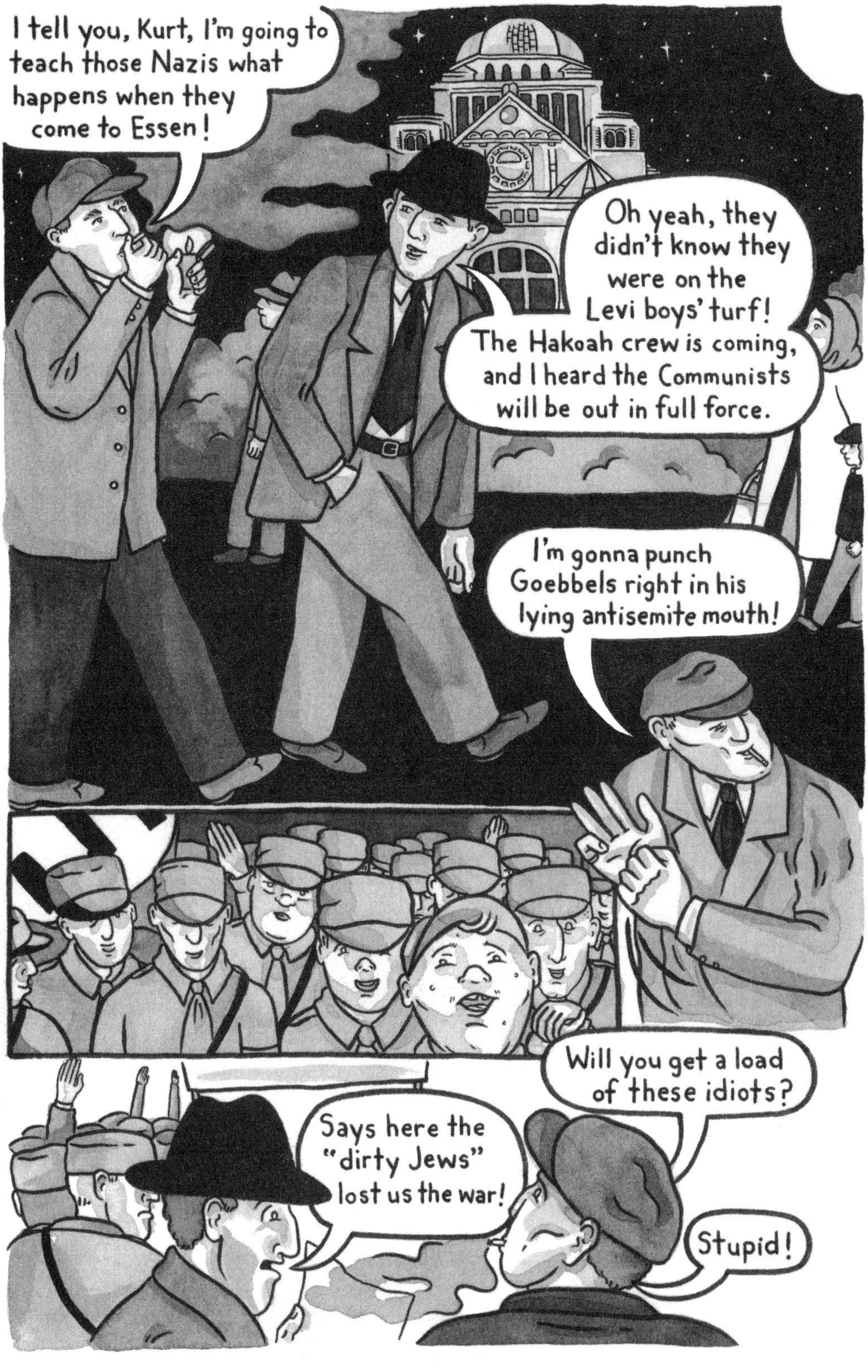
I tell you, Kurt, I'm going to teach those Nazis what happens when they come to Essen!
Oh yeah, they didn't know they were on the Levi boys' turf!
The Hakoah crew is coming, and I heard the Communists will be out in full force.
I'm gonna punch Goebbels right in his lying antisemite mouth!
Will you get a load of these idiots?
Says here the "dirty Jews" lost us the war!
Stupid!

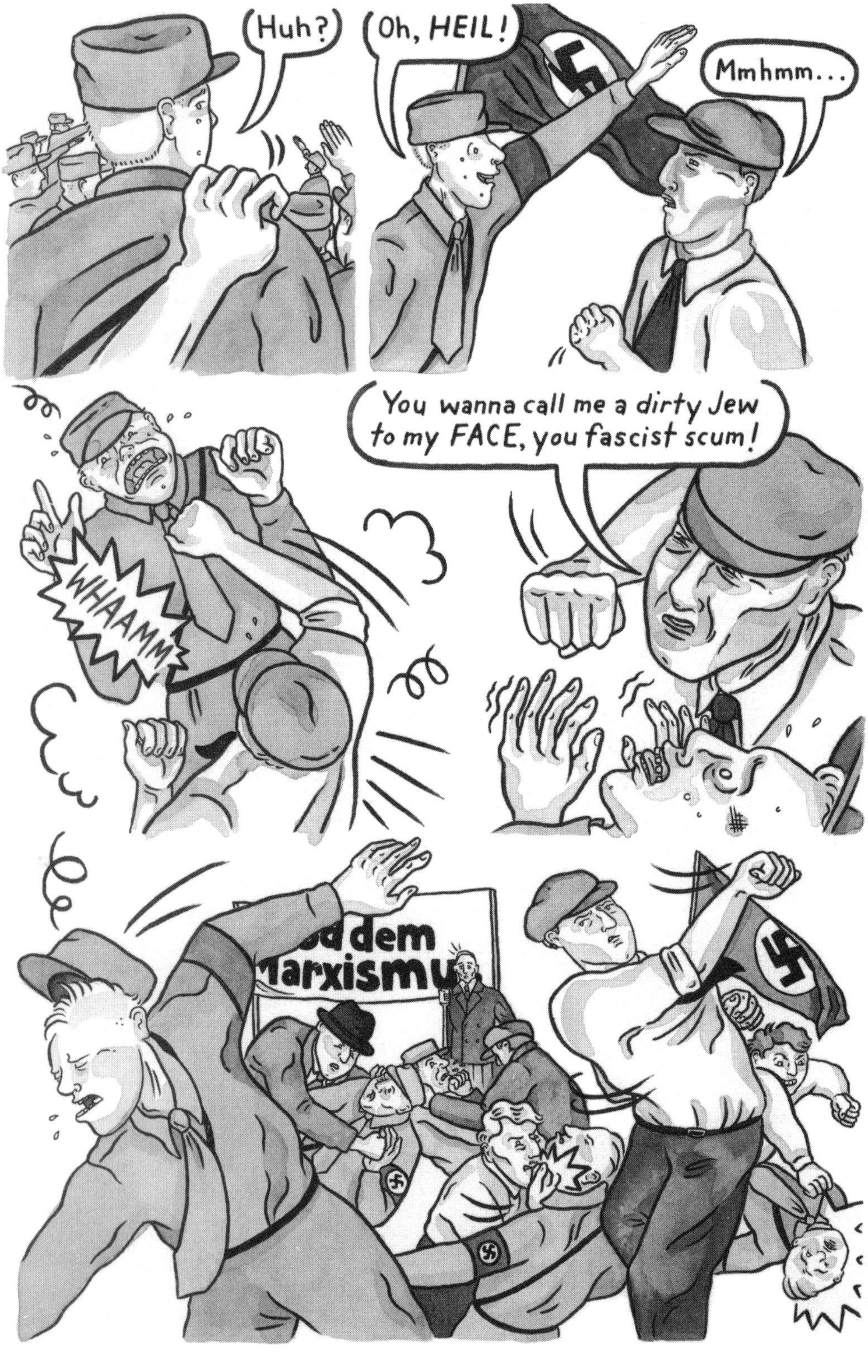
Huh?
Oh, HEIL!
Mmhmm...
WHAAMM
You wanna call me a dirty Jew to my FACE, you fascist scum!
dem

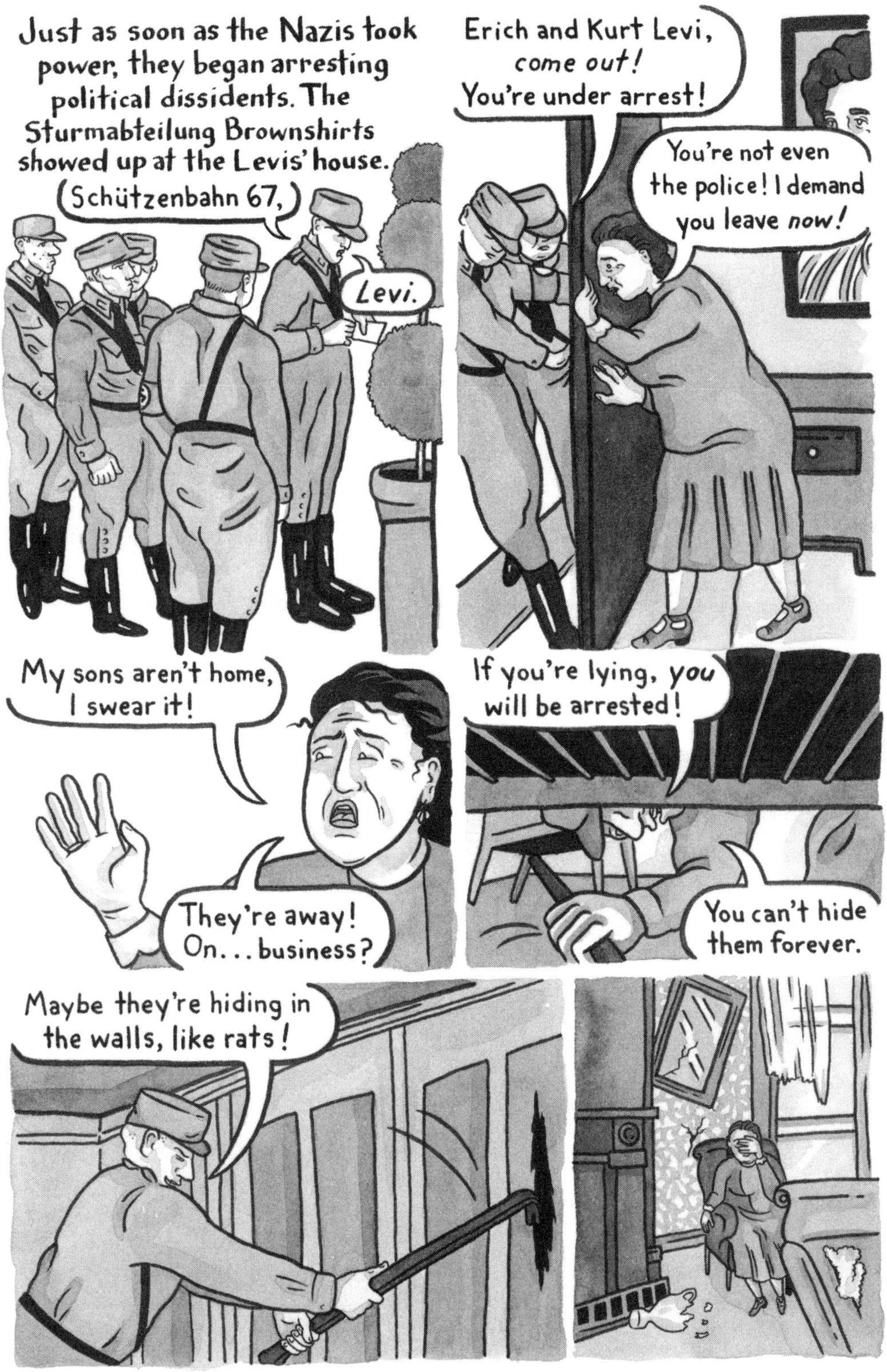
Just as soon as the Nazis took power, they began arresting political dissidents. The Sturmabteilung Brownshirts showed up at the Levis' house.
Schützenbahn 67,
Levi.
Erich and Kurt Levi, come out! You're under arrest!
You're not even the police! I demand you leave now!
My sons aren't home, I swear it!
They're away! On... business?
If you're lying, you will be arrested!
You can't hide them forever.
Maybe they're hiding in the walls, like rats!

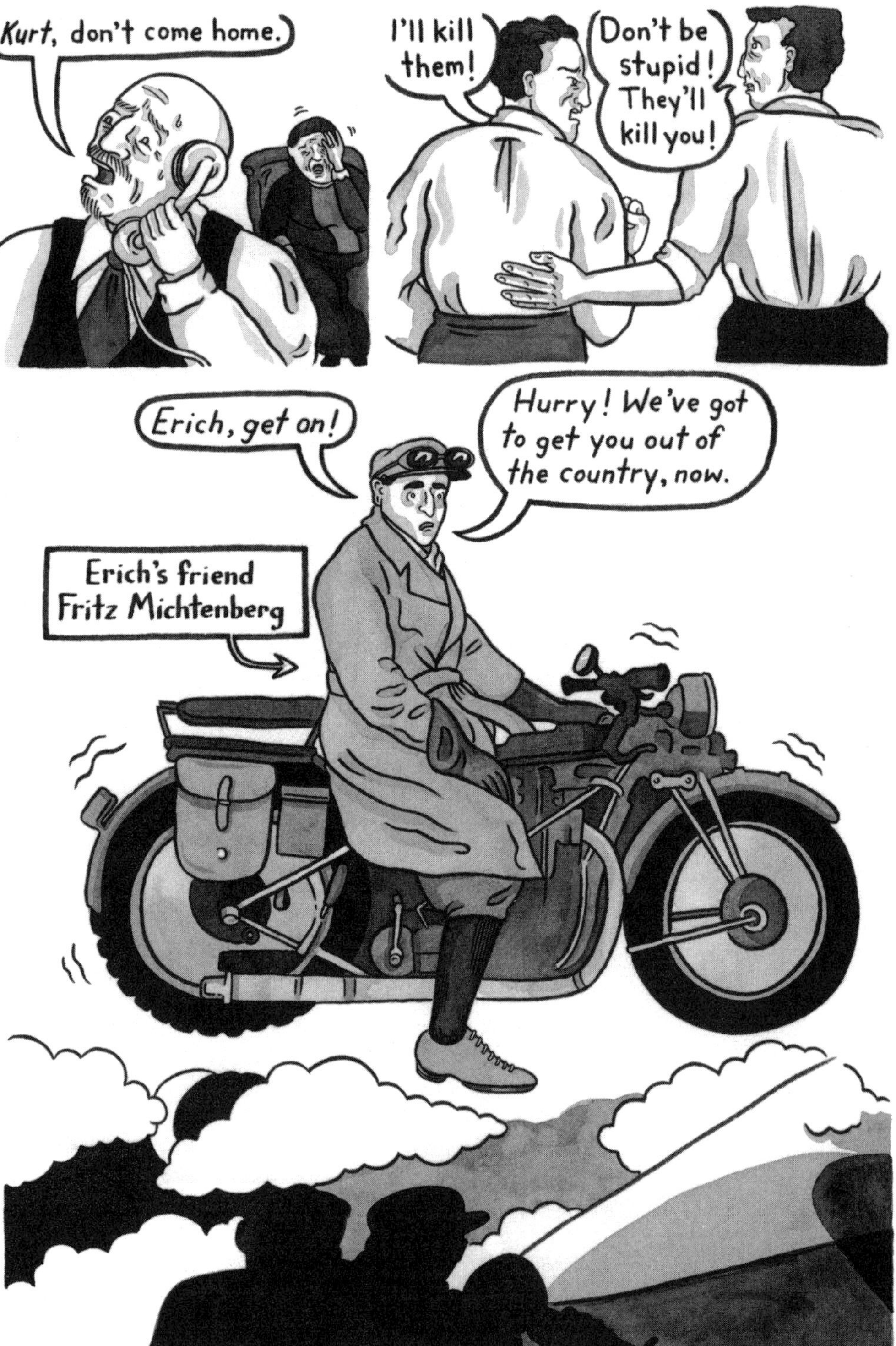
Kurt, don't come home.
I'll kill them!
Don't be stupid! They'll kill you!
Erich, get on!
Hurry! We've got to get you out of the country, now.
Erich's friend Fritz Michtenberg

They drove through the night to Paris.

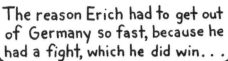

The reason Erich had to get out of Germany so fast, because he had a fight, which he did win. . .

. . .which did go to court, with a man who became very known in the Nazi organization. . .

1996 testimony

. . .by the name of Goebbels.

. . .BY THE NAME OF GOEBBELS. . .

GOEBBELS? Does she mean,

In 1924, Joseph Goebbels, a blossoming antisemite, becomes the Nazi Party representative for Rhineland-Westphalia (including the city of Essen).

He later became the Nazi propaganda minister.

It's not hard to believe that Erich would pick fights with Nazis.

The locations do line up—

109

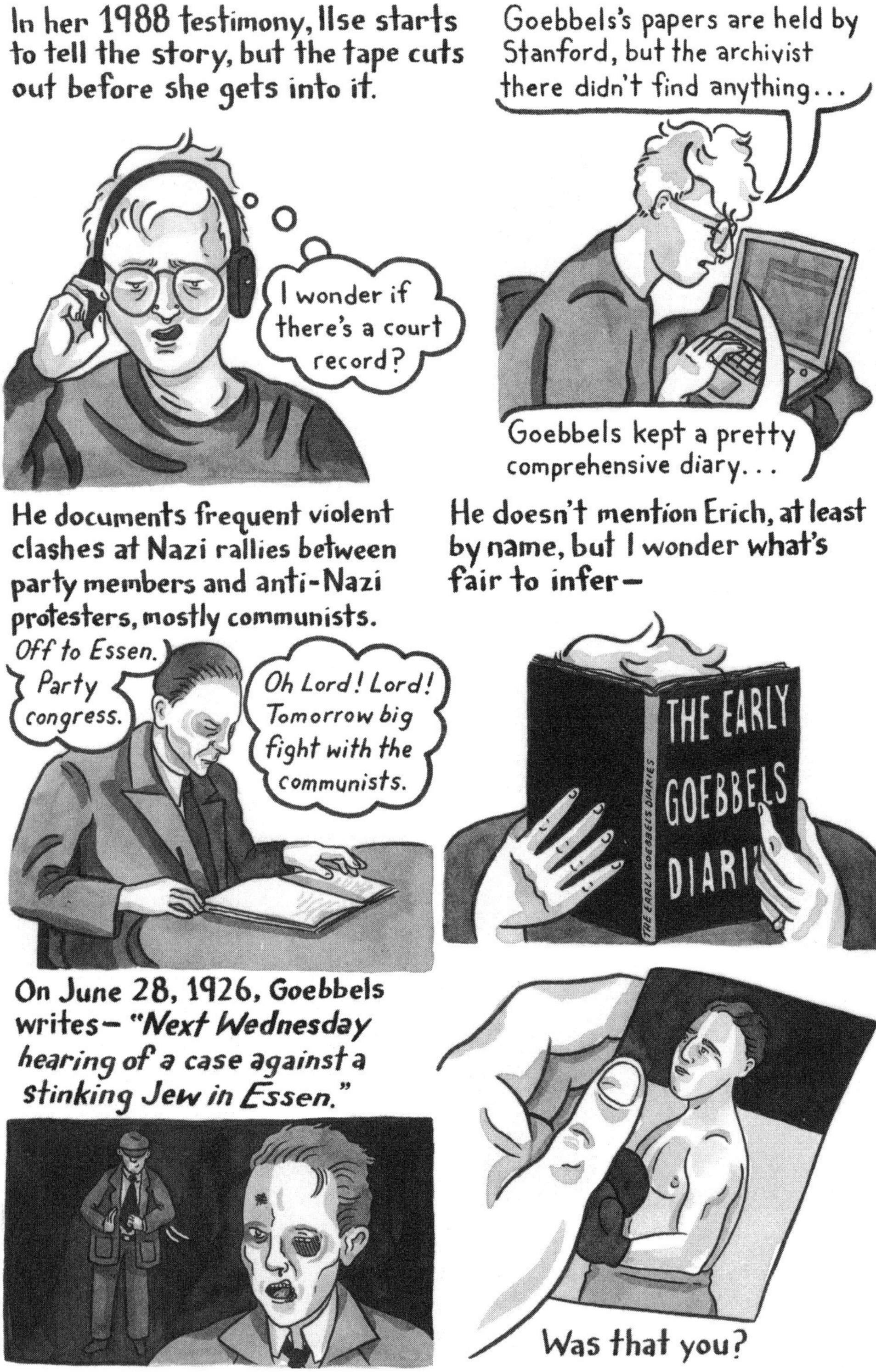
In her 1988 testimony, Ilse starts to tell the story, but the tape cuts out before she gets into it.
I wonder if there's a court record?
Goebbels's papers are held by Stanford, but the archivist there didn't find anything...
Goebbels kept a pretty comprehensive diary...
He documents frequent violent clashes at Nazi rallies between party members and anti-Nazi protesters, mostly communists.
Off to Essen. Party congress.
Oh Lord! Lord! Tomorrow big fight with the communists.
He doesn't mention Erich, at least by name, but I wonder what's fair to infer—
THE EARLY GOEBBELS DIARI
THE EARLY GOEBBELS DIARIES
On June 28, 1926, Goebbels writes— "Next Wednesday hearing of a case against a stinking Jew in Essen."
Was that you?

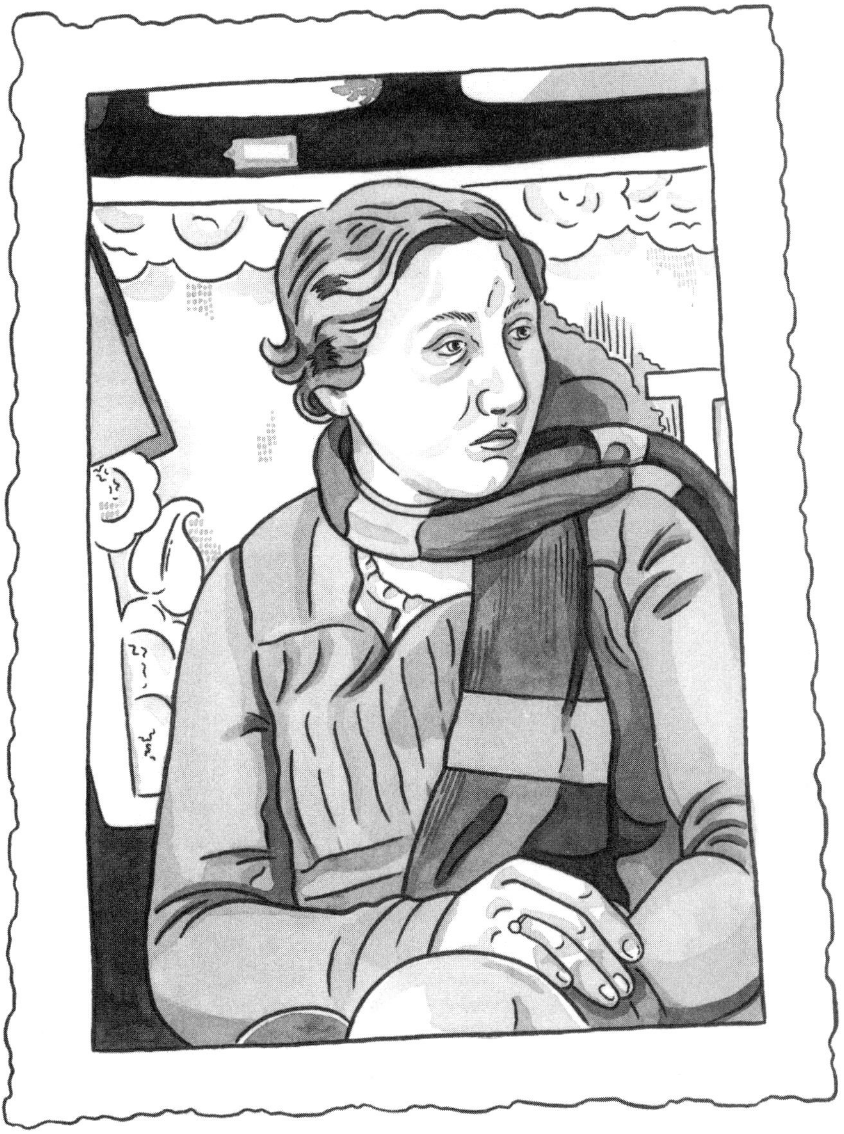

PART 4

ET ES WIE ET ES

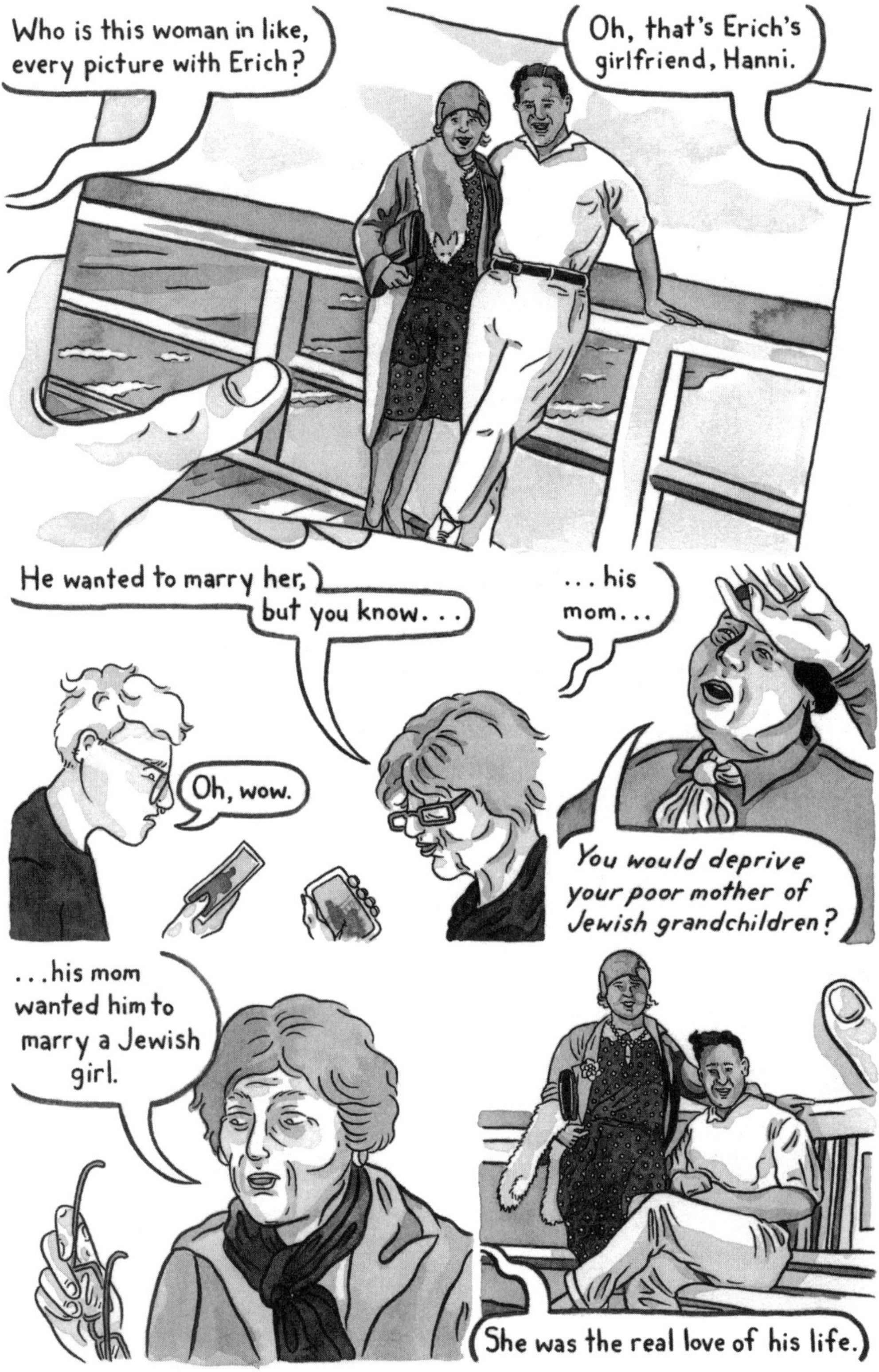
Who is this woman in like, every picture with Erich?
Oh, that's Erich's girlfriend, Hanni.
He wanted to marry her, but you know. . .
. . . his mom. . .
Oh, wow.
You would deprive your poor mother of Jewish grandchildren?
. . .his mom wanted him to marry a Jewish girl.
She was the real love of his life.

This is how my great-grandparents met...

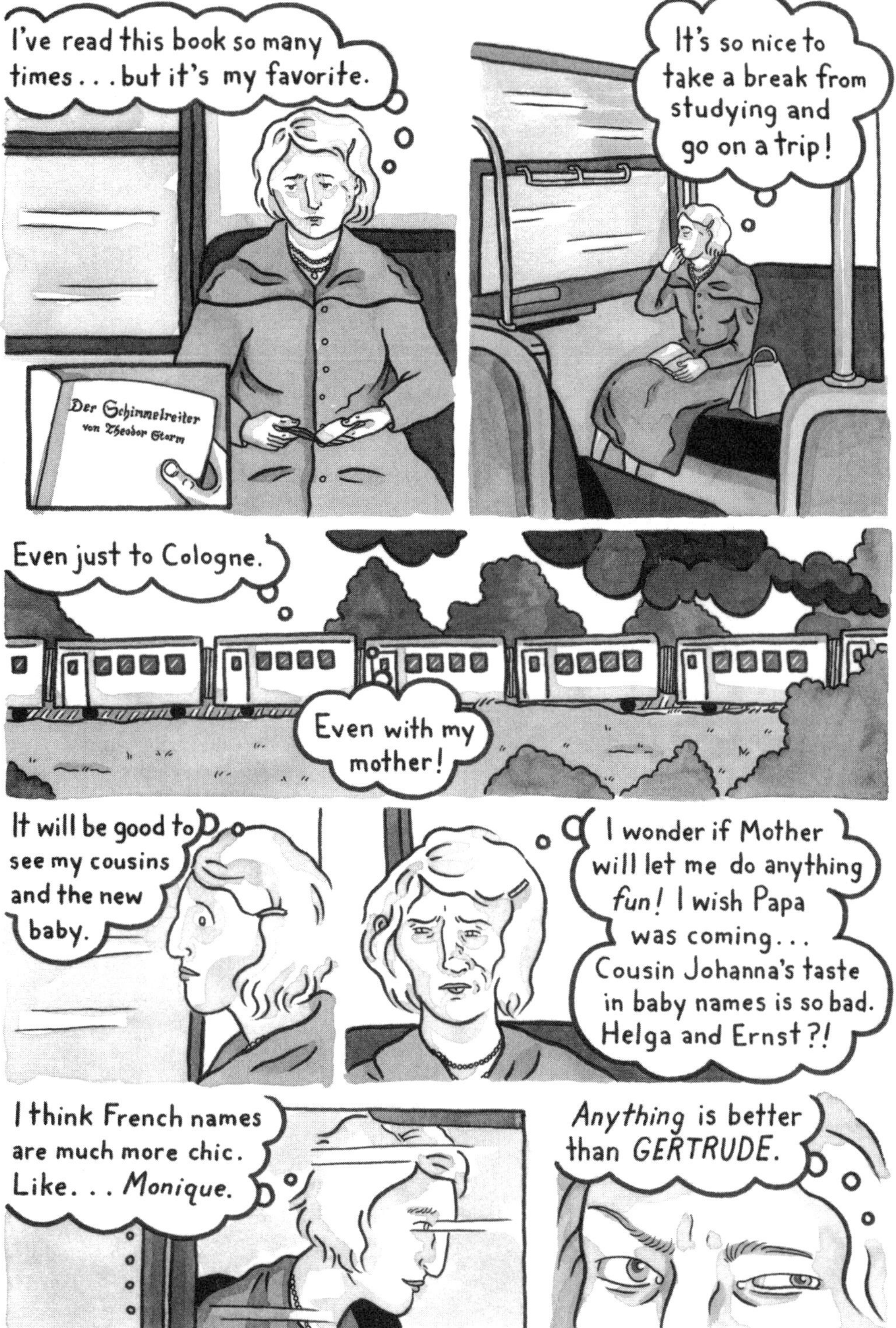

I've read this book so many times... but it's my favorite.
Der Schimmelreiter von Theodor Storm
It's so nice to take a break from studying and go on a trip!
Even just to Cologne.
Even with my mother!
It will be good to see my cousins and the new baby.
I wonder if Mother will let me do anything *fun*! I wish Papa was coming... Cousin Johanna's taste in baby names is so bad. Helga and Ernst?!
I think French names are much more chic. Like... *Monique*.
Anything is better than *GERTRUDE*.

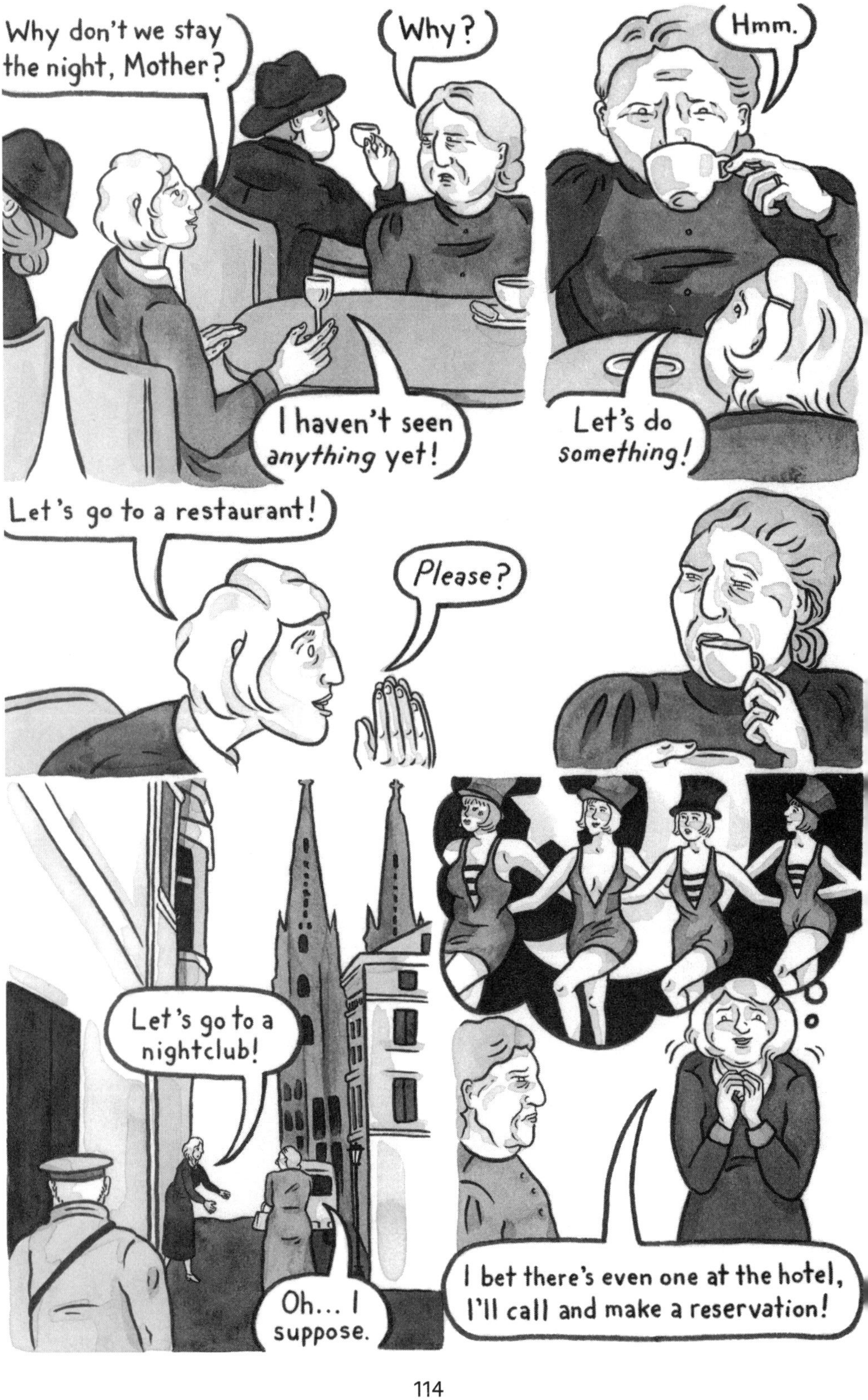
Why don't we stay the night, Mother?
Why?
I haven't seen *anything* yet!
Hmm.
Let's do *something*!
Let's go to a restaurant!
Please?
Let's go to a nightclub!
Oh... I suppose.
I bet there's even one at the hotel, I'll call and make a reservation!

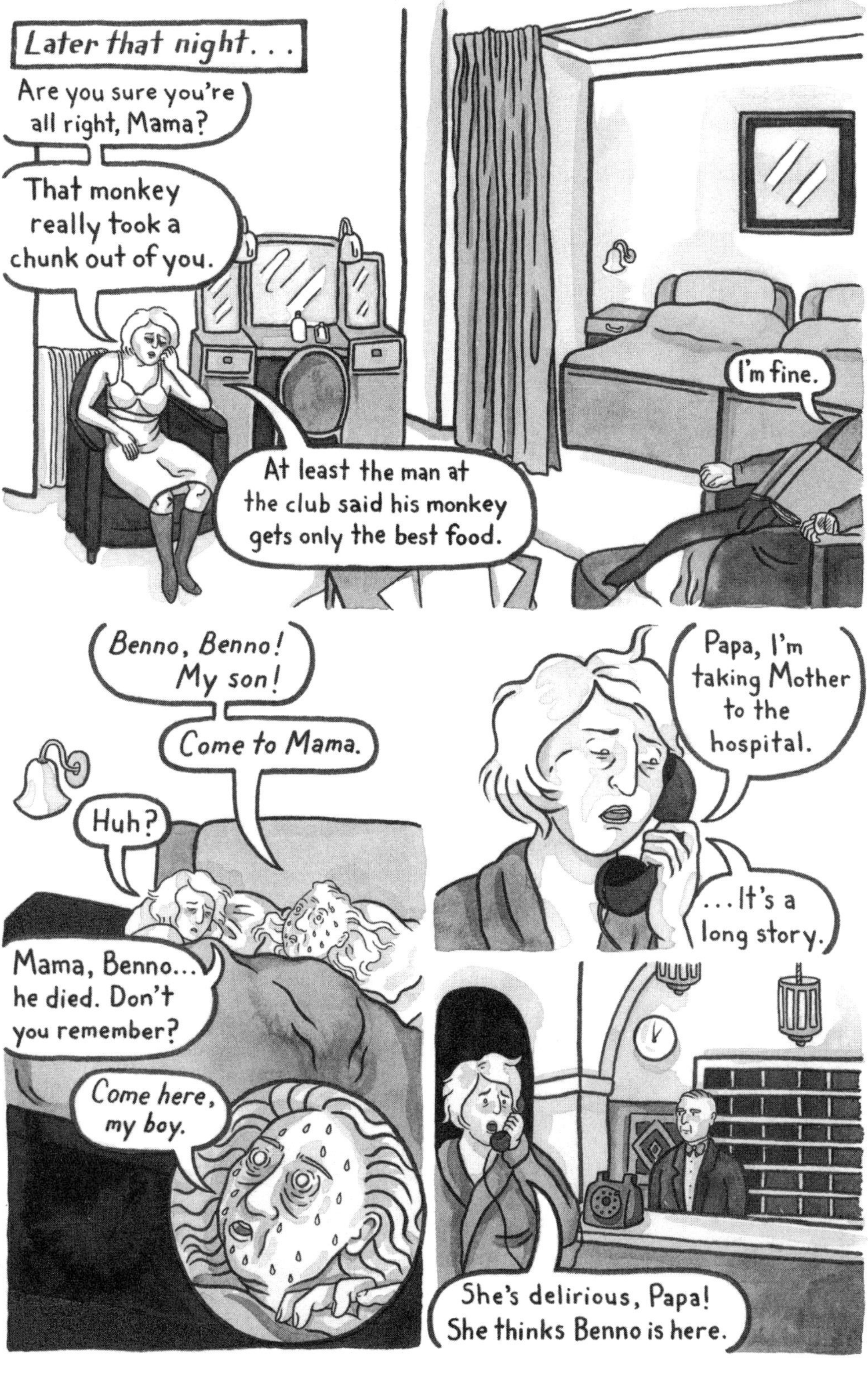
Later that night...
Are you sure you're all right, Mama?
That monkey really took a chunk out of you.
At least the man at the club said his monkey gets only the best food.
I'm fine.
Benno, Benno! My son!
Come to Mama.
Huh?
Mama, Benno... he died. Don't you remember?
Come here, my boy.
Papa, I'm taking Mother to the hospital.
...It's a long story.
She's delirious, Papa! She thinks Benno is here.

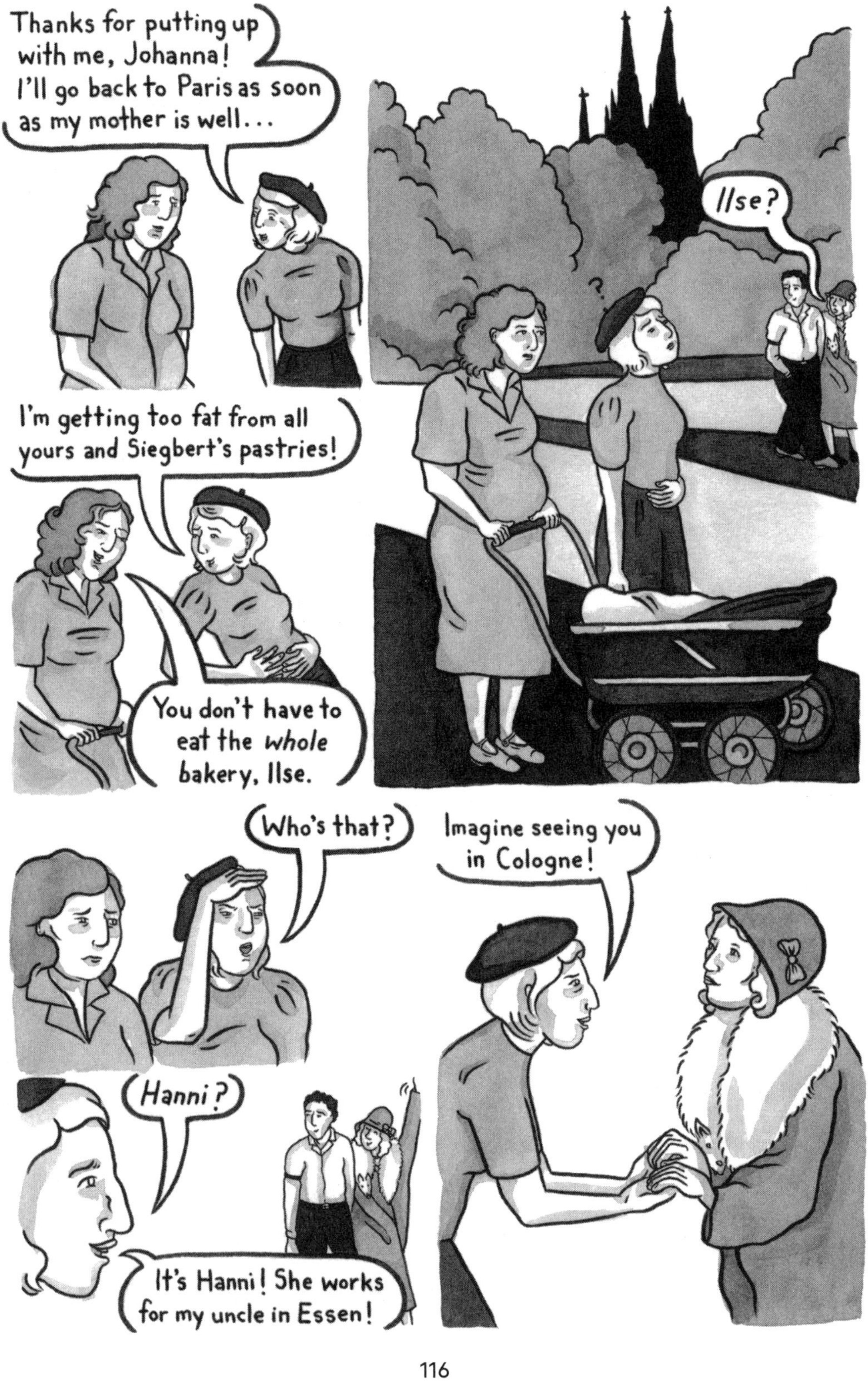
Thanks for putting up with me, Johanna! I'll go back to Paris as soon as my mother is well...
I'm getting too fat from all yours and Siegbert's pastries!
You don't have to eat the *whole* bakery, Ilse.
Ilse?
Who's that?
Hanni?
It's Hanni! She works for my uncle in Essen!
Imagine seeing you in Cologne!

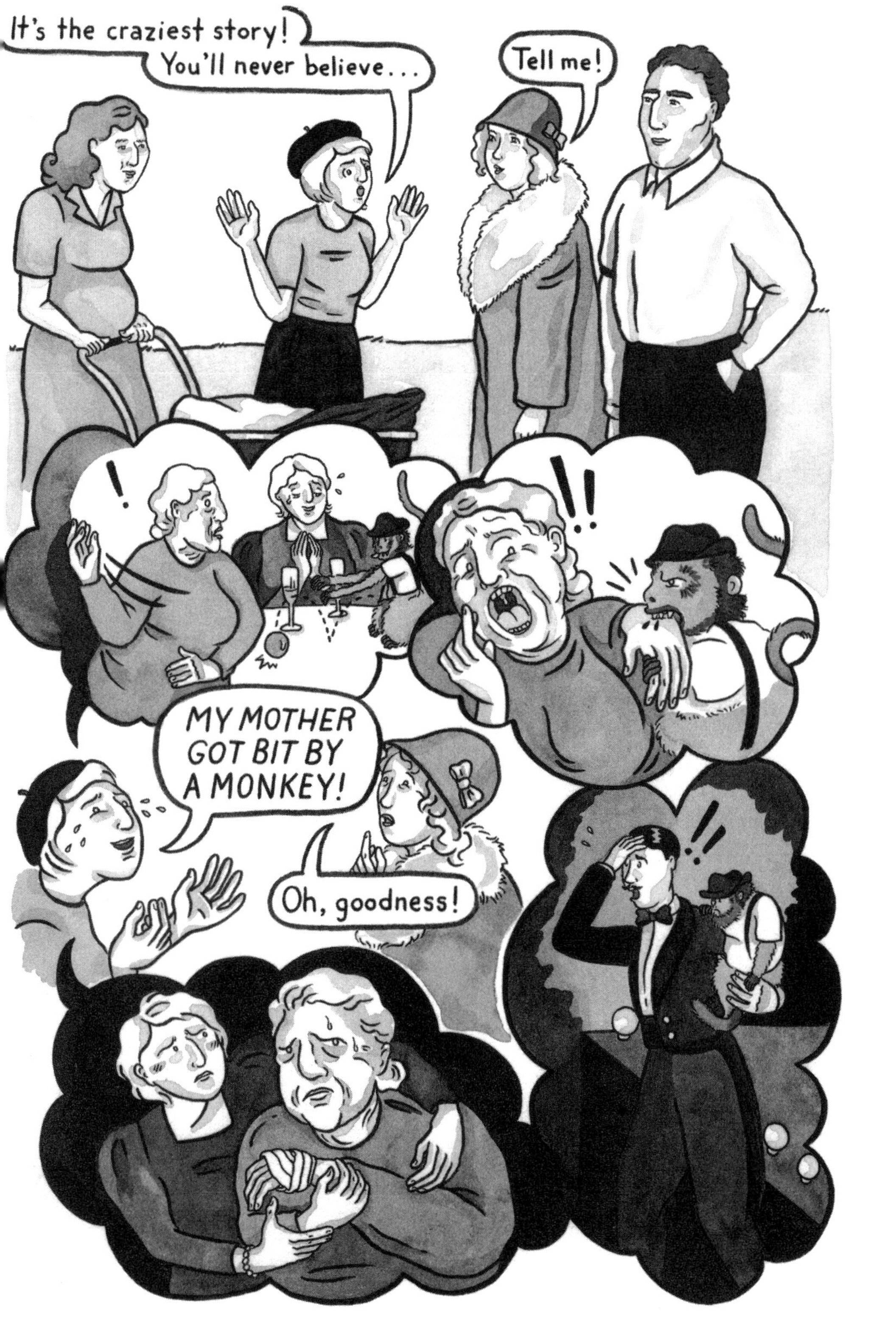
It's the craziest story!
You'll never believe...
Tell me!
!
!!
MY MOTHER GOT BIT BY A MONKEY!
Oh, goodness!
!

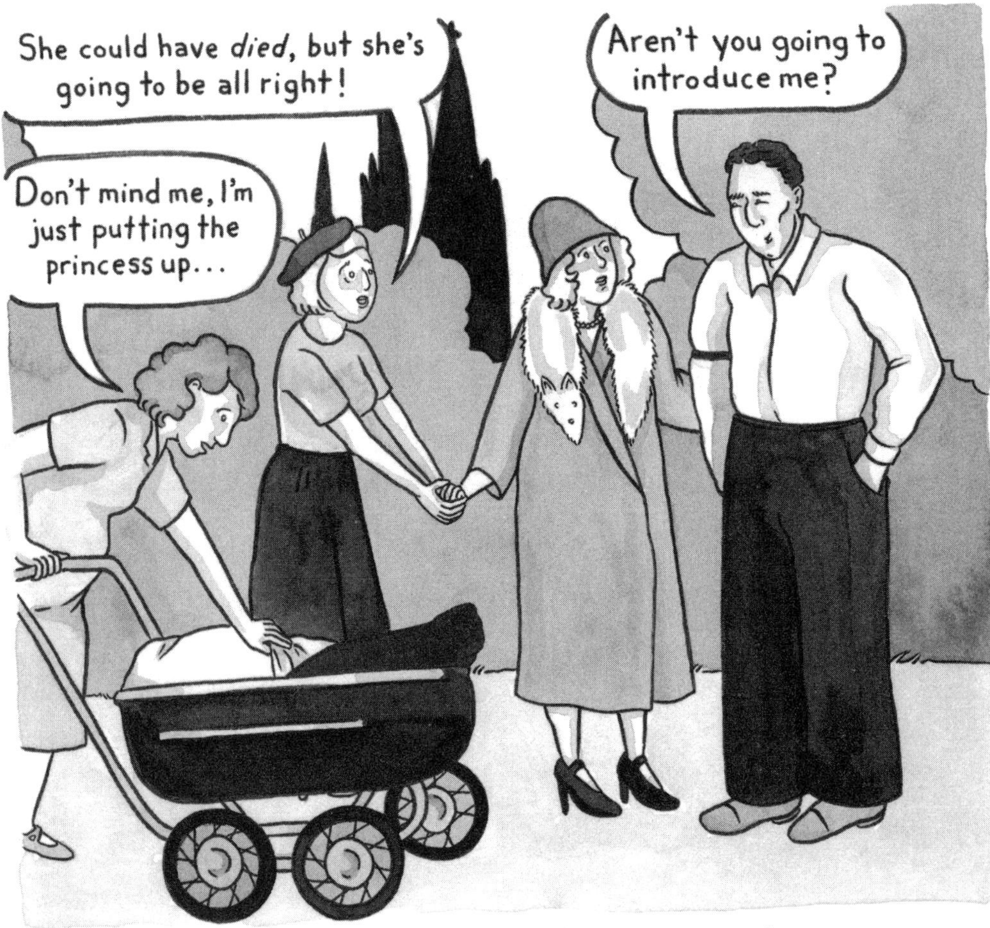
She could have *died*, but she's going to be all right!
Don't mind me, I'm just putting the princess up...
Aren't you going to introduce me?

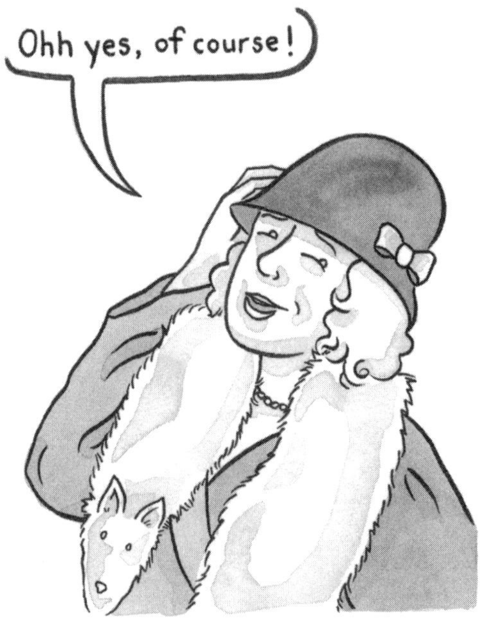
Ohh yes, of course!

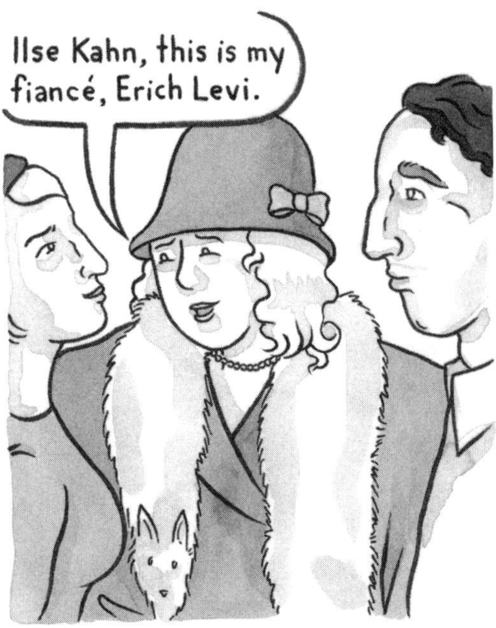
Ilse Kahn, this is my fiancé, Erich Levi.

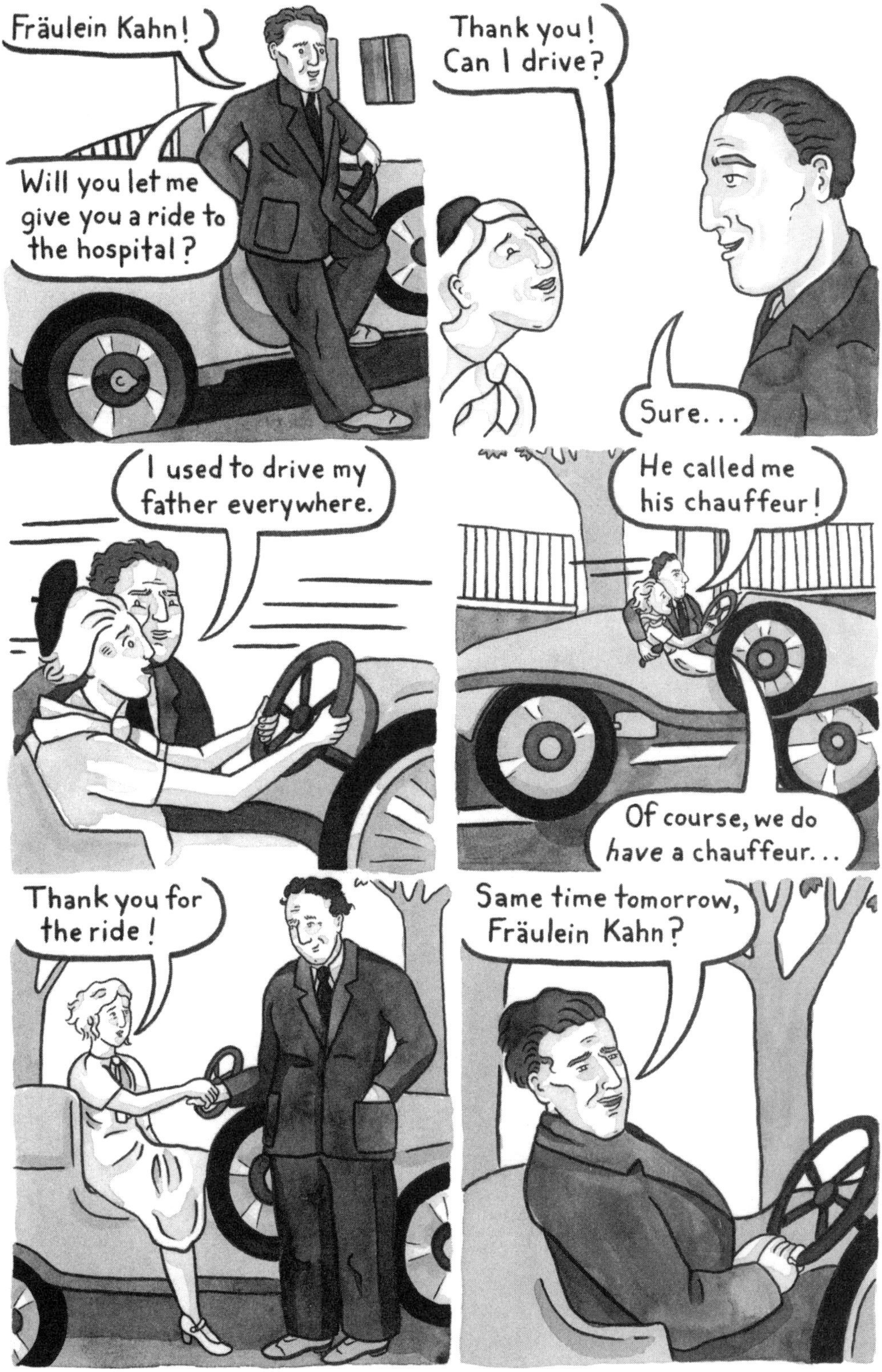
Fräulein Kahn!
Will you let me give you a ride to the hospital?
Thank you! Can I drive?
Sure...
I used to drive my father everywhere.
He called me his chauffeur!
Of course, we do *have* a chauffeur...
Thank you for the ride!
Same time tomorrow, Fräulein Kahn?

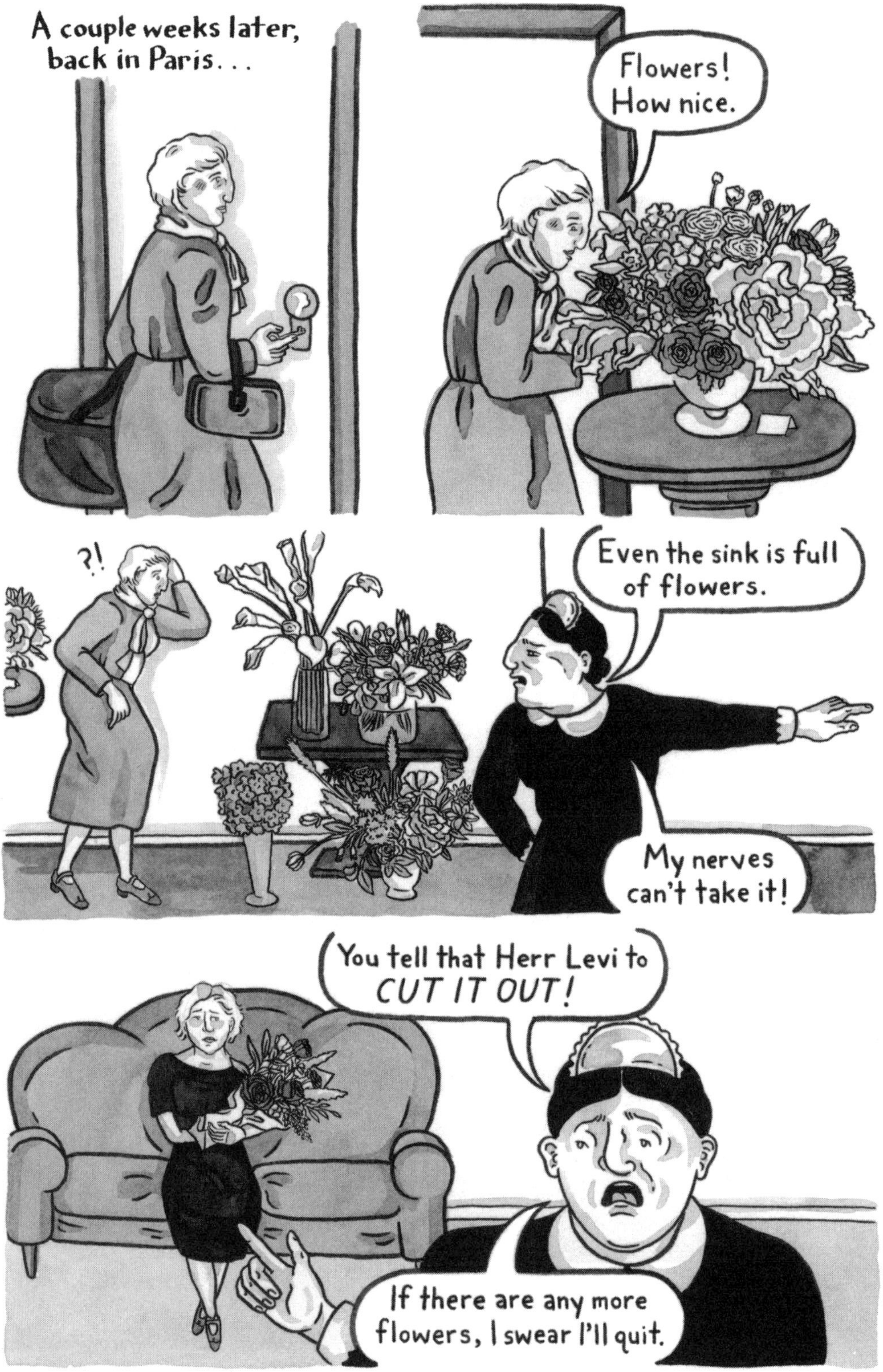
A couple weeks later, back in Paris...
Flowers! How nice.
?!
Even the sink is full of flowers.
My nerves can't take it!
You tell that Herr Levi to CUT IT OUT!
If there are any more flowers, I swear I'll quit.

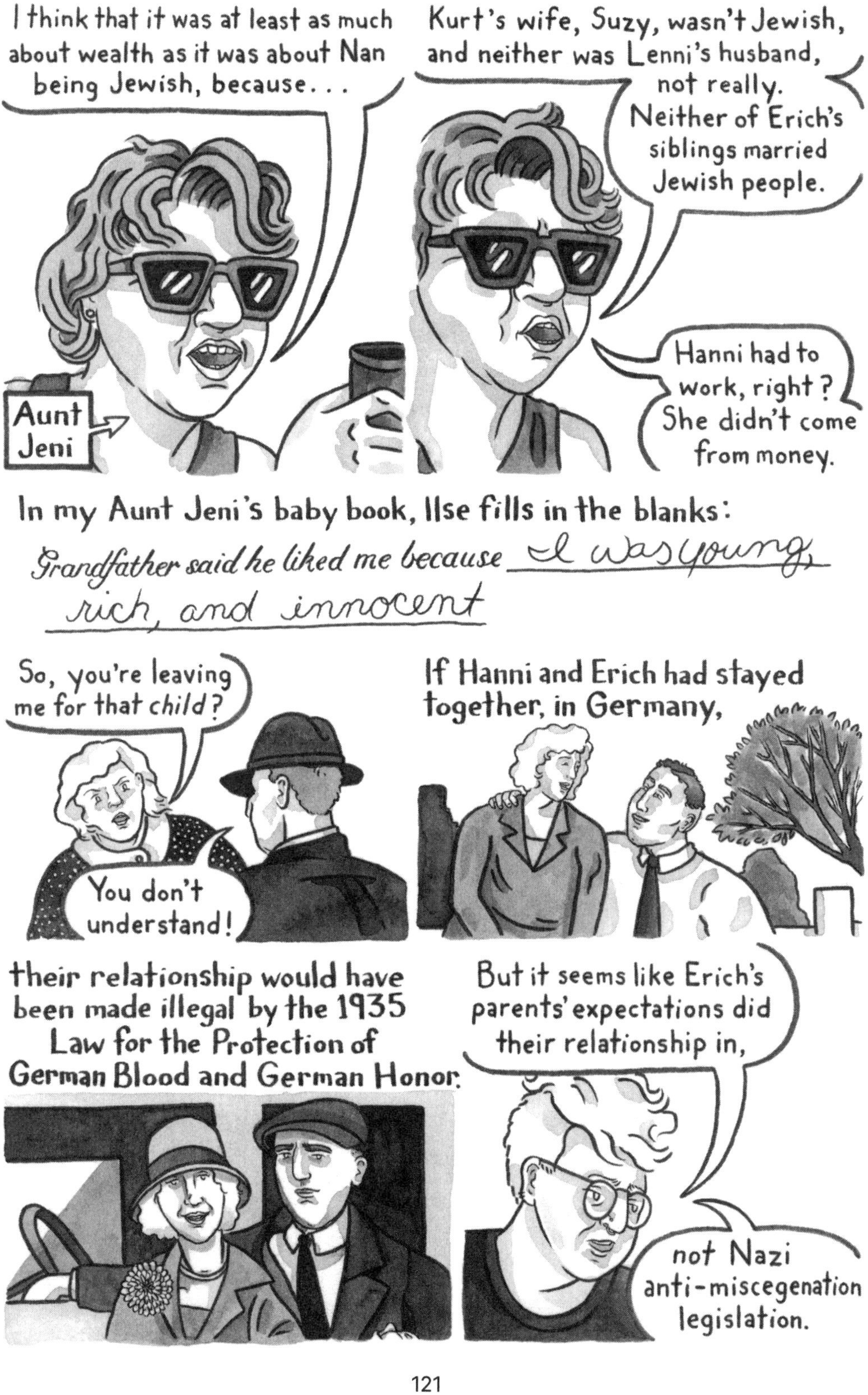
I think that it was at least as much about wealth as it was about Nan being Jewish, because...
Aunt Jeni
Kurt's wife, Suzy, wasn't Jewish, and neither was Lenni's husband, not really. Neither of Erich's siblings married Jewish people.
Hanni had to work, right? She didn't come from money.
In my Aunt Jeni's baby book, Ilse fills in the blanks:
Grandfather said he liked me because I was young, rich, and innocent
So, you're leaving me for that child?
You don't understand!
If Hanni and Erich had stayed together, in Germany,
their relationship would have been made illegal by the 1935 Law for the Protection of German Blood and German Honor.
But it seems like Erich's parents' expectations did their relationship in,
not Nazi anti-miscegenation legislation.

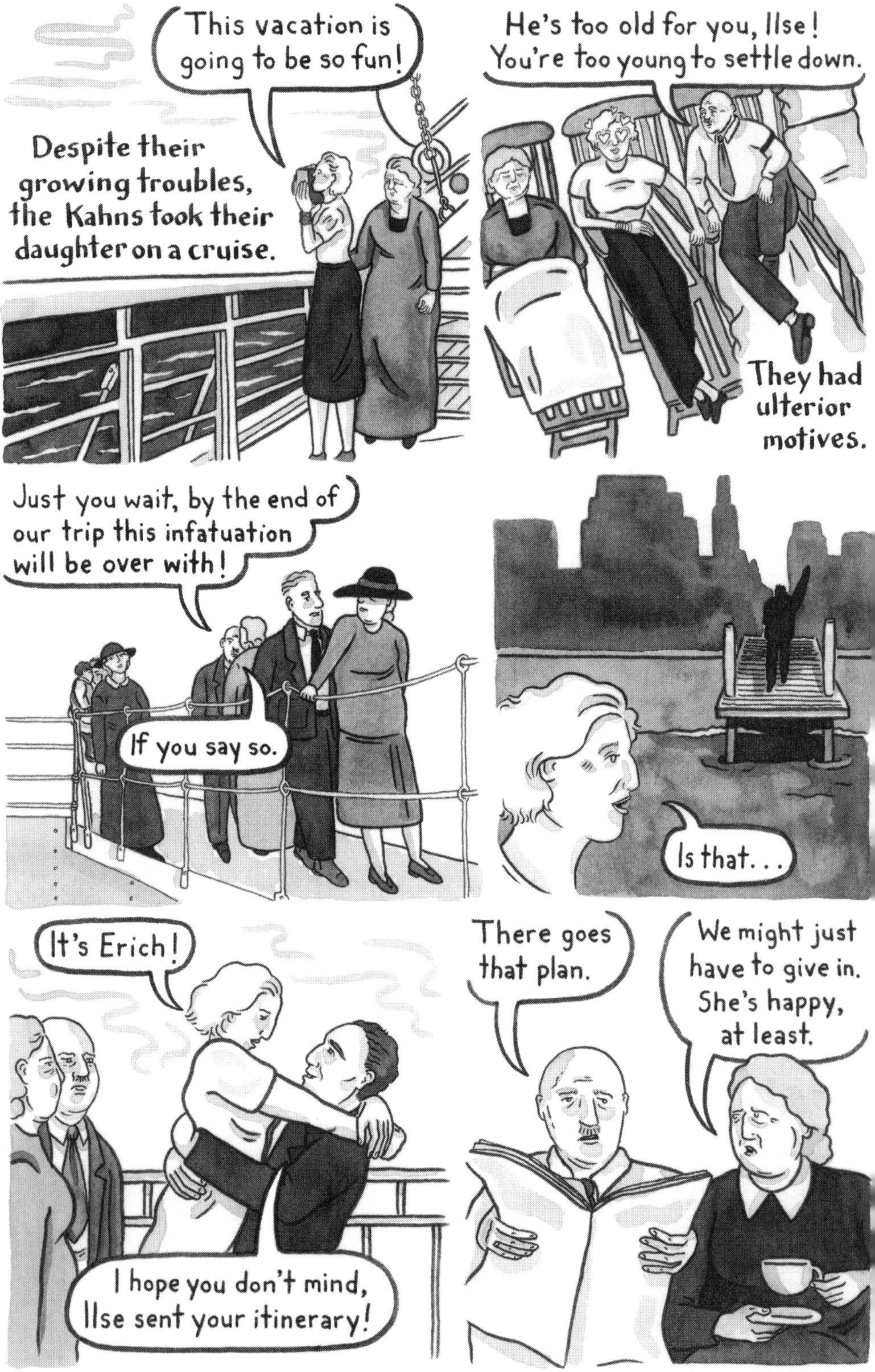
This vacation is going to be so fun!
Despite their growing troubles, the Kahns took their daughter on a cruise.
He's too old for you, Ilse! You're too young to settle down.
They had ulterior motives.
Just you wait, by the end of our trip this infatuation will be over with!
If you say so.
Is that. . .
It's Erich!
I hope you don't mind, Ilse sent your itinerary!
There goes that plan.
We might just have to give in. She's happy, at least.

PART 5

STUMBLING STONES

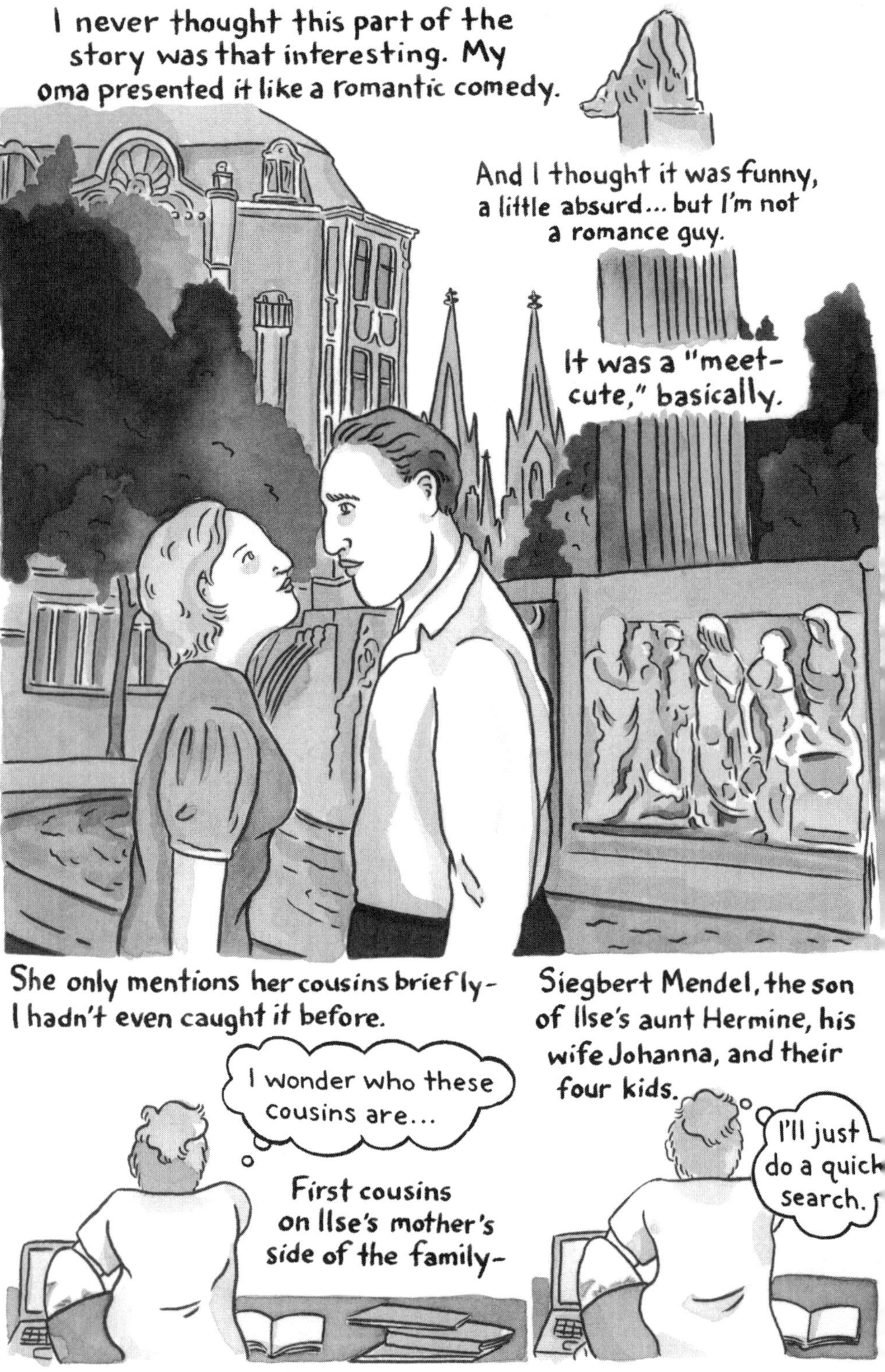
I never thought this part of the story was that interesting. My oma presented it like a romantic comedy.
And I thought it was funny, a little absurd... but I'm not a romance guy.
It was a "meet-cute," basically.
She only mentions her cousins briefly-I hadn't even caught it before.
I wonder who these cousins are...
First cousins on Ilse's mother's side of the family-
Siegbert Mendel, the son of Ilse's aunt Hermine, his wife Johanna, and their four kids.
I'll just do a quick search.

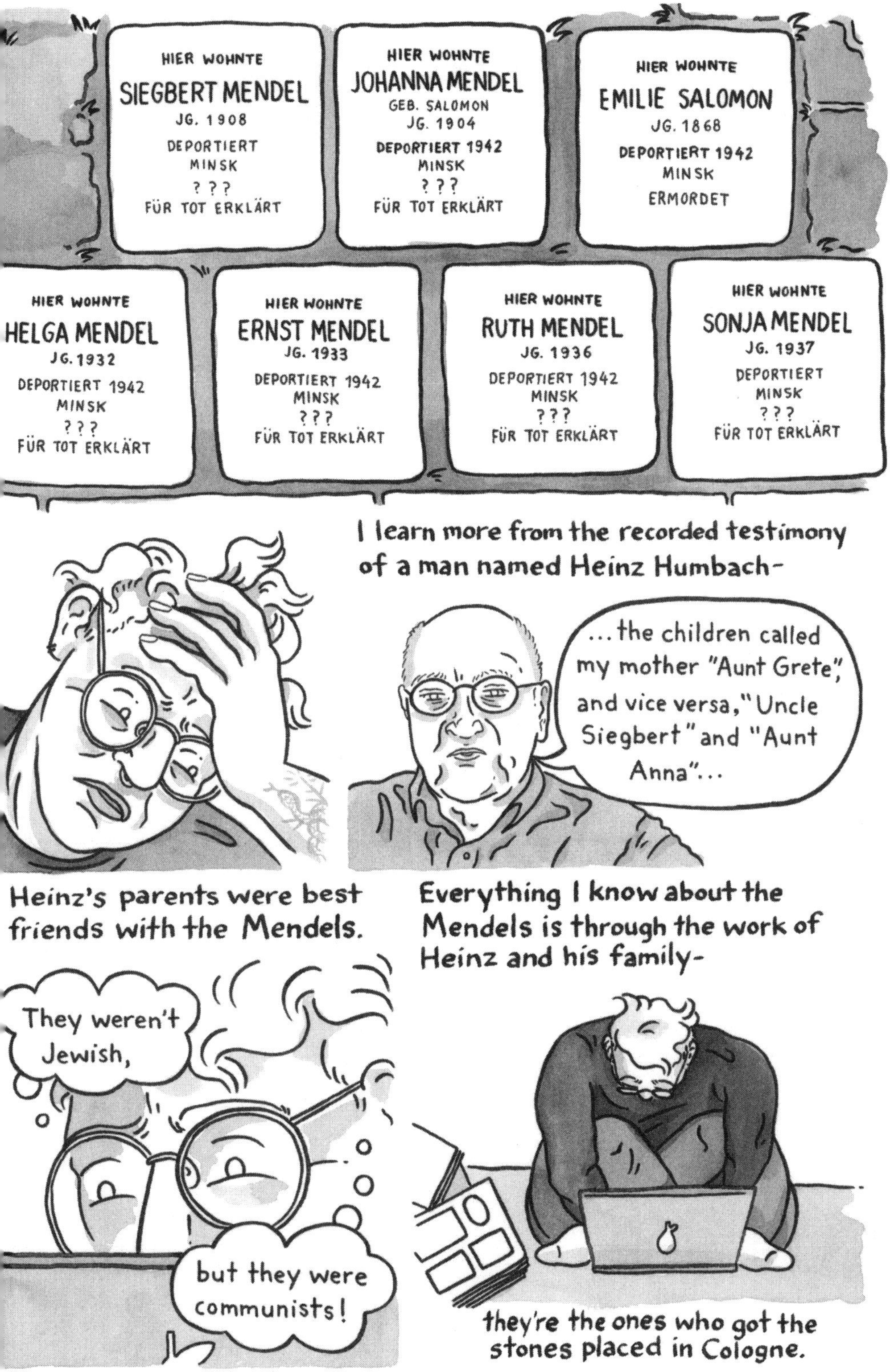
HIER WOHNTE
SIEGBERT MENDEL
JG. 1908
DEPORTIERT
MINSK
???
FÜR TOT ERKLÄRT
HIER WOHNTE
JOHANNA MENDEL
GEB. SALOMON
JG. 1904
DEPORTIERT 1942
MINSK
???
FÜR TOT ERKLÄRT
HIER WOHNTE
EMILIE SALOMON
JG. 1868
DEPORTIERT 1942
MINSK
ERMORDET
HIER WOHNTE
HELGA MENDEL
JG. 1932
DEPORTIERT 1942
MINSK
???
FÜR TOT ERKLÄRT
HIER WOHNTE
ERNST MENDEL
JG. 1933
DEPORTIERT 1942
MINSK
???
FÜR TOT ERKLÄRT
HIER WOHNTE
RUTH MENDEL
JG. 1936
DEPORTIERT 1942
MINSK
???
FÜR TOT ERKLÄRT
HIER WOHNTE
SONJA MENDEL
JG. 1937
DEPORTIERT
MINSK
???
FÜR TOT ERKLÄRT
I learn more from the recorded testimony of a man named Heinz Humbach-
...the children called my mother "Aunt Grete", and vice versa, "Uncle Siegbert" and "Aunt Anna"...
Heinz's parents were best friends with the Mendels.
They weren't Jewish,
but they were communists!
Everything I know about the Mendels is through the work of Heinz and his family-
they're the ones who got the stones placed in Cologne.

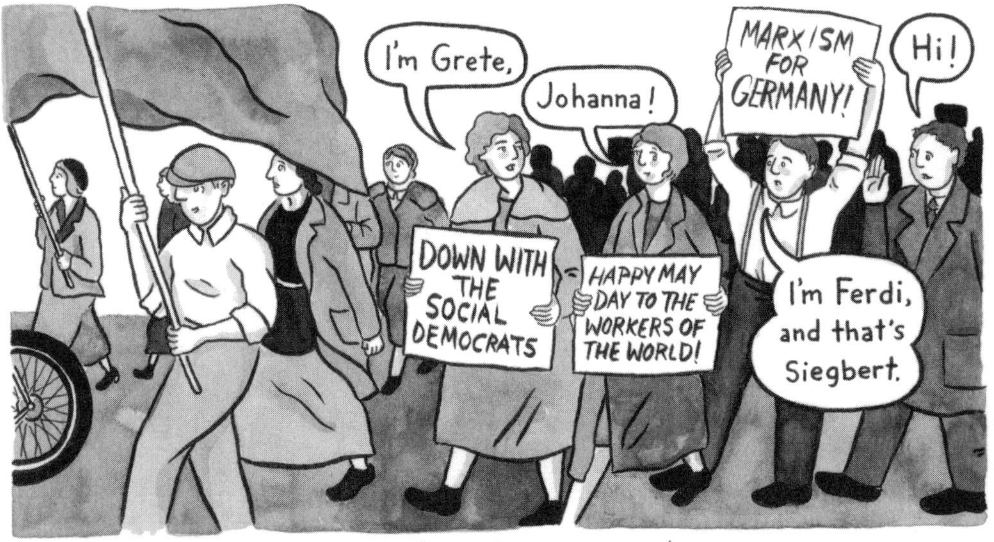
I'm Grete,
Johanna!
DOWN WITH THE SOCIAL DEMOCRATS
HAPPY MAY DAY TO THE WORKERS OF THE WORLD!
MARXISM FOR GERMANY!
Hi!
I'm Ferdi, and that's Siegbert.

They had met in the socialist youth movement.

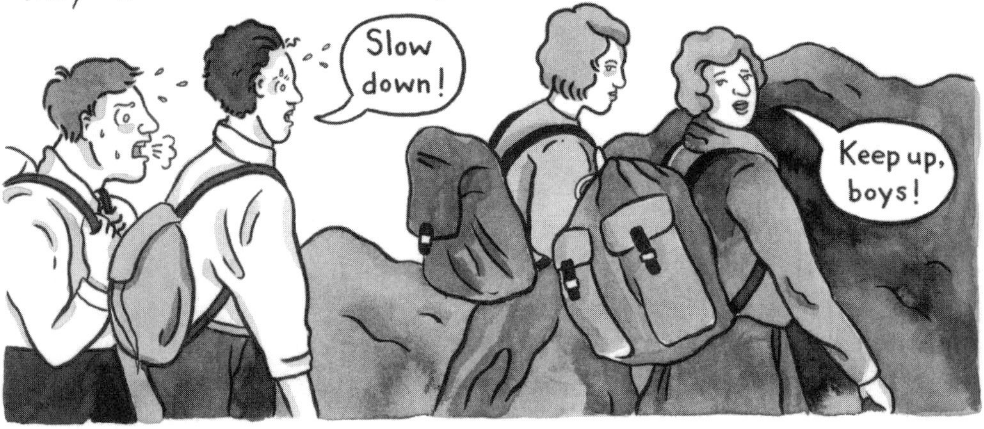
Slow down!
Keep up, boys!

Heinz was older than the Mendel kids, but spent a lot of time with them. Sometimes they would play in the Mendel family bakery after hours.

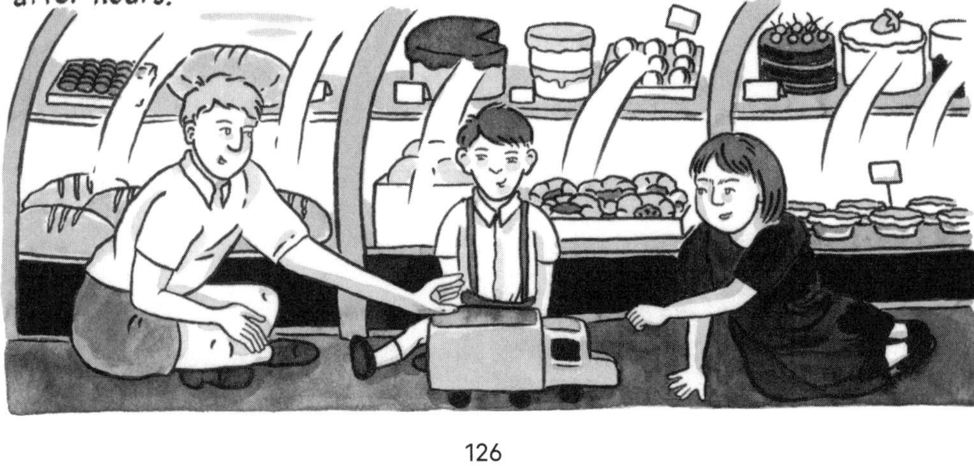

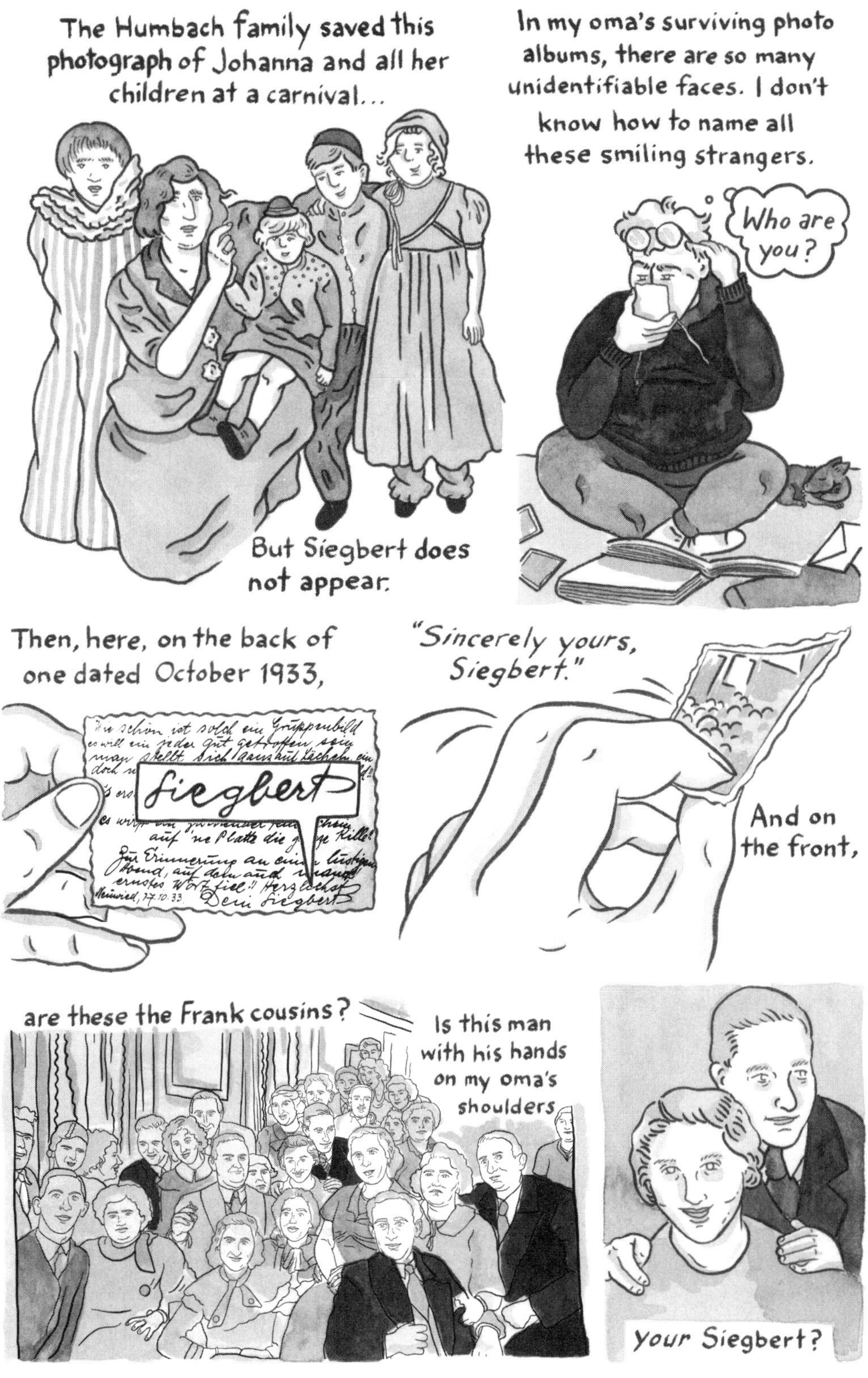

The Humbach family saved this photograph of Johanna and all her children at a carnival...
But Siegbert does not appear.
In my oma's surviving photo albums, there are so many unidentifiable faces. I don't know how to name all these smiling strangers.
Who are you?
Then, here, on the back of one dated October 1933,
Siegbert
"Sincerely yours, Siegbert."
And on the front,
are these the Frank cousins?
Is this man with his hands on my oma's shoulders
your Siegbert?

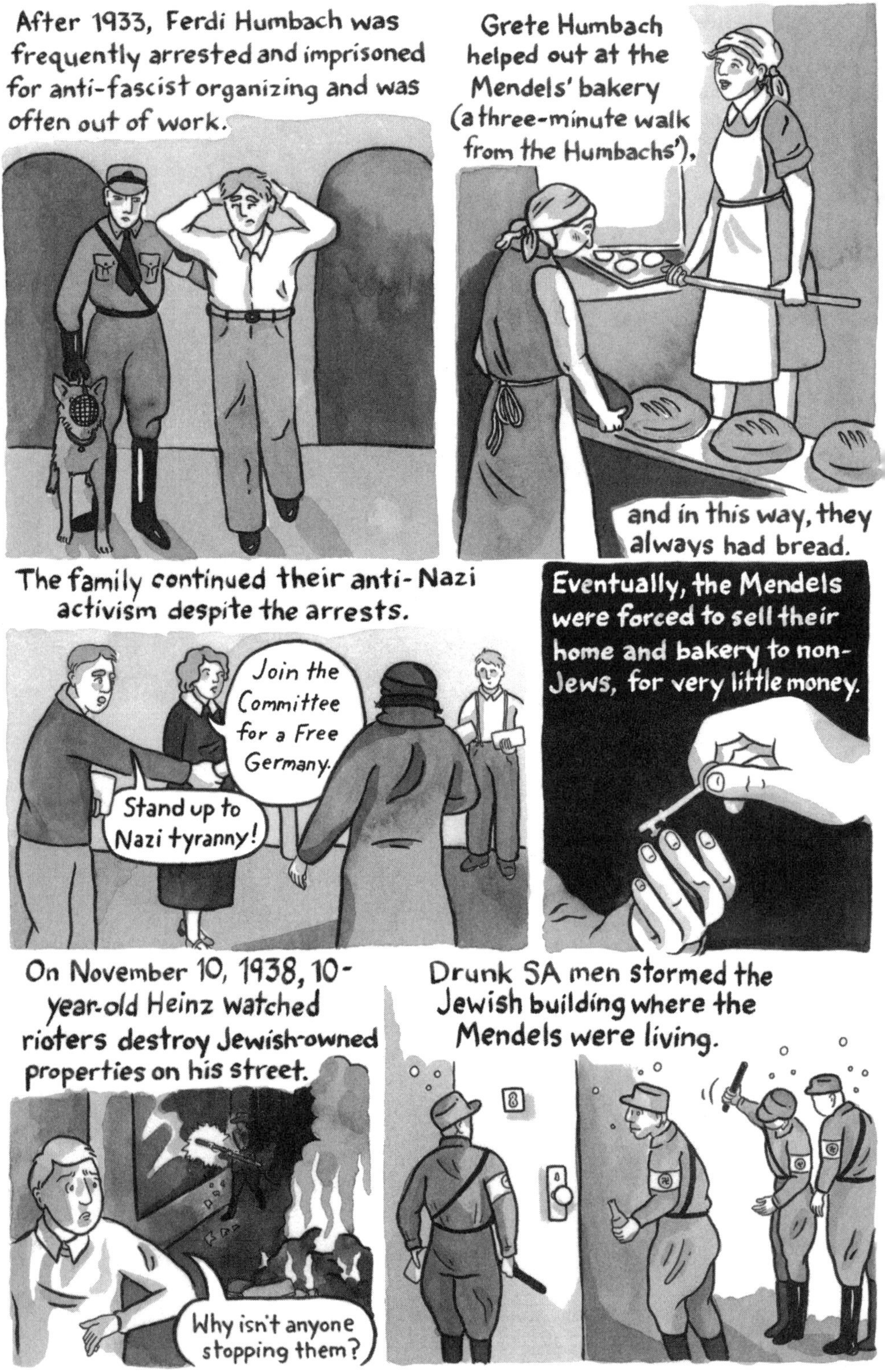
After 1933, Ferdi Humbach was frequently arrested and imprisoned for anti-fascist organizing and was often out of work.
Grete Humbach helped out at the Mendels' bakery (a three-minute walk from the Humbachs'),
and in this way, they always had bread.
The family continued their anti-Nazi activism despite the arrests.
Join the Committee for a Free Germany.
Stand up to Nazi tyranny!
Eventually, the Mendels were forced to sell their home and bakery to non-Jews, for very little money.
On November 10, 1938, 10-year-old Heinz watched rioters destroy Jewish-owned properties on his street.
Why isn't anyone stopping them?
Drunk SA men stormed the Jewish building where the Mendels were living.
8

They went from floor to floor, apartment to apartment. Johanna Mendel could hear them coming.

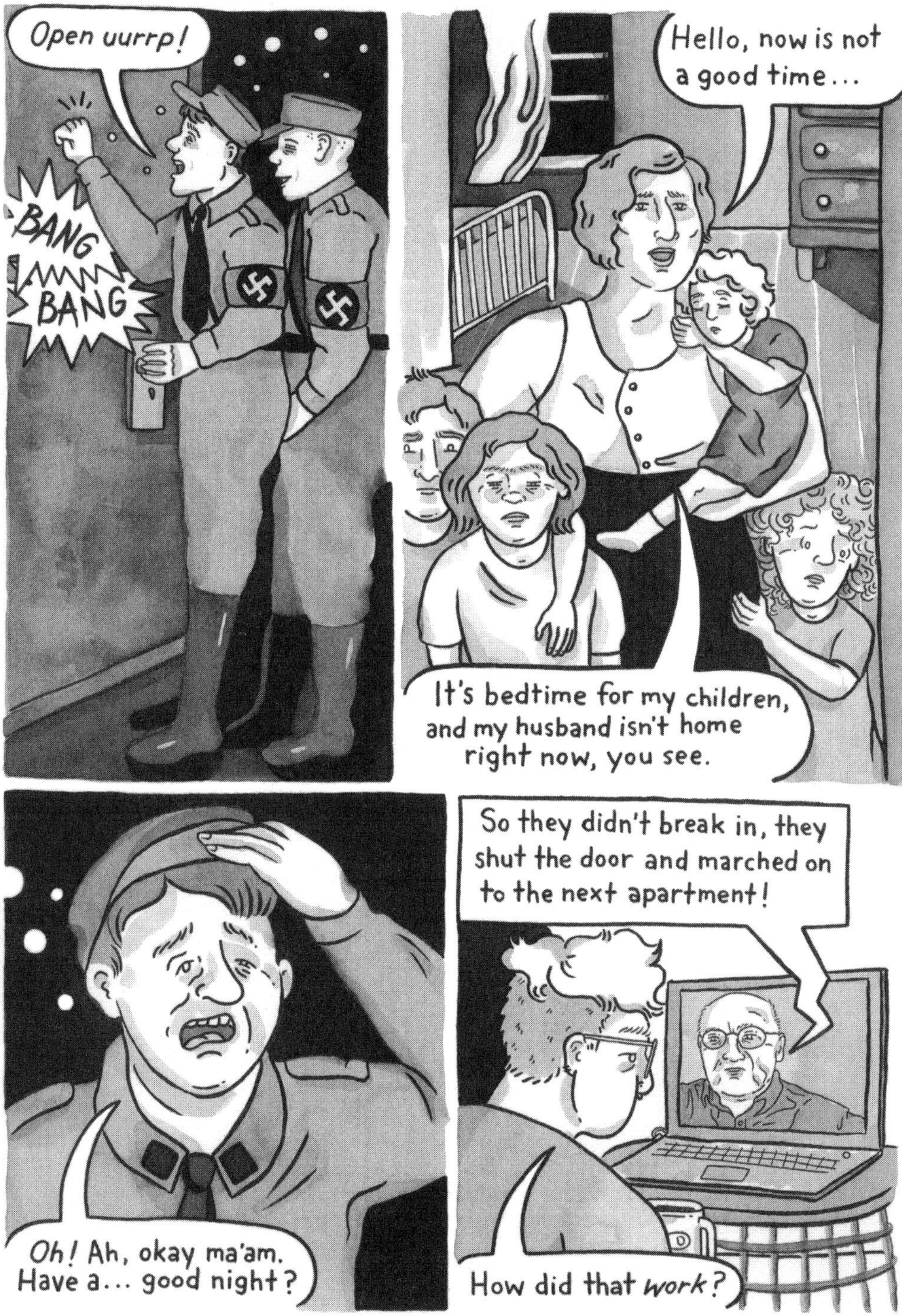
Open uurrp!
BANG BANG
Hello, now is not a good time...
It's bedtime for my children, and my husband isn't home right now, you see.
Oh! Ah, okay ma'am. Have a... good night?
So they didn't break in, they shut the door and marched on to the next apartment!
How did that *work*?

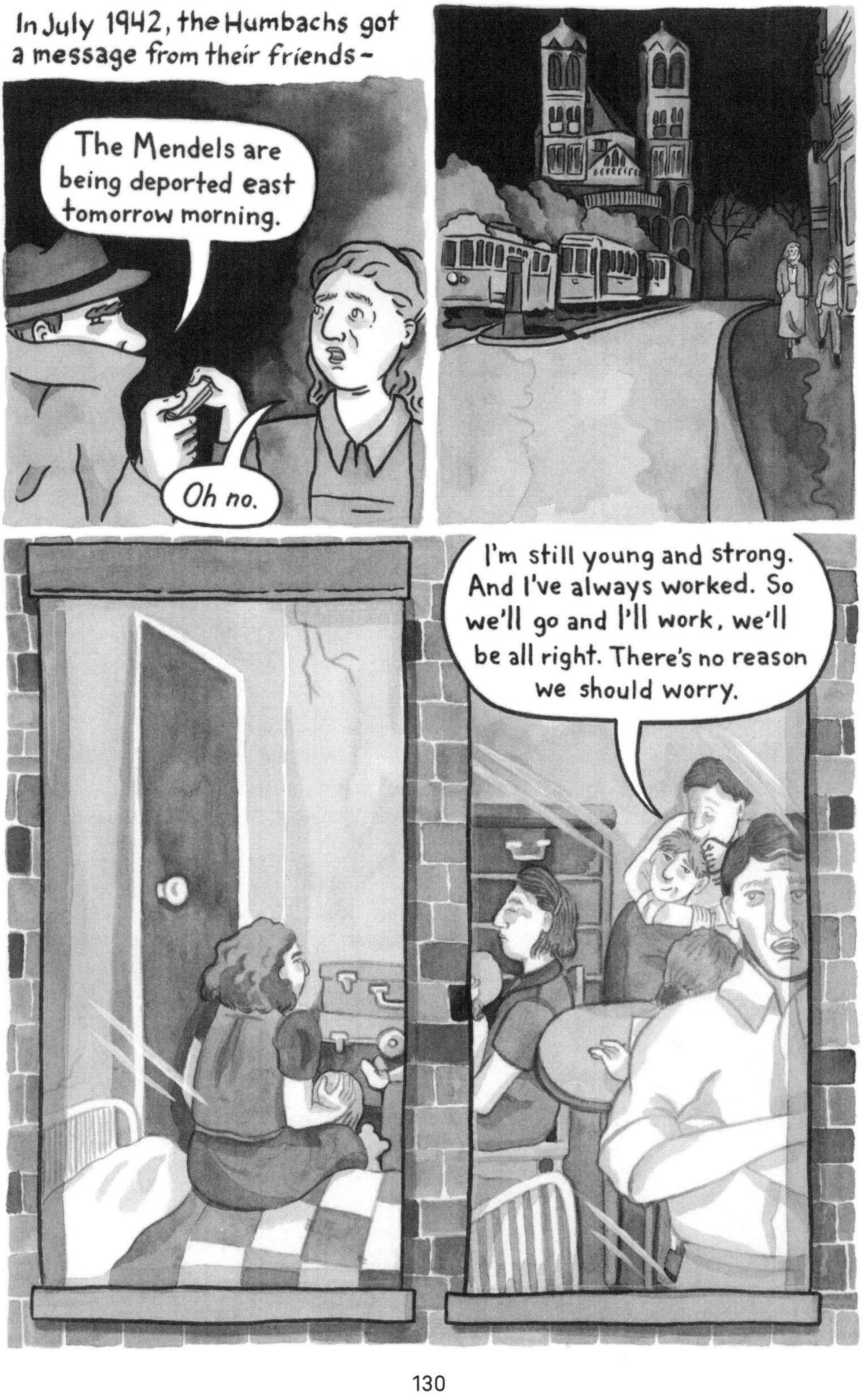
In July 1942, the Humbachs got a message from their friends –
The Mendels are being deported east tomorrow morning.
Oh no.
I'm still young and strong. And I've always worked. So we'll go and I'll work, we'll be all right. There's no reason we should worry.

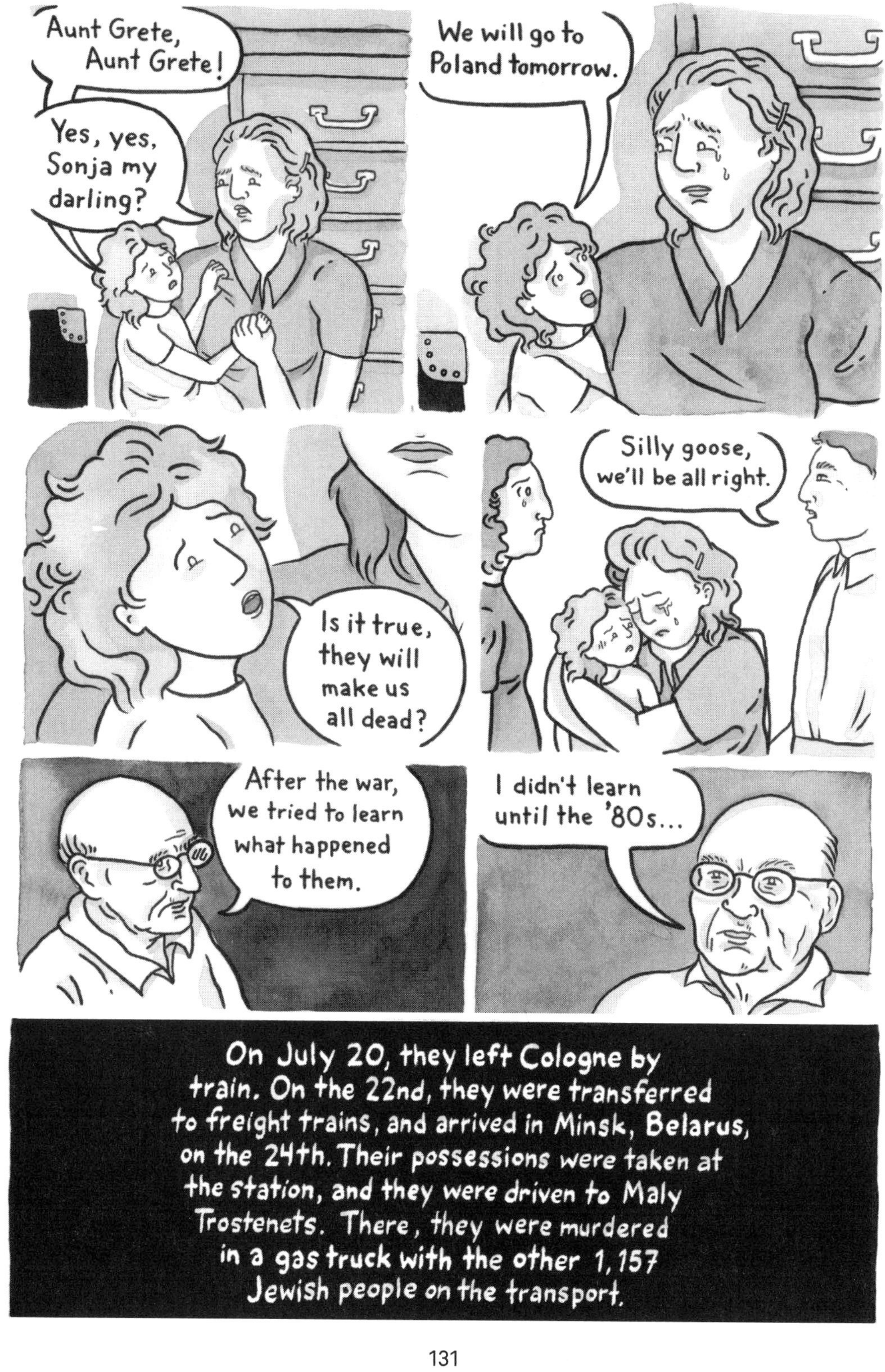
Aunt Grete, Aunt Grete!
Yes, yes, Sonja my darling?
We will go to Poland tomorrow.
Is it true, they will make us all dead?
Silly goose, we'll be all right.
After the war, we tried to learn what happened to them.
I didn't learn until the '80s...

On July 20, they left Cologne by train. On the 22nd, they were transferred to freight trains, and arrived in Minsk, Belarus, on the 24th. Their possessions were taken at the station, and they were driven to Maly Trostenets. There, they were murdered in a gas truck with the other 1,157 Jewish people on the transport.

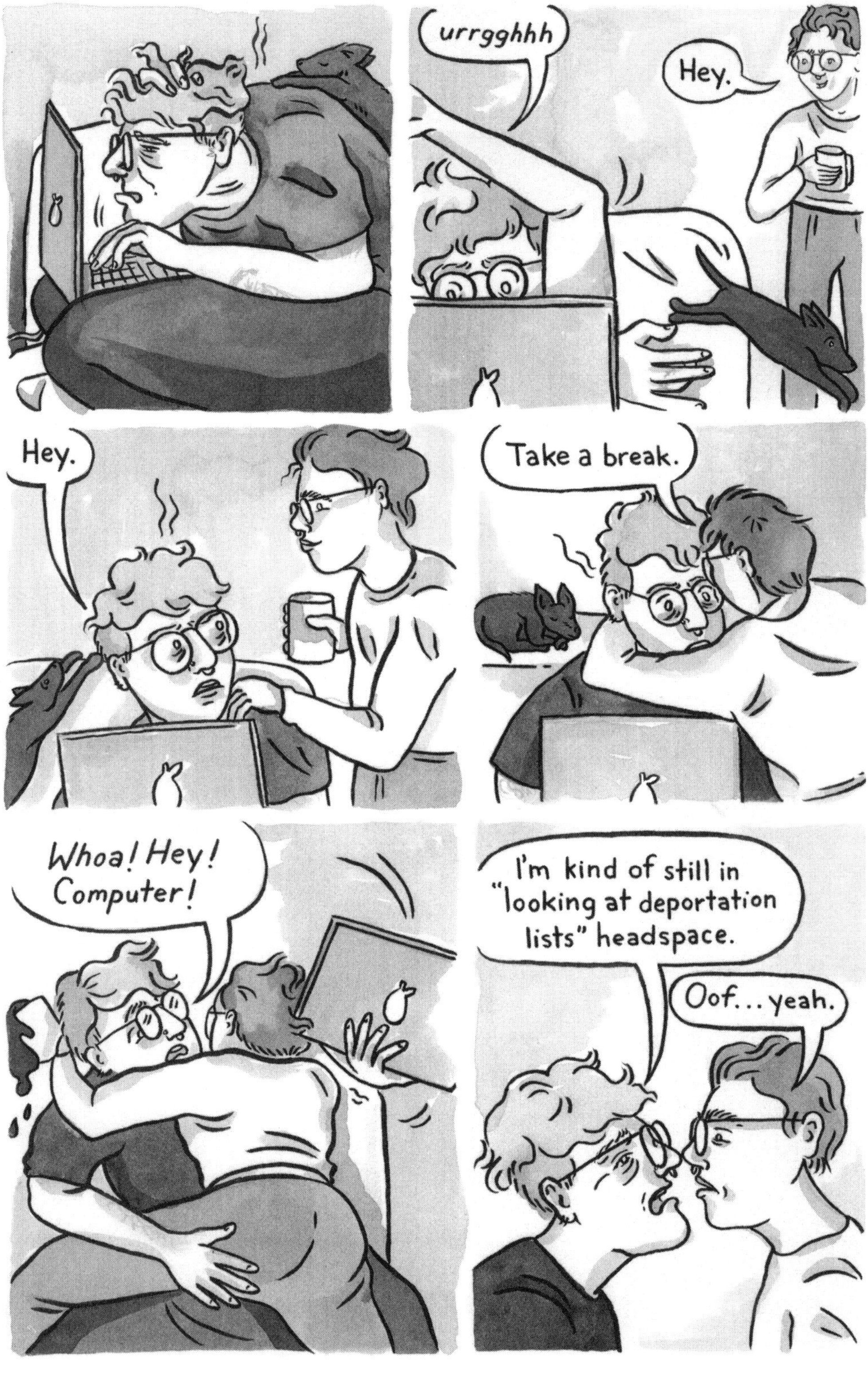
urrgghhh
Hey.
Hey.
Take a break.
Whoa! Hey! Computer!
I'm kind of still in "looking at deportation lists" headspace.
Oof... yeah.

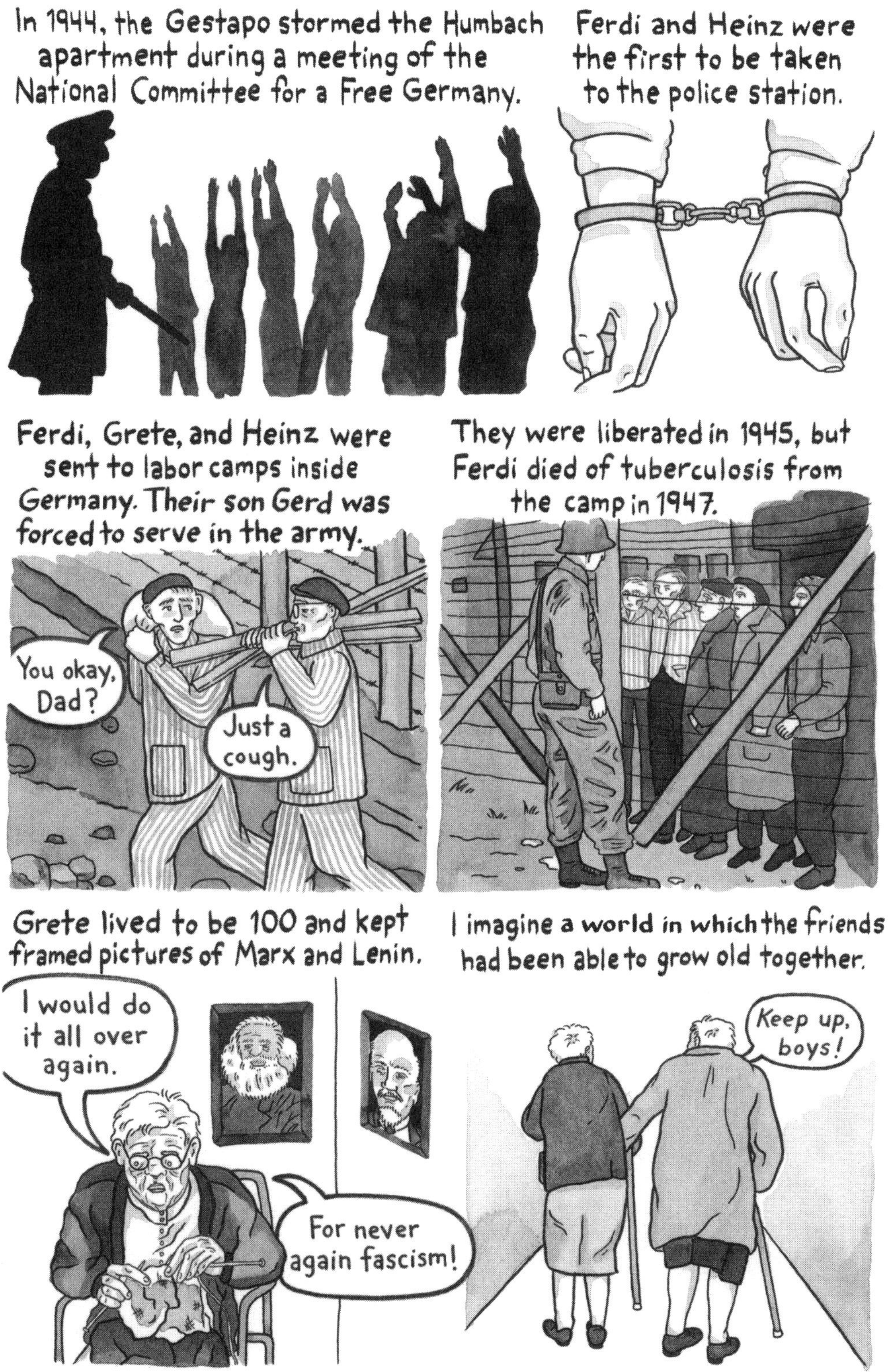
In 1944, the Gestapo stormed the Humbach apartment during a meeting of the National Committee for a Free Germany.
Ferdi and Heinz were the first to be taken to the police station.
Ferdi, Grete, and Heinz were sent to labor camps inside Germany. Their son Gerd was forced to serve in the army.
You okay, Dad?
Just a cough.
They were liberated in 1945, but Ferdi died of tuberculosis from the camp in 1947.
Grete lived to be 100 and kept framed pictures of Marx and Lenin.
I would do it all over again.
For never again fascism!
I imagine a world in which the friends had been able to grow old together.
Keep up, boys!

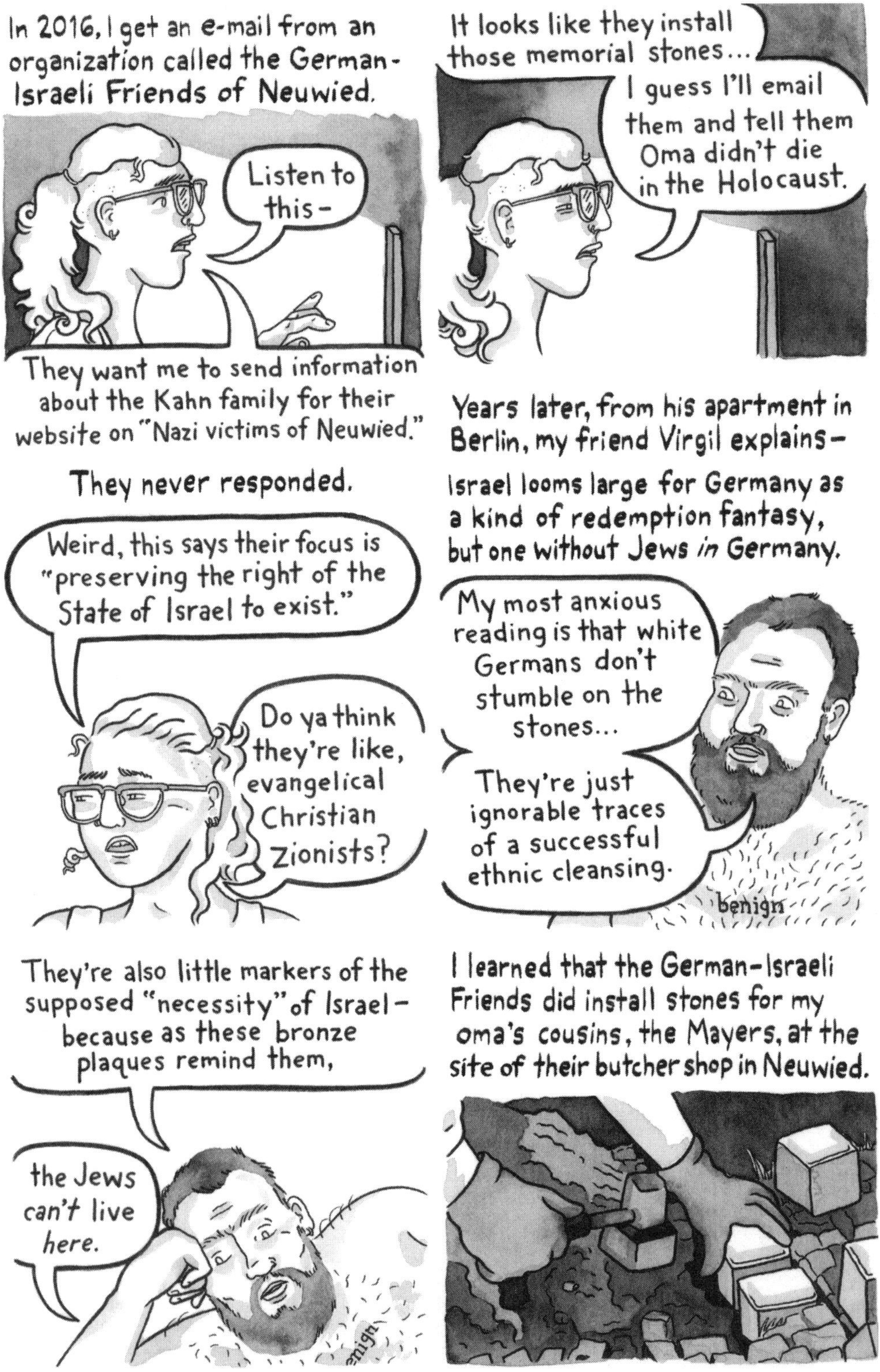
In 2016, I get an e-mail from an organization called the German-Israeli Friends of Neuwied.
Listen to this-
They want me to send information about the Kahn family for their website on "Nazi victims of Neuwied."
It looks like they install those memorial stones...
I guess I'll email them and tell them Oma didn't die in the Holocaust.
They never responded.
Weird, this says their focus is "preserving the right of the State of Israel to exist."
Do ya think they're like, evangelical Christian Zionists?
Years later, from his apartment in Berlin, my friend Virgil explains-
Israel looms large for Germany as a kind of redemption fantasy, but one without Jews *in* Germany.
My most anxious reading is that white Germans don't stumble on the stones...
They're just ignorable traces of a successful ethnic cleansing.
benign
They're also little markers of the supposed "necessity" of Israel-because as these bronze plaques remind them,
the Jews can't live *here*.
I learned that the German-Israeli Friends did install stones for my oma's cousins, the Mayers, at the site of their butcher shop in Neuwied.

Sidonia Mayer, née Frank, was born in 1906 on the family farm in Rockenhausen to Lina's brother Adolf Frank and Jacob's sister Bertha Kahn.

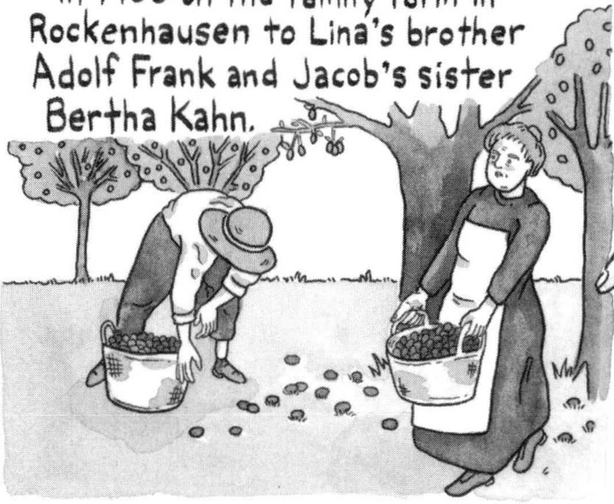

The same farm in the Rhineland where Ilse's mother, Lina Frank, and her nine siblings grew up.

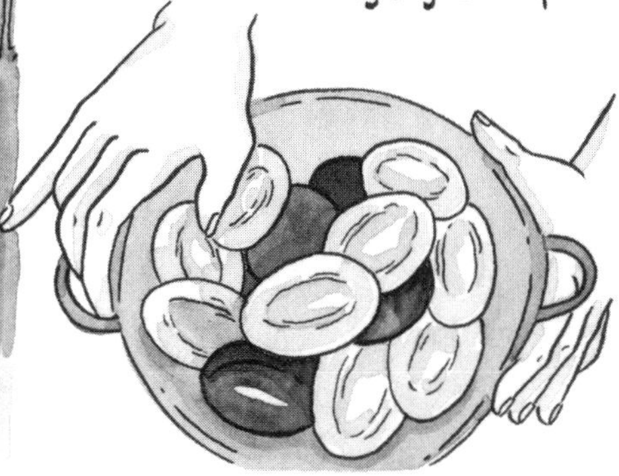

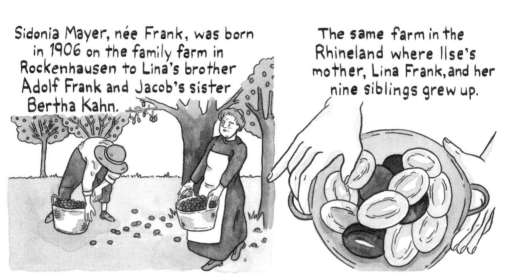

Jacob and his only sibling, Bertha, both married Franks. I don't know what happened to Adolf Frank, but Bertha was murdered at Chełmno, *outside* Łódź, Poland, in 1942.
Ilse grew up visiting the Frank family farm.

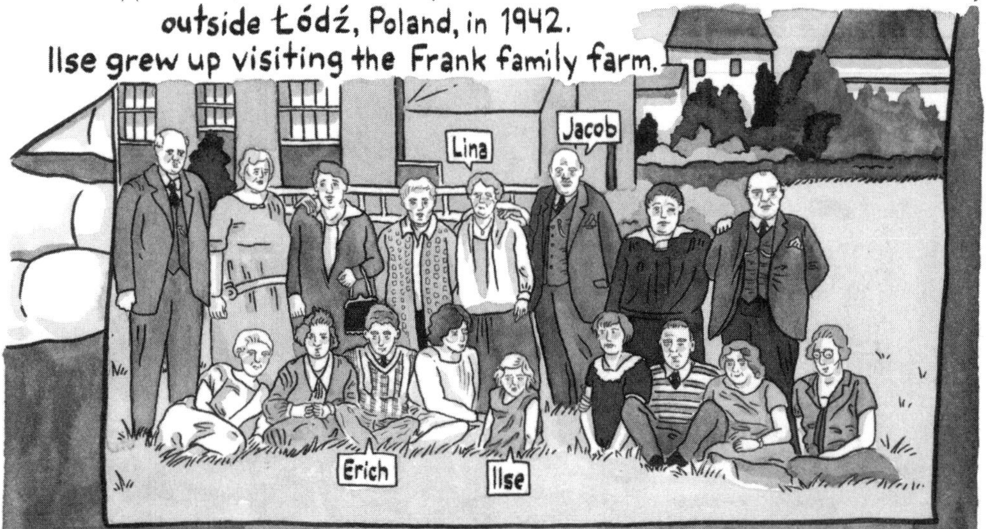
Lina
Jacob
Erich
Ilse

I don't know who most of the people in this photograph are—maybe one of them is Siegbert's mother, Hermine.

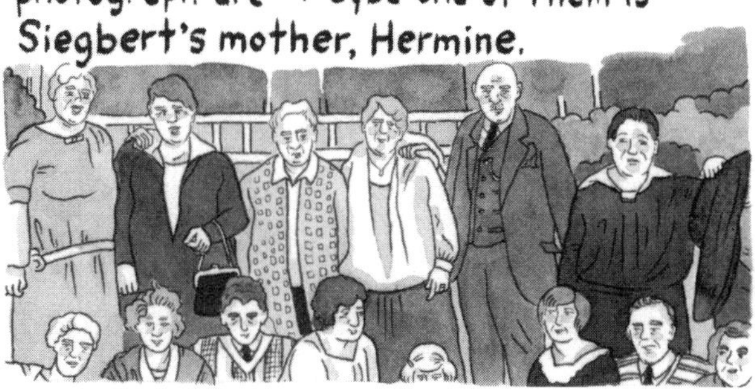

This *might* be Bertha and Adolf Frank.

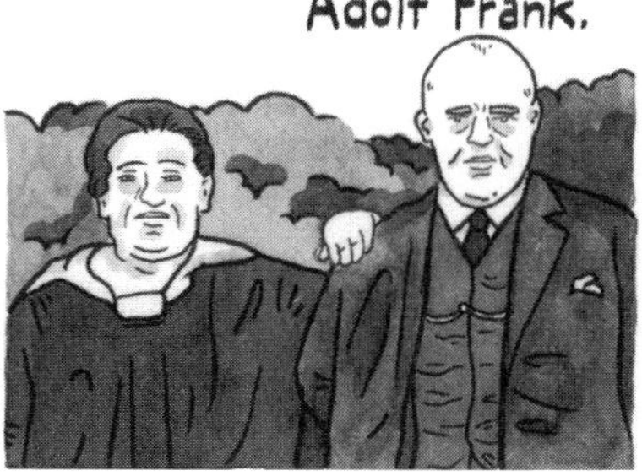

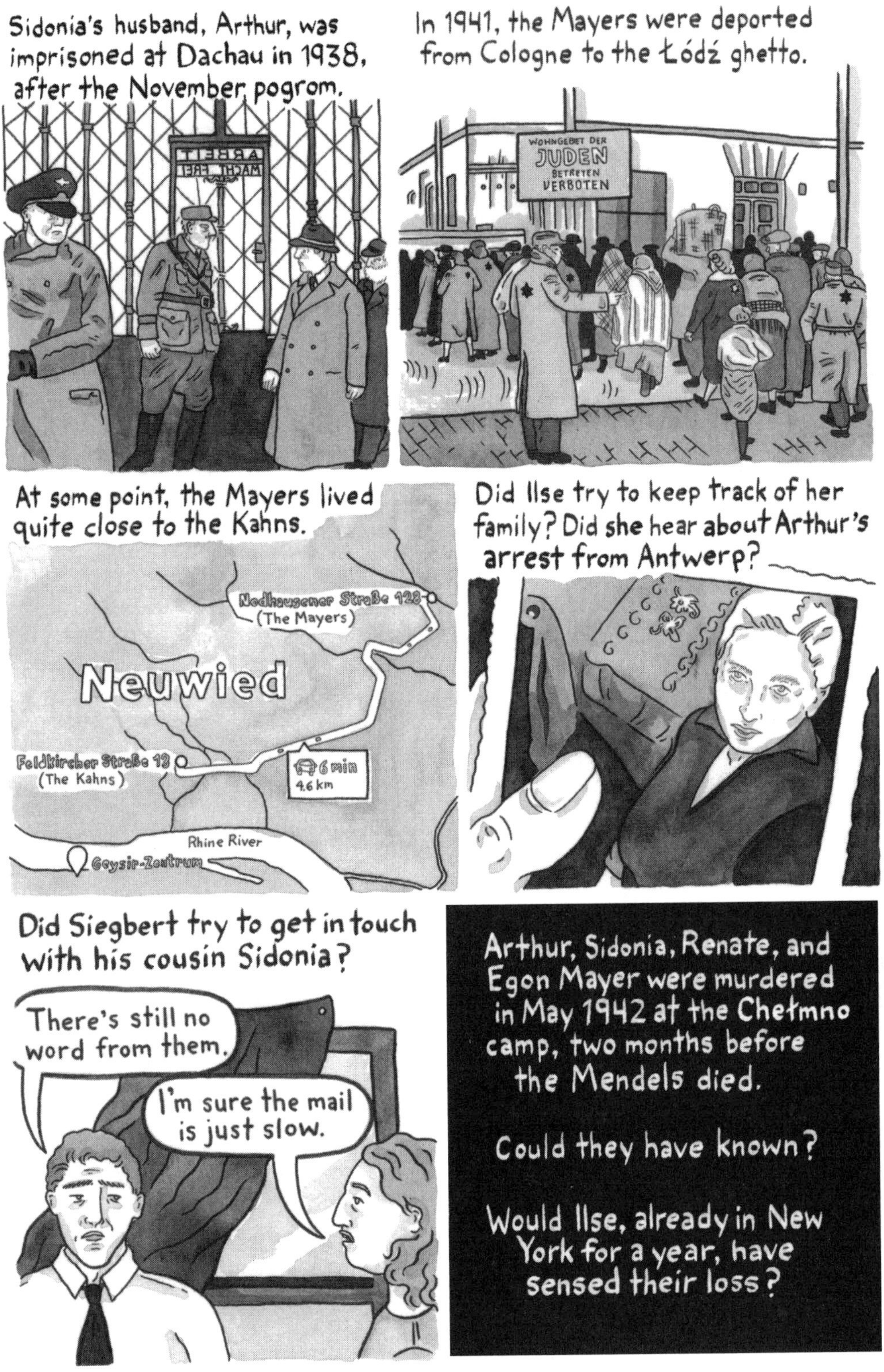
Sidonia's husband, Arthur, was imprisoned at Dachau in 1938, after the November pogrom.
In 1941, the Mayers were deported from Cologne to the Łódź ghetto.
WOHNGEBIET DER JUDEN BETRETEN VERBOTEN
At some point, the Mayers lived quite close to the Kahns.
Nodhausener Straße 128
(The Mayers)
Neuwied
Feldkircher Straße 13
(The Kahns)
6 min
4.6 km
Rhine River
Geysir-Zentrum
Did Ilse try to keep track of her family? Did she hear about Arthur's arrest from Antwerp?
Did Siegbert try to get in touch with his cousin Sidonia?
There's still no word from them.
I'm sure the mail is just slow.
Arthur, Sidonia, Renate, and Egon Mayer were murdered in May 1942 at the Chełmno camp, two months before the Mendels died.
Could they have known?
Would Ilse, already in New York for a year, have sensed their loss?

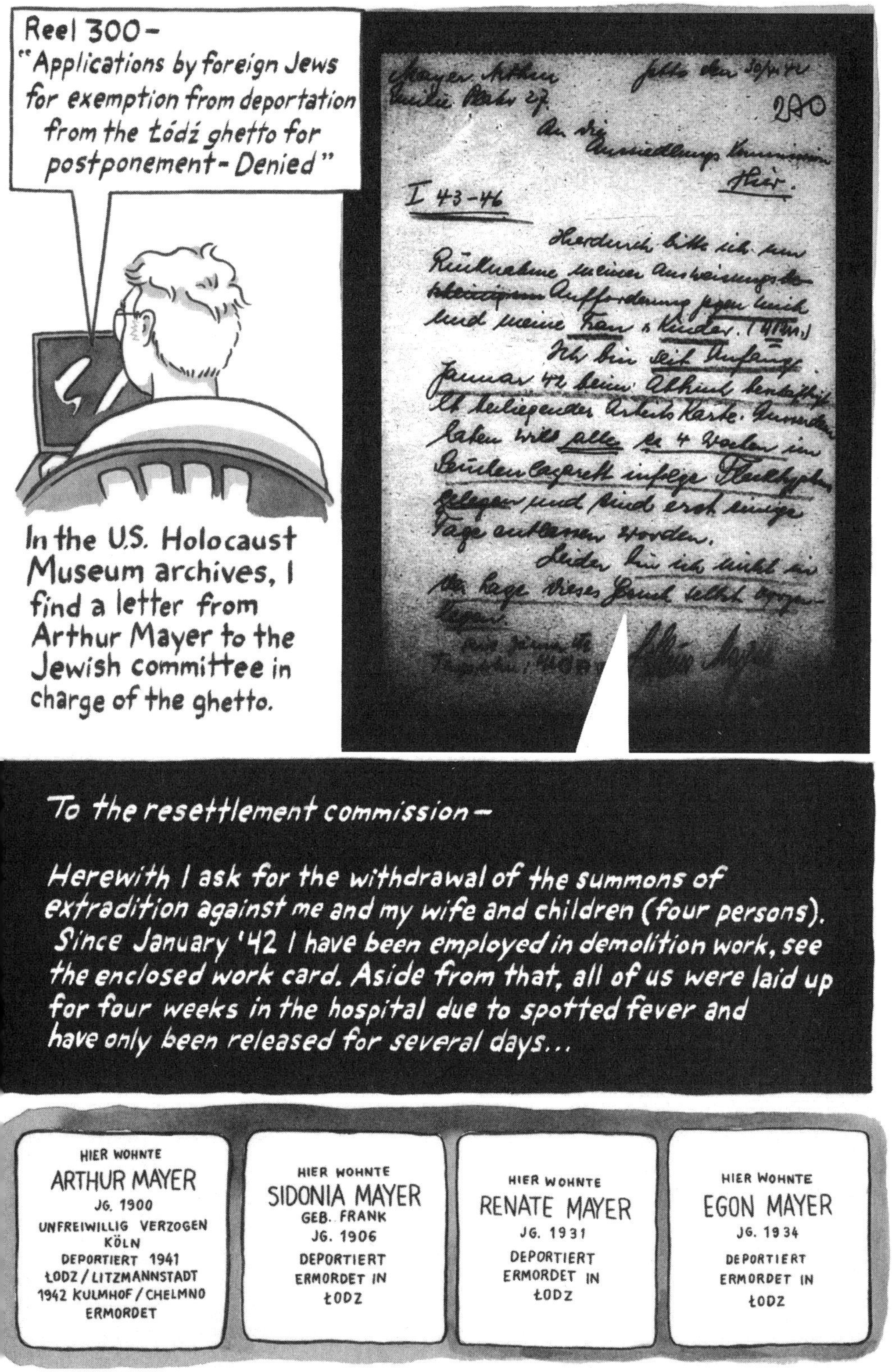

Reel 300 –
"Applications by foreign Jews for exemption from deportation from the Łódź ghetto for postponement – Denied"

In the U.S. Holocaust Museum archives, I find a letter from Arthur Mayer to the Jewish committee in charge of the ghetto.

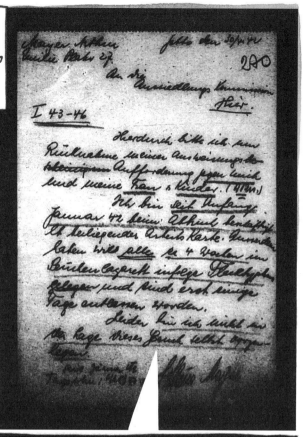

To the resettlement commission –

Herewith I ask for the withdrawal of the summons of extradition against me and my wife and children (four persons). Since January '42 I have been employed in demolition work, see the enclosed work card. Aside from that, all of us were laid up for four weeks in the hospital due to spotted fever and have only been released for several days...

HIER WOHNTE
ARTHUR MAYER
JG. 1900
UNFREIWILLIG VERZOGEN
KÖLN
DEPORTIERT 1941
ŁODZ / LITZMANNSTADT
1942 KULMHOF / CHELMNO
ERMORDET

HIER WOHNTE
SIDONIA MAYER
GEB. FRANK
JG. 1906
DEPORTIERT
ERMORDET IN
ŁODZ

HIER WOHNTE
RENATE MAYER
JG. 1931
DEPORTIERT
ERMORDET IN
ŁODZ

HIER WOHNTE
EGON MAYER
JG. 1934
DEPORTIERT
ERMORDET IN
ŁODZ

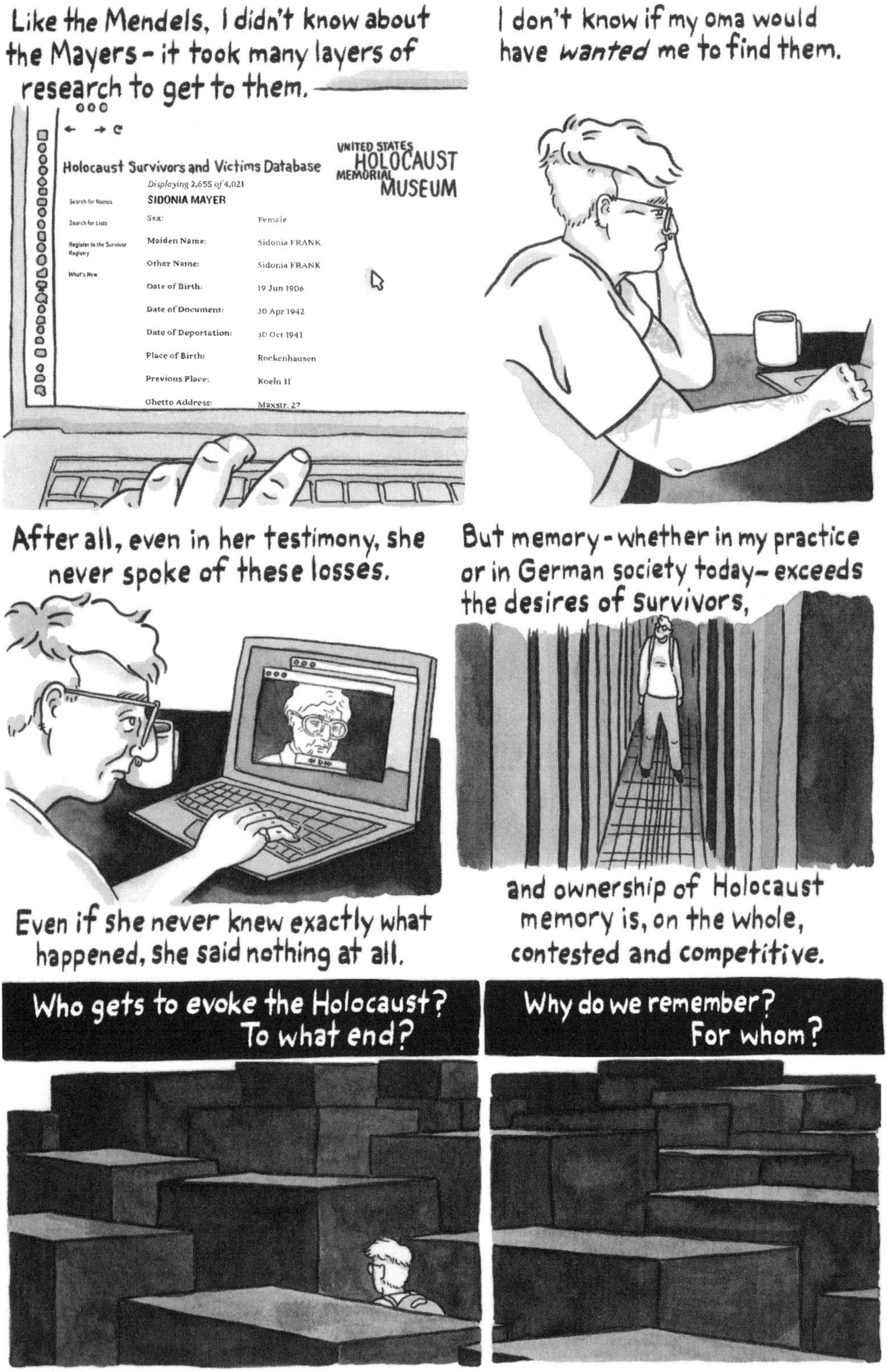
Like the Mendels, I didn't know about the Mayers - it took many layers of research to get to them.
Holocaust Survivors and Victims Database
UNITED STATES HOLOCAUST MEMORIAL MUSEUM
Displaying 2,655 of 4,021
SIDONIA MAYER
Search for Names
Search for Lists
Register in the Survivor Registry
What's New
Sex: Female
Maiden Name: Sidonia FRANK
Other Name: Sidonia FRANK
Date of Birth: 19 Jun 1906
Date of Document: 30 Apr 1942
Date of Deportation: 30 Oct 1941
Place of Birth: Rockenhausen
Previous Place: Koeln II
Ghetto Address: Maxstr. 27
I don't know if my oma would have *wanted* me to find them.
After all, even in her testimony, she never spoke of these losses.
Even if she never knew exactly what happened, she said nothing at all.
But memory - whether in my practice or in German society today - exceeds the desires of survivors,
and ownership of Holocaust memory is, on the whole, contested and competitive.
Who gets to evoke the Holocaust? To what end?
Why do we remember? For whom?

Human rights historian Dirk Moses describes a Holocaust "catechism" that includes a "redemptive philosemitism"—which is to say—

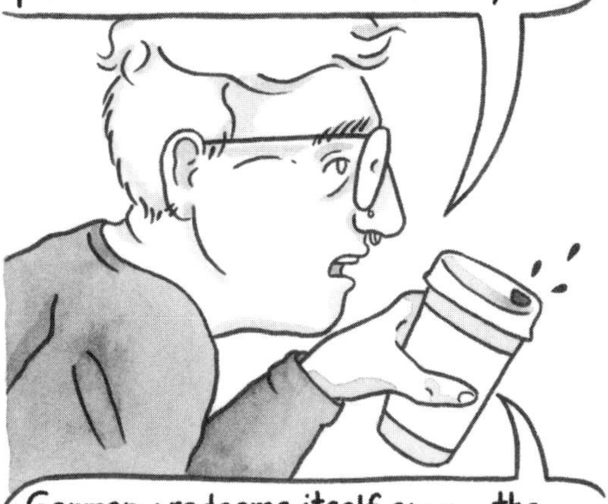

Germany redeems itself among the nations by loving Jews the MOST. But by *Jews*, they often mean Israel, not diaspora Jews.

In 2008, German chancellor Angela Merkel told the Israeli Knesset—

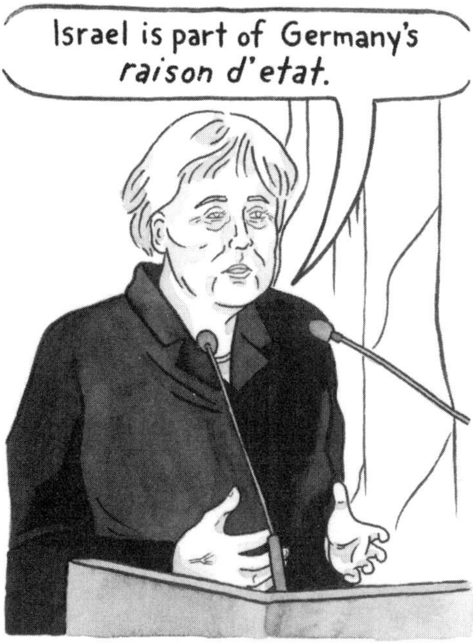
Israel is part of Germany's *raison d'etat.*

Moses describes "the remarkable situation of gentile Germans lecturing American and Israeli Jews with accusing fingers about the correct forms of remembrance and loyalty to Israel."

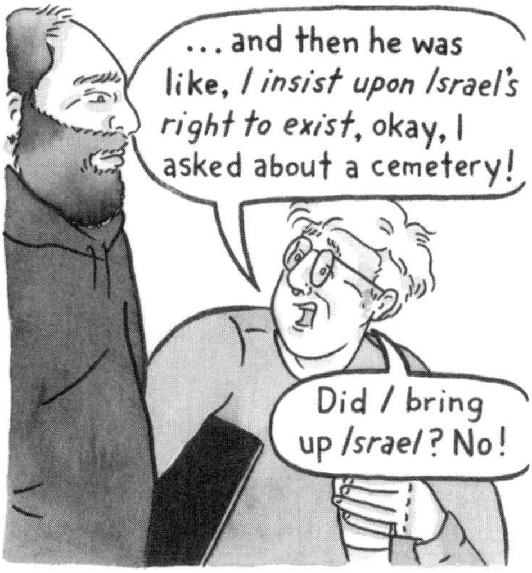
...and then he was like, *I insist upon Israel's right to exist*, okay, I asked about a cemetery!
Did *I* bring up *Israel*? No!

But Jews don't exist to assuage German guilt, and Israel isn't a redemption narrative—it's a contested settler state.

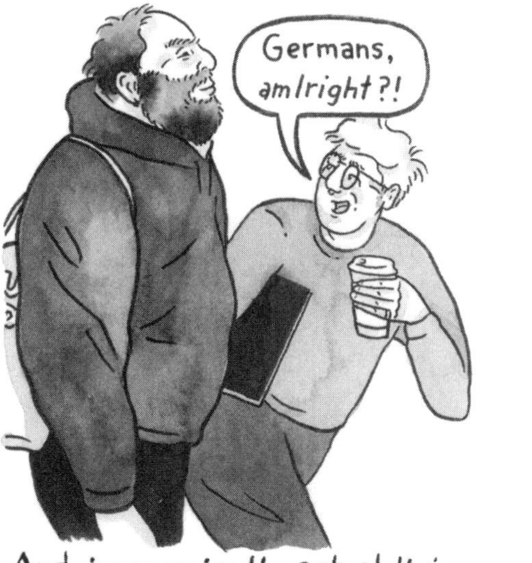
Germans, *am I right*?!

And, *inconveniently*, actual, living Jews aren't all on board.

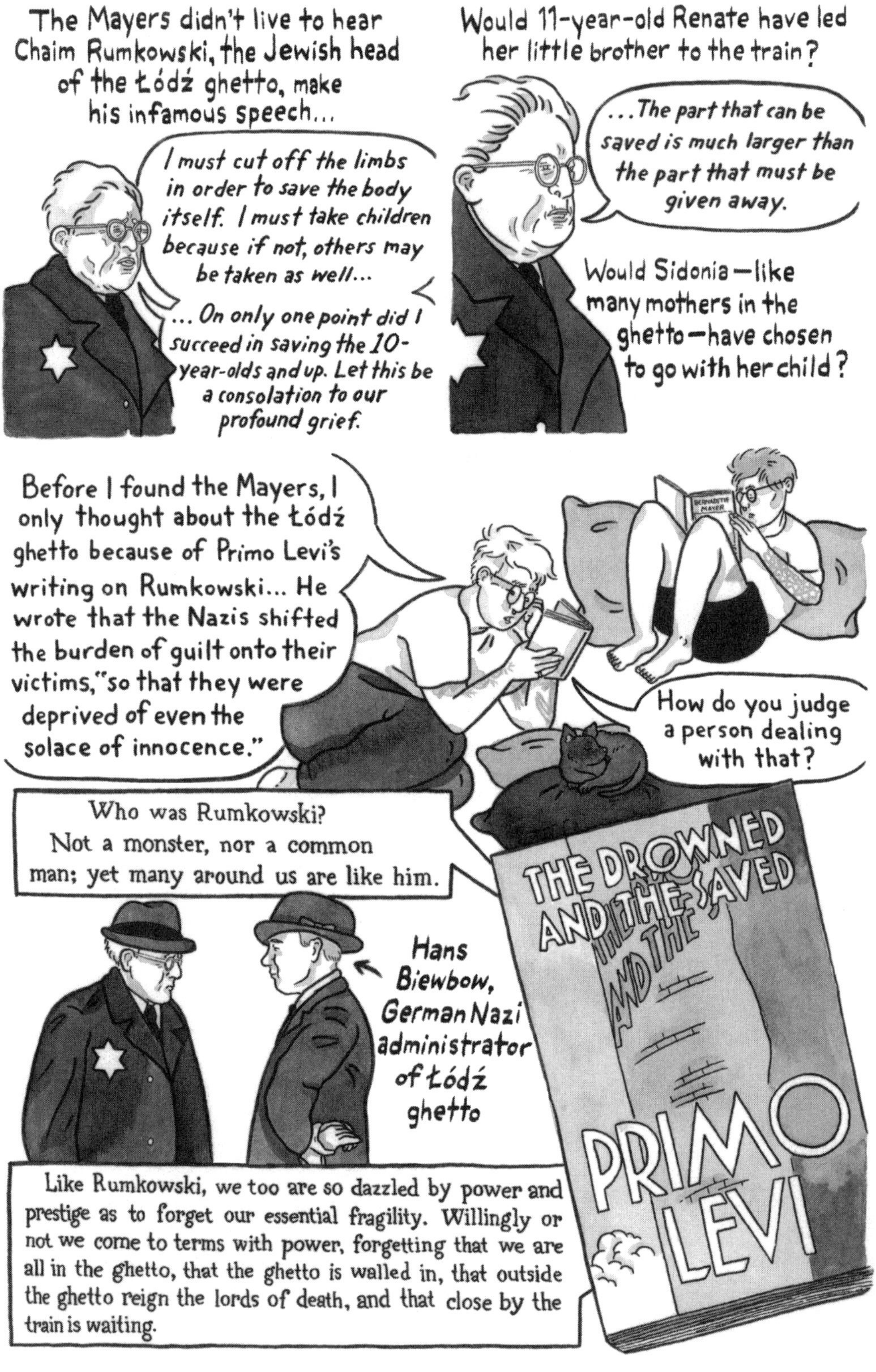

The Mayers didn't live to hear Chaim Rumkowski, the Jewish head of the Łódź ghetto, make his infamous speech...
I must cut off the limbs in order to save the body itself. I must take children because if not, others may be taken as well...
...On only one point did I succeed in saving the 10-year-olds and up. Let this be a consolation to our profound grief.
Would 11-year-old Renate have led her little brother to the train?
...The part that can be saved is much larger than the part that must be given away.
Would Sidonia—like many mothers in the ghetto—have chosen to go with her child?
Before I found the Mayers, I only thought about the Łódź ghetto because of Primo Levi's writing on Rumkowski... He wrote that the Nazis shifted the burden of guilt onto their victims, "so that they were deprived of even the solace of innocence."
How do you judge a person dealing with that?
Who was Rumkowski? Not a monster, nor a common man; yet many around us are like him.
THE DROWNED AND THE SAVED
PRIMO LEVI
Hans Biewbow, German Nazi administrator of Łódź ghetto
Like Rumkowski, we too are so dazzled by power and prestige as to forget our essential fragility. Willingly or not we come to terms with power, forgetting that we are all in the ghetto, that the ghetto is walled in, that outside the ghetto reign the lords of death, and that close by the train is waiting.

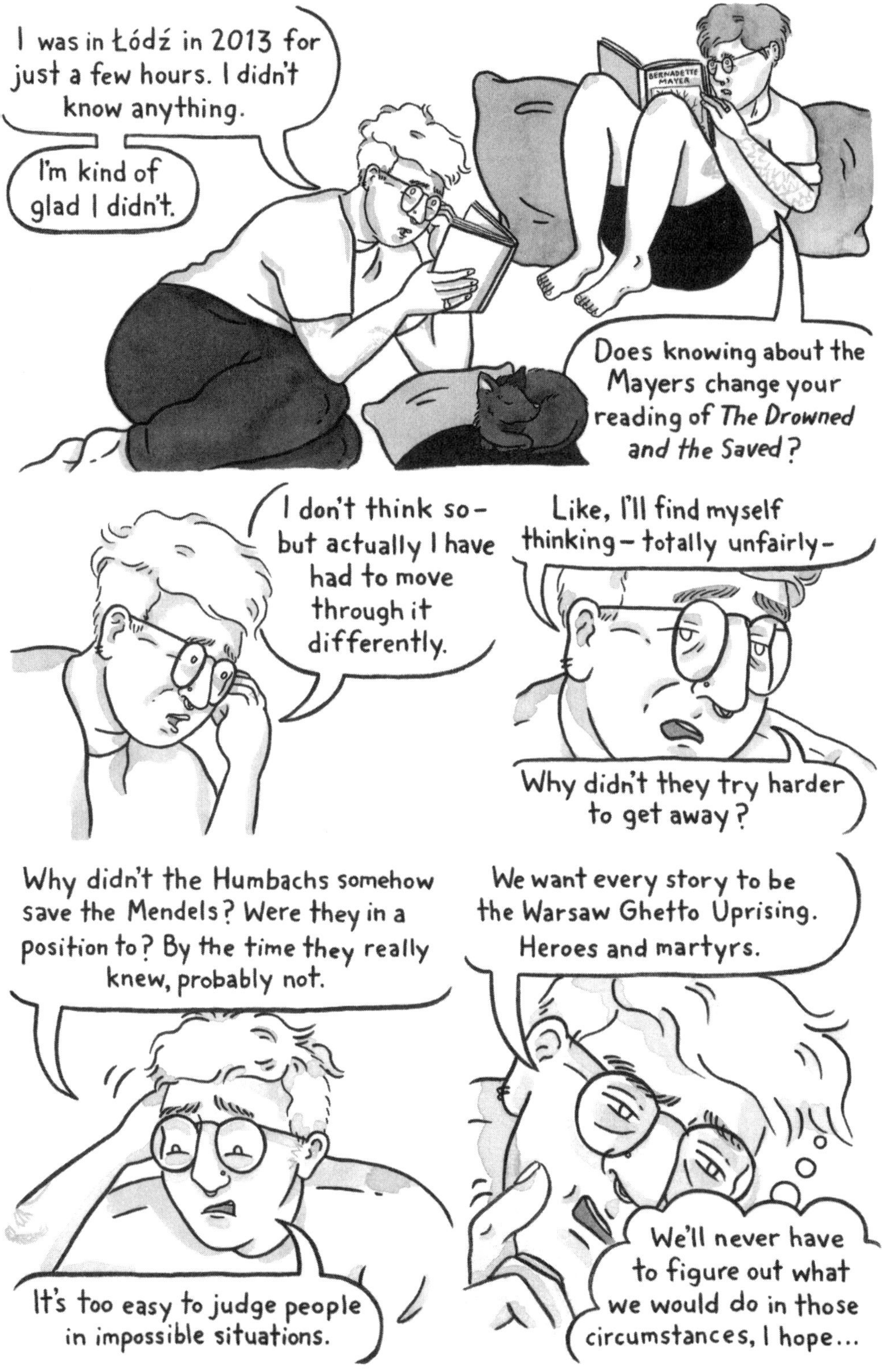
I was in Łódź in 2013 for just a few hours. I didn't know anything.
I'm kind of glad I didn't.
BERNADETTE MAYER
Does knowing about the Mayers change your reading of *The Drowned and the Saved*?
I don't think so– but actually I have had to move through it differently.
Like, I'll find myself thinking – totally unfairly –
Why didn't they try harder to get away?
Why didn't the Humbachs somehow save the Mendels? Were they in a position to? By the time they really knew, probably not.
It's too easy to judge people in impossible situations.
We want every story to be the Warsaw Ghetto Uprising. Heroes and martyrs.
We'll never have to figure out what we would do in those circumstances, I hope...

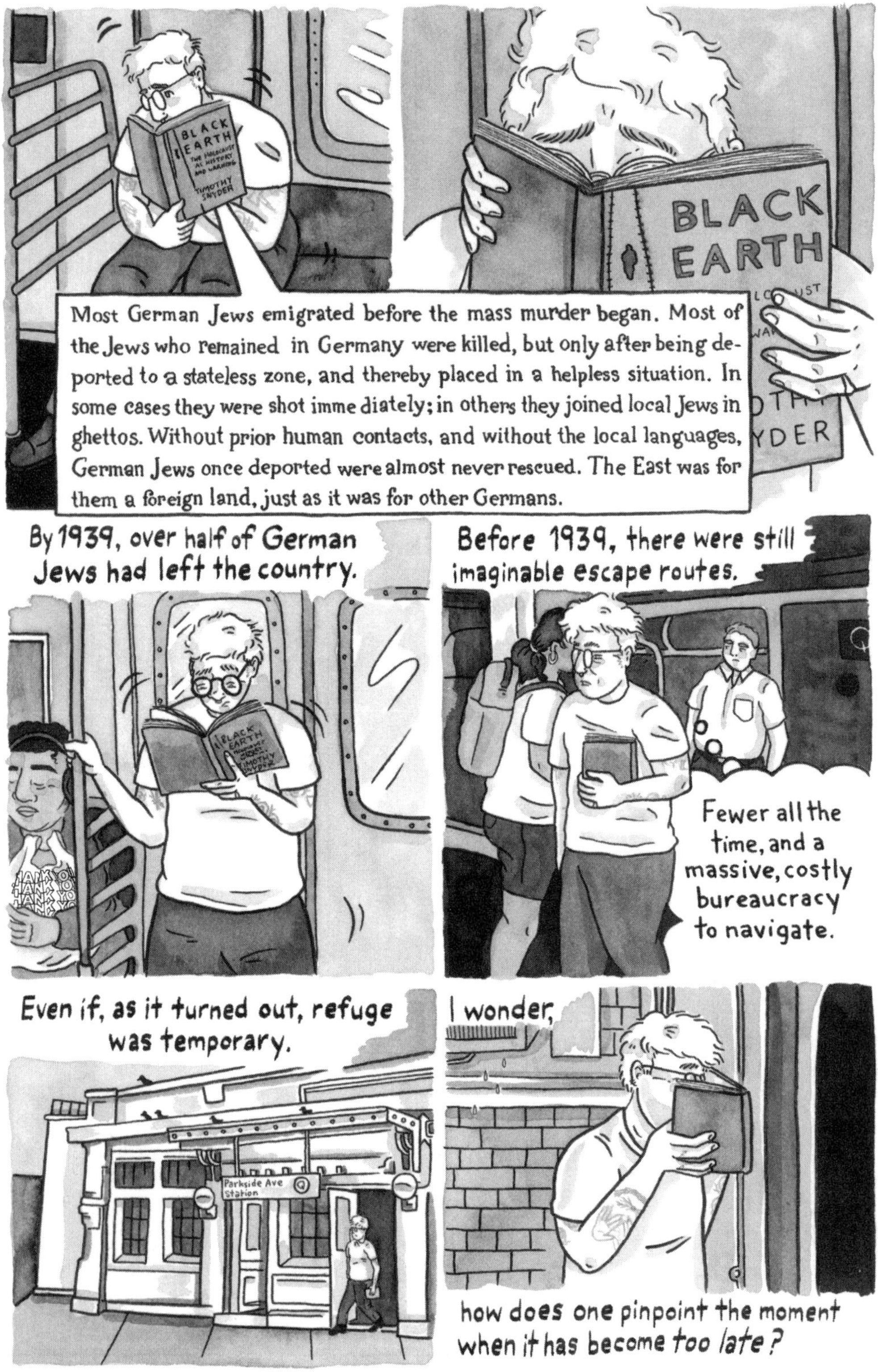
BLACK EARTH
TIMOTHY SNYDER
BLACK EARTH
Most German Jews emigrated before the mass murder began. Most of the Jews who remained in Germany were killed, but only after being deported to a stateless zone, and thereby placed in a helpless situation. In some cases they were shot immediately; in others they joined local Jews in ghettos. Without prior human contacts, and without the local languages, German Jews once deported were almost never rescued. The East was for them a foreign land, just as it was for other Germans.
By 1939, over half of German Jews had left the country.
Before 1939, there were still imaginable escape routes.
Fewer all the time, and a massive, costly bureaucracy to navigate.
Even if, as it turned out, refuge was temporary.
Parkside Ave Station
I wonder,
how does one pinpoint the moment when it has become *too late*?

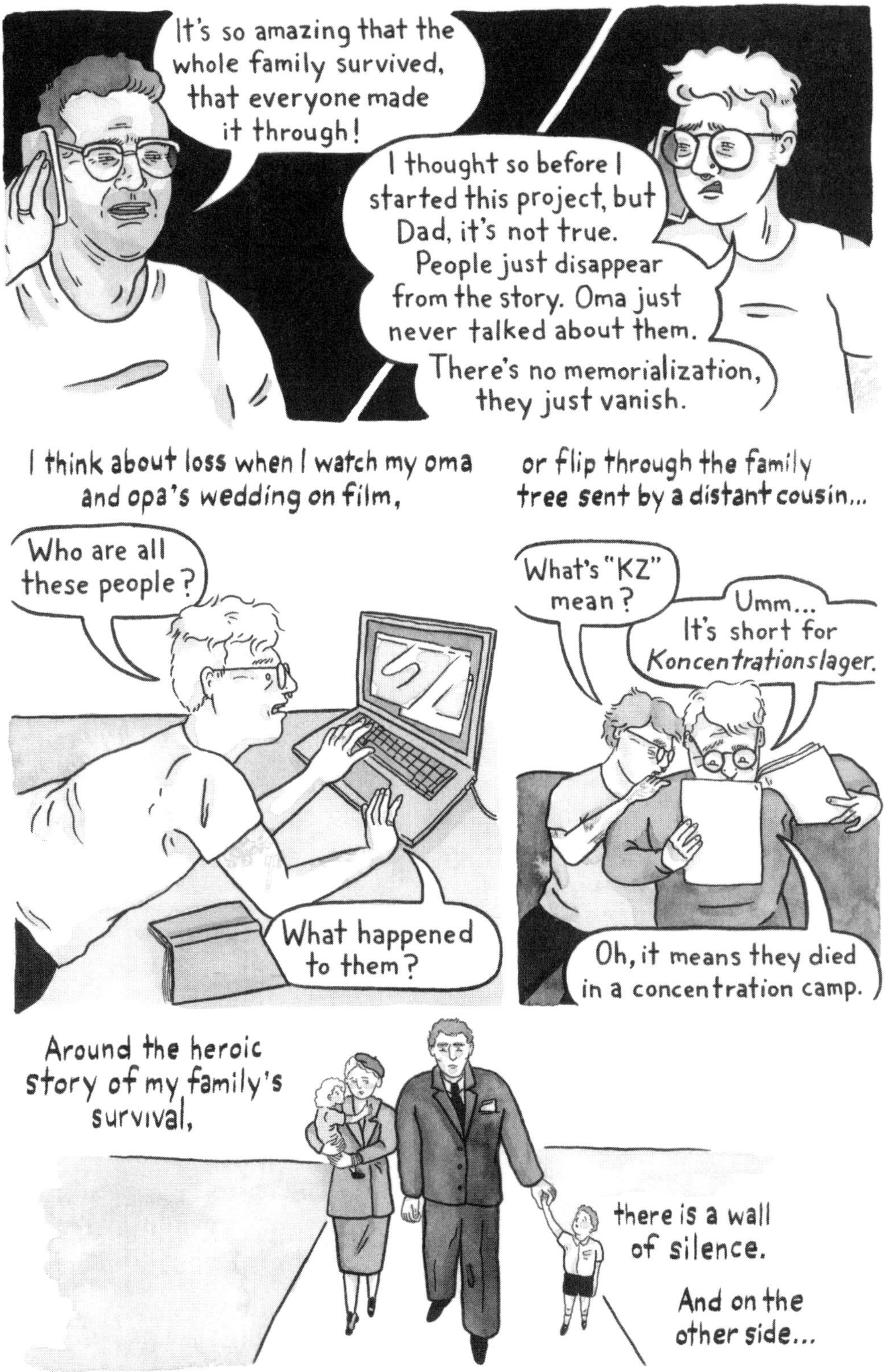
It's so amazing that the whole family survived, that everyone made it through!
I thought so before I started this project, but Dad, it's not true.
People just disappear from the story. Oma just never talked about them.
There's no memorialization, they just vanish.
I think about loss when I watch my oma and opa's wedding on film,
or flip through the family tree sent by a distant cousin...
Who are all these people?
What happened to them?
What's "KZ" mean?
Umm... It's short for Koncentrationslager.
Oh, it means they died in a concentration camp.
Around the heroic story of my family's survival,
there is a wall of silence.
And on the other side...

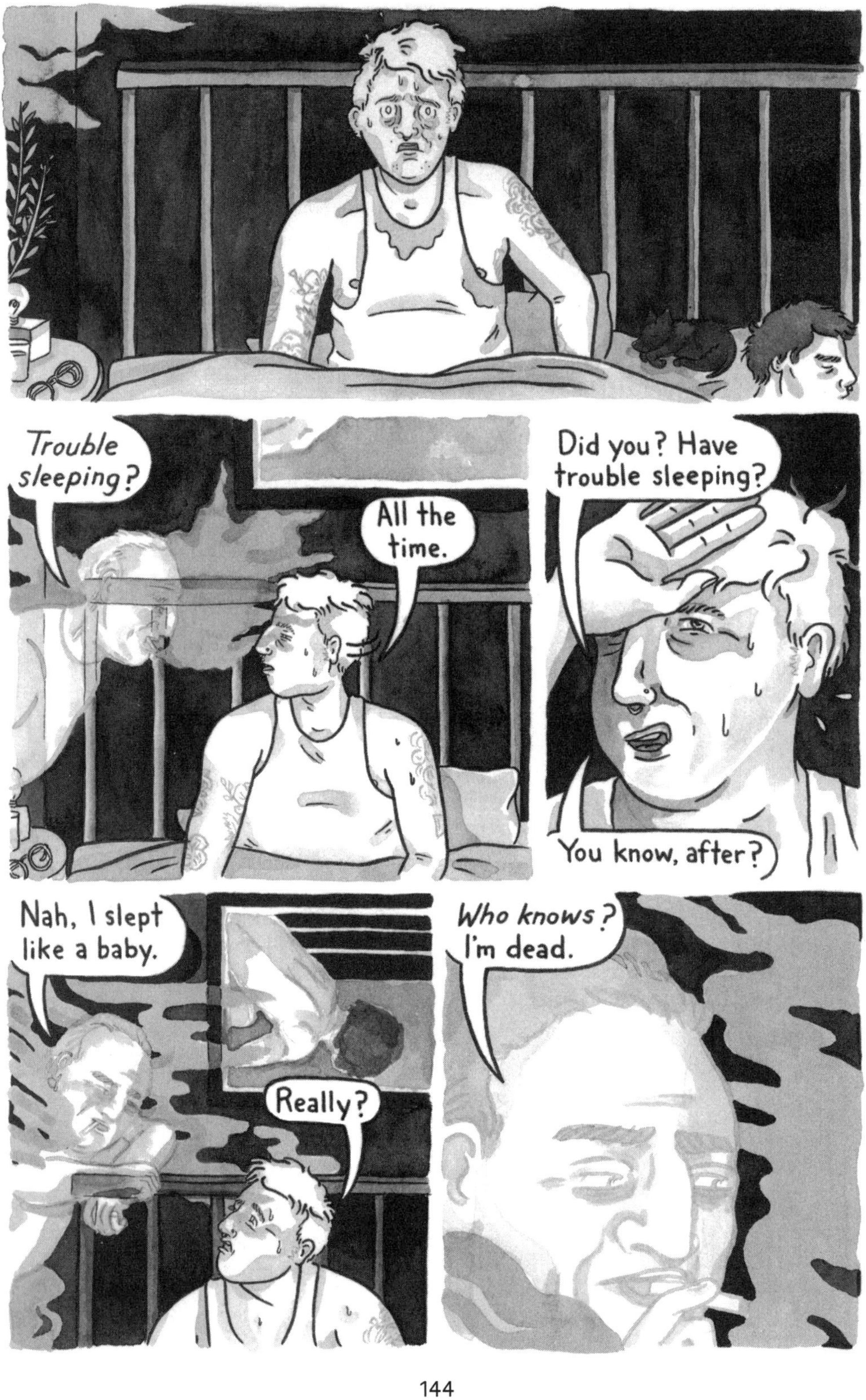
Trouble sleeping?
All the time.
Did you? Have trouble sleeping?
You know, after?
Nah, I slept like a baby.
Really?
Who knows? I'm dead.

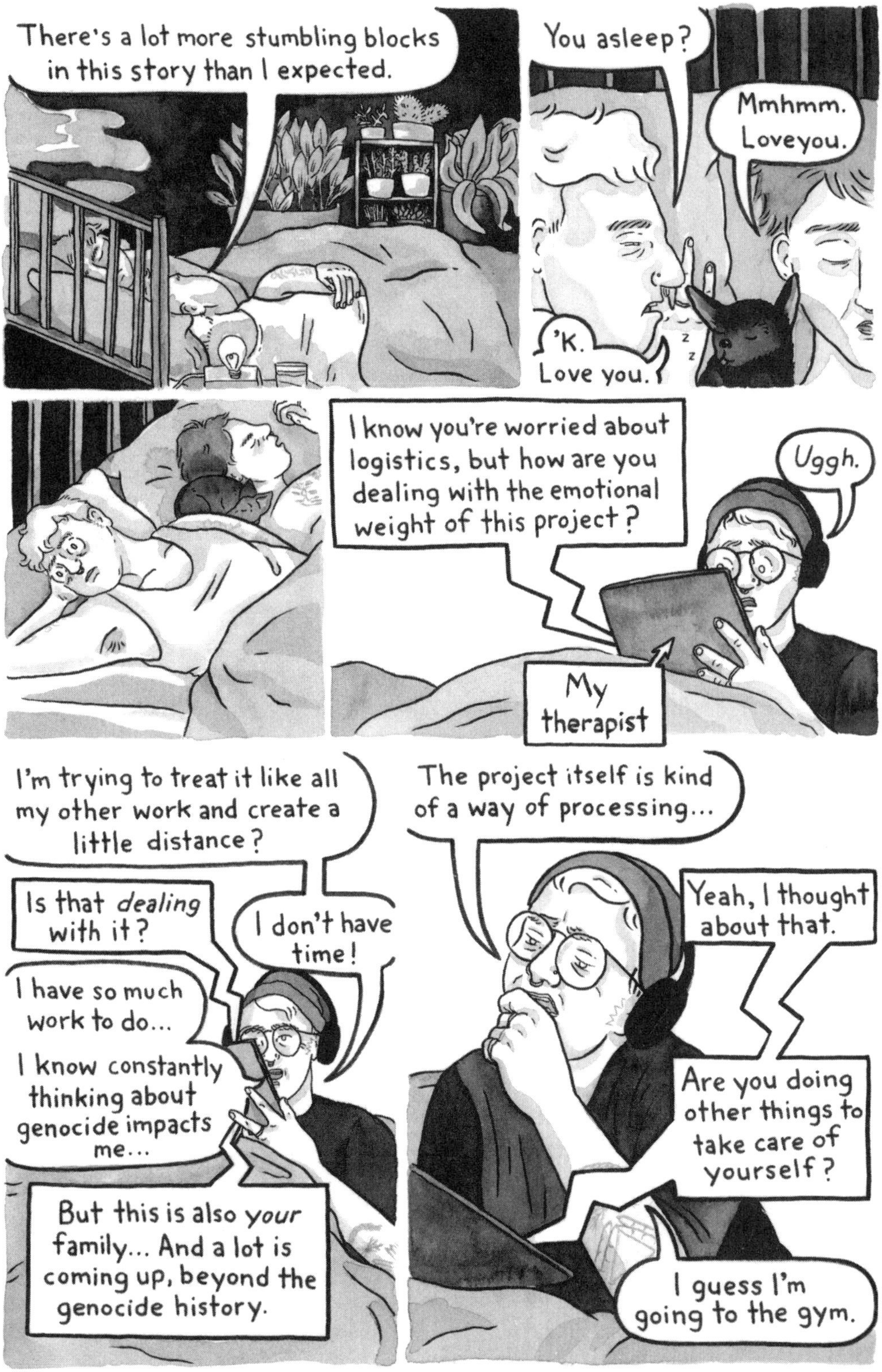
There's a lot more stumbling blocks in this story than I expected.
You asleep?
Mmhmm. Loveyou.
'K. Love you.
z z
I know you're worried about logistics, but how are you dealing with the emotional weight of this project?
Uggh.
My therapist
I'm trying to treat it like all my other work and create a little distance?
Is that *dealing* with it?
I don't have time!
I have so much work to do...
I know constantly thinking about genocide impacts me...
But this is also *your* family... And a lot is coming up, beyond the genocide history.
The project itself is kind of a way of processing...
Yeah, I thought about that.
Are you doing other things to take care of yourself?
I guess I'm going to the gym.

Martina Strehlen from the Old Synagogue in Essen writes to me, *Unfortunately we have no archival material concerning the shops of Salli Levi or his connections to the Jewish community. The old records of the pre-war Jewish community were kept in the synagogue and destroyed by fire during the attack on **November** 10, 1938.*

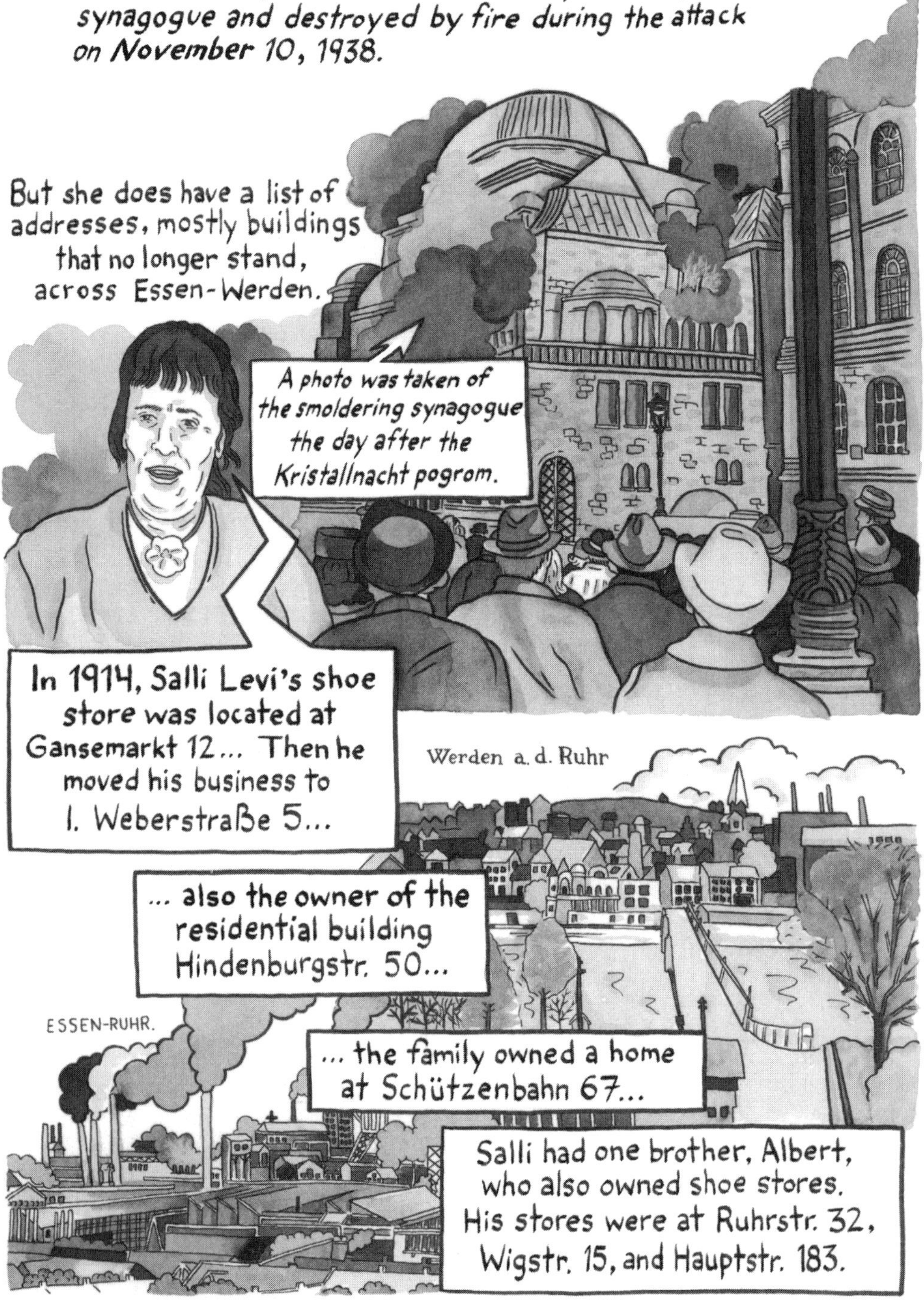

But she does have a list of addresses, mostly buildings that no longer stand, across Essen-Werden.
A photo was taken of the smoldering synagogue the day after the Kristallnacht pogrom.
In 1914, Salli Levi's shoe store was located at Gansemarkt 12... Then he moved his business to I. Weberstraße 5...
Werden a. d. Ruhr
... also the owner of the residential building Hindenburgstr. 50...
ESSEN-RUHR.
... the family owned a home at Schützenbahn 67...
Salli had one brother, Albert, who also owned shoe stores. His stores were at Ruhrstr. 32, Wigstr. 15, and Hauptstr. 183.

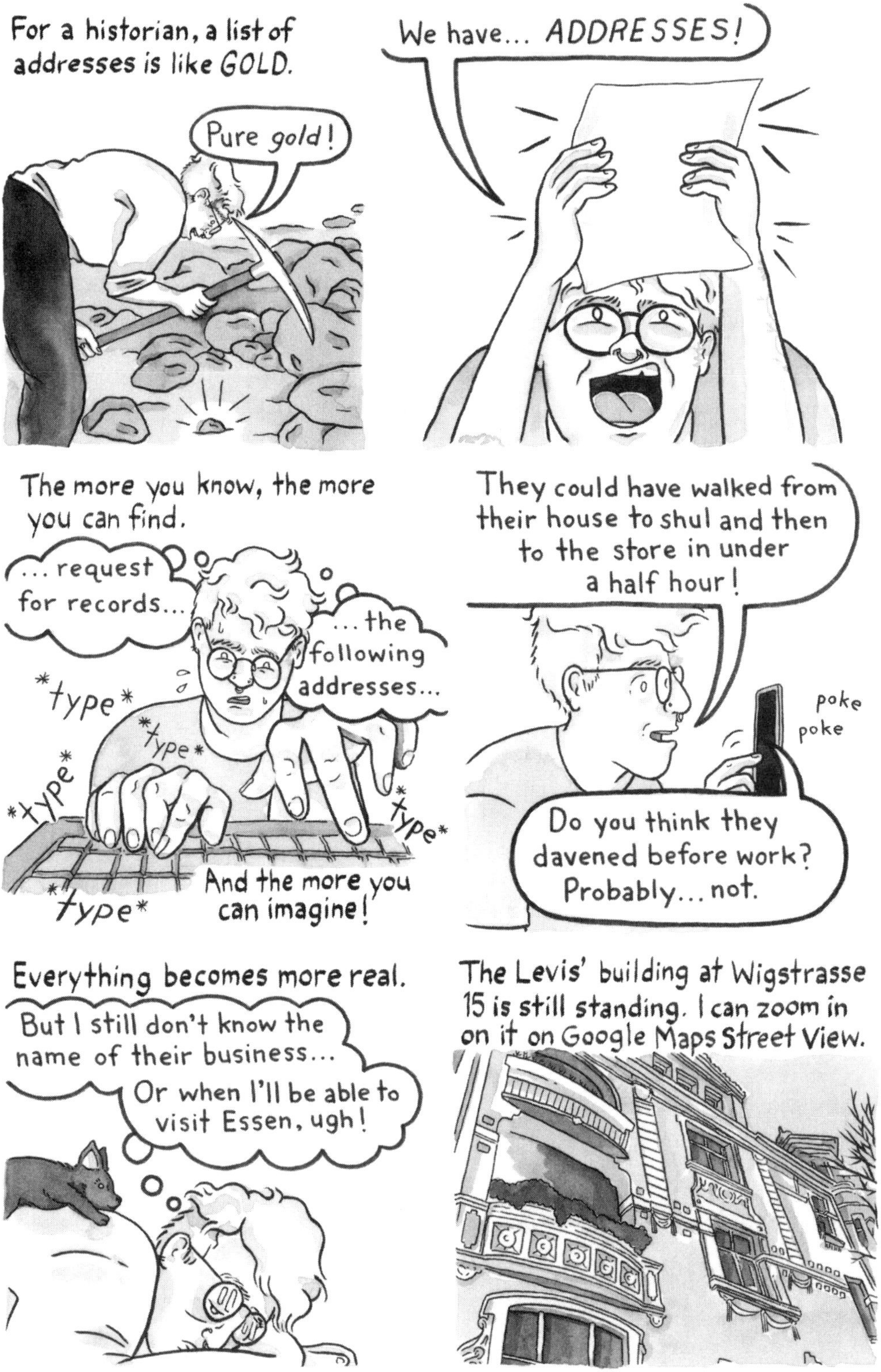

For a historian, a list of addresses is like GOLD.
Pure gold!
We have... ADDRESSES!
The more you know, the more you can find.
... request for records...
... the following addresses...
type
type
type
type
type
And the more you can imagine!
They could have walked from their house to shul and then to the store in under a half hour!
poke poke
Do you think they davened before work? Probably... not.
Everything becomes more real.
But I still don't know the name of their business...
Or when I'll be able to visit Essen, ugh!
The Levis' building at Wigstrasse 15 is still standing. I can zoom in on it on Google Maps Street View.

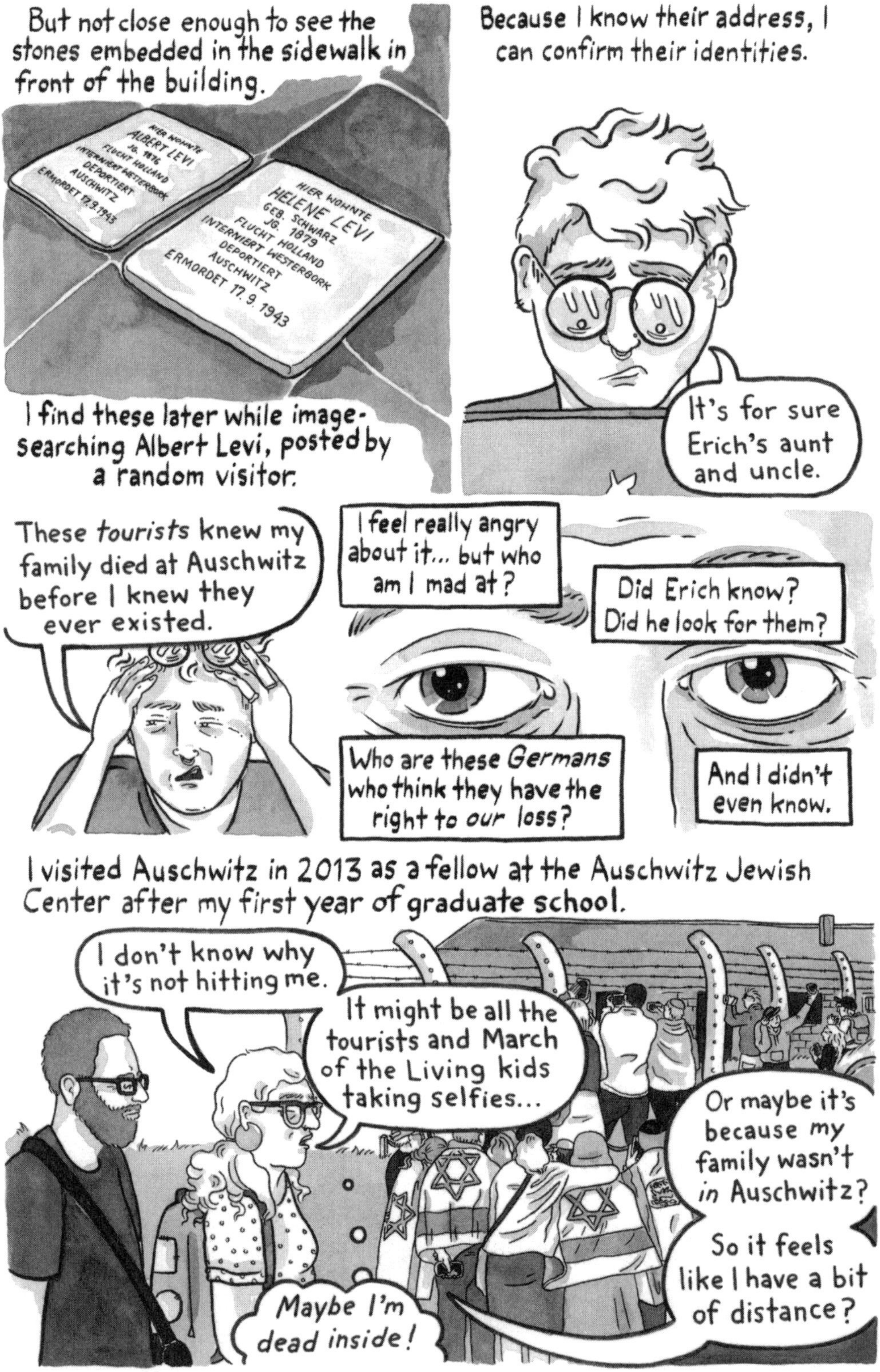
But not close enough to see the stones embedded in the sidewalk in front of the building.
HIER WOHNTE ALBERT LEVI JG. 1876 FLUCHT HOLLAND INTERNIERT WESTERBORK DEPORTIERT AUSCHWITZ ERMORDET 17.9.1943
HIER WOHNTE HELENE LEVI GEB. SCHWARZ JG. 1879 FLUCHT HOLLAND INTERNIERT WESTERBORK DEPORTIERT AUSCHWITZ ERMORDET 17.9.1943
I find these later while image-searching Albert Levi, posted by a random visitor.
Because I know their address, I can confirm their identities.
It's for sure Erich's aunt and uncle.
These *tourists* knew my family died at Auschwitz before I knew they ever existed.
I feel really angry about it... but who am I mad at?
Did Erich know? Did he look for them?
Who are these *Germans* who think they have the right to *our* loss?
And I didn't even know.
I visited Auschwitz in 2013 as a fellow at the Auschwitz Jewish Center after my first year of graduate school.
I don't know why it's not hitting me.
It might be all the tourists and March of the Living kids taking selfies...
Maybe I'm dead inside!
Or maybe it's because *my* family wasn't *in* Auschwitz?
So it feels like I have a bit of distance?

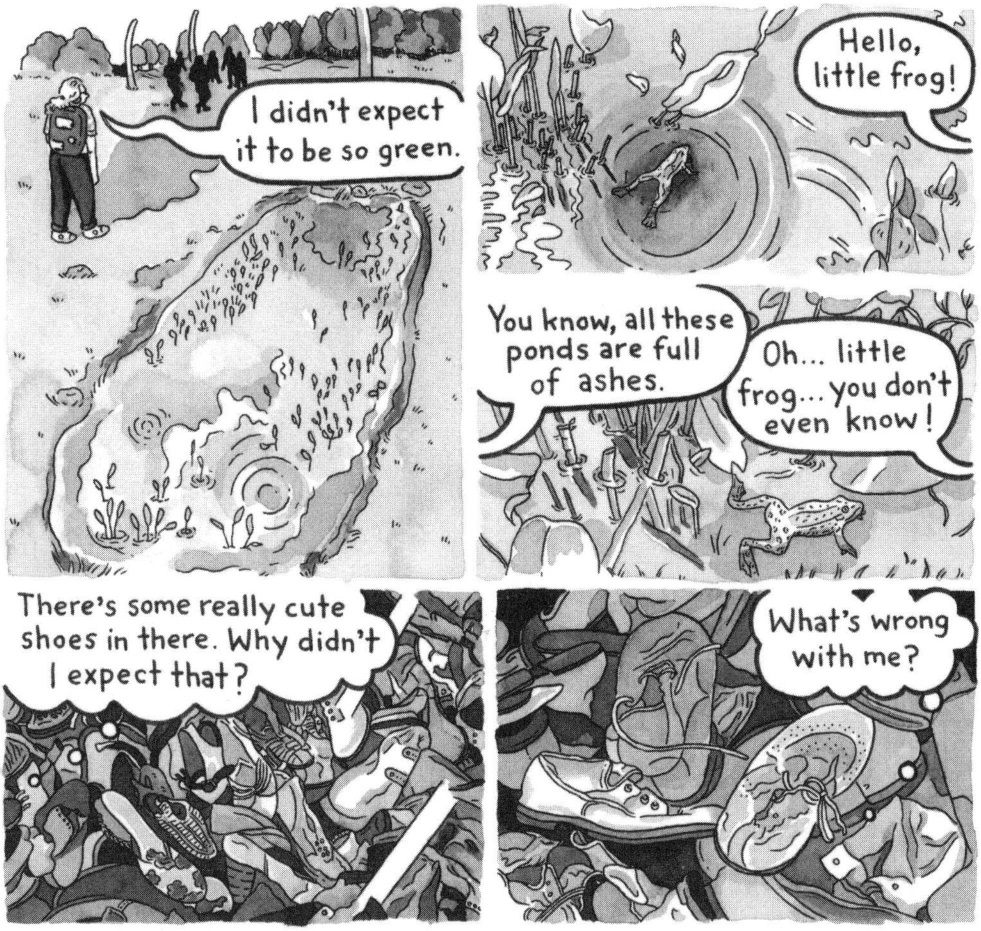
I didn't expect it to be so green.
Hello, little frog!
You know, all these ponds are full of ashes.
Oh... little frog... you don't even know!
There's some really cute shoes in there. Why didn't I expect that?
What's wrong with me?

When I learned that the Levis sold shoes, I wondered how many of those shoes ended up in these piles. And then, whether I had also been looking at Albert and Helene's own shoes.

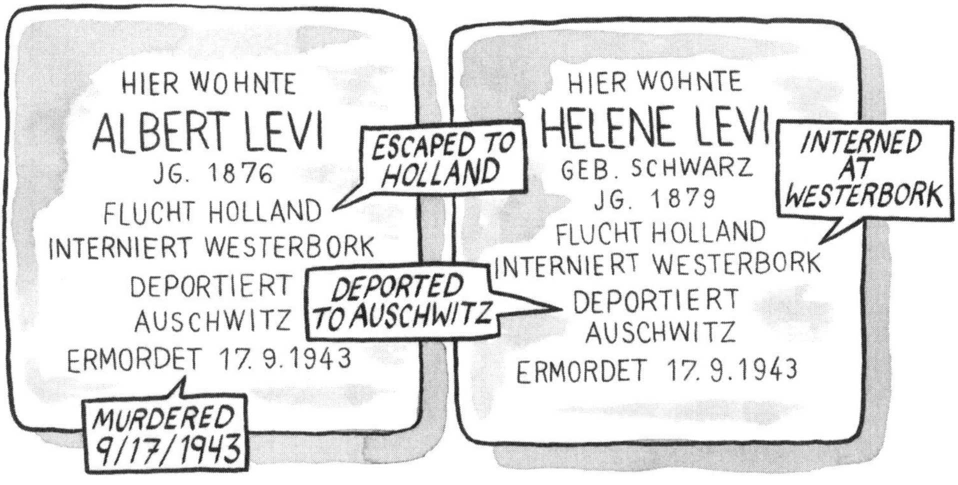
HIER WOHNTE
ALBERT LEVI
JG. 1876
FLUCHT HOLLAND
INTERNIERT WESTERBORK
DEPORTIERT
AUSCHWITZ
ERMORDET 17.9.1943
ESCAPED TO HOLLAND
DEPORTED TO AUSCHWITZ
MURDERED 9/17/1943
HIER WOHNTE
HELENE LEVI
GEB. SCHWARZ
JG. 1879
FLUCHT HOLLAND
INTERNIERT WESTERBORK
DEPORTIERT
AUSCHWITZ
ERMORDET 17.9.1943
INTERNED AT WESTERBORK

Albert and Helene had a daughter, Johanna, who died before she turned five.

Hier ruht
unser liebes
Töchterchen

Johanna Levi

geb. 16. Febr. 1903
gst. 14. Dez. 1907

Their only son, Kurt, lived to adulthood and is presumed to have died at Auschwitz.

That summer I came home with a full-body rash.

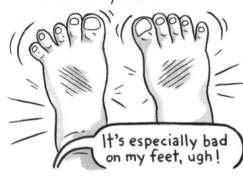

It's especially bad on my feet, ugh!

My ex thought it might be a gluten allergy.

You lived on donuts all summer in Poland!

Well, you've never been *hangry* at AUSCHWITZ!

Maybe it's a *trauma* rash.

It's not gluten!

Just look into it.

As it turns out, not everything is about trauma.

Goodbye, my sweet pierogies...

Stop eating them!

150

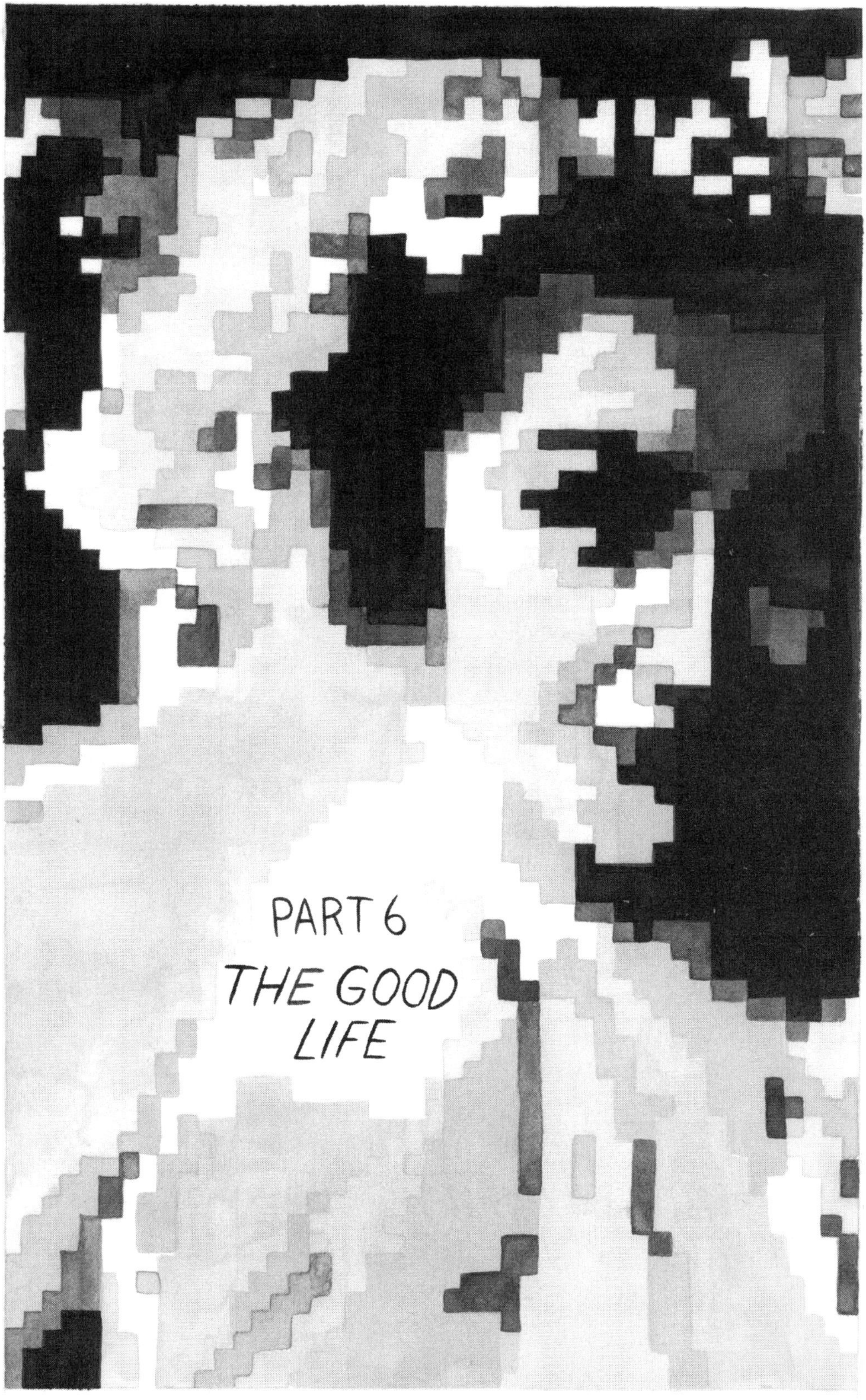
PART 6
THE GOOD LIFE

Ilse and Erich got married twice— their first wedding was at the courthouse in Antwerp.

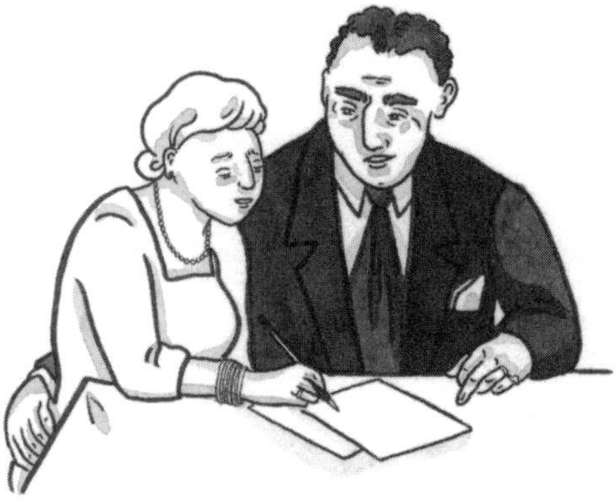

This was strategic: As newlyweds they were permitted to bring household property to Belgium.

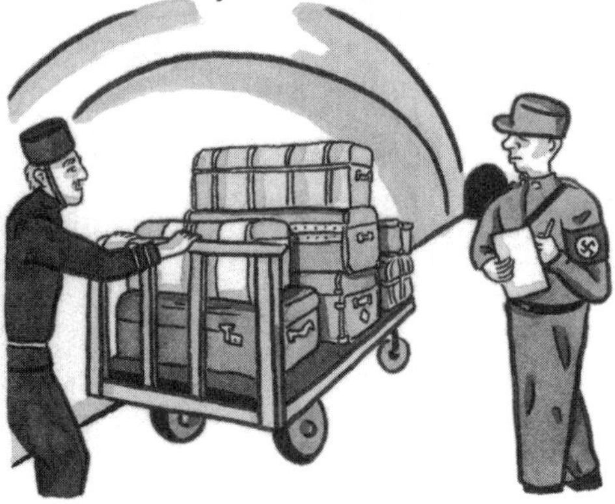

The borders were still relatively open—

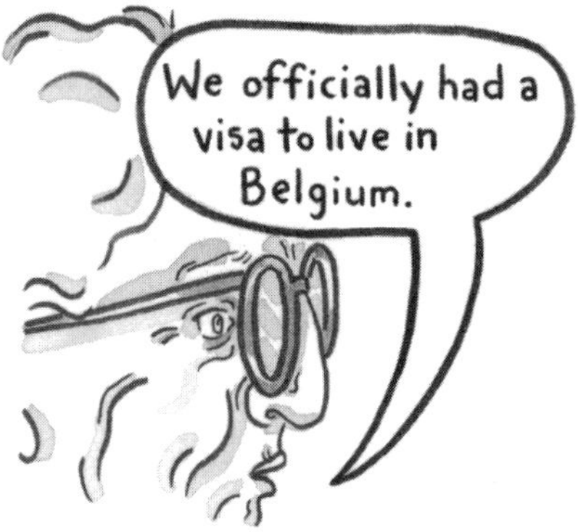
We officially had a visa to live in Belgium.

Erich Kahn opened a branch of the family business in Antwerp and hired Erich Levi.

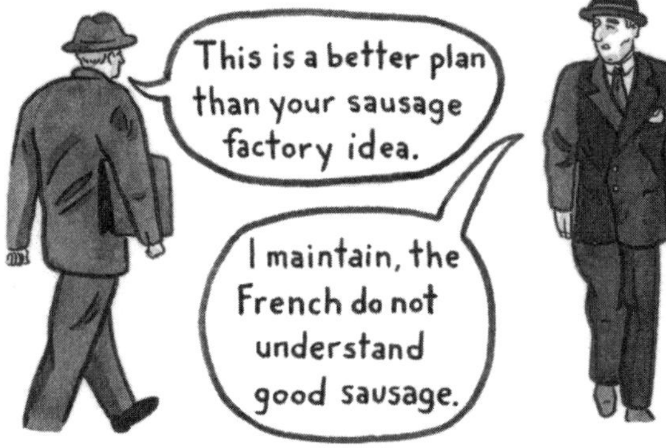
This is a better plan than your sausage factory idea.
I maintain, the French do not understand good sausage.

They shipped a new Mercedes-Benz Cabriolet by train from Germany to Belgium along with linens, furniture, china . . .

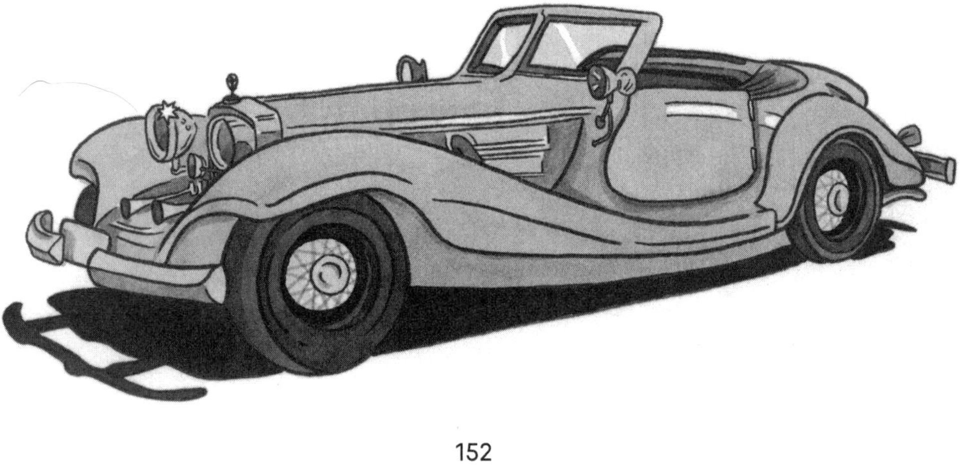

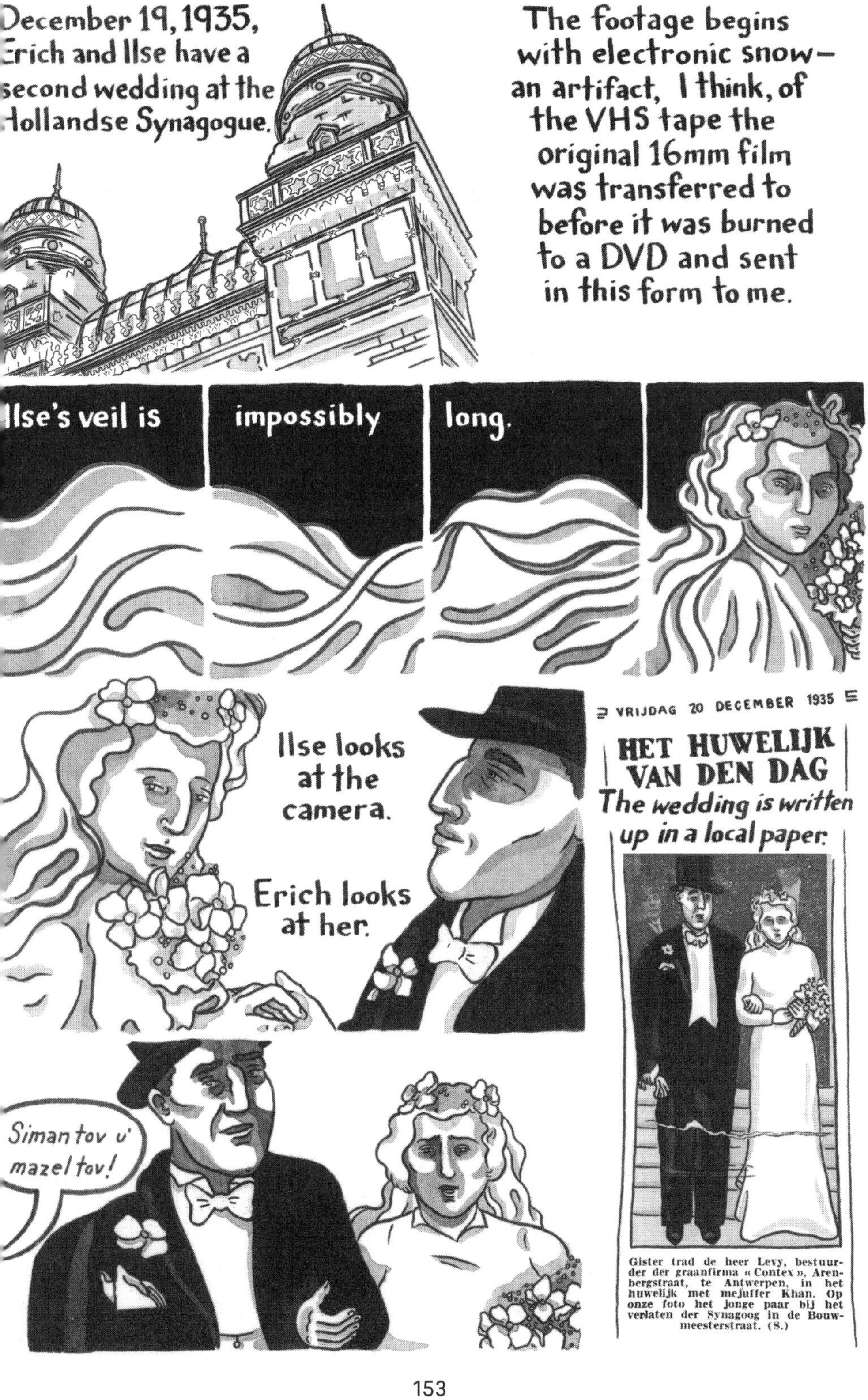
December 19, 1935, Erich and Ilse have a second wedding at the Hollandse Synagogue.
The footage begins with electronic snow— an artifact, I think, of the VHS tape the original 16mm film was transferred to before it was burned to a DVD and sent in this form to me.
Ilse's veil is
impossibly
long.
Ilse looks at the camera.
Erich looks at her.
VRIJDAG 20 DECEMBER 1935
HET HUWELIJK VAN DEN DAG
The wedding is written up in a local paper.
Gister trad de heer Levy, bestuurder der graanfirma « Contex », Arenbergstraat, te Antwerpen, in het huwelijk met mejuffer Khan. Op onze foto het jonge paar bij het verlaten der Synagoog in de Bouwmeesterstraat. (S.)
Siman tov u' mazel tov!

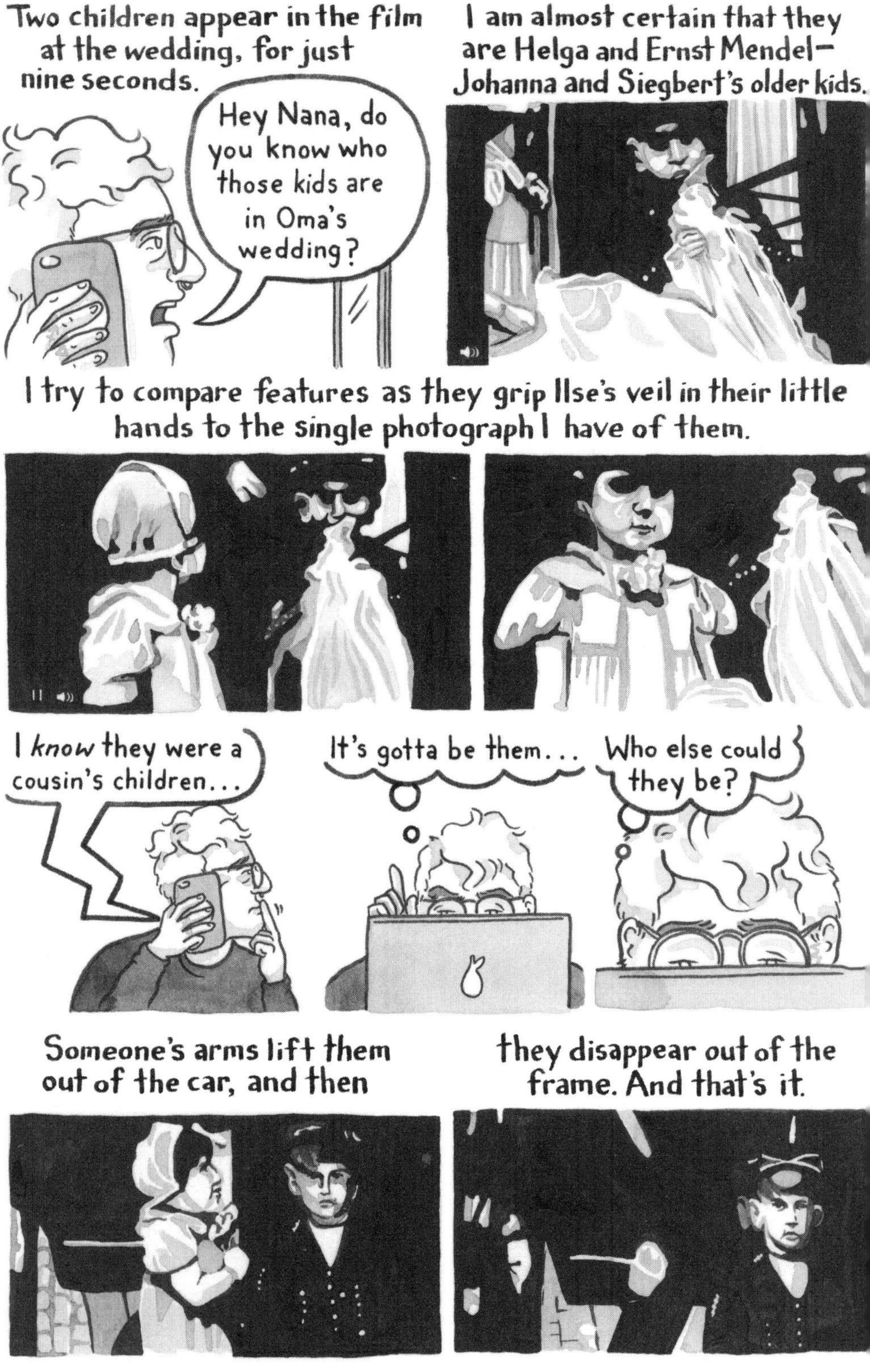
Two children appear in the film at the wedding, for just nine seconds.
Hey Nana, do you know who those kids are in Oma's wedding?
I am almost certain that they are Helga and Ernst Mendel— Johanna and Siegbert's older kids.
I try to compare features as they grip Ilse's veil in their little hands to the single photograph I have of them.
I *know* they were a cousin's children...
It's gotta be them...
Who else could they be?
Someone's arms lift them out of the car, and then
they disappear out of the frame. And that's it.

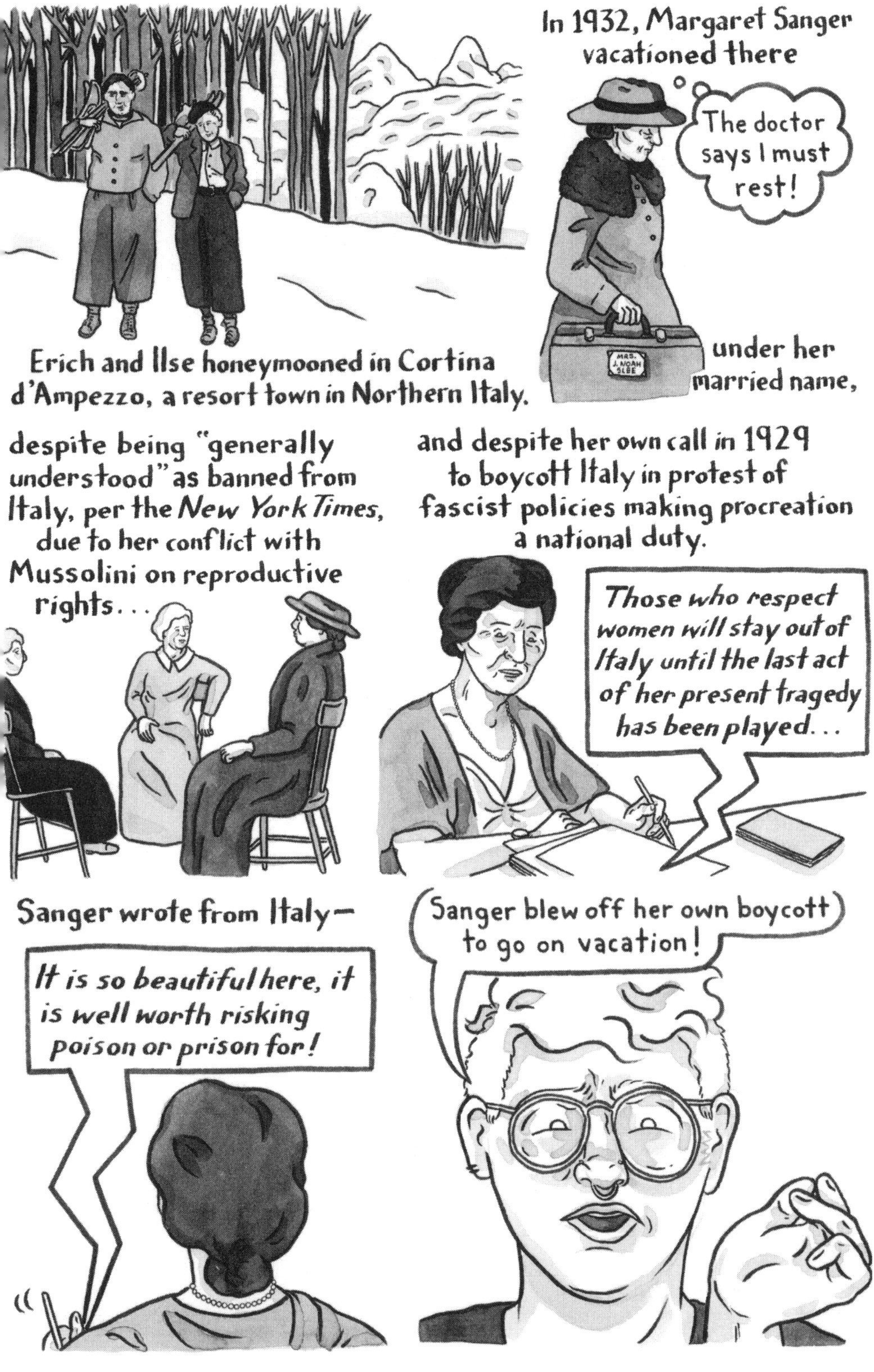
Erich and Ilse honeymooned in Cortina d'Ampezzo, a resort town in Northern Italy.
In 1932, Margaret Sanger vacationed there
The doctor says I must rest!
MRS. J. NOAH SLEE
under her married name,
despite being "generally understood" as banned from Italy, per the *New York Times*, due to her conflict with Mussolini on reproductive rights...
and despite her own call in 1929 to boycott Italy in protest of fascist policies making procreation a national duty.
Those who respect women will stay out of Italy until the last act of her present tragedy has been played...
Sanger wrote from Italy—
It is so beautiful here, it is well worth risking poison or prison for!
Sanger blew off her own boycott to go on vacation!

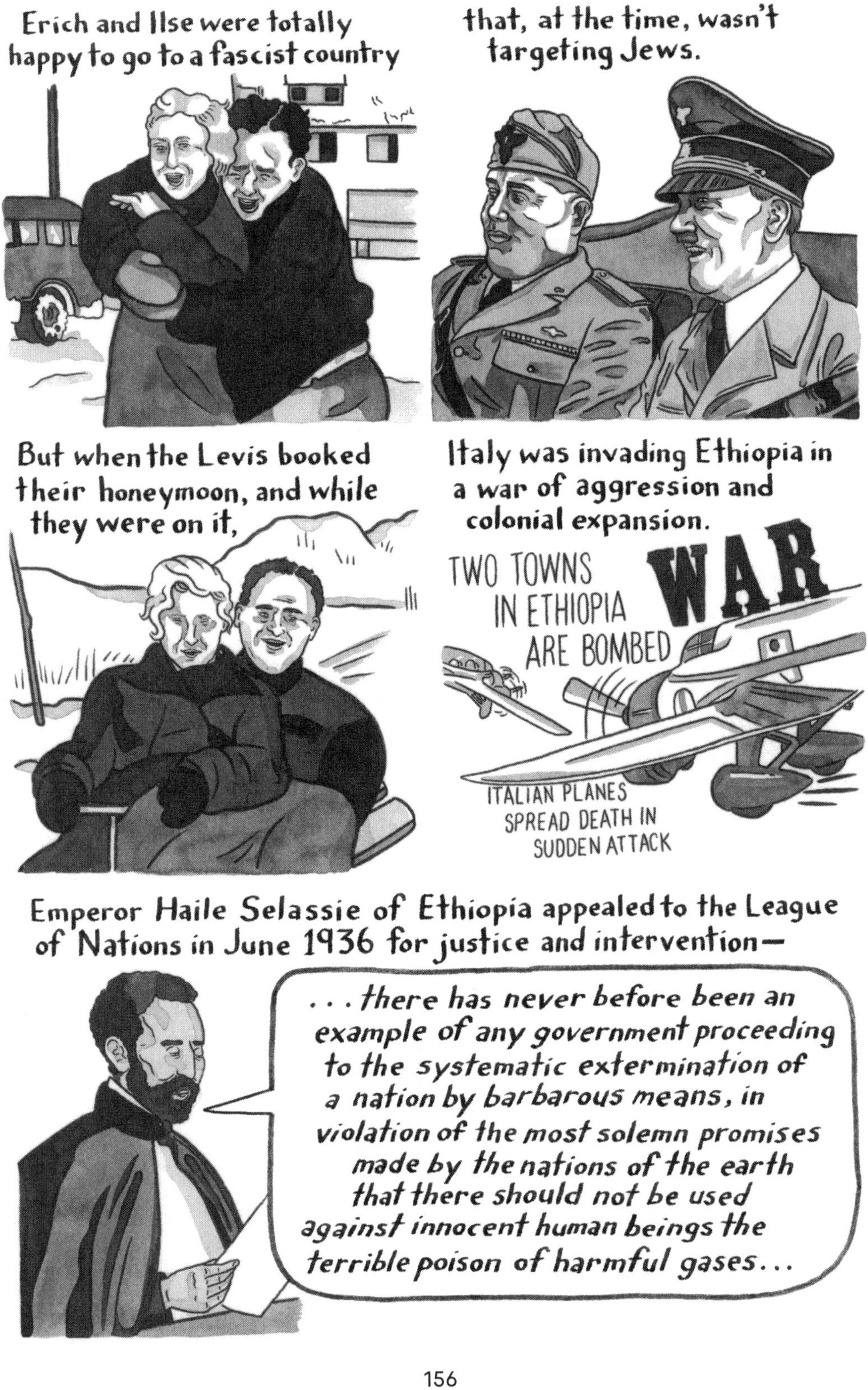
Erich and Ilse were totally happy to go to a fascist country
that, at the time, wasn't targeting Jews.
But when the Levis booked their honeymoon, and while they were on it,
Italy was invading Ethiopia in a war of aggression and colonial expansion.
TWO TOWNS IN ETHIOPIA ARE BOMBED
WAR
ITALIAN PLANES SPREAD DEATH IN SUDDEN ATTACK
Emperor Haile Selassie of Ethiopia appealed to the League of Nations in June 1936 for justice and intervention—
. . . there has never before been an example of any government proceeding to the systematic extermination of a nation by barbarous means, in violation of the most solemn promises made by the nations of the earth that there should not be used against innocent human beings the terrible poison of harmful gases . . .

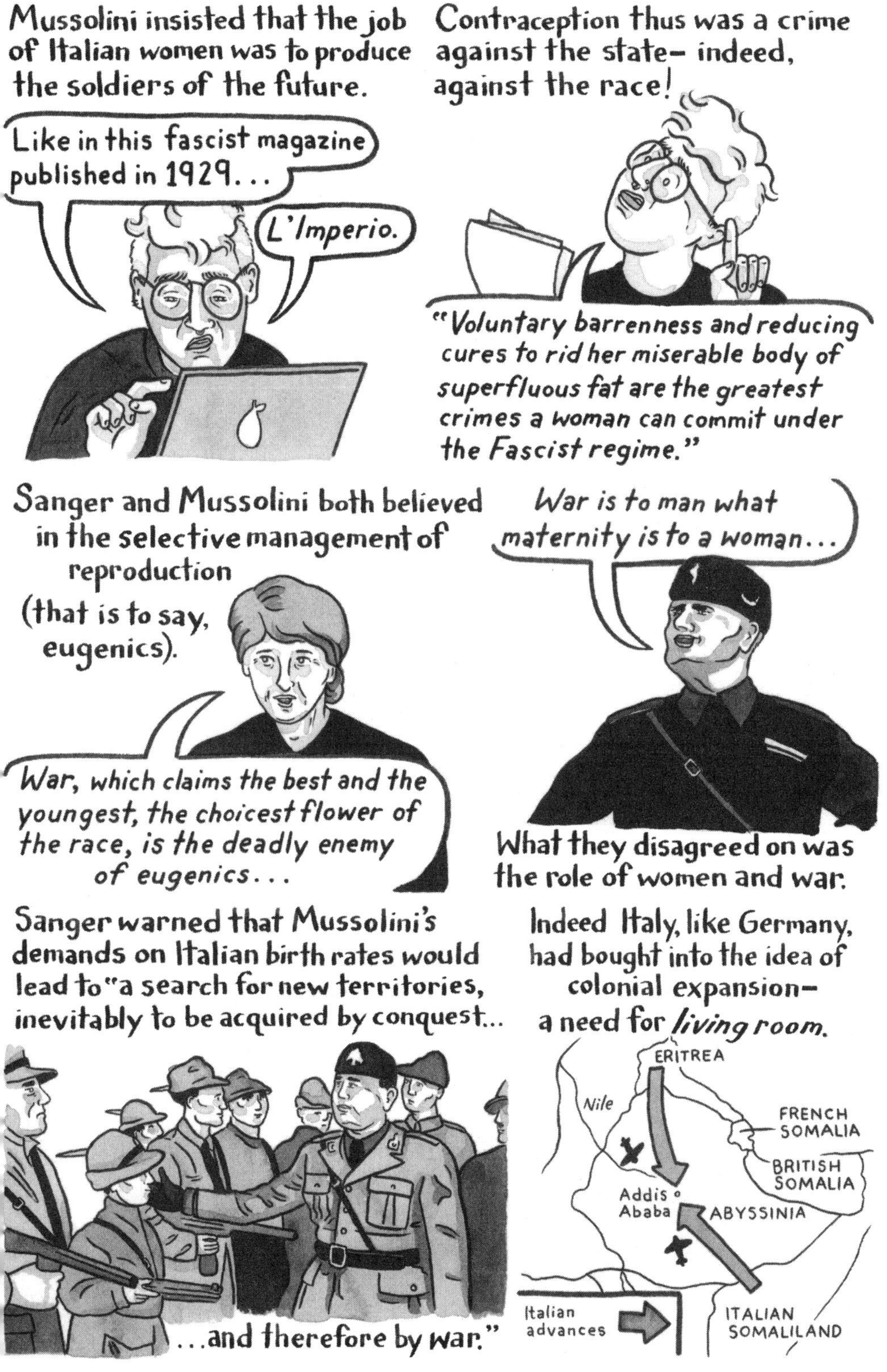

Mussolini insisted that the job of Italian women was to produce the soldiers of the future.
Like in this fascist magazine published in 1929...
L'Imperio.
Contraception thus was a crime against the state– indeed, against the race!
"Voluntary barrenness and reducing cures to rid her miserable body of superfluous fat are the greatest crimes a woman can commit under the Fascist regime."
Sanger and Mussolini both believed in the selective management of reproduction
(that is to say, eugenics).
War, which claims the best and the youngest, the choicest flower of the race, is the deadly enemy of eugenics...
War is to man what maternity is to a woman...
What they disagreed on was the role of women and war.
Sanger warned that Mussolini's demands on Italian birth rates would lead to "a search for new territories, inevitably to be acquired by conquest...
...and therefore by war."
Indeed Italy, like Germany, had bought into the idea of colonial expansion– a need for living room.
ERITREA
Nile
FRENCH SOMALIA
BRITISH SOMALIA
Addis Ababa
ABYSSINIA
Italian advances
ITALIAN SOMALILAND

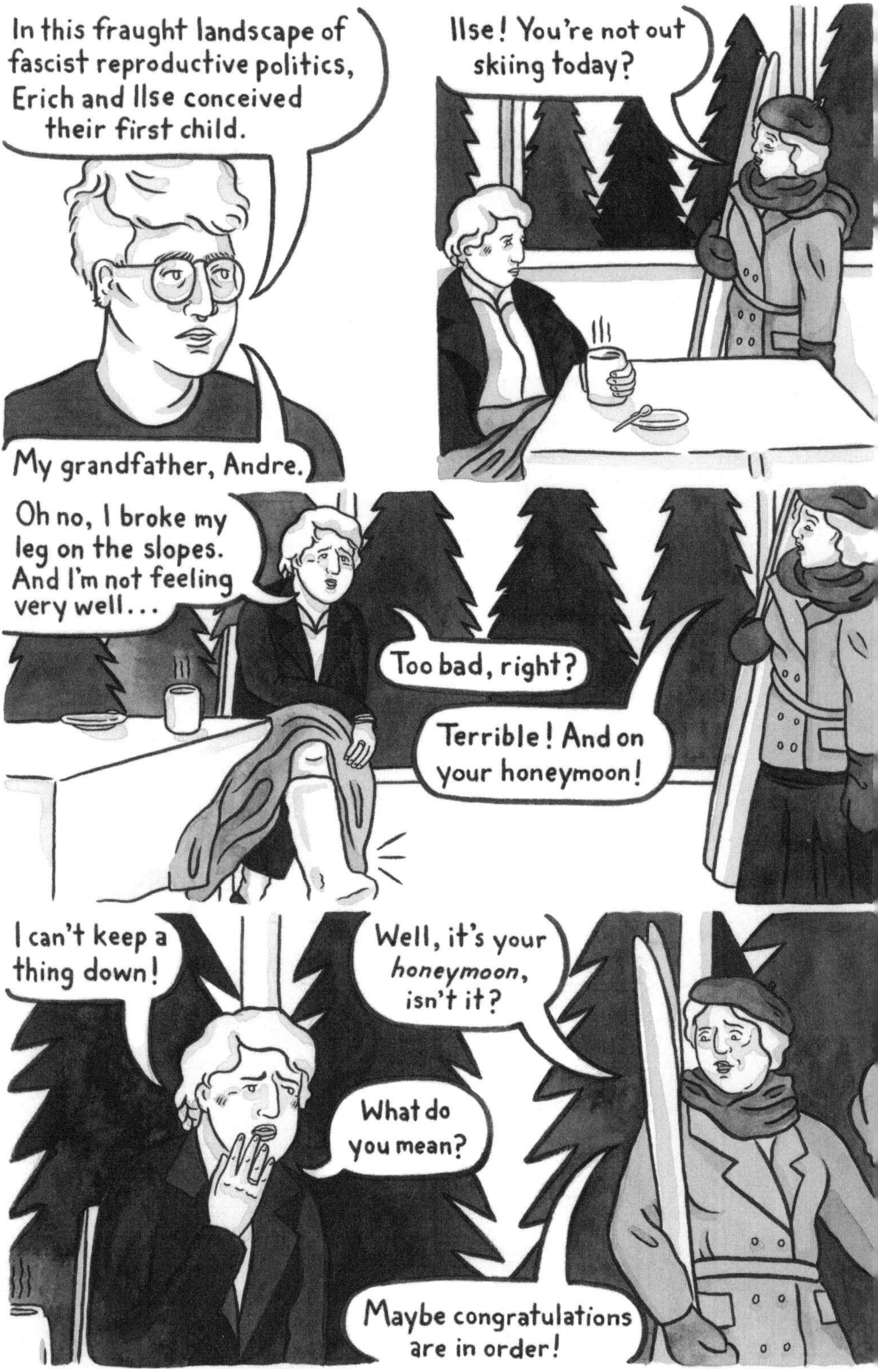
In this fraught landscape of fascist reproductive politics, Erich and Ilse conceived their first child.
My grandfather, Andre.
Ilse! You're not out skiing today?
Oh no, I broke my leg on the slopes. And I'm not feeling very well...
Too bad, right?
Terrible! And on your honeymoon!
I can't keep a thing down!
Well, it's your *honeymoon*, isn't it?
What do you mean?
Maybe congratulations are in order!

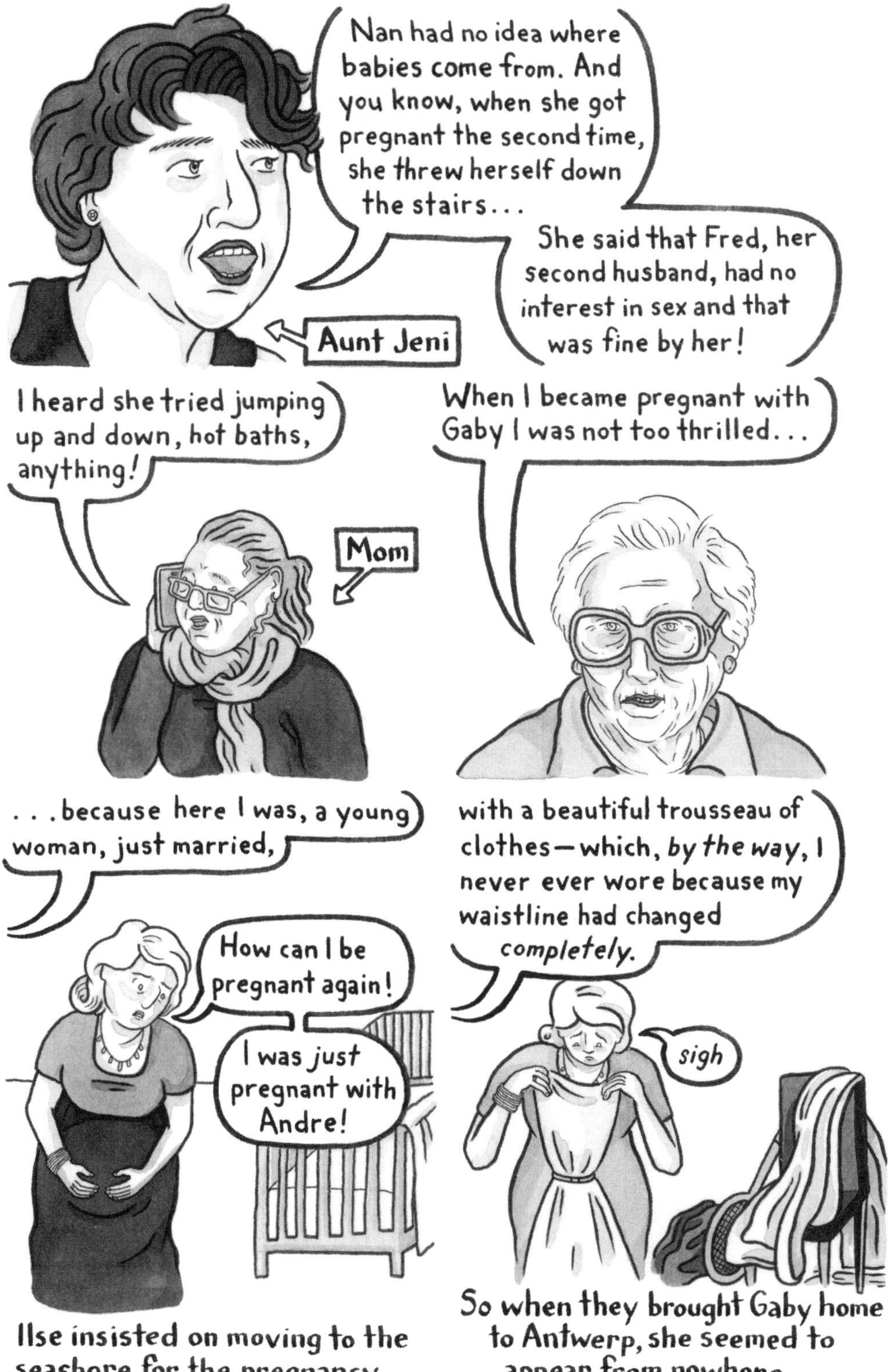
Nan had no idea where babies come from. And you know, when she got pregnant the second time, she threw herself down the stairs...
She said that Fred, her second husband, had no interest in sex and that was fine by her!
Aunt Jeni
I heard she tried jumping up and down, hot baths, anything!
Mom
When I became pregnant with Gaby I was not too thrilled...
...because here I was, a young woman, just married,
with a beautiful trousseau of clothes—which, *by the way*, I never ever wore because my waistline had changed *completely*.
How can I be pregnant again!
I was *just* pregnant with Andre!
sigh
Ilse insisted on moving to the seashore for the pregnancy.
So when they brought Gaby home to Antwerp, she seemed to appear from nowhere.

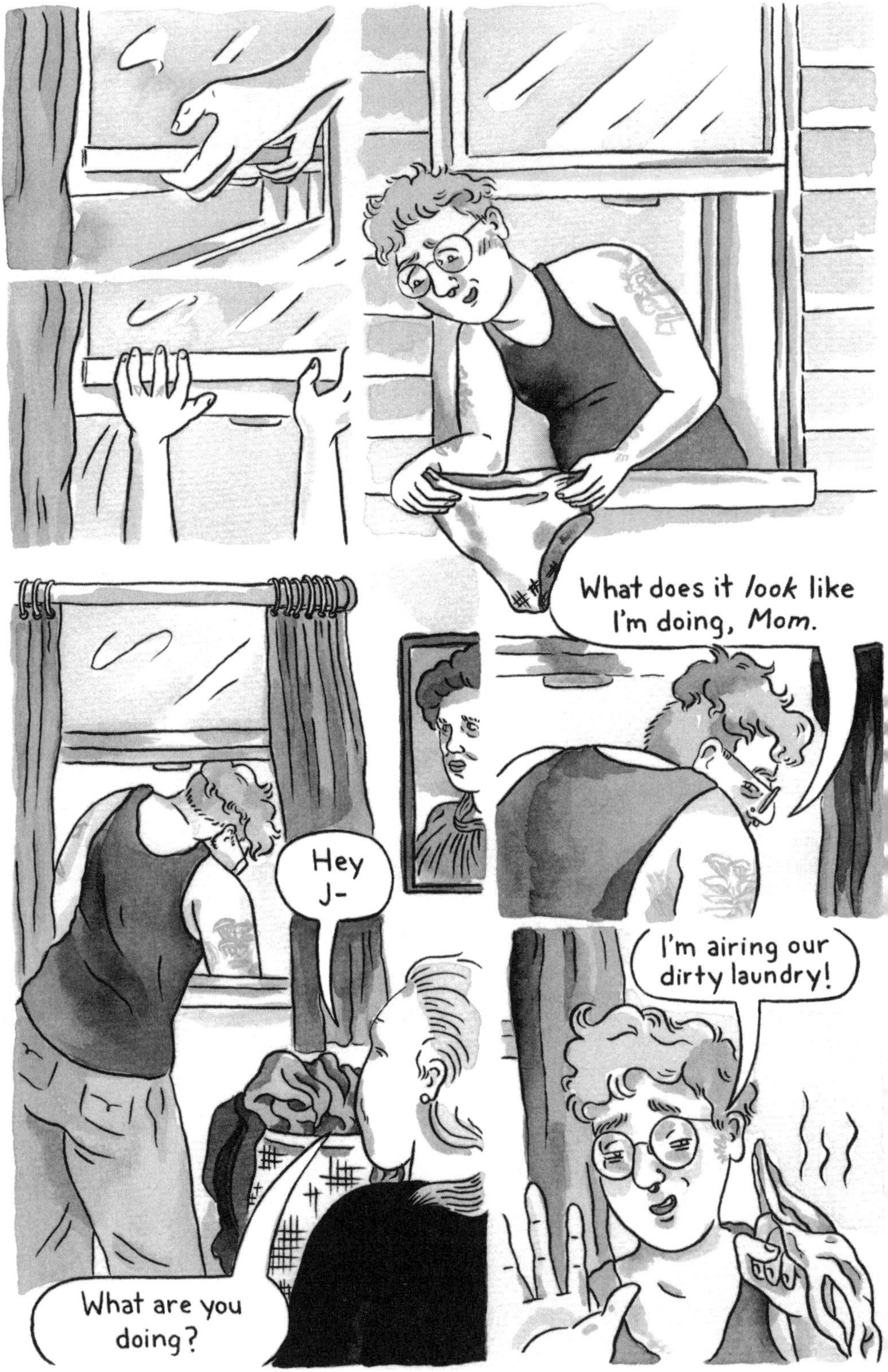
Hey J-
What are you doing?
What does it *look* like I'm doing, *Mom*.
I'm airing our dirty laundry!

My cousin Roxane, in Paris, helps me with the French translation on the documents from this era.

It's shameful the Belgian government made you pay!

I'm shocked!

Did you keep the bill? For them to charge for documents when they sent a whole family to a camp...

We should denounce it!

Eh, paying a government to see documents about how they destroyed your family is a rite of passage in some circles. Anyway...

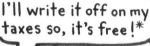

I'll write it off on my taxes so, it's free!*

*A joke!

My oma had fond memories of Belgium, but the archival documents are pretty depressing. They were drowning in hostile bureaucracy.

And Belgium was still a colonial empire that hadn't even started to reckon with their crimes against humanity.

The majority of Jews in Belgium in 1940 weren't Belgian, and they were treated as unwanted foreigners.

161

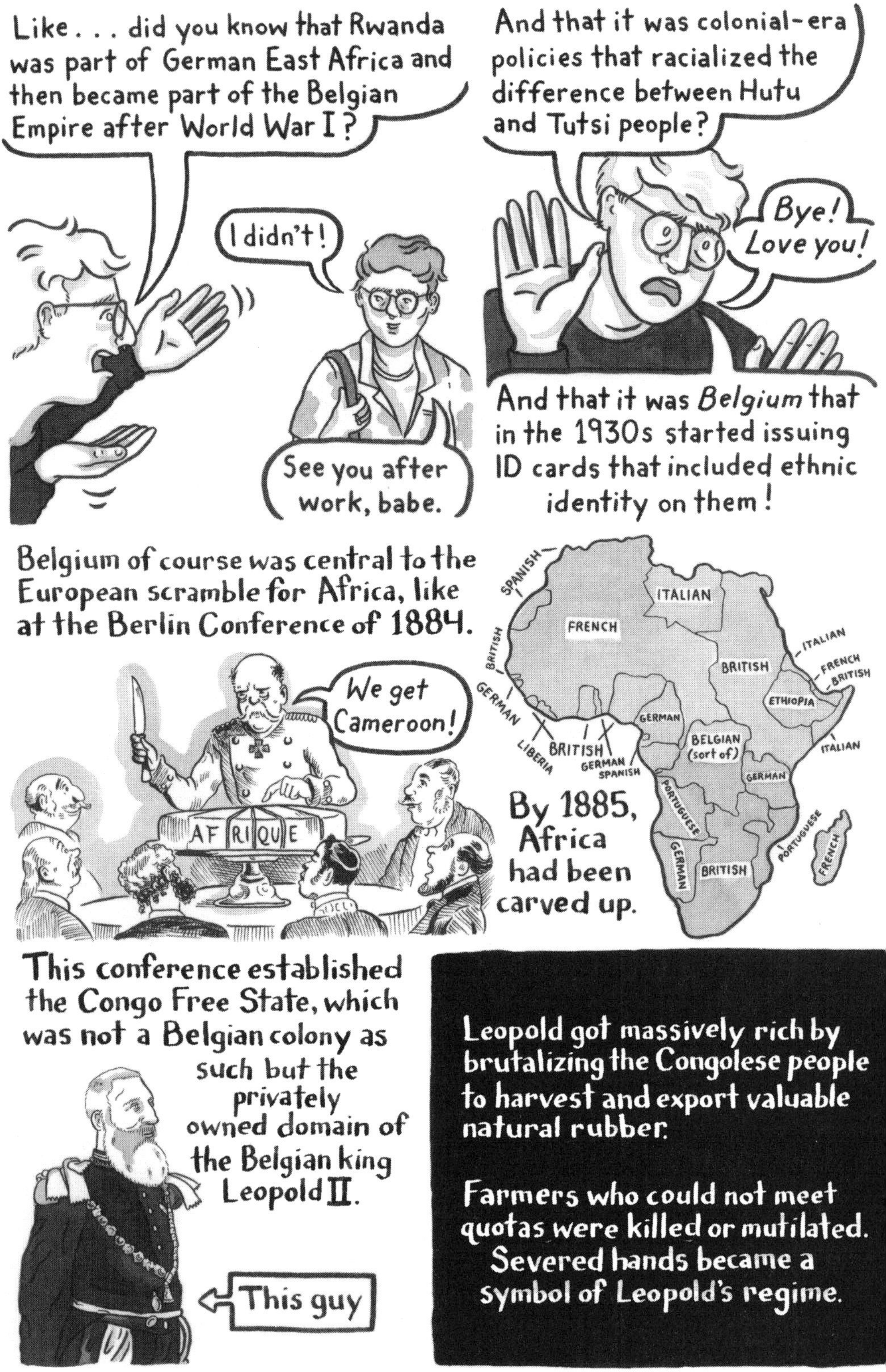

Like . . . did you know that Rwanda was part of German East Africa and then became part of the Belgian Empire after World War I?
I didn't!
See you after work, babe.
And that it was colonial-era policies that racialized the difference between Hutu and Tutsi people?
Bye! Love you!
And that it was *Belgium* that in the 1930s started issuing ID cards that included ethnic identity on them!
Belgium of course was central to the European scramble for Africa, like at the Berlin Conference of 1884.
We get Cameroon!
AFRIQUE
SPANISH
ITALIAN
FRENCH
BRITISH
ITALIAN
FRENCH
BRITISH
BRITISH
ETHIOPIA
GERMAN
GERMAN
LIBERIA
BRITISH
GERMAN
SPANISH
BELGIAN (sort of)
ITALIAN
GERMAN
PORTUGUESE
GERMAN
BRITISH
PORTUGUESE
FRENCH
By 1885, Africa had been carved up.
This conference established the Congo Free State, which was not a Belgian colony as such but the privately owned domain of the Belgian king Leopold II.
This guy
Leopold got massively rich by brutalizing the Congolese people to harvest and export valuable natural rubber.
Farmers who could not meet quotas were killed or mutilated. Severed hands became a symbol of Leopold's regime.

In the pursuit of maximum profit, millions died under Leopold's rule, until 1906, when Belgium bought the Congo from him, which it ruled until 1960.

IN THE RUBBER COILS.

In 1961, the Congolese independence leader Patrice Lumumba was assassinated in a coup backed by Belgium and the United States.

In 2002, Belgium apologized for its role in the assassination.

In 2020, Belgium returned Lumumba's teeth, stolen from his body by a Belgian police officer after his murder.

In addition to rubber, the uranium the U.S. used to create the atom bombs that would be dropped

Mine de radium de Chinkolobwe (Katanga) exploitée par l'Union Minière

on Hiroshima and Nagasaki in August 1945 came from the Belgian Congo.

The year that Erich and Ilse got married there was an International Exposition in the city of Brussels.

Over 20 million people attended the fair, which celebrated the 50th anniversary of Belgian colonization of the Congo.

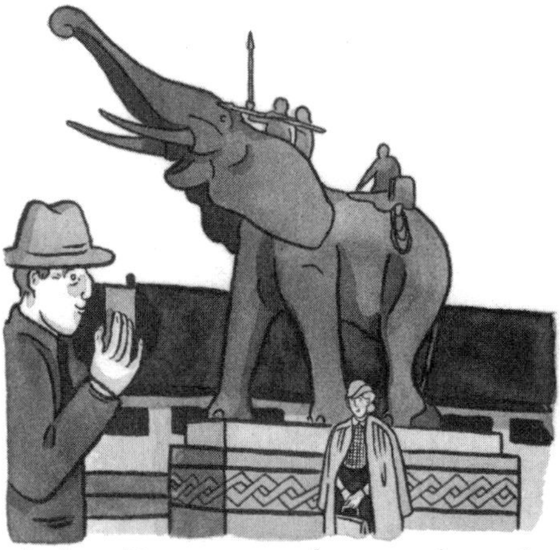

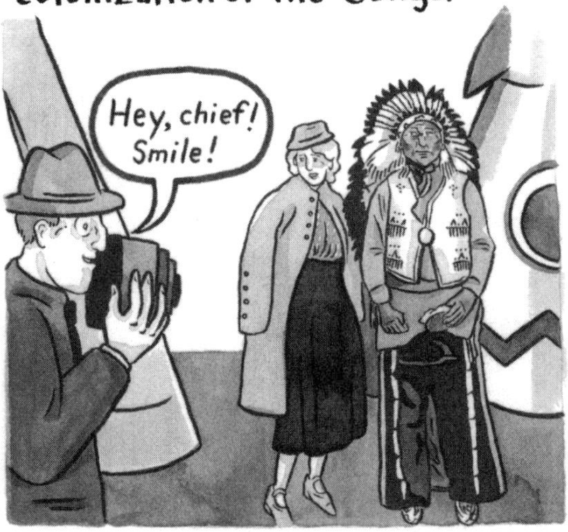

Hey, chief! Smile!

Like the preceding colonial exposition in 1897 and the next one in 1958, this Belgian World Fair featured a human zoo—ethnological exhibits of living people displayed as objects, as curiosities, as animals.

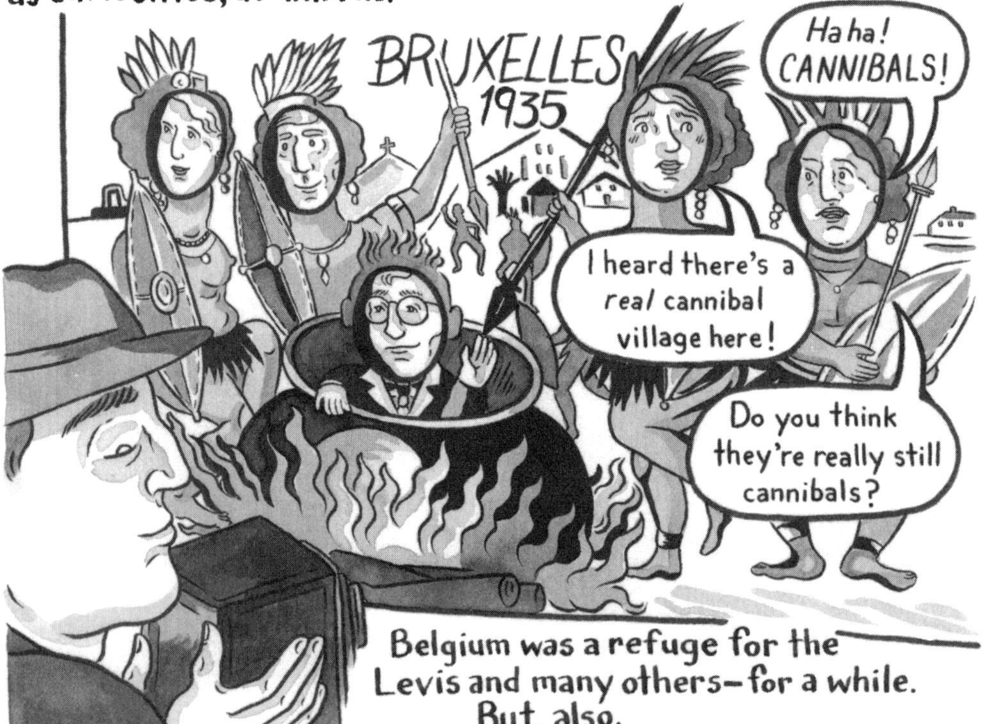

BRUXELLES 1935
Ha ha! CANNIBALS!
I heard there's a *real* cannibal village here!
Do you think they're really still cannibals?
Belgium was a refuge for the Levis and many others—for a while. But, also.

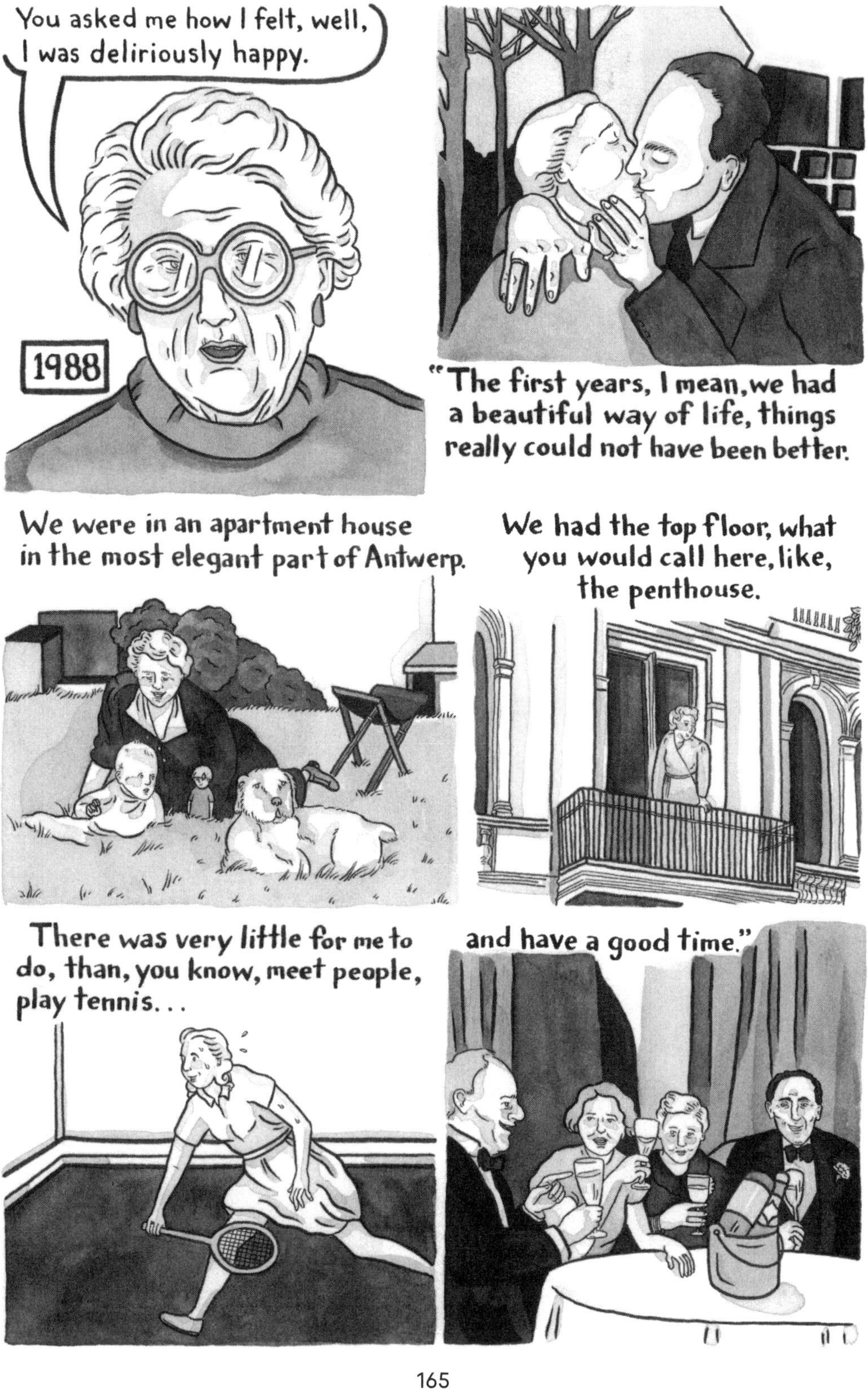
You asked me how I felt, well, I was deliriously happy.
1988
"The first years, I mean, we had a beautiful way of life, things really could not have been better.
We were in an apartment house in the most elegant part of Antwerp.
We had the top floor, what you would call here, like, the penthouse.
There was very little for me to do, than, you know, meet people, play tennis. . .
and have a good time."

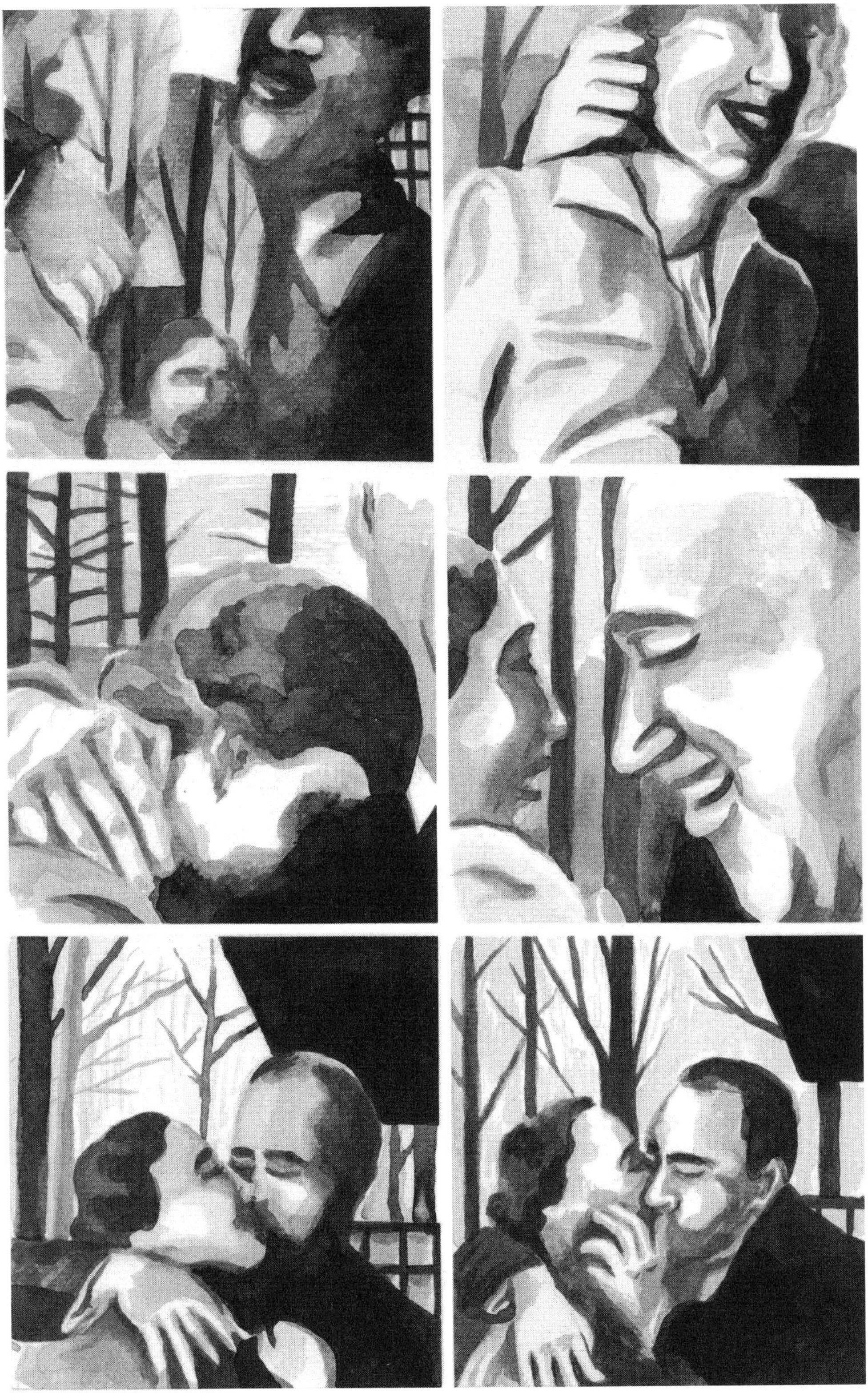

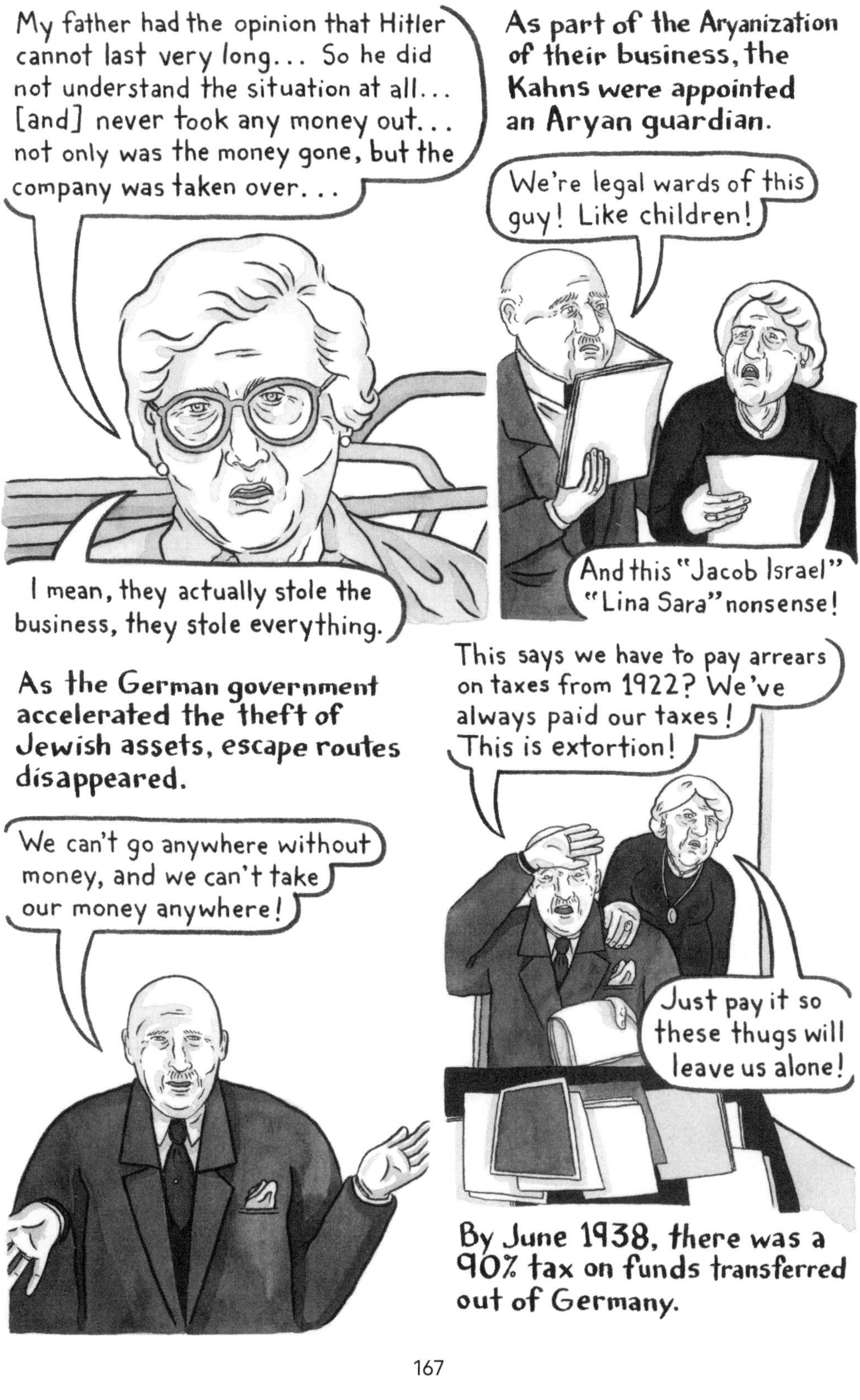
My father had the opinion that Hitler cannot last very long... So he did not understand the situation at all... [and] never took any money out... not only was the money gone, but the company was taken over...
I mean, they actually stole the business, they stole everything.
As part of the Aryanization of their business, the Kahns were appointed an Aryan guardian.
We're legal wards of this guy! Like children!
And this "Jacob Israel" "Lina Sara" nonsense!
As the German government accelerated the theft of Jewish assets, escape routes disappeared.
We can't go anywhere without money, and we can't take our money anywhere!
This says we have to pay arrears on taxes from 1922? We've always paid our taxes! This is extortion!
Just pay it so these thugs will leave us alone!
By June 1938, there was a 90% tax on funds transferred out of Germany.

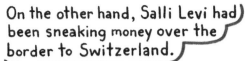
On the other hand, Salli Levi had been sneaking money over the border to Switzerland.

Switzerland is known for its very strict banking secrecy laws.

Please, Mr. Levi, right this way.

One ticket, Frankfurt to Basel, please. First class.

Make it a round trip!

Those criminals won't be able to get to this account at least! We must protect whatever we can until the end of this idiot regime.

Andre, this article says Jews are suing the Swiss banks for stealing their money during the war!

Your grandfather had money there... I wonder...

Oh yeah?

It's probably a waste of time. Or a scam!

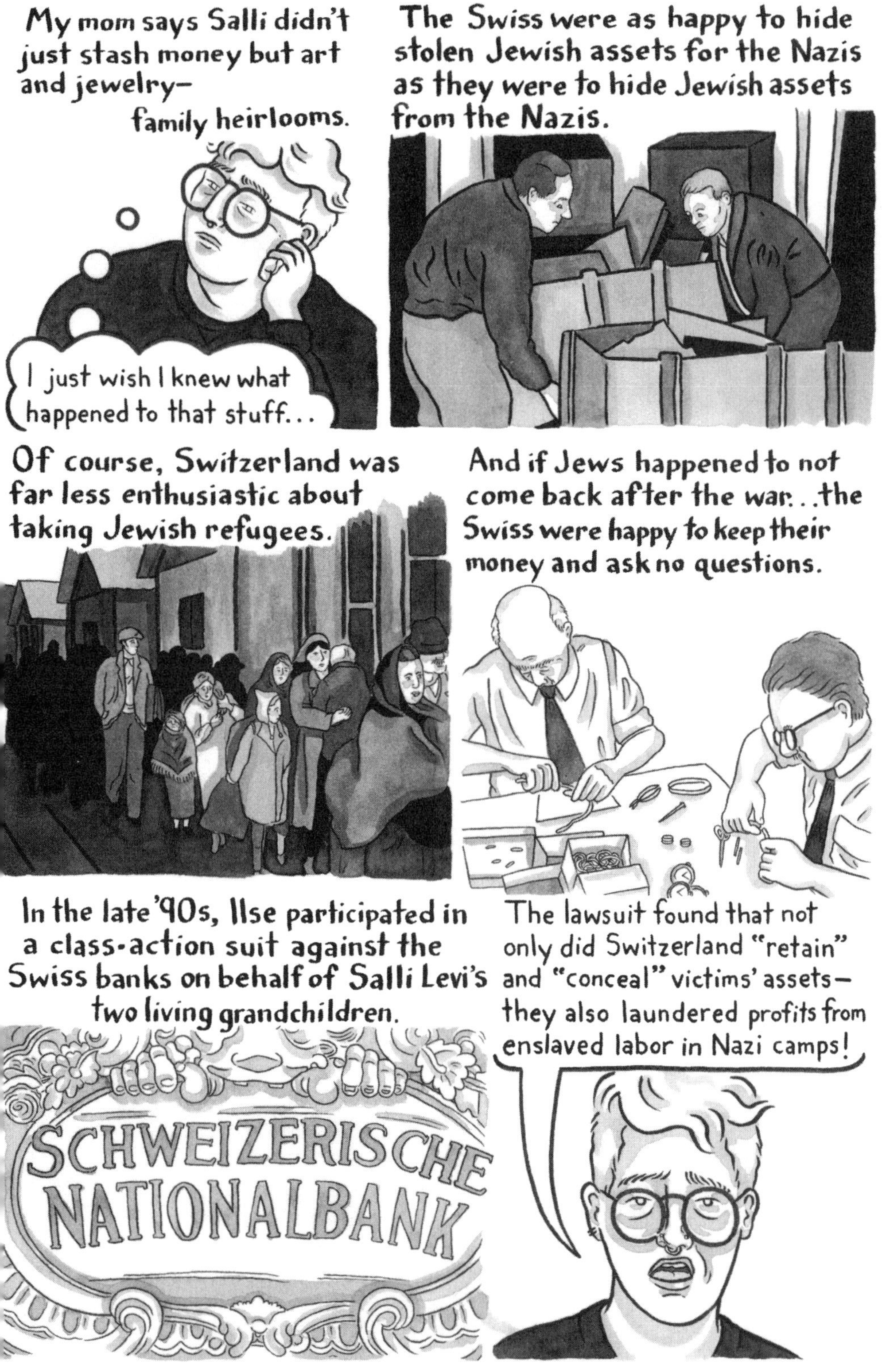

My mom says Salli didn't just stash money but art and jewelry— family heirlooms.
I just wish I knew what happened to that stuff...
The Swiss were as happy to hide stolen Jewish assets for the Nazis as they were to hide Jewish assets from the Nazis.
Of course, Switzerland was far less enthusiastic about taking Jewish refugees.
And if Jews happened to not come back after the war...the Swiss were happy to keep their money and ask no questions.
In the late '90s, Ilse participated in a class-action suit against the Swiss banks on behalf of Salli Levi's two living grandchildren.
SCHWEIZERISCHE NATIONALBANK
The lawsuit found that not only did Switzerland "retain" and "conceal" victims' assets— they also laundered profits from enslaved labor in Nazi camps!

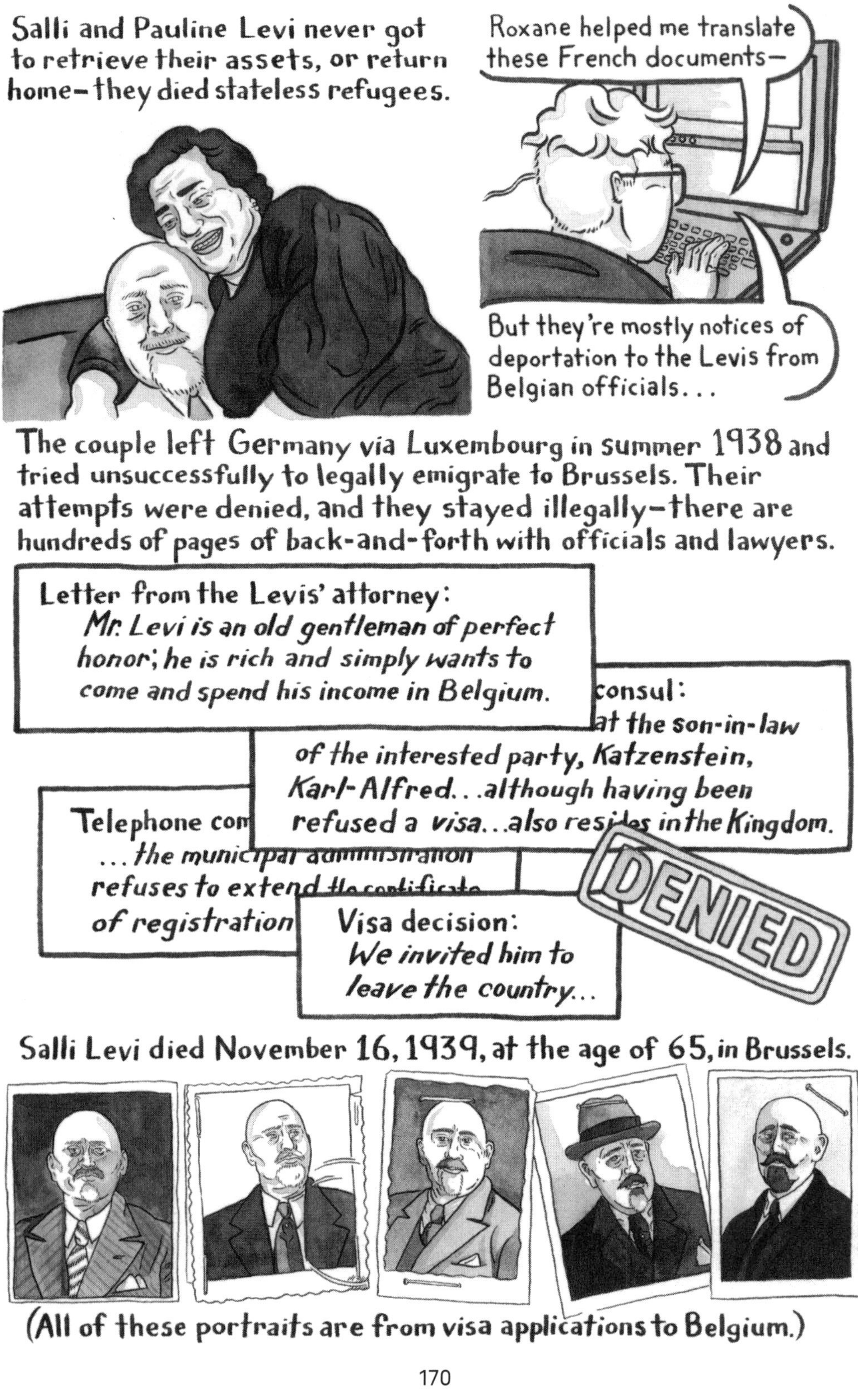
Salli and Pauline Levi never got to retrieve their assets, or return home—they died stateless refugees.
Roxane helped me translate these French documents—
But they're mostly notices of deportation to the Levis from Belgian officials...
The couple left Germany via Luxembourg in summer 1938 and tried unsuccessfully to legally emigrate to Brussels. Their attempts were denied, and they stayed illegally—there are hundreds of pages of back-and-forth with officials and lawyers.
Letter from the Levis' attorney:
Mr. Levi is an old gentleman of perfect honor; he is rich and simply wants to come and spend his income in Belgium.
consul:
at the son-in-law of the interested party, Katzenstein, Karl-Alfred...although having been refused a visa...also resides in the Kingdom.
Telephone com
...the municipal administration refuses to extend
of registration
Visa decision:
We invited him to leave the country...
DENIED
Salli Levi died November 16, 1939, at the age of 65, in Brussels.
(All of these portraits are from visa applications to Belgium.)

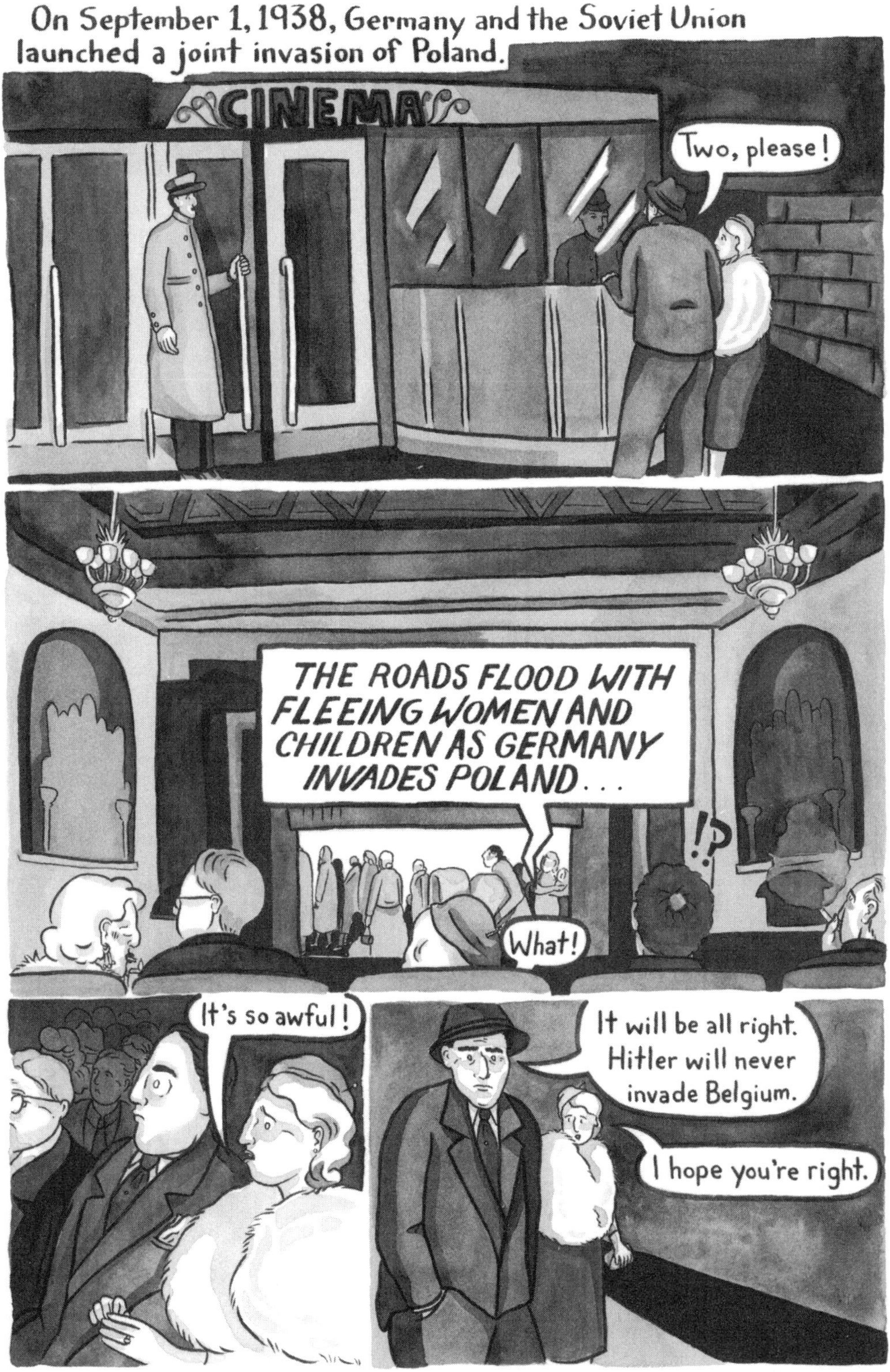
On September 1, 1938, Germany and the Soviet Union launched a joint invasion of Poland.
CINEMA
Two, please!
THE ROADS FLOOD WITH FLEEING WOMEN AND CHILDREN AS GERMANY INVADES POLAND...
!?
What!
It's so awful!
It will be all right. Hitler will never invade Belgium.
I hope you're right.

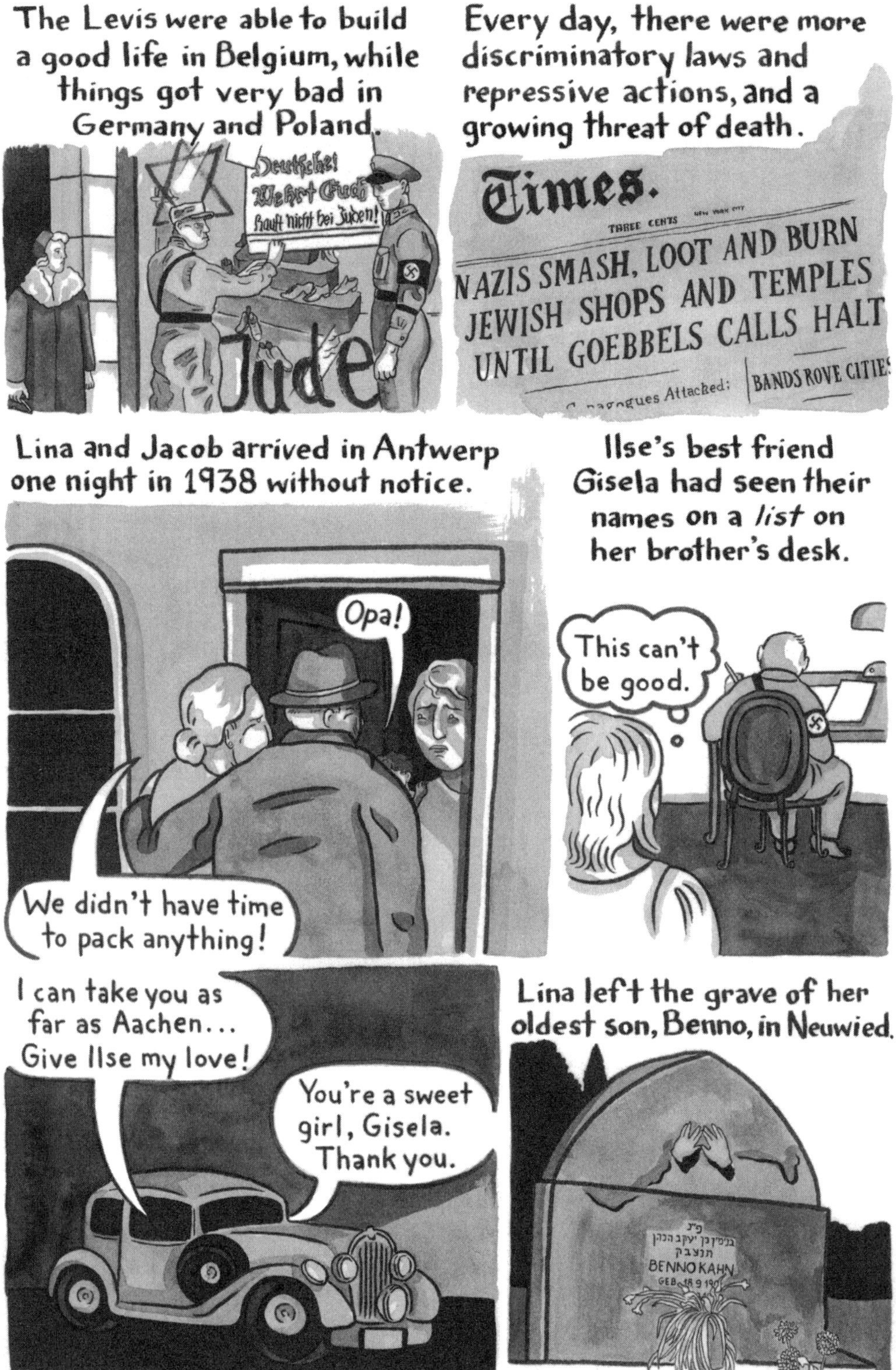

The Levis were able to build a good life in Belgium, while things got very bad in Germany and Poland.
Deutsche! Wehrt Euch kauft nicht bei Juden!
Jude
Every day, there were more discriminatory laws and repressive actions, and a growing threat of death.
Times.
THREE CENTS
NAZIS SMASH, LOOT AND BURN JEWISH SHOPS AND TEMPLES UNTIL GOEBBELS CALLS HALT
nagogues Attacked:
BANDS ROVE CITIE
Lina and Jacob arrived in Antwerp one night in 1938 without notice.
Opa!
We didn't have time to pack anything!
Ilse's best friend Gisela had seen their names on a *list* on her brother's desk.
This can't be good.
I can take you as far as Aachen... Give Ilse my love!
You're a sweet girl, Gisela. Thank you.
Lina left the grave of her oldest son, Benno, in Neuwied.
BENNO KAHN

Ilse's testimonies and the archives contain some contradictions on when Jacob and Lina Kahn got to Belgium—

Ilse to Jeni Leeds, 1988:
This list was for a transport to Poland to a. . . death camp. . . it was on Kristallnacht. . .

Ilse in a short essay, date unknown:
. . . my best friend warned them that they would be deported to Dachau if they did not leave immediately. . .

Ilse in the Shoah Foundation interview, 1996:
My parents came with nothing at the last minute the night before, of Kristallnacht. . . [Gisela] saw on her brother's desk. . . a list for a transport to Dachau. . .

A note from the Hamburg court system, November 11, 1938, the day after the Kristallnacht pogrom—
We have learned that the owner, Kahn, is said to have fled to Holland or Belgium. . .
A response from the secret state police reads,
it can be assumed that [Kahn]. . . was Jewish.

A letter from Kahn & Co. in Hamburg to the foreign exchange office in September 1938—
We would like to inform you that the owners of our company. . . have emigrated to Antwerp without having liquidated the company beforehand. . .

It's confirmable in archives, from Nazi documentation, that the Kahns emigrated abruptly and illegally.

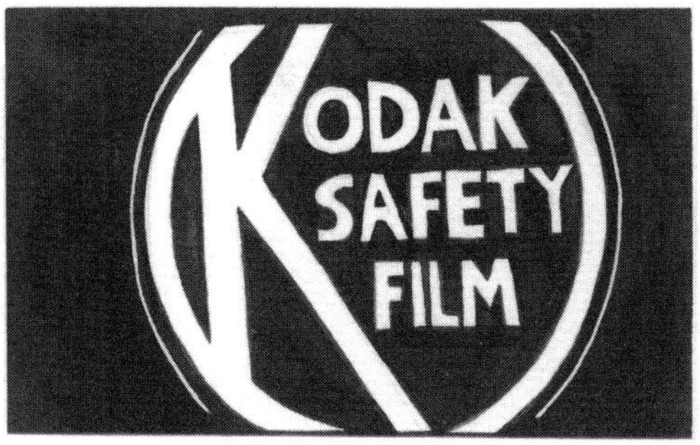
KODAK
SAFETY
FILM

The 21 minutes and 11-odd seconds of surviving home movies are all from these years in Belgium.

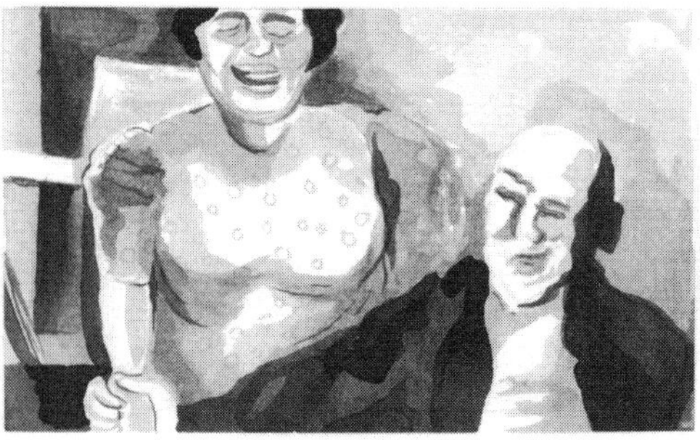

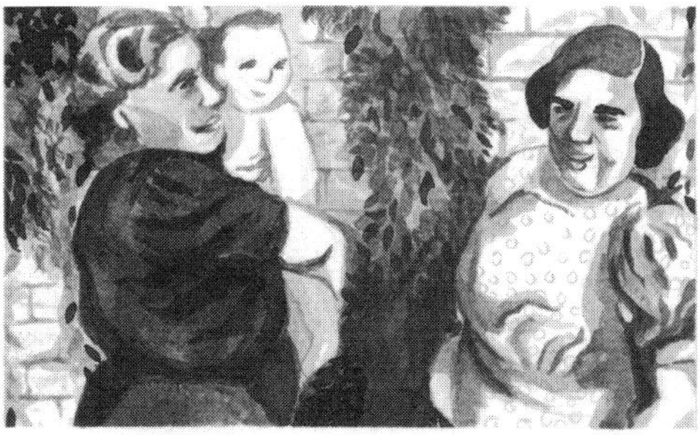

I watch them over and over again, joking around, having fun.

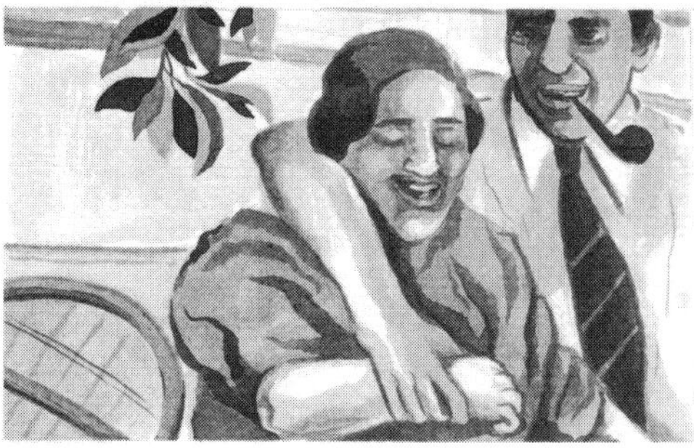

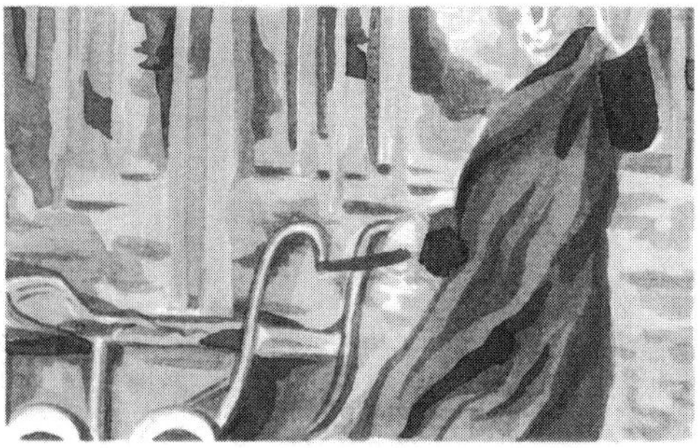

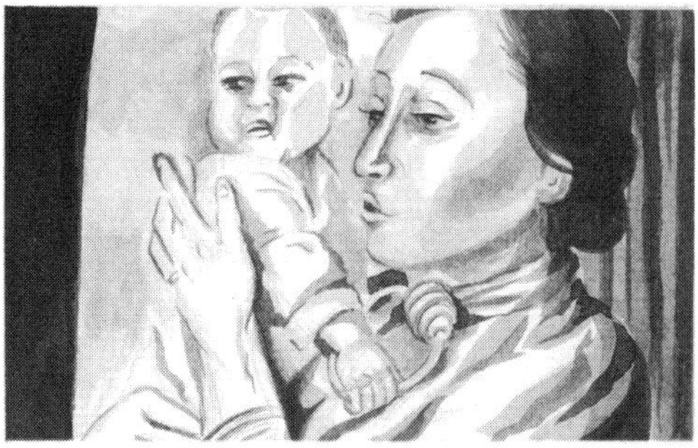

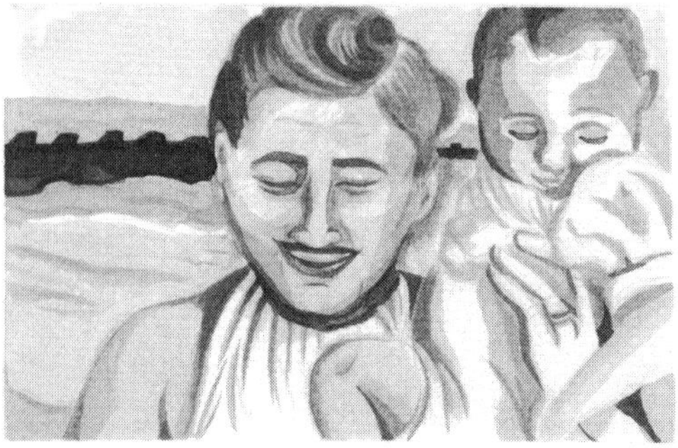

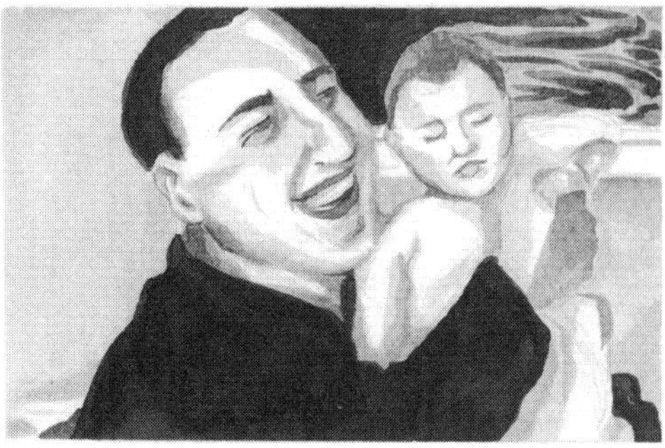

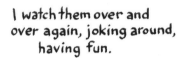

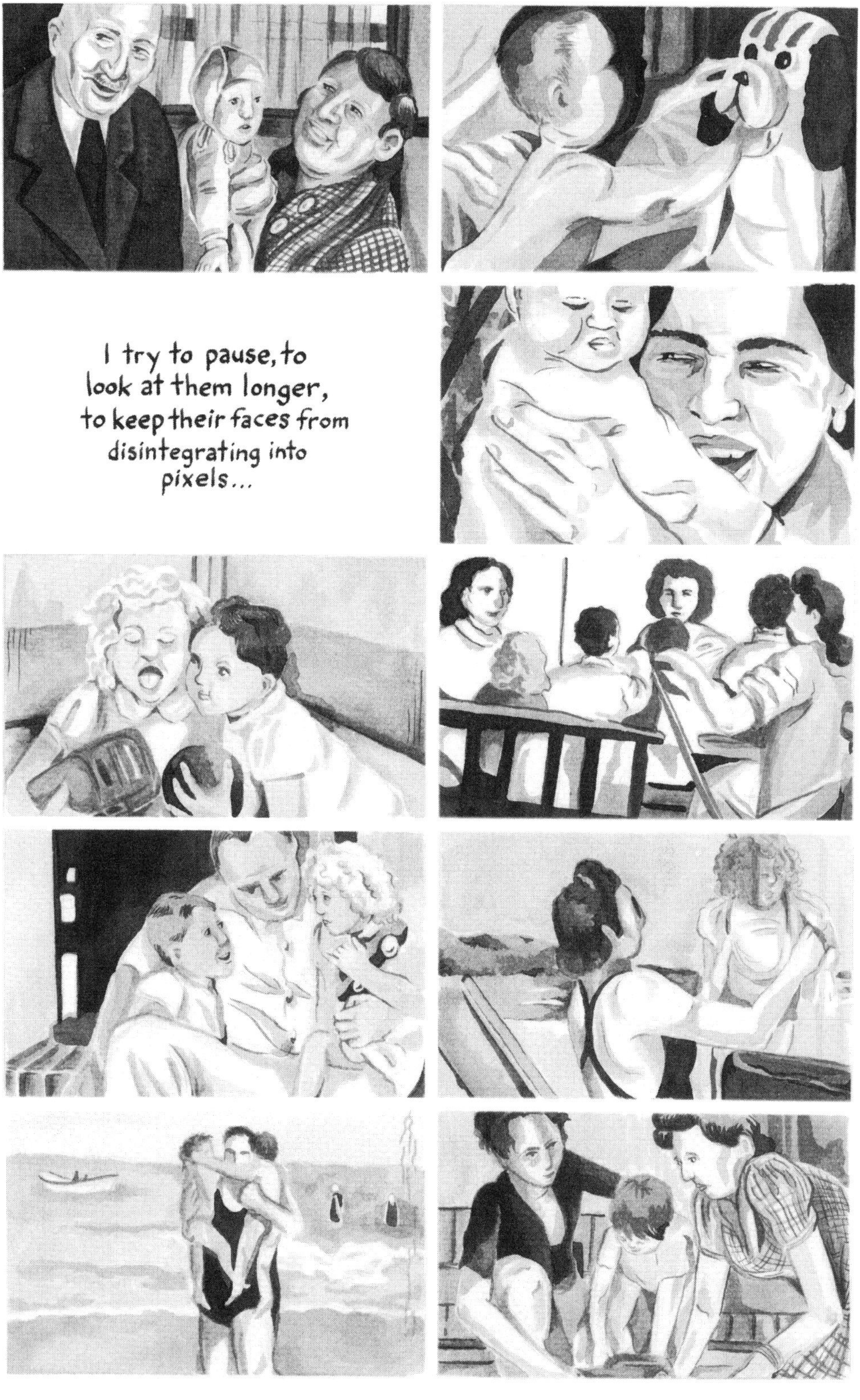
I try to pause, to look at them longer, to keep their faces from disintegrating into pixels...

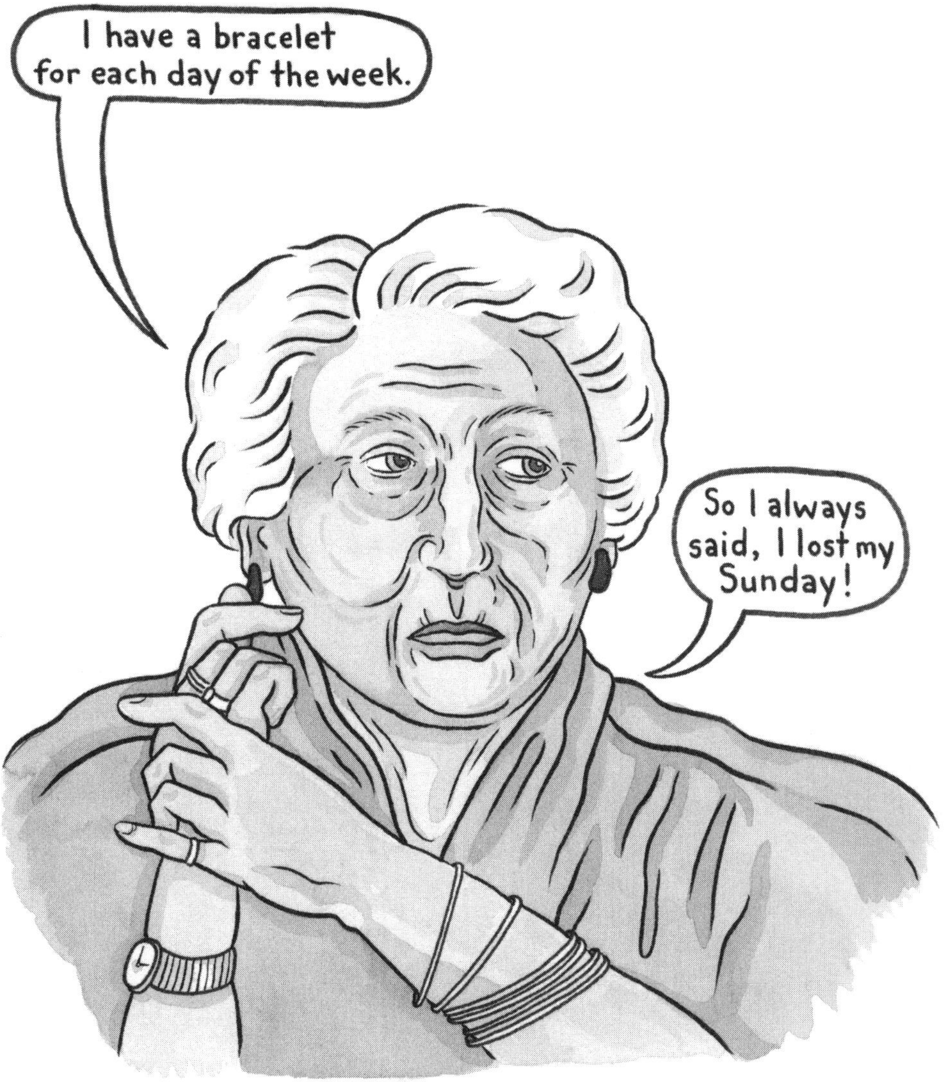
I have a bracelet for each day of the week.
So I always said, I lost my Sunday!

PART 7
LOST SUNDAY

Germany invades Belgium in May 1940. Ilse woke to the sound of bombing.

What is that?

Is that... thunder?

As the Levis prepared to go to the air-raid shelter, Ilse's brother Erich and his wife Trude showed up at their building.

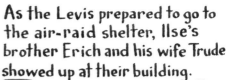

NOTICE! ALL MALE GERMAN CITIZENS UND THE AGE O MUST REPO

There are notices posted everywhere — all German men under 60 must report to the Belgian police!

It's a good thing Hitler expatriated you, Erich! Since you're stateless, you won't have to register. And Dad's almost 60, he'll be left alone...

I'm not sure.

I'll leave Trude with you, it will be safer for her here.

Ilse, whatever you do, don't leave Trude alone.

I won't!

But you're just going to the station to register, right? You'll be back before the baby comes, certainly!

"We sat like frightened birds in a cage, each one busy with their own worries."

We have to leave Antwerp. But not without my brother!

As soon as Erich comes home.

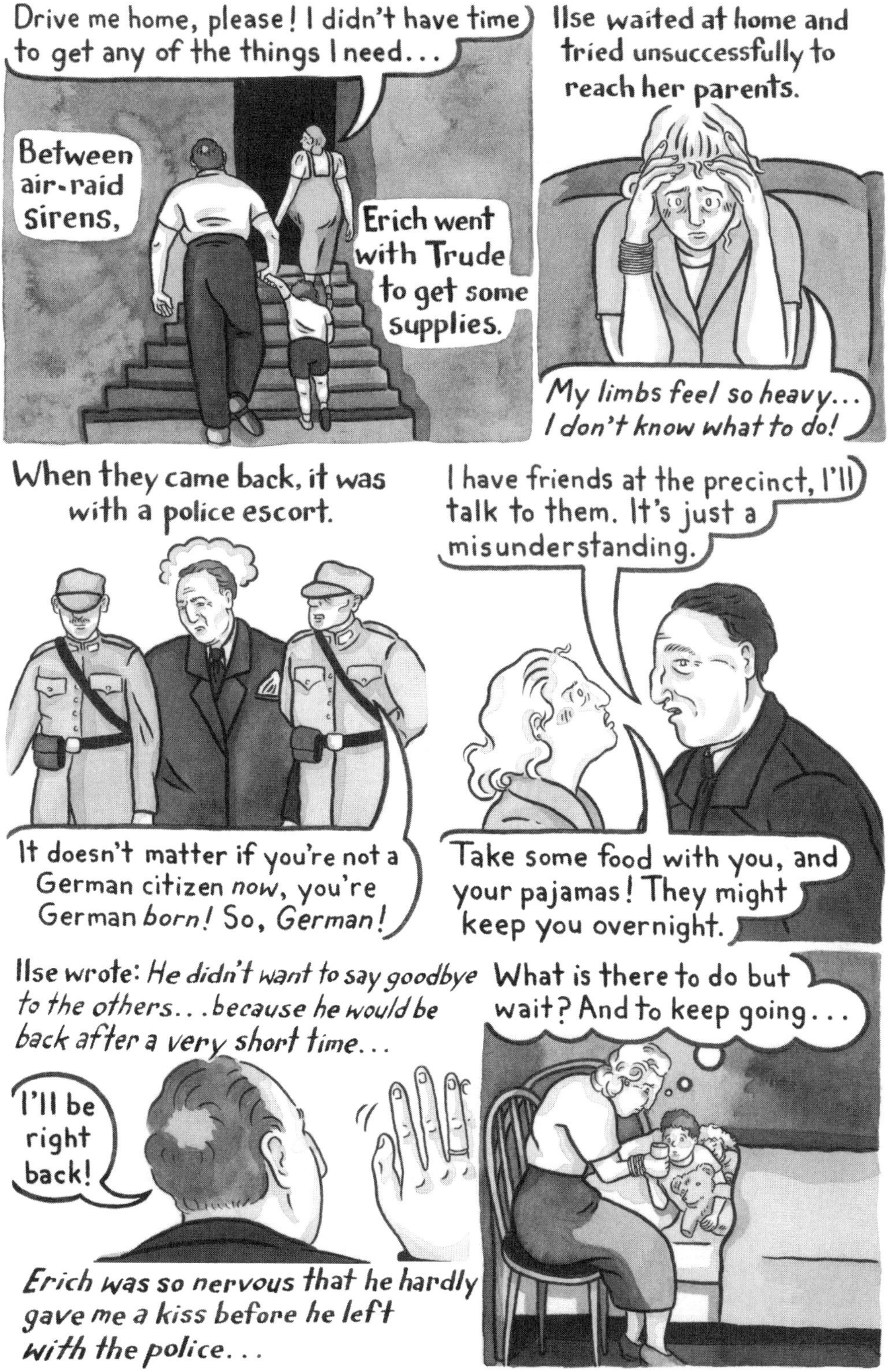
Drive me home, please! I didn't have time to get any of the things I need...
Between air-raid sirens,
Erich went with Trude to get some supplies.
Ilse waited at home and tried unsuccessfully to reach her parents.
My limbs feel so heavy... I don't know what to do!
When they came back, it was with a police escort.
It doesn't matter if you're not a German citizen *now*, you're German *born*! So, *German*!
I have friends at the precinct, I'll talk to them. It's just a misunderstanding.
Take some food with you, and your pajamas! They might keep you overnight.
Ilse wrote: *He didn't want to say goodbye to the others...because he would be back after a very short time...*
I'll be right back!
Erich was so nervous that he hardly gave me a kiss before he left with the police...
What is there to do but wait? And to keep going...

Very late the following night, there was a knock at the door.

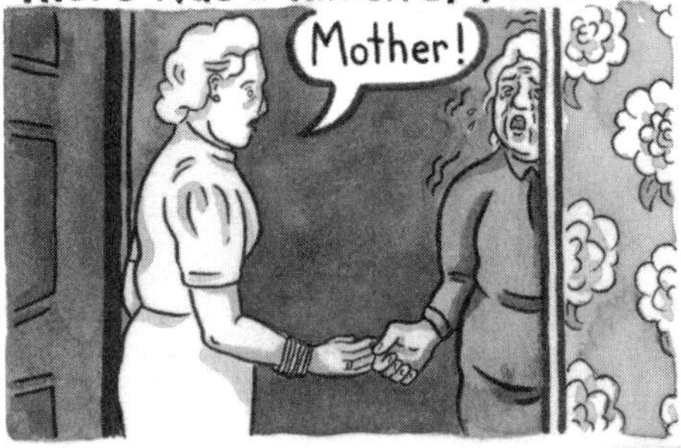
Mother!

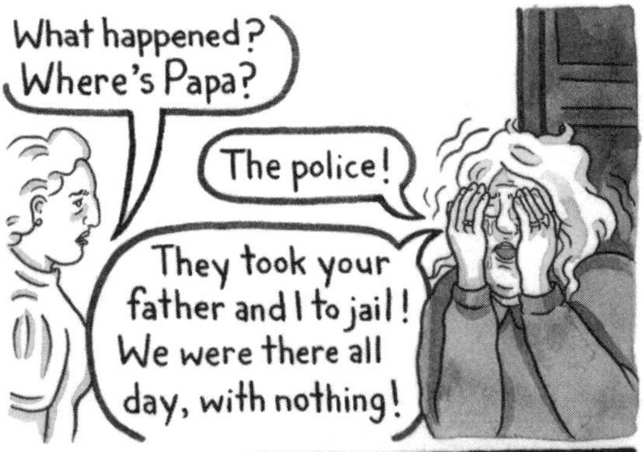
What happened? Where's Papa?
The police!
They took your father and I to jail! We were there all day, with nothing!

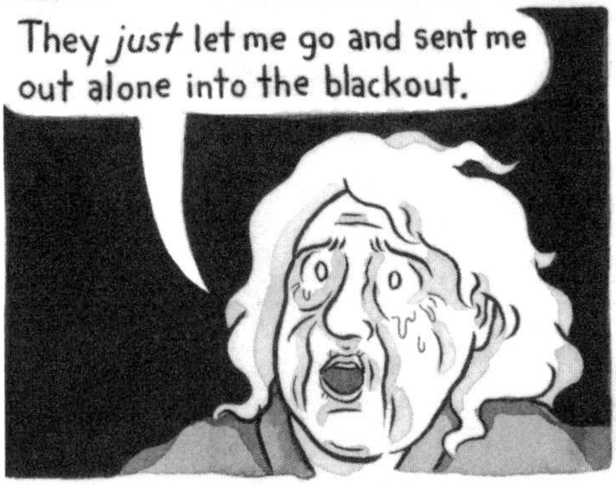
They *just* let me go and sent me out alone into the blackout.

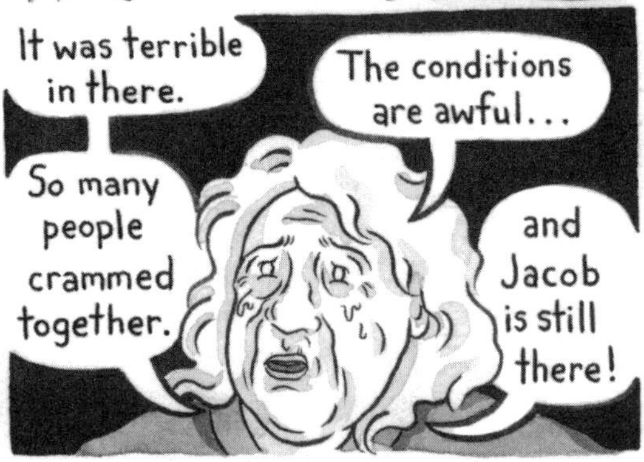
It was terrible in there.
So many people crammed together.
The conditions are awful...
and Jacob is still there!

"Neither my father, brother, brother-in-law, nor my husband returned after they went to register.

...I joined hundreds of women waiting outside the police station. The police did not provide us with any information..."

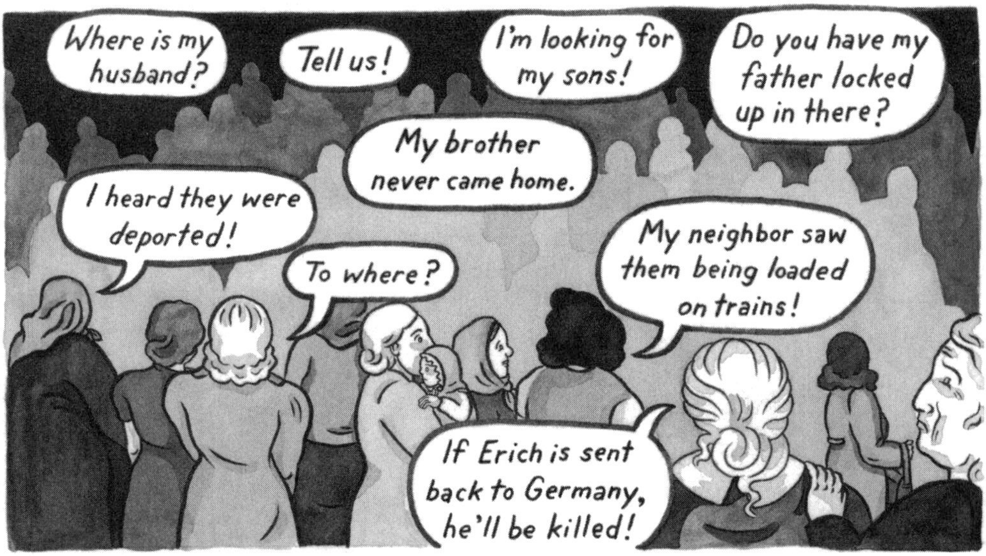
Where is my husband?
Tell us!
I'm looking for my sons!
Do you have my father locked up in there?
My brother never came home.
I heard they were deported!
To where?
My neighbor saw them being loaded on trains!
If Erich is sent back to Germany, he'll be killed!

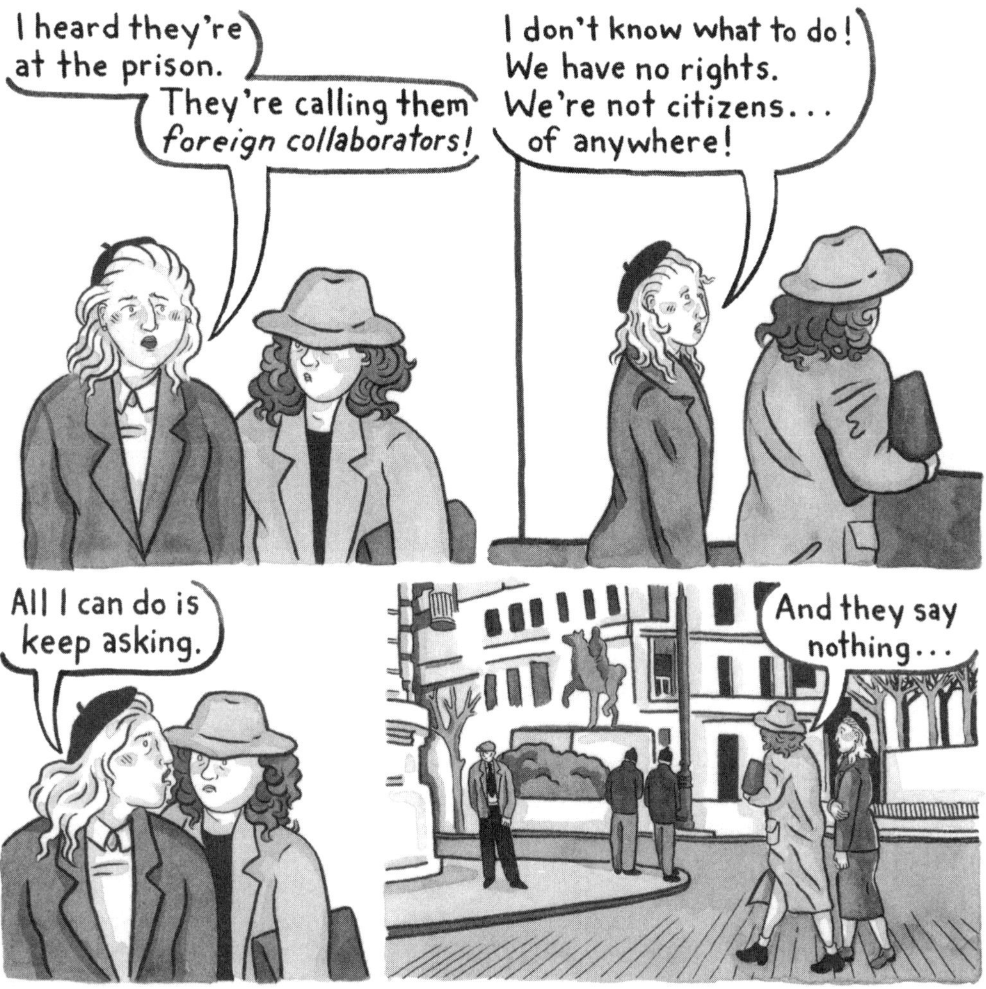
I heard they're at the prison.
They're calling them *foreign collaborators!*
I don't know what to do! We have no rights. We're not citizens... of anywhere!
All I can do is keep asking.
And they say nothing...

As the fighting escalated, Ilse, Trude, and Lina were distracted from their missing husbands by the more immediate threat of air raids and invasion.

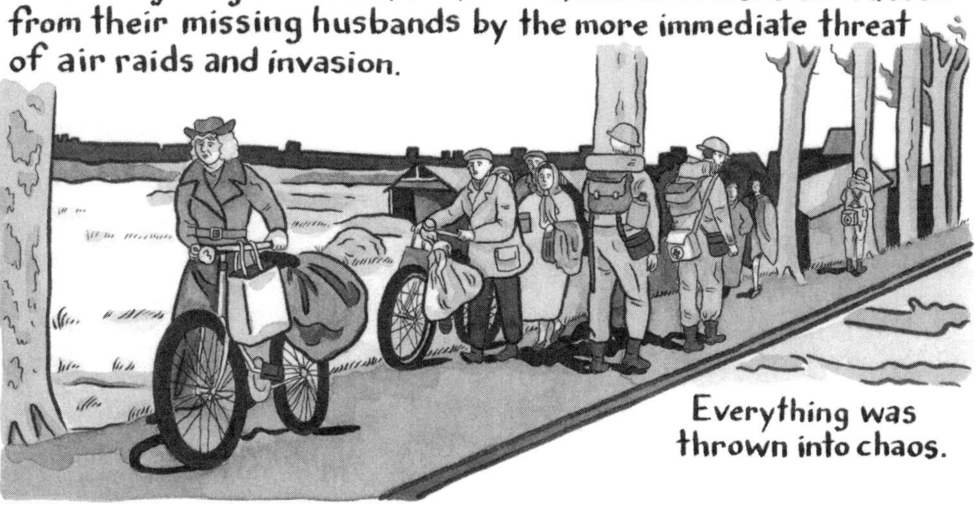
Everything was thrown into chaos.

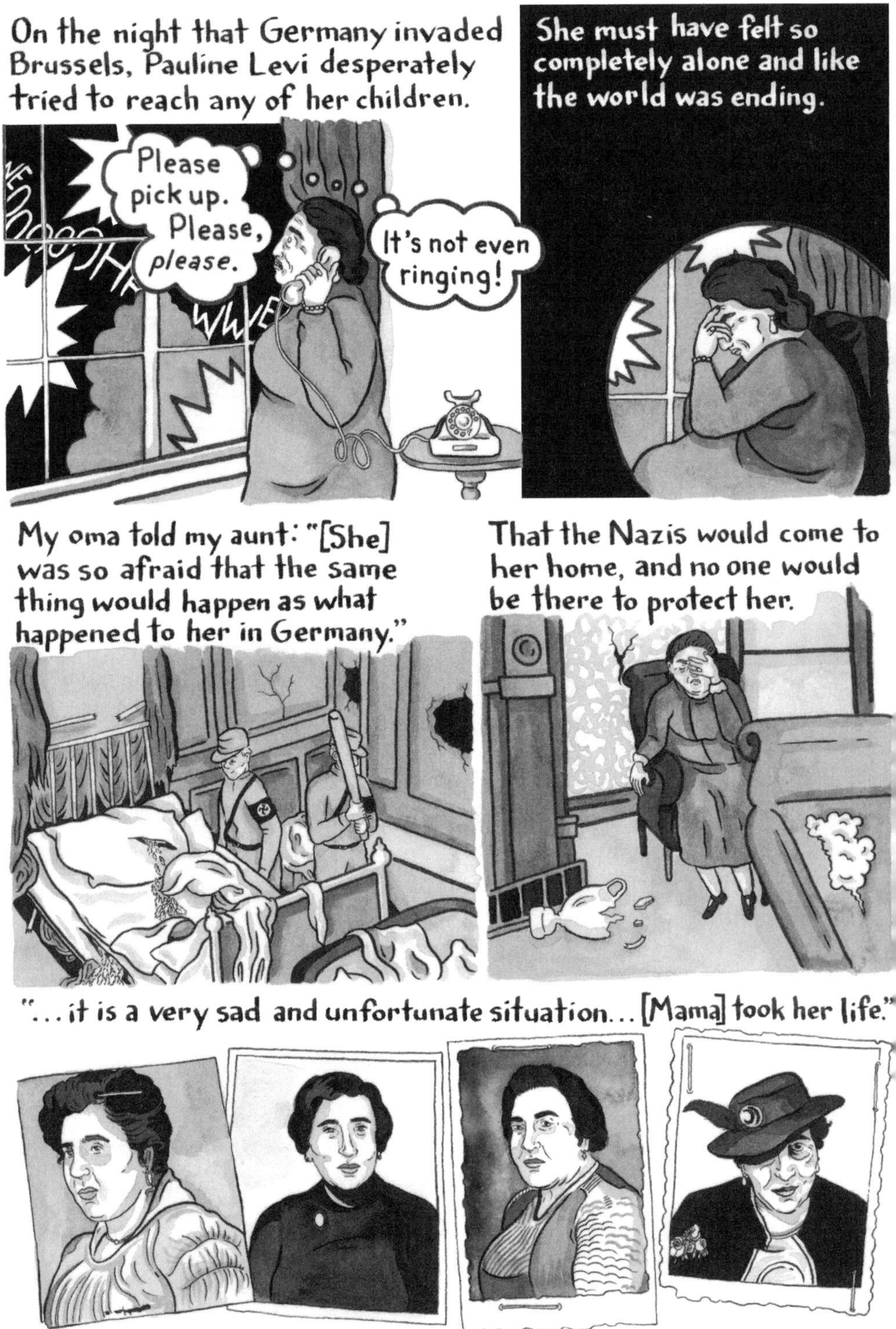
On the night that Germany invaded Brussels, Pauline Levi desperately tried to reach any of her children.
Please pick up. Please, *please*.
It's not even ringing!
She must have felt so completely alone and like the world was ending.
My oma told my aunt: "[She] was so afraid that the same thing would happen as what happened to her in Germany."
That the Nazis would come to her home, and no one would be there to protect her.
"... it is a very sad and unfortunate situation... [Mama] took her life."
[*Pauline Cohen Levi's Belgian visa photos*]

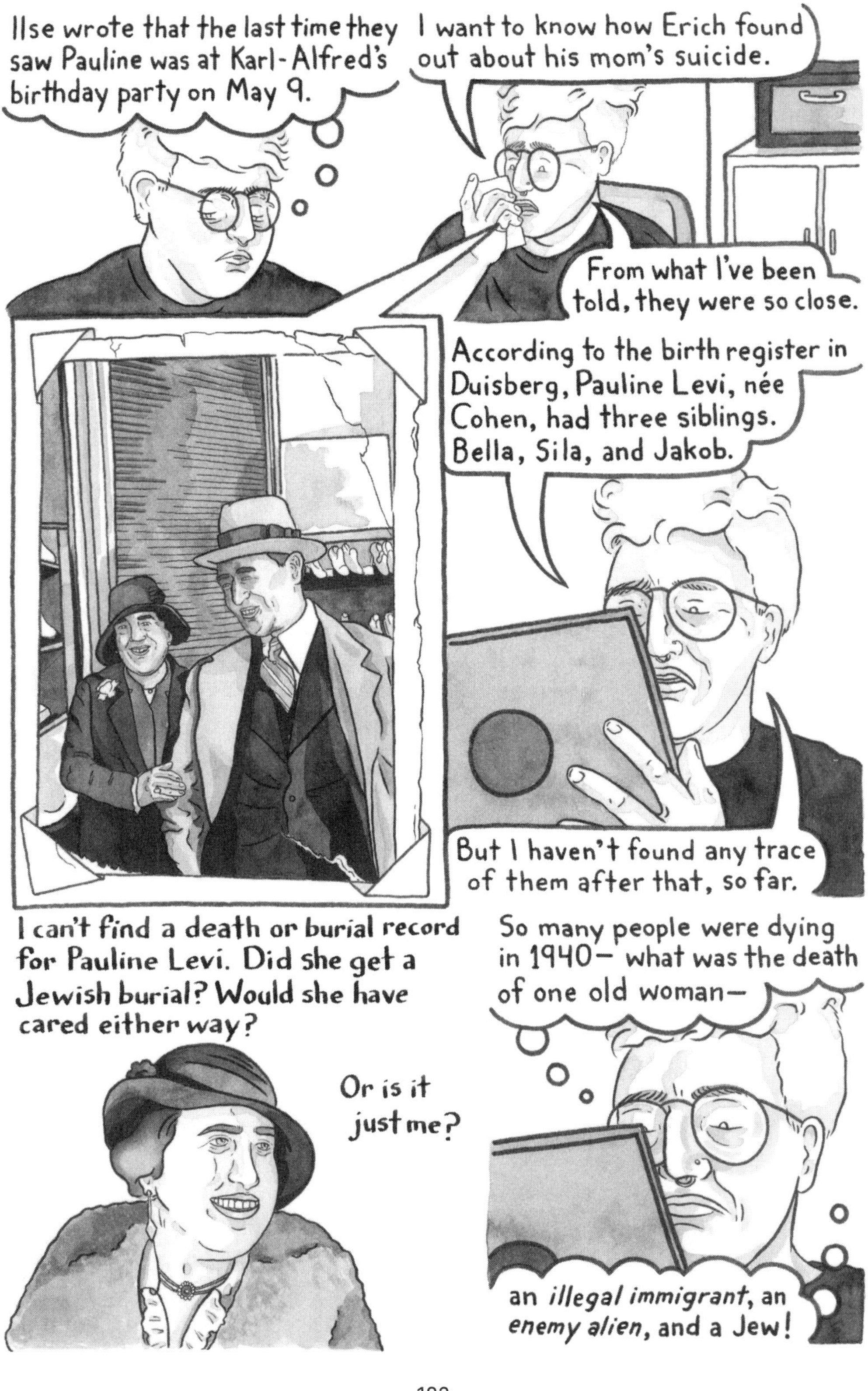

Ilse wrote that the last time they saw Pauline was at Karl-Alfred's birthday party on May 9.
I want to know how Erich found out about his mom's suicide.
From what I've been told, they were so close.
According to the birth register in Duisberg, Pauline Levi, née Cohen, had three siblings. Bella, Sila, and Jakob.
But I haven't found any trace of them after that, so far.
I can't find a death or burial record for Pauline Levi. Did she get a Jewish burial? Would she have cared either way?
Or is it just me?
So many people were dying in 1940— what was the death of one old woman—
an *illegal immigrant*, an *enemy alien*, and a Jew!

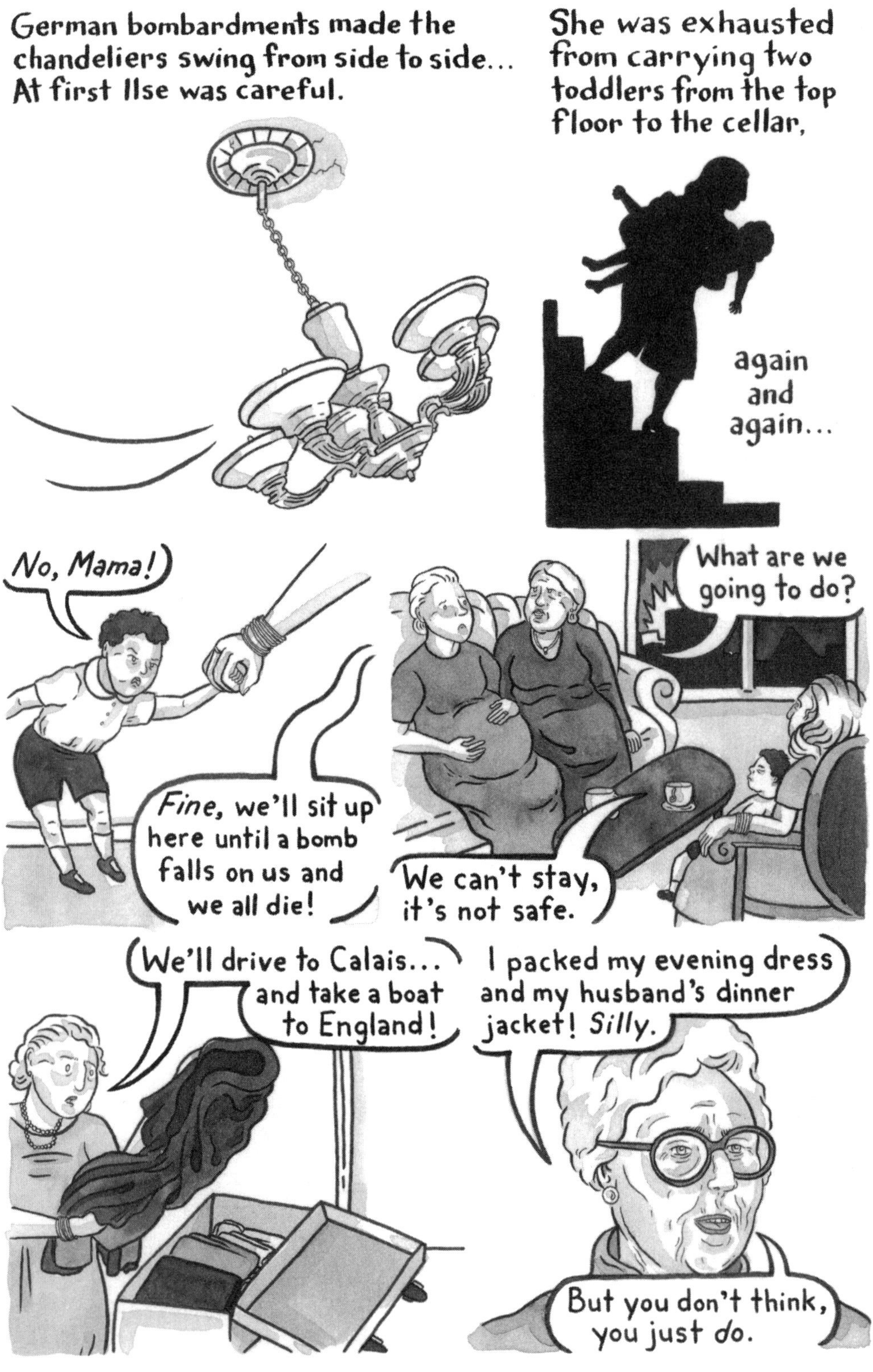
German bombardments made the chandeliers swing from side to side... At first Ilse was careful.
She was exhausted from carrying two toddlers from the top floor to the cellar,
again and again...
No, Mama!
Fine, we'll sit up here until a bomb falls on us and we all die!
What are we going to do?
We can't stay, it's not safe.
We'll drive to Calais... and take a boat to England!
I packed my evening dress and my husband's dinner jacket! *Silly*.
But you don't think, you just *do*.

They loaded Erich Kahn's car with everything they needed for Ilse's sister-in-law Trude's baby.

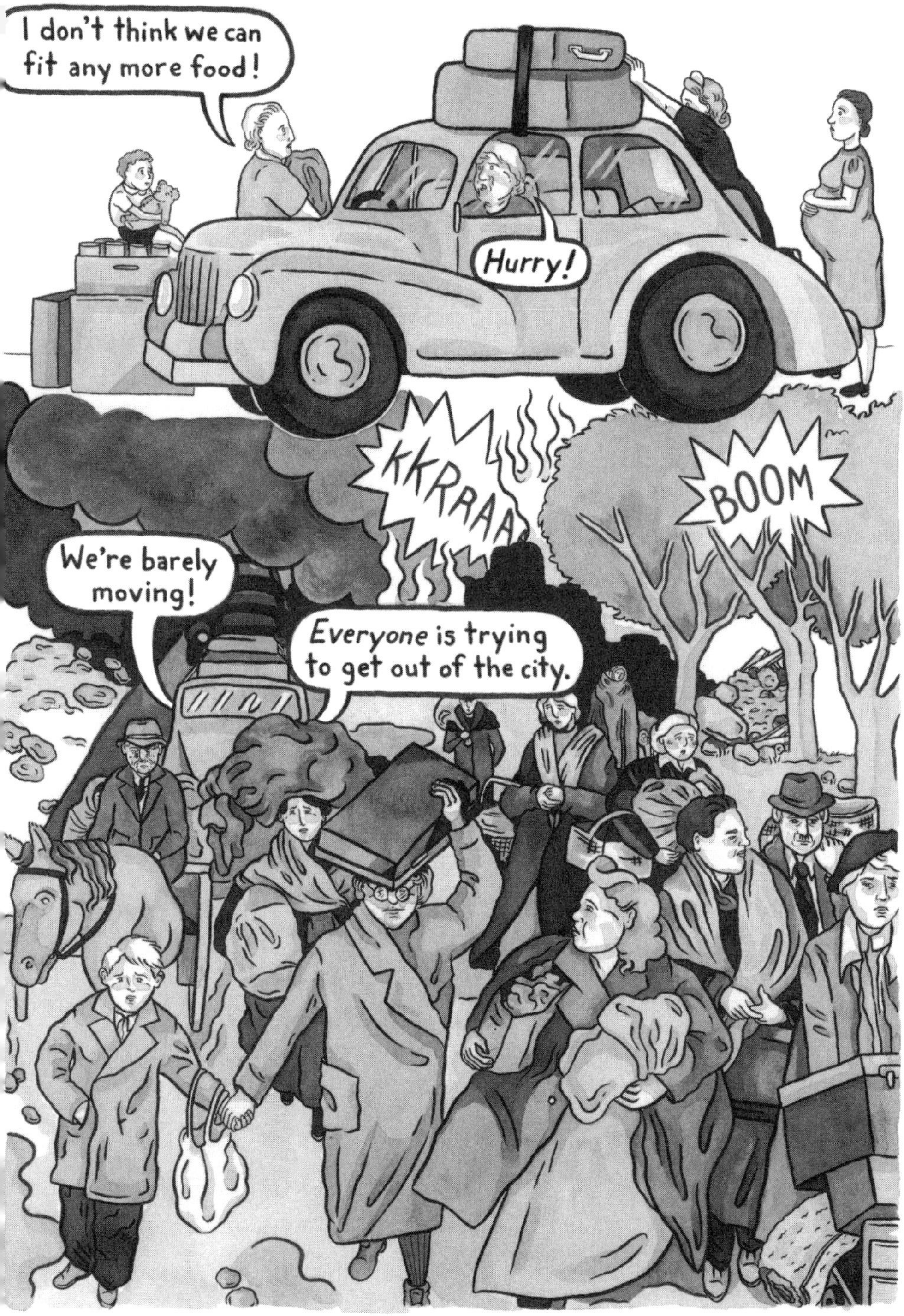
I don't think we can fit any more food!
Hurry!
KKRRAAA
BOOM
We're barely moving!
Everyone is trying to get out of the city.

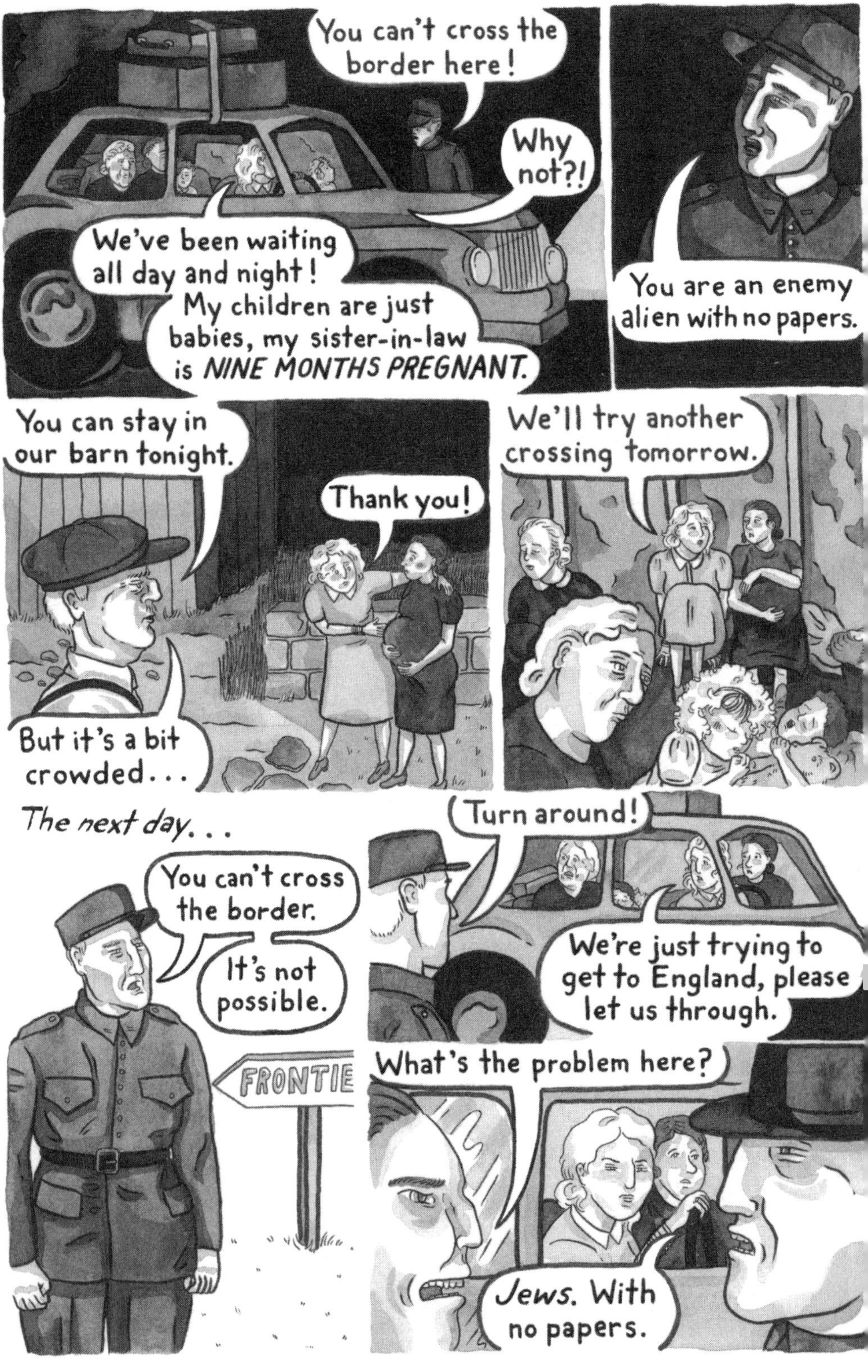
You can't cross the border here!
Why not?!
We've been waiting all day and night! My children are just babies, my sister-in-law is NINE MONTHS PREGNANT.
You are an enemy alien with no papers.
You can stay in our barn tonight.
But it's a bit crowded...
Thank you!
We'll try another crossing tomorrow.
The next day...
You can't cross the border.
It's not possible.
FRONTIE
Turn around!
We're just trying to get to England, please let us through.
What's the problem here?
Jews. With no papers.

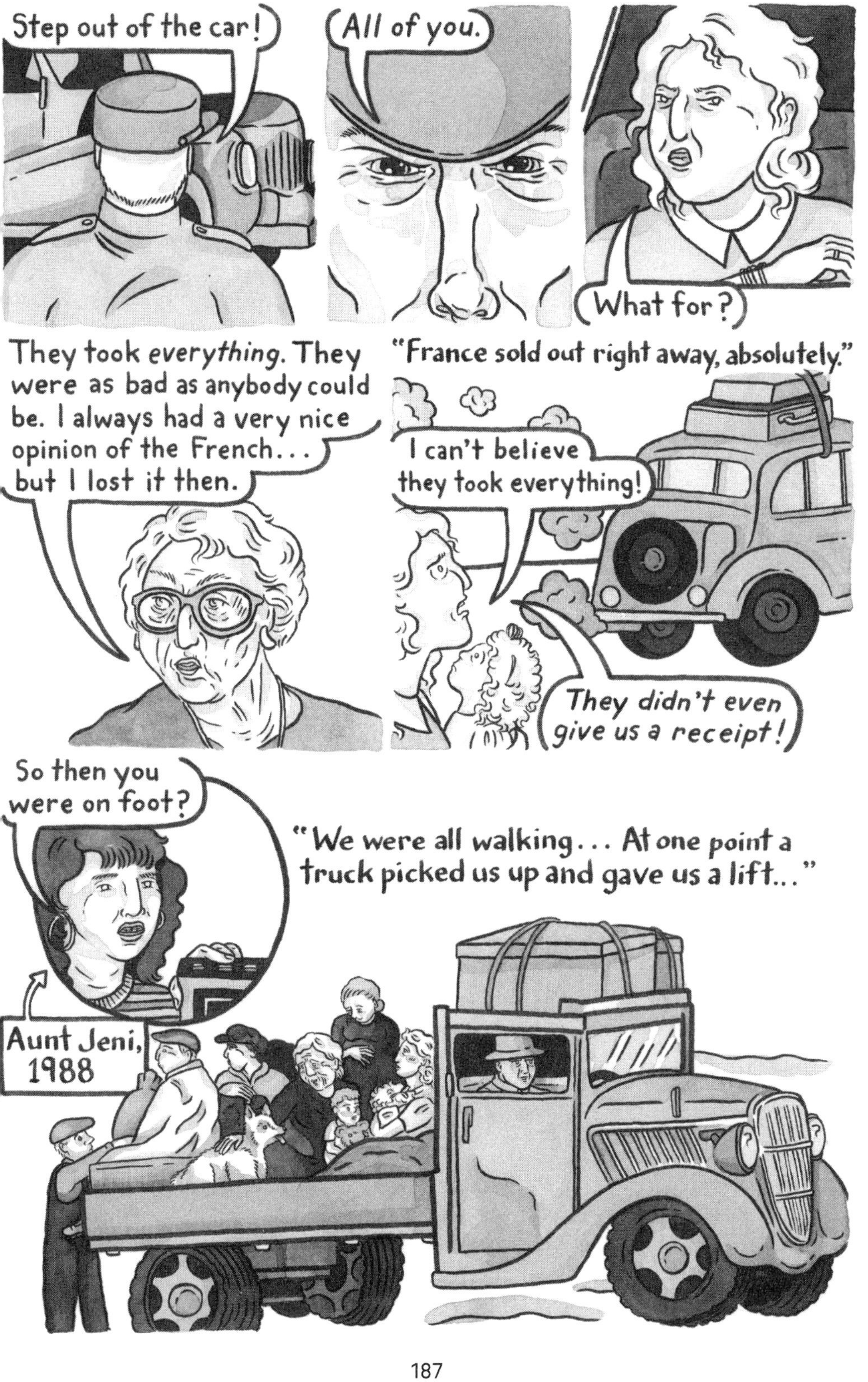
Step out of the car!
All of you.
What for?
They took *everything*. They were as bad as anybody could be. I always had a very nice opinion of the French... but I lost it then.
"France sold out right away, absolutely."
I can't believe they took everything!
They didn't even give us a receipt!
So then you were on foot?
Aunt Jeni, 1988
"We were all walking... At one point a truck picked us up and gave us a lift..."

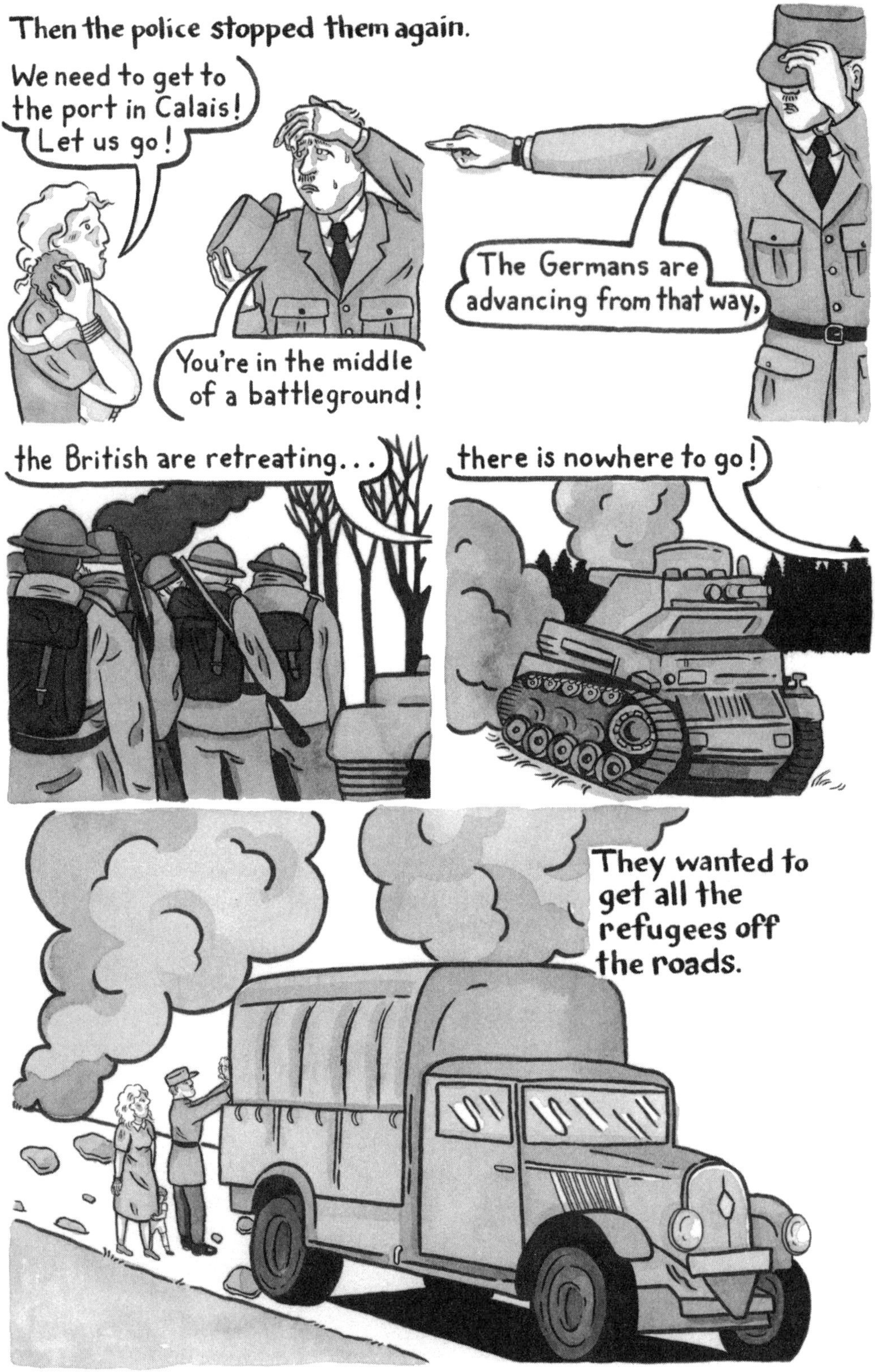
Then the police stopped them again.
We need to get to the port in Calais! Let us go!
You're in the middle of a battleground!
The Germans are advancing from that way,
the British are retreating...
there is nowhere to go!
They wanted to get all the refugees off the roads.

Ilse said: "They took us to a place which was a holding camp in a place called Ambleteuse."
"There were only women and children and gypsies."

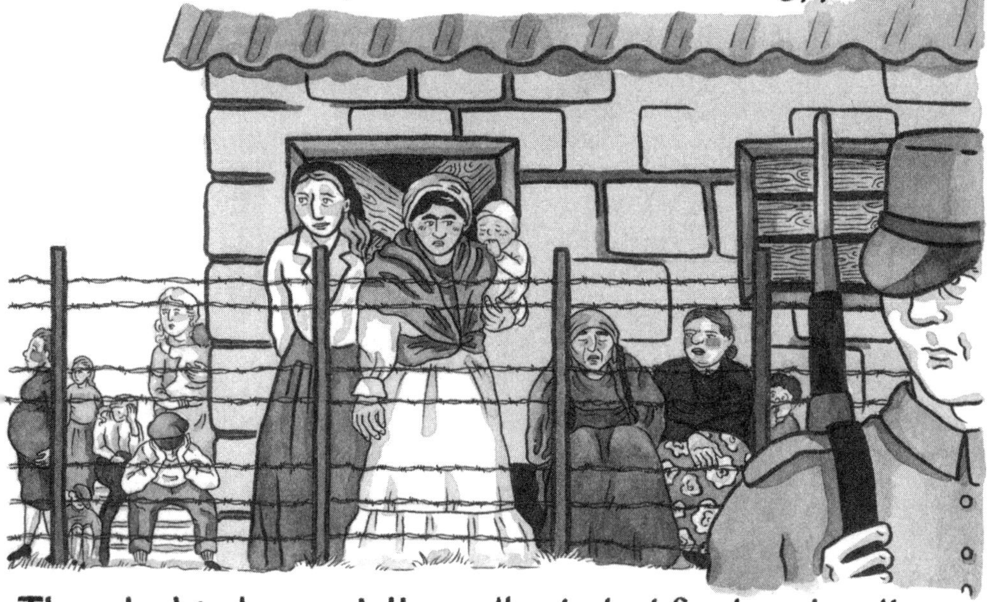

They slept in horse stalls.

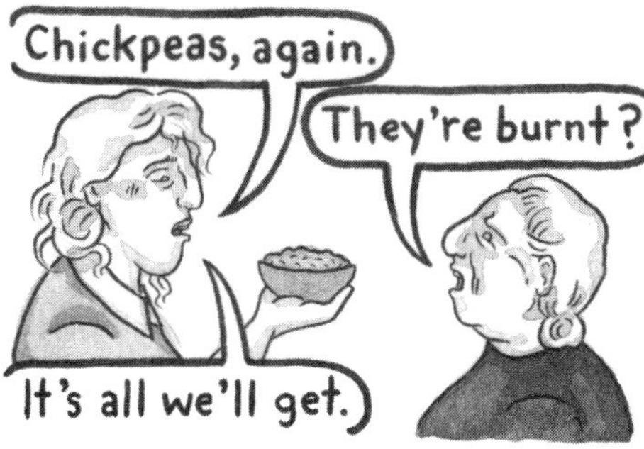
Chickpeas, again.
They're burnt?
It's all we'll get.

Ilse looked for bread on the ground and in the trash.

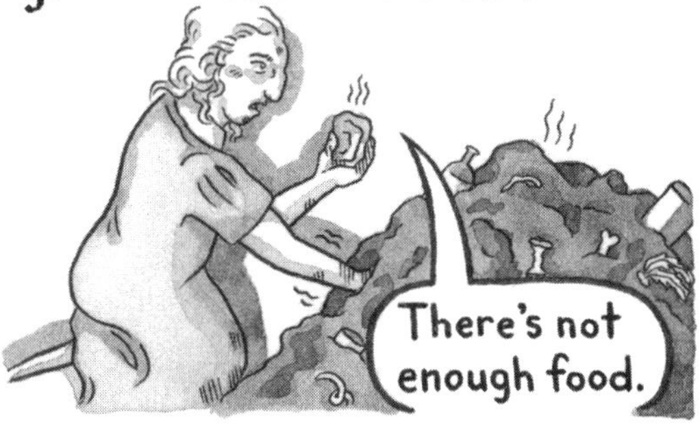
There's not enough food.

Ilse says they were not . . . mistreated . . . but . . .

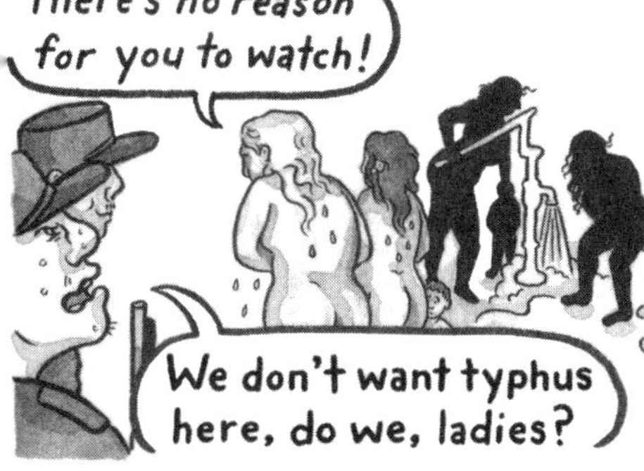
There's no reason for you to watch!
We don't want typhus here, do we, ladies?

Gaby got very ill at the camp, but they wouldn't do anything about it.

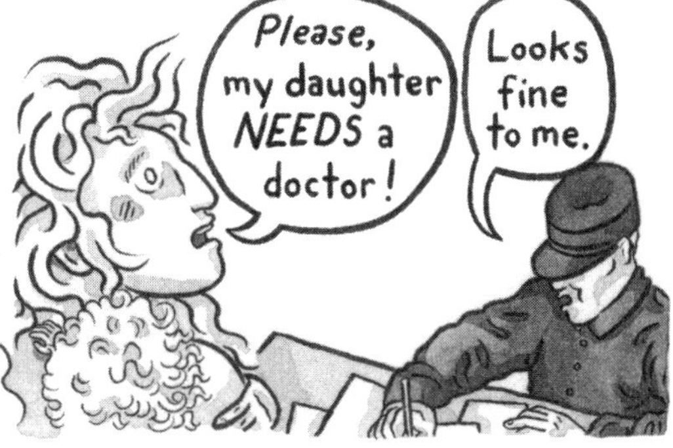
Please, my daughter *NEEDS* a doctor!
Looks fine to me.

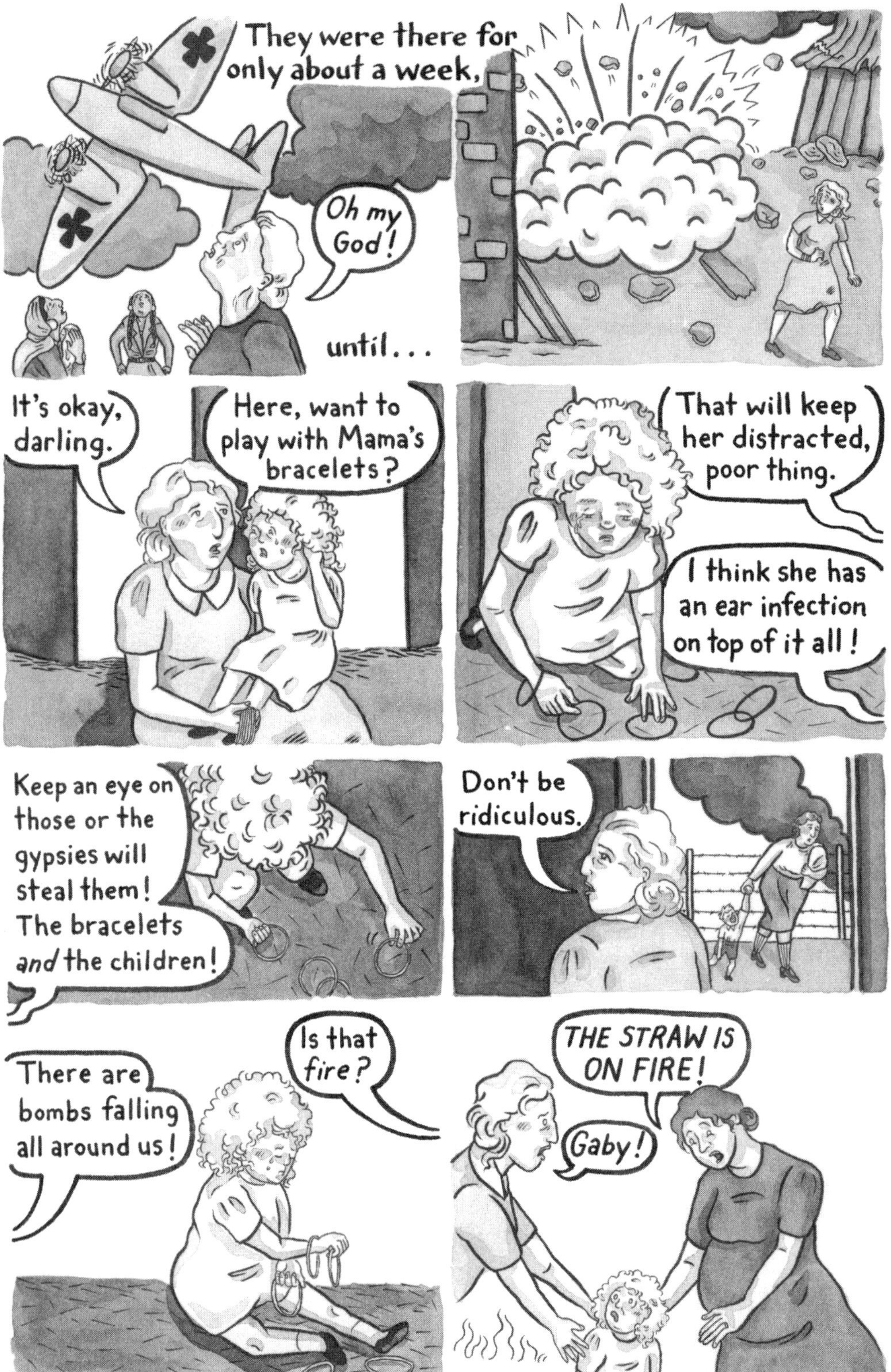
They were there for only about a week,
Oh my God!
until...
It's okay, darling.
Here, want to play with Mama's bracelets?
That will keep her distracted, poor thing.
I think she has an ear infection on top of it all!
Keep an eye on those or the gypsies will steal them! The bracelets *and* the children!
Don't be ridiculous.
There are bombs falling all around us!
Is that fire?
THE STRAW IS ON FIRE!
Gaby!

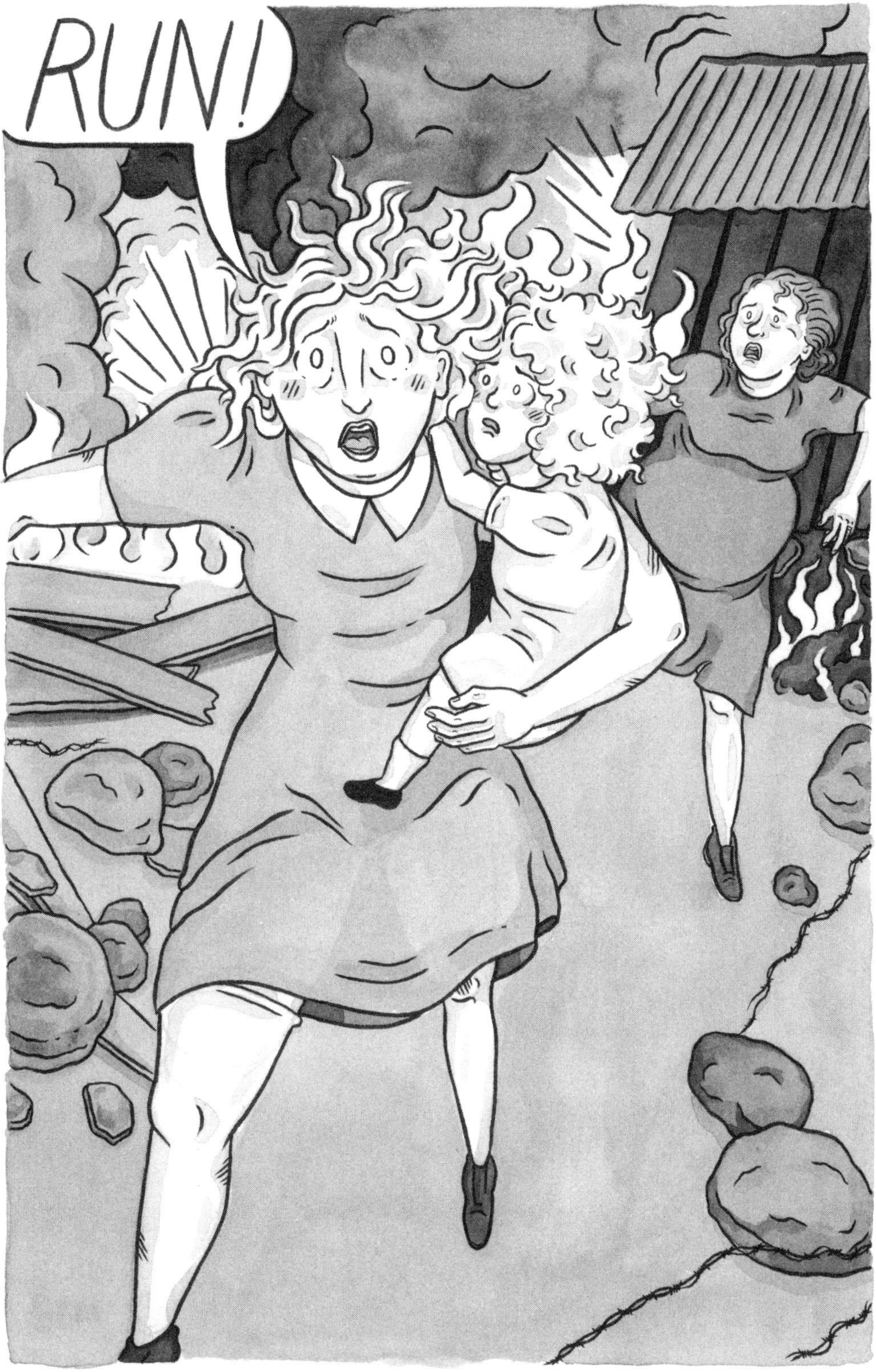
RUN!

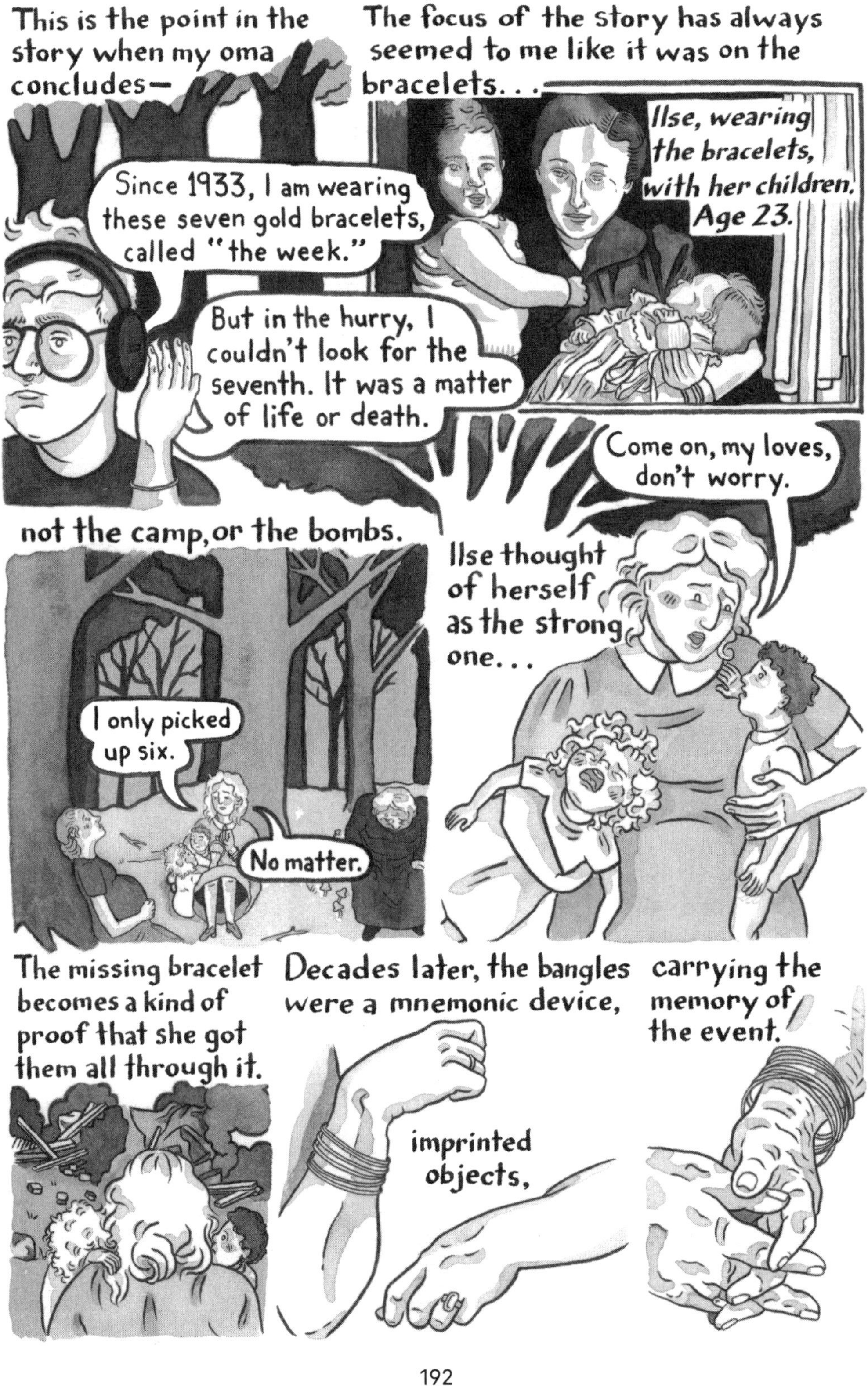

This is the point in the story when my oma concludes—
Since 1933, I am wearing these seven gold bracelets, called "the week."
But in the hurry, I couldn't look for the seventh. It was a matter of life or death.
The focus of the story has always seemed to me like it was on the bracelets. . .
Ilse, wearing the bracelets, with her children. Age 23.
not the camp, or the bombs.
I only picked up six.
No matter.
Ilse thought of herself as the strong one. . .
Come on, my loves, don't worry.
The missing bracelet becomes a kind of proof that she got them all through it.
Decades later, the bangles were a mnemonic device,
imprinted objects,
carrying the memory of the event.

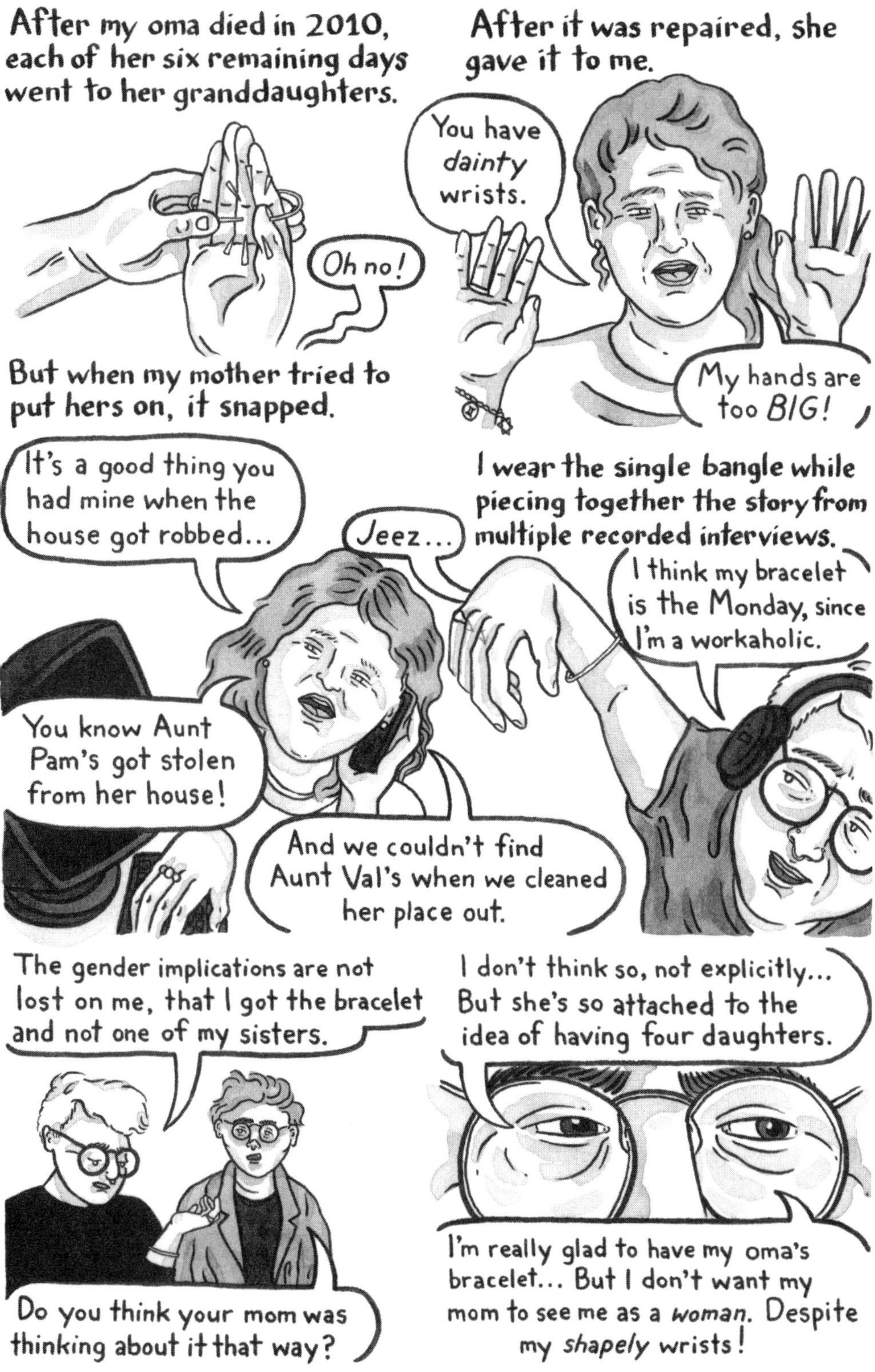
After my oma died in 2010, each of her six remaining days went to her granddaughters.
Oh no!
But when my mother tried to put hers on, it snapped.
After it was repaired, she gave it to me.
You have *dainty* wrists.
My hands are too *BIG*!
It's a good thing you had mine when the house got robbed...
Jeez...
I wear the single bangle while piecing together the story from multiple recorded interviews.
I think my bracelet is the Monday, since I'm a workaholic.
You know Aunt Pam's got stolen from her house!
And we couldn't find Aunt Val's when we cleaned her place out.
The gender implications are not lost on me, that I got the bracelet and not one of my sisters.
Do you think your mom was thinking about it that way?
I don't think so, not explicitly... But she's so attached to the idea of having four daughters.
I'm really glad to have my oma's bracelet... But I don't want my mom to see me as a *woman*. Despite my *shapely* wrists!

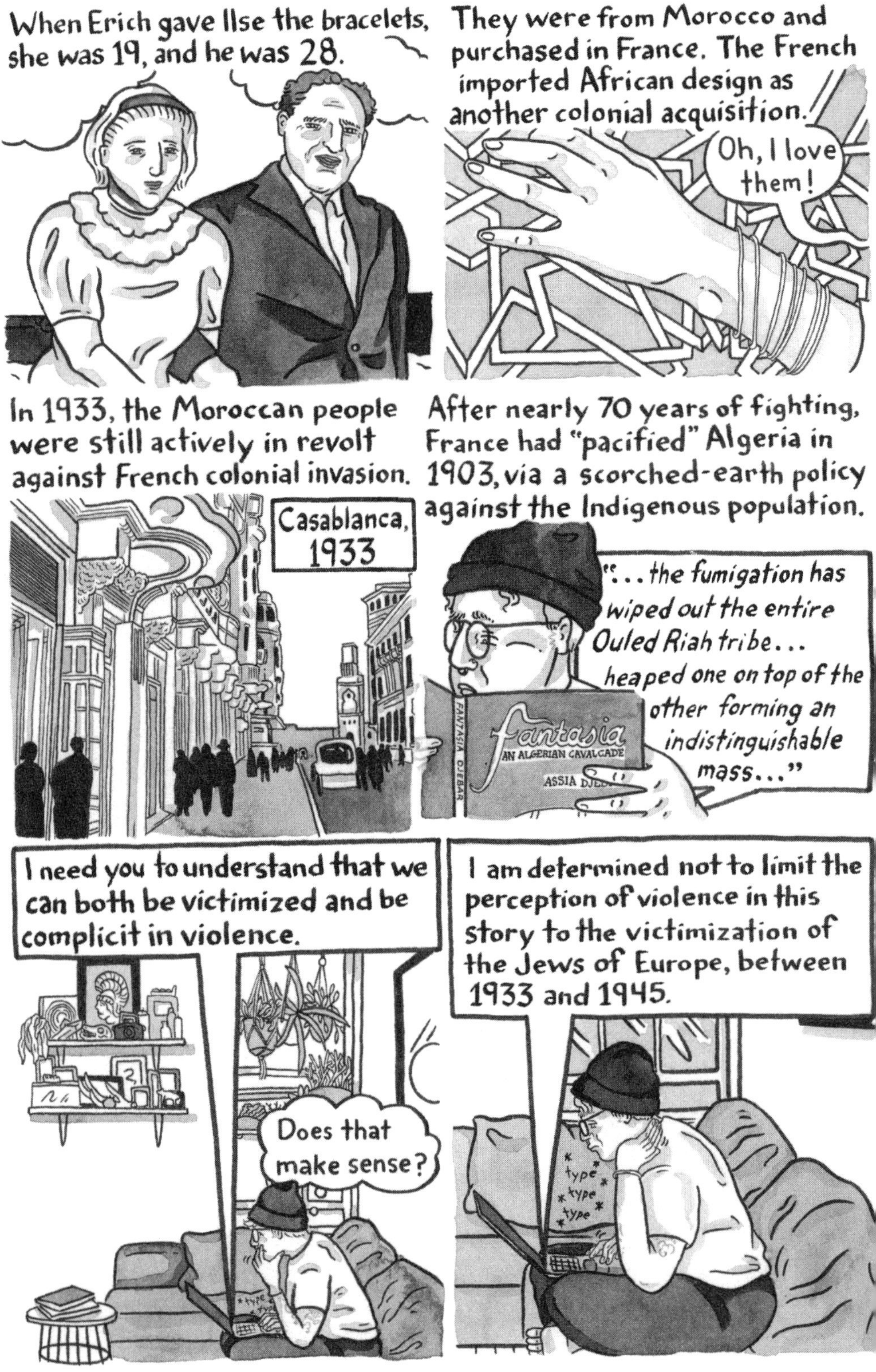
When Erich gave Ilse the bracelets, she was 19, and he was 28.
They were from Morocco and purchased in France. The French imported African design as another colonial acquisition.
Oh, I love them!
In 1933, the Moroccan people were still actively in revolt against French colonial invasion.
Casablanca, 1933
After nearly 70 years of fighting, France had "pacified" Algeria in 1903, via a scorched-earth policy against the Indigenous population.
"...the fumigation has wiped out the entire Ouled Riah tribe... heaped one on top of the other forming an indistinguishable mass..."
Fantasia
AN ALGERIAN CAVALCADE
FANTASIA DJEBAR
I need you to understand that we can both be victimized and be complicit in violence.
Does that make sense?
I am determined not to limit the perception of violence in this story to the victimization of the Jews of Europe, between 1933 and 1945.
type
type
type

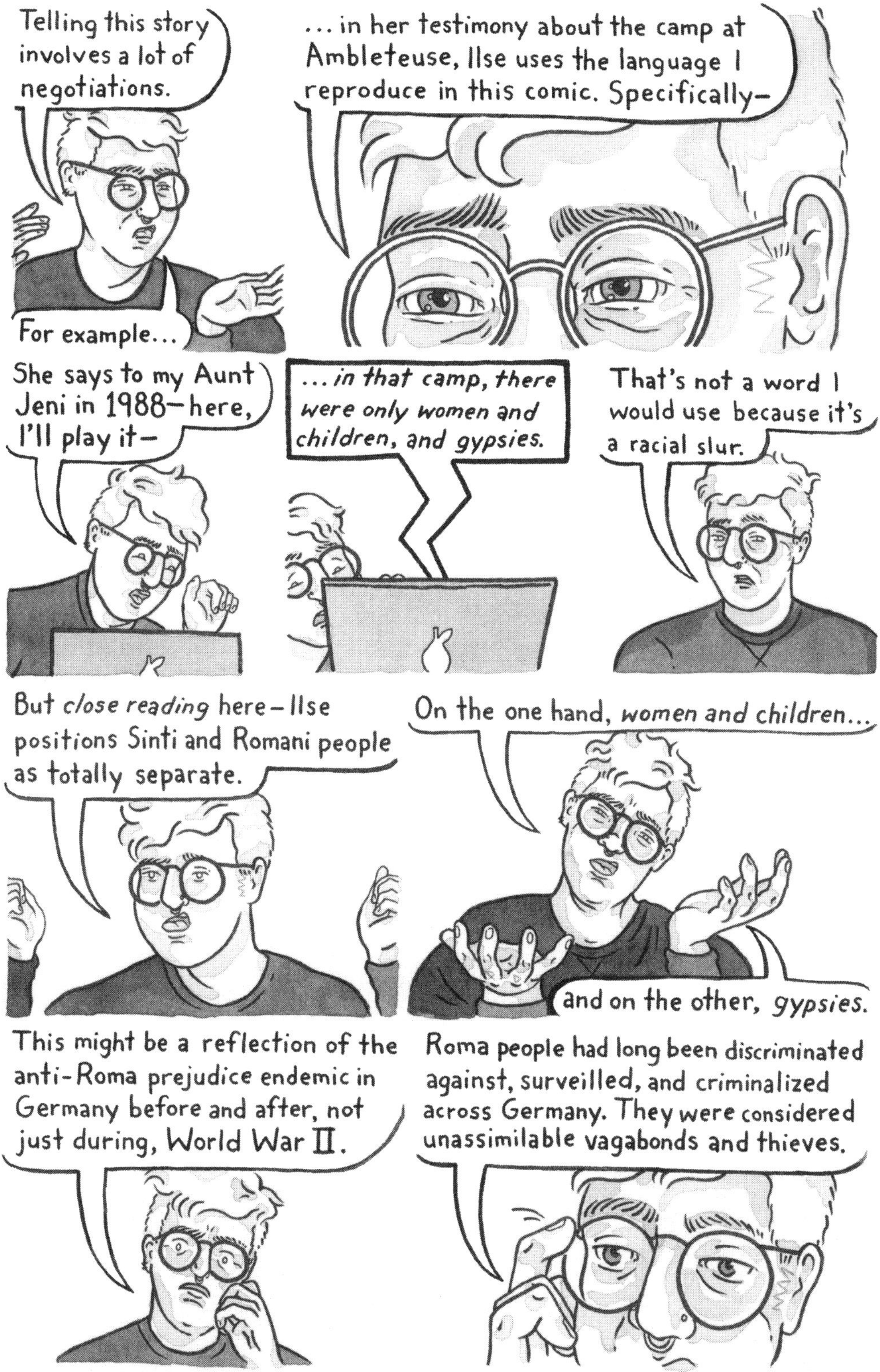
Telling this story involves a lot of negotiations.
For example...
...in her testimony about the camp at Ambleteuse, Ilse uses the language I reproduce in this comic. Specifically—
She says to my Aunt Jeni in 1988—here, I'll play it—
...in that camp, there were only women and children, and gypsies.
That's not a word I would use because it's a racial slur.
But close reading here—Ilse positions Sinti and Romani people as totally separate.
On the one hand, women and children...
and on the other, gypsies.
This might be a reflection of the anti-Roma prejudice endemic in Germany before and after, not just during, World War II.
Roma people had long been discriminated against, surveilled, and criminalized across Germany. They were considered unassimilable vagabonds and thieves.

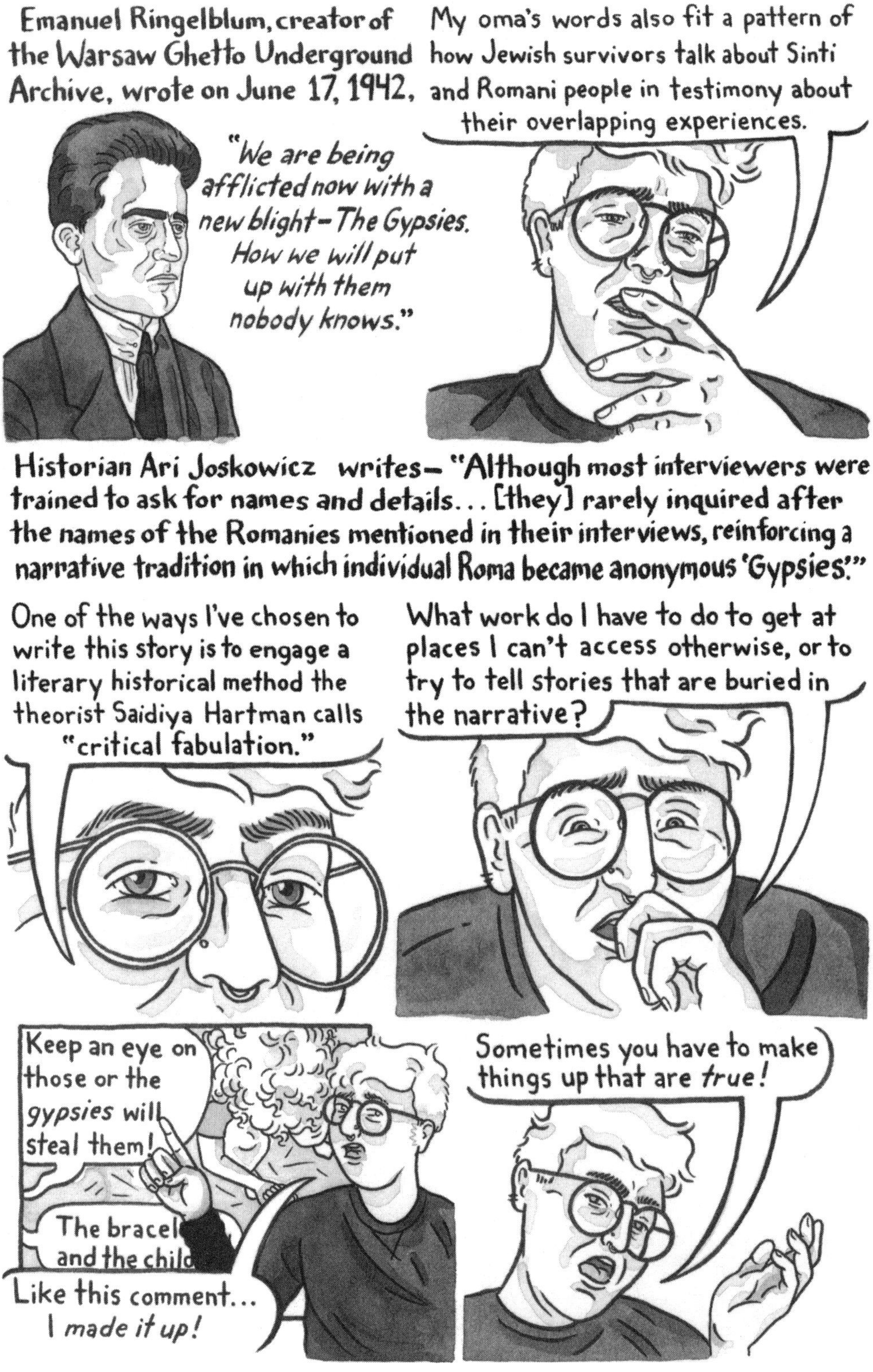
Emanuel Ringelblum, creator of the Warsaw Ghetto Underground Archive, wrote on June 17, 1942,
"We are being afflicted now with a new blight–The Gypsies. How we will put up with them nobody knows."
My oma's words also fit a pattern of how Jewish survivors talk about Sinti and Romani people in testimony about their overlapping experiences.
Historian Ari Joskowicz writes– "Although most interviewers were trained to ask for names and details... [they] rarely inquired after the names of the Romanies mentioned in their interviews, reinforcing a narrative tradition in which individual Roma became anonymous 'Gypsies.'"
One of the ways I've chosen to write this story is to engage a literary historical method the theorist Saidiya Hartman calls "critical fabulation."
What work do I have to do to get at places I can't access otherwise, or to try to tell stories that are buried in the narrative?
Keep an eye on those or the *gypsies* will steal them!
The bracel
and the chil
Like this comment... I *made it up*!
Sometimes you have to make things up that are *true*!

PART 8
ESCAPES

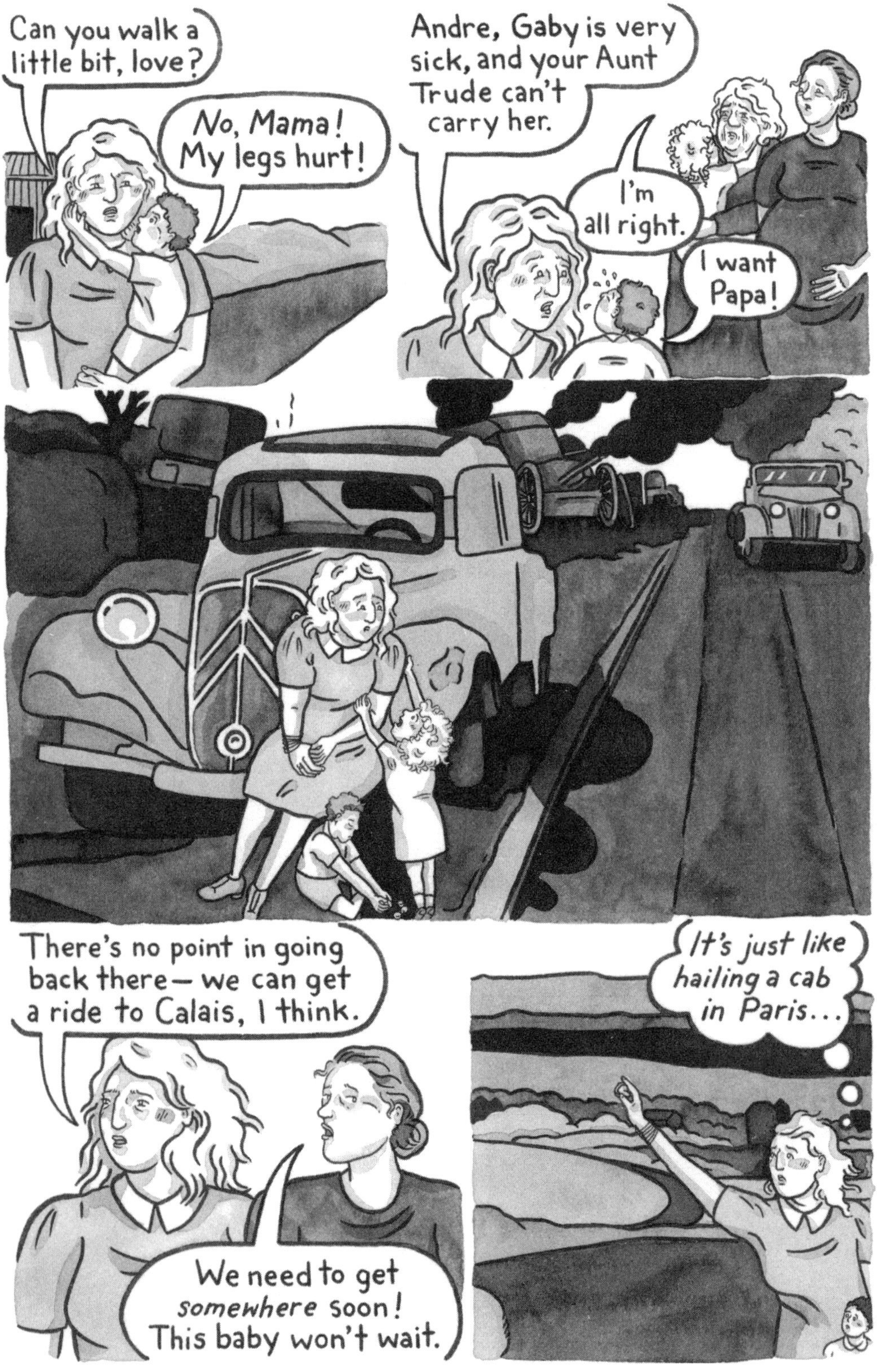
Can you walk a little bit, love?
No, Mama! My legs hurt!
Andre, Gaby is very sick, and your Aunt Trude can't carry her.
I'm all right.
I want Papa!
There's no point in going back there— we can get a ride to Calais, I think.
We need to get *somewhere* soon! This baby won't wait.
It's just like hailing a cab in Paris...

They got back on the road, hitchhiking from Ambleteuse to Calais, a city under German siege.

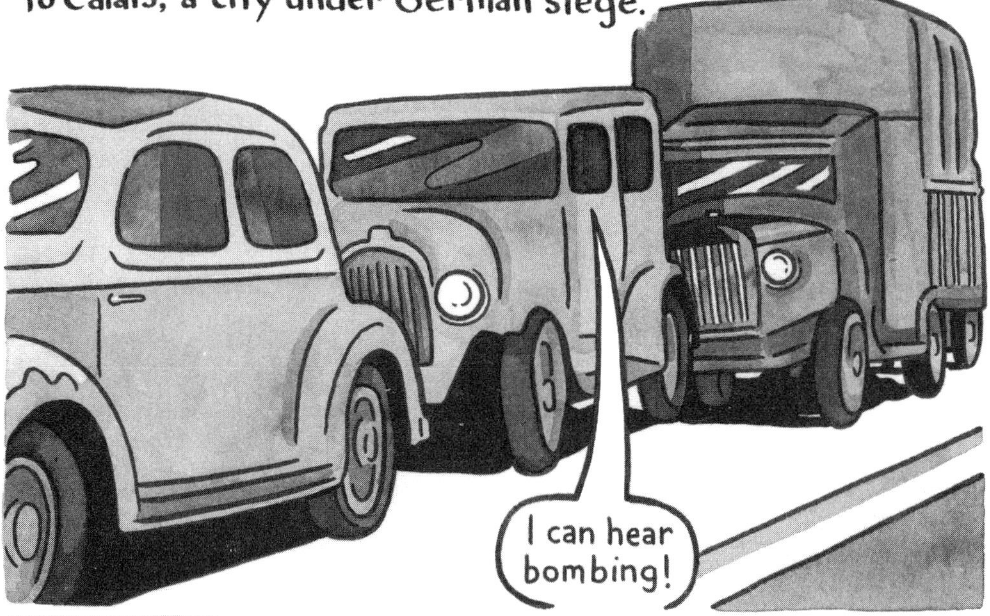
I can hear bombing!

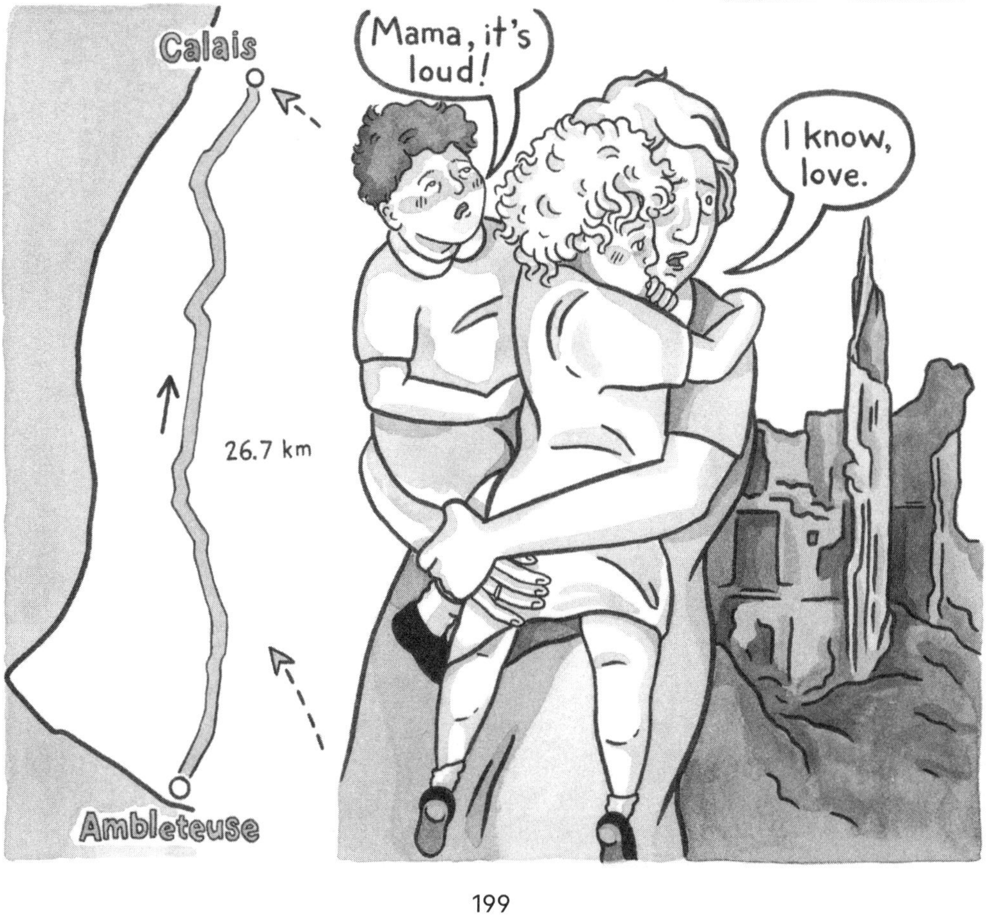
Calais
26.7 km
Ambleteuse
Mama, it's loud!
I know, love.

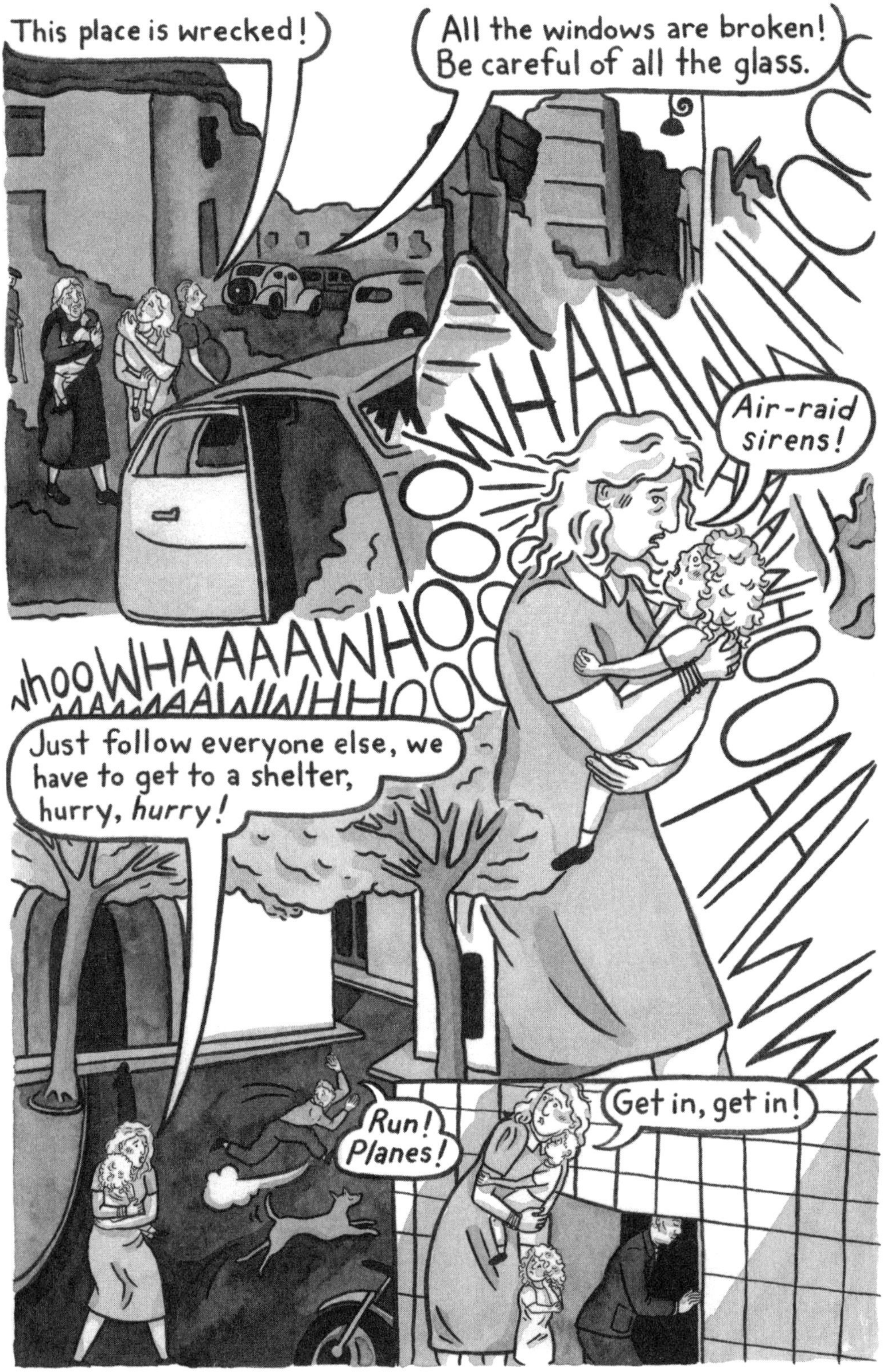
This place is wrecked!
All the windows are broken! Be careful of all the glass.
Air-raid sirens!
whooWHAAAAWHOOOO
Just follow everyone else, we have to get to a shelter, hurry, *hurry*!
Run! Planes!
Get in, get in!

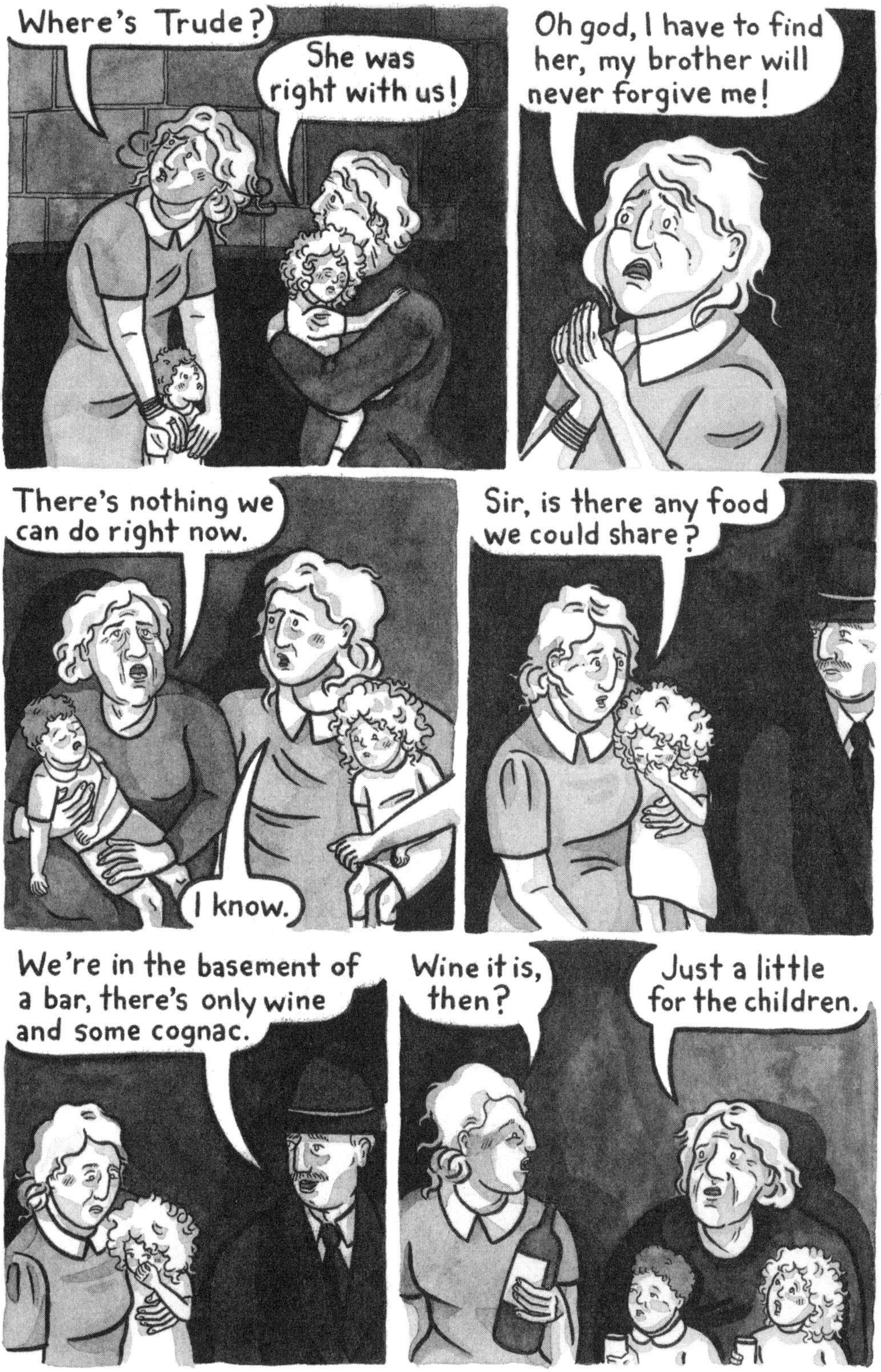
Where's Trude?
She was right with us!
Oh god, I have to find her, my brother will never forgive me!
There's nothing we can do right now.
I know.
Sir, is there any food we could share?
We're in the basement of a bar, there's only wine and some cognac.
Wine it is, then?
Just a little for the children.

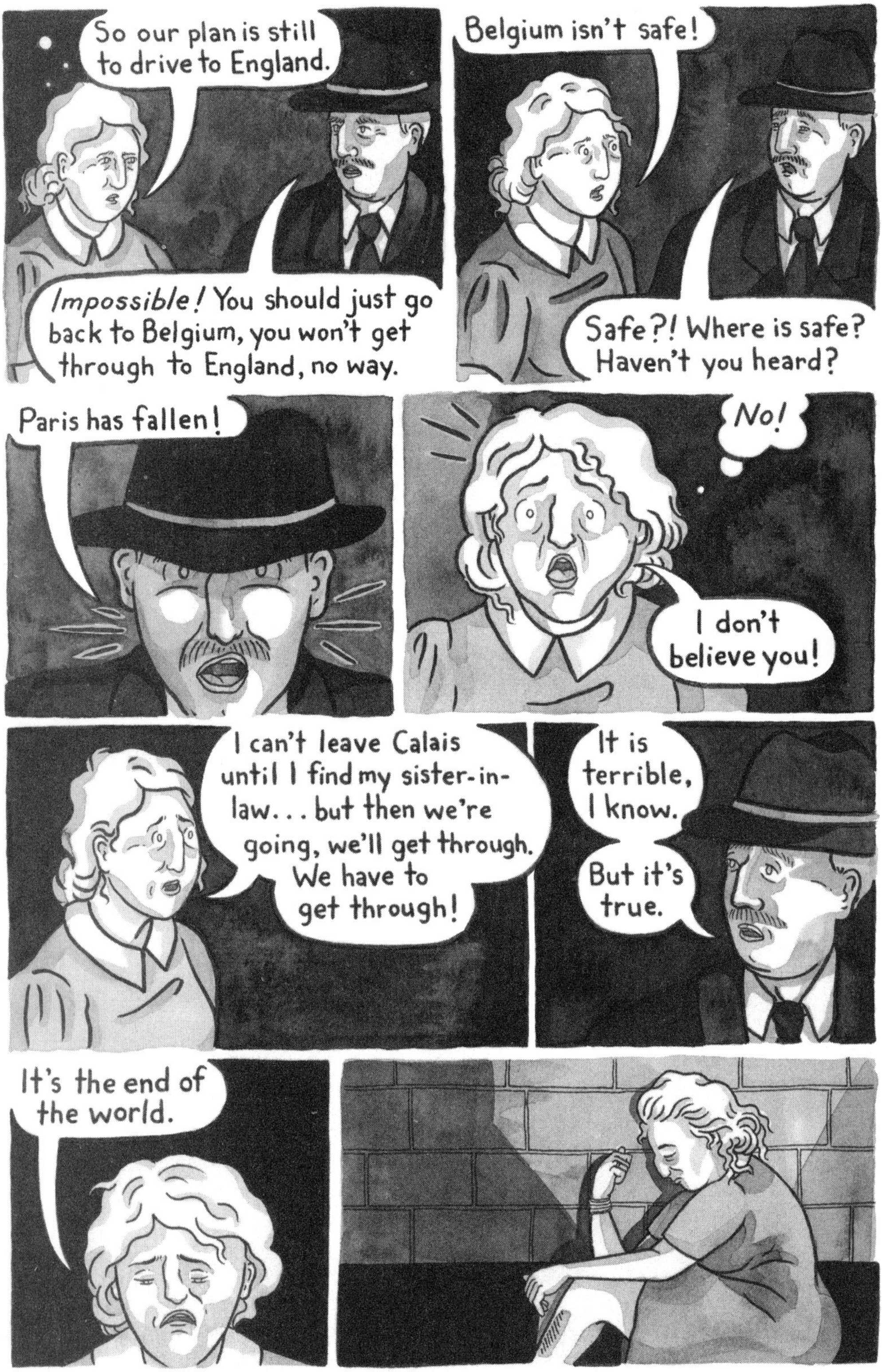
So our plan is still to drive to England.
Impossible! You should just go back to Belgium, you won't get through to England, no way.
Belgium isn't safe!
Safe?! Where is safe? Haven't you heard?
Paris has fallen!
No!
I don't believe you!
I can't leave Calais until I find my sister-in-law... but then we're going, we'll get through. We have to get through!
It is terrible, I know.
But it's true.
It's the end of the world.

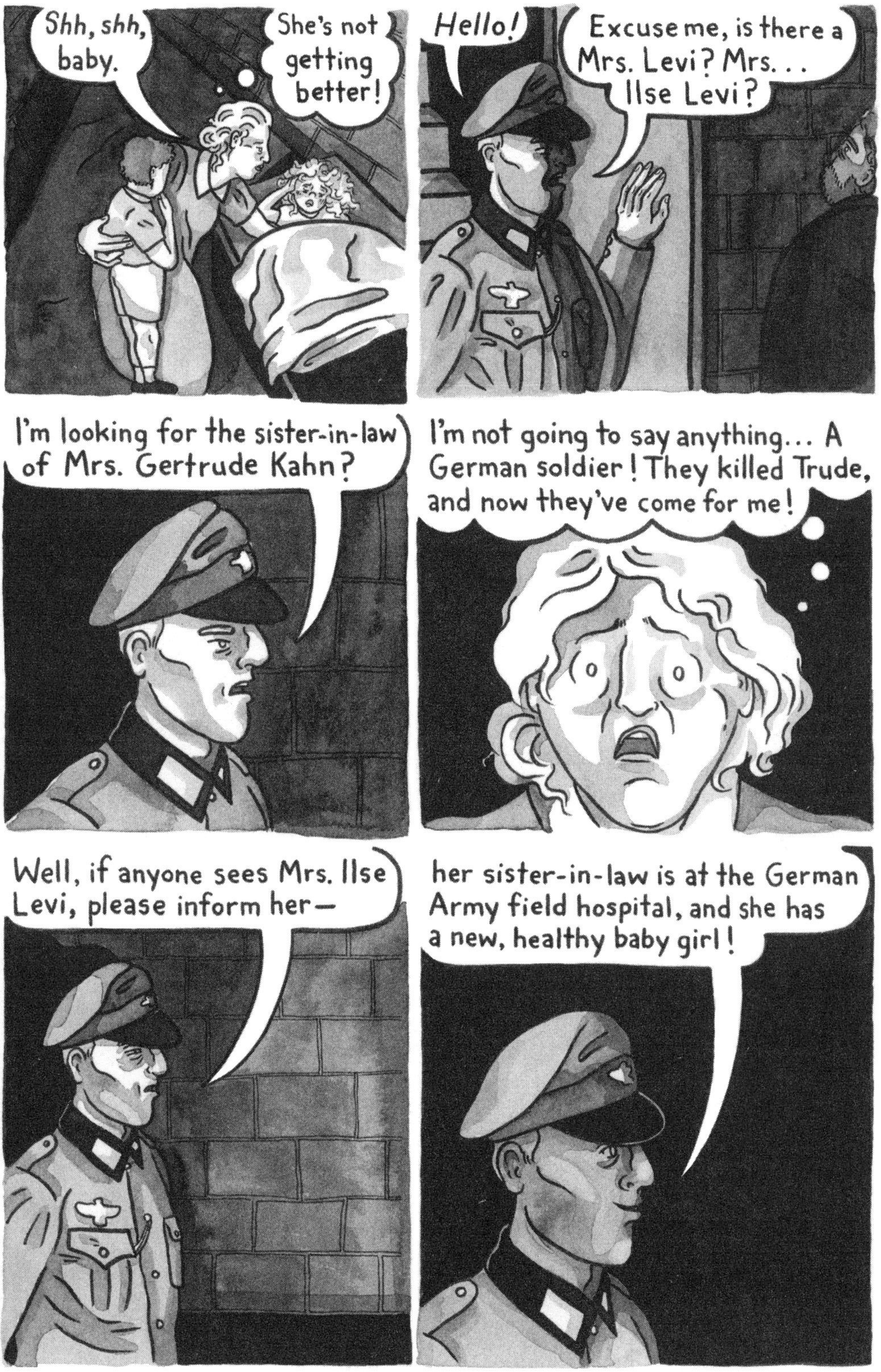

Shh, shh, baby.
She's not getting better!
Hello!
Excuse me, is there a Mrs. Levi? Mrs. . . Ilse Levi?
I'm looking for the sister-in-law of Mrs. Gertrude Kahn?
I'm not going to say anything... A German soldier! They killed Trude, and now they've come for me!
Well, if anyone sees Mrs. Ilse Levi, please inform her—
her sister-in-law is at the German Army field hospital, and she has a new, healthy baby girl!

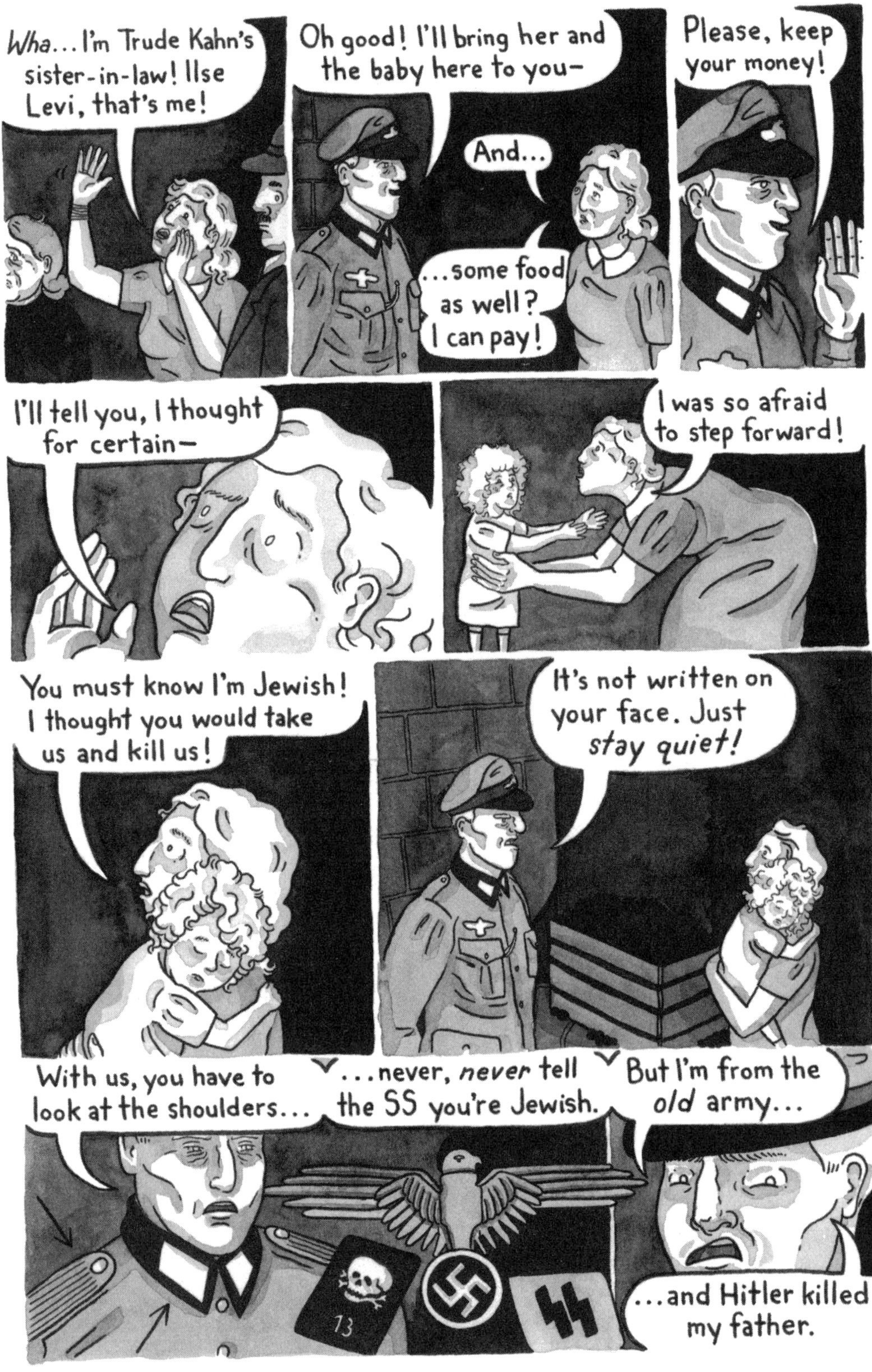
Wha... I'm Trude Kahn's sister-in-law! Ilse Levi, that's me!
Oh good! I'll bring her and the baby here to you–
And...
...some food as well? I can pay!
Please, keep your money!
I'll tell you, I thought for certain–
I was so afraid to step forward!
You must know I'm Jewish! I thought you would take us and kill us!
It's not written on your face. Just *stay quiet!*
With us, you have to look at the shoulders...
...never, *never* tell the SS you're Jewish.
But I'm from the *old* army...
...and Hitler killed my father.

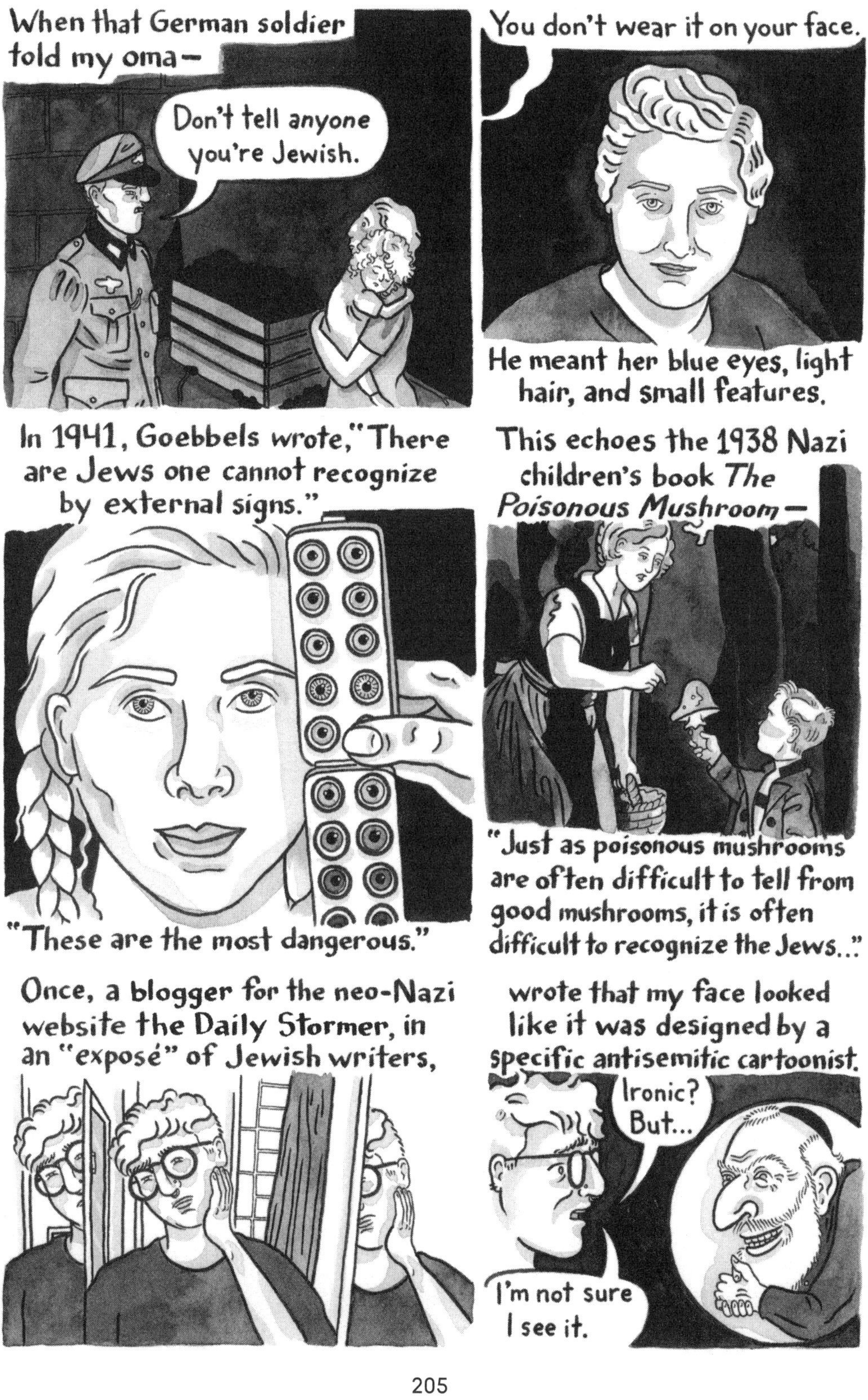
When that German soldier told my oma—
Don't tell anyone you're Jewish.
You don't wear it on your face.
He meant her blue eyes, light hair, and small features.
In 1941, Goebbels wrote, "There are Jews one cannot recognize by external signs."
"These are the most dangerous."
This echoes the 1938 Nazi children's book *The Poisonous Mushroom*—
"Just as poisonous mushrooms are often difficult to tell from good mushrooms, it is often difficult to recognize the Jews..."
Once, a blogger for the neo-Nazi website the Daily Stormer, in an "exposé" of Jewish writers,
wrote that my face looked like it was designed by a specific antisemitic cartoonist.
Ironic? But...
I'm not sure I see it.

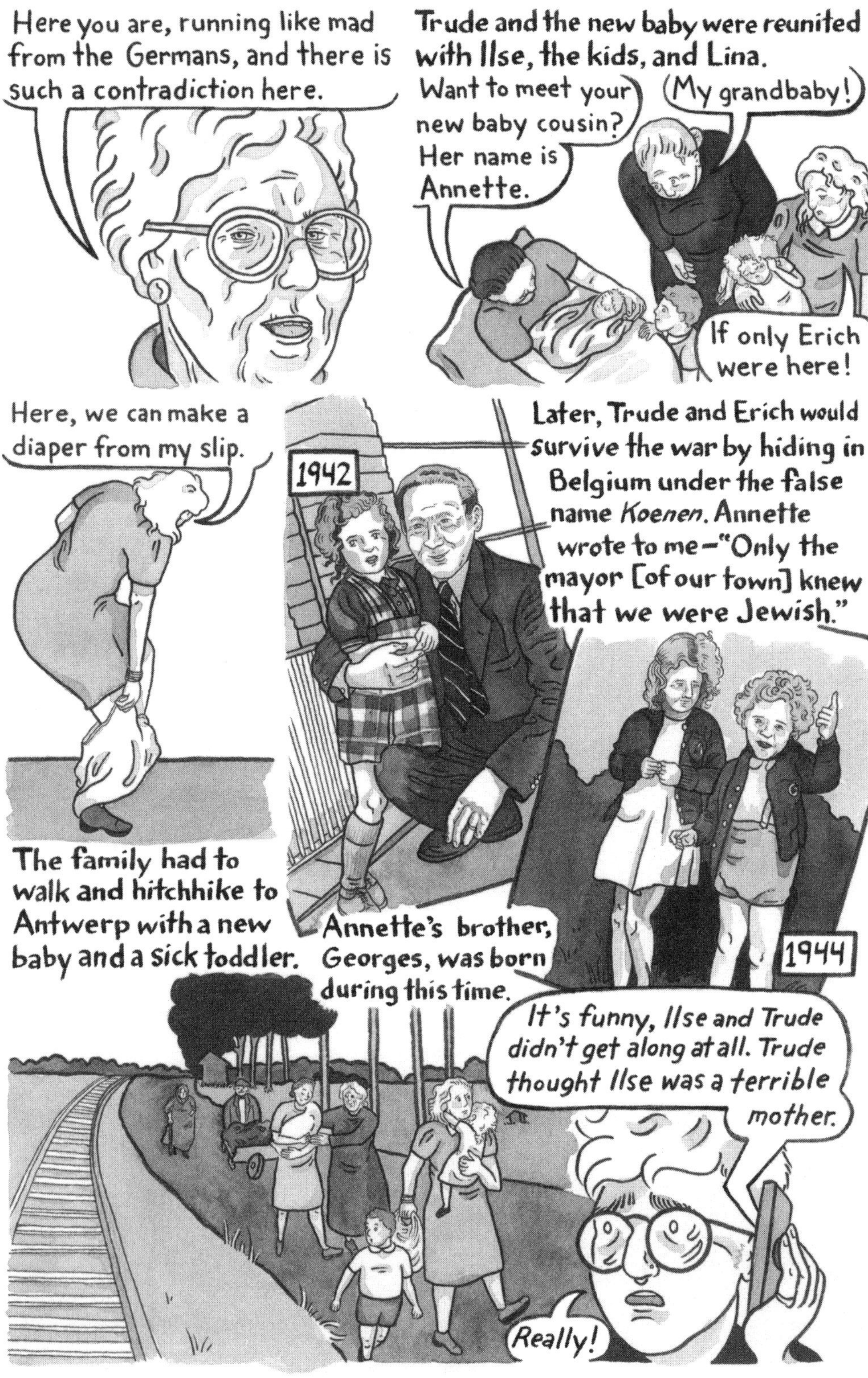

Here you are, running like mad from the Germans, and there is such a contradiction here.
Trude and the new baby were reunited with Ilse, the kids, and Lina.
Want to meet your new baby cousin? Her name is Annette.
My grandbaby!
If only Erich were here!
Here, we can make a diaper from my slip.
1942
Later, Trude and Erich would survive the war by hiding in Belgium under the false name *Koenen*. Annette wrote to me—"Only the mayor [of our town] knew that we were Jewish."
1944
The family had to walk and hitchhike to Antwerp with a new baby and a sick toddler.
Annette's brother, Georges, was born during this time.
It's funny, Ilse and Trude didn't get along at all. Trude thought Ilse was a terrible mother.
Really!

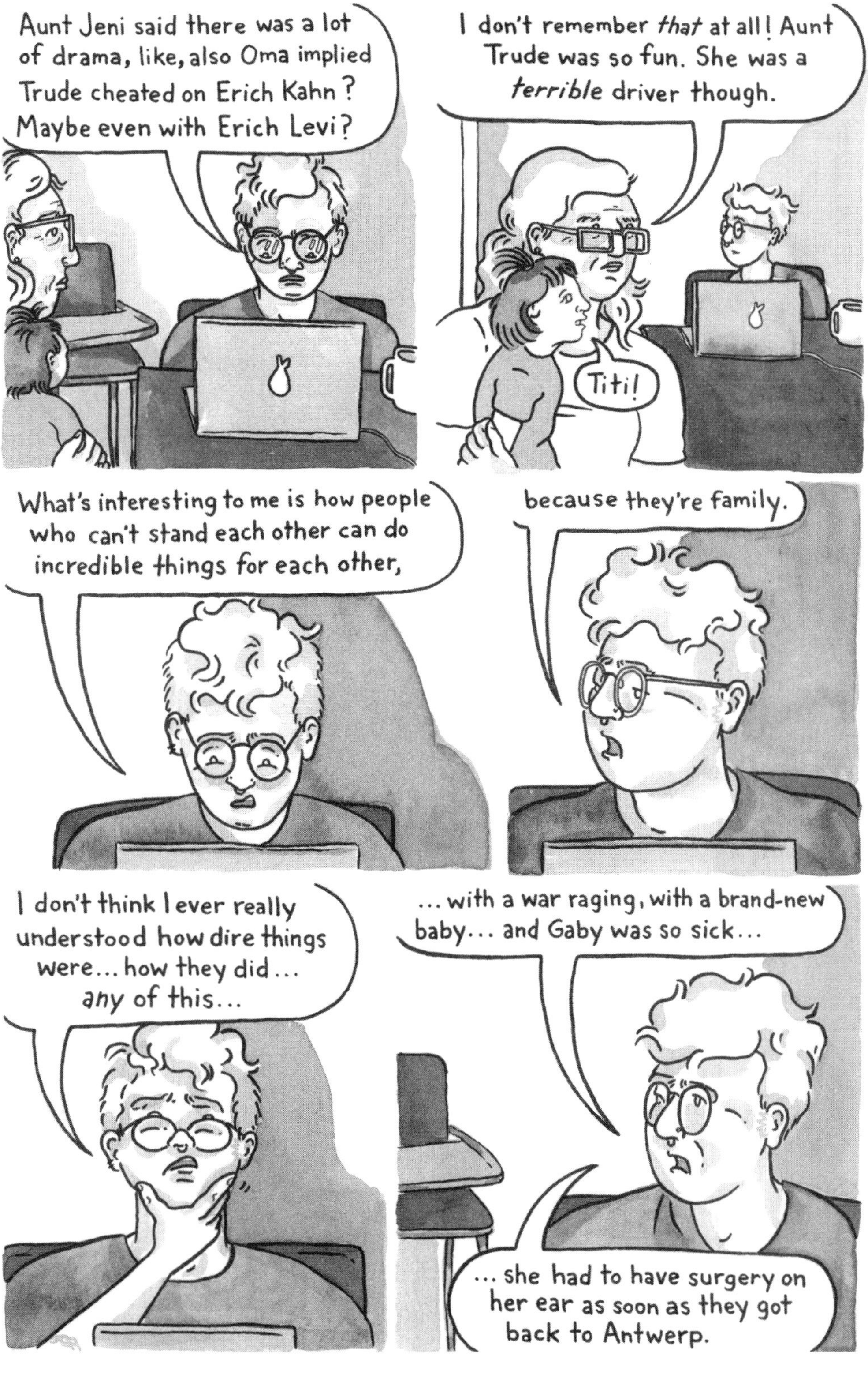
Aunt Jeni said there was a lot of drama, like, also Oma implied Trude cheated on Erich Kahn? Maybe even with Erich Levi?
I don't remember *that* at all! Aunt Trude was so fun. She was a *terrible* driver though.
Titi!
What's interesting to me is how people who can't stand each other can do incredible things for each other,
because they're family.
I don't think I ever really understood how dire things were... how they did... *any* of this...
... with a war raging, with a brand-new baby... and Gaby was so sick...
... she had to have surgery on her ear as soon as they got back to Antwerp.

After they returned to Antwerp, in one of my oma's testimonies, the doorbell rings. In another, there is only a furtive knock.

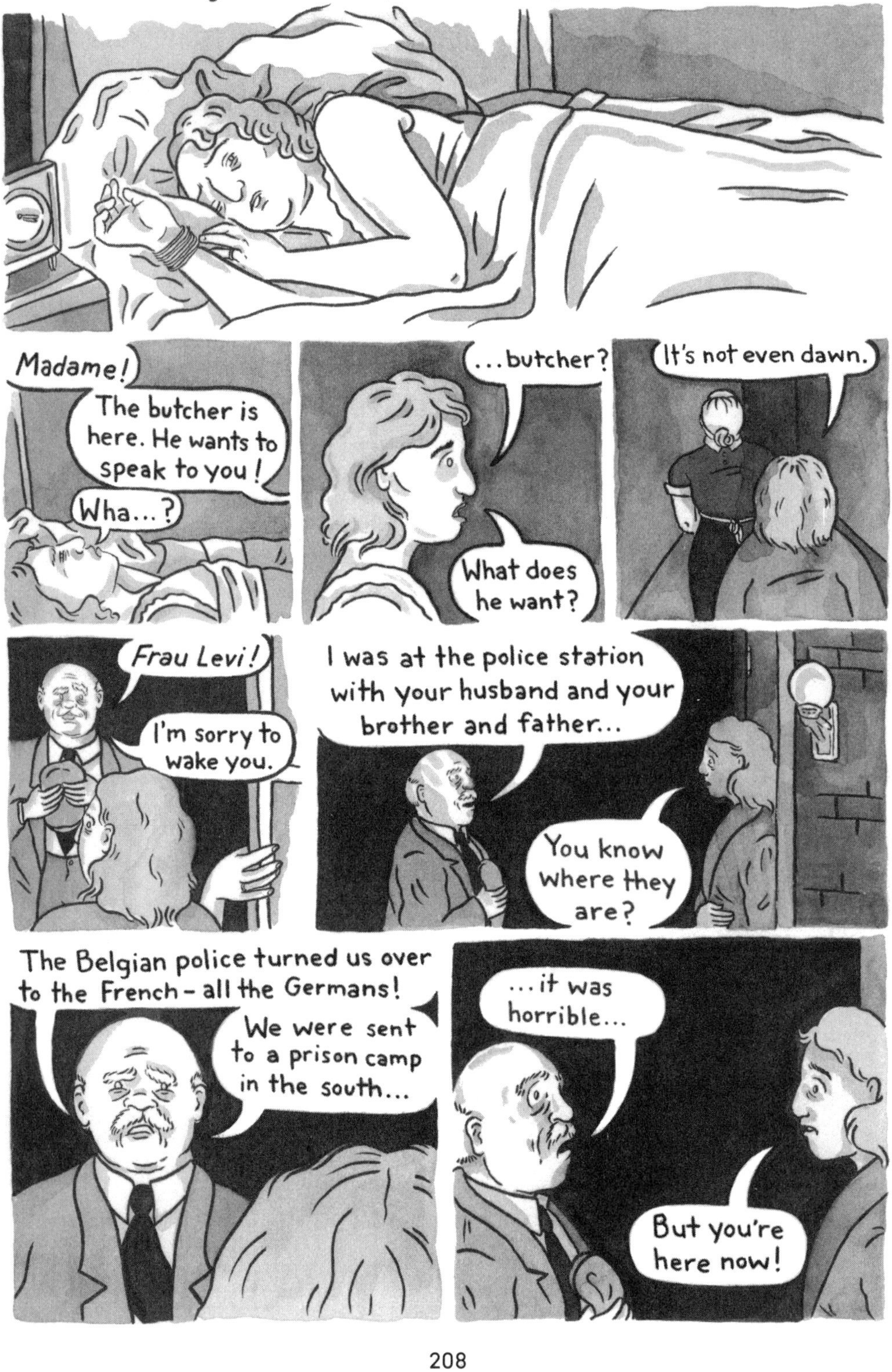

Madame!
The butcher is here. He wants to speak to you!
Wha...?
...butcher?
What does he want?
It's not even dawn.
Frau Levi!
I'm sorry to wake you.
I was at the police station with your husband and your brother and father...
You know where they are?
The Belgian police turned us over to the French – all the Germans!
We were sent to a prison camp in the south...
...it was horrible...
But you're here now!

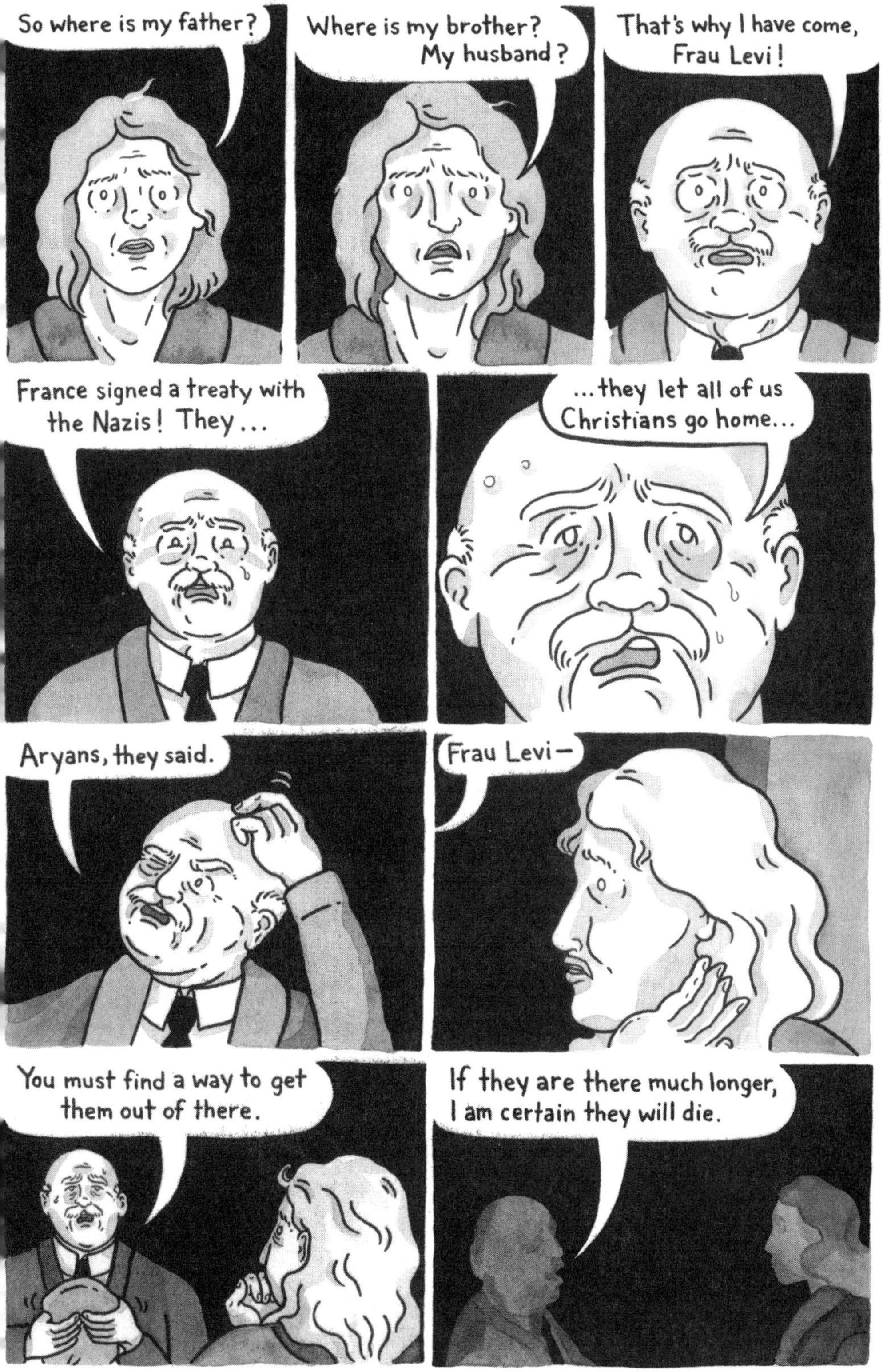
So where is my father?
Where is my brother? My husband?
That's why I have come, Frau Levi!
France signed a treaty with the Nazis! They...
...they let all of us Christians go home...
Aryans, they said.
Frau Levi—
You must find a way to get them out of there.
If they are there much longer, I am certain they will die.

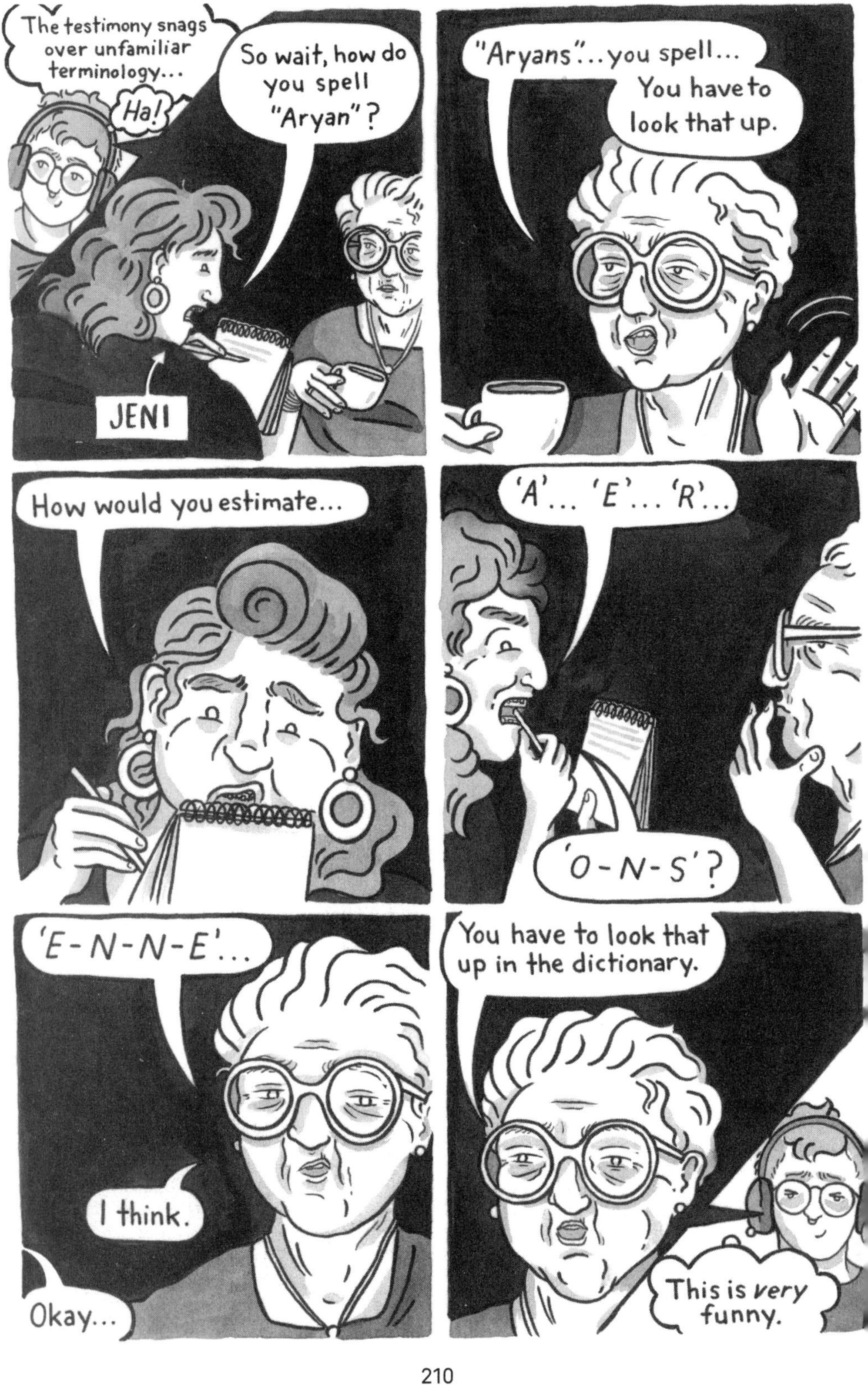
The testimony snags over unfamiliar terminology...
Ha!
So wait, how do you spell "Aryan"?
JENI
"Aryans"... you spell...
You have to look that up.
How would you estimate...
'A'... 'E'... 'R'...
'O-N-S'?
'E-N-N-E'...
I think.
Okay...
You have to look that up in the dictionary.
This is *very* funny.

The men had been sent by cattle car to St.-Cyprien, an internment camp on the southern coast of France.

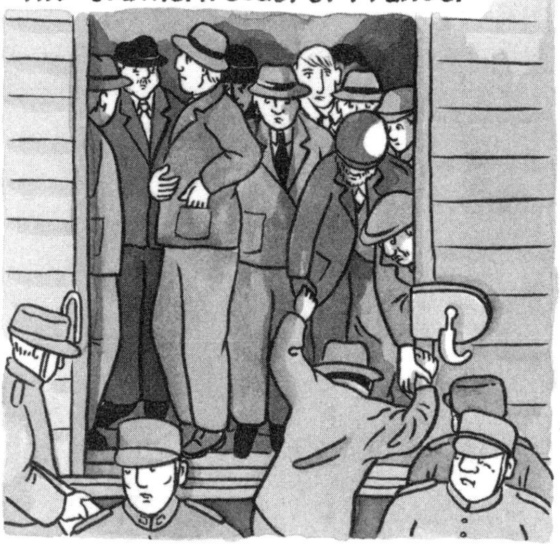

At the Leo Baeck Institute in New York, I read a letter from an aid organization about St.-Cyprien.

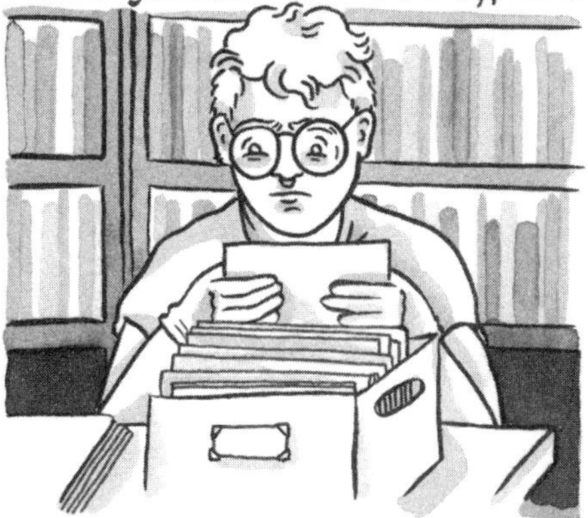

The camp inmates experienced *"hunger, illness, and psychological misery."*

The Levis' Aryan butcher's warning was not wrong – in 1940, inmates at St.-Cyprien had little access to food and no drinking water.

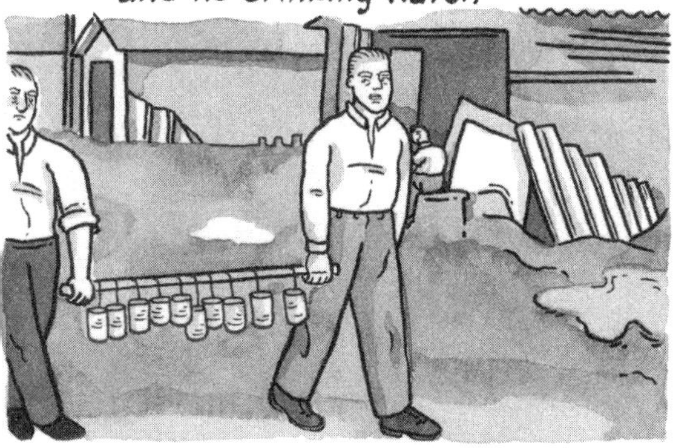

The archived letter describes widespread dysentery and an outbreak of typhoid.

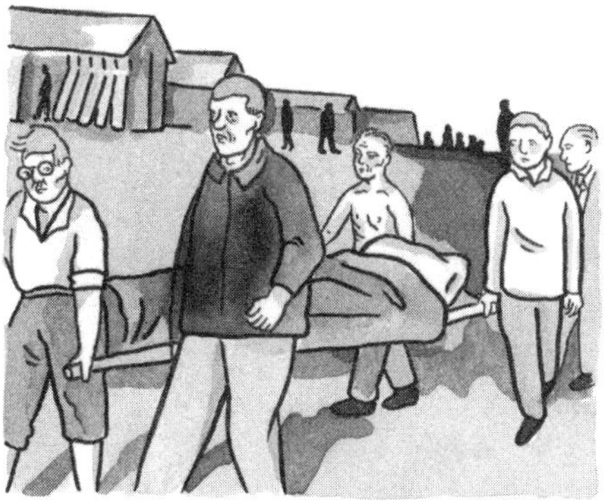

"Fleas, lice, mice, rats are the constant inhabitants of the hell of St.-Cyprien."

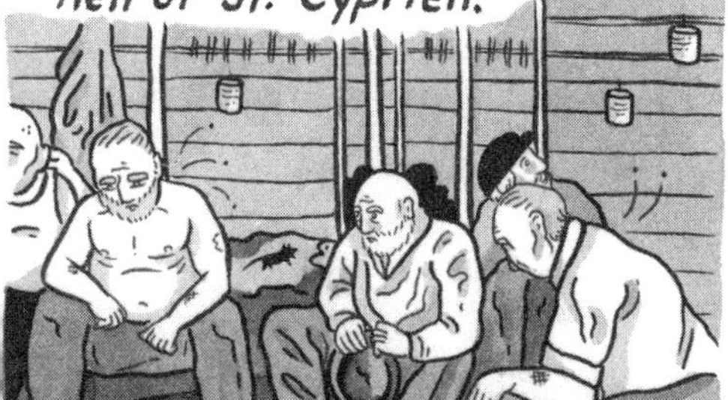

Prisoners lived in sheds and tents open to exposure, within sight of the beautiful Mediterranean.

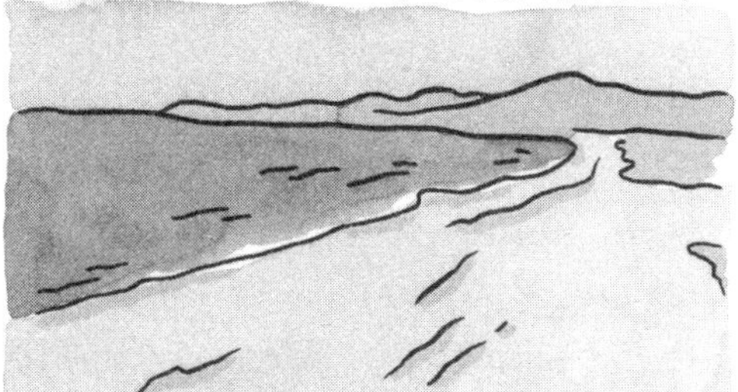

Originally opened to intern refugees from fascist Spain,

the camp known as the "pesthole of the Pyrenees" was basically a warehouse for the unwanted.

At the end of October 1940, the Jewish prisoners at St.-Cyprien were transferred to Camp Gurs.

In 1942, Vichy France turned many of the Jewish inmates of Gurs over to Germany.

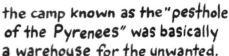

Most of these individuals were sent through the Drancy transit camp, in the suburbs of Paris, to Auschwitz and other killing centers in the occupied East.

We have to do something. I'm going to figure it out.

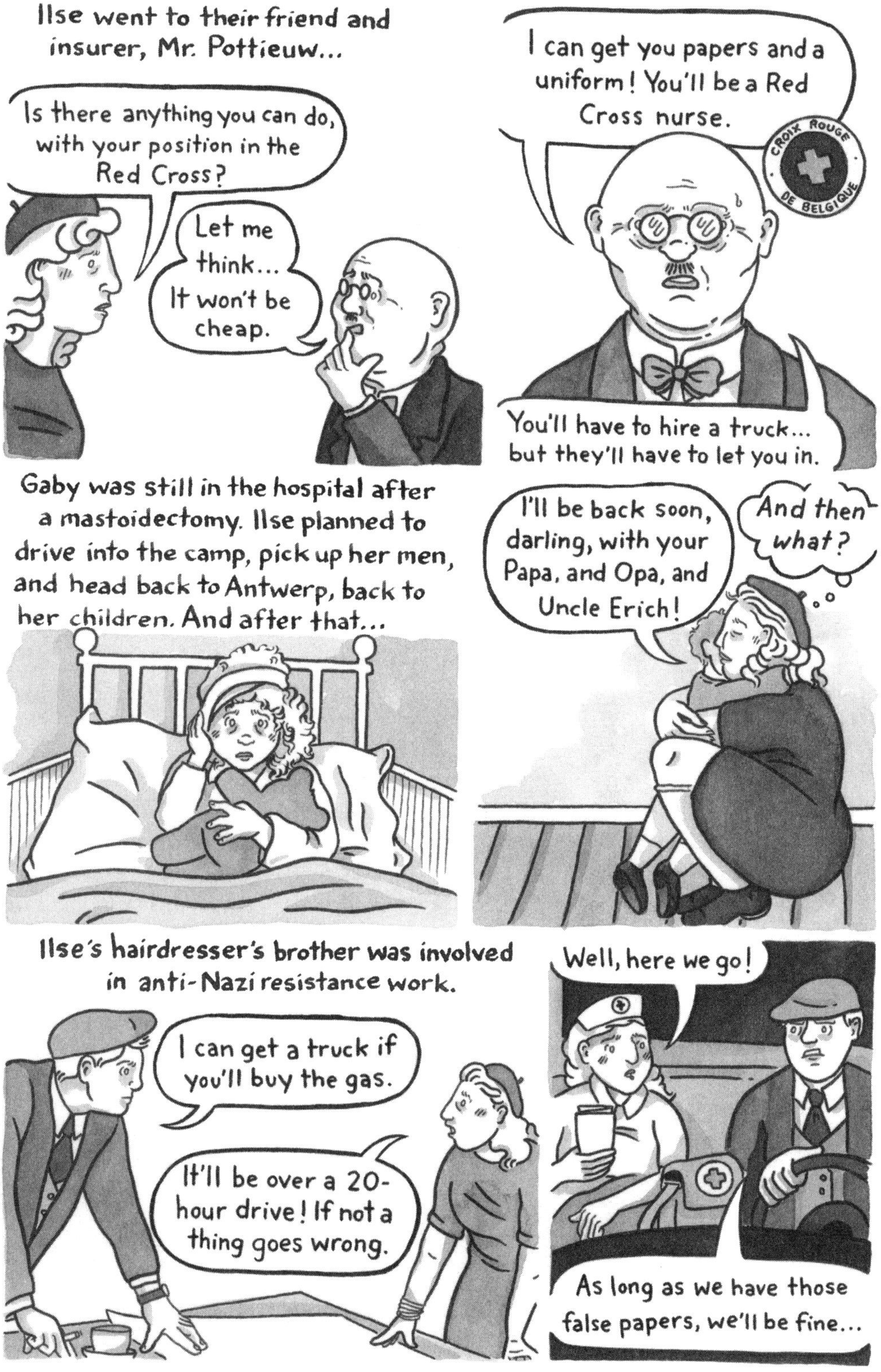
Ilse went to their friend and insurer, Mr. Pottieuw...
Is there anything you can do, with your position in the Red Cross?
Let me think... It won't be cheap.
I can get you papers and a uniform! You'll be a Red Cross nurse.
CROIX ROUGE DE BELGIQUE
You'll have to hire a truck... but they'll have to let you in.
Gaby was still in the hospital after a mastoidectomy. Ilse planned to drive into the camp, pick up her men, and head back to Antwerp, back to her children. And after that...
I'll be back soon, darling, with your Papa, and Opa, and Uncle Erich!
And then what?
Ilse's hairdresser's brother was involved in anti-Nazi resistance work.
I can get a truck if you'll buy the gas.
It'll be over a 20-hour drive! If not a thing goes wrong.
Well, here we go!
As long as we have those false papers, we'll be fine...

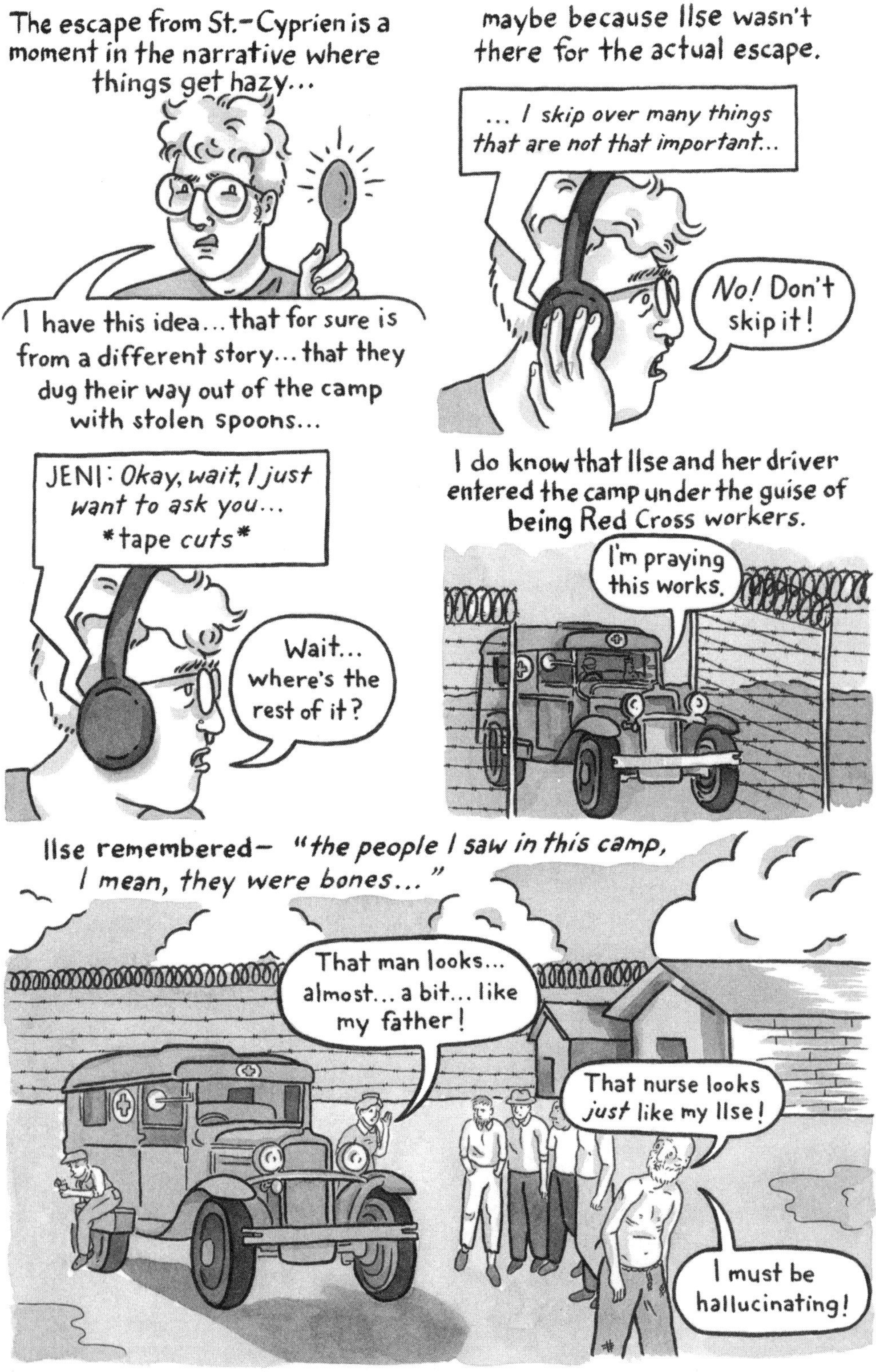
The escape from St.-Cyprien is a moment in the narrative where things get hazy...
I have this idea... that for sure is from a different story... that they dug their way out of the camp with stolen spoons...
maybe because Ilse wasn't there for the actual escape.
... I skip over many things that are not that important...
No! Don't skip it!
JENI: Okay, wait, I just want to ask you... *tape cuts*
Wait... where's the rest of it?
I do know that Ilse and her driver entered the camp under the guise of being Red Cross workers.
I'm praying this works.
Ilse remembered— "the people I saw in this camp, I mean, they were bones..."
That man looks... almost... a bit... like my father!
That nurse looks just like my Ilse!
I must be hallucinating!

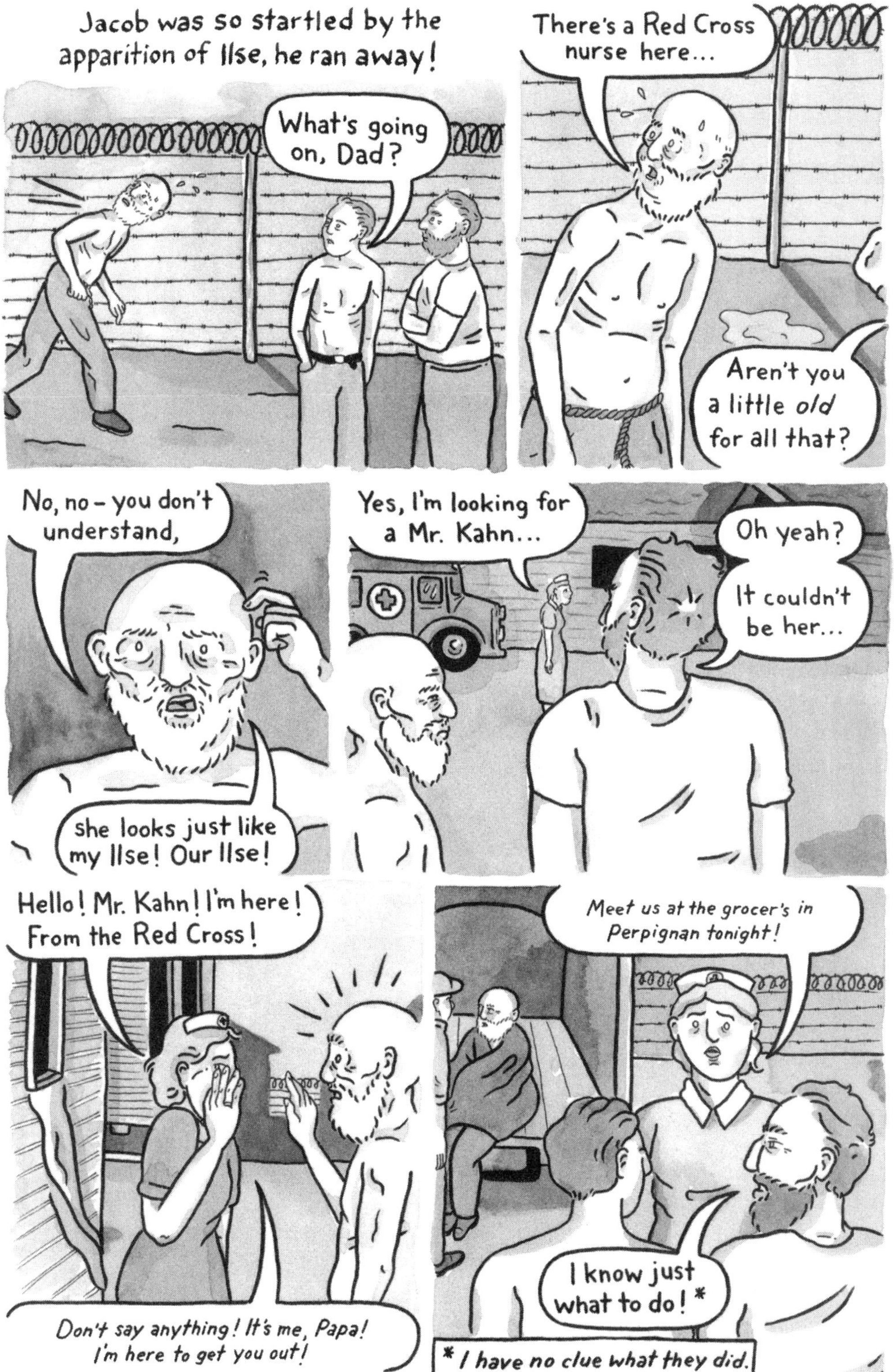
Jacob was so startled by the apparition of Ilse, he ran away!
What's going on, Dad?
There's a Red Cross nurse here...
Aren't you a little *old* for all that?
No, no – you don't understand,
she looks just like my Ilse! Our Ilse!
Yes, I'm looking for a Mr. Kahn...
Oh yeah?
It couldn't be her...
Hello! Mr. Kahn! I'm here! From the Red Cross!
Don't say anything! It's me, Papa! I'm here to get you out!
Meet us at the grocer's in Perpignan tonight!
I know just what to do! *
* I have no clue what they did.

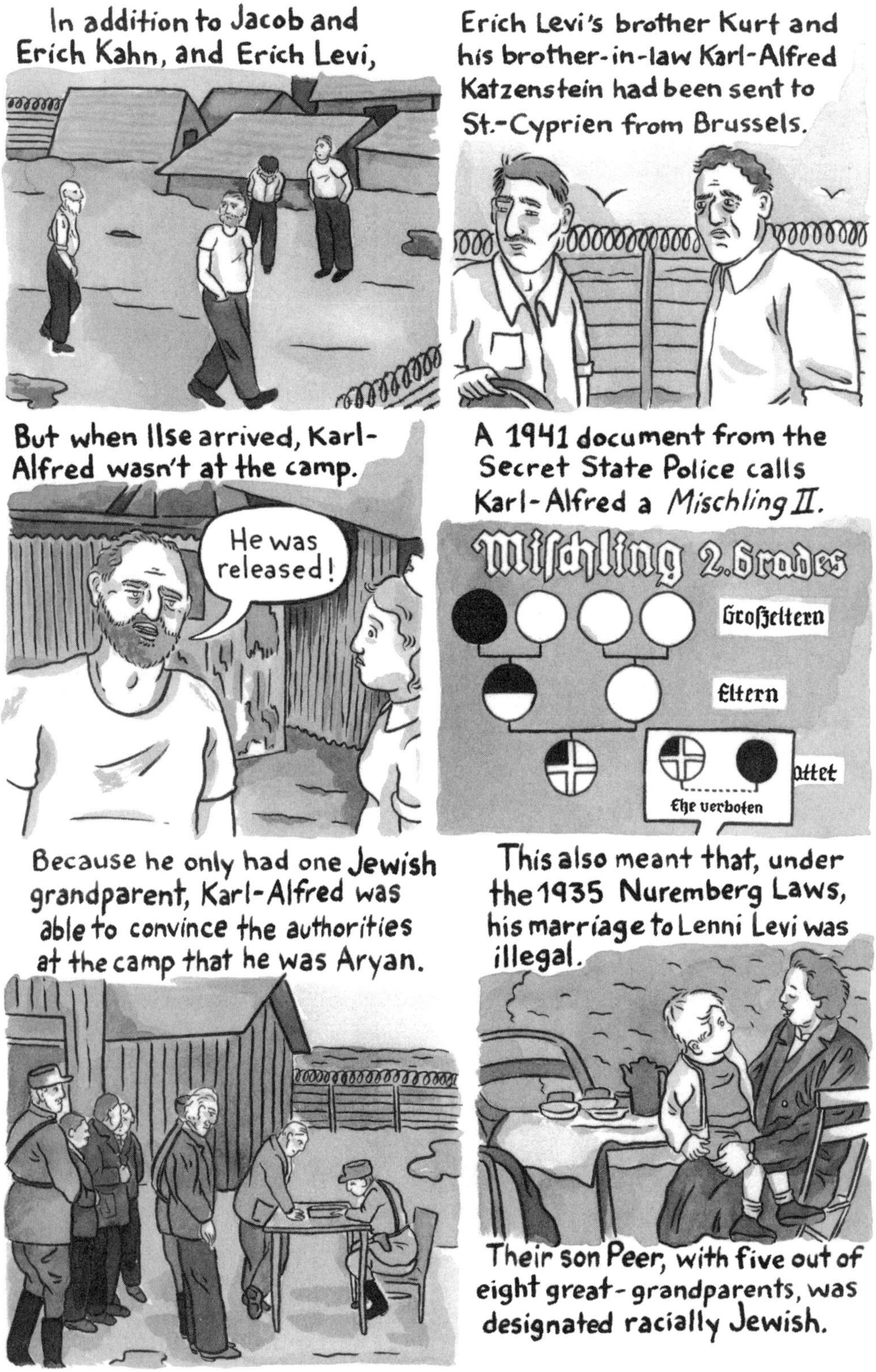
In addition to Jacob and Erich Kahn, and Erich Levi,
Erich Levi's brother Kurt and his brother-in-law Karl-Alfred Katzenstein had been sent to St.-Cyprien from Brussels.
But when Ilse arrived, Karl-Alfred wasn't at the camp.
He was released!
A 1941 document from the Secret State Police calls Karl-Alfred a *Mischling II*.
Mischling 2. Grades
Großeltern
Eltern
Ehe verboten
Because he only had one Jewish grandparent, Karl-Alfred was able to convince the authorities at the camp that he was Aryan.
This also meant that, under the 1935 Nuremberg Laws, his marriage to Lenni Levi was illegal.
Their son Peer, with five out of eight great-grandparents, was designated racially Jewish.

I can't believe he just *left* them there.

Returning to Primo Levi —

...an infernal order such as National Socialism exercises a frightful power of corruption, against which it is difficult to guard oneself. It degrades its victims and makes them similar to itself, because it needs both great and small complicities. To resist it requires a truly solid moral armature...

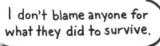

I don't blame anyone for what they did to survive.

But Dad, he abandoned them! While Oma was running *into* the fire to save them.

He's right, of course!

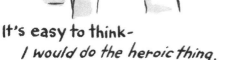

It's easy to think— *I would do the heroic thing.*

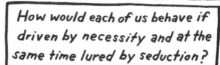

How would each of us behave if driven by necessity and at the same time lured by seduction?

THE DROWNED AND THE SAVED

PRIMO LEVI

But Primo Levi demands a deeper probing—

217

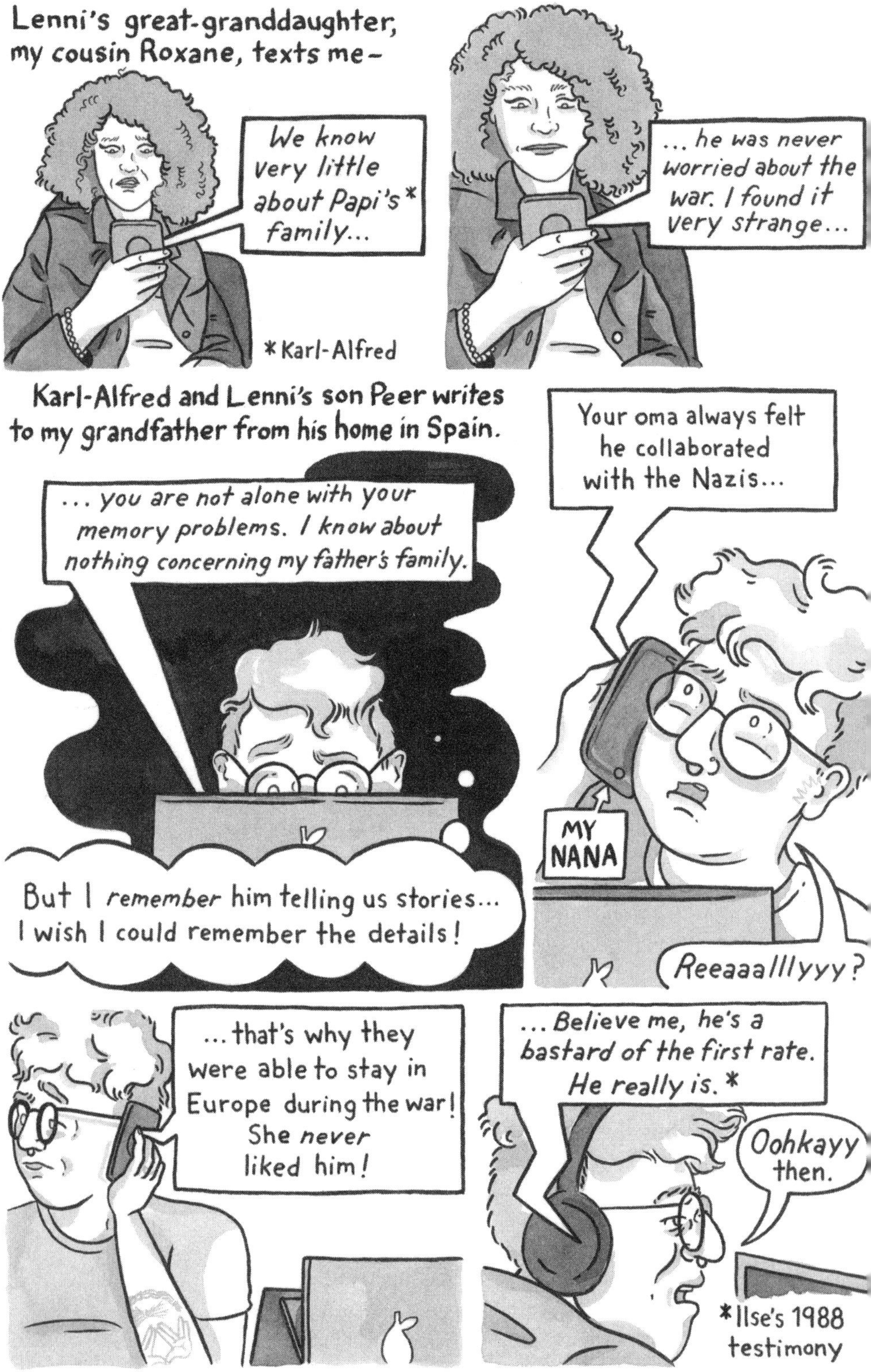

Lenni's great-granddaughter, my cousin Roxane, texts me–
We know very little about Papi's* family...
*Karl-Alfred
... he was never worried about the war. I found it very strange...
Karl-Alfred and Lenni's son Peer writes to my grandfather from his home in Spain.
... you are not alone with your memory problems. I know about nothing concerning my father's family.
But I remember him telling us stories... I wish I could remember the details!
Your oma always felt he collaborated with the Nazis...
MY NANA
Reeaaalllyyy?
... that's why they were able to stay in Europe during the war! She never liked him!
... Believe me, he's a bastard of the first rate. He really is.*
Oohkayy then.
*Ilse's 1988 testimony

So, one way or another, they got away from the camp.

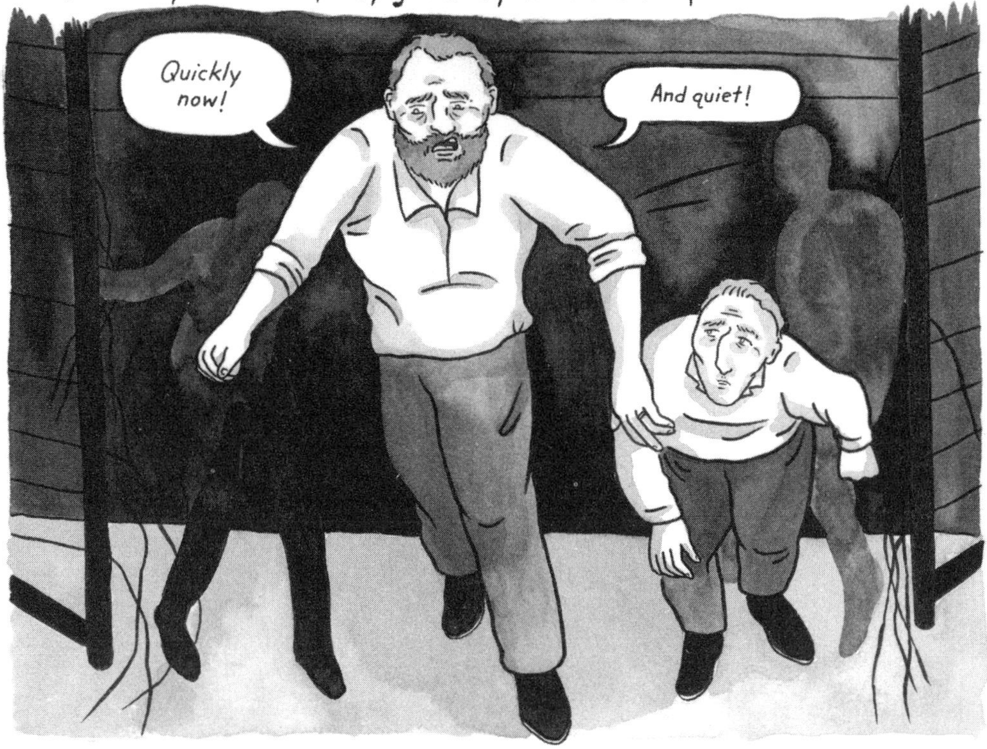
Quickly now!
And quiet!

They were sheltered first by a local grocer. It was decided that Ilse would take her brother and father back to Antwerp and return to Perpignan with the kids while Erich and Kurt stayed in hiding.

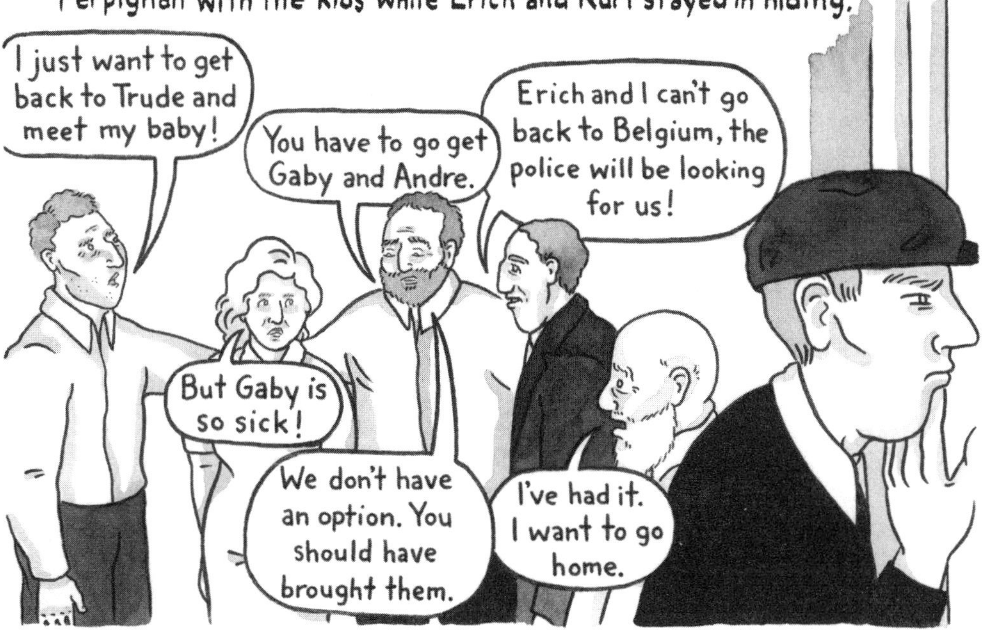
I just want to get back to Trude and meet my baby!
You have to go get Gaby and Andre.
Erich and I can't go back to Belgium, the police will be looking for us!
But Gaby is so sick!
We don't have an option. You should have brought them.
I've had it. I want to go home.

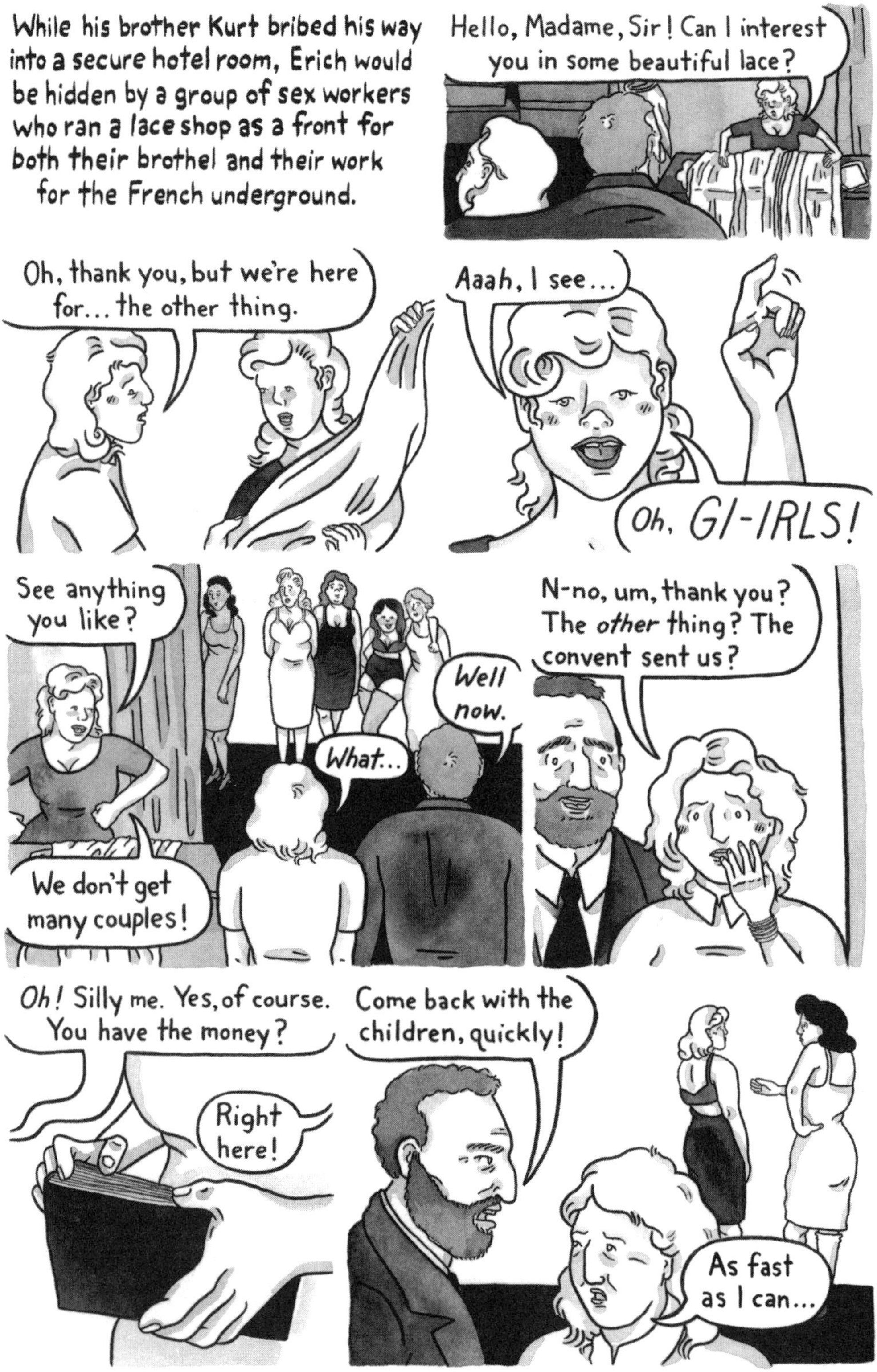
While his brother Kurt bribed his way into a secure hotel room, Erich would be hidden by a group of sex workers who ran a lace shop as a front for both their brothel and their work for the French underground.
Hello, Madame, Sir! Can I interest you in some beautiful lace?
Oh, thank you, but we're here for... the other thing.
Aaah, I see...
Oh, GI-IRLS!
See anything you like?
We don't get many couples!
What...
Well now.
N-no, um, thank you? The *other* thing? The convent sent us?
Oh! Silly me. Yes, of course. You have the money?
Right here!
Come back with the children, quickly!
As fast as I can...

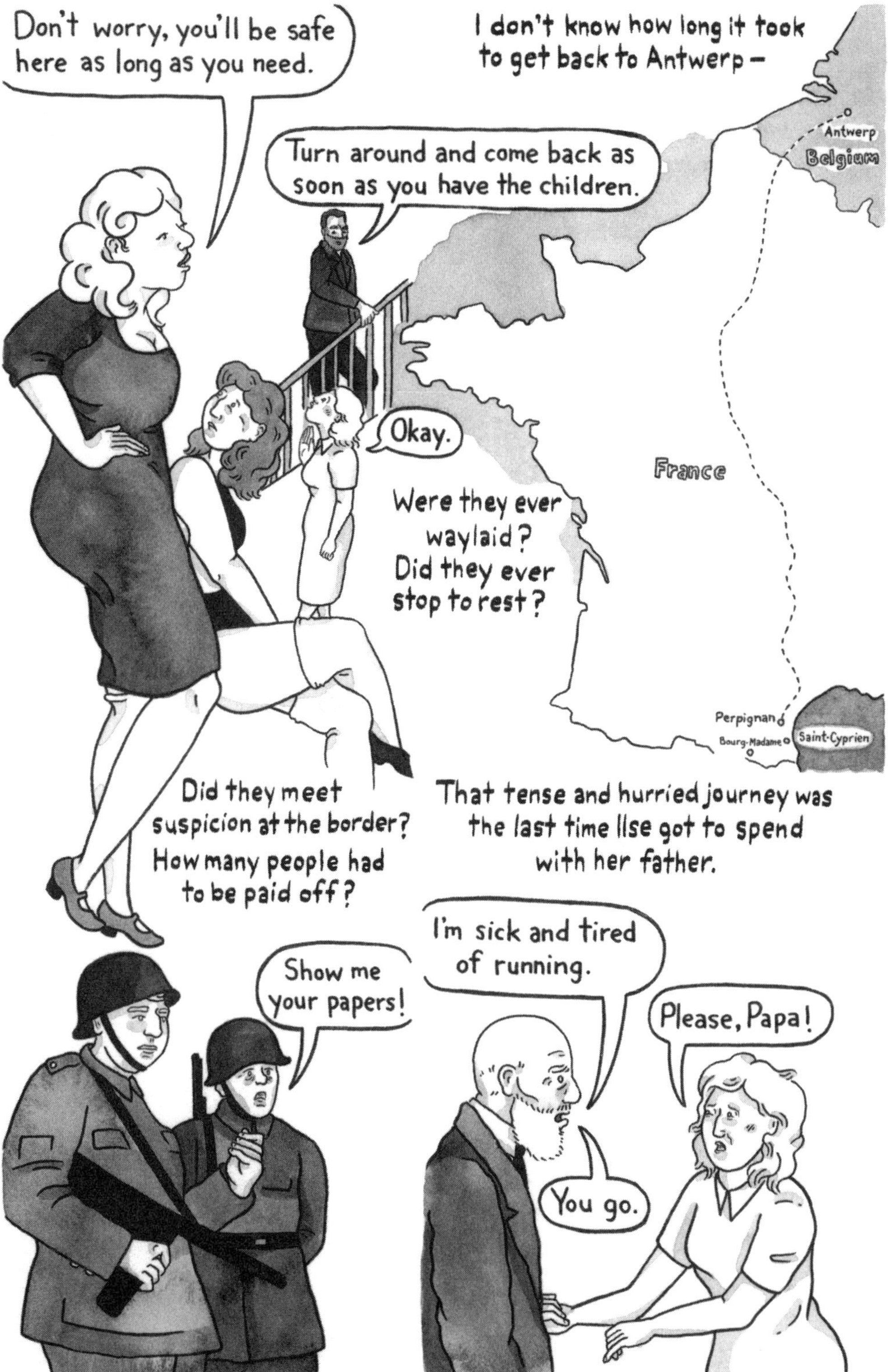
Don't worry, you'll be safe here as long as you need.
I don't know how long it took to get back to Antwerp –
Turn around and come back as soon as you have the children.
Antwerp
Belgium
Okay.
France
Were they ever waylaid? Did they ever stop to rest?
Perpignan
Bourg-Madame
Saint-Cyprien
Did they meet suspicion at the border? How many people had to be paid off?
That tense and hurried journey was the last time Ilse got to spend with her father.
Show me your papers!
I'm sick and tired of running.
Please, Papa!
You go.

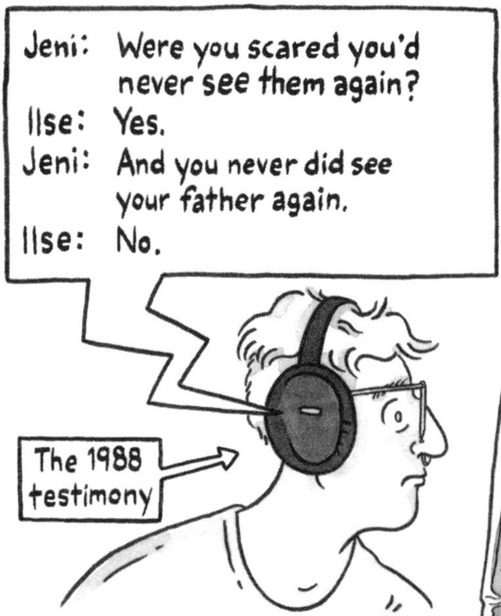
Jeni: Were you scared you'd never see them again?
Ilse: Yes.
Jeni: And you never did see your father again.
Ilse: No.
The 1988 testimony

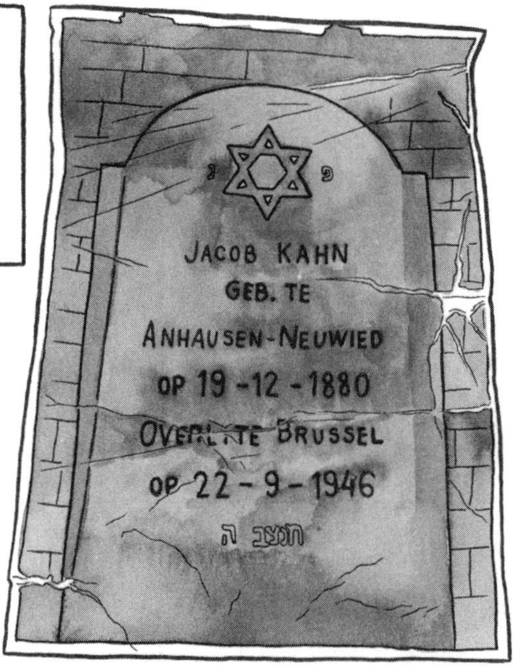
JACOB KAHN
GEB. TE
ANHAUSEN-NEUWIED
OP 19-12-1880
OVERL TE BRUSSEL
OP 22-9-1946

At some point the Kahns moved to Brussels, where it was slightly less dangerous.

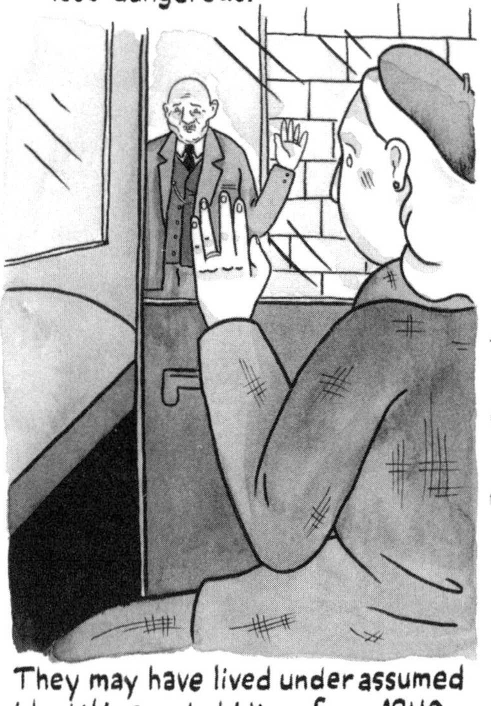

They may have lived under assumed identities or in hiding, from 1940, when Ilse left, to 1945, when the war finally ended.

Ilse received word in 1946 that her father was very ill, but after five years in the U.S., Ilse hadn't gotten citizenship.

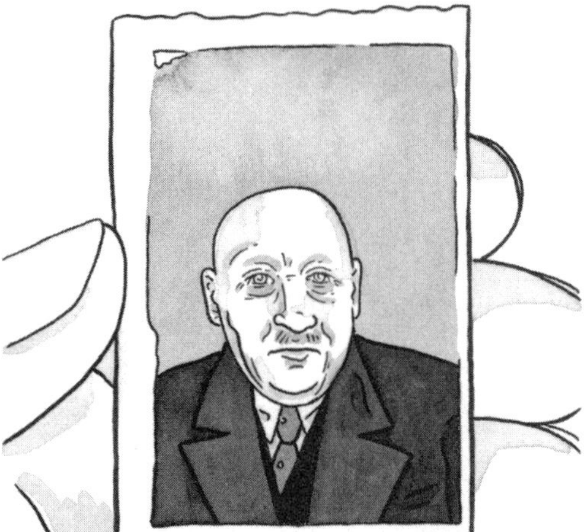

By the time she arranged to leave and come back to the U.S. legally, Jacob Kahn had died at the age of 65.

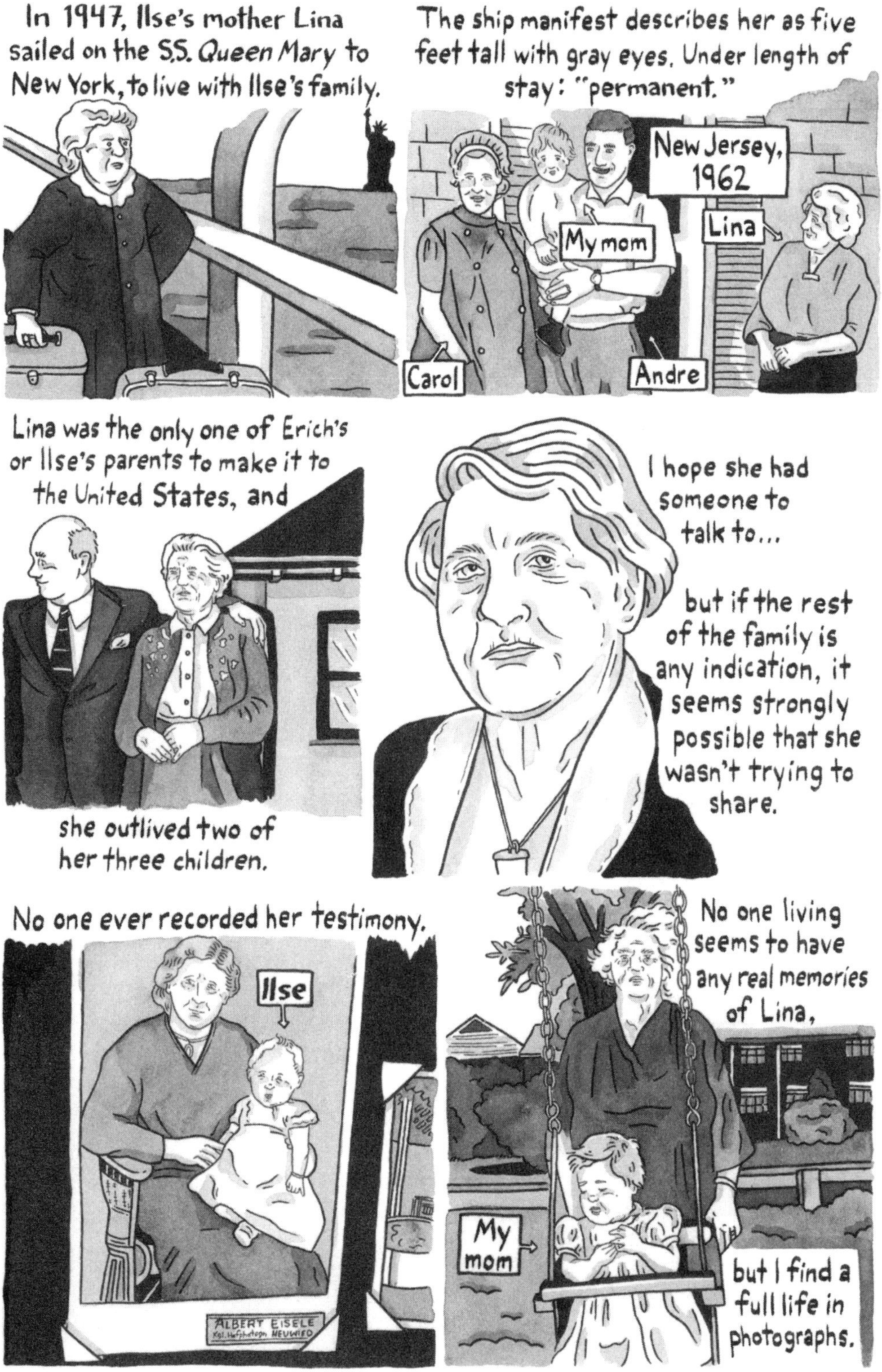
In 1947, Ilse's mother Lina sailed on the S.S. *Queen Mary* to New York, to live with Ilse's family.
The ship manifest describes her as five feet tall with gray eyes. Under length of stay: "permanent."
New Jersey, 1962
My mom
Lina
Carol
Andre
Lina was the only one of Erich's or Ilse's parents to make it to the United States, and
she outlived two of her three children.
I hope she had someone to talk to...
but if the rest of the family is any indication, it seems strongly possible that she wasn't trying to share.
No one ever recorded her testimony.
Ilse
ALBERT EISELE
No one living seems to have any real memories of Lina,
My mom
but I find a full life in photographs.

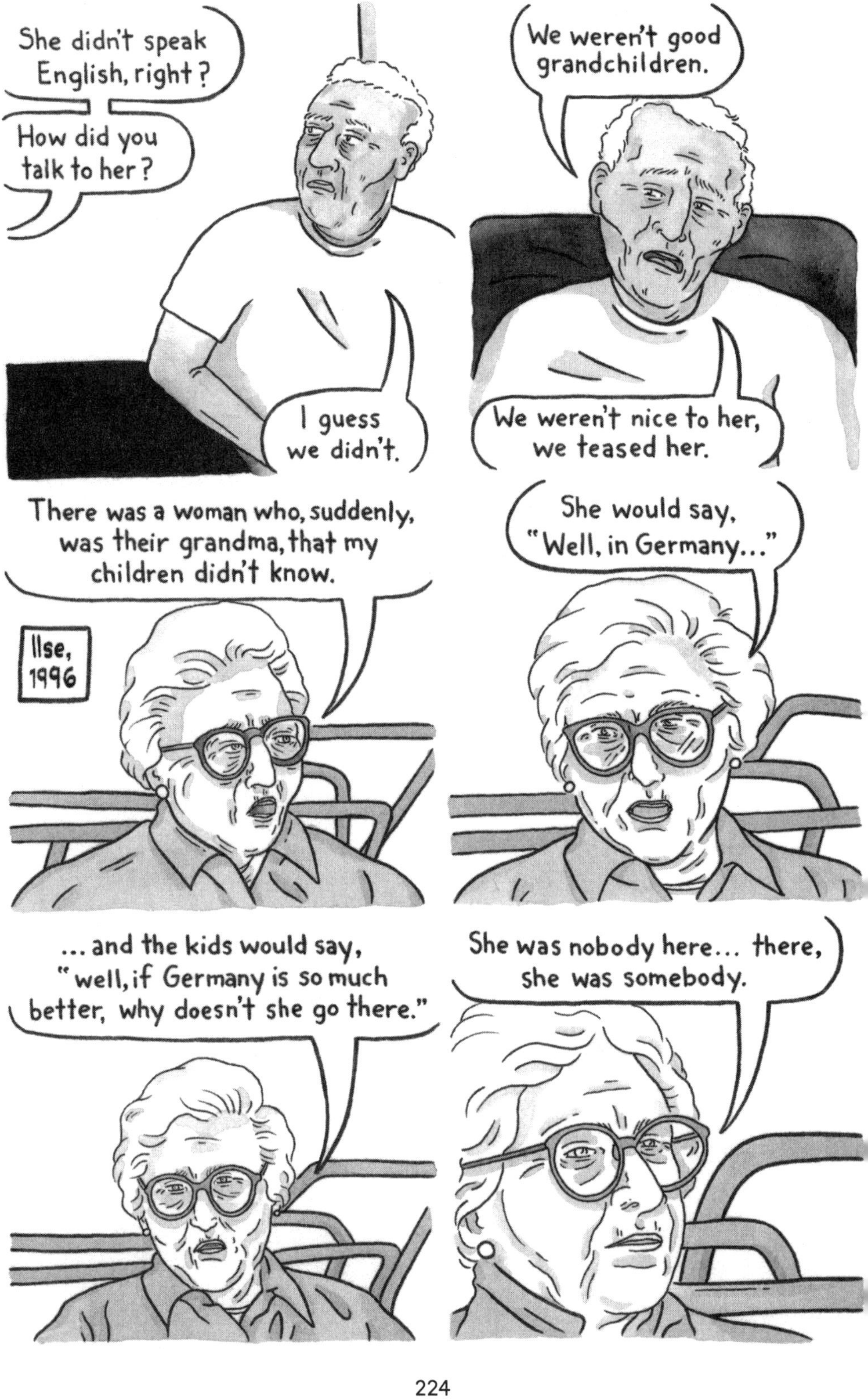
She didn't speak English, right?
How did you talk to her?
I guess we didn't.
We weren't good grandchildren.
We weren't nice to her, we teased her.
There was a woman who, suddenly, was their grandma, that my children didn't know.
Ilse, 1996
She would say, "Well, in Germany..."
... and the kids would say, "well, if Germany is so much better, why doesn't she go there."
She was nobody here... there, she was somebody.

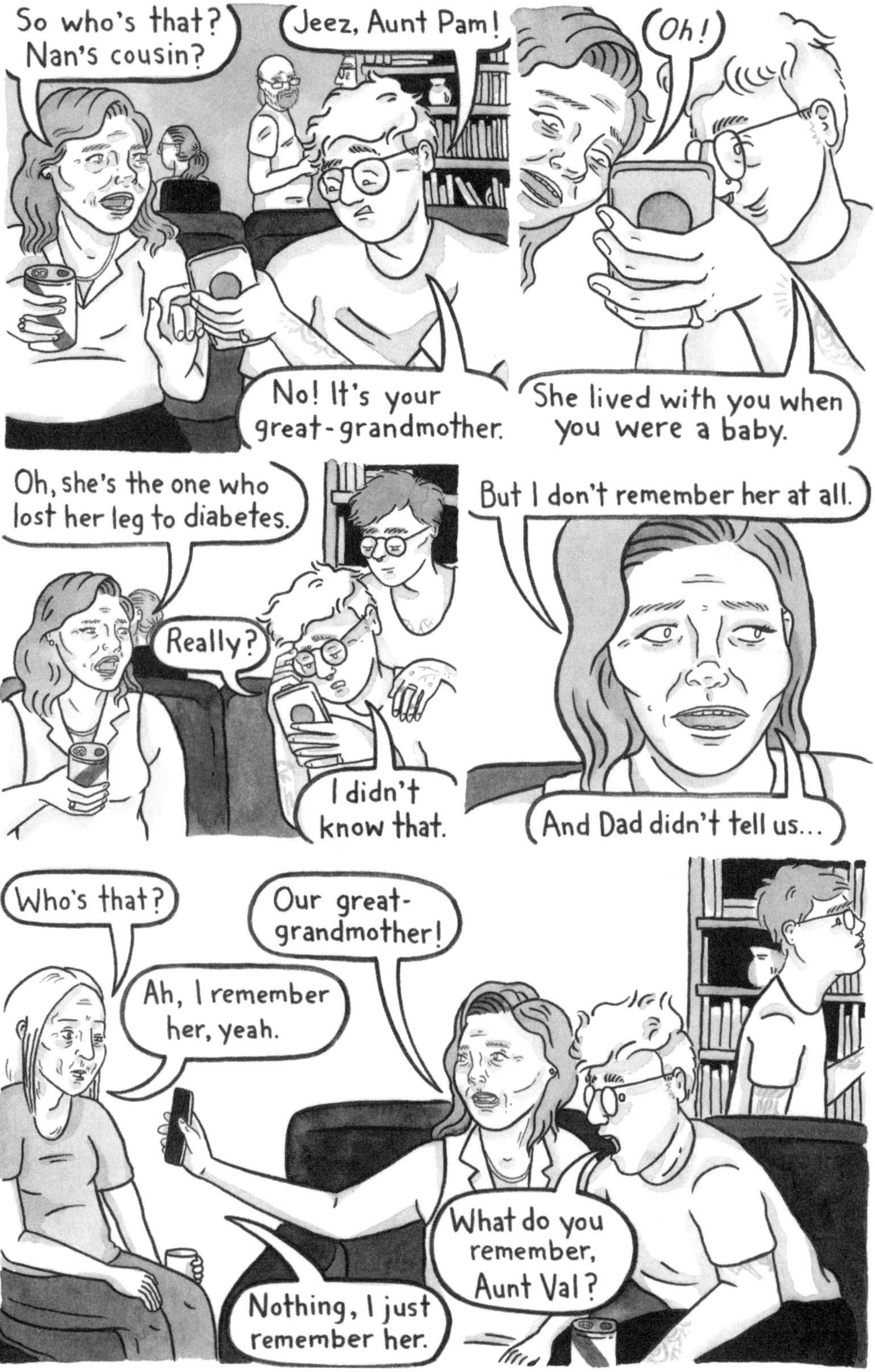
So who's that? Nan's cousin?
Jeez, Aunt Pam!
No! It's your great-grandmother.
Oh!
She lived with you when you were a baby.
Oh, she's the one who lost her leg to diabetes.
Really?
I didn't know that.
But I don't remember her at all.
And Dad didn't tell us...
Who's that?
Our great-grandmother!
Ah, I remember her, yeah.
What do you remember, Aunt Val?
Nothing, I just remember her.

PART 9

PEARLS AND GOLD

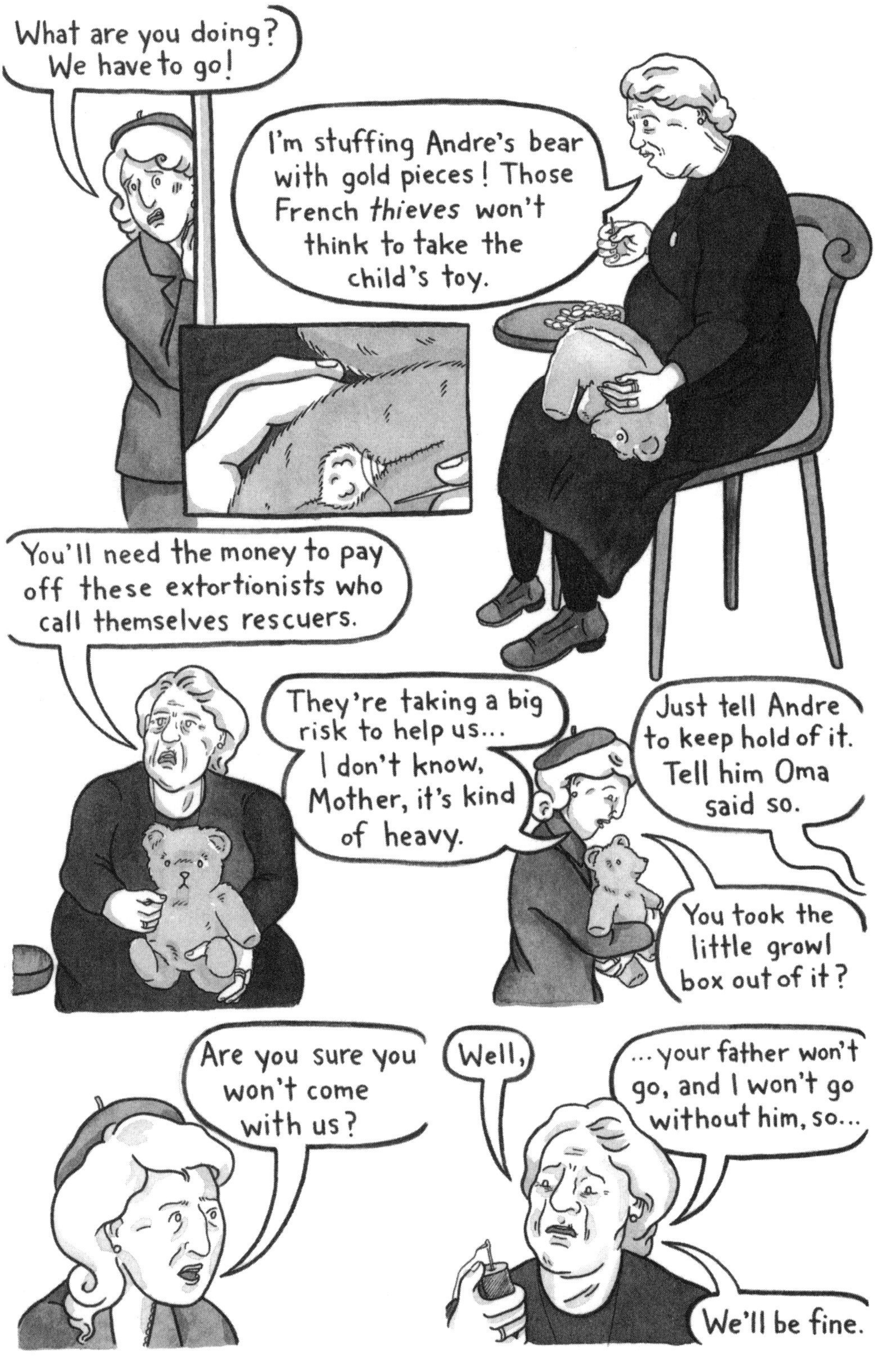
What are you doing? We have to go!
I'm stuffing Andre's bear with gold pieces! Those French *thieves* won't think to take the child's toy.
You'll need the money to pay off these extortionists who call themselves rescuers.
They're taking a big risk to help us... I don't know, Mother, it's kind of heavy.
Just tell Andre to keep hold of it. Tell him Oma said so.
You took the little growl box out of it?
Are you sure you won't come with us?
Well,
...your father won't go, and I won't go without him, so...
We'll be fine.

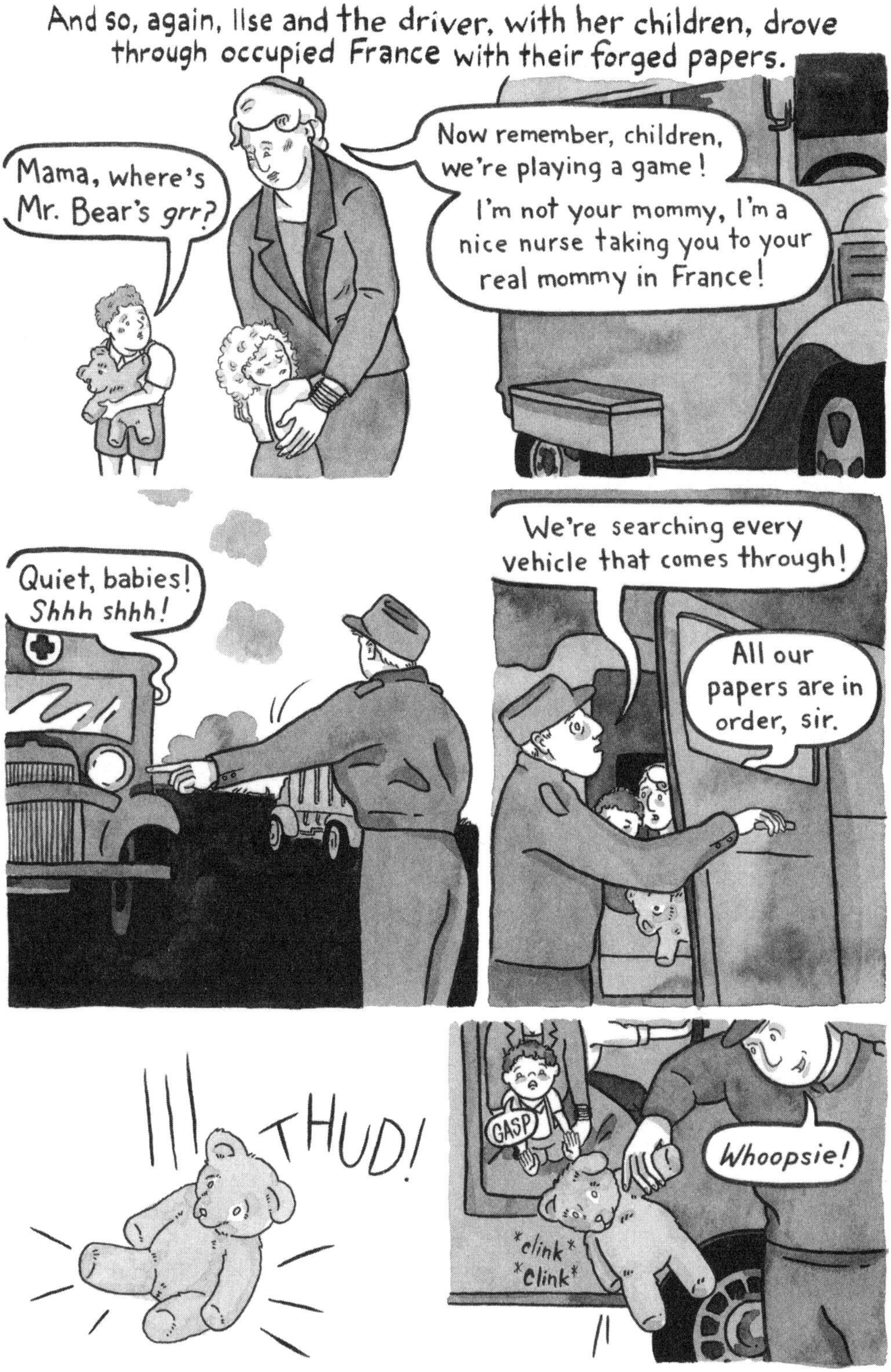
And so, again, Ilse and the driver, with her children, drove through occupied France with their forged papers.
Mama, where's Mr. Bear's grrr?
Now remember, children, we're playing a game!
I'm not your mommy, I'm a nice nurse taking you to your real mommy in France!
Quiet, babies! Shhh shhh!
We're searching every vehicle that comes through!
All our papers are in order, sir.
THUD!
GASP
Whoopsie!
clink
clink

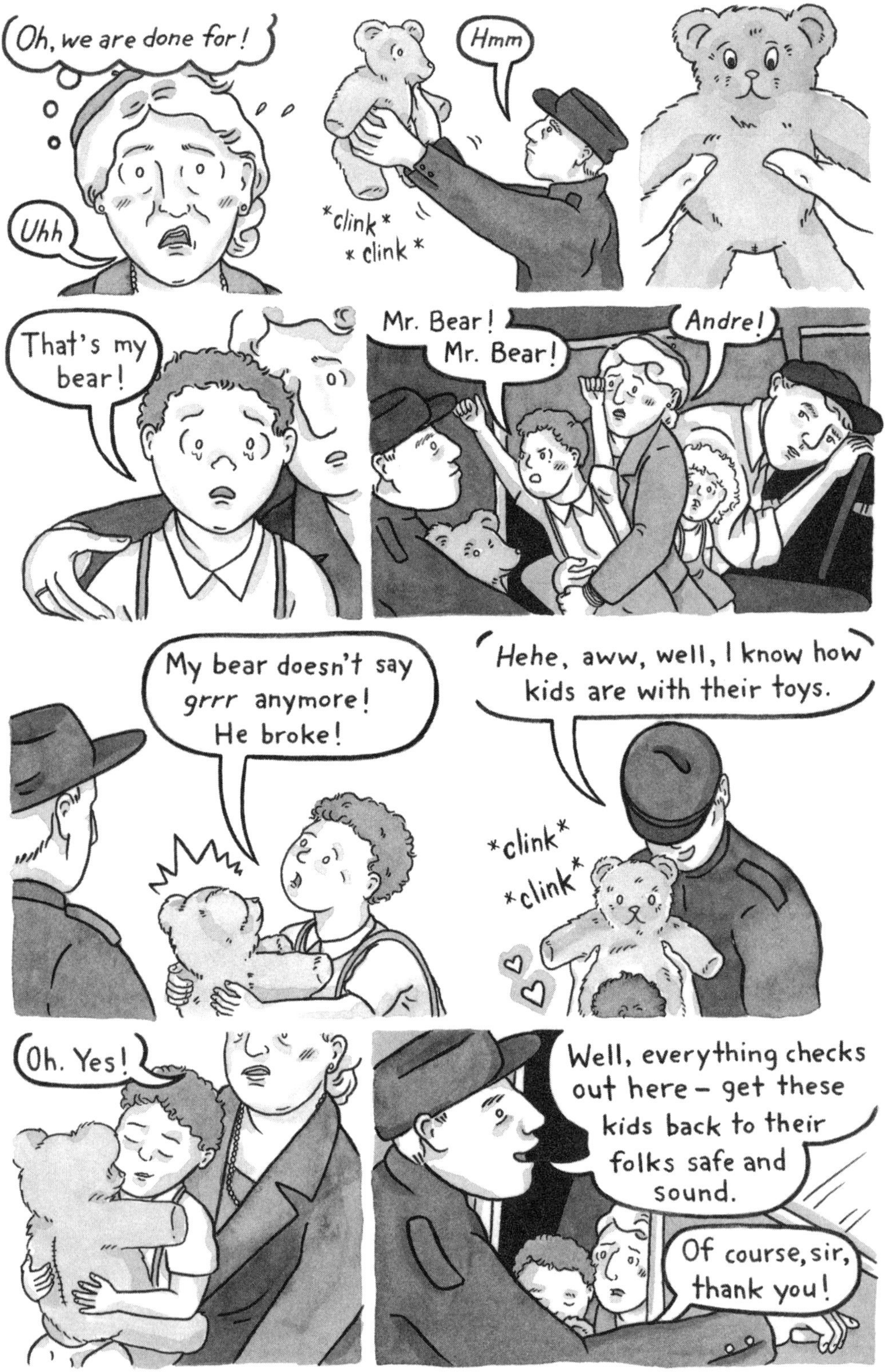
Oh, we are done for!
Uhh
Hmm
clink
clink
That's my bear!
Mr. Bear! Mr. Bear!
Andre!
My bear doesn't say *grrr* anymore! He broke!
Hehe, aww, well, I know how kids are with their toys.
clink
clink
Oh. Yes!
Well, everything checks out here – get these kids back to their folks safe and sound.
Of course, sir, thank you!

I thought for sure we were going to be lined up and shot.

The driver was killed, by the way. He was shot, later on.

From the 1988 tape

They found out what he was doing...

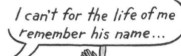

I can't for the life of me remember his name...

He did it as long as he could, he helped people out, and he was killed.

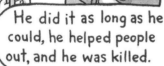

Bye-bye!

Rather than asking—What *would* I do if I was in their place—we might ask: What am I doing, right now in the present, that mirrors these actions?

tap
tap
tap

I keep returning to Primo Levi, who turns the mirror back on ourselves.

Less... would I drive the Levis to Free France in 1940 and more, who needs assistance and refuge right *now*.

231

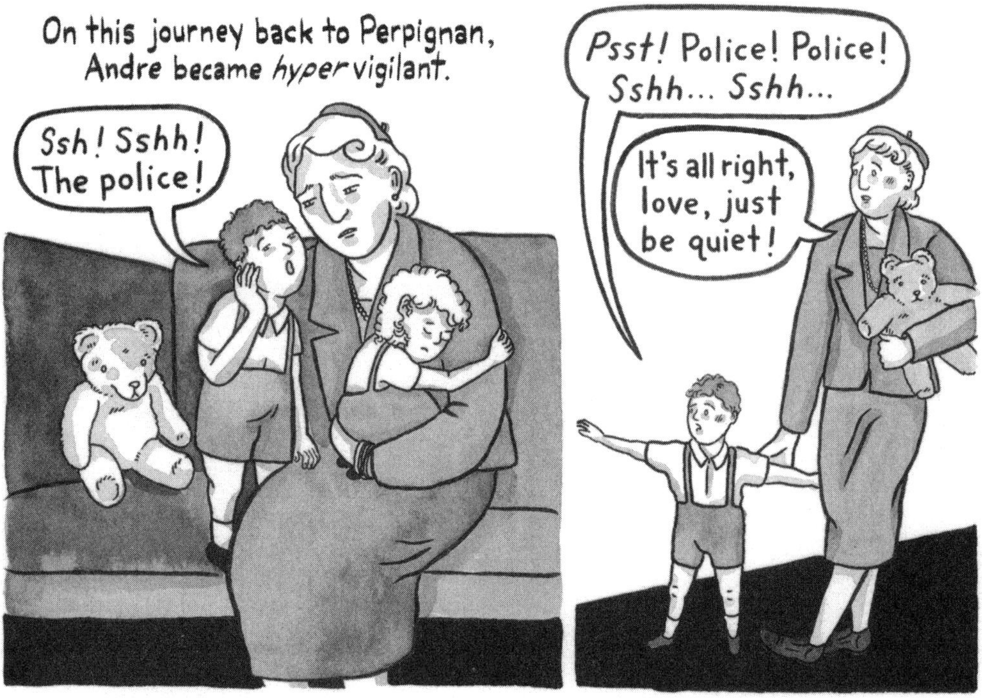
On this journey back to Perpignan, Andre became *hyper* vigilant.
Ssh! Sshh! The police!
Psst! Police! Police! Sshh... Sshh...
It's all right, love, just be quiet!

Nathan Durst, writing on child-survivors of the Holocaust in the *American Journal of Psychotherapy*, describes survivors of my grandfather's age as having developed *"chameleonlike features that were connected to the continuing demands of having to adapt to ever new frightening situations."*

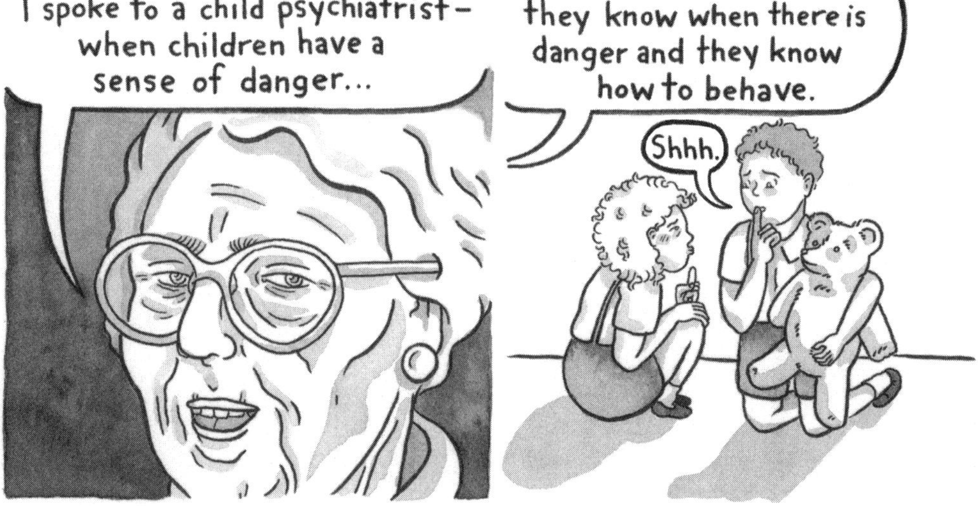
I spoke to a child psychiatrist– when children have a sense of danger...
they know when there is danger and they know how to behave.
Shhh.

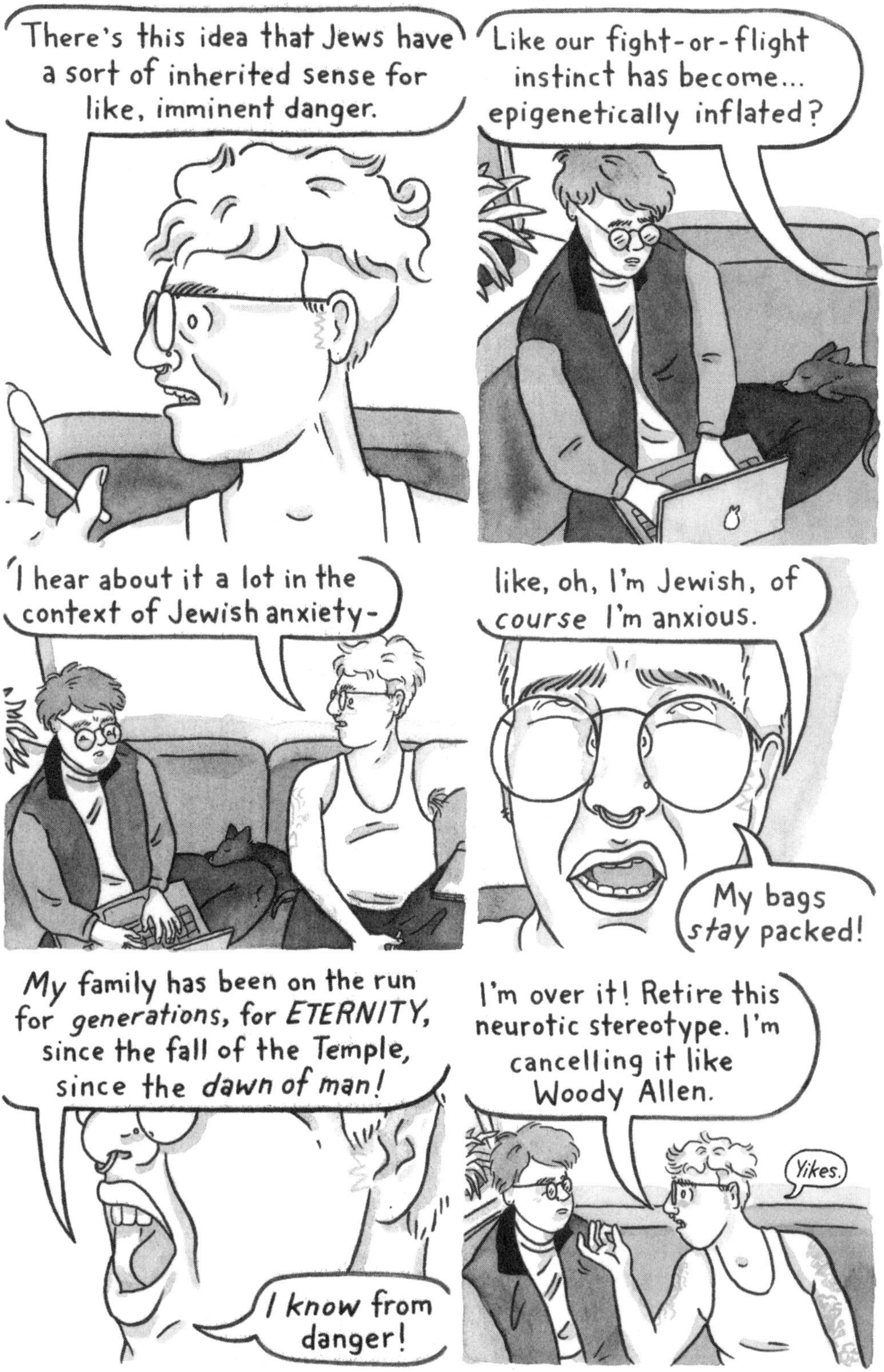
There's this idea that Jews have a sort of inherited sense for like, imminent danger.
Like our fight-or-flight instinct has become... epigenetically inflated?
I hear about it a lot in the context of Jewish anxiety-
like, oh, I'm Jewish, of *course* I'm anxious.
My bags *stay* packed!
My family has been on the run for *generations*, for *ETERNITY*, since the fall of the Temple, since the *dawn of man*!
I know from danger!
I'm over it! Retire this neurotic stereotype. I'm cancelling it like Woody Allen.
Yikes.

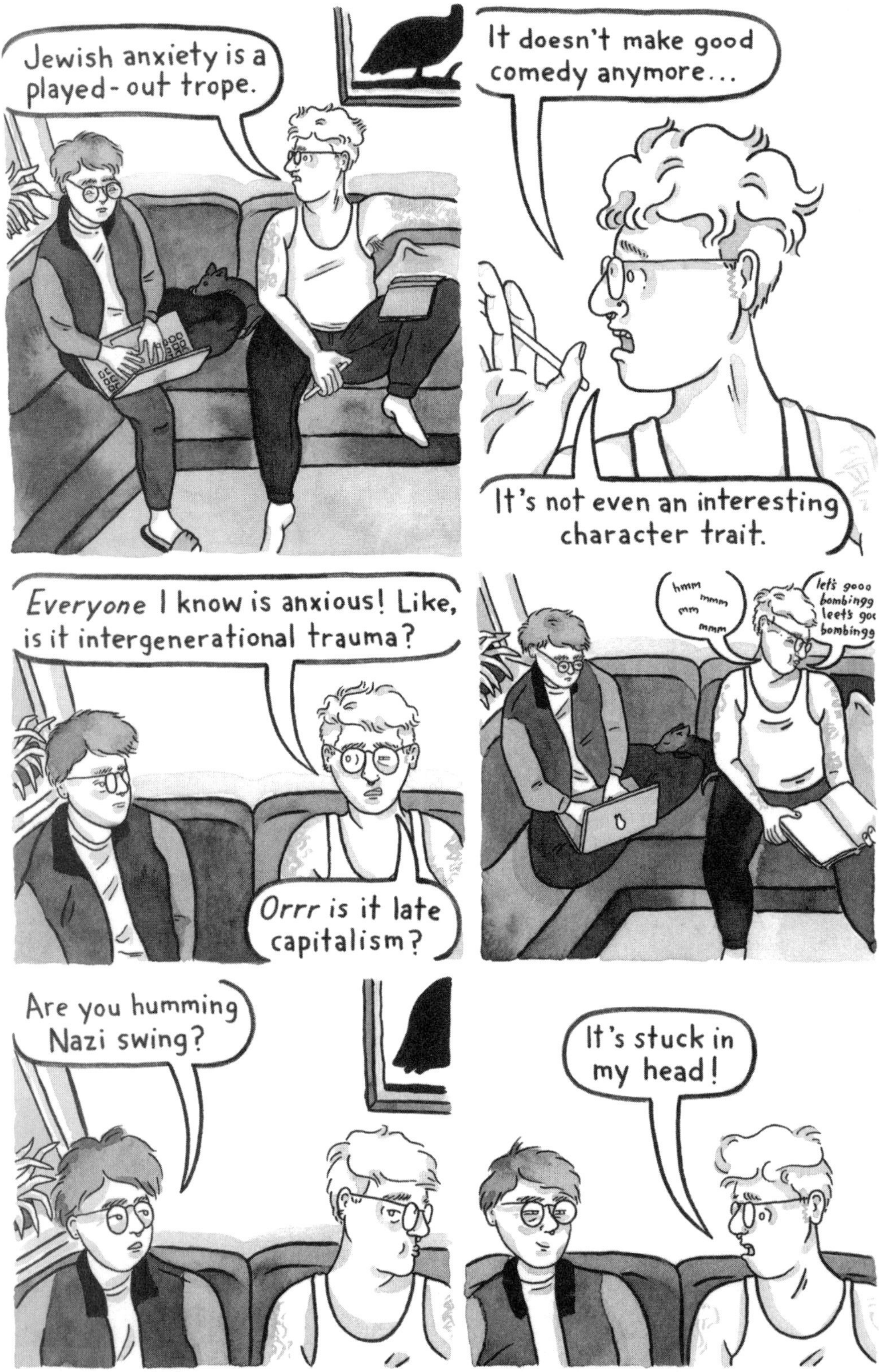
Jewish anxiety is a played-out trope.
It doesn't make good comedy anymore...
It's not even an interesting character trait.
Everyone I know is anxious! Like, is it intergenerational trauma?
Orrr is it late capitalism?
hmm mmm mm mmm
let's gooo bombingg leet's go bombingg
Are you humming Nazi swing?
It's stuck in my head!

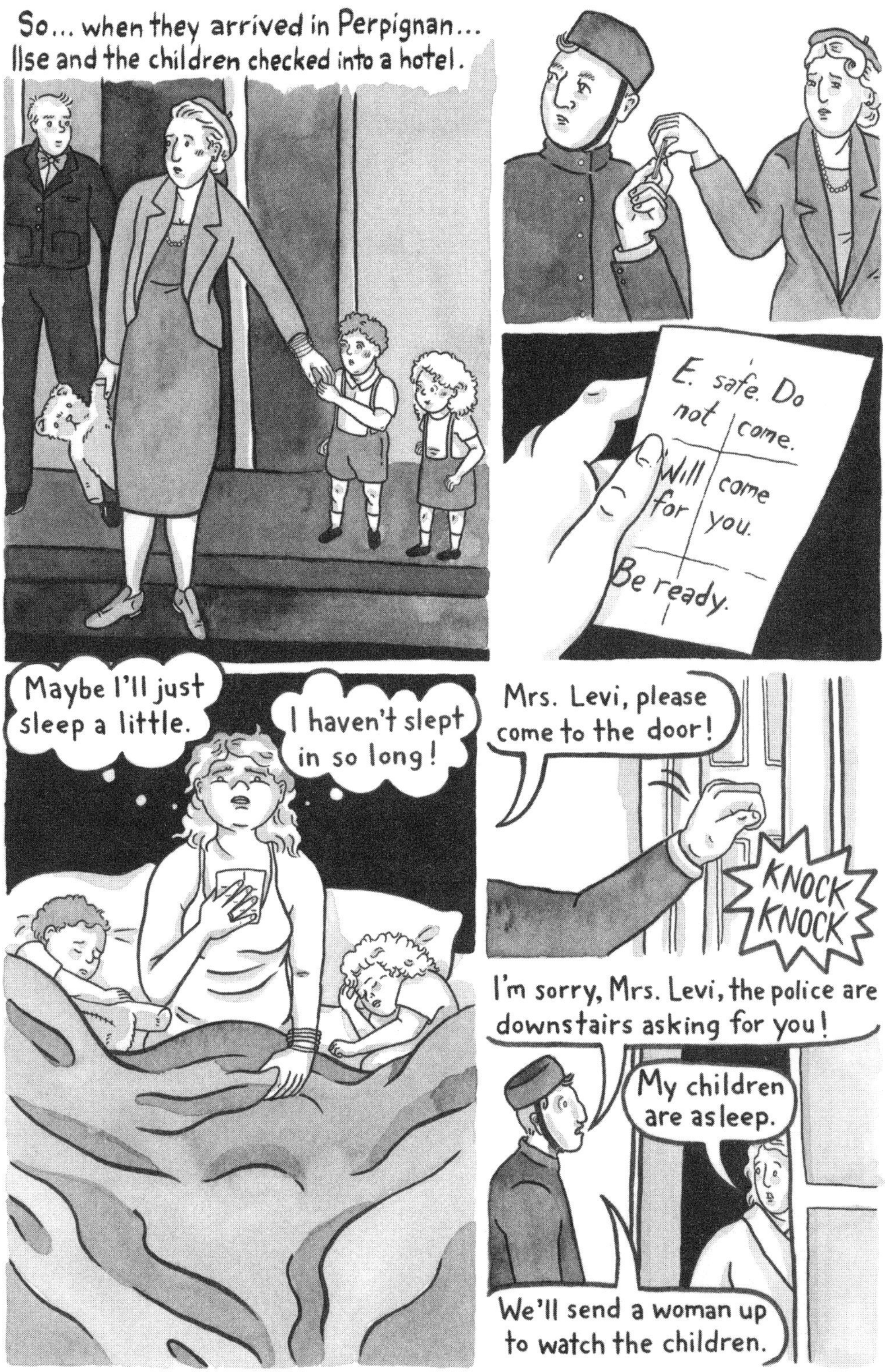

So... when they arrived in Perpignan... Ilse and the children checked into a hotel.
E. safe. Do not come.
Will come for you.
Be ready.
Maybe I'll just sleep a little.
I haven't slept in so long!
Mrs. Levi, please come to the door!
KNOCK KNOCK
I'm sorry, Mrs. Levi, the police are downstairs asking for you!
My children are asleep.
We'll send a woman up to watch the children.

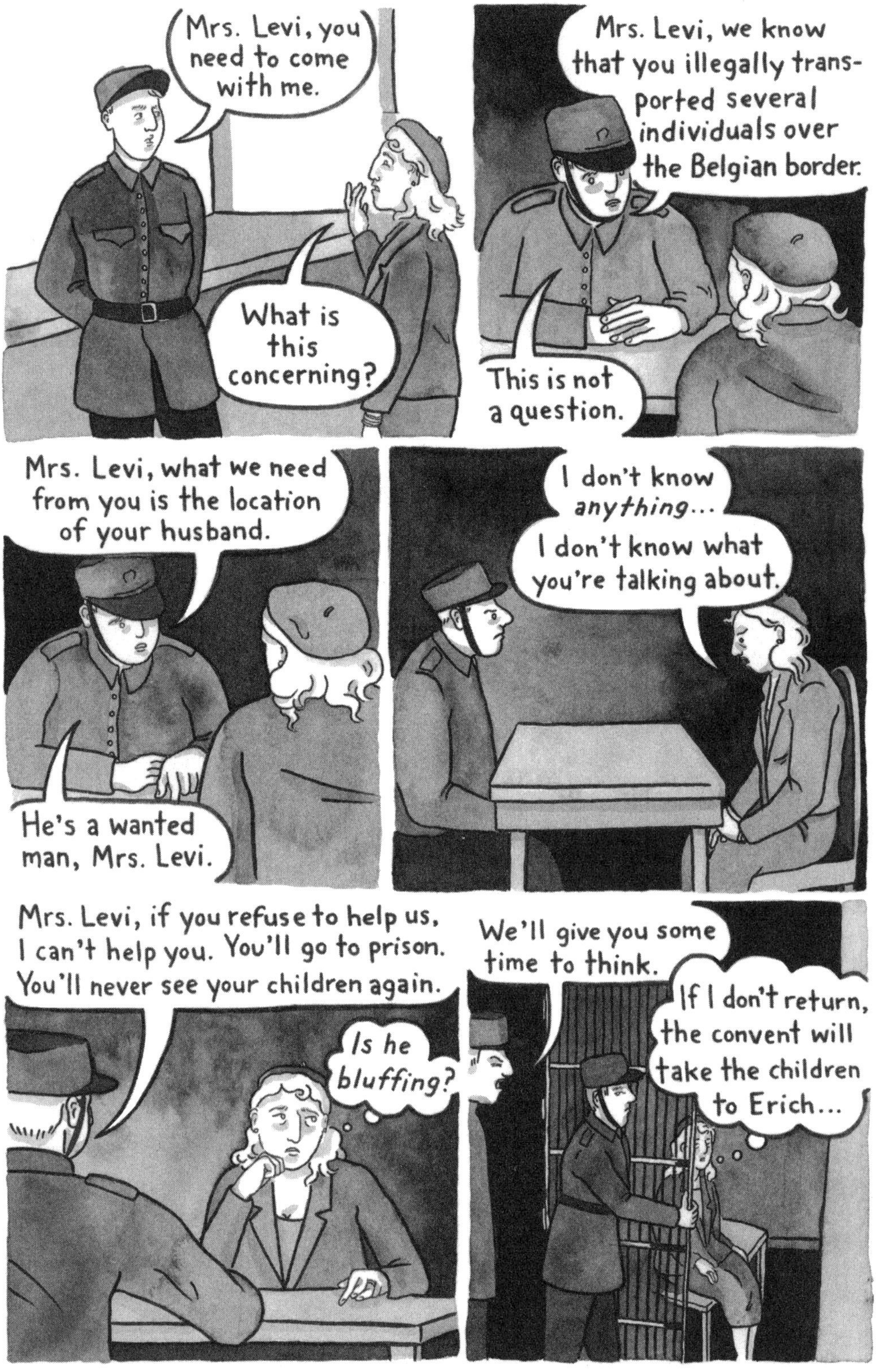

Mrs. Levi, you need to come with me.
What is this concerning?
Mrs. Levi, we know that you illegally transported several individuals over the Belgian border.
This is not a question.
Mrs. Levi, what we need from you is the location of your husband.
He's a wanted man, Mrs. Levi.
I don't know *anything*...
I don't know what you're talking about.
Mrs. Levi, if you refuse to help us, I can't help you. You'll go to prison. You'll never see your children again.
Is he bluffing?
We'll give you some time to think.
If I don't return, the convent will take the children to Erich...

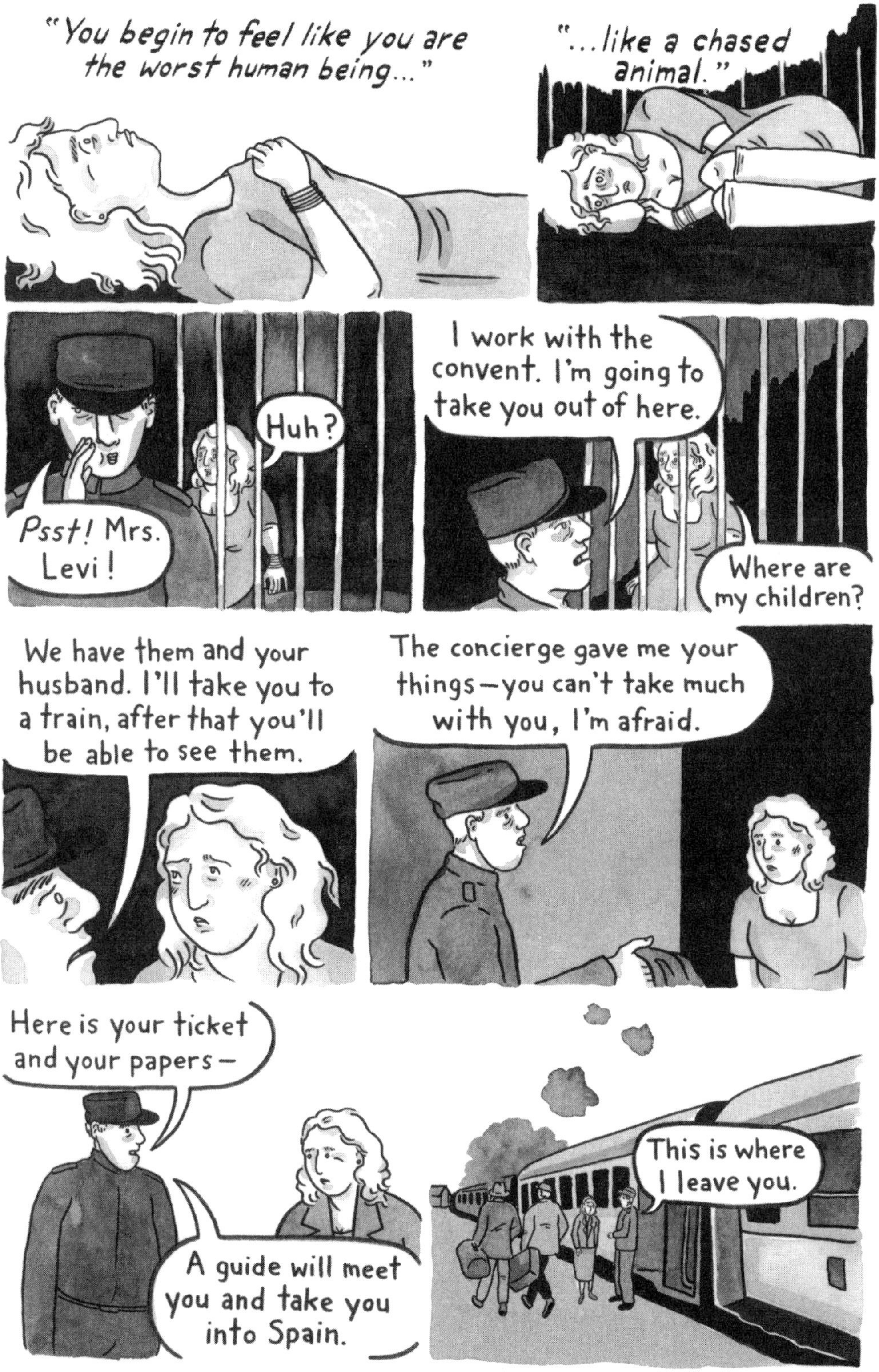
"You begin to feel like you are the worst human being..."
"...like a chased animal."
Psst! Mrs. Levi!
Huh?
I work with the convent. I'm going to take you out of here.
Where are my children?
We have them and your husband. I'll take you to a train, after that you'll be able to see them.
The concierge gave me your things—you can't take much with you, I'm afraid.
Here is your ticket and your papers—
A guide will meet you and take you into Spain.
This is where I leave you.

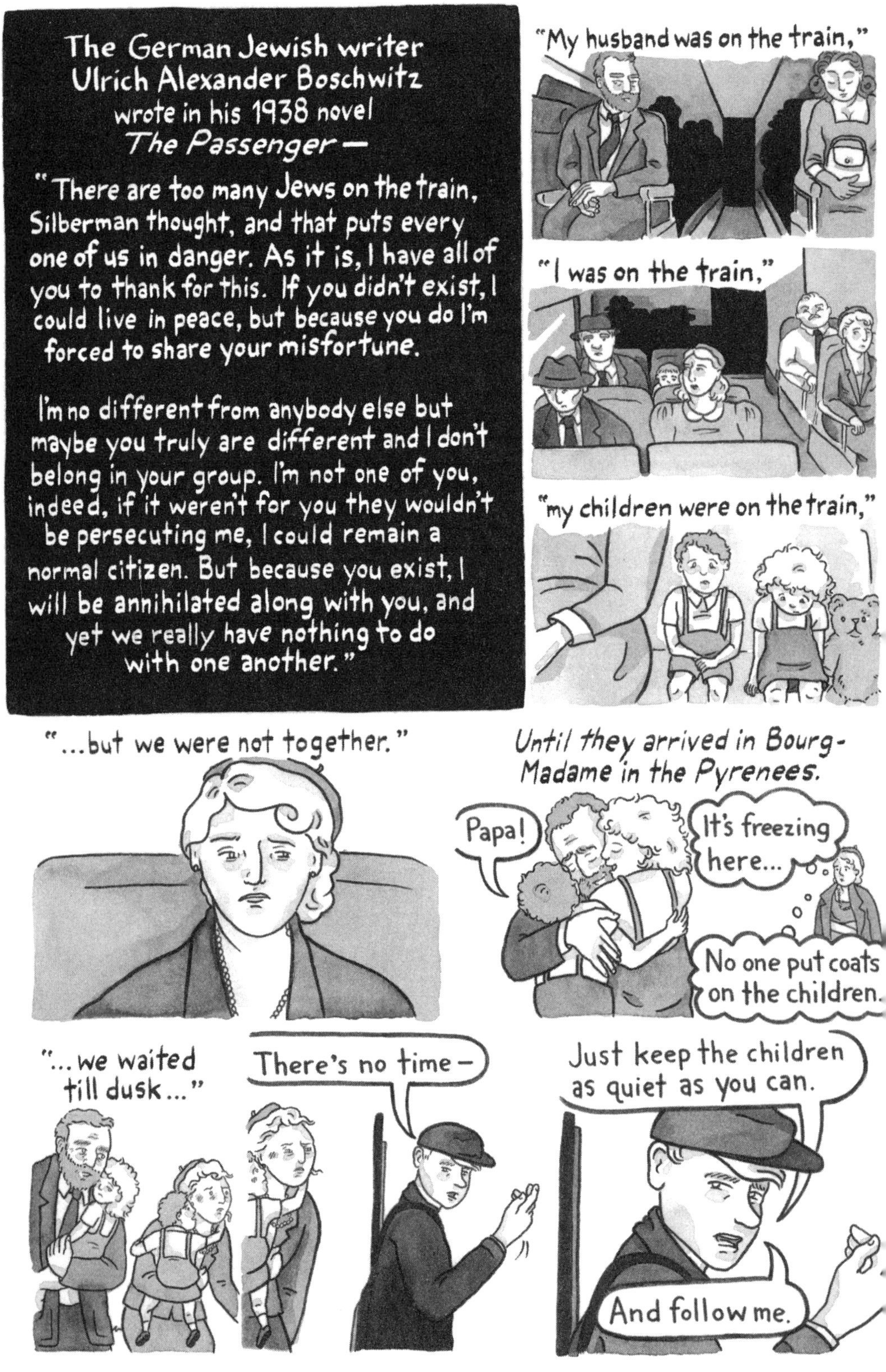
The German Jewish writer Ulrich Alexander Boschwitz wrote in his 1938 novel *The Passenger*—
"There are too many Jews on the train, Silberman thought, and that puts every one of us in danger. As it is, I have all of you to thank for this. If you didn't exist, I could live in peace, but because you do I'm forced to share your misfortune.
I'm no different from anybody else but maybe you truly are different and I don't belong in your group. I'm not one of you, indeed, if it weren't for you they wouldn't be persecuting me, I could remain a normal citizen. But because you exist, I will be annihilated along with you, and yet we really have nothing to do with one another."
"My husband was on the train,"
"I was on the train,"
"my children were on the train,"
"...but we were not together."
Until they arrived in Bourg-Madame in the Pyrenees.
Papa!
It's freezing here...
No one put coats on the children.
"...we waited till dusk..."
There's no time—
Just keep the children as quiet as you can.
And follow me.

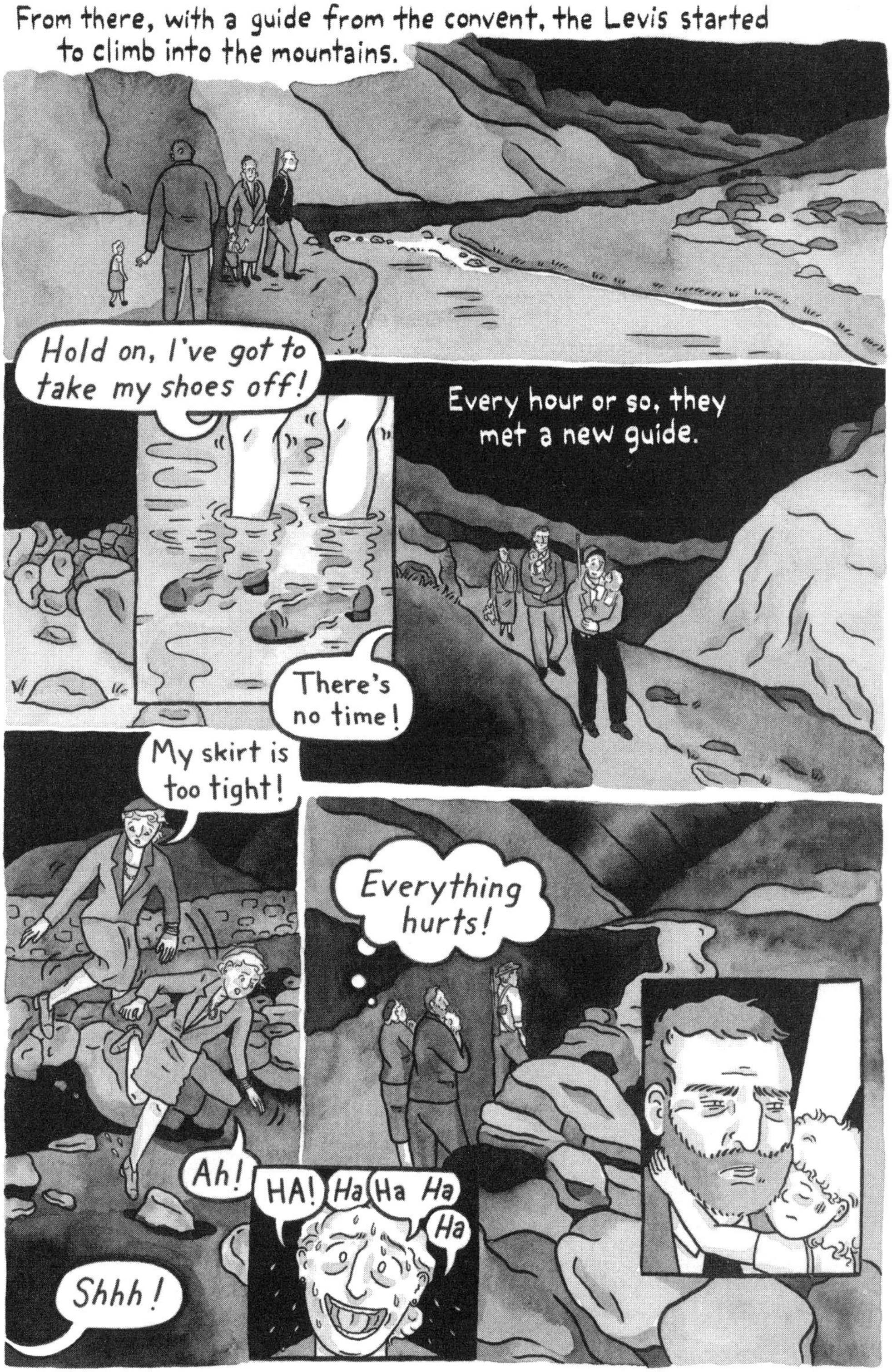
From there, with a guide from the convent, the Levis started to climb into the mountains.
Hold on, I've got to take my shoes off!
There's no time!
Every hour or so, they met a new guide.
My skirt is too tight!
Everything hurts!
Ah!
HA! Ha Ha Ha Ha
Shhh!

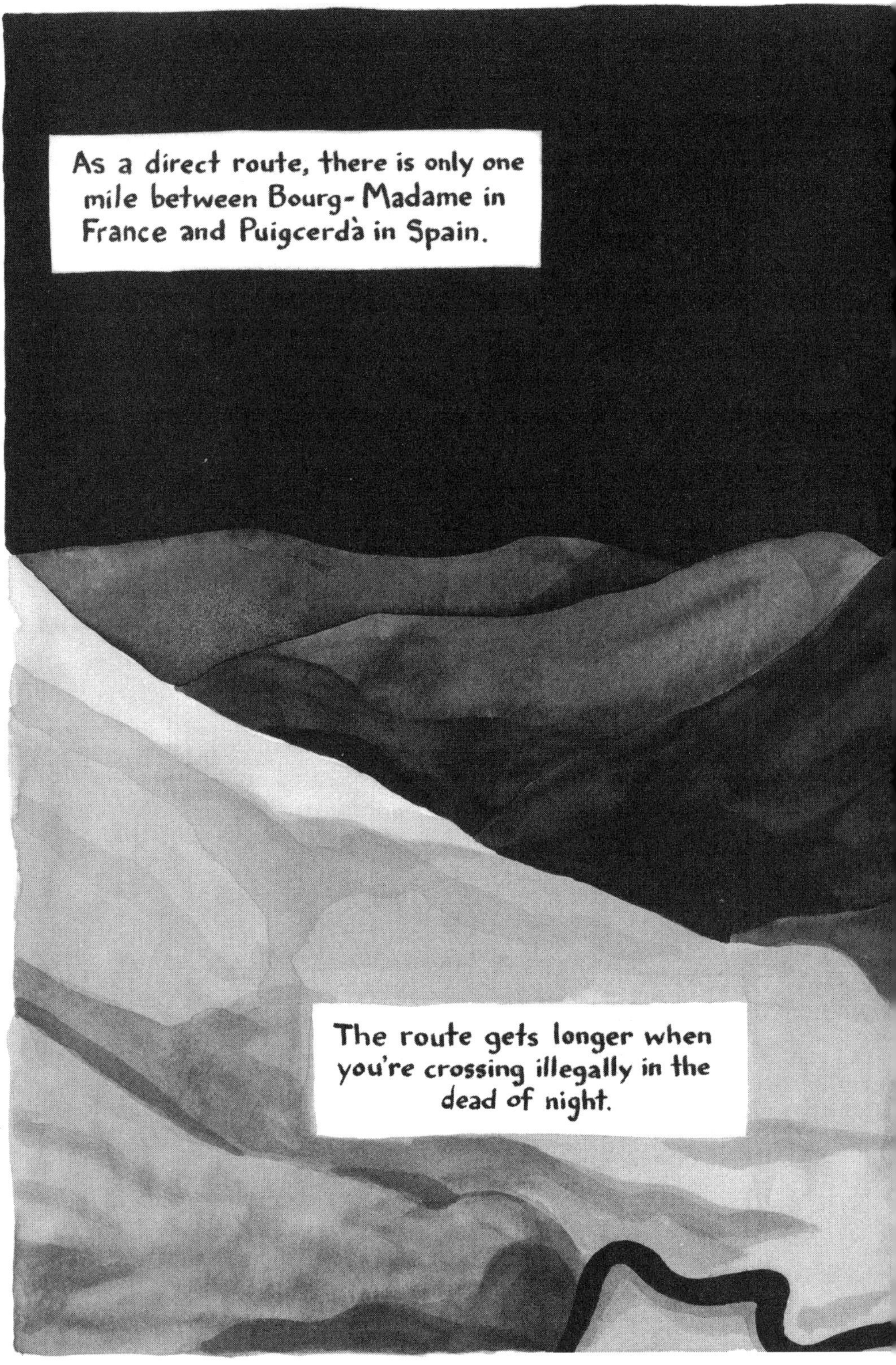
As a direct route, there is only one mile between Bourg-Madame in France and Puigcerdà in Spain.
The route gets longer when you're crossing illegally in the dead of night.

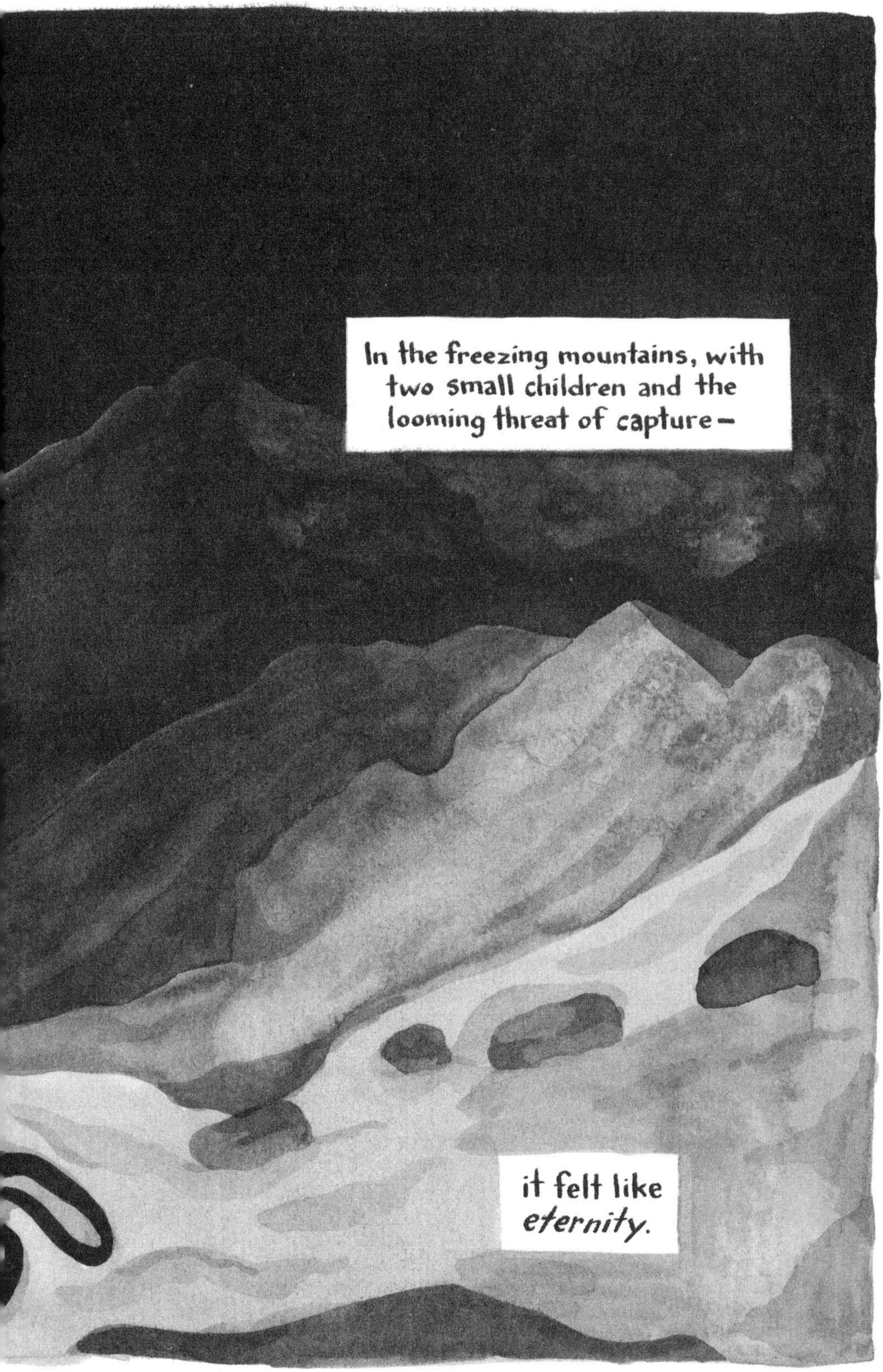
In the freezing mountains, with two small children and the looming threat of capture—
it felt like *eternity*.

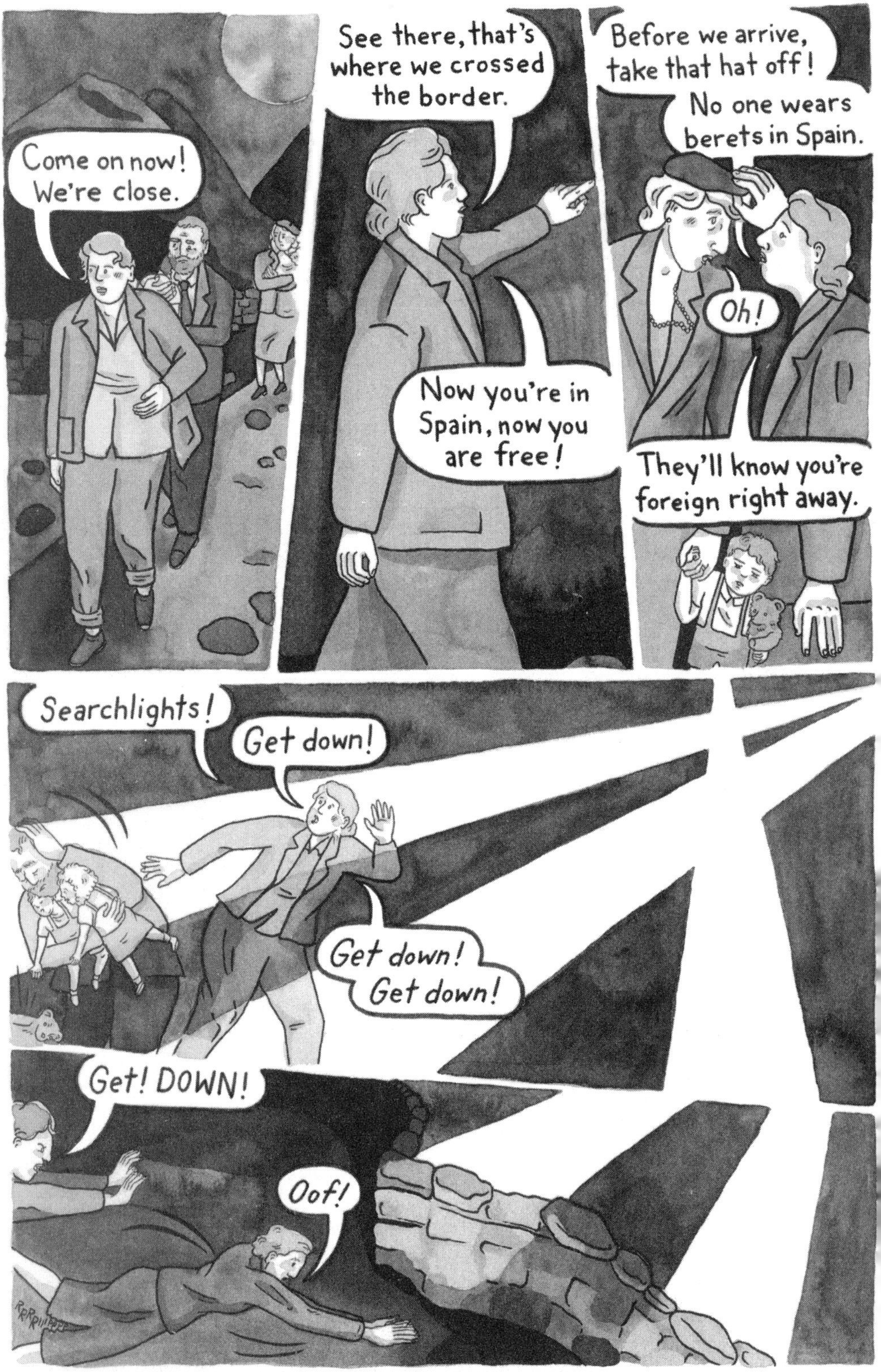
Come on now! We're close.
See there, that's where we crossed the border.
Now you're in Spain, now you are free!
Before we arrive, take that hat off!
No one wears berets in Spain.
Oh!
They'll know you're foreign right away.
Searchlights!
Get down!
Get down! Get down!
Get! DOWN!
Oof!
RRRRIIPP

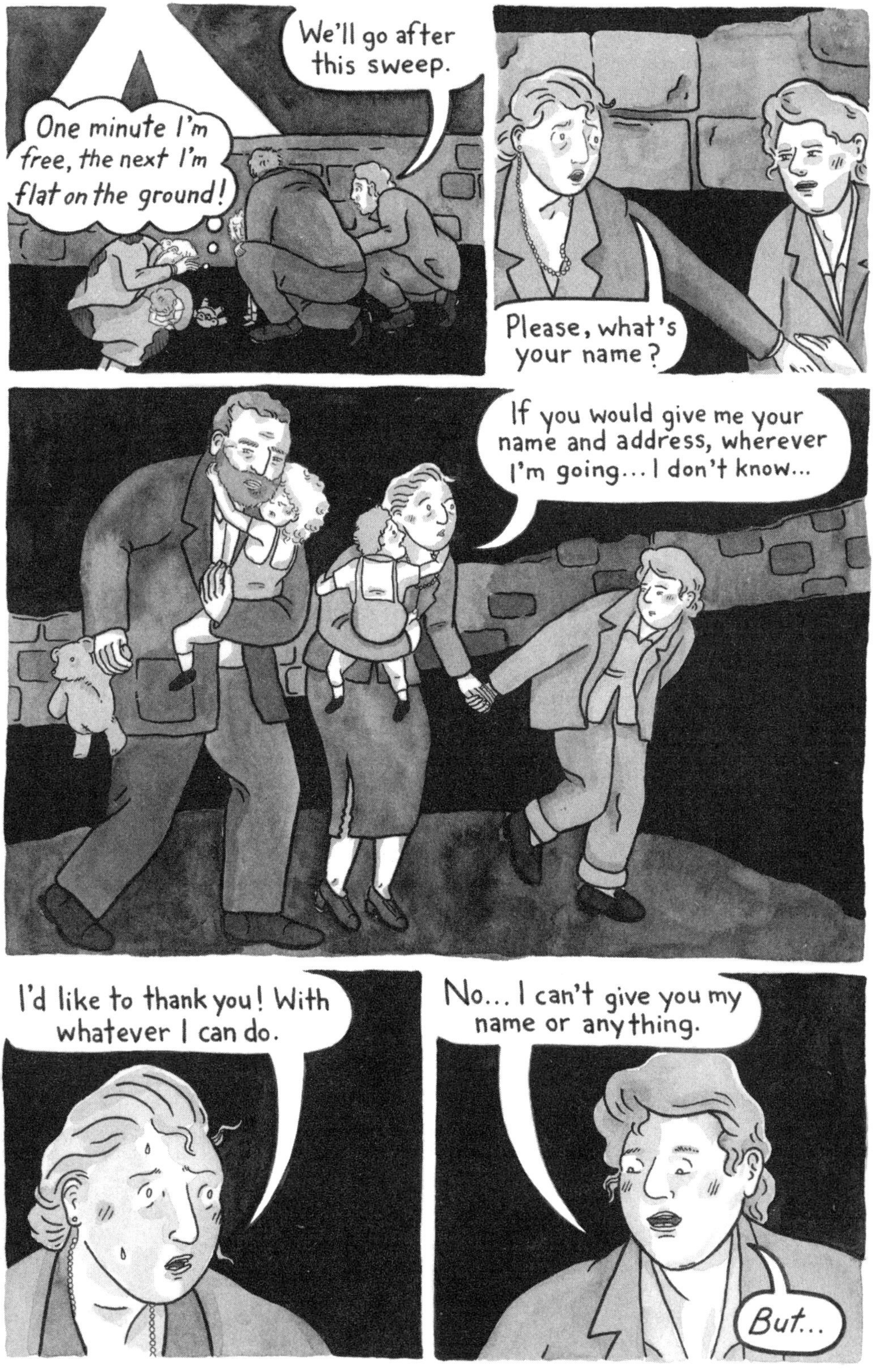
One minute I'm free, the next I'm flat on the ground!
We'll go after this sweep.
Please, what's your name?
If you would give me your name and address, wherever I'm going... I don't know...
I'd like to thank you! With whatever I can do.
No... I can't give you my name or anything.
But...

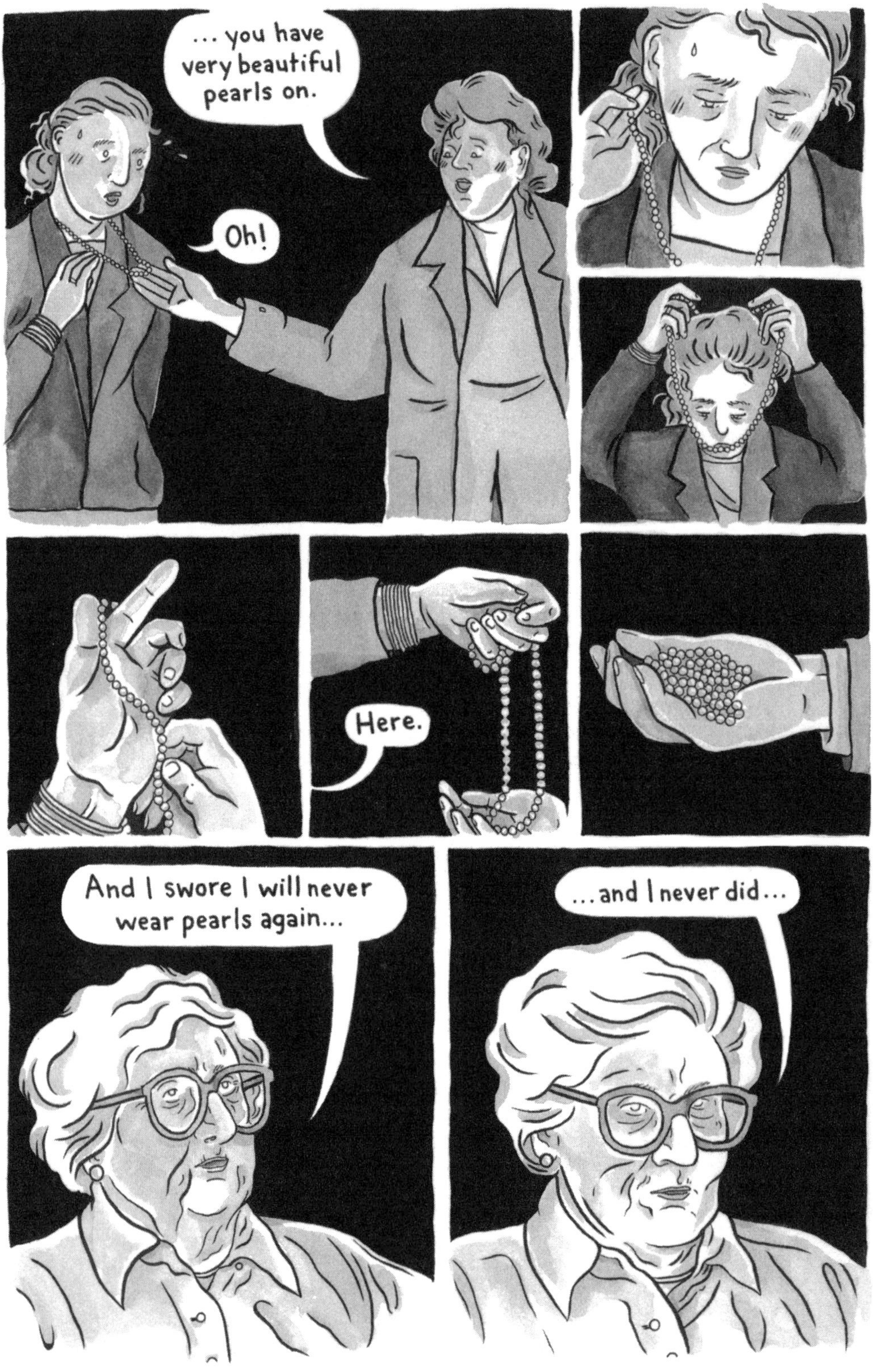
... you have very beautiful pearls on.
Oh!
Here.
And I swore I will never wear pearls again...
...and I never did...

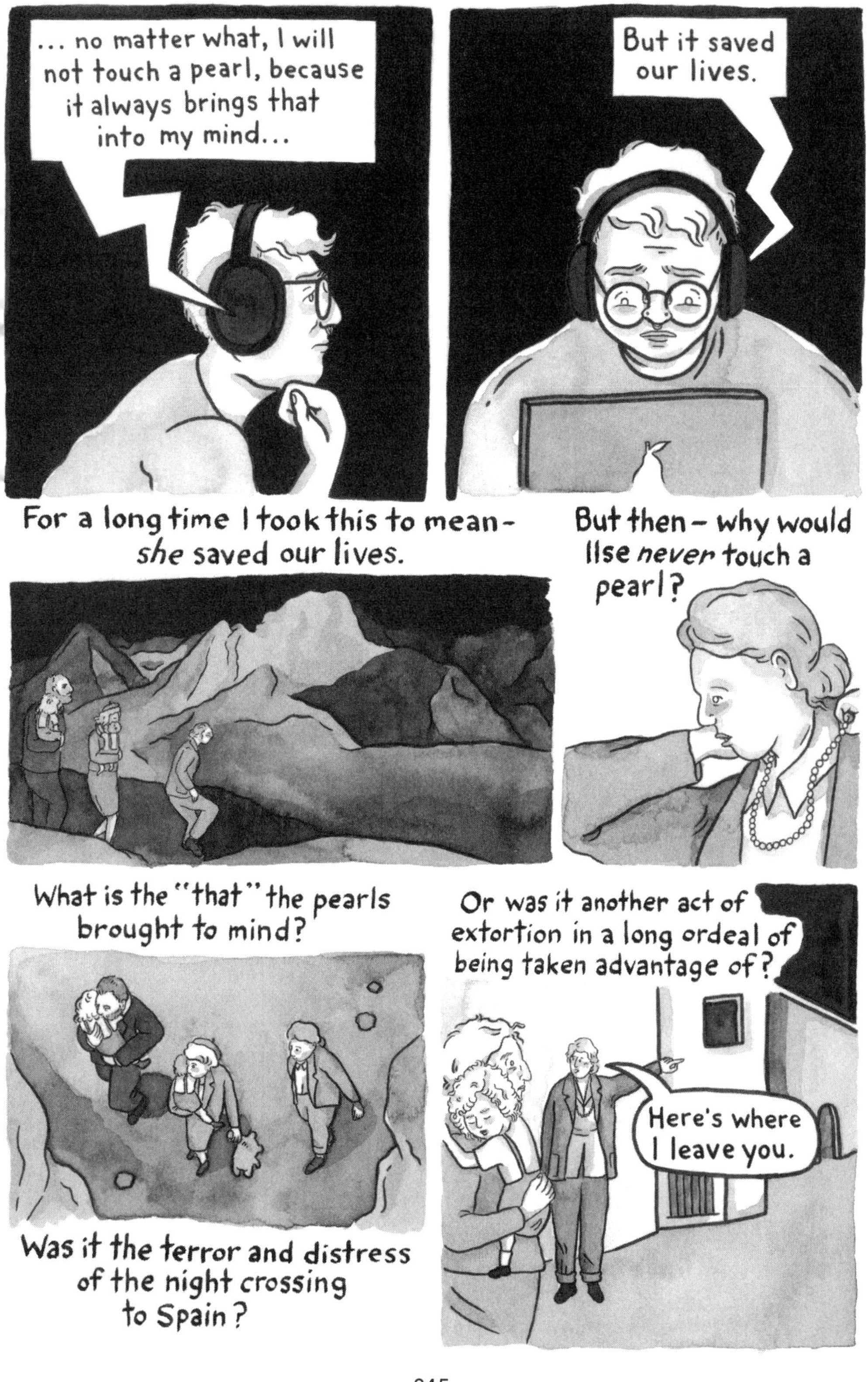

... no matter what, I will not touch a pearl, because it always brings that into my mind...
But it saved our lives.
For a long time I took this to mean– *she* saved our lives.
But then – why would Ilse *never* touch a pearl?
What is the "that" the pearls brought to mind?
Was it the terror and distress of the night crossing to Spain?
Or was it another act of extortion in a long ordeal of being taken advantage of?
Here's where I leave you.

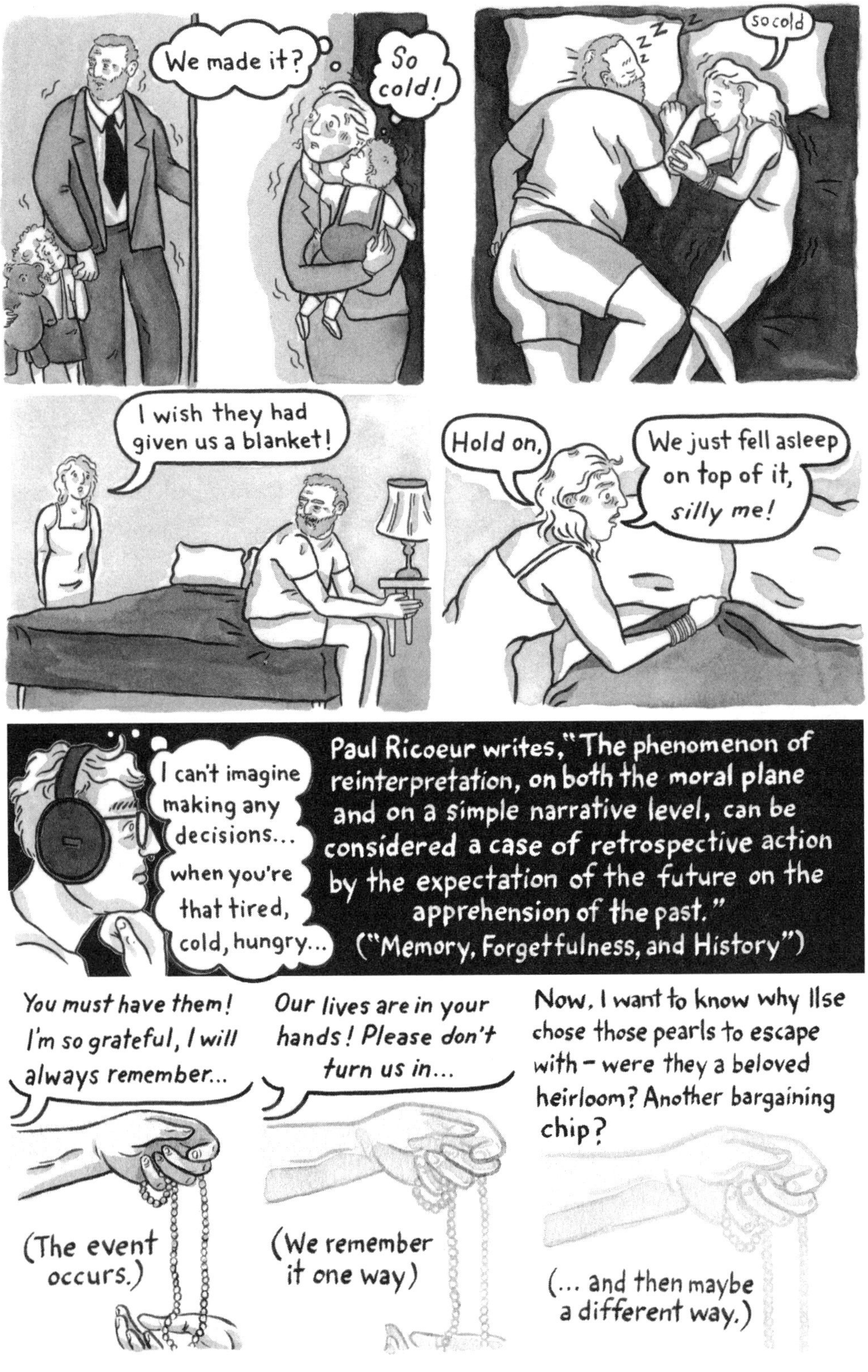

We made it?
So cold!
so cold
I wish they had given us a blanket!
Hold on,
We just fell asleep on top of it, *silly me!*
I can't imagine making any decisions... when you're that tired, cold, hungry...
Paul Ricoeur writes, "The phenomenon of reinterpretation, on both the moral plane and on a simple narrative level, can be considered a case of retrospective action by the expectation of the future on the apprehension of the past." ("Memory, Forgetfulness, and History")
You must have them! I'm so grateful, I will always remember...
(The event occurs.)
Our lives are in your hands! Please don't turn us in...
(We remember it one way)
Now, I want to know why Ilse chose those pearls to escape with – were they a beloved heirloom? Another bargaining chip?
(... and then maybe a different way.)

PART 10

*TRANSATLANTIC
FALANGISTS*

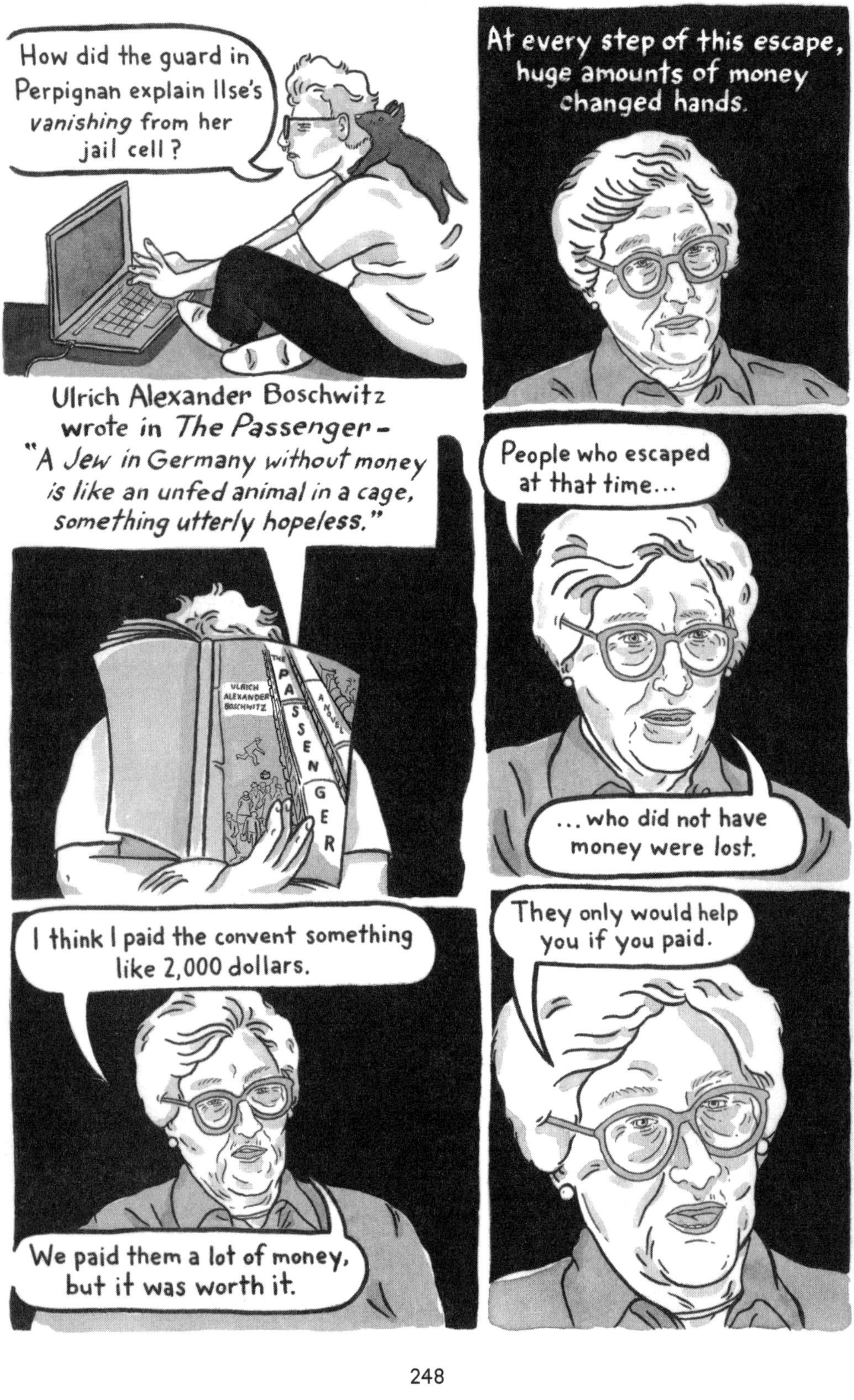
How did the guard in Perpignan explain Ilse's *vanishing* from her jail cell?
At every step of this escape, huge amounts of money changed hands.
Ulrich Alexander Boschwitz wrote in *The Passenger* – "A *Jew* in Germany *without money is like an unfed animal in a cage, something utterly hopeless.*"
People who escaped at that time...
ULRICH ALEXANDER BOSCHWITZ
THE PASSENGER
A NOVEL
...who did not have money were lost.
I think I paid the convent something like 2,000 dollars.
We paid them a lot of money, but it was worth it.
They only would help you if you paid.

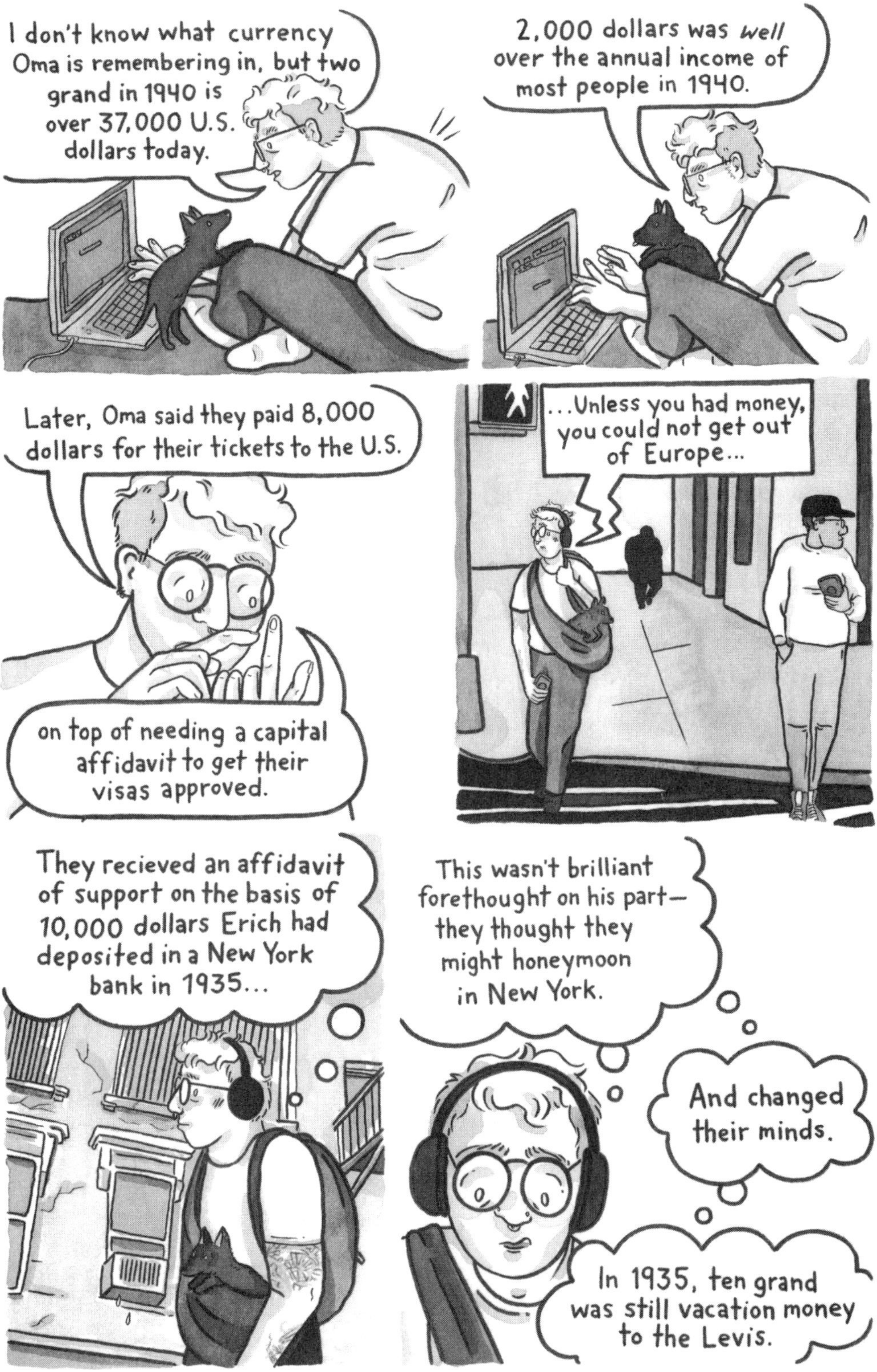
I don't know what currency Oma is remembering in, but two grand in 1940 is over 37,000 U.S. dollars today.
2,000 dollars was *well* over the annual income of most people in 1940.
Later, Oma said they paid 8,000 dollars for their tickets to the U.S.
on top of needing a capital affidavit to get their visas approved.
...Unless you had money, you could not get out of Europe...
They recieved an affidavit of support on the basis of 10,000 dollars Erich had deposited in a New York bank in 1935...
This wasn't brilliant forethought on his part— they thought they might honeymoon in New York.
And changed their minds.
In 1935, ten grand was still vacation money to the Levis.

After arriving in Spain, the Levis took a train to Barcelona...

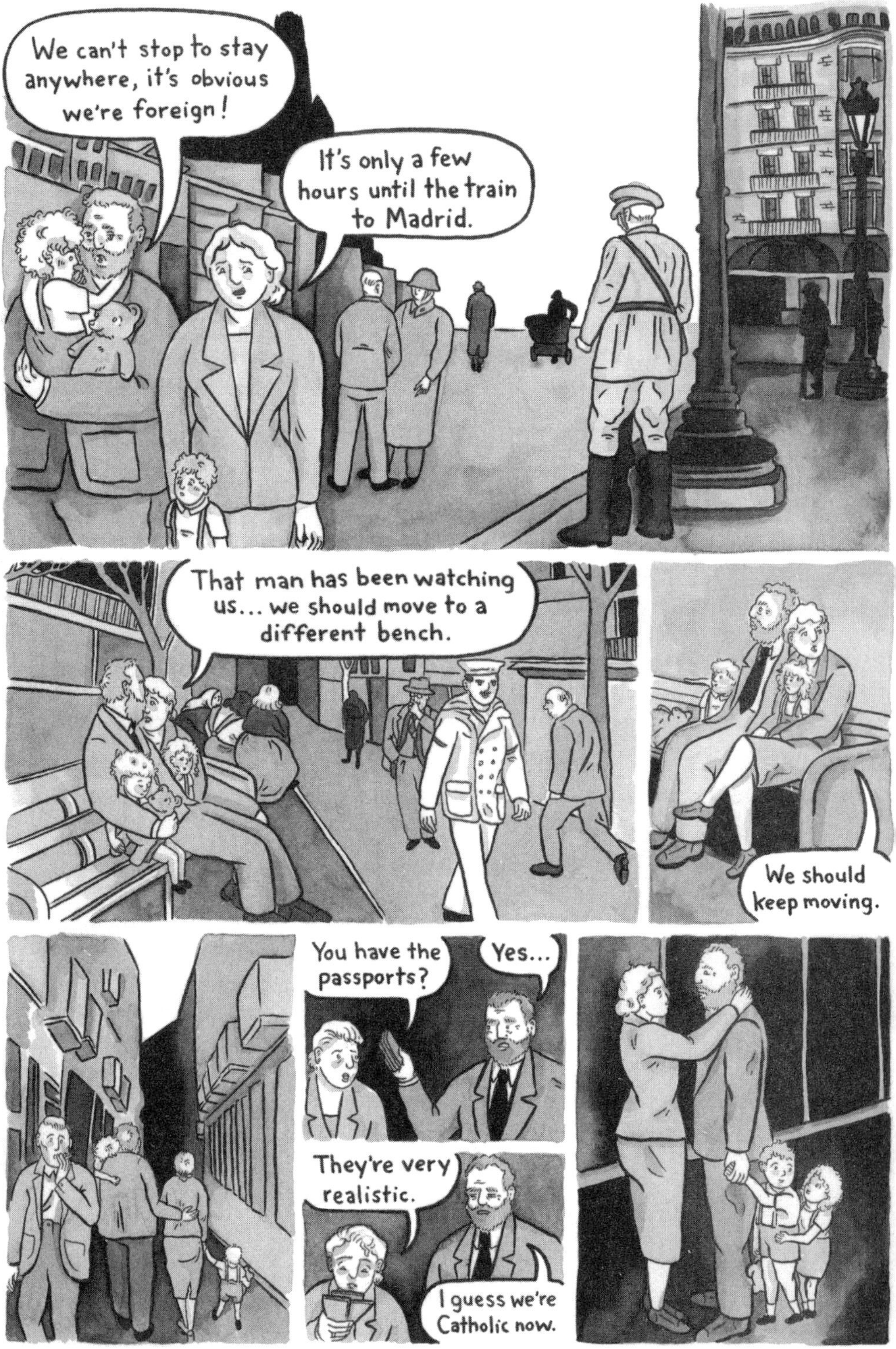

We can't stop to stay anywhere, it's obvious we're foreign!
It's only a few hours until the train to Madrid.
That man has been watching us... we should move to a different bench.
We should keep moving.
You have the passports?
Yes...
They're very realistic.
I guess we're Catholic now.

In Madrid, they caught a train to Lisbon – out of neutral (but friendly to Germany) fascist Spain, into neutral (but allied to England) authoritarian Portugal.

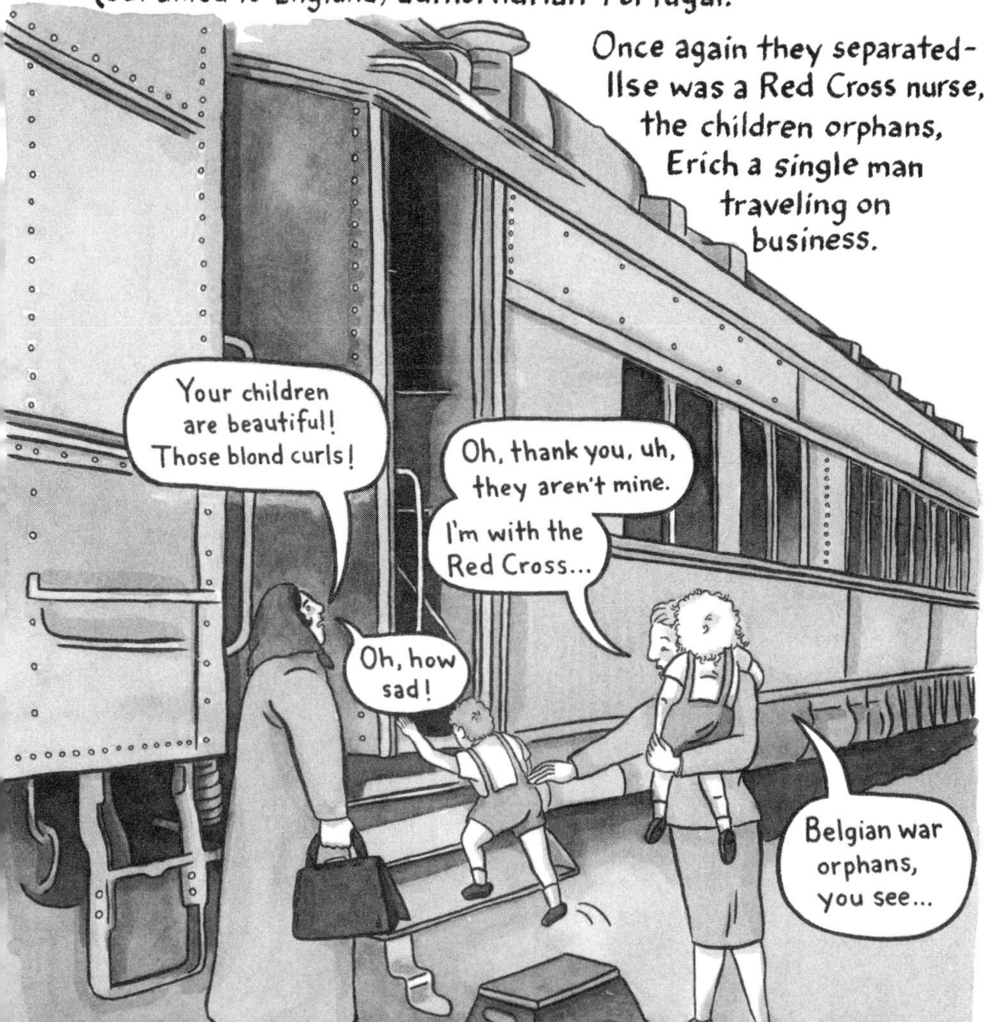
Once again they separated- Ilse was a Red Cross nurse, the children orphans, Erich a *single* man traveling on business.
Your children are beautiful! Those blond curls!
Oh, thank you, uh, they aren't mine.
I'm with the Red Cross...
Oh, how sad!
Belgian war orphans, you see...

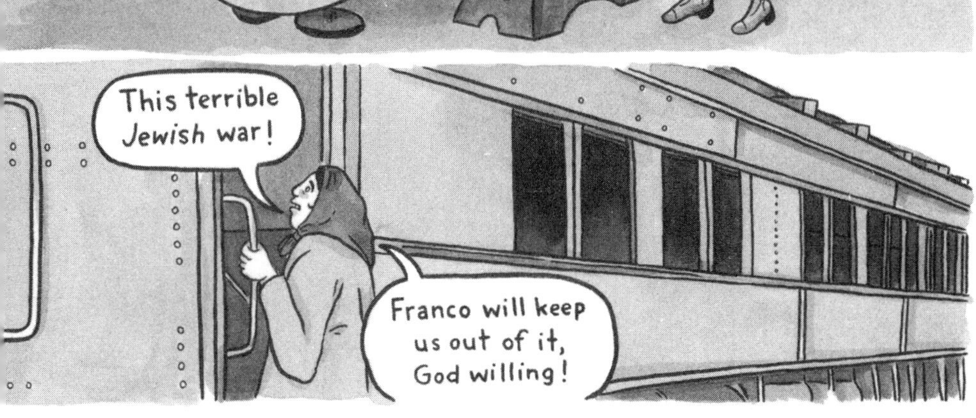
This terrible *Jewish* war!
Franco will keep us out of it, God willing!

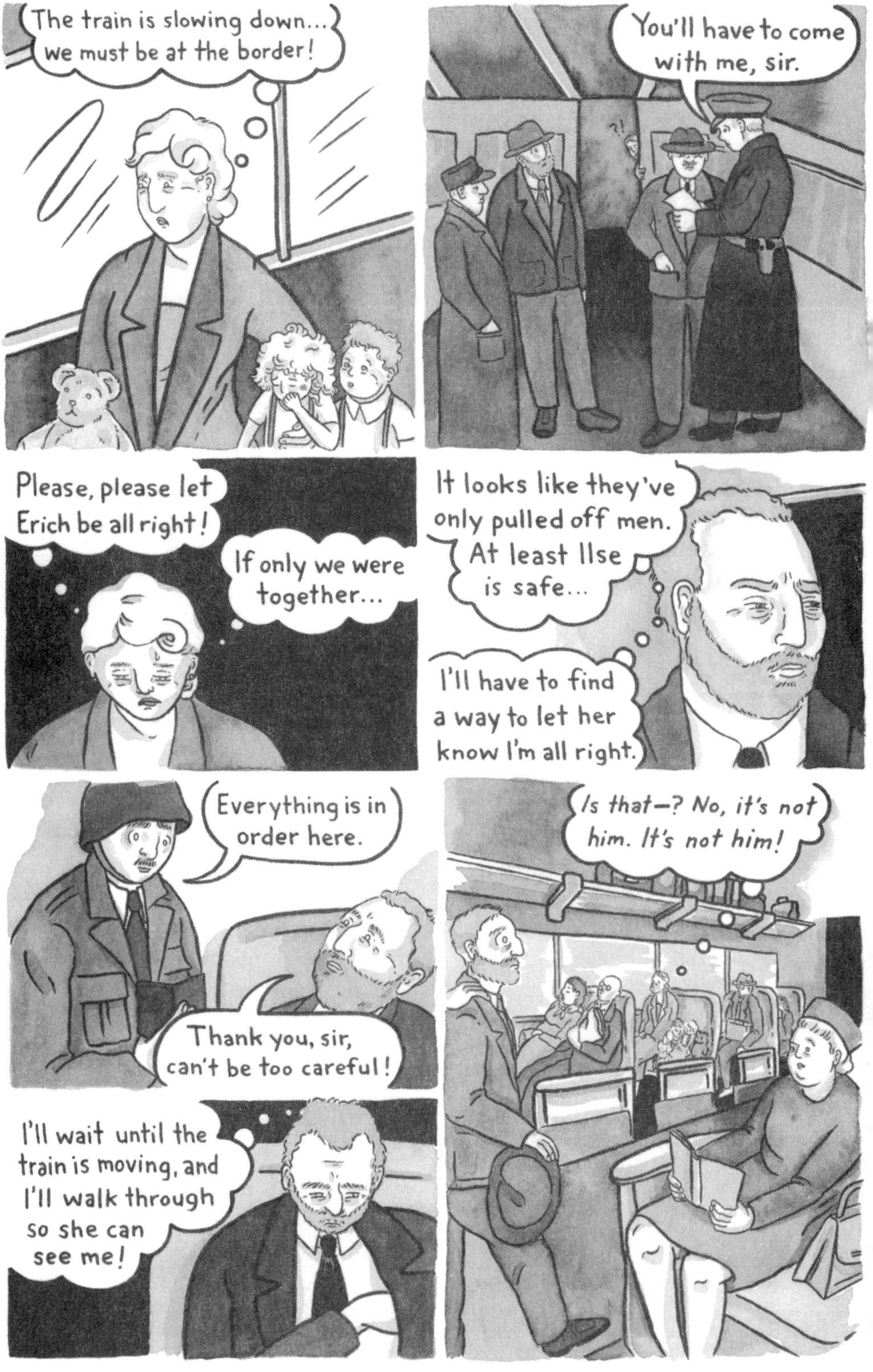
The train is slowing down... we must be at the border!
You'll have to come with me, sir.
?!
Please, please let Erich be all right!
If only we were together...
It looks like they've only pulled off men. At least Ilse is safe...
I'll have to find a way to let her know I'm all right.
Everything is in order here.
Thank you, sir, can't be too careful!
I'll wait until the train is moving, and I'll walk through so she can see me!
Is that—? No, it's not him. It's not him!

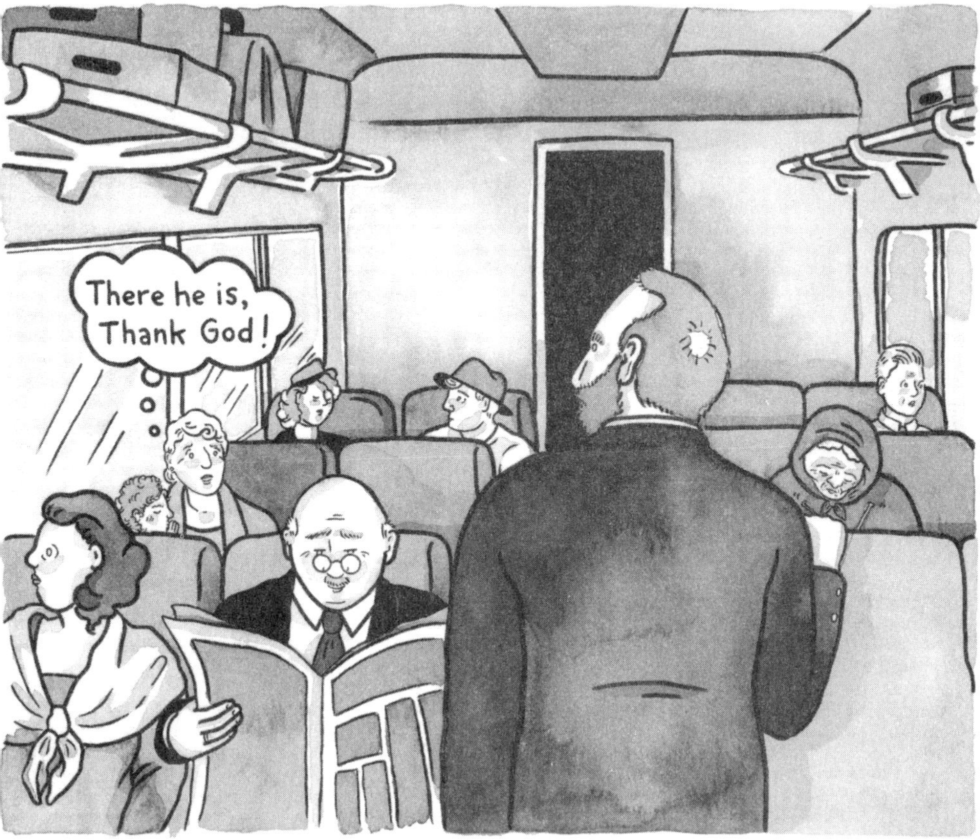
There he is, Thank God!

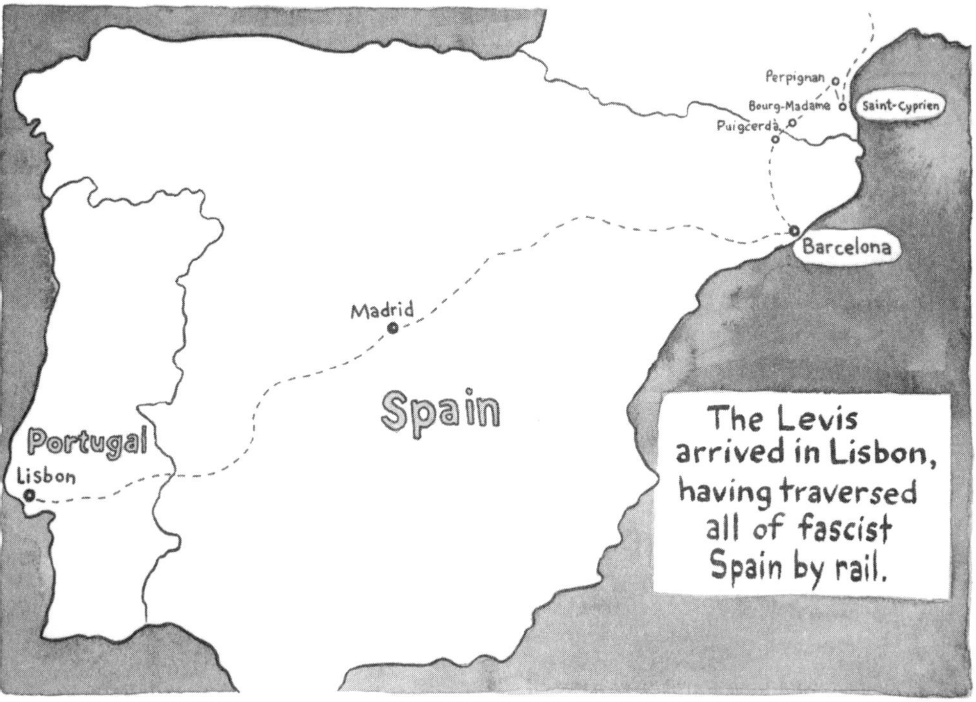
Perpignan
Bourg-Madame
Saint-Cyprien
Puigcerdà
Barcelona
Madrid
Spain
Portugal
Lisbon
The Levis arrived in Lisbon, having traversed all of fascist Spain by rail.

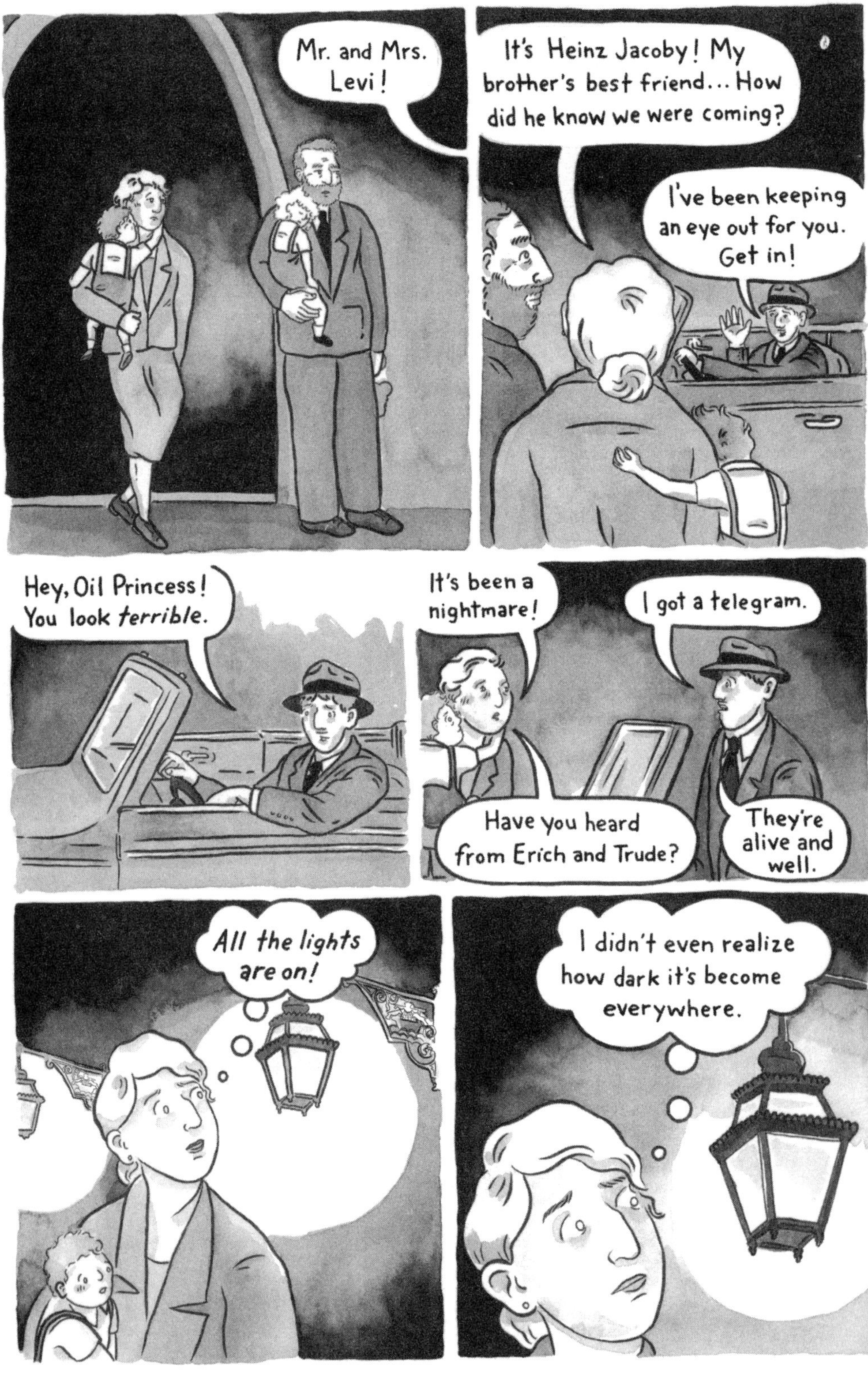
Mr. and Mrs. Levi!
It's Heinz Jacoby! My brother's best friend... How did he know we were coming?
I've been keeping an eye out for you. Get in!
Hey, Oil Princess! You look *terrible*.
It's been a nightmare!
I got a telegram.
Have you heard from Erich and Trude?
They're alive and well.
All the lights are on!
I didn't even realize how dark it's become everywhere.

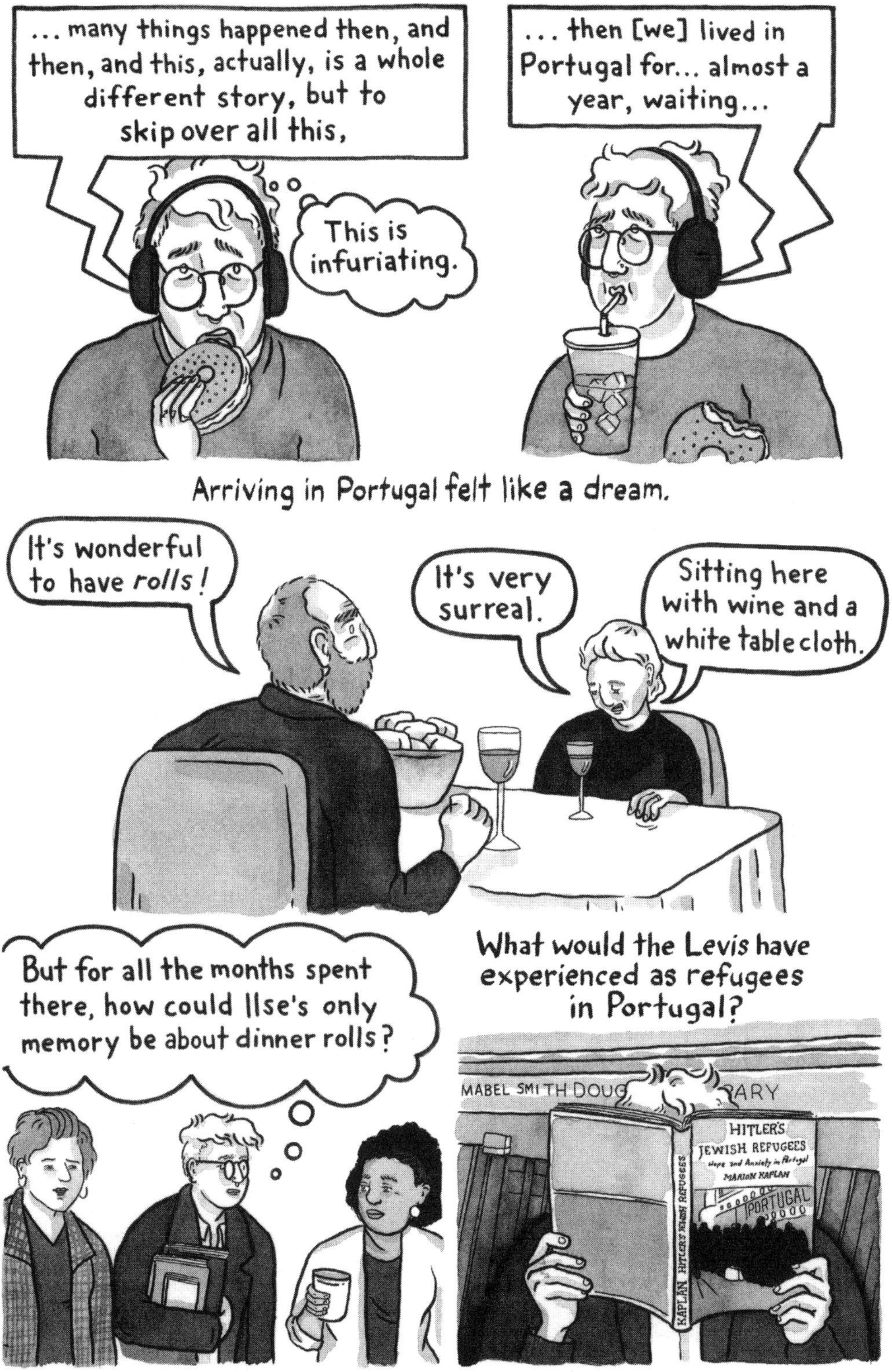

... many things happened then, and then, and this, actually, is a whole different story, but to skip over all this,
This is infuriating.
... then [we] lived in Portugal for... almost a year, waiting...
Arriving in Portugal felt like a dream.
It's wonderful to have *rolls*!
It's very surreal.
Sitting here with wine and a white table cloth.
But for all the months spent there, how could Ilse's only memory be about dinner rolls?
What would the Levis have experienced as refugees in Portugal?
MABEL SMITH DOUG
ARY
HITLER'S JEWISH REFUGEES
Hope and Anxiety in Portugal
MARION KAPLAN
PORTUGAL
KAPLAN HITLER'S JEWISH REFUGEES

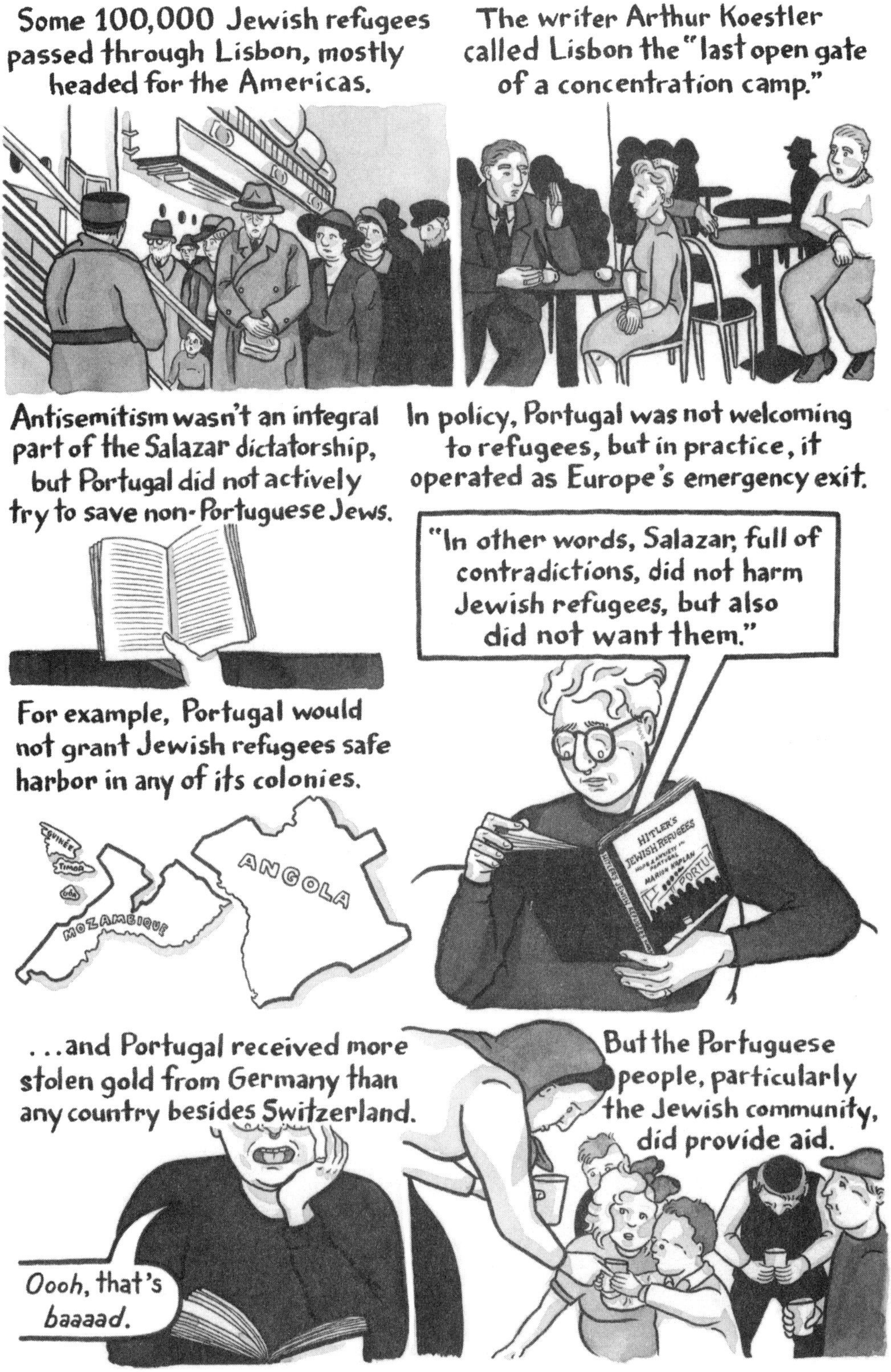
Some 100,000 Jewish refugees passed through Lisbon, mostly headed for the Americas.
The writer Arthur Koestler called Lisbon the "last open gate of a concentration camp."
Antisemitism wasn't an integral part of the Salazar dictatorship, but Portugal did not actively try to save non-Portuguese Jews.
In policy, Portugal was not welcoming to refugees, but in practice, it operated as Europe's emergency exit.
"In other words, Salazar, full of contradictions, did not harm Jewish refugees, but also did not want them."
For example, Portugal would not grant Jewish refugees safe harbor in any of its colonies.
ANGOLA
MOZAMBIQUE
HITLER'S JEWISH REFUGEES
MARION KAPLAN
...and Portugal received more stolen gold from Germany than any country besides Switzerland.
Oooh, that's *baaaad.*
But the Portuguese people, particularly the Jewish community, did provide aid.

James B. Reston wrote for the *New York Times* in December 1940-

One sees them all over Central Lisbon—in the Café Lisboa, on Avenida da Liberdade, where they gather to console one another, and in the Rocio, a main square, where they stand each day watching news bulletins for information about the course of the war.

Today at noon, for example, they made their daily trek up the Lisbon hills to the Cosinha Economica on Travessa do Noronha, where about 500 of them eat communal meals paid for by the American Jewish Distribution Committee. As usual, they came down to the docks to say farewell to their friends on the Excambion as the ship headed for Bermuda, and tomorrow and the next day, as for the last few months, they will go through the same tedious routine while waiting for passage and permission to enter other countries.

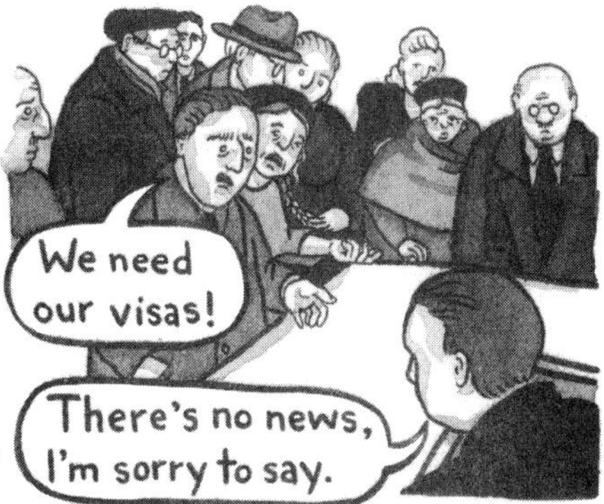

We need our visas!
There's no news, I'm sorry to say.

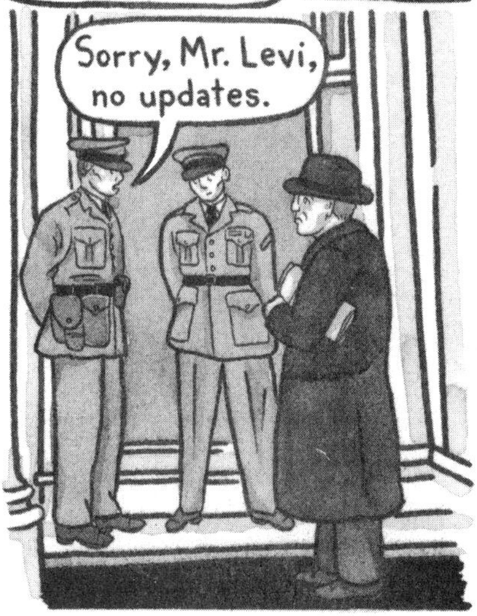

Sorry, Mr. Levi, no updates.

Lisbon was full of Nazi infiltrators, British agents, not to mention Salazar's secret police.

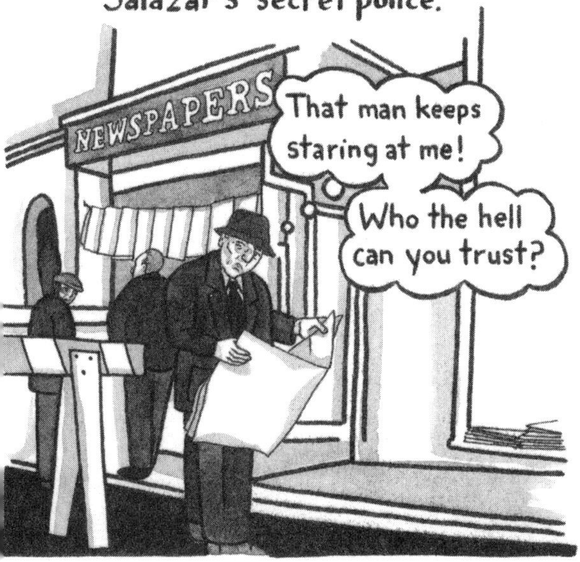

NEWSPAPERS
That man keeps staring at me!
Who the hell can you trust?

Without travel papers, the Levis were stuck in this fraught place—they couldn't go home, or find a new one.

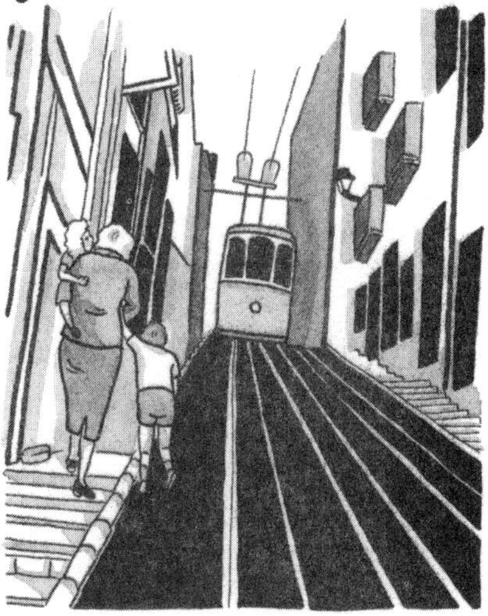

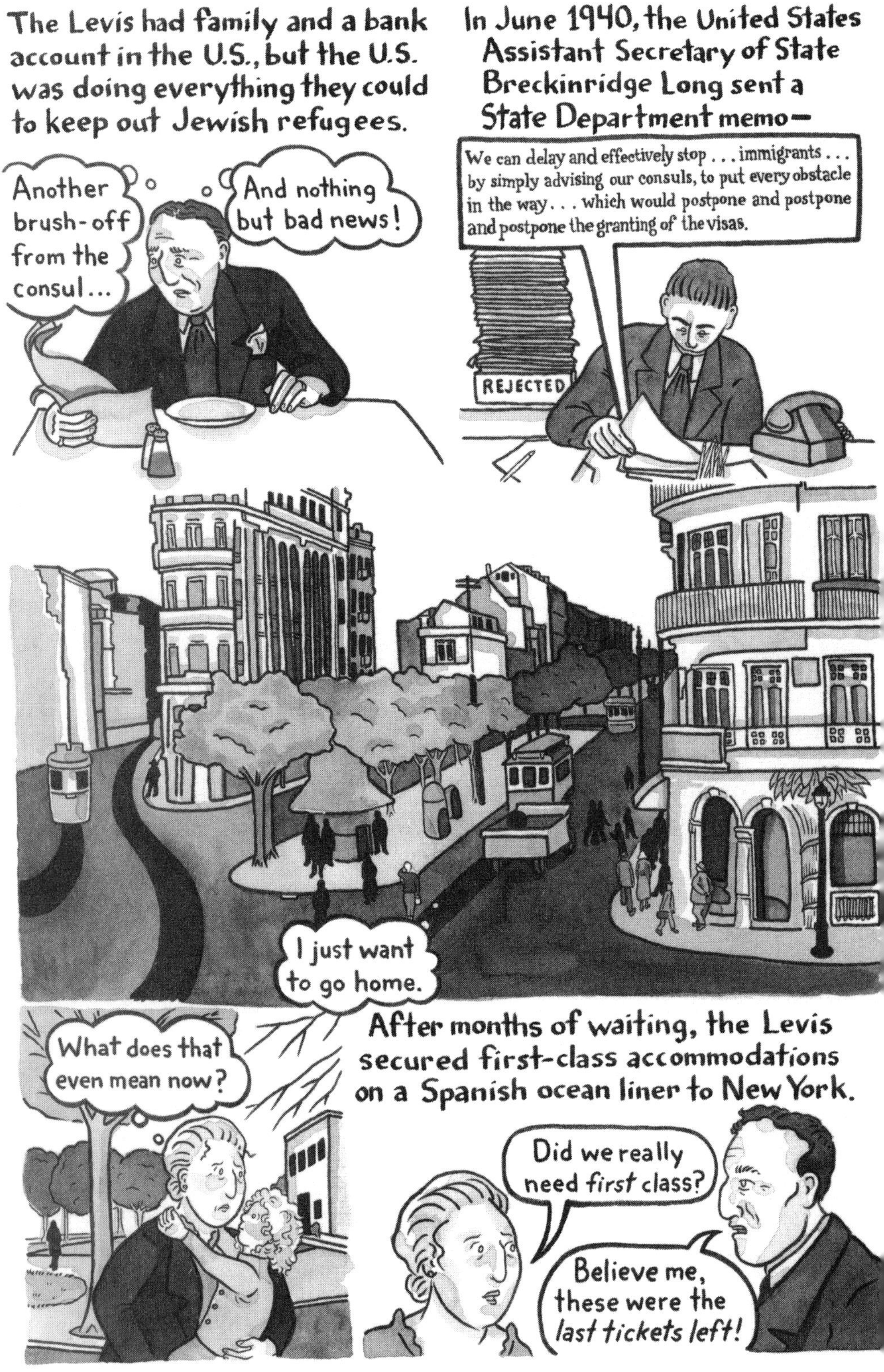

The Levis had family and a bank account in the U.S., but the U.S. was doing everything they could to keep out Jewish refugees.
Another brush-off from the consul...
And nothing but bad news!
In June 1940, the United States Assistant Secretary of State Breckinridge Long sent a State Department memo—
We can delay and effectively stop . . . immigrants . . . by simply advising our consuls, to put every obstacle in the way. . . which would postpone and postpone and postpone the granting of the visas.
REJECTED
I just want to go home.
What does that even mean now?
After months of waiting, the Levis secured first-class accommodations on a Spanish ocean liner to New York.
Did we really need *first* class?
Believe me, these were the *last tickets left!*

The *Magallanes* was a flagship vessel of the Spanish state-backed shipping line Compañía Transatlántica.

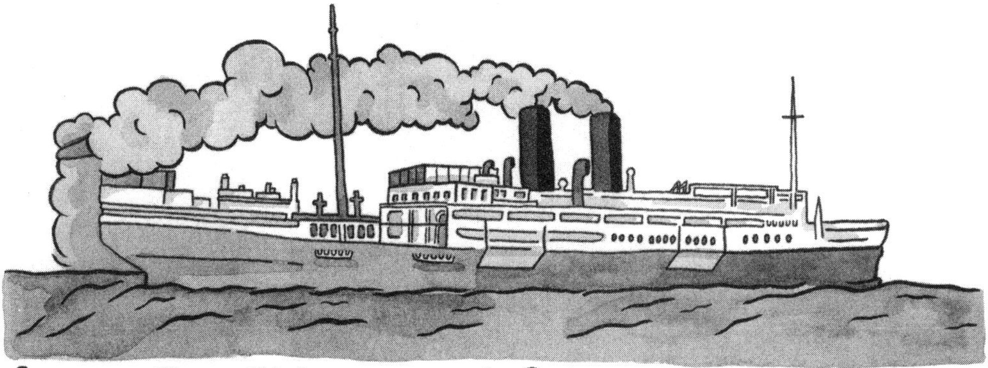

Compañía Transatlántica's U.S. routes were handled by two Falangists (the far right nationalist movement that became the party of Franco)—

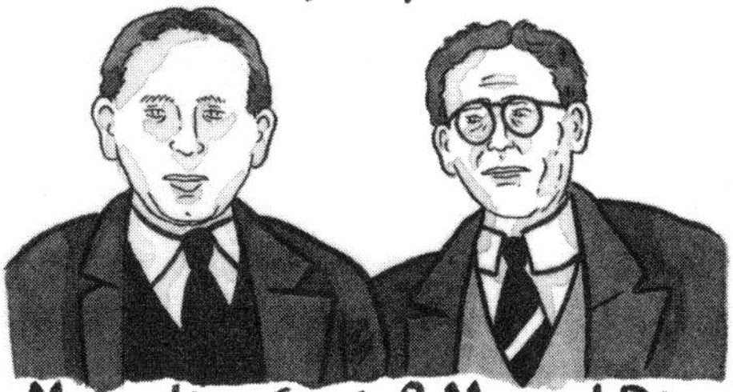

Marcelino Garcia & Manuel Diaz.

As British and American ship and air lines limited or stopped service, Spanish and Portuguese vessels gained a monopoly on transatlantic service.

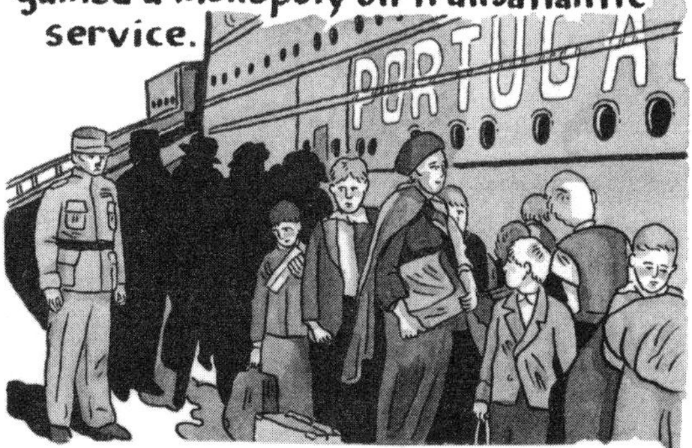

Historian Brooke L. Blower writes, "They were charging refugees *staggering prices* and subjecting them to *monstrous* treatment."

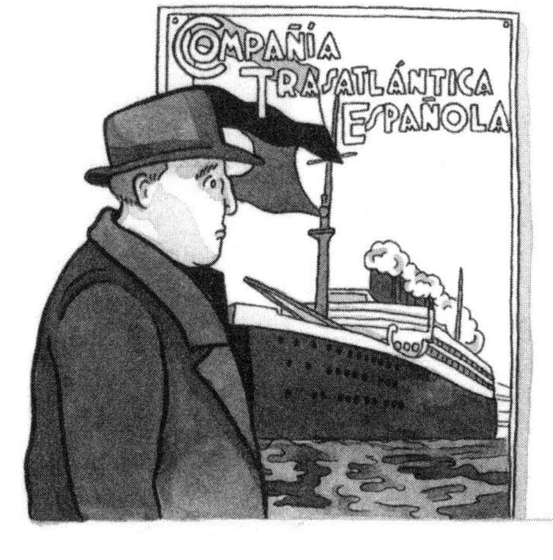
COMPAÑIA
TRASATLÁNTICA
ESPAÑOLA

Where it would normally cost between $160 and 450 for the Spain to U.S. route, prices went up into the thousands.

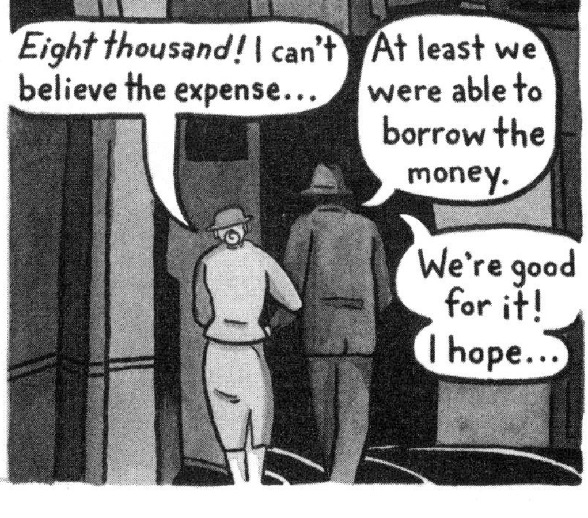
Eight thousand! I can't believe the expense...
At least we were able to borrow the money.
We're good for it! I hope...

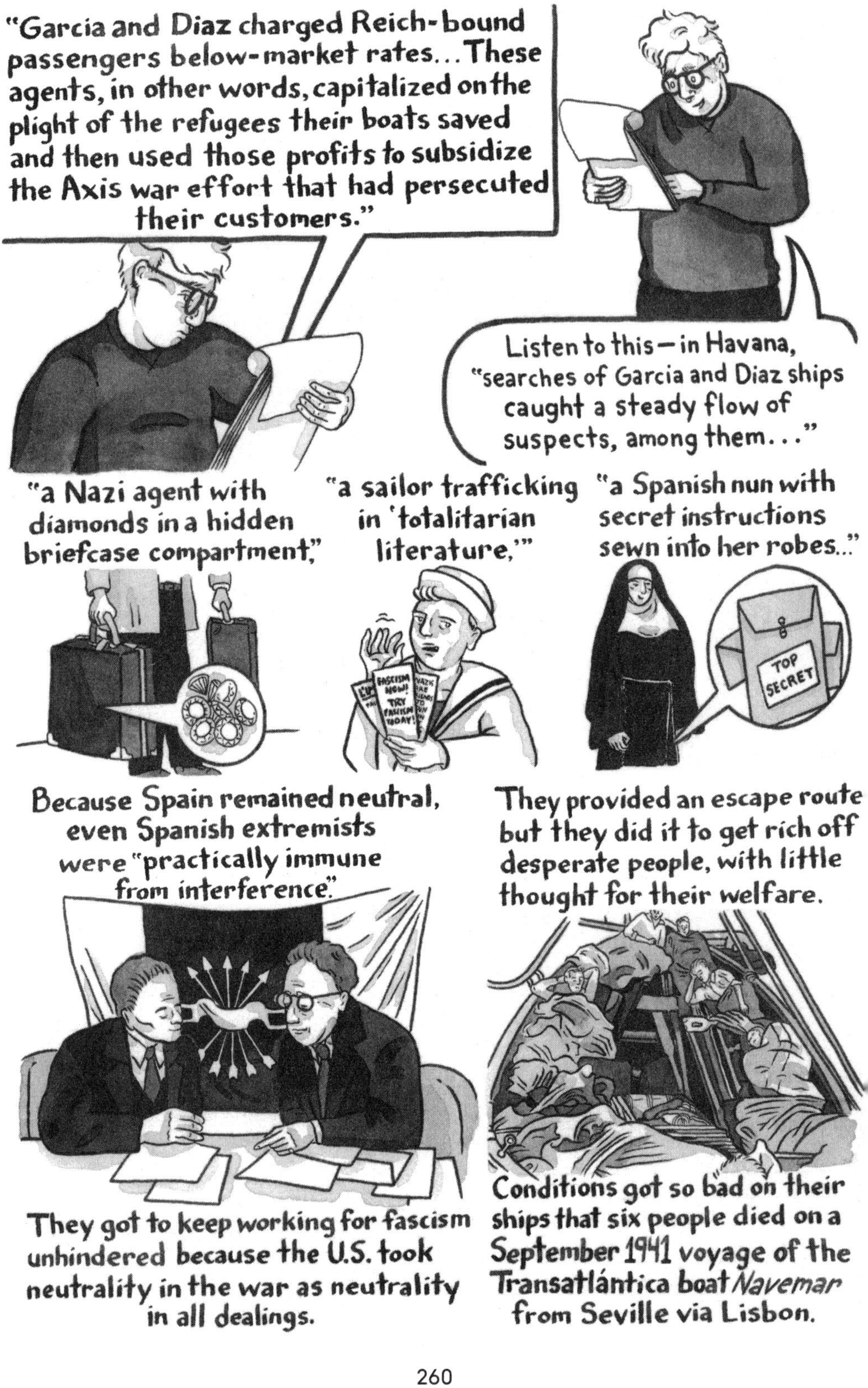
"Garcia and Diaz charged Reich-bound passengers below-market rates... These agents, in other words, capitalized on the plight of the refugees their boats saved and then used those profits to subsidize the Axis war effort that had persecuted their customers."
Listen to this—in Havana, "searches of Garcia and Diaz ships caught a steady flow of suspects, among them..."
"a Nazi agent with diamonds in a hidden briefcase compartment,"
"a sailor trafficking in 'totalitarian literature,'"
FASCISM NOW! TRY FASCISM TODAY!
"a Spanish nun with secret instructions sewn into her robes..."
TOP SECRET
Because Spain remained neutral, even Spanish extremists were "practically immune from interference."
They provided an escape route but they did it to get rich off desperate people, with little thought for their welfare.
They got to keep working for fascism unhindered because the U.S. took neutrality in the war as neutrality in all dealings.
Conditions got so bad on their ships that six people died on a September 1941 voyage of the Transatlántica boat *Navemar* from Seville via Lisbon.

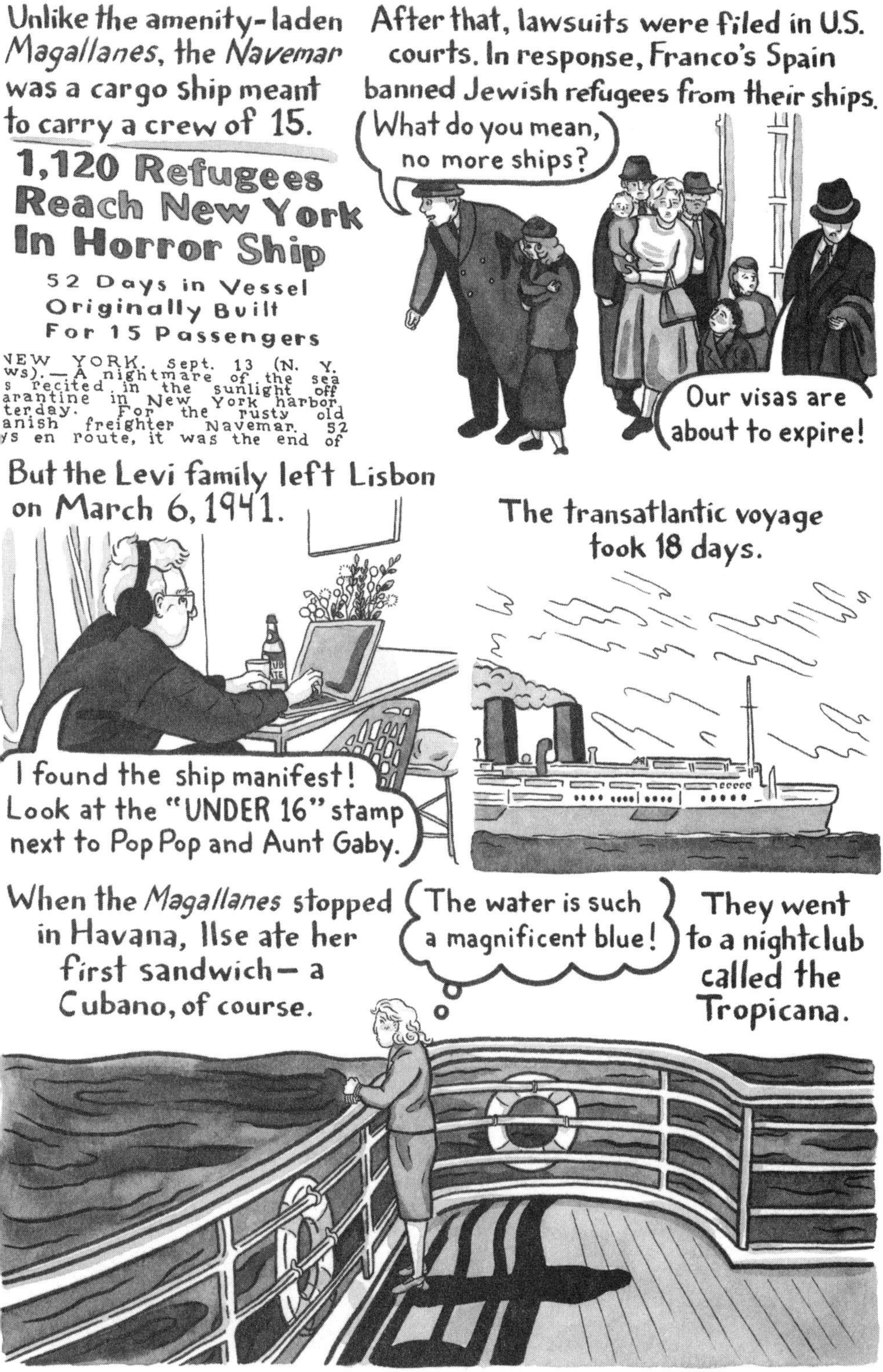
Unlike the amenity-laden *Magallanes*, the *Navemar* was a cargo ship meant to carry a crew of 15.
1,120 Refugees Reach New York In Horror Ship
52 Days in Vessel Originally Built For 15 Passengers
NEW YORK, Sept. 13 (N. Y. ws).—A nightmare of the sea s recited in the sunlight off arantine in New York harbor terday. For the rusty old anish freighter Navemar, 52 ys en route, it was the end of
After that, lawsuits were filed in U.S. courts. In response, Franco's Spain banned Jewish refugees from their ships.
What do you mean, no more ships?
Our visas are about to expire!
But the Levi family left Lisbon on March 6, 1941.
I found the ship manifest! Look at the "UNDER 16" stamp next to Pop Pop and Aunt Gaby.
The transatlantic voyage took 18 days.
When the *Magallanes* stopped in Havana, Ilse ate her first sandwich—a Cubano, of course.
The water is such a magnificent blue!
They went to a nightclub called the Tropicana.

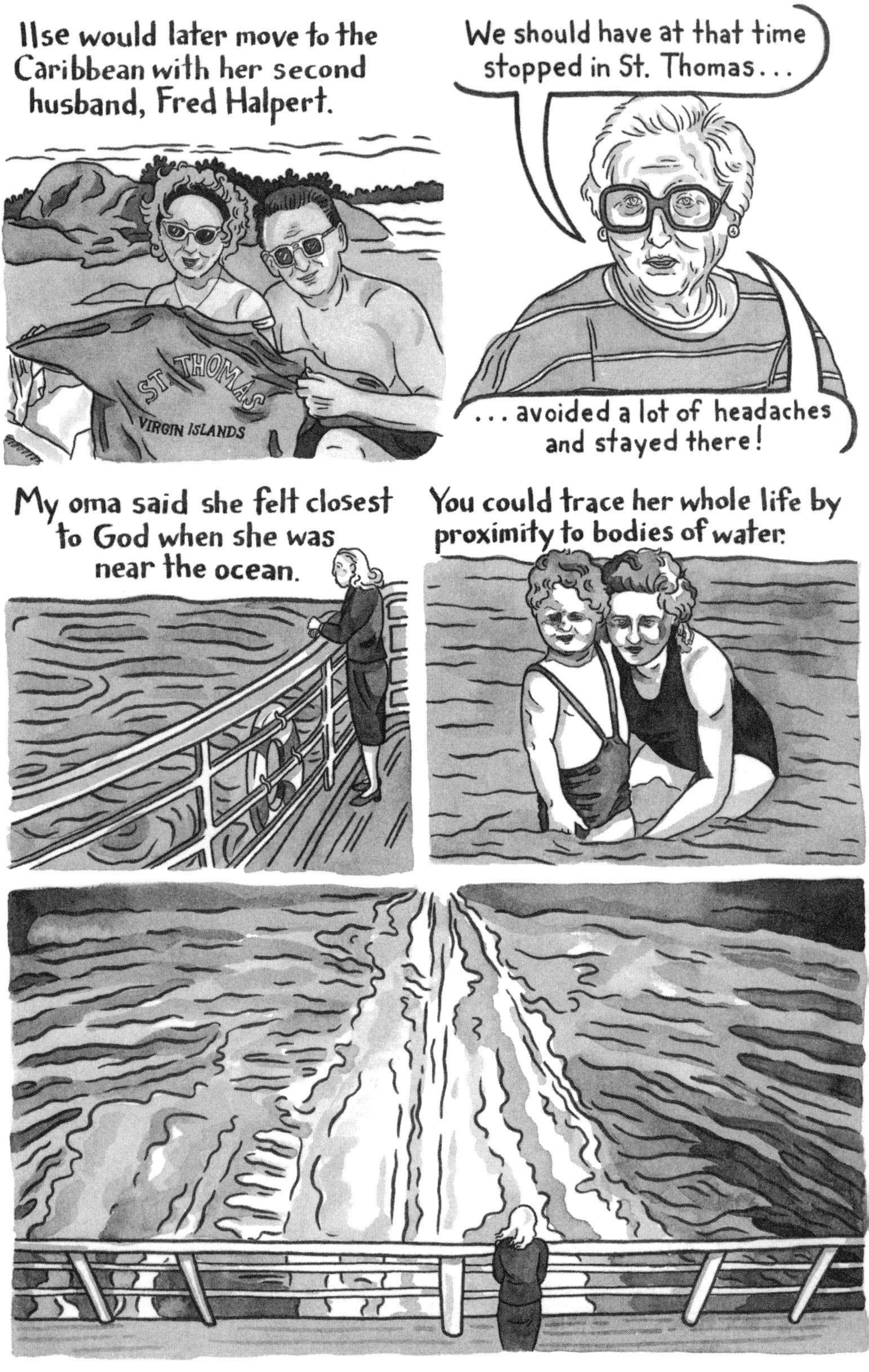
Ilse would later move to the Caribbean with her second husband, Fred Halpert.
ST. THOMAS
VIRGIN ISLANDS
We should have at that time stopped in St. Thomas . . .
. . . avoided a lot of headaches and stayed there!
My oma said she felt closest to God when she was near the ocean.
You could trace her whole life by proximity to bodies of water.

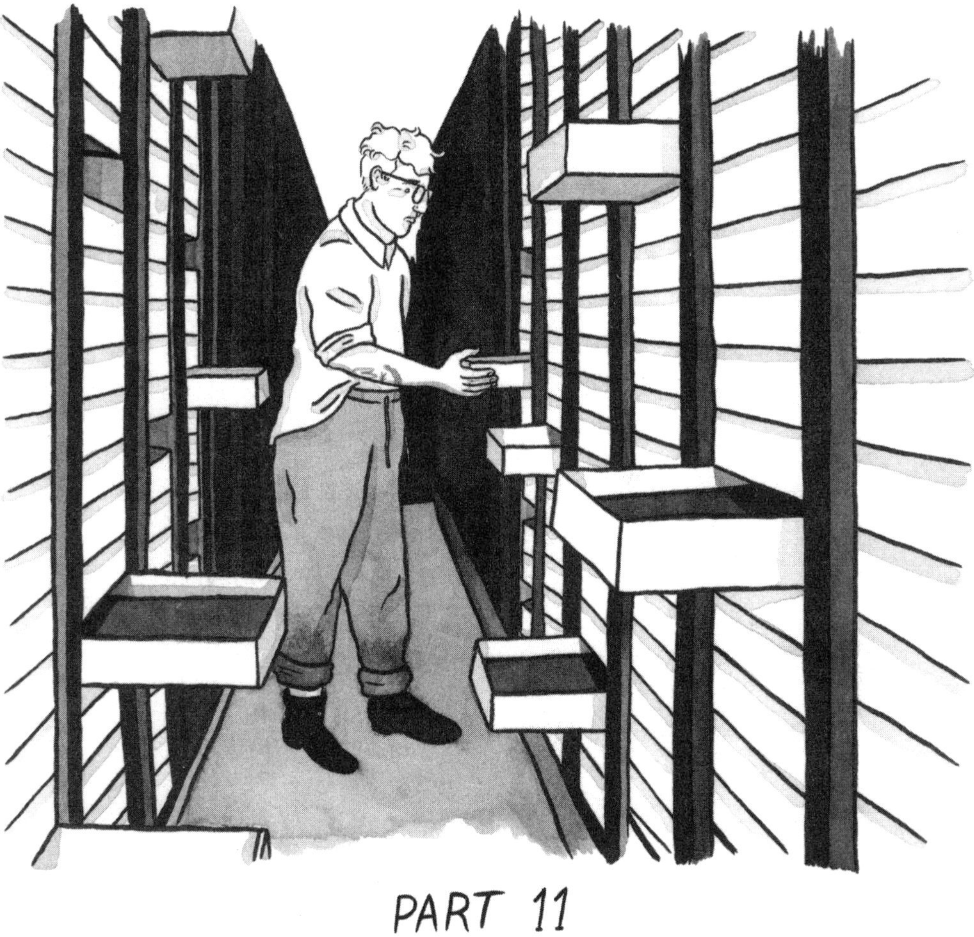

PART 11

HOARDERS

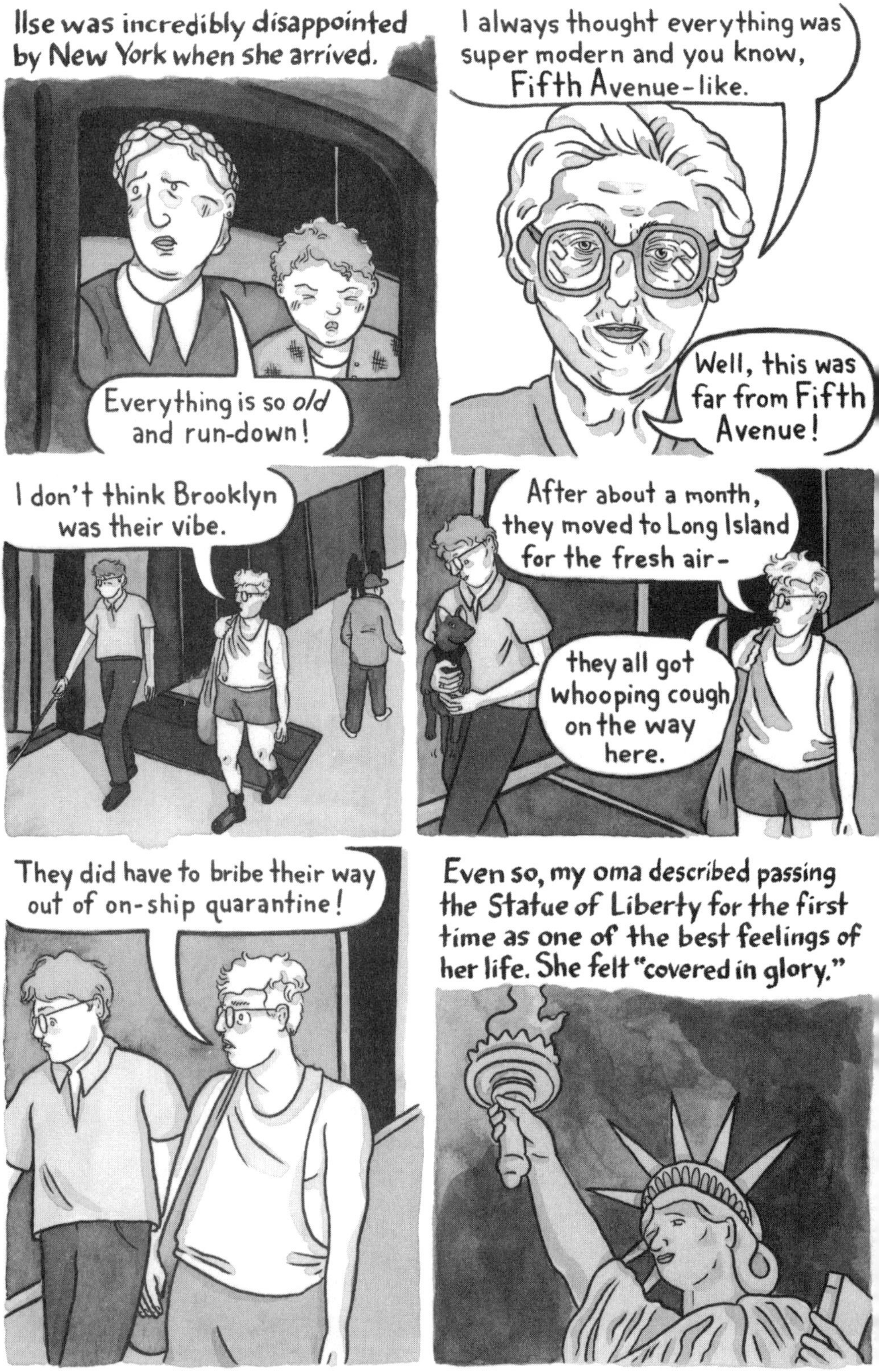
Ilse was incredibly disappointed by New York when she arrived.
Everything is so *old* and run-down!
I always thought everything was super modern and you know, Fifth Avenue-like.
Well, this was far from Fifth Avenue!
I don't think Brooklyn was their vibe.
After about a month, they moved to Long Island for the fresh air-
they all got whooping cough on the way here.
They did have to bribe their way out of on-ship quarantine!
Even so, my oma described passing the Statue of Liberty for the first time as one of the best feelings of her life. She felt "covered in glory."

The Levi family ended in 1941 in New York City when the surviving Levis changed their name to *Leeds*.

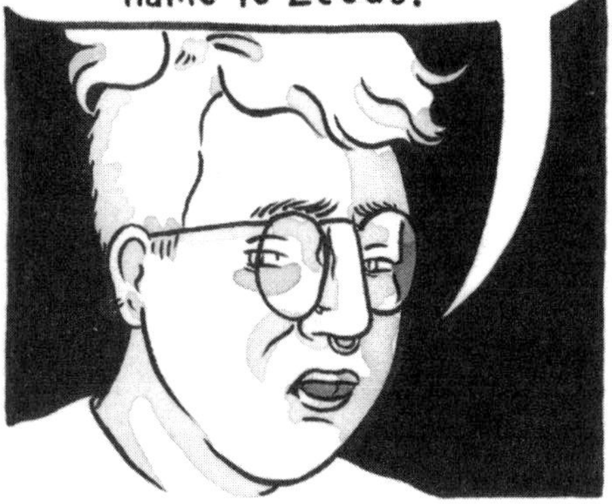

LEGAL NOTICE

At a Special Term, Part II of the City Court of the City of New York held at the Old County Courthouse, No. 52 Chambers Street, City Hall Park, County of New York, on the 3rd day of September, 1941.

Present:

Hon. Henry S. Schimmel

In the Matter of the Application of ERICH LEVI for Leave to Change his Name to ERIC STANLEY LEEDS

Upon reading and filing the petition of ERICH LEVI, duly verified the 3rd day of September, 1941, and entitled as above praying for leave of the petitioner and his wife GERTRUDE ILSE LEVI and their children, ANDRE GEORGE LEVI and GABRIELLA MONIQUE LEVI to assume the names of ERIC STANLEY LEEDS, ILSE JOAN LEEDS, ANDRE GEORGE LEEDS and GABY MONIQUE LEEDS respectively, in place and instead of their

They set about leaving the past behind

and becoming Americans.

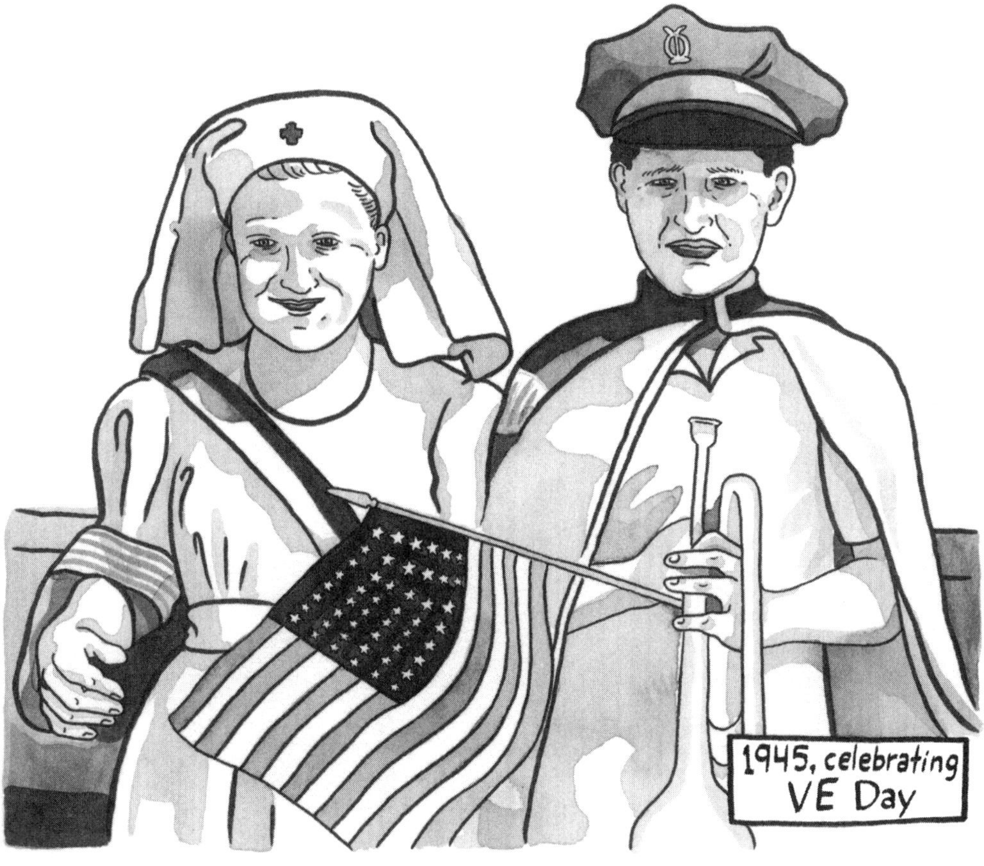
1945, celebrating VE Day

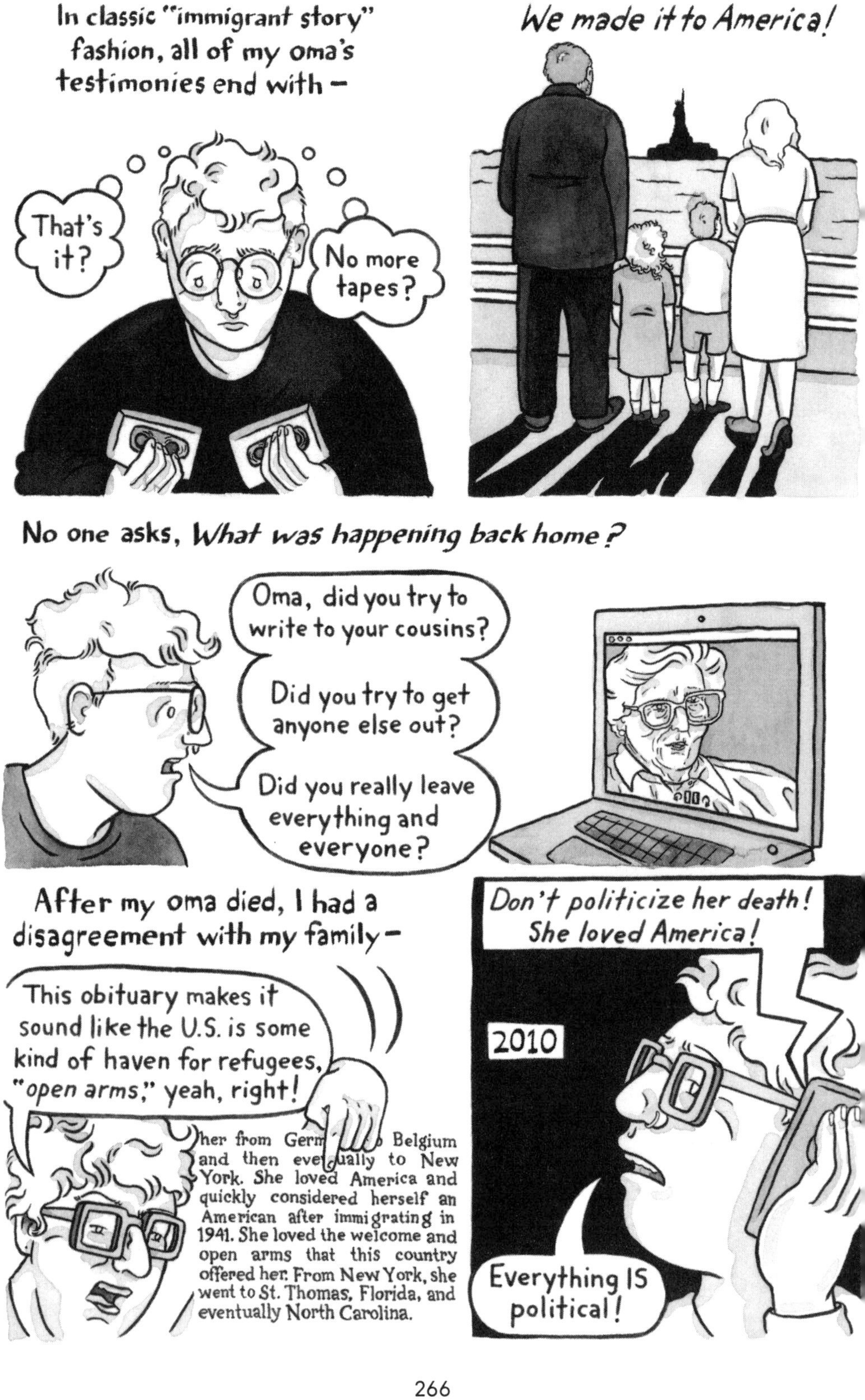

In classic "immigrant story" fashion, all of my oma's testimonies end with –
That's it?
No more tapes?
We made it to America!
No one asks, What was happening back home?
Oma, did you try to write to your cousins?
Did you try to get anyone else out?
Did you really leave everything and everyone?
After my oma died, I had a disagreement with my family –
This obituary makes it sound like the U.S. is some kind of haven for refugees, "open arms," yeah, right!
her from Germ[...] Belgium and then eve[...]ually to New York. She loved America and quickly considered herself an American after immigrating in 1941. She loved the welcome and open arms that this country offered her. From New York, she went to St. Thomas, Florida, and eventually North Carolina.
Don't politicize her death! She loved America!
2010
Everything IS political!

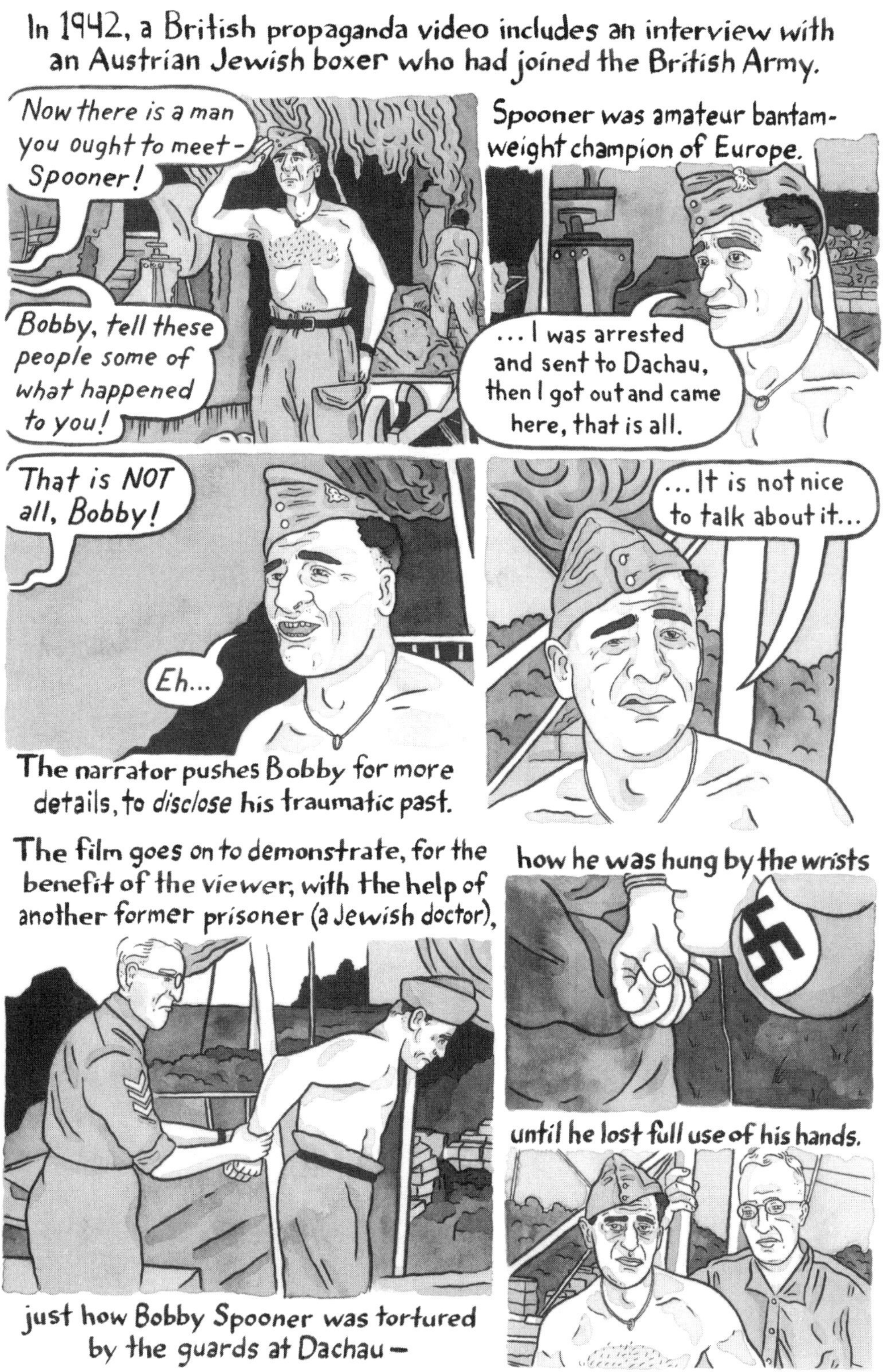

In 1942, a British propaganda video includes an interview with an Austrian Jewish boxer who had joined the British Army.
Now there is a man you ought to meet - Spooner!
Bobby, tell these people some of what happened to you!
Spooner was amateur bantam-weight champion of Europe.
... I was arrested and sent to Dachau, then I got out and came here, that is all.
That is NOT all, Bobby!
Eh...
The narrator pushes Bobby for more details, to *disclose* his traumatic past.
... It is not nice to talk about it...
The film goes on to demonstrate, for the benefit of the viewer, with the help of another former prisoner (a Jewish doctor),
just how Bobby Spooner was tortured by the guards at Dachau –
how he was hung by the wrists
until he lost full use of his hands.

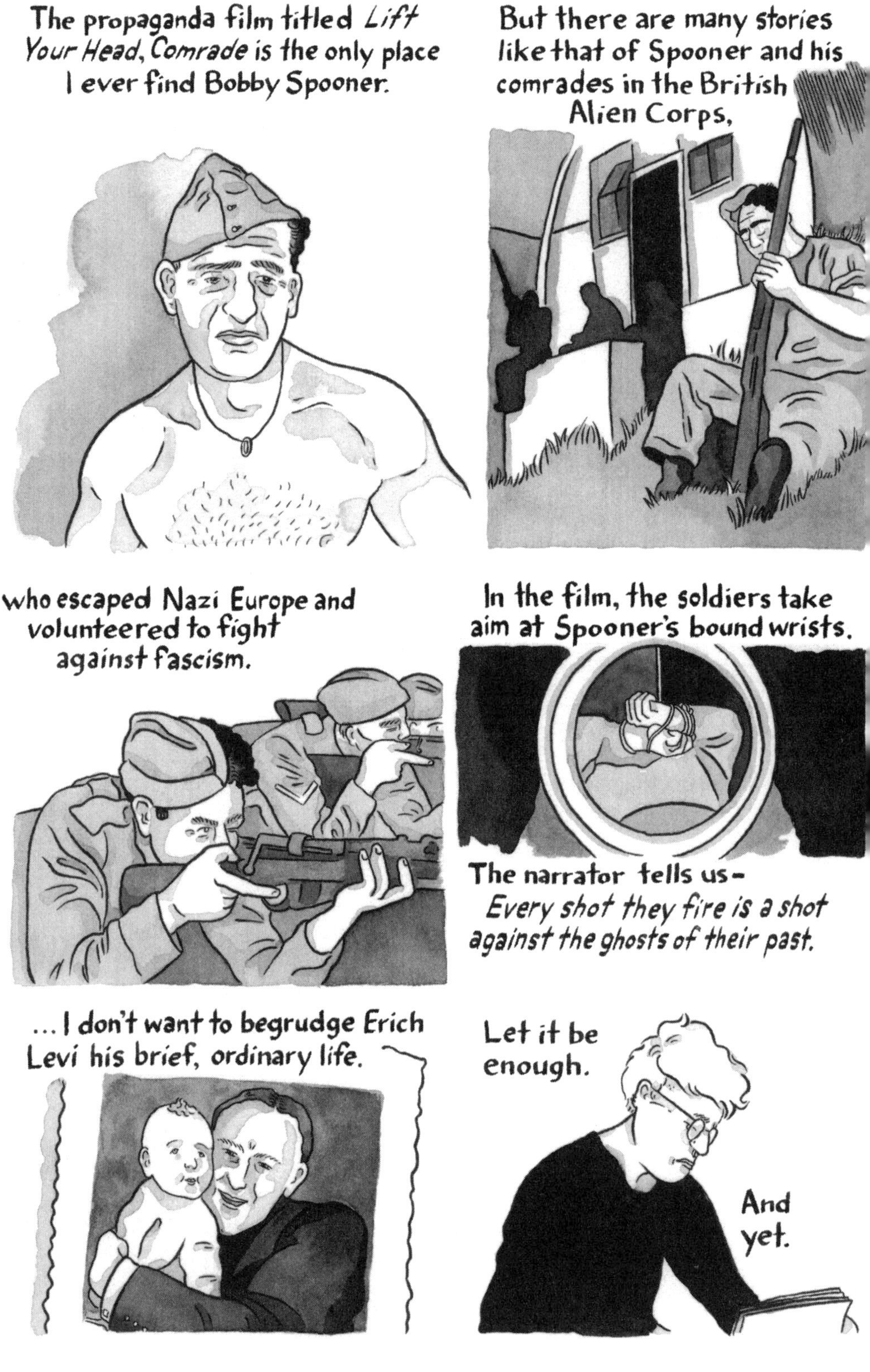
The propaganda film titled *Lift Your Head, Comrade* is the only place I ever find Bobby Spooner.
But there are many stories like that of Spooner and his comrades in the British Alien Corps,
who escaped Nazi Europe and volunteered to fight against fascism.
In the film, the soldiers take aim at Spooner's bound wrists.
The narrator tells us- *Every shot they fire is a shot against the ghosts of their past.*
...I don't want to begrudge Erich Levi his brief, ordinary life.
Let it be enough.
And yet.

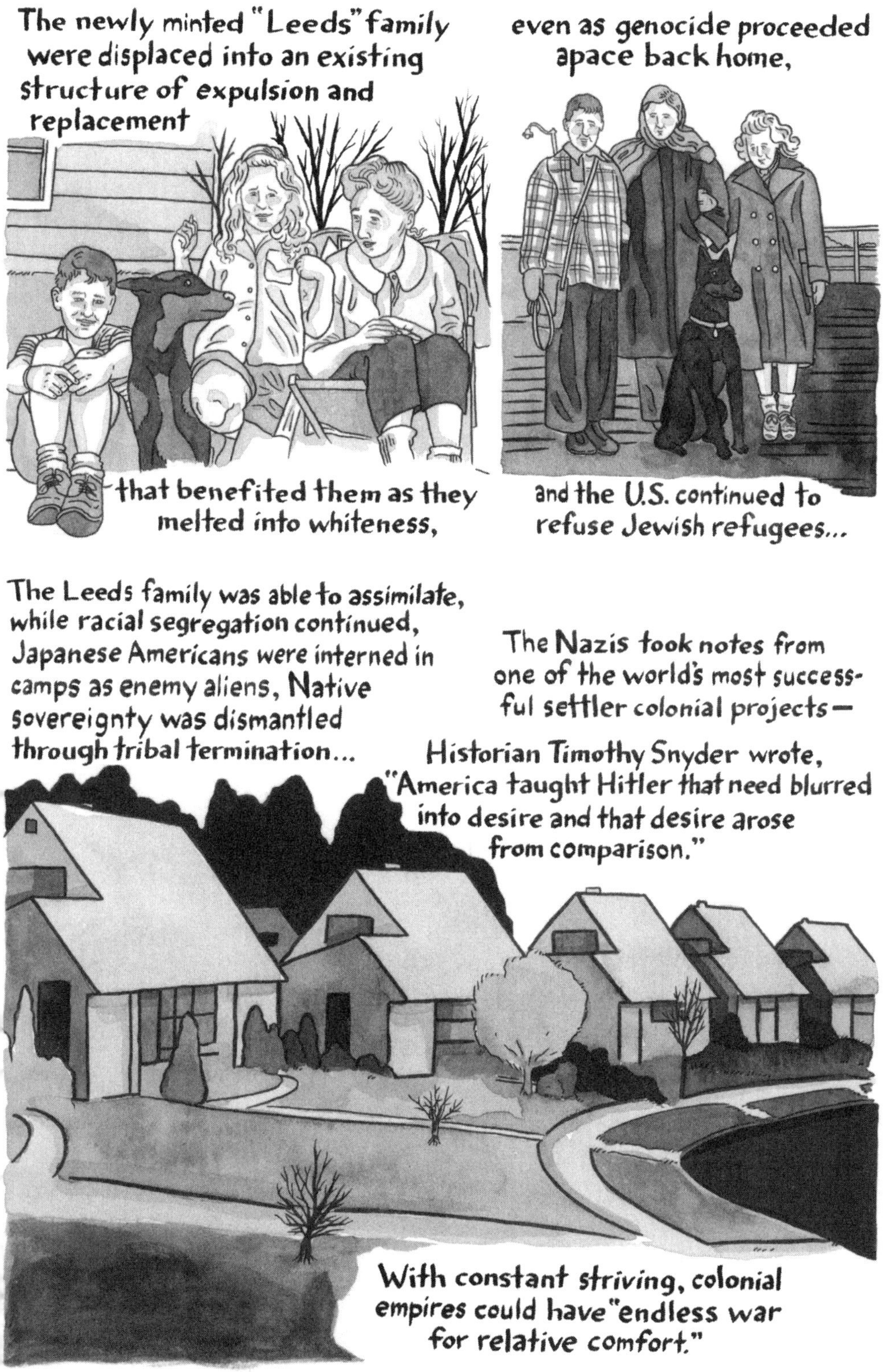
The newly minted "Leeds" family were displaced into an existing structure of expulsion and replacement
that benefited them as they melted into whiteness,
even as genocide proceeded apace back home,
and the U.S. continued to refuse Jewish refugees...
The Leeds family was able to assimilate, while racial segregation continued, Japanese Americans were interned in camps as enemy aliens, Native sovereignty was dismantled through tribal termination...
The Nazis took notes from one of the world's most successful settler colonial projects—
Historian Timothy Snyder wrote, "America taught Hitler that need blurred into desire and that desire arose from comparison."
With constant striving, colonial empires could have "endless war for relative comfort."

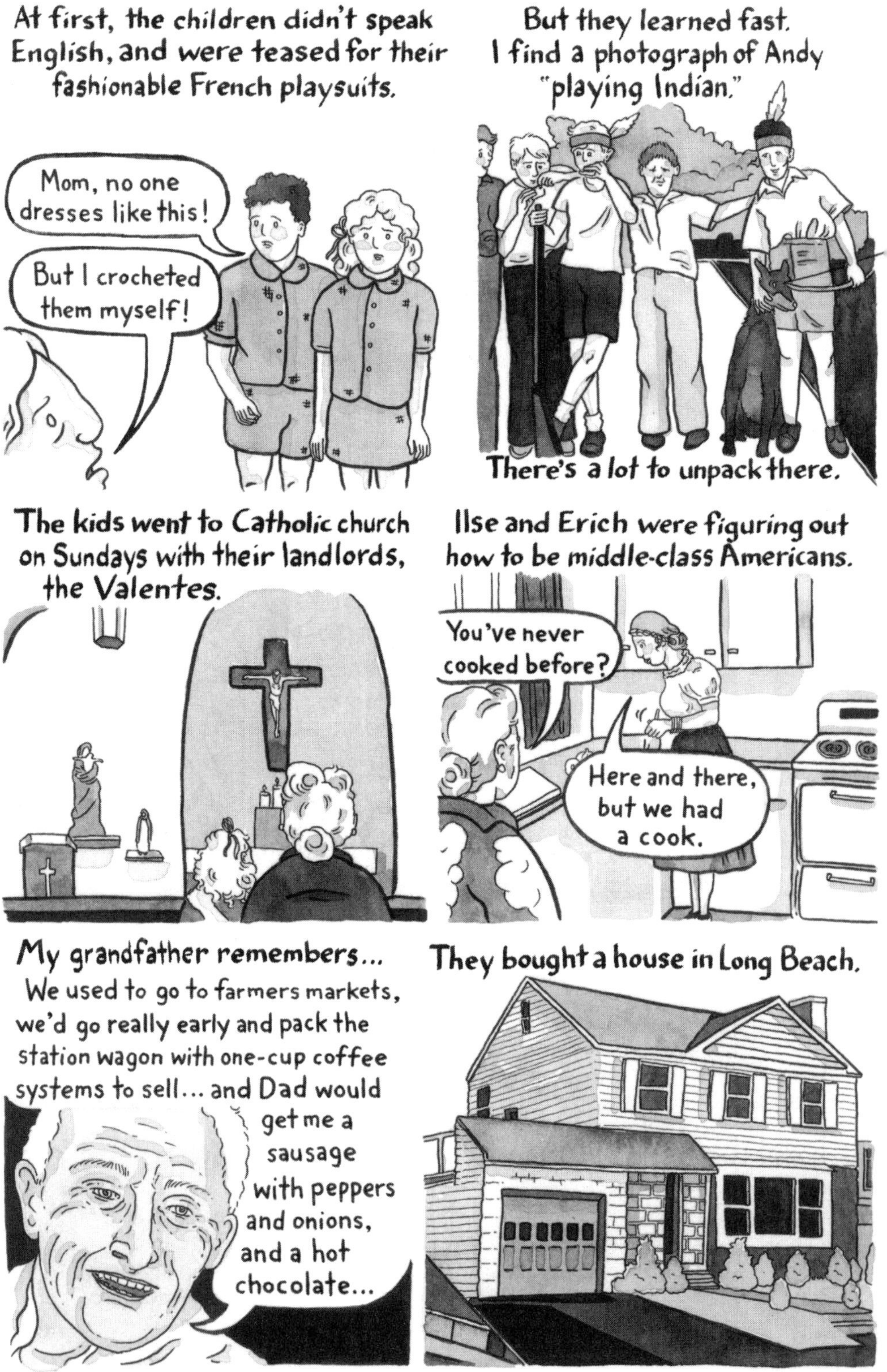
At first, the children didn't speak English, and were teased for their fashionable French playsuits.
Mom, no one dresses like this!
But I crocheted them myself!
But they learned fast. I find a photograph of Andy "playing Indian."
There's a lot to unpack there.
The kids went to Catholic church on Sundays with their landlords, the Valentes.
Ilse and Erich were figuring out how to be middle-class Americans.
You've never cooked before?
Here and there, but we had a cook.
My grandfather remembers...
We used to go to farmers markets, we'd go really early and pack the station wagon with one-cup coffee systems to sell... and Dad would get me a sausage with peppers and onions, and a hot chocolate...
They bought a house in Long Beach.

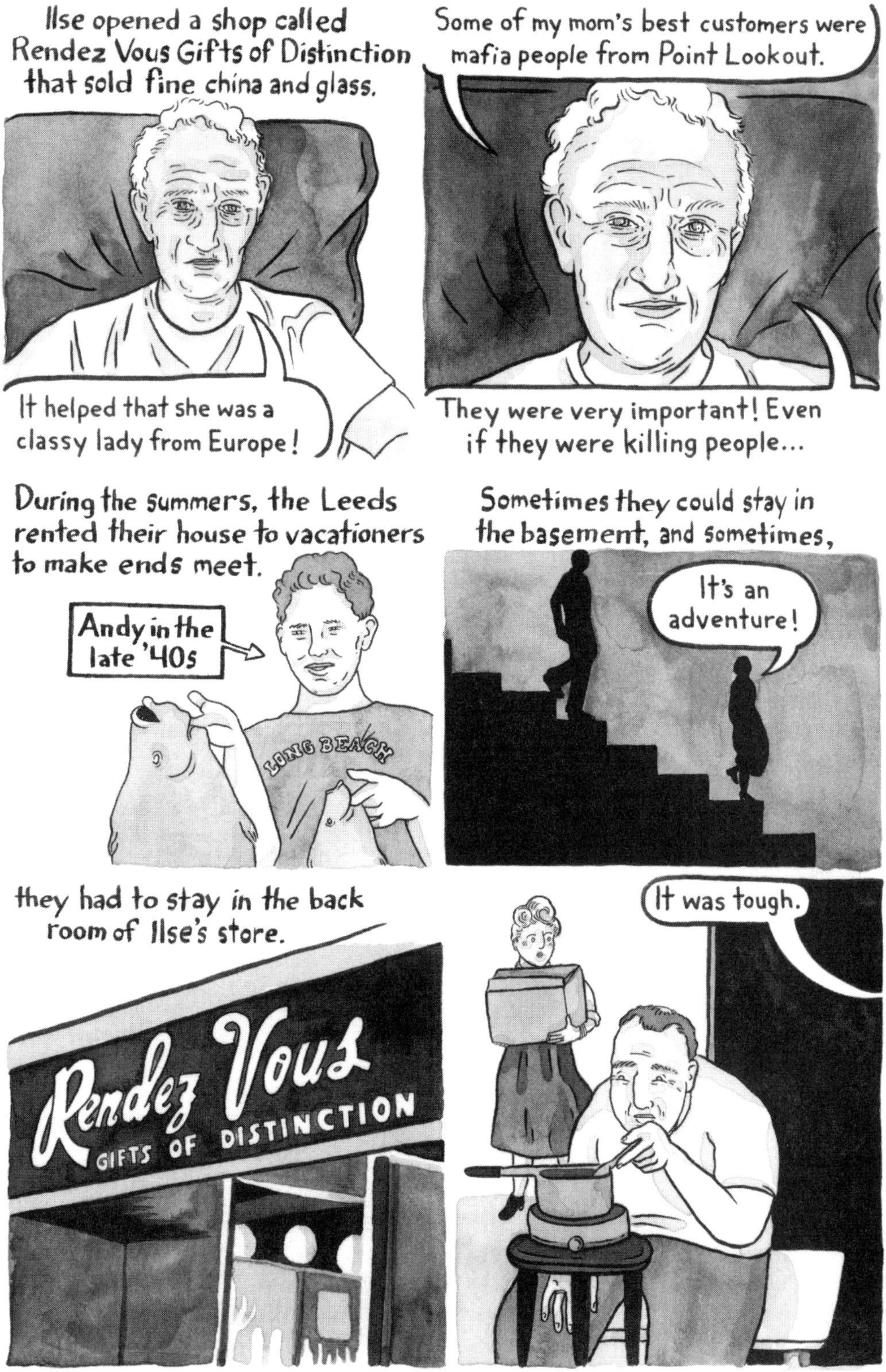
Ilse opened a shop called Rendez Vous Gifts of Distinction that sold fine china and glass.
Some of my mom's best customers were mafia people from Point Lookout.
It helped that she was a classy lady from Europe!
They were very important! Even if they were killing people...
During the summers, the Leeds rented their house to vacationers to make ends meet.
Andy in the late '40s
LONG BEACH
Sometimes they could stay in the basement, and sometimes,
It's an adventure!
they had to stay in the back room of Ilse's store.
Rendez Vous
GIFTS OF DISTINCTION
It was tough.

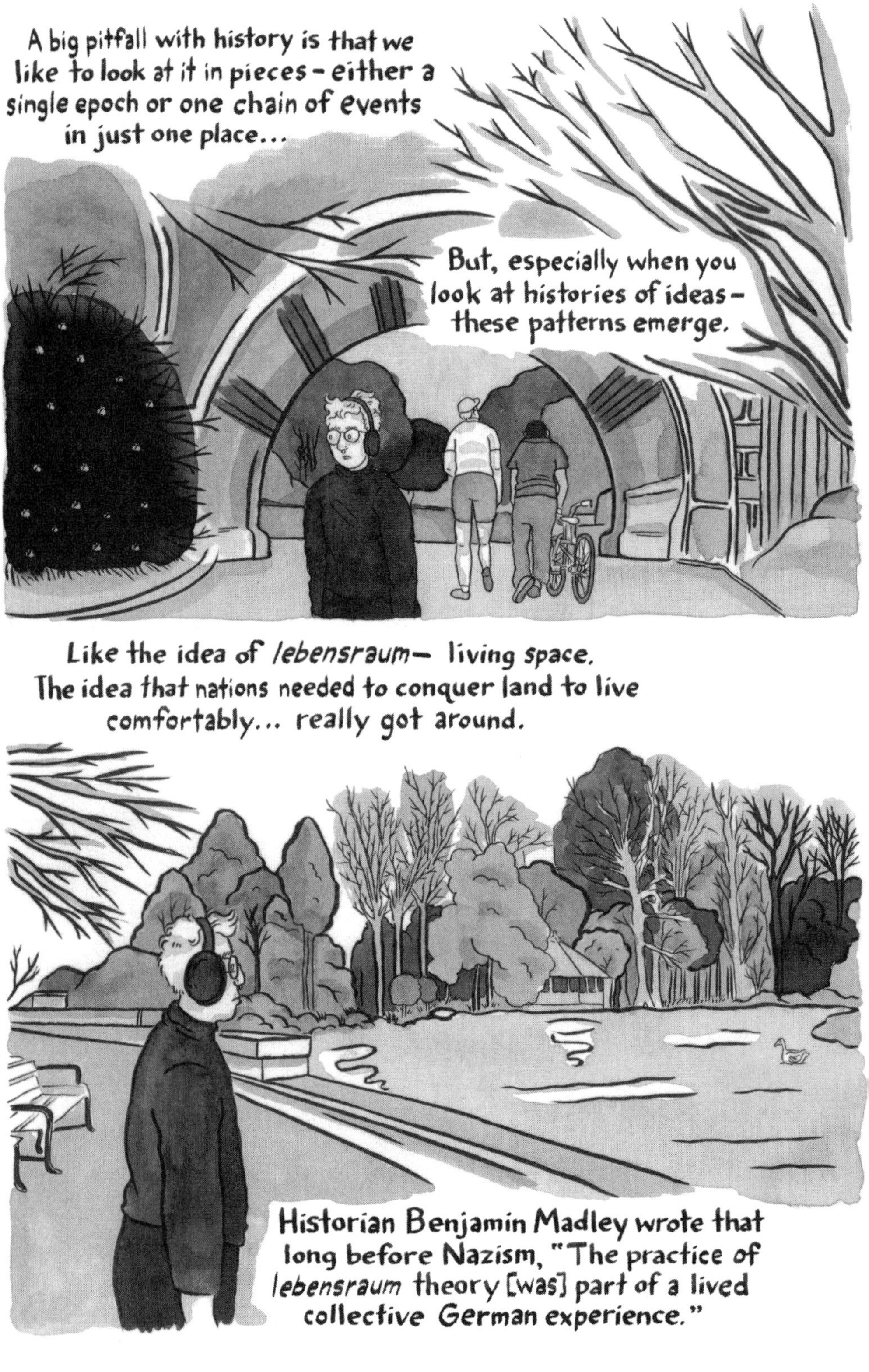
A big pitfall with history is that we like to look at it in pieces – either a single epoch or one chain of events in just one place...
But, especially when you look at histories of ideas – these patterns emerge.
Like the idea of *lebensraum* – living space. The idea that nations needed to conquer land to live comfortably... really got around.
Historian Benjamin Madley wrote that long before Nazism, "The practice of *lebensraum* theory [was] part of a lived collective German experience."

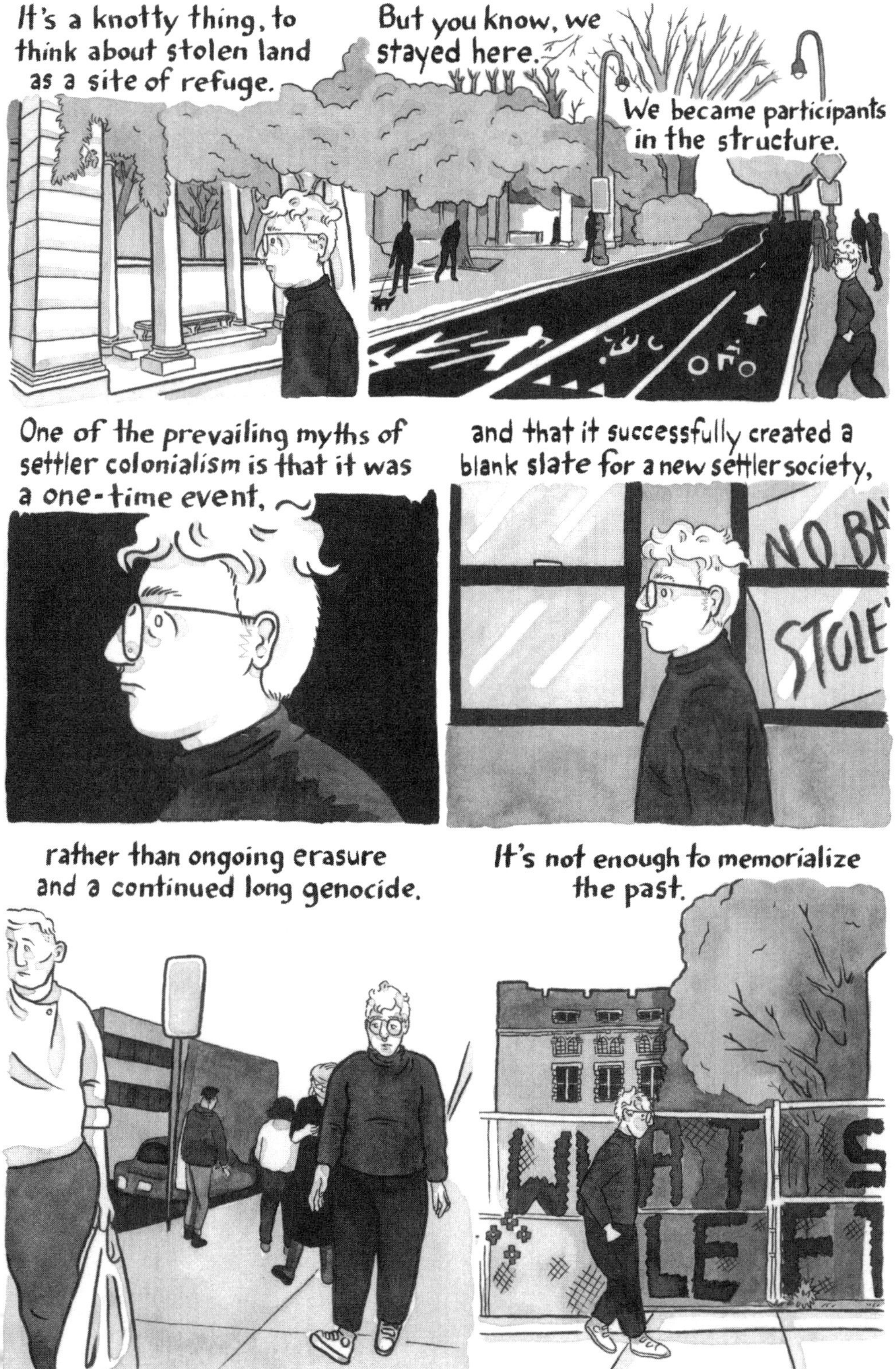
It's a knotty thing, to think about stolen land as a site of refuge.
But you know, we stayed here.
We became participants in the structure.
One of the prevailing myths of settler colonialism is that it was a one-time event,
and that it successfully created a blank slate for a new settler society,
NO BA
STOLE
rather than ongoing erasure and a continued long genocide.
It's not enough to memorialize the past.
WHAT S
LEFT

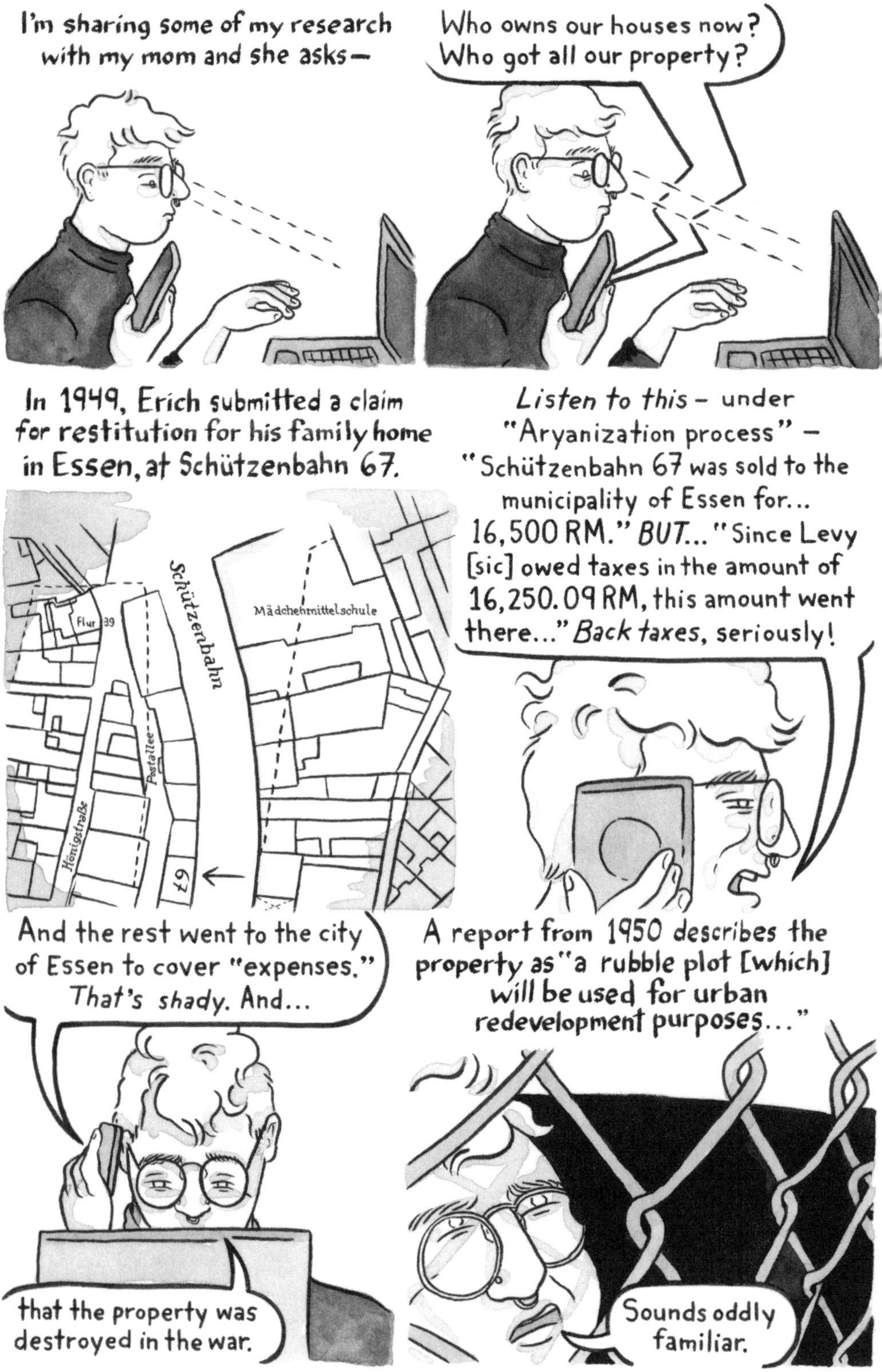

I'm sharing some of my research with my mom and she asks—
Who owns our houses now? Who got all our property?
In 1949, Erich submitted a claim for restitution for his family home in Essen, at Schützenbahn 67.
Schützenbahn
Mädchenmittelschule
Flur 39
Postallee
Königstraße
67
Listen to this – under "Aryanization process" – "Schützenbahn 67 was sold to the municipality of Essen for... 16,500 RM." *BUT*... "Since Levy [sic] owed taxes in the amount of 16,250.09 RM, this amount went there..." *Back taxes*, seriously!
And the rest went to the city of Essen to cover "expenses." *That's shady.* And...
that the property was destroyed in the war.
A report from 1950 describes the property as "a rubble plot [which] will be used for urban redevelopment purposes..."
Sounds oddly familiar.

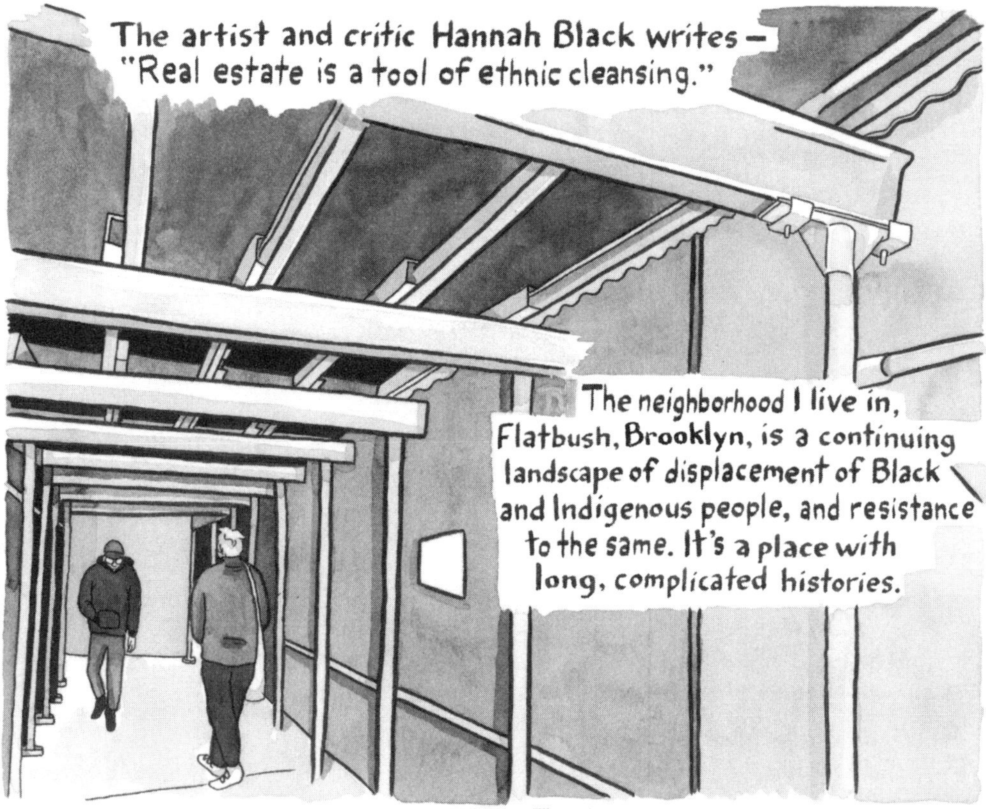
The artist and critic Hannah Black writes – "Real estate is a tool of ethnic cleansing."
The neighborhood I live in, Flatbush, Brooklyn, is a continuing landscape of displacement of Black and Indigenous people, and resistance to the same. It's a place with long, complicated histories.

New York's reckoning with historical dispossession is so tied up with present-day gentrification and development –

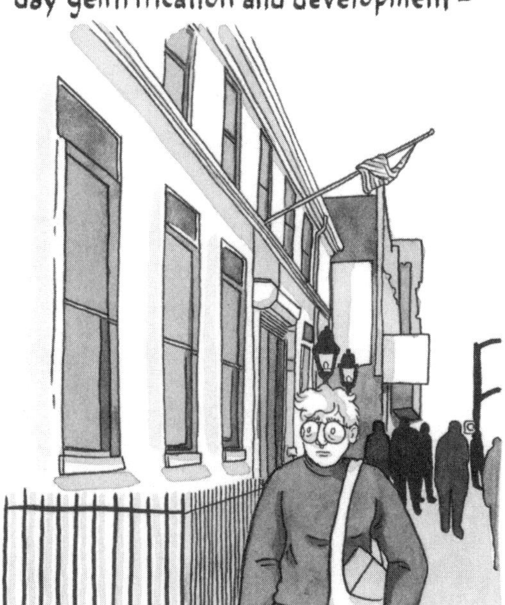

The Flatbush post office is across the street from an empty lot where the city wants to put more "affordable" housing.

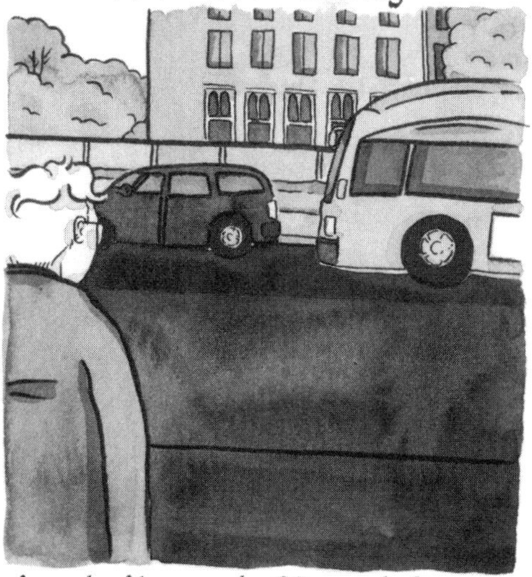

I go to the post office a lot, so I pass it all the time.

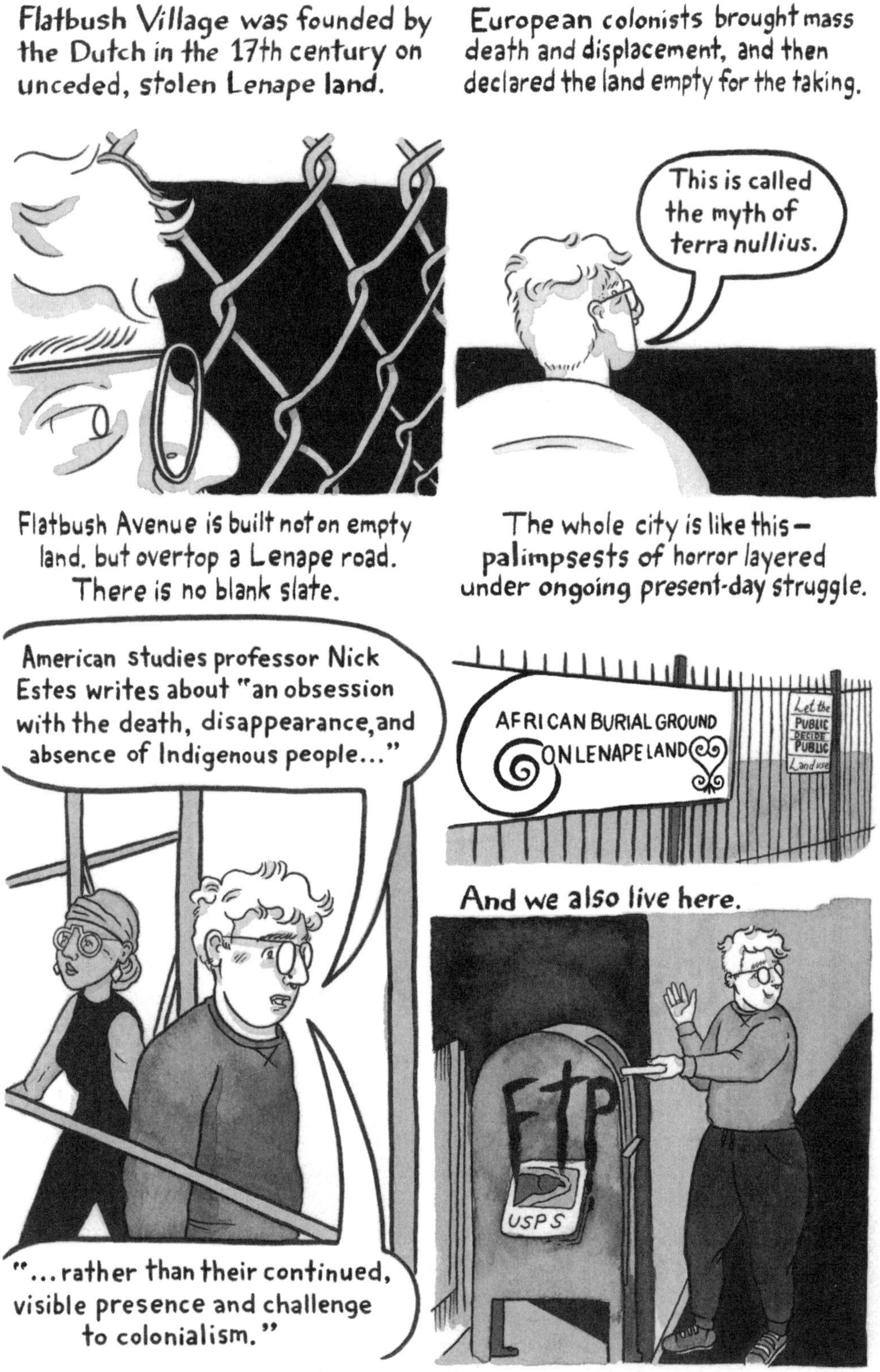
Flatbush Village was founded by the Dutch in the 17th century on unceded, stolen Lenape land.
European colonists brought mass death and displacement, and then declared the land empty for the taking.
This is called the myth of terra nullius.
Flatbush Avenue is built not on empty land. but overtop a Lenape road. There is no blank slate.
The whole city is like this— palimpsests of horror layered under ongoing present-day struggle.
American studies professor Nick Estes writes about "an obsession with the death, disappearance, and absence of Indigenous people..."
"...rather than their continued, visible presence and challenge to colonialism."
AFRICAN BURIAL GROUND ON LENAPE LAND
Let the PUBLIC DECIDE PUBLIC Land use
And we also live here.
FTP
USPS

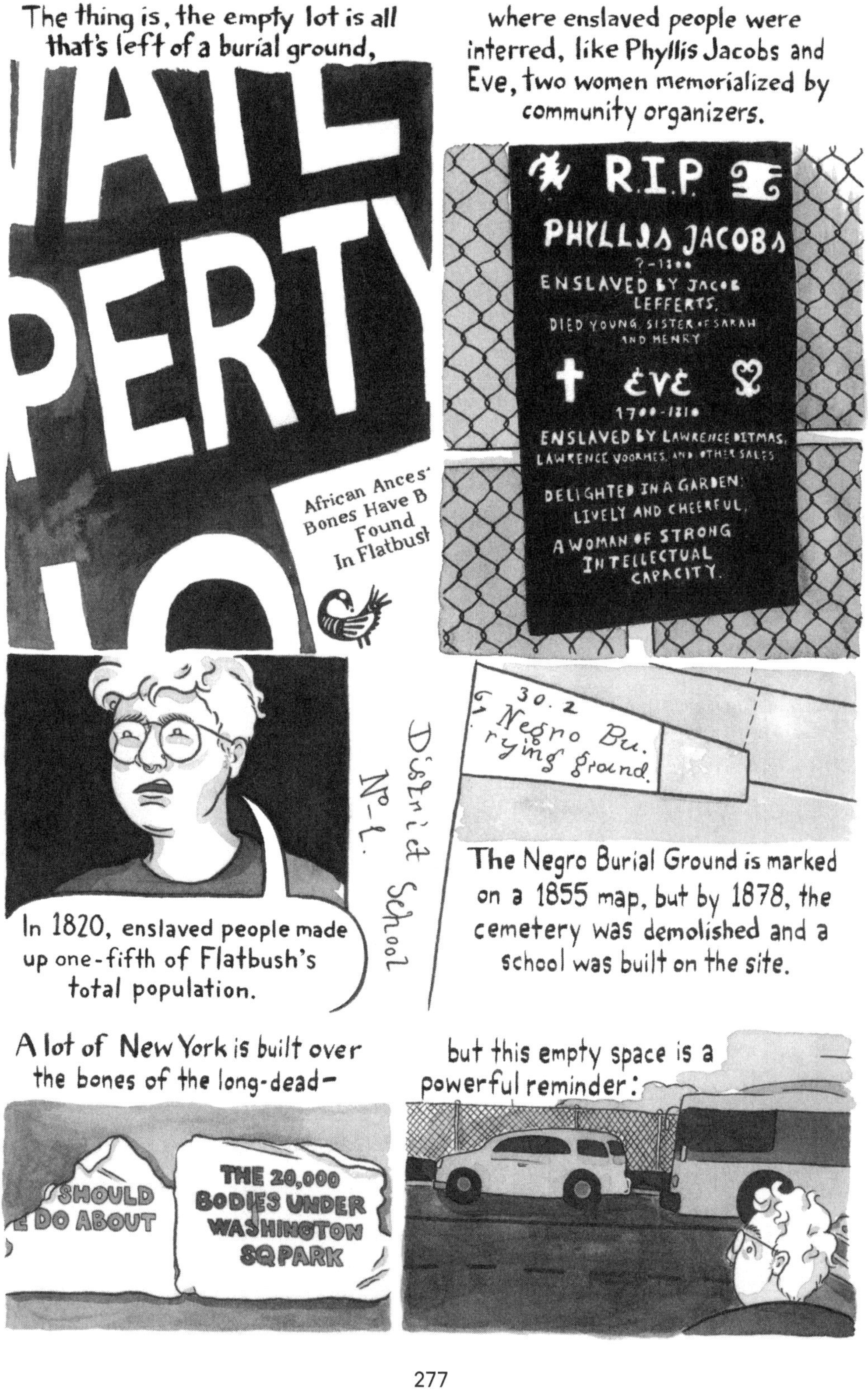

The thing is, the empty lot is all that's left of a burial ground,
African Ances
Bones Have B
Found
In Flatbusl
where enslaved people were interred, like Phyllis Jacobs and Eve, two women memorialized by community organizers.
R.I.P.
PHYLLIS JACOBS
?-1800
ENSLAVED BY JACOB LEFFERTS.
DIED YOUNG. SISTER OF SARAH AND HENRY
EVE
1700-1810
ENSLAVED BY LAWRENCE DITMAS, LAWRENCE VOORHES, AND OTHER SALES
DELIGHTED IN A GARDEN; LIVELY AND CHEERFUL, A WOMAN OF STRONG INTELLECTUAL CAPACITY.
In 1820, enslaved people made up one-fifth of Flatbush's total population.
District School No 1.
30.2
Negro Bu. rying ground.
The Negro Burial Ground is marked on a 1855 map, but by 1878, the cemetery was demolished and a school was built on the site.
A lot of New York is built over the bones of the long-dead—
SHOULD
DO ABOUT
THE 20,000 BODIES UNDER WASHINGTON SQ PARK
but this empty space is a powerful reminder:

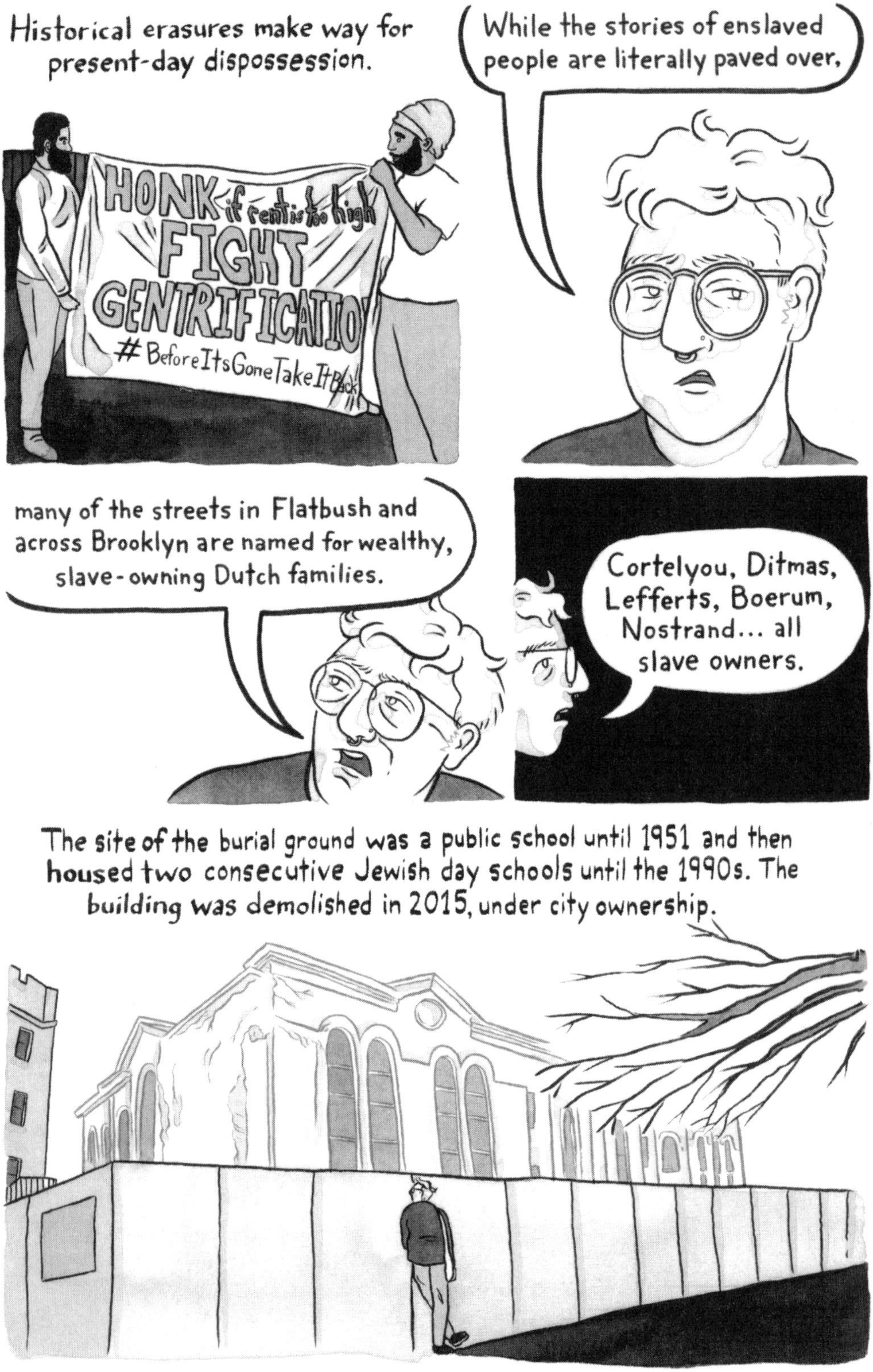
Historical erasures make way for present-day dispossession.
HONK if rent is too high
FIGHT GENTRIFICATIO
#BeforeItsGoneTakeItBack
While the stories of enslaved people are literally paved over,
many of the streets in Flatbush and across Brooklyn are named for wealthy, slave-owning Dutch families.
Cortelyou, Ditmas, Lefferts, Boerum, Nostrand... all slave owners.
The site of the burial ground was a public school until 1951 and then housed two consecutive Jewish day schools until the 1990s. The building was demolished in 2015, under city ownership.

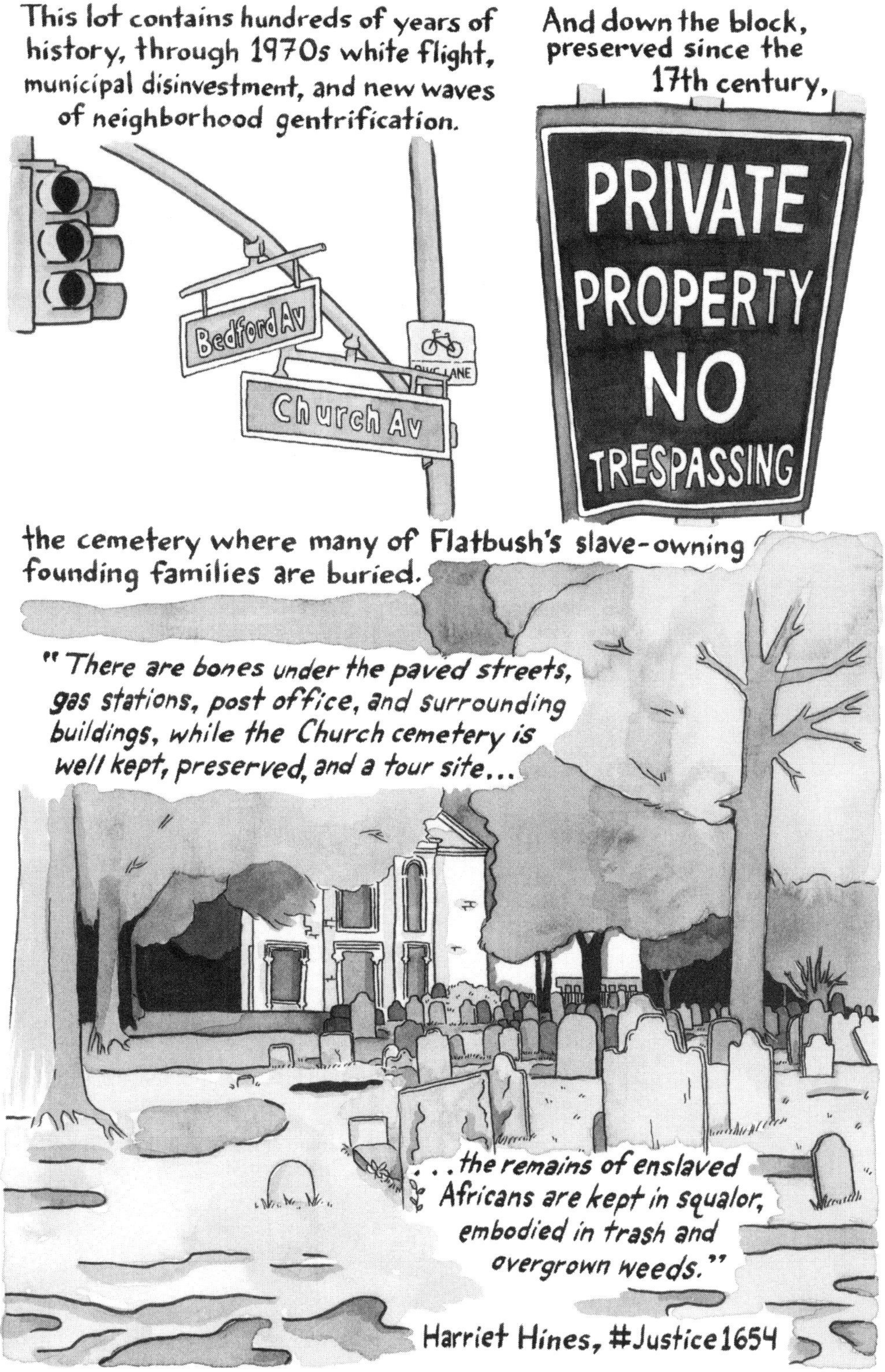
This lot contains hundreds of years of history, through 1970s white flight, municipal disinvestment, and new waves of neighborhood gentrification.
Bedford Av
Church Av
And down the block, preserved since the 17th century,
PRIVATE PROPERTY NO TRESPASSING
the cemetery where many of Flatbush's slave-owning founding families are buried.
"There are bones under the paved streets, gas stations, post office, and surrounding buildings, while the Church cemetery is well kept, preserved, and a tour site...
...the remains of enslaved Africans are kept in squalor, embodied in trash and overgrown weeds."
Harriet Hines, #Justice1654

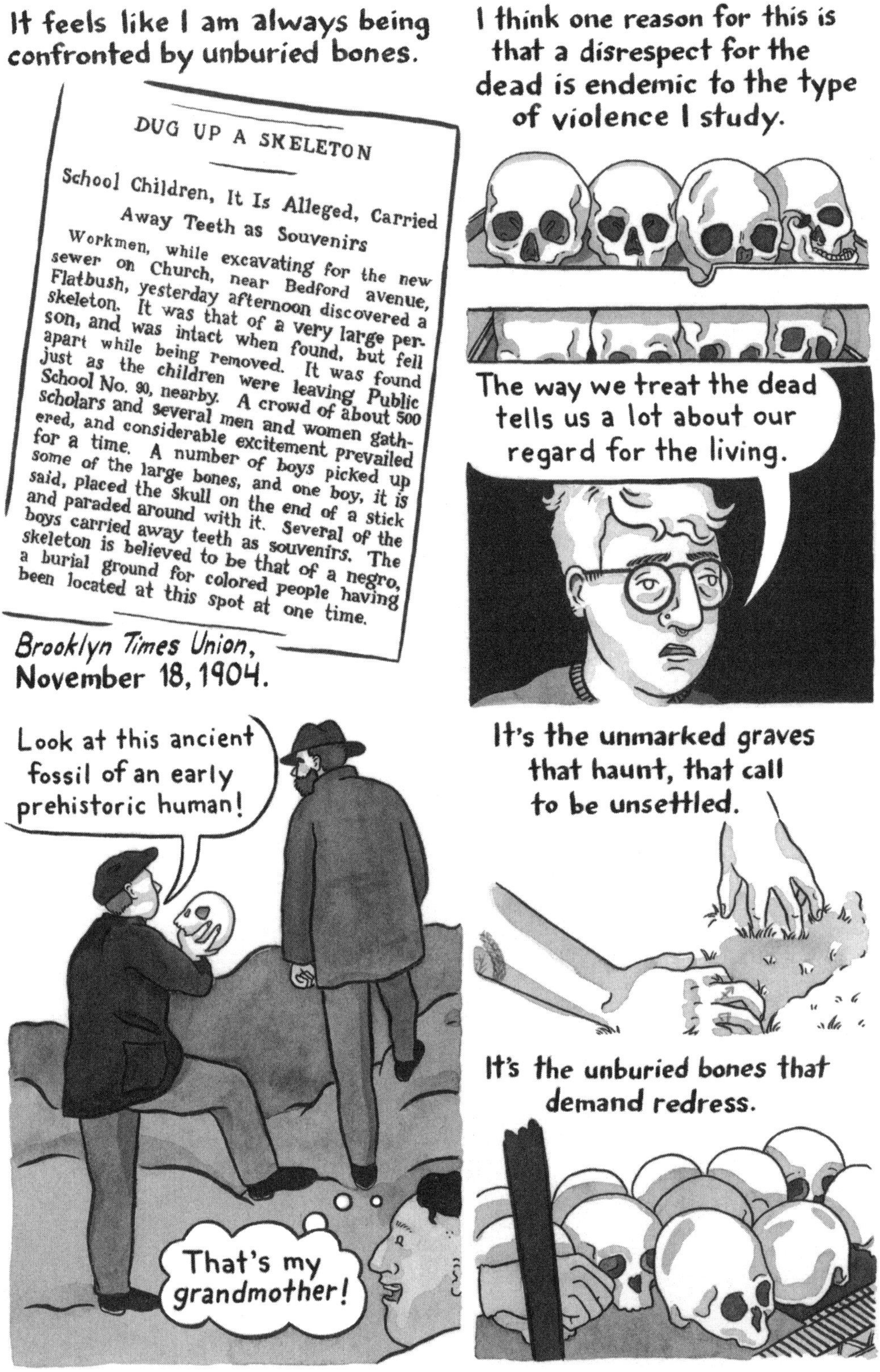
It feels like I am always being confronted by unburied bones.
DUG UP A SKELETON
School Children, It Is Alleged, Carried Away Teeth as Souvenirs
Workmen, while excavating for the new sewer on Church, near Bedford avenue, Flatbush, yesterday afternoon discovered a skeleton. It was that of a very large person, and was intact when found, but fell apart while being removed. It was found just as the children were leaving Public School No. 90, nearby. A crowd of about 500 scholars and several men and women gathered, and considerable excitement prevailed for a time. A number of boys picked up some of the large bones, and one boy, it is said, placed the skull on the end of a stick and paraded around with it. Several of the boys carried away teeth as souvenirs. The skeleton is believed to be that of a negro, a burial ground for colored people having been located at this spot at one time.
Brooklyn Times Union, November 18, 1904.
Look at this ancient fossil of an early prehistoric human!
That's my grandmother!
I think one reason for this is that a disrespect for the dead is endemic to the type of violence I study.
The way we treat the dead tells us a lot about our regard for the living.
It's the unmarked graves that haunt, that call to be unsettled.
It's the unburied bones that demand redress.

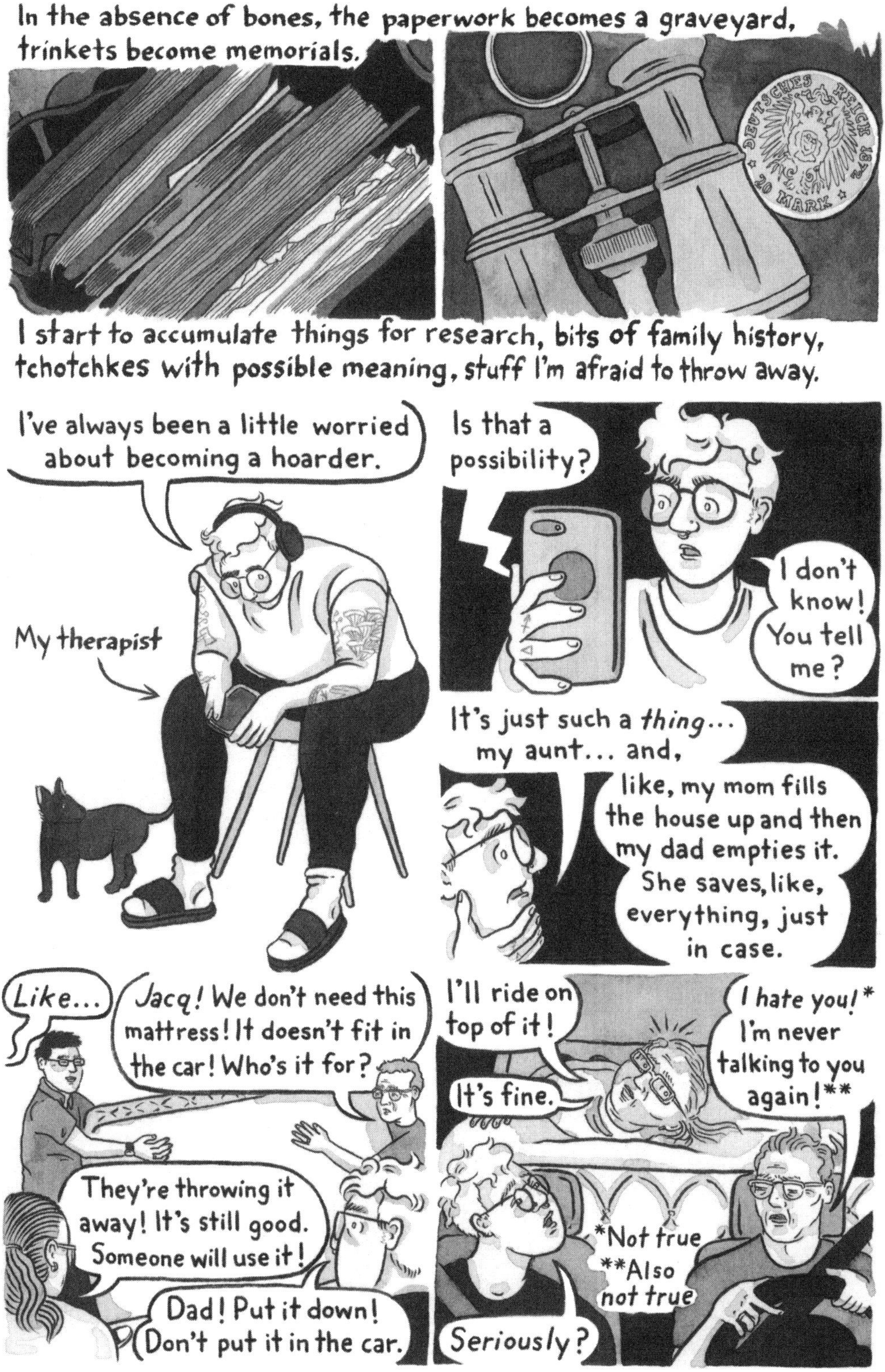

In the absence of bones, the paperwork becomes a graveyard, trinkets become memorials.
DEUTSCHES REICH 1872 20 MARK
I start to accumulate things for research, bits of family history, tchotchkes with possible meaning, stuff I'm afraid to throw away.
I've always been a little worried about becoming a hoarder.
My therapist
Is that a possibility?
I don't know! You tell me?
It's just such a *thing*... my aunt... and,
like, my mom fills the house up and then my dad empties it. She saves, like, everything, just in case.
Like...
Jacq! We don't need this mattress! It doesn't fit in the car! Who's it for?
They're throwing it away! It's still good. Someone will use it!
Dad! Put it down! Don't put it in the car.
I'll ride on top of it!
It's fine.
*I hate you!** I'm never talking to you again!***
Seriously?
*Not true
**Also not true

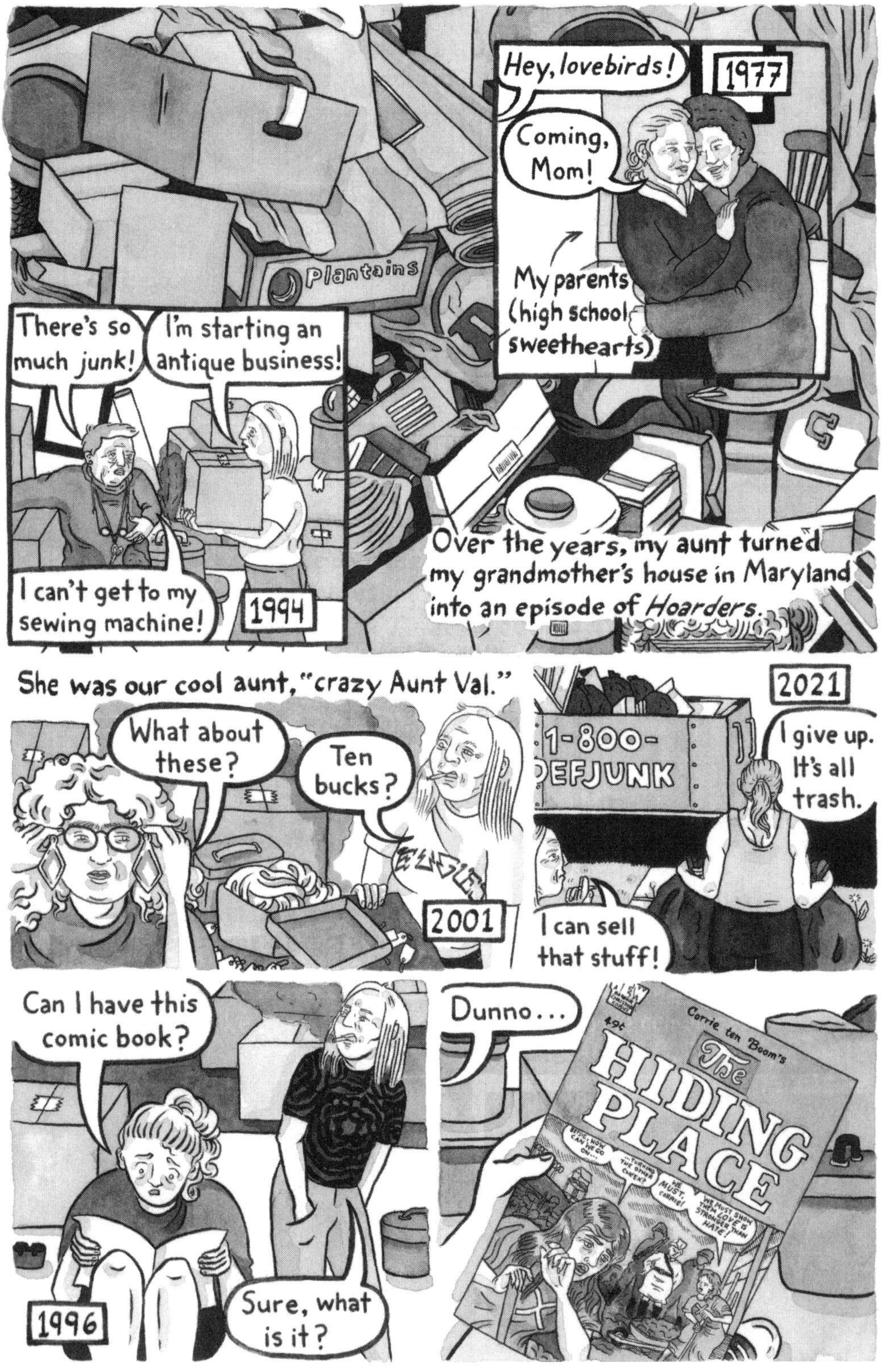

Hey, lovebirds!
1977
Coming, Mom!
My parents (high school sweethearts)
plantains
There's so much *junk*!
I'm starting an antique business!
I can't get to my sewing machine!
1994
Over the years, my aunt turned my grandmother's house in Maryland into an episode of *Hoarders*.
She was our cool aunt, "crazy Aunt Val."
What about these?
Ten bucks?
2001
2021
1-800-
DEFJUNK
I give up. It's all trash.
I can sell that stuff!
Can I have this comic book?
1996
Sure, what is it?
Dunno...
Corrie ten Boom's
49¢
The HIDING PLACE
BETSIE, HOW CAN WE GO ON...
...TURNING THE OTHER CHEEK?
WE MUST, CARRIE!
WE MUST SHOW THEM LOVE IS STRONGER THAN HATE!

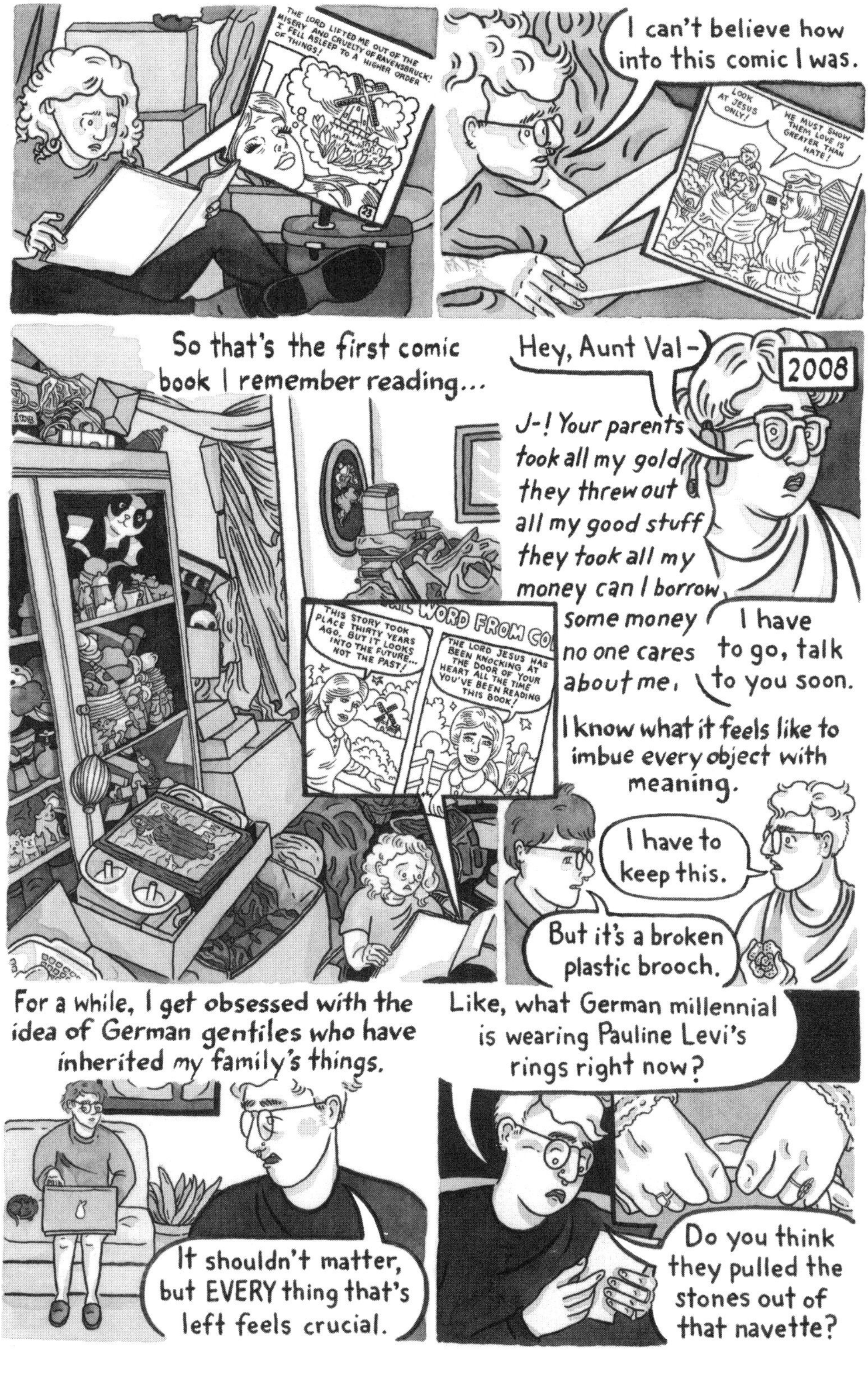

THE LORD LIFTED ME OUT OF THE MISERY AND CRUELTY OF RAVENSBRUCK! I FELL ASLEEP TO A HIGHER ORDER OF THINGS!
I can't believe how into this comic I was.
LOOK AT JESUS ONLY!
WE MUST SHOW THEM LOVE IS GREATER THAN HATE!
So that's the first comic book I remember reading...
Hey, Aunt Val-
2008
J-! Your parents took all my gold they threw out all my good stuff they took all my money can I borrow some money no one cares about me.
I have to go, talk to you soon.
THIS STORY TOOK PLACE THIRTY YEARS AGO, BUT IT LOOKS INTO THE FUTURE... NOT THE PAST!
THE LORD JESUS HAS BEEN KNOCKING AT THE DOOR OF YOUR HEART ALL THE TIME YOU'VE BEEN READING THIS BOOK!
I know what it feels like to imbue every object with meaning.
I have to keep this.
But it's a broken plastic brooch.
For a while, I get obsessed with the idea of German gentiles who have inherited my family's things.
It shouldn't matter, but EVERY thing that's left feels crucial.
Like, what German millennial is wearing Pauline Levi's rings right now?
Do you think they pulled the stones out of that navette?

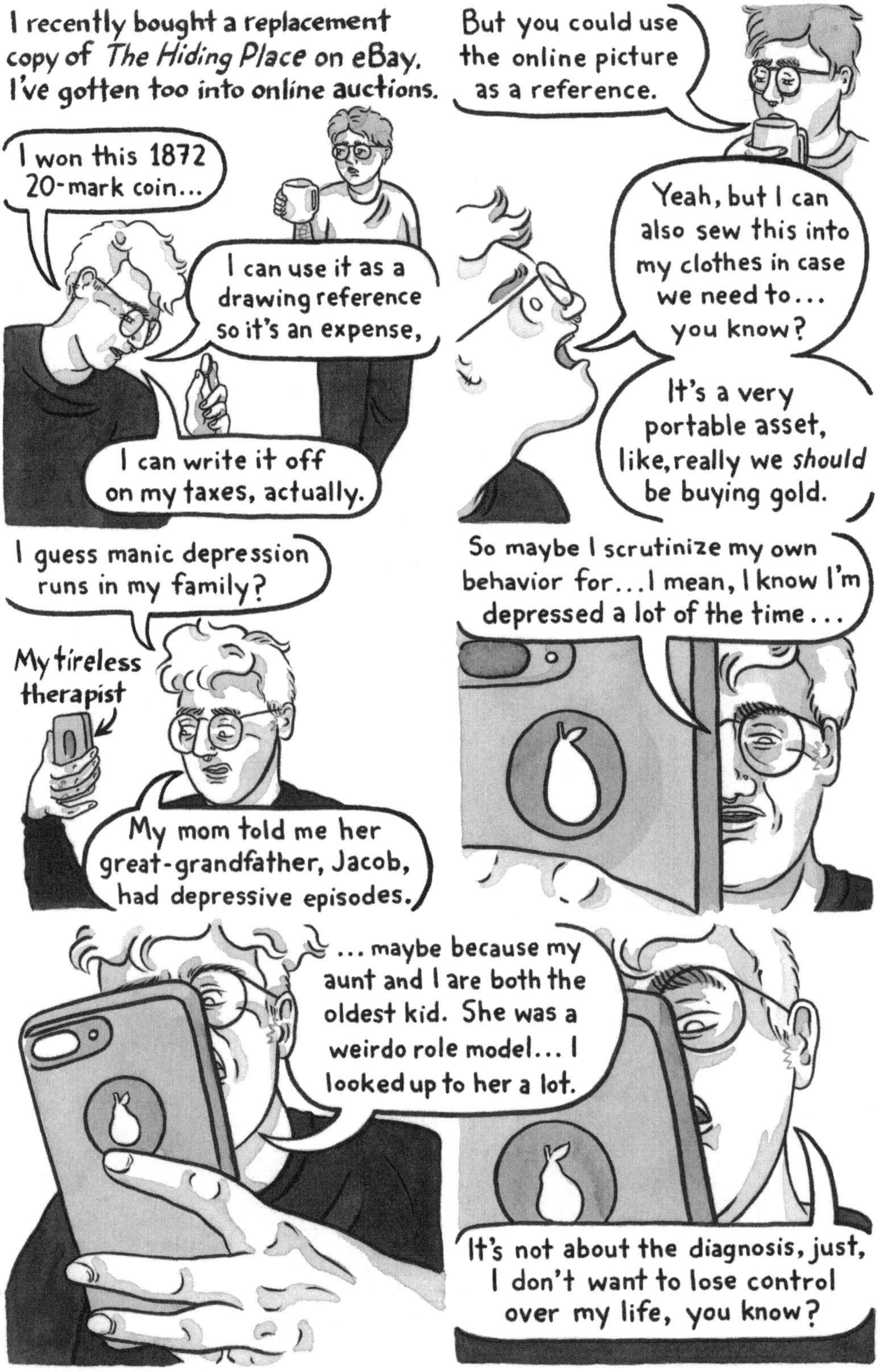

I recently bought a replacement copy of *The Hiding Place* on eBay. I've gotten too into online auctions.
But you could use the online picture as a reference.
I won this 1872 20-mark coin...
I can use it as a drawing reference so it's an expense,
I can write it off on my taxes, actually.
Yeah, but I can also sew this into my clothes in case we need to... you know?
It's a very portable asset, like, really we *should* be buying gold.
I guess manic depression runs in my family?
My tireless therapist
My mom told me her great-grandfather, Jacob, had depressive episodes.
So maybe I scrutinize my own behavior for... I mean, I know I'm depressed a lot of the time...
... maybe because my aunt and I are both the oldest kid. She was a weirdo role model... I looked up to her a lot.
It's not about the diagnosis, just, I don't want to lose control over my life, you know?

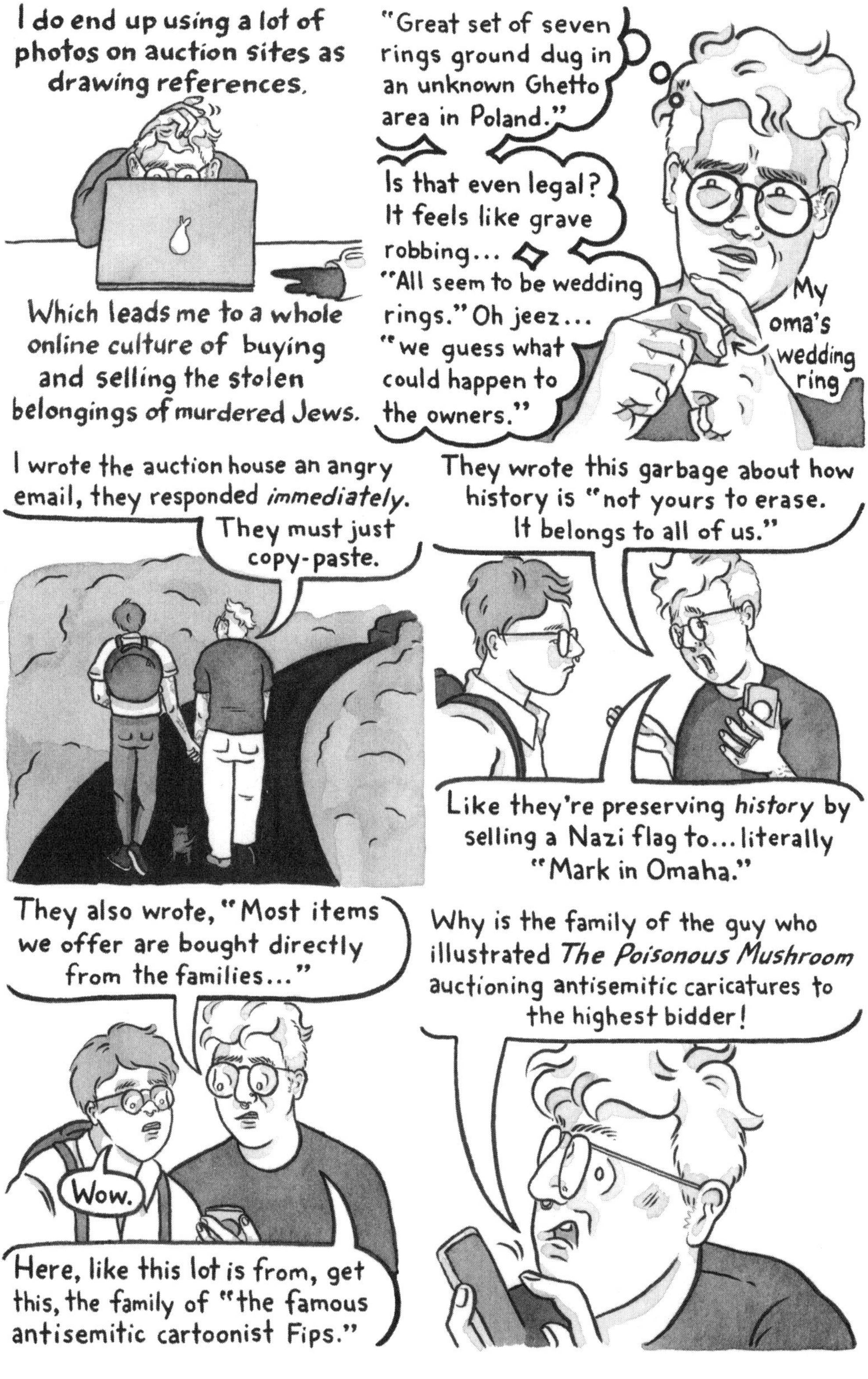
I do end up using a lot of photos on auction sites as drawing references.
Which leads me to a whole online culture of buying and selling the stolen belongings of murdered Jews.
"Great set of seven rings ground dug in an unknown Ghetto area in Poland."
Is that even legal? It feels like grave robbing...
"All seem to be wedding rings." Oh jeez... "we guess what could happen to the owners."
My oma's wedding ring
I wrote the auction house an angry email, they responded *immediately*.
They must just copy-paste.
They wrote this garbage about how history is "not yours to erase. It belongs to all of us."
Like they're preserving *history* by selling a Nazi flag to... literally "Mark in Omaha."
They also wrote, "Most items we offer are bought directly from the families..."
Wow.
Here, like this lot is from, get this, the family of "the famous antisemitic cartoonist Fips."
Why is the family of the guy who illustrated *The Poisonous Mushroom* auctioning antisemitic caricatures to the highest bidder!

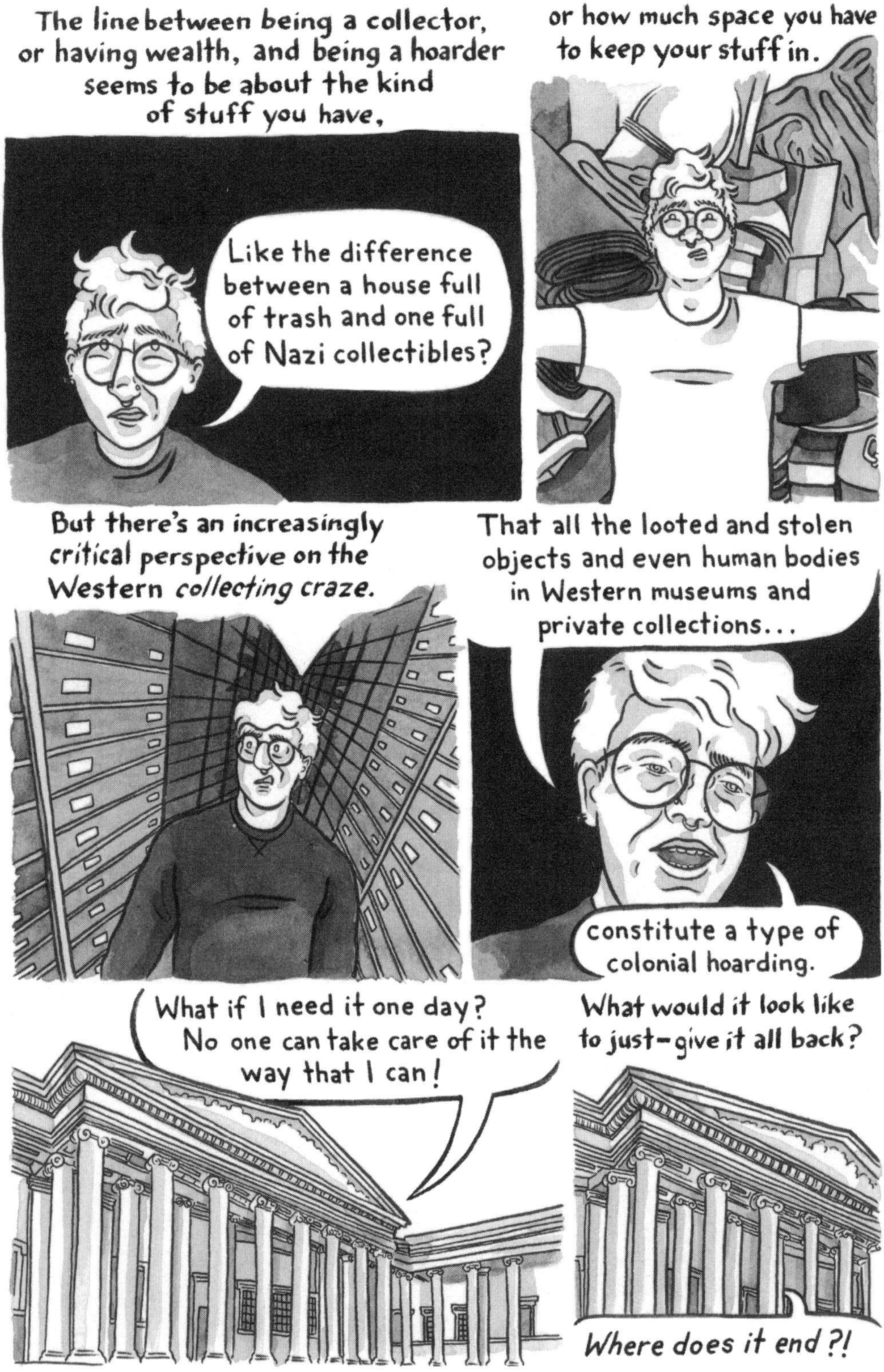

The line between being a collector, or having wealth, and being a hoarder seems to be about the kind of stuff you have,
Like the difference between a house full of trash and one full of Nazi collectibles?
or how much space you have to keep your stuff in.
But there's an increasingly critical perspective on the Western *collecting craze.*
That all the looted and stolen objects and even human bodies in Western museums and private collections...
constitute a type of colonial hoarding.
What if I need it one day? No one can take care of it the way that I can!
What would it look like to just—give it all back?
Where does it end?!

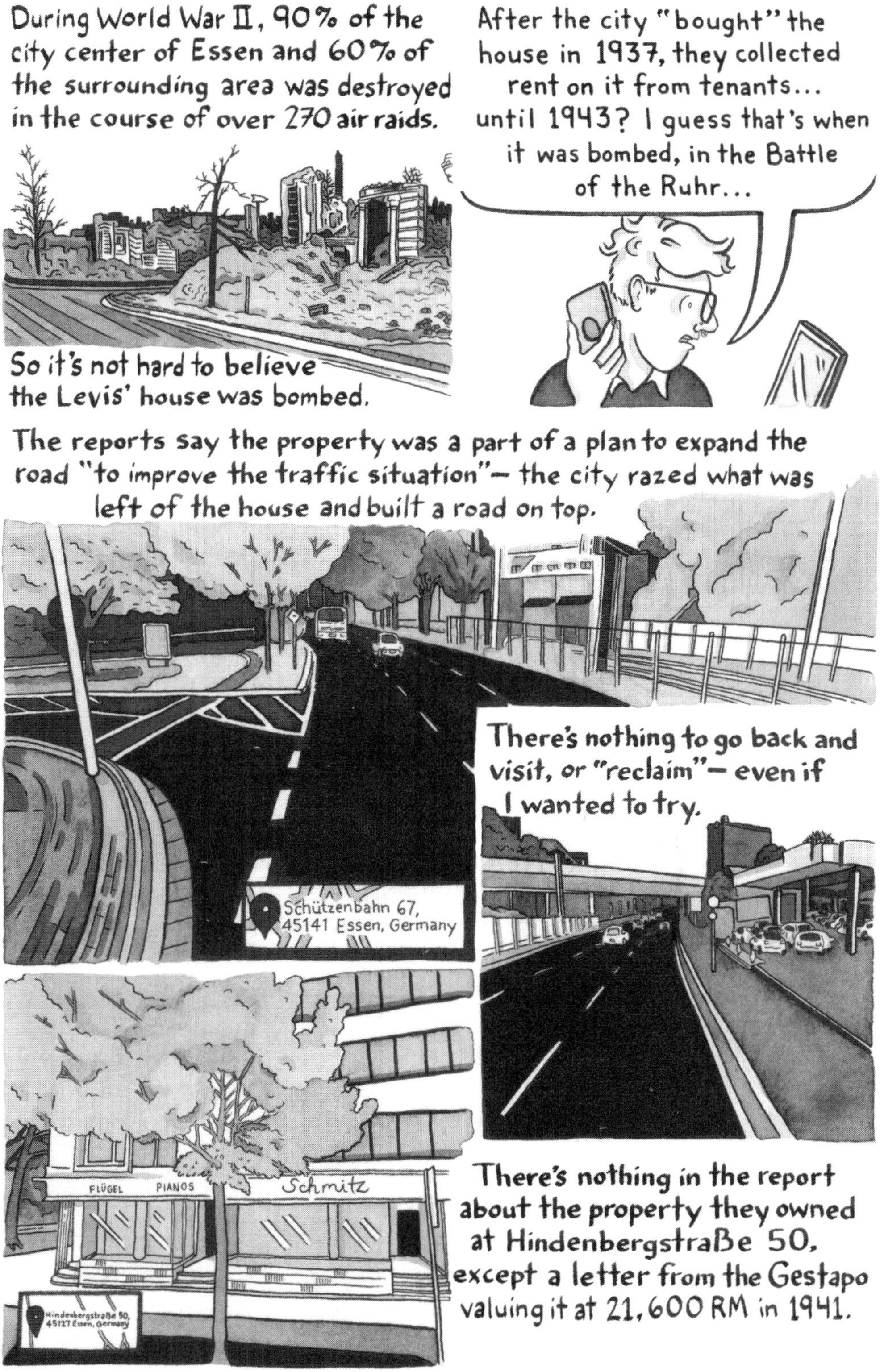
During World War II, 90% of the city center of Essen and 60% of the surrounding area was destroyed in the course of over 270 air raids.
After the city "bought" the house in 1937, they collected rent on it from tenants... until 1943? I guess that's when it was bombed, in the Battle of the Ruhr...
So it's not hard to believe the Levis' house was bombed.
The reports say the property was a part of a plan to expand the road "to improve the traffic situation"— the city razed what was left of the house and built a road on top.
Schützenbahn 67,
45141 Essen, Germany
There's nothing to go back and visit, or "reclaim"— even if I wanted to try.
FLÜGEL
PIANOS
Schmitz
Hindenbergstraße 50,
45127 Essen, Germany
There's nothing in the report about the property they owned at Hindenbergstraße 50, except a letter from the Gestapo valuing it at 21,600 RM in 1941.

The Levi heirs settle for about 2,500 U.S. dollars in 1950 — Kurt dies of ALS later that year.

Neither of the Levi boys lived to be 50.

There's an easy outrage and clear target to material loss —

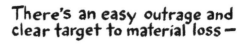

Hey! Where's my stuff!

You took it, give it back!

Yeah, I'm talking to you, Germany!

But from the perspective of reparations, which is to say— *repair* — what's the goal?

I think the question of reclamation of property or citizenship rights— *anything* in Europe— can't ethically be considered...

... without a deep consideration of all the connected legacies of theft and dispossession that created *Europe*,

and the continuity of injustice or inequality right now.

This of course is not a new set of questions.

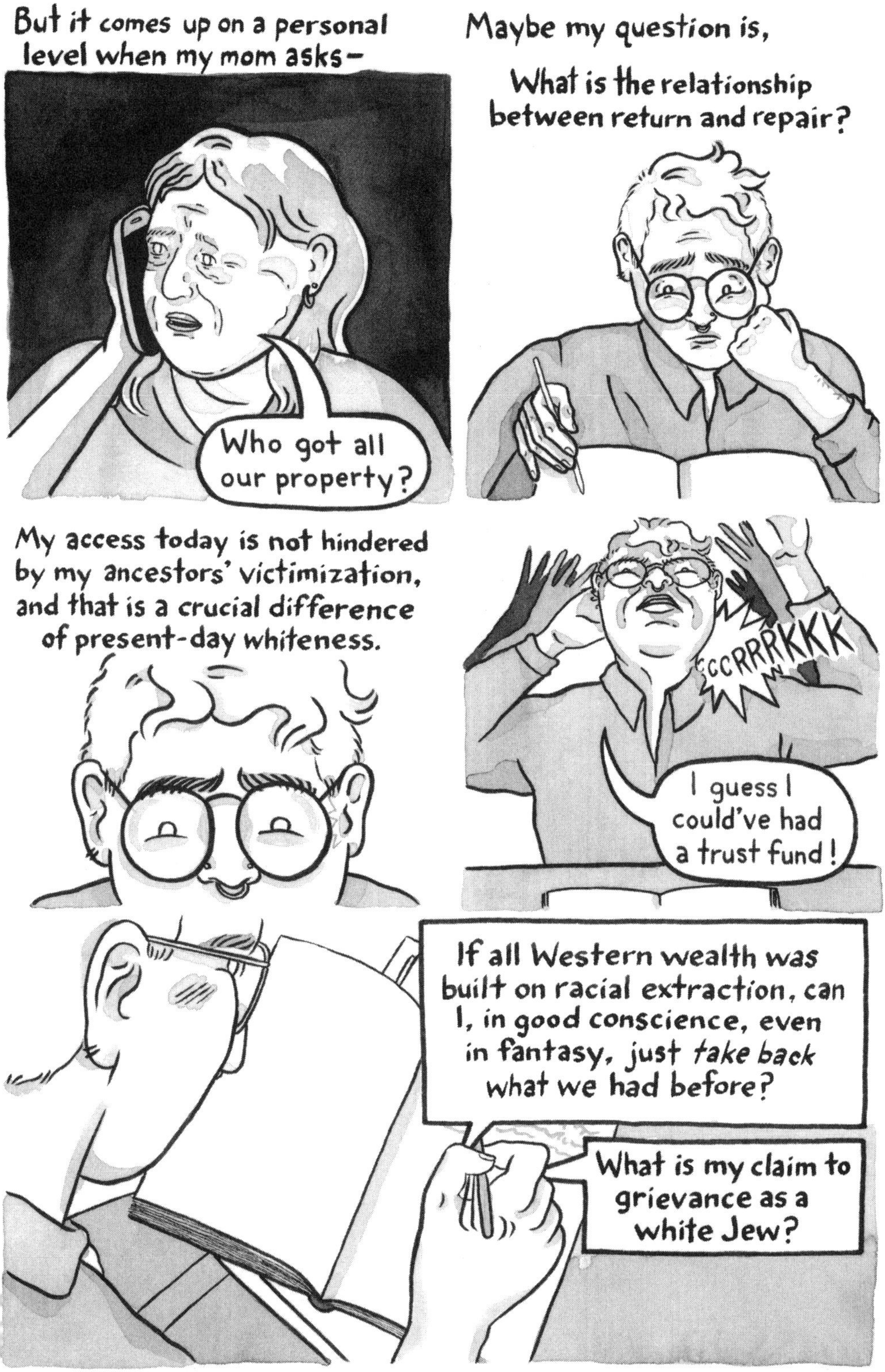

But it comes up on a personal level when my mom asks—
Who got all our property?
Maybe my question is,
What is the relationship between return and repair?
My access today is not hindered by my ancestors' victimization, and that is a crucial difference of present-day whiteness.
CCRRRKKK
I guess I could've had a trust fund!
If all Western wealth was built on racial extraction, can I, in good conscience, even in fantasy, just *take back* what we had before?
What is my claim to grievance as a white Jew?

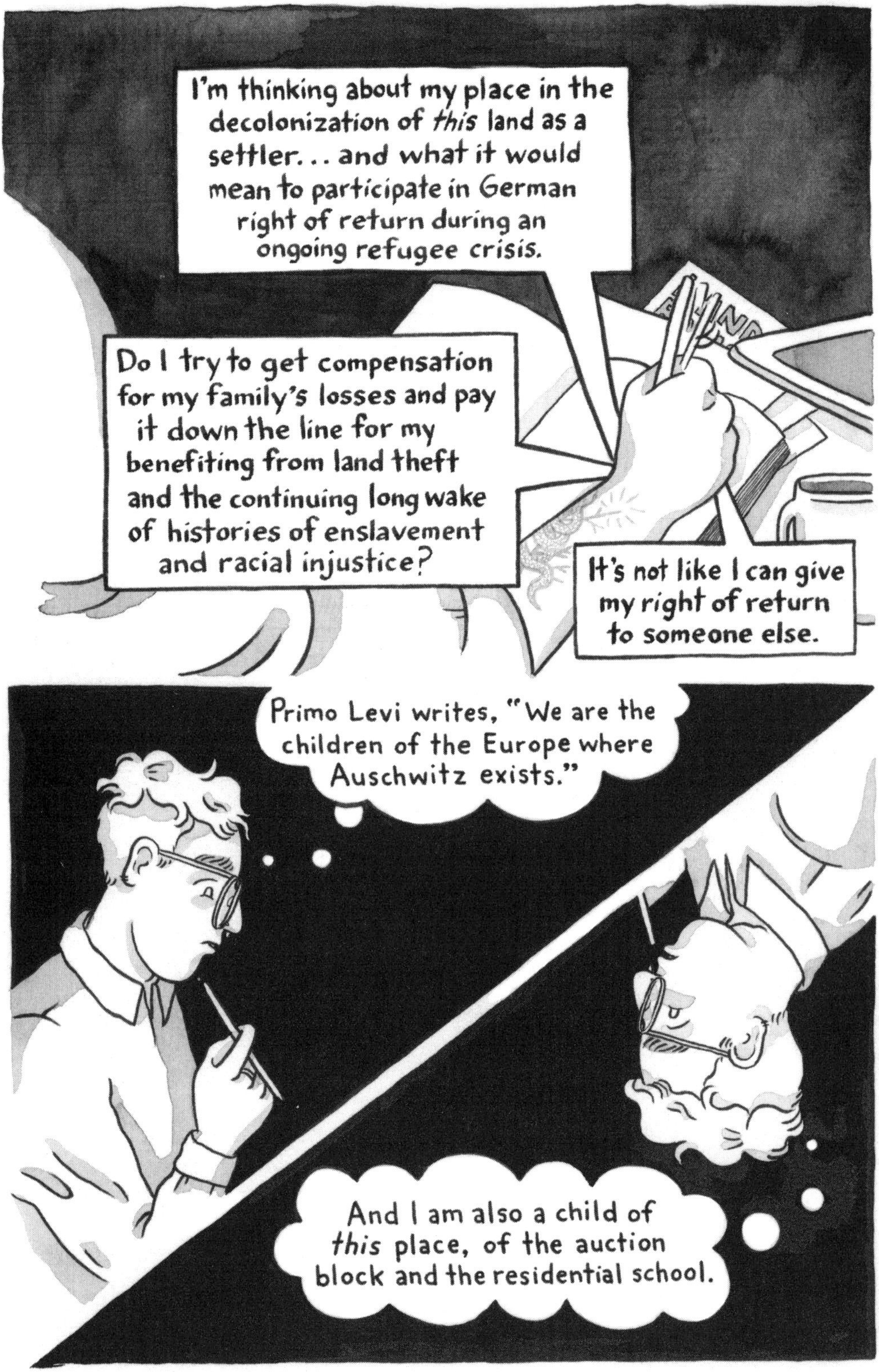
I'm thinking about my place in the decolonization of *this* land as a settler... and what it would mean to participate in German right of return during an ongoing refugee crisis.
Do I try to get compensation for my family's losses and pay it down the line for my benefiting from land theft and the continuing long wake of histories of enslavement and racial injustice?
It's not like I can give my *right* of return to someone else.
Primo Levi writes, "We are the children of the Europe where Auschwitz exists."
And I am also a child of *this* place, of the auction block and the residential school.

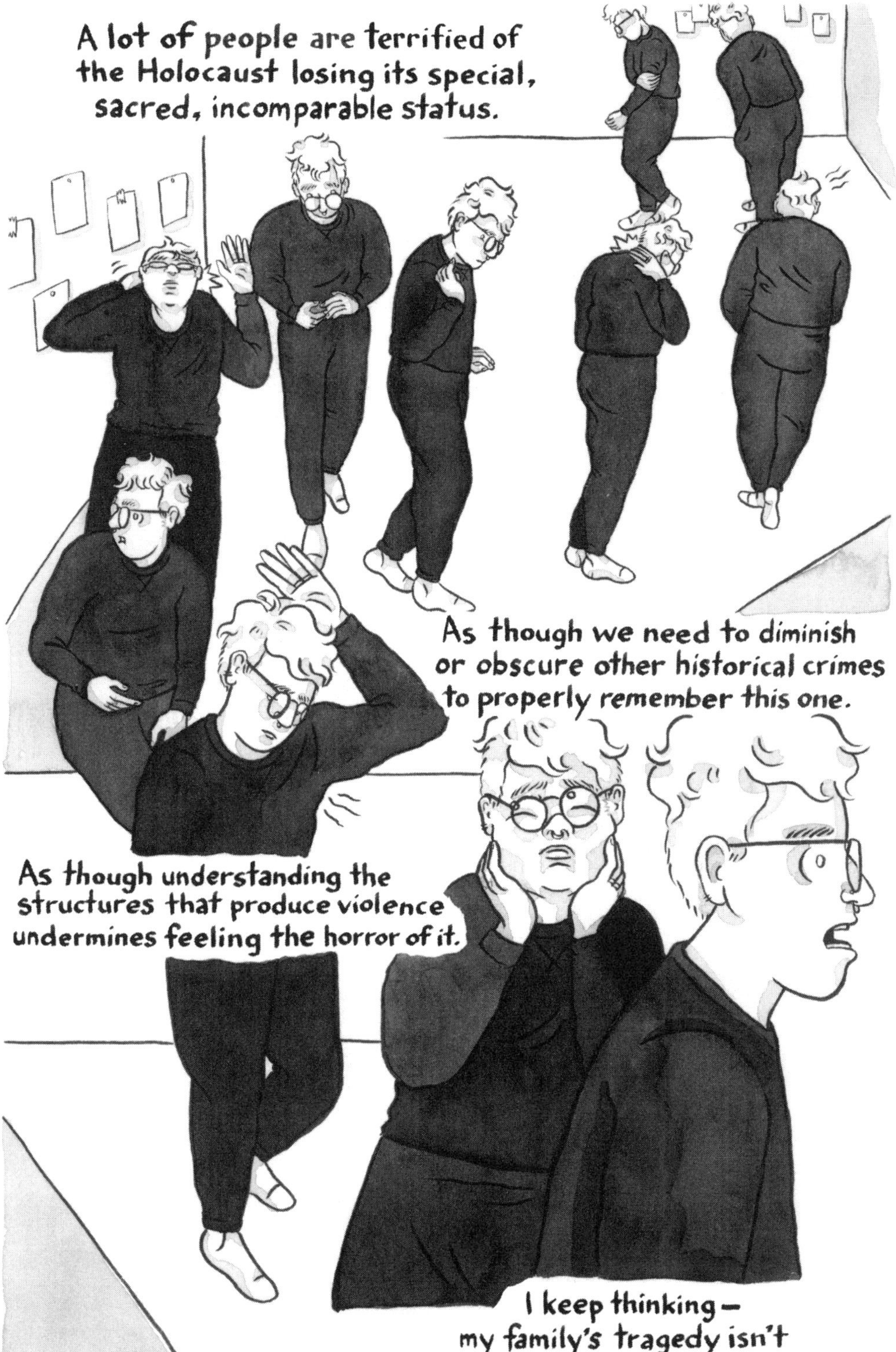
A lot of people are terrified of the Holocaust losing its special, sacred, incomparable status.
As though we need to diminish or obscure other historical crimes to properly remember this one.
As though understanding the structures that produce violence undermines feeling the horror of it.
I keep thinking — my family's tragedy isn't unique, only specific.

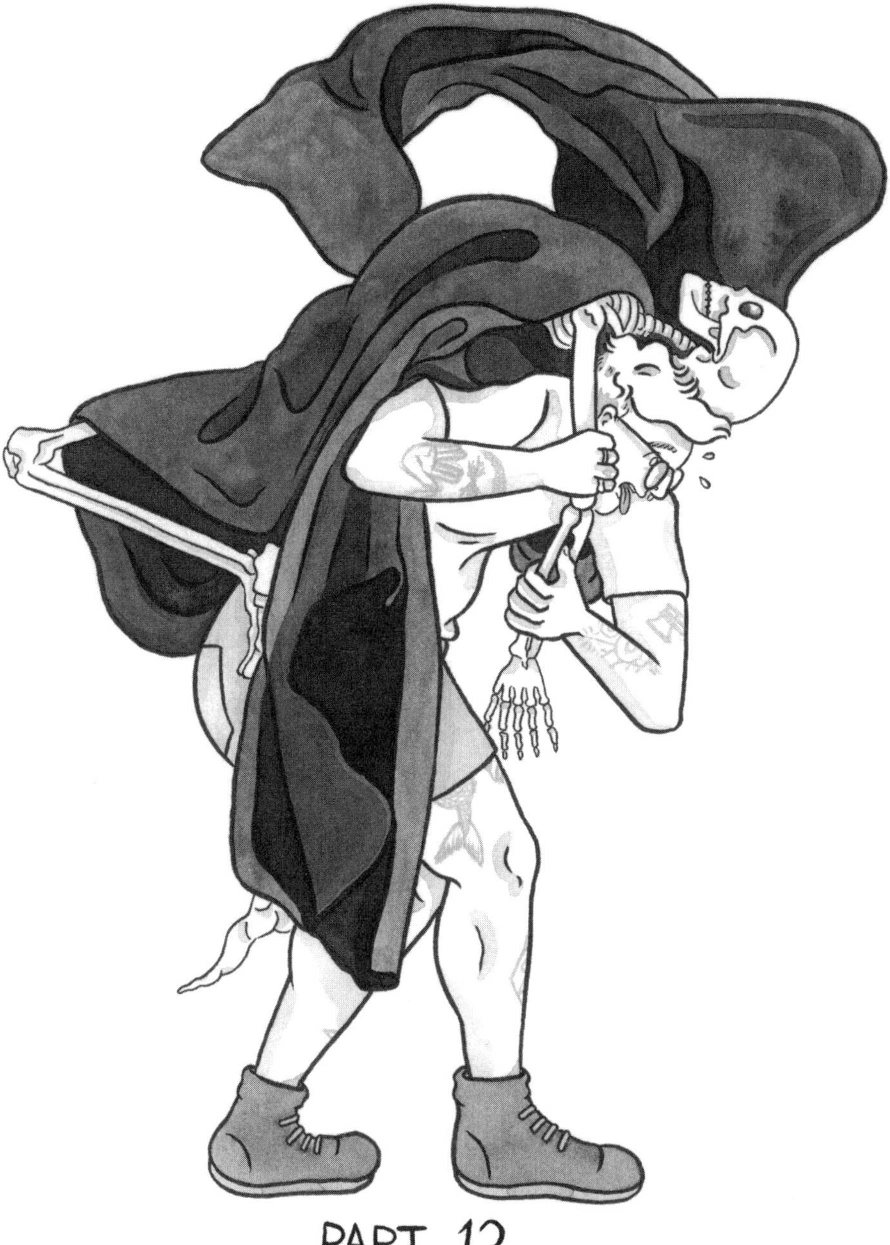

PART 12

AFTERLIVES, WHICH IS TO SAY, GHOSTS

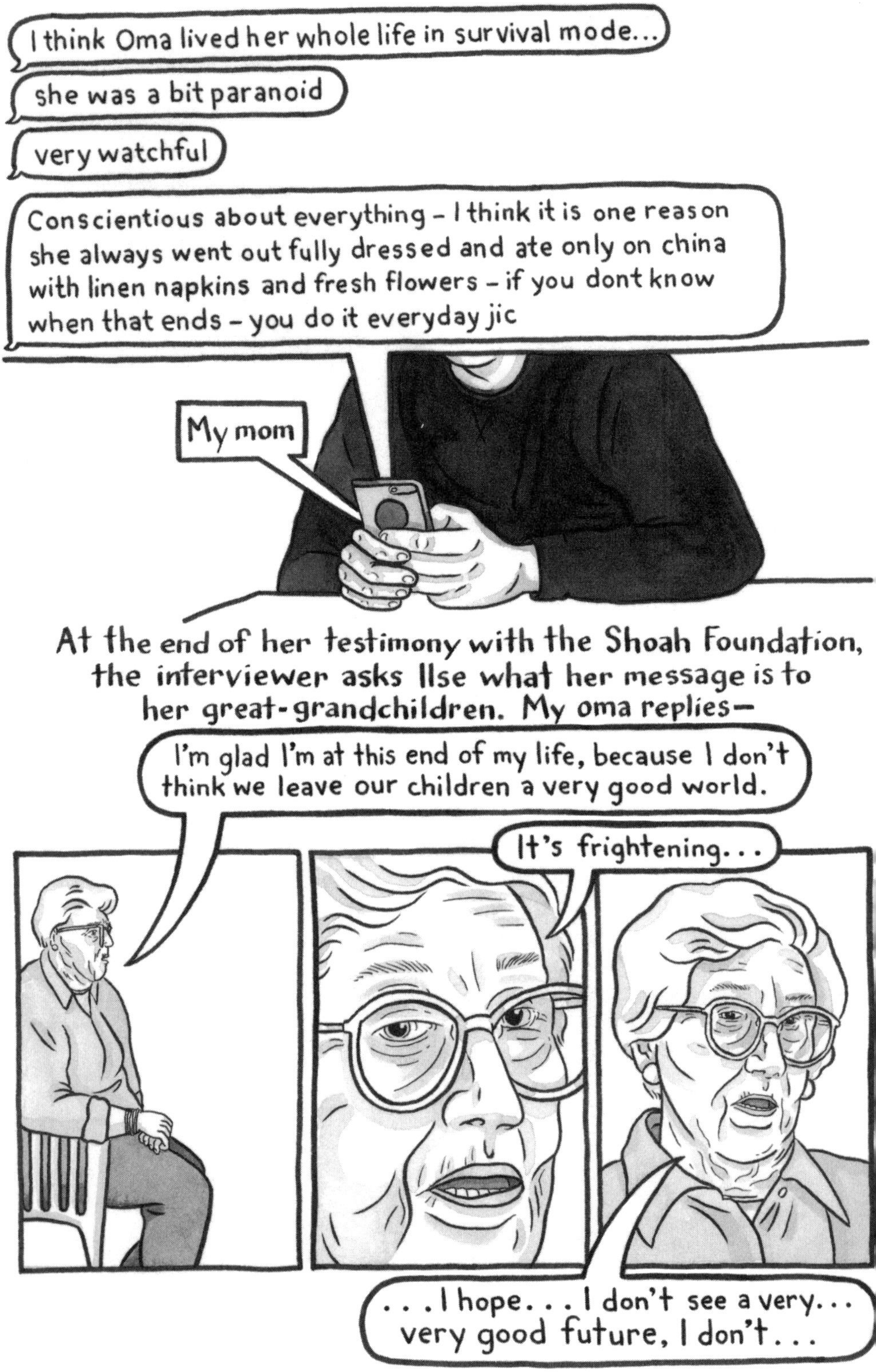

I think Oma lived her whole life in survival mode...
she was a bit paranoid
very watchful
Conscientious about everything - I think it is one reason she always went out fully dressed and ate only on china with linen napkins and fresh flowers - if you dont know when that ends - you do it everyday jic
My mom
At the end of her testimony with the Shoah Foundation, the interviewer asks Ilse what her message is to her great-grandchildren. My oma replies—
I'm glad I'm at this end of my life, because I don't think we leave our children a very good world.
It's frightening...
...I hope...I don't see a very... very good future, I don't...

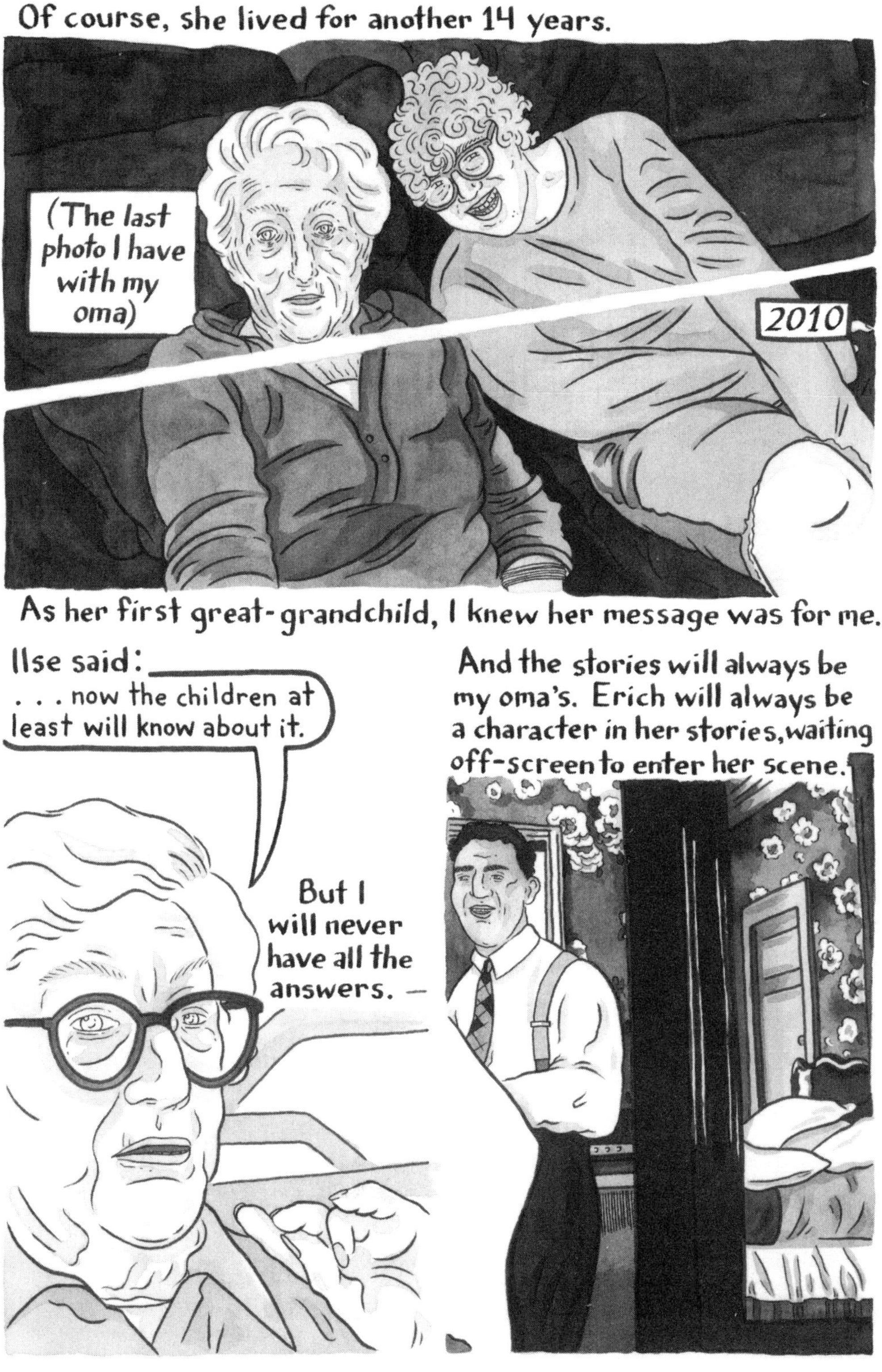
Of course, she lived for another 14 years.
(The last photo I have with my oma)
2010
As her first great-grandchild, I knew her message was for me.
Ilse said:
. . . now the children at least will know about it.
But I will never have all the answers. —
And the stories will always be my oma's. Erich will always be a character in her stories, waiting off-screen to enter her scene.

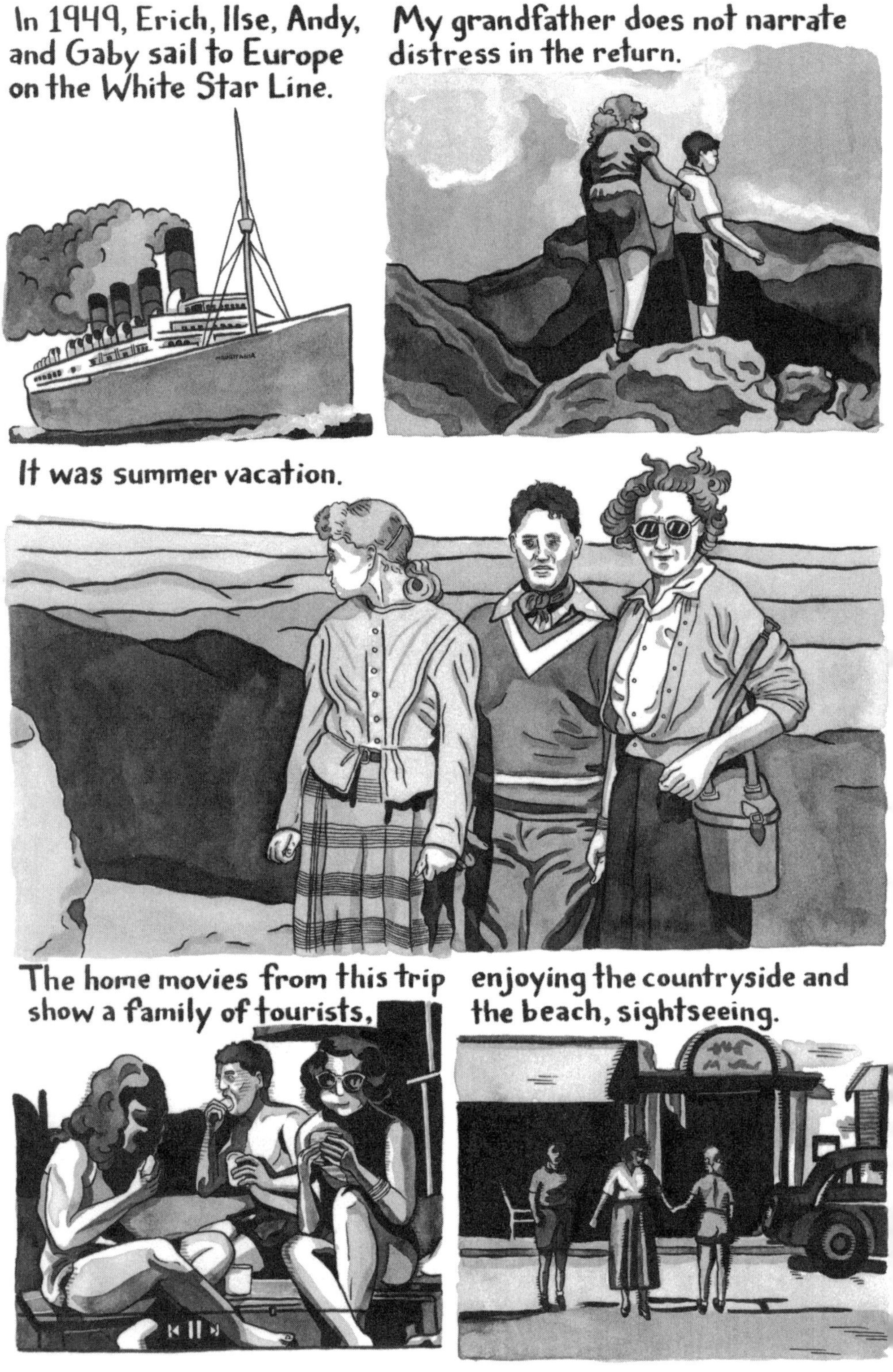
In 1949, Erich, Ilse, Andy, and Gaby sail to Europe on the White Star Line.
My grandfather does not narrate distress in the return.
It was summer vacation.
The home movies from this trip show a family of tourists,
enjoying the countryside and the beach, sightseeing.

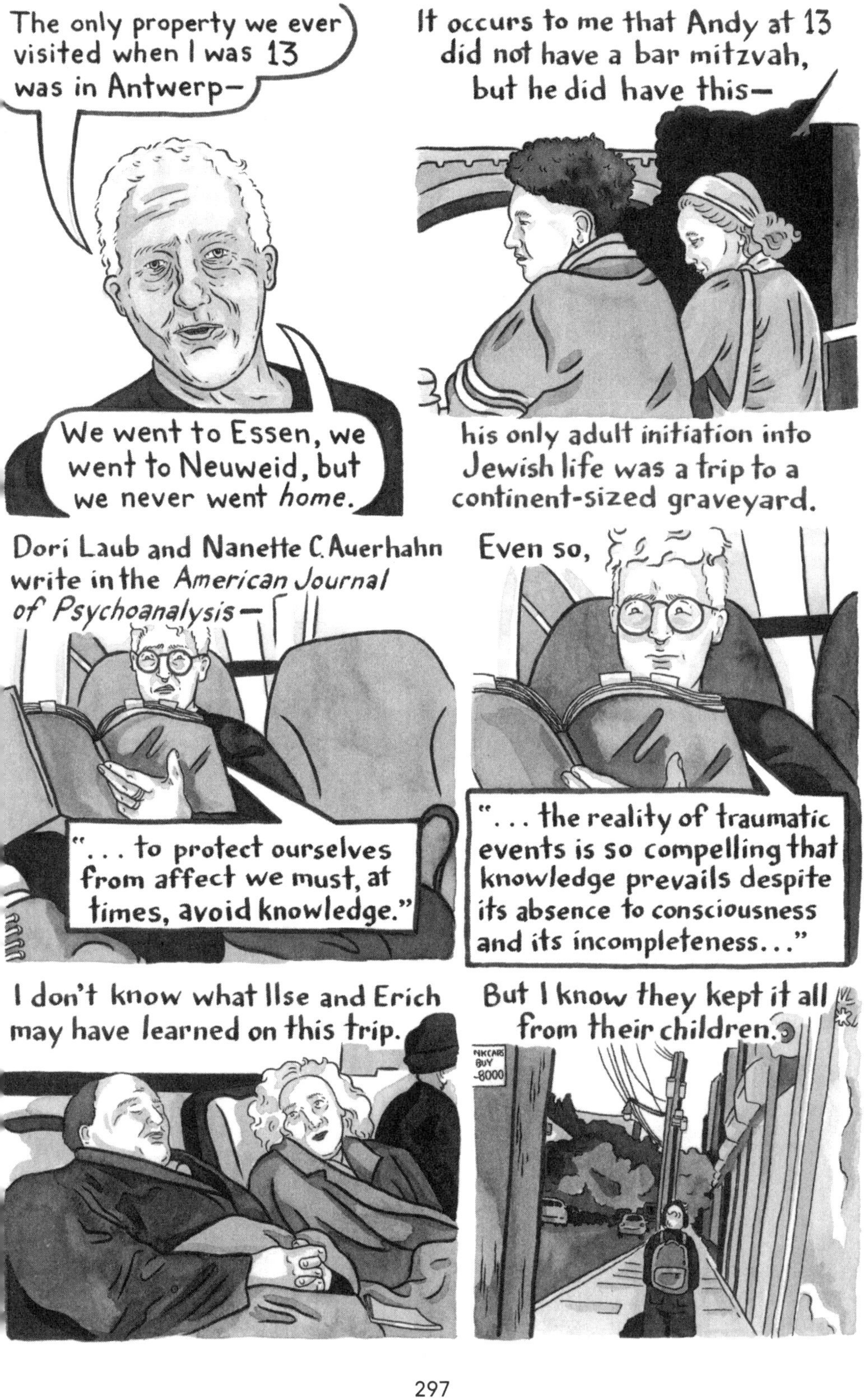
The only property we ever visited when I was 13 was in Antwerp—
We went to Essen, we went to Neuweid, but we never went *home.*
It occurs to me that Andy at 13 did not have a bar mitzvah, but he did have this—
his only adult initiation into Jewish life was a trip to a continent-sized graveyard.
Dori Laub and Nanette C. Auerhahn write in the *American Journal of Psychoanalysis*—
". . . to protect ourselves from affect we must, at times, avoid knowledge."
Even so,
". . . the reality of traumatic events is so compelling that knowledge prevails despite its absence to consciousness and its incompleteness. . ."
I don't know what Ilse and Erich may have learned on this trip.
But I know they kept it all from their children.

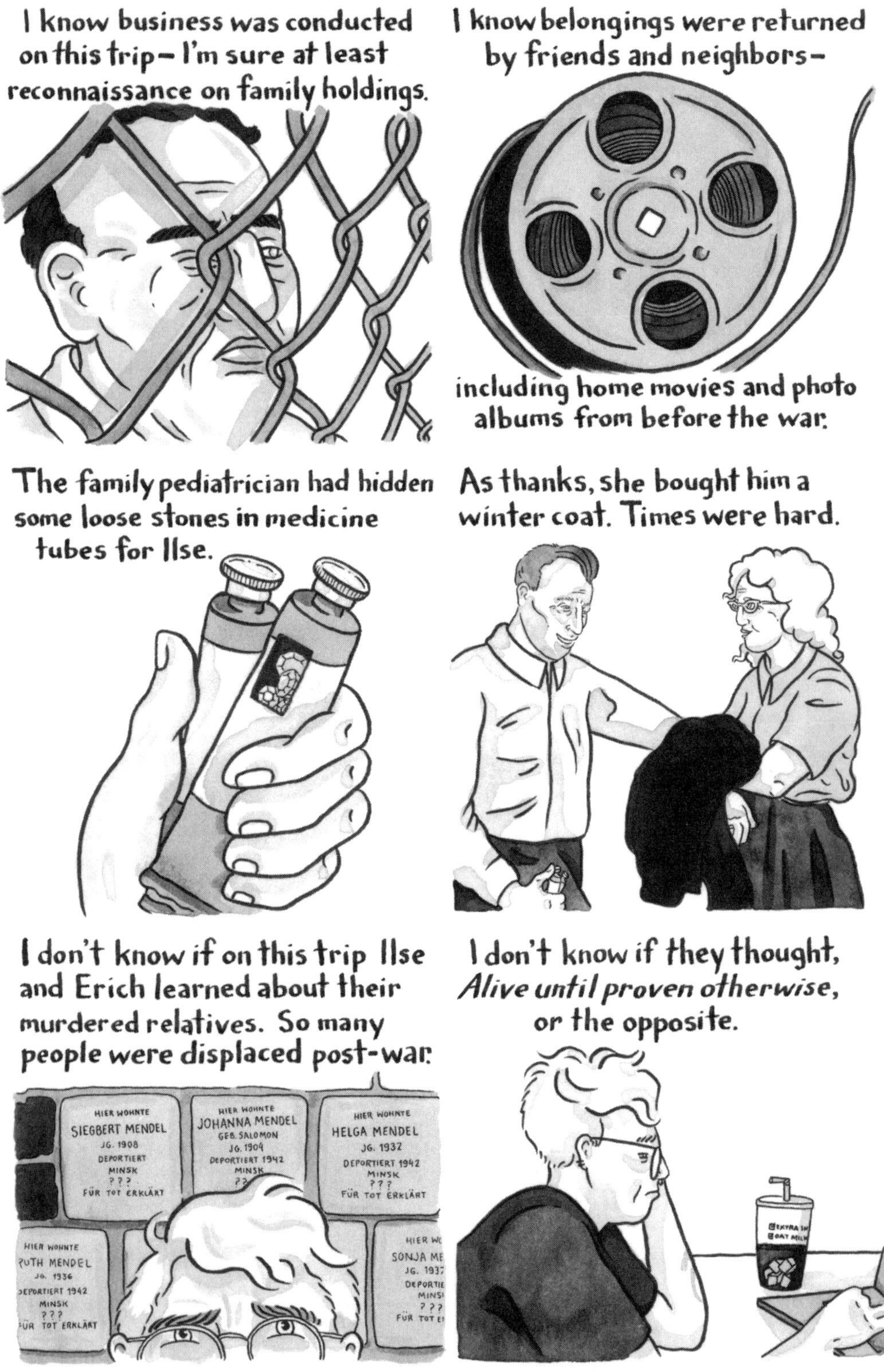
I know business was conducted on this trip— I'm sure at least reconnaissance on family holdings.
I know belongings were returned by friends and neighbors—
including home movies and photo albums from before the war.
The family pediatrician had hidden some loose stones in medicine tubes for Ilse.
As thanks, she bought him a winter coat. Times were hard.
I don't know if on this trip Ilse and Erich learned about their murdered relatives. So many people were displaced post-war.
HIER WOHNTE
SIEGBERT MENDEL
JG. 1908
DEPORTIERT
MINSK
???
FÜR TOT ERKLÄRT
HIER WOHNTE
JOHANNA MENDEL
GEB. SALOMON
JG. 1904
DEPORTIERT 1942
HIER WOHNTE
HELGA MENDEL
JG. 1932
DEPORTIERT 1942
MINSK
???
FÜR TOT ERKLÄRT
HIER WOHNTE
JG. 1936
DEPORTIERT 1942
MINSK
???
I don't know if they thought, *Alive until proven otherwise*, or the opposite.

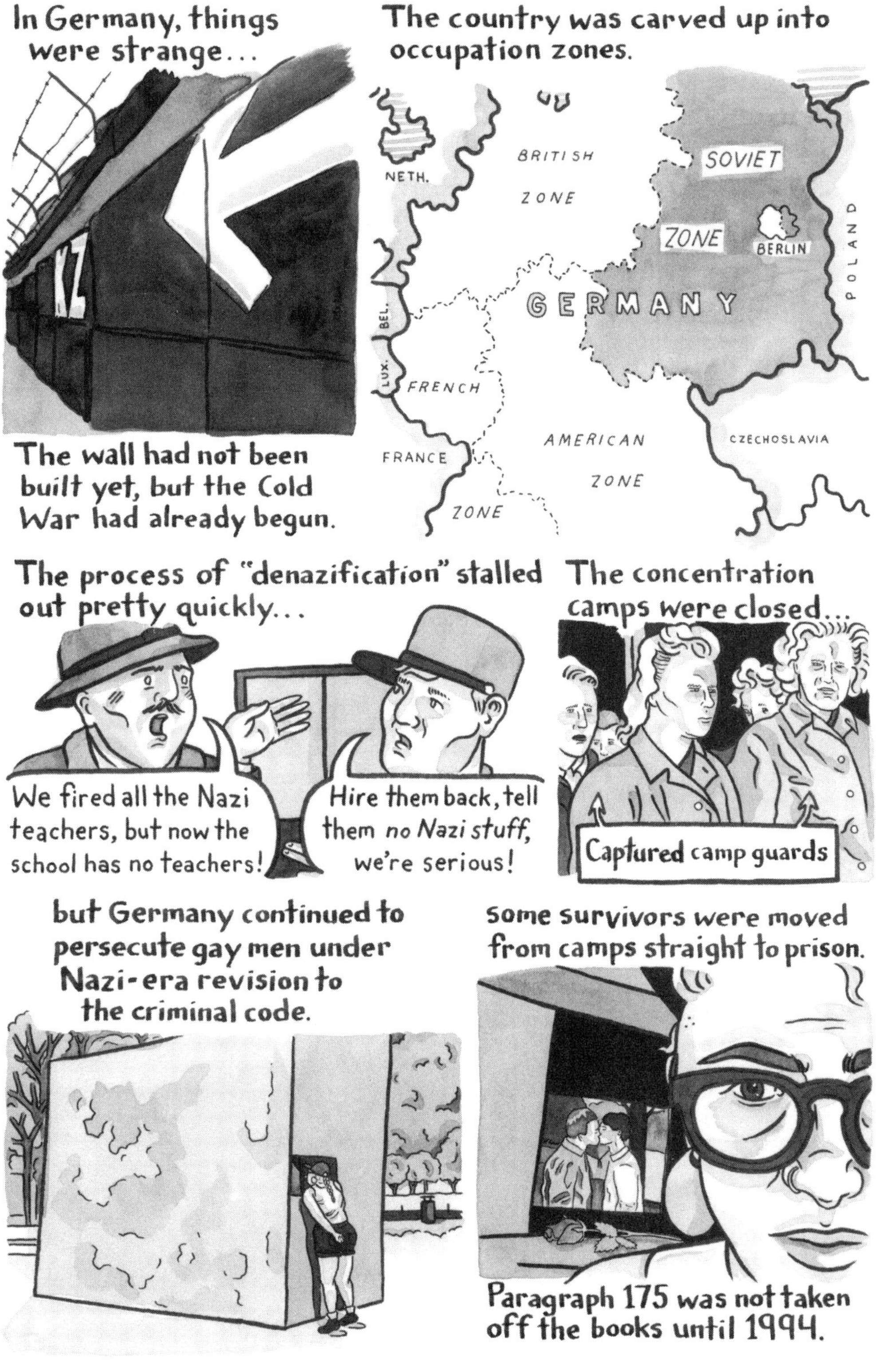
In Germany, things were strange...
KZ
The wall had not been built yet, but the Cold War had already begun.
The country was carved up into occupation zones.
NETH.
BRITISH ZONE
SOVIET ZONE
BERLIN
POLAND
GERMANY
BEL.
LUX.
FRENCH ZONE
FRANCE
AMERICAN ZONE
CZECHOSLAVIA
The process of "denazification" stalled out pretty quickly...
We fired all the Nazi teachers, but now the school has no teachers!
Hire them back, tell them *no Nazi stuff*, we're serious!
The concentration camps were closed...
Captured camp guards
but Germany continued to persecute gay men under Nazi-era revision to the criminal code.
Some survivors were moved from camps straight to prison.
Paragraph 175 was not taken off the books until 1994.

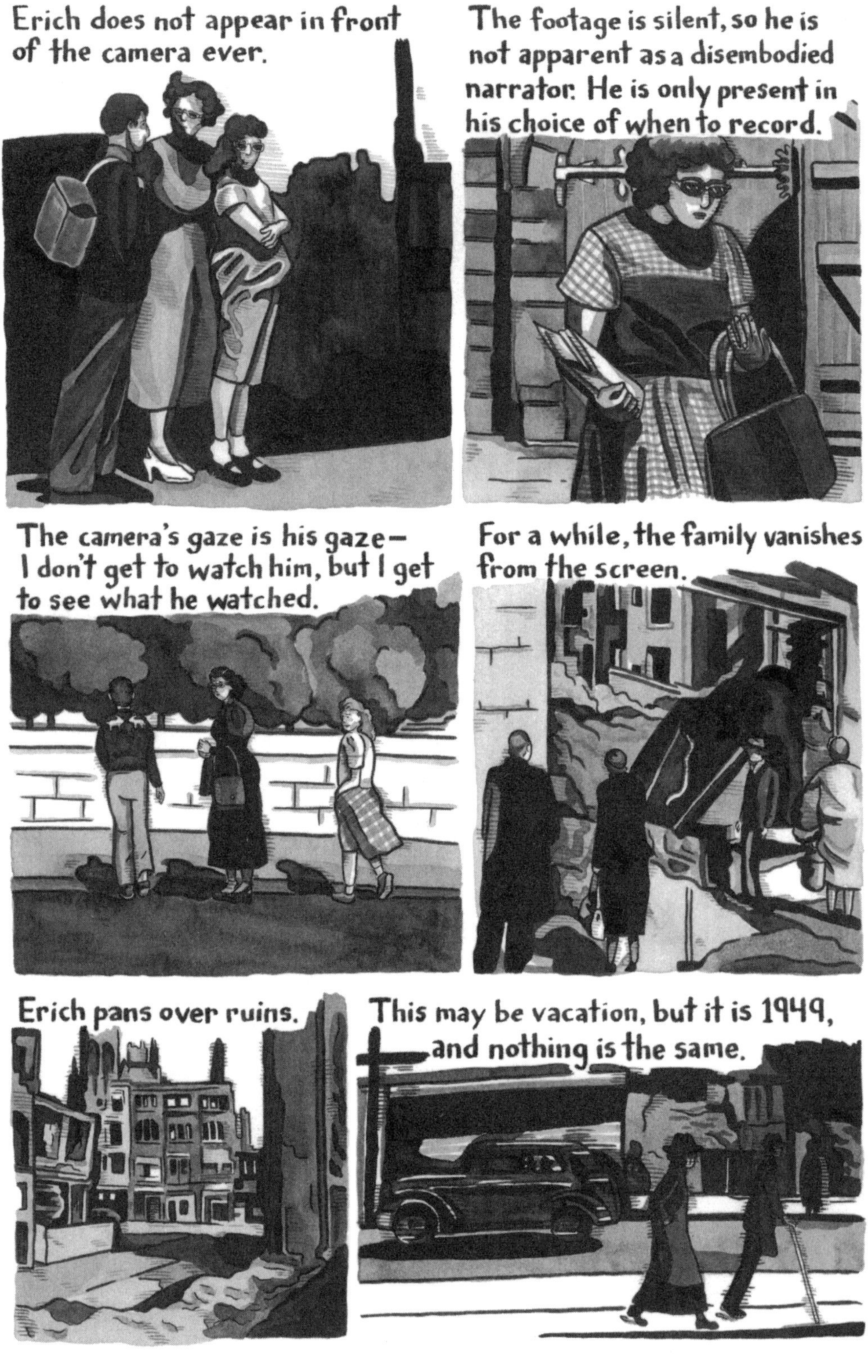
Erich does not appear in front of the camera ever.
The footage is silent, so he is not apparent as a disembodied narrator. He is only present in his choice of when to record.
The camera's gaze is his gaze— I don't get to watch him, but I get to see what he watched.
For a while, the family vanishes from the screen.
Erich pans over ruins.
This may be vacation, but it is 1949, and nothing is the same.

Here's the wreckage of Cologne, where Erich and Ilse met, the spires of the cathedral rising above the debris.

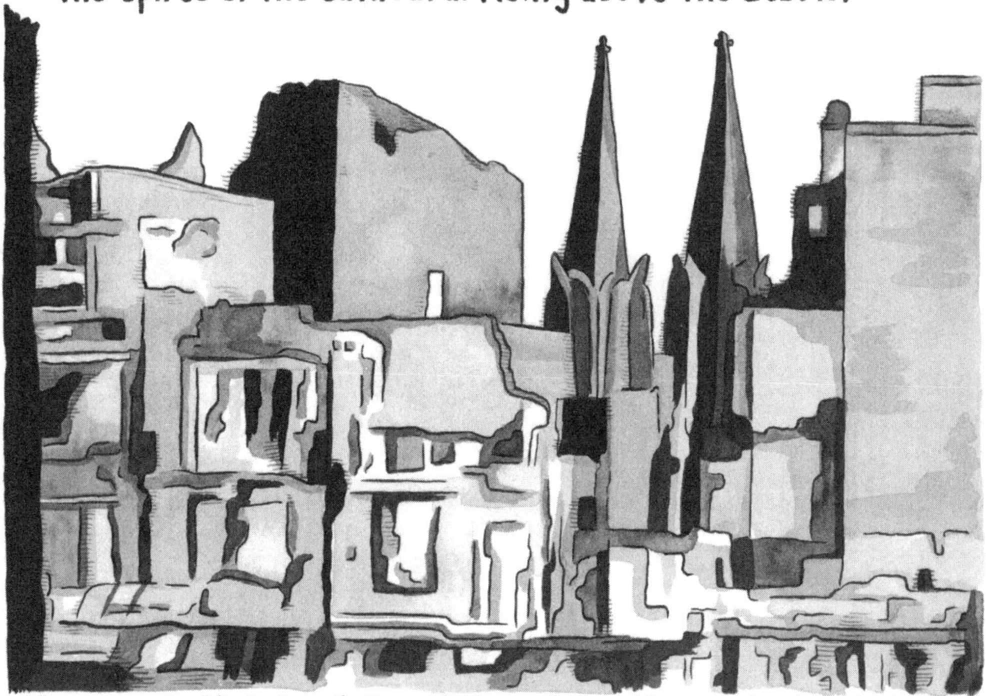

Here's what's left of Erich's hometown, the smoked-out shell of the synagogue of his youth.

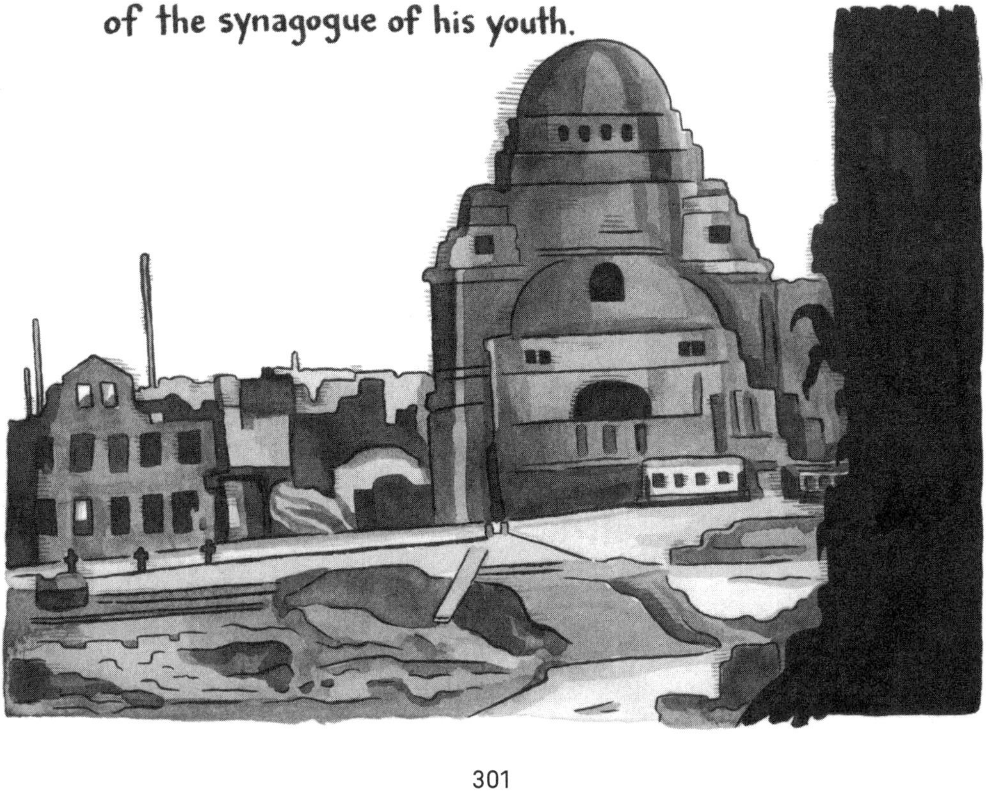

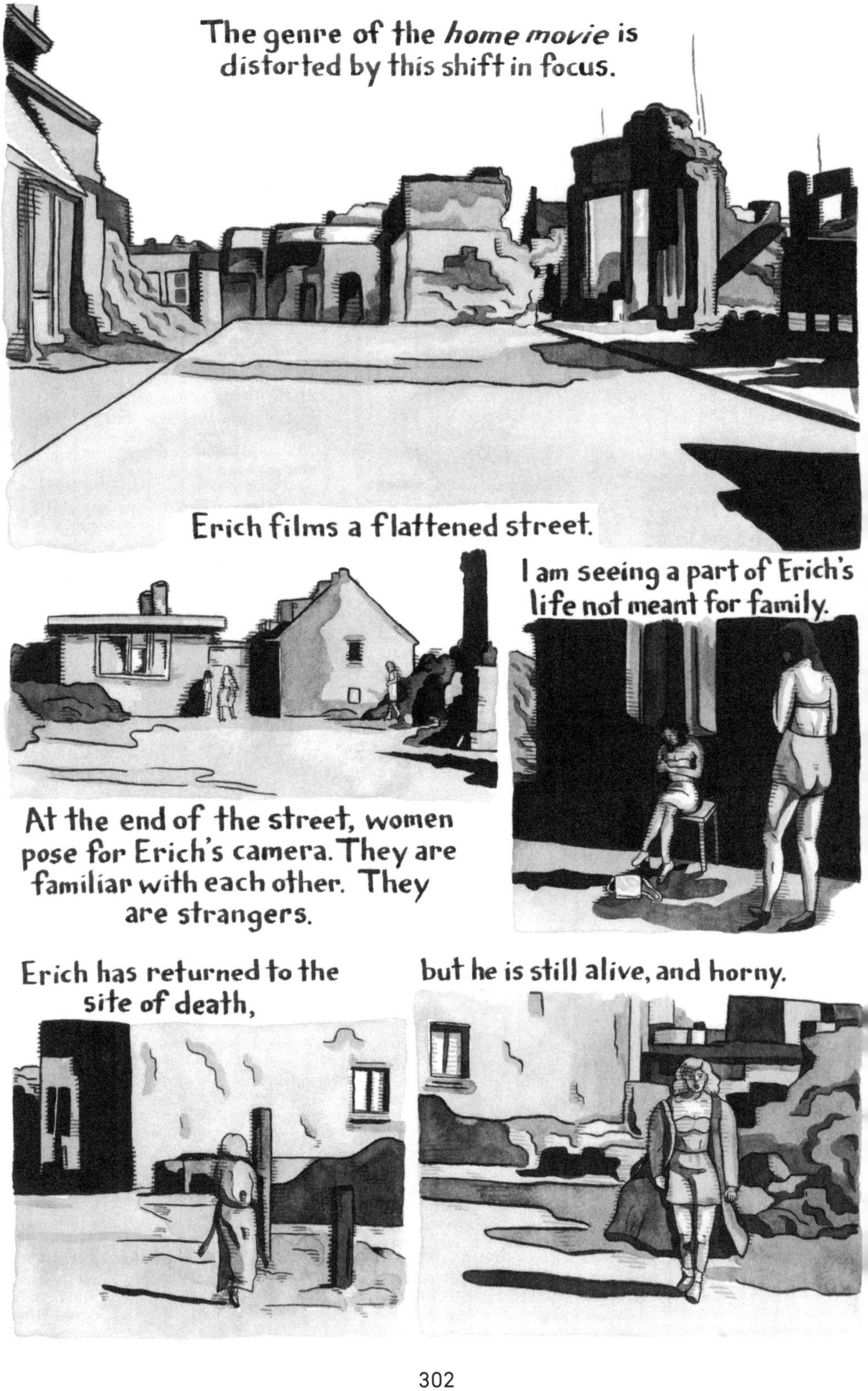
The genre of the *home movie* is distorted by this shift in focus.
Erich films a flattened street.
At the end of the street, women pose for Erich's camera. They are familiar with each other. They are strangers.
I am seeing a part of Erich's life not meant for family.
Erich has returned to the site of death,
but he is still alive, and horny.

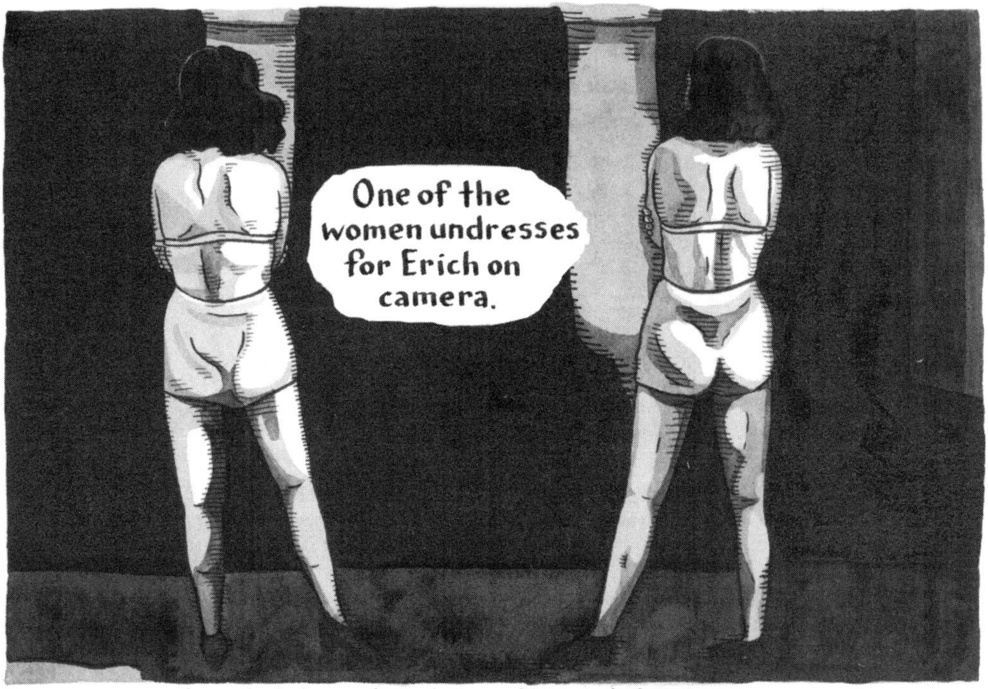
One of the women undresses for Erich on camera.

I watch her striptease through his eyes.
I'm privy to his desire, but I want something else.

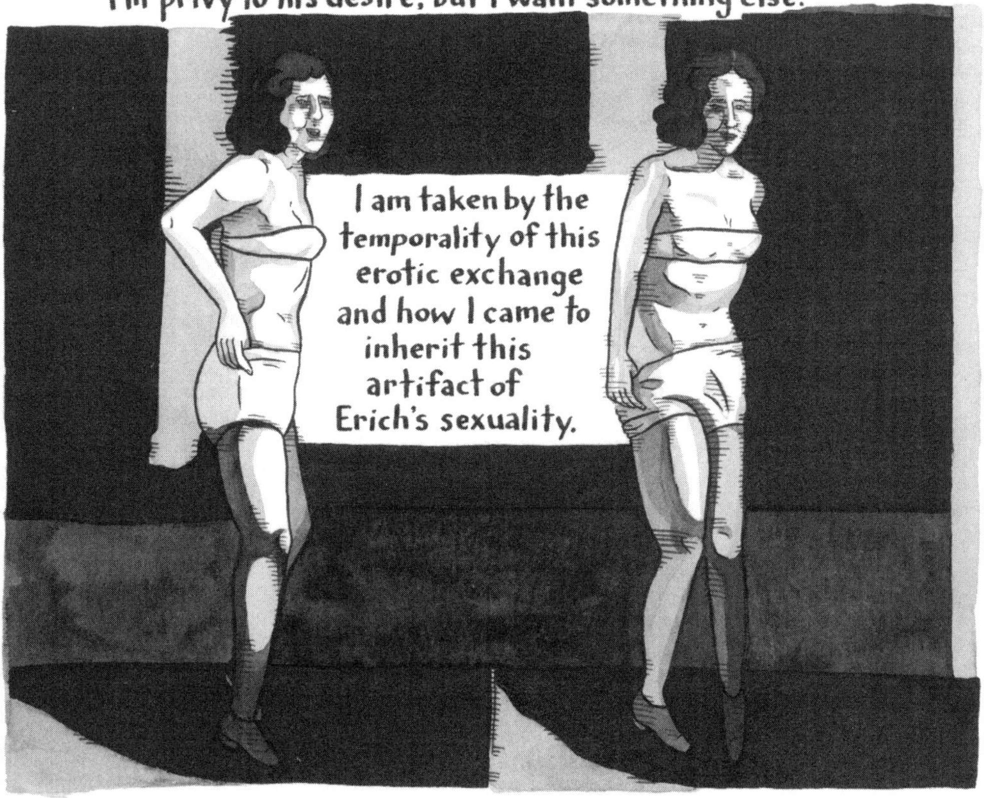
I am taken by the temporality of this erotic exchange and how I came to inherit this artifact of Erich's sexuality.

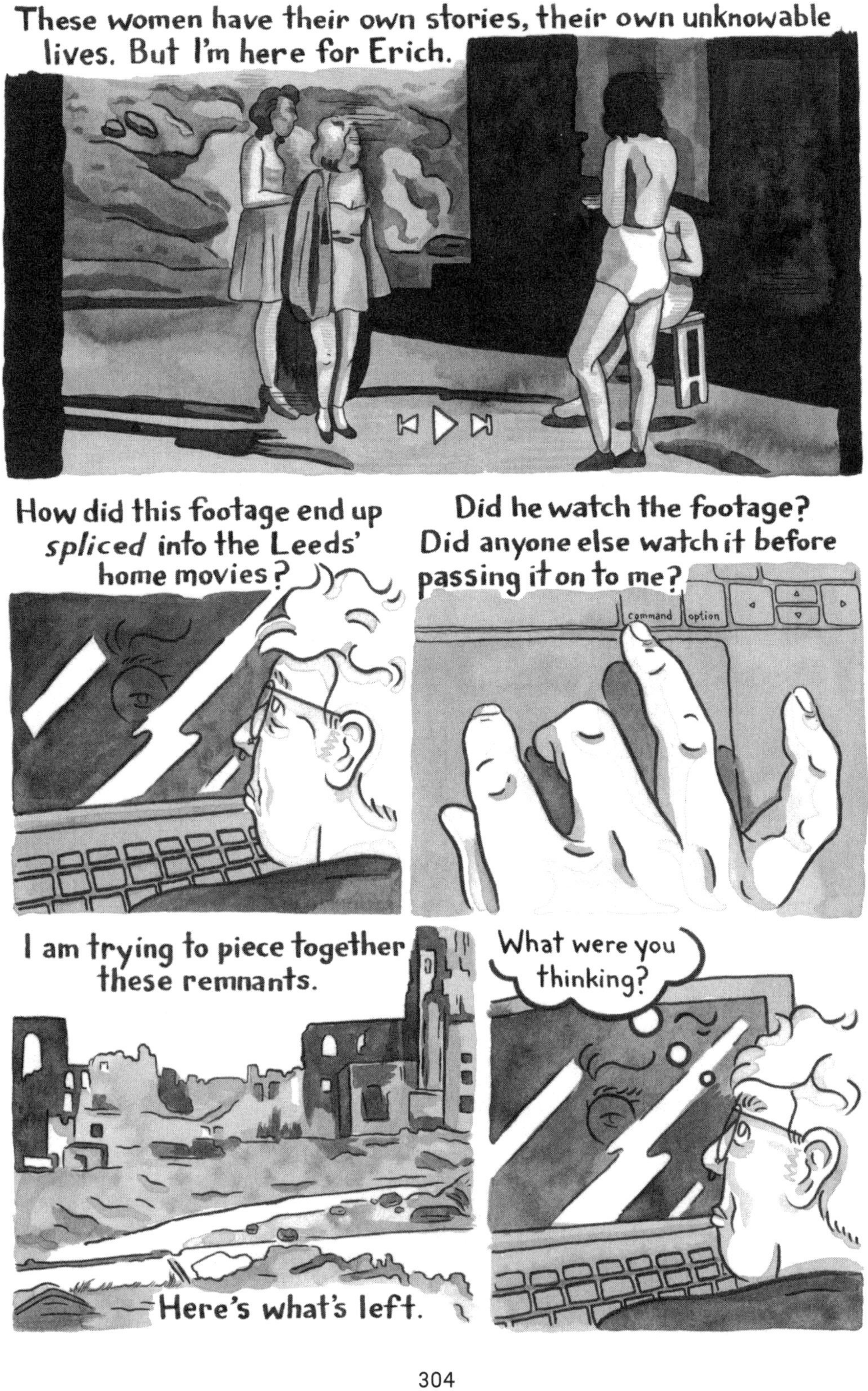
These women have their own stories, their own unknowable lives. But I'm here for Erich.
How did this footage end up *spliced* into the Leeds' home movies?
Did he watch the footage? Did anyone else watch it before passing it on to me?
command
option
I am trying to piece together these remnants.
Here's what's left.
What were you thinking?

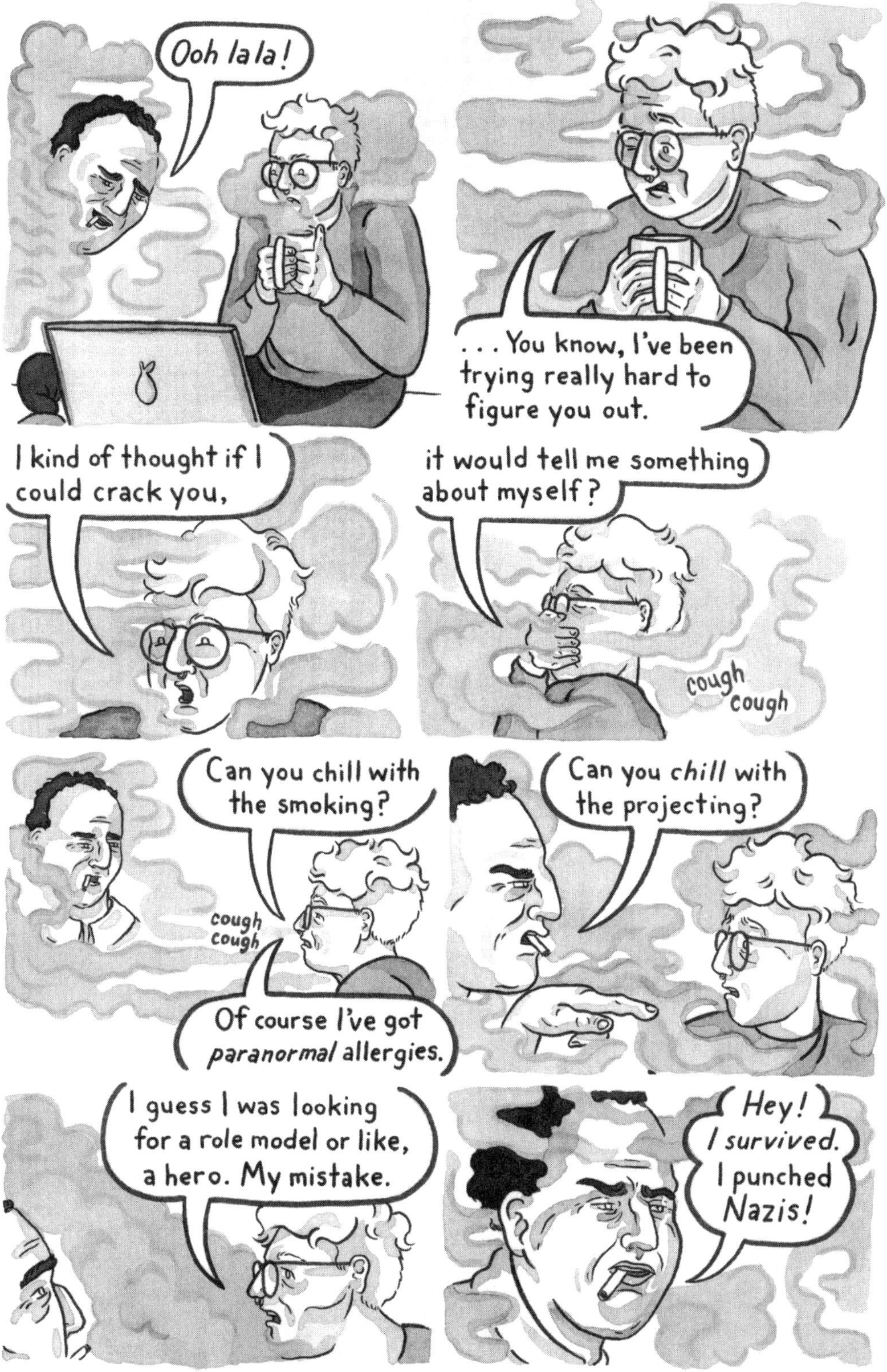
Ooh la la!
. . . You know, I've been trying really hard to figure you out.
I kind of thought if I could crack you,
it would tell me something about myself?
cough cough
Can you chill with the smoking?
cough cough
Of course I've got *paranormal* allergies.
Can you *chill* with the projecting?
I guess I was looking for a role model or like, a hero. My mistake.
Hey! I survived. I punched Nazis!

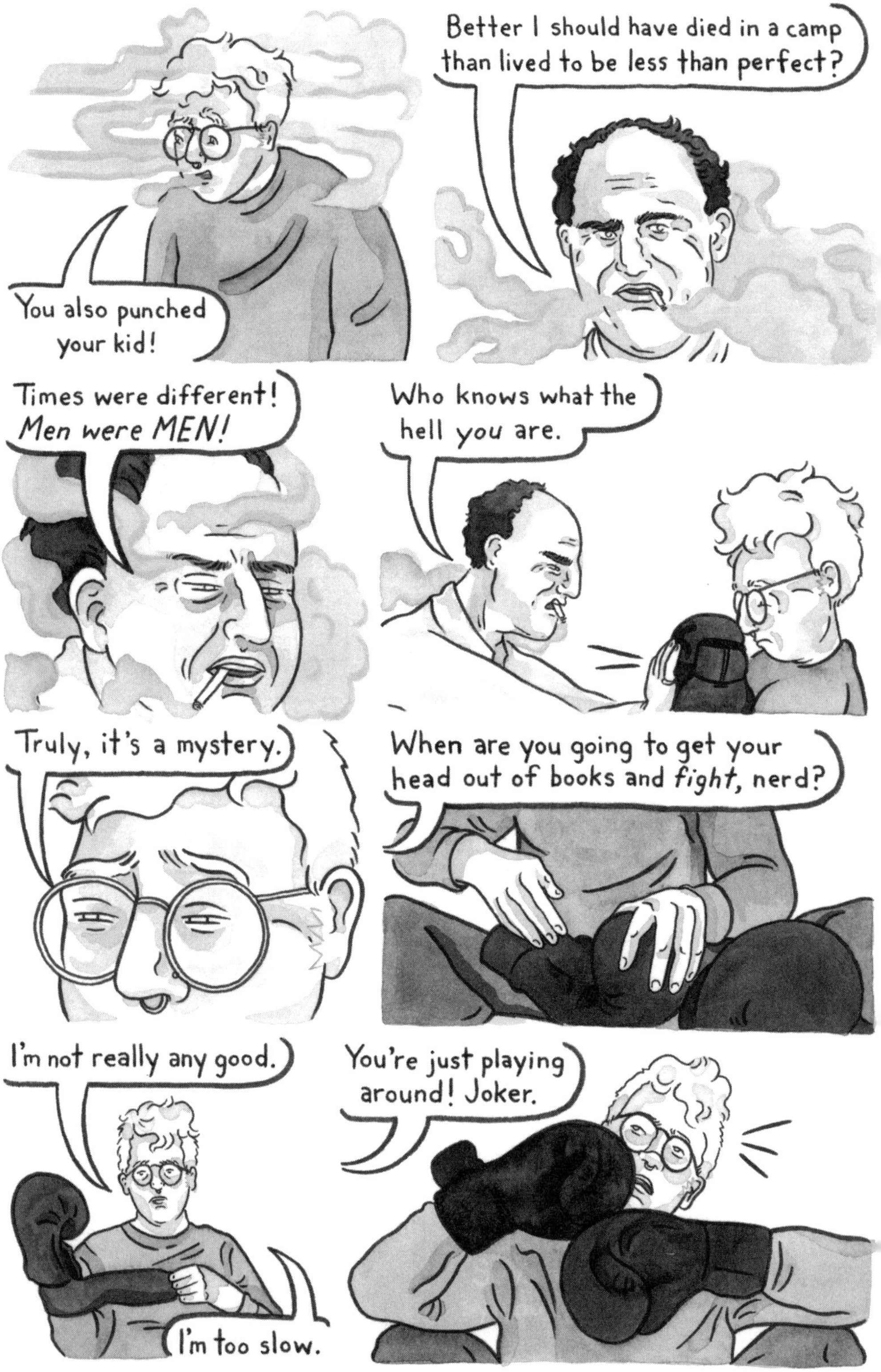

You also punched your kid!
Better I should have died in a camp than lived to be less than perfect?
Times were different! *Men were MEN!*
Who knows what the hell *you* are.
Truly, it's a mystery.
When are you going to get your head out of books and *fight*, nerd?
I'm not really any good.
I'm too slow.
You're just playing around! Joker.

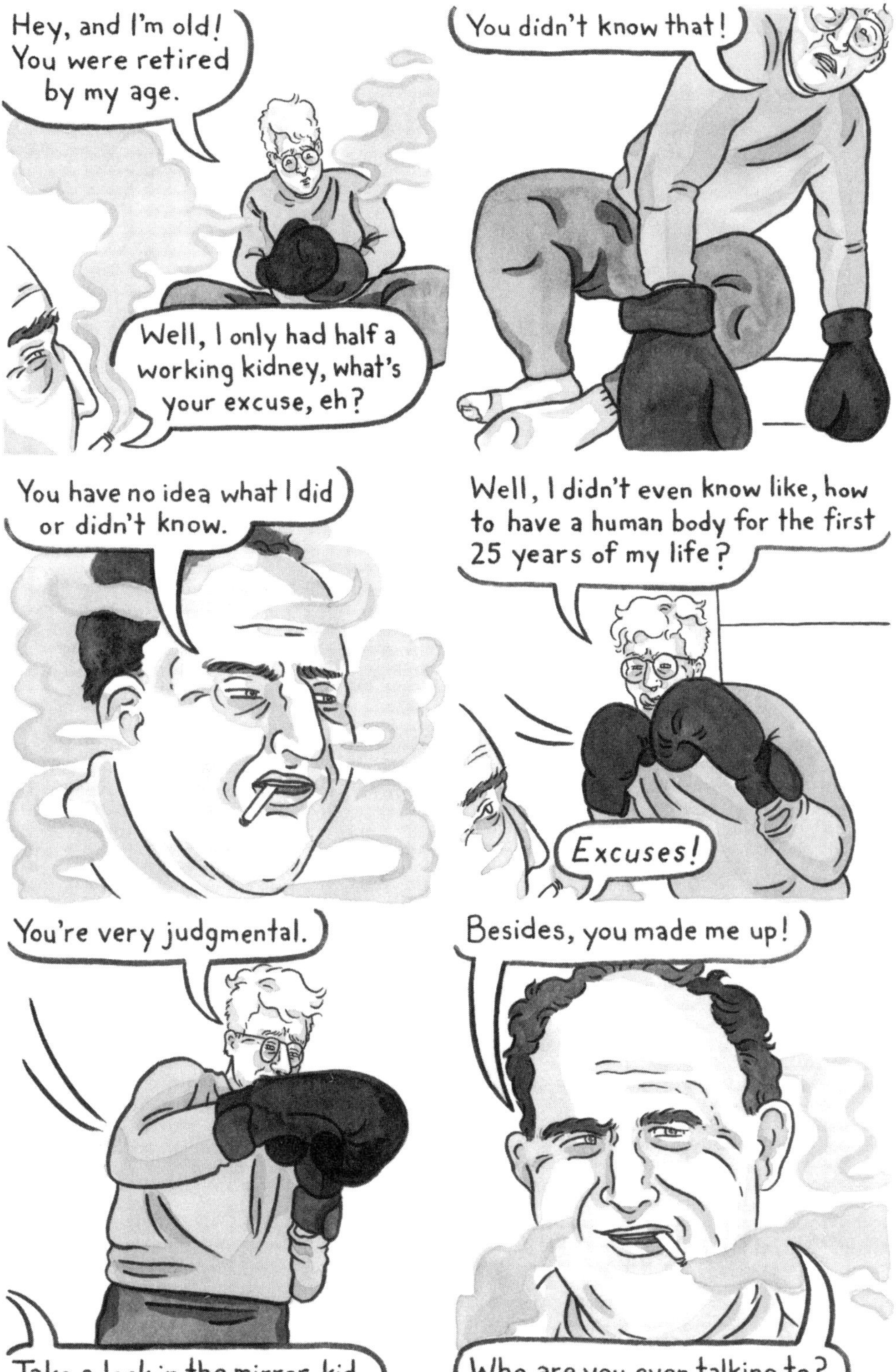
Hey, and I'm old! You were retired by my age.
Well, I only had half a working kidney, what's your excuse, eh?
You didn't know that!
You have no idea what I did or didn't know.
Well, I didn't even know like, how to have a human body for the first 25 years of my life?
Excuses!
You're very judgmental.
Take a look in the mirror, kid.
Besides, you made me up!
Who are you even talking to?

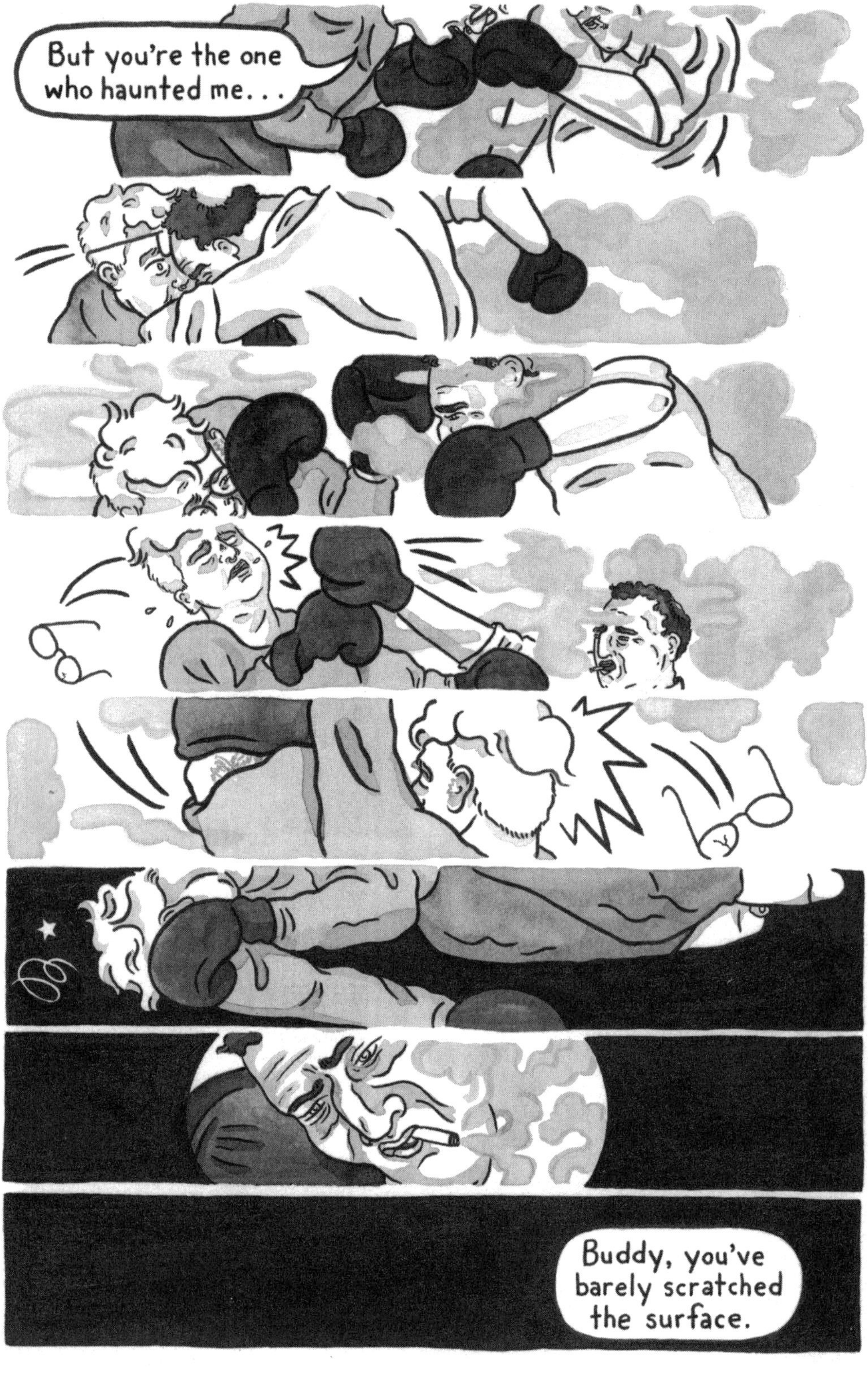
But you're the one who haunted me. . .
Buddy, you've barely scratched the surface.

Acknowledgments

Special thank-you to Andre and Donna Leeds, Jennifer Pruitt, Roxane Kansten, Annette Vandow, and Jacqueline Brager for all your help recovering and remembering, and everyone in the family, close and distant, who answered my endless questions.

charles theonia, here for it all. I'm glad we ended up on the same timeline, and on the same couch with pony and the loverboys.

To everyone who kept me alive and built me up over the long duration of this project, read drafts, guided me through, delivered coffee, erased pencil lines, stuck around—Vivianne Salgado, Judy Gerson, Gina Apostol, virgil b/g taylor, ray ferreira, Cesario Lavery, Steven Crane z"l, Abigail Lloyd, Bell Kauffmann, Elle Pérez, Lou Cornum, Maysam Taher, Cat Fitzpatrick, Ali Howell, Che Gossett, Katie Fricas, Bishakh Som, Jeanne Thornton, Sara Lautman, Hal Schrieve, Tina Horn, Jordy Silverstein, Danny Cohen, Ethel Brooks, my Doctoral Wrecking Crew, and all my other people past and present. Sina Lene Lutscher provided translation support, Max Fox fixed my messy citations, a number of archivists and librarians helped me with finding materials, including Birte Klarzyk at the National Socialism Documentation Center of the City of Cologne and Martina Strehlen at the Old Synagogue in Essen. At various points in the development of the book, I had the opportunity to take workshops with Paul Karasik, Dan Nott, Tom Hart, Jake Goldwasser, and Morgan Bassichis—thank you for providing the space and to everyone who made it what it was.

The first iteration of *Heavyweight* was published by *Jewish Currents* in 2020, thanks to Arielle Angel. Ross Harris and Vedika Khanna first saw and believed in the project before I knew I could write a book; Aemilia Phillips, Rachel Kahan, and Ariana Sinclair saw it through. A residency at Tin House in 2021 jumpstarted my writing with the invaluable gift of time to work. The Jerome Hill Artist Fellowship came in and saw me through to the end. Endless gratitude.

Citations and Notes

P. 3

Panel 1: Mariam Fraser and Nirmal Puwal, "Introduction: Intimacy in Research," *History of the Human Sciences* 21, no. 4 (2008).

P. 6

Panel 3: The concept of a "conspiracy of silence" has become almost a common-sense usage in the context of Holocaust memory, but it is usually, when credited, attributed to the work of Yael Danieli; Yael Danieli, "Psychotherapist's Participation in the Conspiracy of Silence about the Holocaust," *Psychoanalytic Psychology* 1, no. 1 (1984): 23–42.

Panel 6: Primo Levi with Leonardo de Benedetti, "Anniversary [1955]," in *Auschwitz Testimonies 1945–1986,* translated by Judith Woolfe (Cambridge, UK: Polity, 2017), 67–69.

P. 7

Panel 1: Robert Krell, "Child Survivors of the Holocaust: 40 Years Later Introduction," *Journal of the American Academy of Child Psychiatry* 24, no. 4 (1985).

P. 8

Panel 2: My thoughts on haunting are deeply informed by Avery F. Gordon's *Ghostly Matters: Haunting and the Sociological Imagination* (Minneapolis: University of Minnesota Press, 1997).

P. 9

Ilse Halpert, "Shoah Foundation Testimony," January 30, 1996, USC Shoah Foundation's Visual History Archive, University of Southern California, transcript and digital audio, https://vhaonline.usc.edu/viewingPage? testimonyID=11014&returnIndex=0#.

P. 11

Marianne Hirsch, *The Generation of Postmemory: Writing and Visual Culture after the Holocaust* (New York: Columbia University Press, 2012).

P. 16

The plot described here is based on the plot of *The Devil's Arithmetic* by Jane Yolen (New York: Puffin Modern Classics, 1988).

P. 17

Panel 1: An origin point for the concept of intergenerational trauma is found in Vivian Rakoff, John J. Sigal, and Nathan B. Epstein, "Children and Families of Concentration Camp Survivors," *Canada's Mental Health* 14, no. 4 (1966): 24–26. I am also thinking here about the concept of epigenetic trauma, of which I am skeptical, despite finding it emotionally compelling. I prefer thinking about the concept of trauma as chronic, repetitive, or transferred not genetically, but rather behaviorally.

P. 19
Panel 4: "Shoah," which translates to "catastrophe" or "total destruction," is the commonly used Hebrew term for the mass murder of European Jewry under National Socialism. While "Holocaust" is broadly used to describe the total destruction under Nazism, exactly which devastation it refers to is sometimes up for debate. Different impacted communities often utilize their own language, centering their own experience. Romani communities, for example, use the term "Samudaripen," which translates to "mass murder."

P. 21
Panel 4: "Yom HaShoah" is Holocaust Remembrance Day, secularly observed in Israel. Jewish communities in the United States frequently follow this observance; when I was growing up, it was marked in my community by acts of mourning and awareness raising, which included wearing reproductions of the yellow stars worn by Jews under Nazi occupation after 1941.

P. 22
I assume that the "6 million Jews" written on my arm was a child's attempt at participation in these memorial activities.

P. 23
Panel 3: I found this personal essay in my grandmother's papers after she passed away.

P. 24
Panel 2: Throughout this book, I follow contemporary guidance on the spelling of "antisemitism"; while the oft-used spelling "anti-Semitism" accurately captures the historical scientific racism active in anti-Jewish hatred, to continue to use it falsely "legitimizes the pseudo-scientific category of Semitism." Jewish Voice for Peace, *On Antisemitism: Solidarity and the Struggle for Justice* (Chicago: Haymarket Books, 2017).

Panel 3: Harold Bloom, foreword to *Zakhor: Jewish History and Jewish Memory* by Yosef Hayim Yerushalmi (Seattle and London: University of Washington Press, 1996).

P. 37
Panel 4: "Slummin' on Park Avenue (Let's Go Bombing)" (Charlie and His Orchestra), German Propaganda Swing, Harlequin 1990.

Panel 8: A regional Nazi official in Czechoslovakia issued rules for the performance of jazz, which are reproduced in J. J. Gould, "Josef Skvorecky on the Nazis' Control-Freak Hatred of Jazz," *The Atlantic*, January 3, 2012, https://www.theatlantic.com /entertainment/ archive/2012/01/josef-skvorecky-nazis-jazz/250837/.

P. 42
For more information on colonial postcards like those reproduced here, see David Ciarlo, *Advertising Empire: Race and Visual Culture in Imperial Germany* (Boston: Harvard University Press, 2011); George Steinmetz and Julia Hell, "The Visual Archive of Colonialism: Germany and Namibia," *Public Culture* 18, no. 1 (2006): 147–83.

P. 44
Michael Zimmermann, *Jüdisches Leben in Essen 1800–1933* (Essen, Germany: Klartext Verlag, 1993).

P. 45
Panel 4: The "Old Synagogue" in Essen was originally dedicated in 1913; beginning in the 1950s, the interior of the building was used as a museum for industrial design. In 1980, the focus turned to remembrance of Essen's Jewish community, and in 2008 the Old Synagogue became a "House of Jewish Culture"; Martina Strehlen is the Deputy Head of Research Collections. "History of the House," Stadt Essen, last modified July 15, 2020, https://www.essen.de/leben/kultur_/alte_synagoge/geschichte_des_hauses_.en.html.

PP. 46–47
Casper W. Erichsen and Larissa Forster, *What the Elders Used to Say: Namibian Perspectives on the Last Decade of German Colonial Rule* (Windhoek: Namibia Institute for Democracy, 2008); Jan-Bart Gewald and Jeremy Silvester, *Words Cannot Be Found. German Colonial Rule in Namibia: An Annotated Report of the 1918 Blue Book* (Leiden: Brill, 2004); David Olusoga and Casper Erichsen, *The Kaiser's Holocaust: Germany's Forgotten Genocide and the Colonial Roots of Nazism* (London: Faber & Faber, 2011); George Steinmetz, *The Devil's Handwriting: Precoloniality and the German Colonial State In Qingdao, Samoa, and Southwest Africa* (Chicago: University of Chicago Press, 2007); Daniel Joseph Walther, *Creating Germans Abroad: Cultural Policies and National Identity in Namibia* (Athens, OH: Ohio University Press, 2002); Joachim Zeller and Jürgen Zimmerer, *Genocide in German South-West Africa: The Colonial War (1904–1908) in Namibia and Its Aftermath* (Monmouth, NJ: Merlin Press, 2008); and James Giblin and Jamie Monson, *Maji Maji: Lifting the Fog of War* (Leiden: Brill, 2010).

P. 48
Panel 1: Robin D.G. Kelley, "A Poetics of Anticolonialism," foreword to Aimé Césaire, *Discourse on Colonialism,* translated by Joan Pinkham (New York: Monthly Review Press, 2000).

P. 49
Ralph Bunche, "French and British Imperialism in West Africa," *The Journal of Negro History* 21, no. 1 (1936): 31–46; Aimé Césaire, *Discourse on Colonialism,* translated by Joan Pinkham (New York: Monthly Review Press, 2000); W.E.B. Du Bois, *The World and Africa: An Inquiry into the Part Which Africa Has Played in World History* (New York: International Publishers, 1947).

P. 50

Doron Avraham, "Between Concern and Difference: German Jews and the Colonial 'Other' in South West Africa," *German History* 40, no. 1 (March 2022): 38–60.

P. 51

Panel 3: My thinking here is beholden to the work of M. Jacqui Alexander, *Pedagogies of Crossing: Meditations on Feminism, Sexual Politics, Memory, and the Sacred* (Durham, NC: Duke University Press, 2005).

P. 53

Panel 6: Hamburg State Archives (Staatsarchiv Hamburg), File 232–5_889; File 313–3 C c 1622; File 351–11_34651.

P. 54

Panel 1: Jürgen Zimmerer, "The History of Globalization Is the History of Colonialism," interview by Daniel Meßner, June 1, 2017, https://www.uni-hamburg.de/news room/forschung/2017-06-01-zimmerer-kolonialismus.html.

P. 55

Panel 1: Eugen Fischer, *Die Rehobother bastards und das bastardierungsproblem beim menschen* ["The Rehoboth Bastards and the Problem of Miscegenation among Humans"] (Jena: Fischer, 1913). The image of Eugen Fischer here is reproduced from a historical photograph of Eugen Fischer photographing a woman and child in German South West Africa, accessed via the Archives of the Max Planck Society in Berlin-Dahlem.

Panel 2: This image is copied from a photograph of Eugen Fischer studying racial portraits in his office at the Kaiser Wilhelm Institute for Anthropology, Human Heredity, and Eugenics in Berlin, accessed via the Archives of the Max Planck Society.

Panel 3: Hugh Jedell, "Denies Reich Seeks to Improve Race; Scientist Says Purity Rather Than Superiority of Stock Is Aim of Hitlerites. Move a Boon to Science; Government Liberal in Its Aid to Anthropological and Ethnological Study," *New York Times*, September 3, 1933.

Panel 4: The images in the bottom panel appear in the United States Holocaust Memorial Museum archive and are from Fischer's research in German South West Africa. The images are featured on a slide used for a lecture in 1936 by Dr. B. K. Schultz in Dresden. The caption on the slide reads, "Batardfrauen aus Südwestafrika; die eine hnelt dem europichen, die andere dem hottentottichen Ercheinungsbild"—"Bastard women from South West Africa; one resembles the European, the other the Hottentott."

P. 56

David Fine, *Jewish Integration in the German Army in the First World War* (Berlin: De Gruyter, 2012); Tim Grady, *A Deadly Legacy: German Jews and the Great War* (New Haven, CT: Yale University Press, 2017); Werner T. Angress, "The German Army's 'Judenzählung' of 1916: Genesis–Consequences–Significance," *The Leo Baeck Institute Year Book* 23 (1978): 117–38.

P. 57
Among other texts, I recommend Kate Evans, *Red Rosa: A Graphic Biography of Rosa Luxemburg* (New York: Verso, 2015).

P. 58
Panel 4: Margaret Sanger, *The Selected Papers of Margaret Sanger,* Volume 4: *Round the World for Birth Control, 1920–1966* (Champaign, IL: University of Illinois Press, 2016). A note on milk: Germany was required to give 90,000 cows to France as reparations for cows taken during the First World War ("French See No Wrong in Demanding Cows: Germany Having Taken 500,000 from Them They Think They Should Have 90,000 Back," *New York Times*, November 12, 1919, https://nyti .ms/457asdt).

P. 59
Panel 2: This image is based on a photograph of Senegalese infantrymen of the French colonial army taken in 1914.
Panel 3: The postcard referenced here is digitally archived at https://bildpostkarten .uni-osnabrueck.de/frontend/index.php/Detail/objects/os_ub_0015404; Iris Wigger, *The "Black Horror on the Rhine": Intersections of Race, Nation, Gender and Class in 1920s Germany* (London: Palgrave Macmillan, 2017).

P. 60
Panel 2: "They Called Them 'The Children of Shame,'" *DW*, November 20, 2020, https://www.dw.com/en/they-called-them- the-children-of-shame/a-55680718.
Panel 4: The images in this panel are satirical cartoons, including a cartoon from the satirical German newspaper *Kladderadatsch*—"Der schwarze Terror in deutschen Landen" ["The Black Terror in German Lands"], no. 18–22, May 30, 1920; Universitätsbibliothek Heidelberg, https://doi.org/10.11588/diglit.2300#0317; as well as "Die Schwarze Schmach! (The Black Shame)," published in "Franzosen im Ruhrgebiet," A. M. Cay, Berlin, 1923. I found this illustration in Iris Wigger, Alexander Yendell, and David Herbert, "The End of 'Welcome Culture'? How the Cologne Assaults Reframed Germany's Immigration Discourse," *European Journal of Communication* 37 (2021), https://www.researchgate.net/figure/Illustration -Die-Schwarze-Schmach-The-Black-Shame-Franzosen-im-Ruhrgebiet-AM-Cay _fig2_352463178.
Panel 5: *The Birth of a Nation*, directed by D. W. Griffith, 1915.

P. 61
Panel 1: Peter Campbell, "The 'Black Horror on the Rhine': Idealism, Pacifism, and Racism in Feminism and the Left in the Aftermath of the First World War," *Social History* XLVII, no. 94 (June 2014): 471–96. See writings by Ray Beveridge: Ray Beveridge, "The Black Terror in Germany," *The American Monthly* (1920–1933), December 1920; Ray Beveridge, "Negro Reign of Terror in Germany: Testimony of an American Woman Who Has Personally Investigated the French Outrages," *The American Monthly* (1920–1933), November 1920.
Panels 3–5: W.E.B Du Bois, "Returning Soldiers," *The Crisis*, May 1919.

P. 62

The photographs referenced here were discovered in a photo album by a French collector, Baptiste Garin. Stéphanie Trouillard, "The Nazi Massacre of African Soldiers in French Army, 80 Years On," *France24*, June 21, 2020, https://www.france24.com/en/20200621-the-nazi-massacre-of-senegalese-soldiers-in-french-army-80-years-on.

P. 63

See Robert Reinders, "Racialism on the Left: E. D. Morel and the 'Black Horror on the Rhine,'" *International Review of Social History* 13 (1968): 1–28.

Panel 1: E. D. Morel, "Black Scourge in Europe," *The Daily Herald,* April 10, 1920.

Panel 2: Paul von Hindenburg, *Out of My Life* (London: Cassell, 1920).

Panel 3: Friedrich Ebert, Darmstadt speech, February 13, 1923, in Christian Koller, *"Von Wilden aller Rassen Niedergemetzelt": Die Diskussion um die Verwendung von Kolonialtruppen in Europa Zwischen Rassismus, Kolonial- und Militärpolitik (1914–1930)* (Stuttgart: Franz Steiner Verlag, 2001).

Panel 4: Adolf Hitler, *Mein Kampf* (Munich: Franz Eher Nachfolger, 1925).

Panel 5: Alfred Rosenberg, *The Myth of the Twentieth Century* (1930; repr., Torrance, CA: Noontide Press, 1982).

P. 64

Panel 1: The photograph referenced here is featured on the cover of Iris Wigger's book *The "Black Horror on the Rhine": Intersections of Race, Nation, Gender and Class in 1920s Germany* (London: Palgrave Macmillan, 2017). The image source is credited to Stadtarchiv Mainz BPSF/8904 17.

Panel 2: Tina Campt, *Other Germans: Black Germans and the Politics of Race, Gender, and Memory in the Third Reich* (Ann Arbor: University of Michigan Press, 2004).

Panel 3: *Black Survivors of the Holocaust*, directed by David Okuefuna (Afro Wisdom Films, Channel 4), 1997; Paul Weindling, "The Dangers of White Supremacy: Nazi Sterilization and Its Mixed-Race Adolescent Victims," *American Journal of Public Health* 112 (2022): 248–54.

P. 65

Panel 1: Sharon Gillerman, *Germans into Jews: Remaking the Jewish Social Body in the Weimar Republic*, (Palo Alto, CA: Stanford University Press, 2009). The language of "unwanted migrants" reflects societal attitudes toward asylum seekers and refugees that is very familiar in our own time and place. Sara Ahmed notes that "the politics of fear is often narrated as a border anxiety: fear speaks the language of 'floods' and 'swamps,' of being invaded by inappropriate others, against whom the nation must defend itself." In Ahmed's *The Cultural Politics of Emotion* (New York: Routledge, 2004).

Panel 2: The image of the Neuwied synagogue is based on an image archived digitally at the National Library of Israel, https://www.nli.org.il/en/items/ NNL_EPHEMERA700347938/NLI.

P. 66

Panels 2–3: See research on Taglit-Birthright and the so-called continuity crisis in Jewish communities. Hadas Binyamini writes, "The so-called Jewish continuity crisis reached disaster proportions in the 1990s, when philanthropy-funded studies revealed that 52 percent of American Jews married non-Jewish partners. In 1999, Jewish leaders responded to this sense of crisis by fusing Zionism and Jewish endogamy in the form of Birthright." From Binyamini's "Philanthropy and the 'Jewish Continuity Crisis,'" *Public Books*, 2021, https://www.publicbooks.org/philanthropy -and-the-jewish-continuity-crisis/.

P. 69

Panel 1: "Law Against Overcrowding," USHMM, https://perspectives.ushmm.org /item/law-against-overcrowding.

Panels 2–4: "The Sorbonne in the 20th Century," The History of the Sorbonne, The Chancellerie des Universités de Paris, https:/www.sorbonne.fr/en/the-sorbonne /history-of-the-sorbonne/la-sorbonne-au-xxe-siecle-de-lancienne-universite-de -paris-aux-13-universites-parisiennes/.

Panels 5–6: Regarding the Institute of Sexology, I am not interested in romanticizing the contributions of Magnus Hirschfeld and his colleagues, but it remains the case that the Nazis targeted the Institute as a site of sexual and gender liberation. On this romanticization, see Jules Gill-Peterson, "Our Weimar, Our Selves," August 20, 2021, https://open.substack.com/pub/sadbrowngirl/p/our-weimar-our-selves?utm _campaign=post&utm_medium=web.

P. 70

See: Helen MacDonald, *Human Remains: Dissection and Its Histories* (New Haven, CT: Yale University Press, 2011); Jennifer L. Muller, Kristen E. Pearlstein, and Carlina de la Cova, "Dissection and Documented Skeletal Collections: Embodiments of Legalized Inequality," *The Bioarchaeology of Dissection and Autopsy in the United States*, edited by Kenneth C. Nystrom (Cham, Switzerland: Springer International Publishing, 2017), 185–201; Andrew Zimmerman, *Anthropology and Antihumanism in Imperial Germany* (Chicago: University of Chicago Press, 2001); Laura Briggs, "The Race of Hysteria: 'Overcivilization' and the 'Savage' Woman in Late Nineteenth-Century Obstetrics and Gynecology," *American Quarterly* 52, no. 2 (June 2000): 246–73.

Panel 3: The image of Sarah Baartman on this page is based on an 1811 engraving published by Lewis Delin et Sculp; it must be noted that all existing images of Baartman were made in the context of compromised consent, and we do not know what role Baartman might have had in her own self-styling.

P. 71

Panel 1: Pascal Blanchard, *Human Zoos: Science and Spectacle in the Age of Colonial Empires* (Liverpool: Liverpool University Press, 2008).

Panel 2: A regulation passed in Germany in May 1942 that prohibited Jews from owning dogs, cats, or birds. In her graphic memoir *We Are on Our Own* (Montreal: Drawn & Quarterly, 2006), Miriam Katin recounts her mother being forced to turn the family dog, Rexy, over to Nazi authorities in Hungary in 1944.

Panel 3: Wendy Lower, *Hitler's Furies: German Women in the Nazi Killing Fields* (New York: Houghton Mifflin Harcourt, 2013).

PP. 80-82
Erik Jensen, *Body by Weimar: Athletes, Gender, and German Modernity* (New York: Oxford University Press, 2010). Further thanks to Erik Jensen for corresponding with me about my research.

P. 83
Ronald Schechter and Liz Clarke, *Mendoza the Jew: Boxing, Manliness and Nationalism, A Graphic History* (New York: Oxford University Press, 2013).

P. 84
Erik Jensen, *Body by Weimar: Athletes, Gender, and German Modernity* (New York: Oxford University Press, 2010).

P. 85
Hermann Schröter, *Geschichte und Schicksal der Essener Juden* (Essen: Stadt Essen, 1980).

P. 86
Panel 3: Max Nordau, opening speech at the Second Zionist Congress in Basel on August 28, 1898. Todd Samuel Presner, "'Clear Heads, Solid Stomachs, and Hard Muscles': Max Nordau and the Aesthetics of Jewish Regeneration," *Modernism/modernity* 10, no. 2 (2003): 269–96.

P. 92
Gerald Gems, "Joe Louis–Max Schmeling Fight, Clem Mccarthy, Announcer (June 22, 1938)," Library of Congress National Recording Registry, https://www.loc.gov/static/programs/national-recording-preservation-board/documents/JoeLouisMaxSchmelingFight.pdf.

PP. 97-101
Lorely French, *Roma Voices in the German-Speaking World* (London: Bloomsbury 2015); "Johann 'Rukeli' Trollmann," German Resistance Memorial Center, https://www.gdw-berlin.de/en/recess/biographies/index_of_persons/biographie/view-bio/johann- rukeli-trollmann/?no_cache=1.

P. 102
Jack Johnson, "How and Why I Lost My Title," *Big Book of Boxing* (1977).

P. 103
The bulletin shown here is the *Reich Gazette*, in which the names of expatriated Germans were published in compliance with the Law on the Repeal of Naturalisation and Recognition of German Citizenship enacted on July 14, 1933; see more at "Reichsausbürgerungskartei," Deutsche National Bibliothek, last updated June 21, 2019, https://www.dnb.de/EN/Ueber-uns/DEA/Nachrichten/_content/ausbuergerung.html. I received this document as a creased photocopy from my grandfather.

P. 110
Joseph Goebbels, *The Early Goebbels Diaries, 1925–1926*, edited by Helmut Heiber, translated by Oliver Watson (New York: Prager, 1963).

P. 113
I inherited this slim volume from my oma; I was told it was one of her favorite books and that her father had given it to her. The book is *Der Schimmelreiter* ["Rider of the White Horse"] by Theodor Storm, 1888. The book was later republished in English as *The Dykemaster*.

P. 121
Panel 2: Suzy—Suzanna Catharina Keizer—was born in Voorburg, Holland, in 1910. After Kurt's death in 1950, Suzy cut off contact with Erich and Lenni; my grandparents speculate she was concerned about sharing her inheritance from Kurt's successful American business ventures. Suzy quickly remarried and moved to Brazil.
Panel 6: The 1935 Law for the Protection of German Blood and German Honor, commonly referred to, along with the Reich Citizenship Law, as the Nuremberg race laws, made illegal marriages as well as nonmarital sex "between Jews and citizens of German or related blood," and also forbade Jews from employing "in their households female subjects of the state of Germany or related blood who are under 45 years old." It also made it illegal for Jews to fly or display German or Nazi flags.

P. 123
"Stolpersteine," or "stumbling stones," are a site-specific project by German artist Gunter Demnig, in which a brass plaque is installed in the sidewalk in front of the last known residence of a Holocaust victim—Jewish or not Jewish. The plaque includes the name, date, and place of birth, and date and place of deportation and/or death of the individual. Stumbling stones can be located on the website https://stolpersteine.wdr .de/web/en/map.

PP. 125–33
Heinz Humbach, "History Experienced," interview by Erlebte Geschichte, https:// eg.nsdok.de/default.asp?typ=interview&pid=25&aktion=erstes. Heinz Humbach's testimony is translated from the original German.

P. 127
Photograph courtesy of the Humbach family via Stadt Köln NS-Dokumentationszentrum.

P. 128
Email correspondence with Malle Bensch-Humbach, 2021.

P. 133
Some of this information comes from the obituary of Gerd Humbach, Heinz Humbach's brother, published online by the German Communist Party of Rhineland-Westphalia, "Abschied von Gerd Humbach," Deutsche Kommunistische Partei Rheinland-Westfalen, https://www.dkp-rheinland-westfalen.de/ index.php/partei

/ehrengalerie/1498-abschied-von-gerd-humbach; some is from the article by Pascal Beuker, "A Life for the Resistance," on the occasion of Grete Humbach's 100th birthday, *Die Tageszeitung*, February 22, 2005, https://taz.de/Ein-Leben-fuer-den-Widerstand/!641242/.

P. 134
The German-Israeli Friends of Neuwied website can be found at https://www.dif-neuwied.de/. I do not claim to know the motivations of individual members of that or any organization. Virgil b/g Taylor is an artist whose work frequently contends with memory in the contemporary German landscape; for example, his project *zur Entwicklung der Jüdenstraße* (KW Institute for Contemporary Art, 2023).

P. 136
The Mayers are listed in the United States Holocaust Memorial Museum Holocaust Survivors and Victims Database, on the list "Transport 16 Cologne 2 M."

P. 137
United States Holocaust Memorial Museum, *The Elders of the Jews in the Łódź Ghetto Collection*, REEL 300/ PAGE 270–2.

P. 138
Panels 4–6: The blocks in these images are the stelae of the Memorial to the Murdered Jews of Europe in Berlin, designed by Peter Eisenman and opened in 2005.

P. 139:
Panels 1 and 3: Dirk Moses, "The German Catechism," *Geschichte der Gegenwart*, 2021, https:// geschichtedergegenwart.ch/the-german-catechism/.

Panel 2: "Speech by Federal Chancellor Angela Merkel to the Knesset in Jerusalem" (March 18, 2008), https://m.knesset.gov.il/EN/activity/Documents/SpeechPdf/merkel.pdf.

Panel 3: This exchange was with the German-Israeli Friends of Neuwied member in charge of the stumbling stone project in town. I sent a website inquiry asking if Benno Kahn's headstone was still standing; his response email began, "Dear Sol, Shalom, when I googled you, I found out that—in spite of your first name, that sounded to me like Salomon—you are a young lady. And I was fascinated to read about the little scandal you caused. Congratulations. I insist on Israel's right of existence, but I do not agree with the governments of the past years, especially not with the settlement policy and its consequences."

Panel 4: My conceptualization of settler colonialism and the settler state is informed by a broad array of scholarship that includes Patrick Wolfe, "Settler Colonialism and the Elimination of the Native," *Journal of Genocide Research* 8, no. 4 (2006): 387–409.

P. 140
Panels 1–2: *The Chronicle of the Łódź Ghetto, 1941–1944*, edited by Lucjan Dobroszycki, translated by Richard Lourie, Joachim Neugroschel, and others (New Haven, CT: Yale University Press, 1987).

Panels 3–4: Primo Levi, *The Drowned and the Saved* (New York: Summit Books, 1988), 67.

P. 141
Panel 1: Thank you to charles theonia for being a willing and brilliant interlocutor and also sometimes acting as a mouthpiece in this comic.

P. 142
Timothy Snyder, *Black Earth: The Holocaust as History and Warning* (New York: Penguin Random House, 2015).

P. 146
Panel 2: Image drawn from a historical photograph of the Essen Synagogue in the aftermath of Kristallnacht, via Stadtbildstelle Essen.

P. 148
One of the places I found the stumbling stones online was in an article written by a local freelance reporter, Daniel Henschke, titled "A Tragic End," in the *Stadtspiegel Essen*, 2017, https://www.lokalkompass.de/essen-werden/c-ueberregionales/ein-tragisches- ende_a793773. Another is on the photo blog of German photographer Thomas Thomitzek: https://www.fotocommunity.de/photo/albert-levi-helene-levi-thomas-thomitzek/21431418.

P. 152
Panel 4: According to family lore, Erich Levi tried to start a sausage factory in Paris. It did not take off.

P. 155
New York Times, September 22, 1932; Margaret Sanger, *The Selected Papers of Margaret Sanger,* Volume 4: *Round the World for Birth Control, 1920–1966* (Champaign, IL: University of Illinois Press, 2016).

P. 156
Panel 2: Image reference is "Adolph Hitler and Benito Mussolini in 1940," AP Photo.
Panel 5: Haile Selassie, "Appeal to the League of Nations," June 1936.

P. 157
Panels 1–2: Mario Carli (editor of *L'Imperio*) in "Italy, Thin Ladies Flayed," *Time* 13, no. 3, January 21, 1929.

P. 162
Panels 1–2: Mahmood Mamdani, *When Victims Become Killers: Colonialism, Nativism, and the Genocide in Rwanda* (Princeton and Oxford: Princeton University Press, 2002).
Panel 3: The reference for this panel is an unattributed cartoon in the French newspaper *L'illustration* (January 3, 1885).

Panels 5–6: Adam Hochschild, *King Leopold's Ghost: A Story of Greed, Terror and Heroism in Colonial Africa* (New York: HarperCollins, 1998).

P. 163
Panel 1: The reference for this panel is a cartoon by Linley Sambourne titled "In the Rubber Coils," *Punch Magazine* (November 28, 1906).

Panel 3: The image is based on a 1960 photograph of Patrice Lumumba being welcomed on a visit to Belgium. Percy Zvomuya, "Lumumba's Remains Return Home to Find Rest at Last," *New Frame*, September 16, 2020, https://www.newframe .com/lumumbas-remains-return-home-to-find-rest-at- last/; Jason Burke, "Belgium Returns Patrice Lumumba's Tooth to Family 61 Years after His Murder," *The Guardian*, June 20, 2022, https://www.theguardian.com/world/2022/jun/20/belgium -returns-patrice-lumumba-tooth-congolese-independence.

Panel 4: Frank Swain, "The Forgotten Mine That Built the Atomic Bomb," *BBC Future*, August 3, 2020, https://www.bbc.com/future/article/20200803-the-forgotten -mine-that-built-the-atomic-bomb.

P. 164
The images on this page are based on photographs from the Clemens Radauer Collection on human zoos. See M. G. Stanard, "Selling the Empire between the Wars: Colonial Expositions in Belgium, 1920–1940," *French Colonial History* 6 (2005): 159–78.

P. 167
Dispossession: Plundering German Jewry, 1933–1953, edited by C. Kreutzmüller and J. R. Zatlin, (Ann Arbor: University of Michigan Press, 2020).

PP. 168–69
M. R. Marrus, *Some Measure of Justice: The Holocaust Era Restitution Campaign of the 1990s,* with a foreword by W. A. Schabas (Madison: University of Wisconsin Press, 2009).

P. 170
Belgian State Archives File A125557.

P. 172
Panel 2: "Nazis Smash, Loot and Burn Jewish Shops and Temples Until Goebbels Calls Halt," *New York Times*, November 11, 1938.

Panel 6: Benno Kahn is buried in the Neuwied Jewish cemetery, in what is now Niederbieber. Although the cemetery was vandalized in 1938, Benno Kahn's headstone still stands, albeit damaged.

P. 178
This story is based on the narration from Ilse Halpert's 1988 and 1996 testimonies as well as a document partly typewritten and partly handwritten by Ilse in 1949 on the stationery of a Belgian company—I assume—on the family's first return trip to Europe. The document contains much more detail than the later testimonies.

P. 185

I felt conflicted about this: For narrative flow, I removed a couple of Ilse's passengers; Ilse says that she took with her "my mother, my housekeeper, my sister-in-law Trude, her sister-in-law Laura, and my two children." In the 1988 tape, Jeni asks and Ilse confirms that everyone, including the housekeeper, who remains unnamed, was Jewish. The housekeeper and Laura had valid paperwork to cross the border but wouldn't leave the group. In the 1996 Shoah Foundation interview, Ilse tells Benbasat, "My housekeeper, before we were taken into Ambleteuse, went back to Antwerp. I don't know how she got back but I know she got back well because I had news from her." However, in the 1988 interview with Jennifer Leeds, Ilse remembers the housekeeper being with her at Ambleteuse and afterward, in Calais.

P. 189

Notably, in their 1996 interview, Joan Benbasat does not understand that Ilse is not describing a concentration camp. This camp in Ambleteuse was likely an informal holding camp for refugees to get them out of the way of army operations.

Panel 1: I have chosen to retain the use of the racial slur in this quote and when referring to the quote, as well as other, primarily historical, references in which sources refer to Romani people as "gypsies." I tried out several methods of obscuring the slur and they all, ultimately, felt like a concealment of the complexities of prejudice in the context I try to capture here. Although my decision is set in text, I don't feel set in my decision. I would also like to point readers to the work of the European Roma Rights Centre (http://www.errc.org/) and the scholarship of Dr. Ethel Brooks.

Panel 4: Marianne Hirsch in *The Generation of Postmemory* writes that the visual archive of the Holocaust is ruled by a "Nazi gaze," in which "the photographer, the perpetrator, and the spectator share the same space of looking at the victim. . . . The camera itself embodies the gaze of the perpetrator." Marianne Hirsch, *The Generation of Postmemory: Writing and Visual Culture after the Holocaust* (New York: Columbia University Press, 2012), 133–34. In the scene at Ambleteuse, the perpetrator gaze is not explicitly genocidal, but you are placed in the position of harmful looking; I have made you complicit.

P. 192

Carol Kidron describes the ways in which "material traces are depicted [by descendents of Holocaust survivors] as integral 'actors' in the drama of survivor-descendant interaction, functioning as bridges to the Holocaust past" (9). The bracelet represents an ambiguous function, as both an inconspicuous piece of rather ordinary jewelry and a "sanctified repositor[y] for the presence of the absent past" (6). Kidron argues, "a person-object interaction semiotically and sensuously resurrects the past" in a mode that shifts from the meaning the object holds for the original owner, who experiences the events associated with the object, to the meaning that the object holds for those who inherit that object and the memory it indexes. Carol A. Kidron, "Toward an Ethnography of Silence: The Lived Presence of the Past in the Everyday Life of Holocaust Trauma Survivors and Their Descendants in Israel," *Current Anthropology* 50, no. 1 (2009): 5–27.

P. 194
Panel 4: Assia Djebar, *Fantasia: An Algerian Cavalcade* (Portsmouth, NH: Heinemann, 2003).

P. 195
Simon Constantine, *Sinti and Roma in Germany (1871–1933): Gypsy Policy in the Second Empire and Weimar Republic* (London: Routledge, 2020)

P. 196
Panels 1–3: Ari Joskowicz, "Separate Suffering, Shared Archives: Jewish and Romani Histories of Nazi Persecution," *History and Memory* 28, no. 1 (2016): 110–40.
Panel 4: Saidiya Hartman, "Venus in Two Acts," *Small Axe* 12, no. 2 (2008).

P. 205
Panel 3: Joseph Goebbels, "The Jews Are Guilty!" German Propaganda Archive, 1943. Translation by Randall Bytwerk, https://www.jewishvirtuallibrary.org/joseph-goebbels-quot-the-jews-are-guilty-quot.
Panel 4: Julius Streicher, *The Poisonous Mushroom*, 1938.
Panels 5–6: The Daily Stormer piece, which I will not link to, was targeting the writer Malcolm Harris, to "expose" that he works with and is friends with a lot of Jews. The article, written by American Nazi Andrew Anglin, was titled "Jew Terrorist Malcolm 'The Hammer' Harris Must Explain Why His Entire Network of Subversives Is Jew," The Daily Stormer, 2015.

P. 211
Marcel Bervoets-Tragholz, *La liste de Saint-Cyprien* (Brussels: Alice Editions, 2006), accessed via the United States Holocaust Memorial Museum.
Panel 2: "4000 in Need—Silent Organisations," Saint-Cyprien/Gurs folder at the Center for Jewish History, 1940.

P. 216
Panel 4: This image is drawn from a 1935 chart titled "Die Nürnberger Gesetze" (Nuremberg Race Laws), accessed via the United States Holocaust Memorial Museum, https://encyclopedia.ushmm.org/content/en/photo/chart-with-the-title-die-nuernberger-gesetze-nuremberg-race-laws.

P. 222
My mother had this photograph of Jacob Kahn's gravestone, but I don't know exactly where the grave is located—presumably in Brussels.

P. 232
Nathan Durst, "Child-Survivors of the Holocaust: Age-Specific Traumatization and the Consequences for Therapy," *American Journal of Psychotherapy* 57, no. 4 (2003).

P. 233
Ulrich Alexander Boschwitz, *The Passenger* (New York: Metropolitan Books, 1938).

P. 246
Panel 5: Paul Ricoeur, "Memory, Forgetfulness, and History," *Iyyun: The Jerusalem Philosophical Quarterly* 45 (1996): 13–24.

PP. 255–57
Marion Kaplan, *Hitler's Jewish Refugees: Hope and Anxiety in Portugal* (New Haven, CT: Yale University Press, 2020).

P. 257
James B. Reston, "Lisbon's Refugees Now Put at 8,000," *New York Times*, December 15, 1940.

P. 258
Panel 2: "Personal Story: Breckinridge Long," The Americans and the Holocaust, United States Holocaust Memorial Museum, https://exhibitions.ushmm.org/americans-and-the-holocaust/personal-story/breckinridge-long.

PP. 259–60
Brooke L. Blower, "New York City's Spanish Shipping Agents and the Practice of State Power in the Atlantic Borderlands of World War II," *The American Historical Review* 119, no. 1 (February 2014).

P. 261
Panel 1: "1,120 Refugees Reach New York in Horror Ship," *N.Y. News*, September 13, 1941, accessed via the Cincinatti Center for Holocaust & Humanity Education, https://www.cincinnatijudaicafund.com/Detail/objects/2619. The original article calls the journey of the *Navemar* "one of the most horror-stricken voyages since the days when slaves were shipped below-decks from Africa." A Jewish Telegraphic Agency bulletin released the next day calls the *Navemar* "The Floating Concentration Camp" (*JTA Daily News Bulletin* VIII, no. 230, September 14, 1941, http://pdfs.jta.org/1941/1941-09-14_230.pdf?_ga=2.193713001.531126073.1695836930-911480388.1695836930).

P. 262
The Levis' transatlantic crossing is, for me, haunted by the history of the transatlantic slave trade, and while writing this section, I was thinking about Christina Sharpe's *In the Wake: On Blackness and Being* (Durham, NC: Duke University Press, 2016) and particularly the concept of residence time—"the amount of time it takes for a substance to enter the ocean and then leave the ocean." In the case of the salt in human blood, 260 million years (41). For my oma, the ocean was about God; for me, it's about a collapsing of time.

P. 266
"Ilse Halpert Obituary," *Charlotte Observer*, December 21, 2010.

PP. 267–68
"Into Battle No. 1: Lift Your Head Comrade," 1942, accessed at United States Ho-

locaust Memorial Museum, courtesy of Imperial War Museums, https://collections
.ushmm.org/search/catalog/irn1004401.

P. 269
Timothy Snyder, *Black Earth: The Holocaust as History and Warning* (New York: Penguin Random House, 2015), 12.

P. 272
Benjamin Madley, "From Africa to Auschwitz: How German South West Africa Incubated Ideas and Methods Adopted and Developed by the Nazis in Eastern Europe," *European History Quarterly* 35, no. 3 (2005).

P. 275
Hannah Black, "From Minneapolis to Jerusalem: On Black-Palestinian Solidarity," *Jewish Currents*, October 25, 2021, https://jewishcurrents.org/from-minneapolis-to
-jerusalem 2021.

P. 276
Nick Estes, "The Empire of All Maladies," *Baffler Magazine* 52, July 2020, https://the
baffler.com/salvos/the-empire-of-all-maladies-estes. Estes here is discussing Michael V. Wilcox's concept of "terminal narratives."

P. 277
This work is beholden to the activism of the Flatbush African Burial Ground Coalition. An archaeological study of the site was prepared in 2021 by Historical Perspectives Inc. for the New York City Economic Development Corporation and is available at http://s-media.nyc.gov/agencies/lpc/arch_reports/1914.pdf.

P. 279
Ben Verde, "2021 Elections: Where Do Flatbush Council Candidates Stand on the PS 90 Project?" *Brooklyn Paper*, June 8, 2021, https://www.brooklynpaper.com/ps90
-project-flatbush- candidates/.

P. 280
See Ricardo Roque, "Human Skulls, Dangerous Wanderers," in *Crawling Doubles: Colonial Collecting and Affect*, edited by Mathieu Kleyebe Abonnenc (Paris: Editions B42, 2016).

P. 282
Corrie Ten Boom, *The Hiding Place* (Old Tappan, NJ: Spire Christian Comics, 1973).

P. 285
"Fips" was the pen name of Philipp Rupprecht, a German artist particularly known for antisemitic caricature and the illustrator of the books *Trau keinem Fuchs auf grüner Heid und keinem Jud auf seinem Eid* ("Don't Trust a Fox in a Green Pasture or a Jew Upon His Oath," 1936) and *Der Giftpilz* ("The Poisonous Mushroom," 1938), published by Stürmer Verlag.

P. 286

My thinking here is informed by the work of scholar Claire Urbanski, who describes the carceral logic of institutional holdings as an "indefinite detention." Claire Urbanski, "Ancestral Detention: Settler Desire and the Carceral Logics of Grave Theft and Museum Containment," Conference Presentation, Spatializing Sovereignty Conference, Mills College (2016). See also Ann Fabian, *The Skull Collectors: Race, Science, and America's Unburied Dead* (Chicago: University of Chicago Press, 2010).

P. 287

Thank you to the Essen City Archives, which sent me everything they could find on the Levi family upon my inquiry and without charge.

P. 291

Michael Rothberg, *Multidirectional Memory: Remembering the Holocaust in the Age of Decolonization* (Palo Alto, CA: Stanford University Press, 2009).

P. 293

This drawing is based on "Dybbuk" by Ephraim Moshe Lilien, in *Die Bücher der Bibel* (Berlin: Benjamin Harz Verlag, 1923).

P. 297

Dori Laub and Nanette C. Auerhahn, "Knowing and Not Knowing Massive Psychic Trauma: Forms of Traumatic Memory," *American Journal of Psychoanalysis* 74 (1993): 287–302.

P. 299

Panel 3: See Mikkel Dack, "Everyday Denazification in Postwar Germany," in *Everyday Denazification in Postwar Germany: The Fragebogen and Political Screening during the Allied Occupation* (Cambridge: Cambridge University Press, 2023).

Panel 4: This image references a photograph of SS women camp guards at Bergen-Belsen after Allied capture on April 19, 1945. The photograph comes from the collections of the Imperial War Museums.

Panels 5–6: Paragraph 175 was German legal code from 1871 to 1994. The core text of the law read, "An unnatural sex act committed between persons of male sex or by humans with animals is punishable by imprisonment; the loss of civil rights might also be imposed." See Jake W. Newsome, *Pink Triangle Legacies* (Ithaca, NY: Cornell University Press, 2022) and Laurie Marhoefer, *Sex and the Weimar Republic: German Homosexual Emancipation and the Rise of the Nazis* (Toronto, ON: University of Toronto Press, 2015). The image in the second-to-last panel is of the Memorial to Homosexuals Persecuted under Nazism in Berlin, designed by Michael Elmgreen and Ingar Dragset. I invite readers to look up the alternative "Celestial Teapot" proposal by Lukas Duwenhogger.